LIABILITY REGIMES IN
CONTEMPORARY
MARITIME LAW

ESSENTIAL MARITIME AND TRANSPORT LAW SERIES

Bills of Lading: Law and Contracts
by Nicholas Gaskell and
Regina Asariotis, Yvonne Baatz
(2000)

Modern Law of Maritime Insurance, Volume 2
Edited by Professor D. Rhidian Thomas
(2002)

Maritime Fraud
by Paul Todd
(2003)

Port State Control
2nd edition
by Dr Z. Oya Özçayir
(2004)

War, Terror and Carriage by Sea
by Keith Michel
(2004)

Freight Forwarding and Multimodal Transport Contracts
by David A. Glass
(2004)

Contracts of Carriage by Land and Air
by Malcolm Clarke and
David Yates
(2004)

Marine Insurance: Law and Practice
by F. D. Rose
(2004)

General Average: Law and Practice
2nd edition
by F. D. Rose
(2005)

Marine Insurance Clauses
4th edition
by N. Geoffrey Hudson and Tim Madge
(2005)

Marine Insurance:
The Law in Transition
Edited by Professor D. Rhidian Thomas
(2006)

LIABILITY REGIMES IN CONTEMPORARY MARITIME LAW

EDITED BY

PROFESSOR D. RHIDIAN THOMAS

informa

LONDON

2007

Informa Law
Mortimer House
37–41 Mortimer Street
London W1T 3JH
law.enquiries@informa.com

An Informa business

British Library Cataloguing in Publication Data
A catalogue record for this book
is available from the
British Library

ISBN 978-184311-654-7

Text set in 10/12pt Postscript Plantin by
Tony Lansbury, Tonbridge, Kent
Printed in Great Britain by
MPG Books, Bodmin, Cornwall

Foreword

BY THE HON. MR JUSTICE DAVID STEEL

As both the Admiralty Judge and Judge in Charge of the Commercial Court, I am better placed than most to recognise the enormous contribution to international commercial law derived from our leading universities. The Institute of International Shipping and Trade Law at Swansea, under its Director, Professor D. Rhidian Thomas, has shot to the forefront of this academic contribution, made all the more worthwhile by the care taken to absorb and incorporate ideas from practitioners and a wide range of shipping and commercial interests.

The present volume represents the work product of the second international colloquium organised by the Institute. The first, which was devoted to marine insurance law, was a notable success. The content of this new volume reveals that the second was equally worthwhile. No doubt the third, on time charters, which will be imminent at the time of publication, will be equally valuable.

DAVID STEEL
Royal Courts of Justice
16 May 2007

Preface

BY PROFESSOR D. RHIDIAN THOMAS

The contributions to this book in their original form saw the light of day as papers delivered at the Second International Colloquium organised by the Institute of International Shipping and Trade Law, Swansea University, and held at Swansea on 14–15 September 2006.

The colloquium title "Maritime Liabilities" is one of considerable breadth and equal topicality. But within the compass of a two-day event it would have been impossible to visit every nook and cranny of the subject, and consequently the agenda selectively identified some of the salient issues in contemporary maritime law, namely pollution liabilities; the liabilities of ports, salvors, classification societies and carriers of passengers; and the liability of claimants for the wrongful arrest of ships. Broader influences on the emergent law, such as the ISM and ISPS Codes, were also analysed; as also was the phenomenon of global limitation of liability. Aspects of the agenda were immeasurably enhanced by comparative insights to US law and the national law of several European states.

Maritime law, with its concepts of "duties" and "liabilities", "exceptions" and "rights of limitation", differs little, except for the embracing marine context, from the corresponding concepts to be found in terrestrial law. There is common to each broad tradition the full range of strict, presumed fault and traditional fault based liabilities, together with accompanying manipulations to the burden of proof and questions of causation and remoteness. Both also share the difficulty in determining the circumstances when human wrongdoing may be attributed to corporate defendants. Equally present is the compelling influence of public policy in the shaping of the law, a fact now recognised with agreeable candour in the common law's development of the tort of negligence. The principle that the polluter pays, widely applicable to both marine and non-marine pollution, connotes strict liability and embodies compensatory, deterrent and regulatory components of policy. Public policy considerations were again to the fore when the question of the duty of care of salvors finally came full-face before the English courts in the latter half of the last century. They are equally to the fore in the contemporary jurisprudential debate about the proper formulation of the duty of care owed by classification societies. As with questions of morality, public policy does not necessarily reveal a clear and unambiguous face, rather a complex equation of counter-balancing considerations. In the result precisely where public policy should stand may be a complex and hotly debated question.

Notwithstanding the substantial and, probably, growing homogeneity of contemporary maritime and terrestrial law, past and present differences in their respective liability regimes continue to be identifiable in the distinctive history and major contemporary source of maritime law.

The history of maritime law, for example, in the context of collisions, reveals the early recognition that contributory negligence was causal rather than an absolute defence, though it took many years for the equal division of loss rule to be displaced by a more sensitive and just apportionment based on the degree of fault. It took many more years for the common law to adopt a similar position. The same strand of maritime legal history reveals how causation came to be recognised as a vital element in the determination of liability, displacing the concept of liability founded on bare fault. In the history of maritime law few, if any, developments loom larger than the early commitment, through legislative intervention in the case of English law, to the concept of global limitation. This concept has expanded over the centuries into a virtual universal concept underpinned by international conventions. Its survival is jealously guarded, notwithstanding that in the contemporary world it is at least arguable that the *raison d'etre* of the concept is questionable. When the horizon of history is surveyed more generally, the nineteenth century is recognised as a period when the potential liabilities of shipowners increased significantly, fuelled by an evolving common law and the emergence of legislation as a significant source of law. The demand for insurance consequently increased and it was responded to and largely satisfied by the emergence of P&I Clubs, which are such a familiar and important part of the modern legal landscape.

International conventions may generate new policy and law, achieve international harmonisation and reform old law. Their influence on the contemporary topography of maritime law is profound. But what is not to be found in this immensely important modern legal source is any commitment to any particular category of liability regime. In this regard international conventions are as various as the law of nation states, they manifest the same range of liability regimes. They are also susceptible to similar evolutionary developments, as may be witnessed when a string of consecutive international conventions revolve about a single subject.

The contributions in this book provide unambiguous evidence of the variety of liability regimes to be found in maritime law. They reveal how the nature and extent of liability may differ significantly as between different subject areas. They also reveal an almost universal attachment to the right to limit liability, in one form or another. With regard to liability regimes diversity, not uniformity, is the hallmark of maritime law.

DRT

Contents

PART 1: SHIP SOURCE POLLUTION – OIL AND
HAZARDOUS AND NOXIOUS SUBSTANCES

PART 2: PORT LIABILITIES

PART 3: CIVIL AND POLLUTION LIABILITIES OF SALVORS

PART 4: LIABILITIES OF CLASSIFICATION SOCIETIES UNDER ENGLISH AND US LAW

PART 5: THE ISM AND ISPS CODES AND MARITIME LIABILITIES

PART 8: SUBSTANTIVE AND JURISDICTIONAL ISSUES RELATING TO LIMITATION OF LIABILITY

APPENDICES

Authors' Biographies

PROFESSOR D. RHIDIAN THOMAS is Professor of Maritime Law and Director of the Institute of the International Shipping and Trade Law at the School of Law, University of Wales, Swansea. His principal research interests are in the fields of maritime law, marine insurance law, international trade and commercial law, and international arbitration law. He has held positions at several universities and lectured internationally. He is the author of *Maritime Liens* (*British Shipping Law Series*, Stevens and Sons, 1980); *The Law and Practice Relating to Appeals from Arbitration Awards* (LLP, 1994), *Default Powers of Arbitrators* (LLP, 1996), and editor of and contributor to Volumes 1 (1996) and 2 (2002) of *Modern Law of Marine Insurance*, and of *Marine Insurance; The Law in Transition* (2006), all published by LLP/Informa, London. He has also published widely in academic journals. He is Editor-in-Chief of the *Journal of International Maritime Law*, and co-editor of *Arbitration International*. He is a member of the CMI and of the Committee on Marine Insurance Law; the British Maritime Law Association and chairman of the Sub-Committee on Mortgages and Ship Arrest; the Chartered Institute of Arbitrators and British Insurance Law Association.

DR PHIL ANDERSON B.A. (Hons), D.Prof. (Middlesex), FNI, MEWI, AMAE, Master Mariner, is Managing Director of Consult ISM Ltd and Immediate Past President of The Nautical Institute. Dr Anderson heads his own company providing specialist consultancy services and expert witnesses in legal actions and disputes where the management of safety may be an issue. He is a Class One Master Mariner with 11 years seagoing experience. He then worked for over 25 years with P&I Clubs – initially handling claims and disputes and latterly pioneering accident prevention initiatives and risk management with the Club. Since the end of 2004 he has worked independently as an ISM expert. He is author (or co-author) of numerous books on the ISM Code and related topics, evidence collection as well as marine insurance and specifically third party liability/P&I insurance. He is the immediate past president of the international professional body for master mariners and others in control of seagoing ships – The Nautical Institute. A member of the Expert Witness Institute and a practicing associate of the. Academy of Experts. He is also a part time lecturer at the World Maritime University, the School of Marine Science and Technology at the University of Newcastle upon Tyne and the School of Law at the University of Northumbria at Newcastle. He is a member of the IMO roster of experts and UK Government, MCA, human element working group.

ARCHIE BISHOP is a Solicitor both in England and Hong Kong, an Examiner in Admiralty and until recently was the Senior Partner of Holman Fenwick & Willan with whom he is now a Consultant. Trained aboard HMS Worcester he served seven years as a deck officer with the P&O Line before joining the firm in 1960. Since that time he has specialised in collision, salvage, total loss and all other casualties. He has considerable experience in the investigation of large casualties, the resultant legal issues, choice and enforcement of appropriate jurisdiction, public enquiries and dealing with claims by government and local authorities concerning oil pollution, and has been involved in many leading cases. He is the Legal Adviser to the International Salvage Union, worked with the International Maritime Organization's Legal Committee in preparing the Salvage Convention, 1989, is a member of the drafting committee of LOF and played a leading role in the development of the SCOPIC Clause. He sits on the Salvage Committee of the British Maritime Law Association and the Salvage Liaison Group and is the Chairman of the Steering Committee of the London Shipping Law Centre. He is a CEDR Accredited Mediator and a visiting lecturer to the International Maritime Law Institute of Malta, and University College London.

PROFESSOR MARTIN DAVIES B.C.L, M.A. (Oxon), LLM (Harvard), Professor of Maritime Law, Director of Maritime Law Center, Tulane Law School. Professor Davies is the Director of the Maritime Law Center based in Tulane Law School. Before coming to Tulane, he was a law professor at The University of Melbourne in Australia and before that he taught at Monash University, The University of Western Australia and Nottingham University. He is author (or co-author) of books on maritime law, international trade law, conflict of laws, and the law of torts. He also has extensive practical experience as a consultant in maritime matters and general international litigation. He has advised on cargo claims, arrest and admiralty matters, drafting bills of lading, sea waybills and charterparties, collisions and limitation of liability, oil pollution, salvage, marine insurance, maritime arbitrations and international sale of goods.

COLIN DE LA RUE, Solicitor, Ince & Co. Colin de la Rue is a partner in Ince & Co whose main areas of practice since 1989 have related to pollution from ships. Working with others in the firm and overseas lawyers he has acted in most major oil spills in modern times. He is legal adviser on pollution matters to a number of shipping, insurance and oil industry bodies, and is acting for industry interests in proceedings to challenge the validity of the EU Directive on Criminal Sanctions. He is co-author of *Shipping and the Environment* (1998) and has twice chaired CMI international working groups concerned with pollution.

PROFESSOR ROBERT FORCE. At Tulane, Professor Force teaches two foundation courses in Maritime Law and advanced courses in Marine Pollution and Regulation of Shipping. He is a member of the Planning Committee of the Tulane Admiralty Law Institute and the Maritime Law Association of the United States. His publications have been cited by various courts including the Supreme Court of the United States.

STEPHEN GIRVIN is Professor of Maritime Law at the University of Birmingham. He has taught previously at the University of Aberdeen, the University of Nottingham, and the National University of Singapore (NUS). He remains associated with NUS as MPA Visiting Professor in Maritime Law and has previously held visiting positions at the Universities of Cape Town and Sydney. His research and teaching currently embrace shipping and maritime law and company law. He also has interests in international sales, legal history and torts. He is the author of *Carriage of Goods by Sea* (OUP, 2007), one of the authors of the 17th edition of *Charlesworth and Morse's Company Law* (Sweet & Maxwell, 2005), and is one of the editors of the looseleaf work, *Palmer's Company Law* (Sweet & Maxwell). He is a member of the Editorial Committee of the *International Maritime and Commercial Law Yearbook* (Informa). He has served as an academic advisor to the Legal Committee of the Singapore Shipping Association and acts from time to time as a consultant. He is a member of the maritime law associations of Singapore (the SMLA) and Britain (BMLA) and is a Supporting Member of the LMAA.

MÅNS JACOBSSON, Director of IOPC Funds. Måns Jacobsson became Director of the International Oil Pollution Compensation Funds on 1 January 1985, following a career in Sweden where he served as a judge and thereafter became Assistant Under-Secretary and Head of Department for International Affairs in the Swedish Ministry of Justice. He was later appointed President of Division of the Stockholm Court of Appeal. He is also Visiting Professor of the World Maritime University in Malmo, Sweden and of Shanghai Maritime University, Shanghai, People's Republic of China.

SIMON KVERNDAL Q.C., M.A. (Cantab.), Barrister at Law, Quadrant Chambers. Simon Kverndal has a broad commercial practice with particular specialism in all aspects of maritime litigation and arbitration. This work typically involves detailed consideration of the many and varied technical issues which arise in the field of maritime transport and he is well known for his hands on co-operation with the consultant experts appointed in such cases. He comes from a family, originally from Norway, which has been involved for many generations in the shipping industry and in particular in maritime claims. He is a qualified mediator and also sits as an arbitrator. As well as being a member of the LMM (supporting member), COMBAR and the LCLBA, he is a Member of the Court of Assistants of the Worshipful Company of Shipwrights.

NIGEL MEESON Q.C., B.A, M.A. (Oxon), Barrister at Law, Quadrant Chambers. Nigel Meeson graduated with 1st Class honours in Jurisprudence from Magdalen College, Oxford in 1981 and was called to the Bar in 1982. After a short time with a London P & I Club and lecturing in International Trade and Commercial law he has been in practice at the Bar in London specialising in shipping, insurance, aviation and other aspects of international trade and transport, commercial litigation and international and domestic arbitration and mediation. He took silk in 2002 and was appointed a Recorder in 2004. He has been a CEDR accredited mediator since 1993, is a Member of the Chartered Institute of Arbitrators and is a supporting

Member of the London Maritime Arbitrators' Association. He is also admitted as an Attorney in California (1990). He was a visiting lecturer at University College London from 1994 to 2005, and is a member of the steering committee of the London Shipping Law Centre. He is the author of *Admiralty Jurisdiction and Practice* (1993), (3rd ed., 2003); *Ship and Aircraft Mortgages* (1989) a contributor to *Ship Sale and Purchase* (2nd ed., 1993), (3rd ed., 1998) and *Jurisdiction and Forum Selection in International Maritime Law*, Essays in Honor of Robert Force (2005).

PROFESSOR PROSHANTO KUMAR MUKHERJEE LL.B (Dalhousie), Ph.D. (Wales) is IFT Professor of Maritime Safety and Environmental Protection, World Maritime University, Malmo. Professor Mukherjee is Honourary Research Fellow of the University of Wales, Swansea, and Academic Coordinator of the joint Ph.D. programme in Maritime and Commercial Law of the World Maritime University and University of Wales, Swansea. He spent 16 years at sea which included command time. He read law at Dalhousie University, obtained his Ph.D. from University of Wales Swansea and was a practicing barrister and solicitor in Ontario. He was Senior Adviser, Maritime Policy and International Affairs of the Canadian Hydrographic Service and later, Senior Deputy Director and Professor of Maritime Law of the IMO International Maritime Law Institute in Malta. He was IMO Legal Adviser for the Caribbean Region and has drafted shipping and marine environmental legislation for numerous jurisdictions worldwide. He is author of *Maritime Legislation* (WMU Publications, 2002). His extensive publications embrace every aspect of public and private maritime law. He is co-editor of *Maritime Violence and Other Security Issues at Sea* (WMU Publications, 2002) and is currently co-authoring *Farthing on International Shipping* (4th ed.). He was a member of the Advisory Board of Editors of the *Journal of Maritime Law and Commerce* and is on the editorial boards of the WMU *Journal of Maritime Affairs* and the *Journal of International Maritime Law*. Professor Mukherjee is a Fellow of the Nautical Institute and an Associate Fellow of the Royal Institute of Navigation in London.

PROFESSOR ERIK ROSAEG is a member of the Scandinavian Institute of Maritime Law based in the University of Oslo. He holds a master degree and doctorate from the same University and has been working there since 1982, except for a period in the Norwegian Ministry of Justice 1995–96. Professor Rosaeg regularly represents his native country Norway at the IMO Legal Committee and similar meetings, and has chaired a number of working groups. For more than a decade he has been a pivotal figure in the development of International Maritime Law Conventions, such as the HNS Convention 1996, the Athens Convention 2002 and the Athens Implementation Guidelines 2006. He has a special interest for compulsory insurance schemes. His teaching and research interests include maritime law, contract law and third party relations in private law (bankruptcy, mortgages and property conflicts). He has also had an interest in diverse subjects like law and economics, electronic commerce, protection of minors (in particular asylum seekers) and health information in insurance. During the academic year 2006–2007, Professor Rosaeg has been a visiting researcher at the Institute of Maritime Law, University of Southampton.

PROFESSOR DR FRANK SMEELE, L.I.M. M.A. (Amsterdam) is Professor of Maritime Law at the Law Faculty, Erasmus University at Rotterdam and Attorney and Partner at Van Traa Advocation, Rotterdam. Professor Smeele (1966) graduated in Law and European Studies at the University of Amsterdam in 1991. In 1998 he received his PhD cum laude from Erasmus University Rotterdam for his thesis on The Identity of the Carrier under Bills of Lading. In 1998 he was admitted as attorney at law to the Rotterdam bar, where he practices maritime law at Van Traa Advocaten, the leading Dutch law firm in the field of maritime and transport law, since 2004 as partner. Also in 2004 Professor Smeele was appointed as part-time professor of Maritime Law at Erasmus University Rotterdam. He is author (or co-author) of various of various books and articles on maritime law, transport law, general private law, conflict of laws and jurisdiction law. His has extensive experience in dealing with and litigating about cargo claims, arrest and admiralty matters, b/i and c/p disputes, collisions and limitation of liability.

DR BARIS SOYER B.A. (Ankara), LL.M, Ph.D (So'ton). Dr Soyer is Reader in Commercial and Maritime Law at the University of Swansea, where he is also a member of the Institute of International Shipping and Trade Law. He is also the director of LLM Programmes. He was previously a lecturer at the University of Exeter. He is the author of *Warranties in Marine Insurance* (Cavendish Publishing, 2001). The second edition of this book was published in 2006. The first edition was the joint winner of the Cavendish Book Prize in 2001 and was awarded the Book Prize of the British Insurance Law Association in 2002. His principal interest is in the field of marine insurance, but his interests extend more broadly throughout maritime and contract law. He has published extensively in these areas. Dr Soyer is an editor of the *Journal of International Maritime Law* and is on the editorial board of *Shipping and Trade Law* and *Baltic Maritime Law Quarterly*.

TOBY STEPHENS, Solicitor, Holman Fenwick & Willan. Toby Stephens is a solicitor specialising in maritime law. Toby worked for a short time as a marine surveyor prior to being admitted as a solicitor in 1999 with another firm. Toby joined Holman Fenwick & Willan's Admiralty and Crisis Management team in 2001 focusing on all aspects of marine casualties, where he was made a partner in 2007. As well as dealing with collisions, pollution, limitation of liability and total loss, Toby has a particular interest in salvage and salvors' liabilities and has been involved in a number of high profile salvage cases, acting for salvors, ship owners, property underwriters and P&I Clubs. Toby has written several papers on the subject and has lectured on a variety of topics within the sphere of marine casualties. Toby has also undertaken a secondment to a leading Lloyd's syndicate as head of the legal department advising on all aspects of marine and insurance law.

PROFESSOR ANDREW TETTENBORN MA, LL.B (Cantab), Barrister, Bracton Professor of Law, University of Exeter. Andrew Tettenborn has been Bracton Professor of Law at Exeter Law School since 1996, having previously taught at the universities of Nottingham and Cambridge. In addition he has held visiting positions at Melbourne University, the University of Connecticut and also Case Law School,

Cleveland, Ohio. He is author (or co-author) of books on torts, damages and maritime law, and of numerous articles and chapters on aspects of common law, commercial law and restitution.

PROFESSOR RICHARD WILLIAMS LLB (Wales) LLM (London), Institute of International Shipping and Trade Law, University of Swansea. Richard Williams retired from private practise at the end of 2000 after 30 years with Ince & Co. He had been a partner for 25 years and was chairman of the firm's dry shipping business group. He is now a Visiting Professor and teaches the law relating to Charterparties and Marine Cargo Claims at the University of Wales, Swansea. Throughout his career he has been involved not only in the litigation of cases to the highest courts of appeal in the UK and abroad but also in the development of policy and documentation within the industry both for clients and international industry bodies. He was closely connected with an agency of the United Nations for over 25 years and has been consulted by them and other international bodies such as UNCTAD, BIMCO and the International Group of Protection and Indemnity Clubs in relation to industry-wide issues and the drafting of standard documents. He is the author of numerous papers and articles on shipping law and is co-author of the text-book *Limitation of Liability of Maritime Claims* (published by Lloyd's of London Press) (4th ed., 2005). He is a regular speaker on maritime law matters at conferences around the world and organises and speaks at training courses for various industry bodies.

Table of Cases

Table of Legislation

*(Where material is reproduced in full, the paragraph number is in **bold**.)*

PART 1

Ship Source Pollution – Oil and Hazardous and Noxious Substances

PART I

CHAPTER 1

Ship source pollution – Oil and hazardous and noxious substances

MÅNS JACOBSSON*

INTRODUCTION

1.1 The international regime for the compensation of pollution damage caused by oil spills from tankers is based on two treaties adopted under the auspices of the International Maritime Organization (IMO), the 1992 International Convention on Civil Liability for Oil Pollution Damage (1992 Civil Liability Convention) and the 1992 International Convention on the Establishment of an International Fund for Compensation for Oil Pollution Damage (1992 Fund Convention). These Conventions replace two corresponding Conventions adopted in 1969 and 1971 respectively.

1.2 The 1992 Civil Liability Convention governs the liability of shipowners for oil pollution damage. The Convention lays down the principle of strict liability for shipowners and creates a system of compulsory liability insurance. Shipowners are normally entitled to limit their liability to an amount which is linked to the tonnage of their ship.

1.3 The 1992 Fund Convention, which is supplementary to the 1992 Civil Liability Convention, set up an intergovernmental organisation, the International Oil Pollution Compensation Fund 1992 (1992 Fund), which provides additional compensation to victims when the compensation under the 1992 Civil Liability Convention is inadequate. By becoming party to the 1992 Fund Convention, a State becomes a member of the 1992 Fund. The Organisation has its headquarters in London.

1.4 The 1992 Fund succeeds a previous organisation, the 1971 Fund, which is at present being wound up.

1.5 A third tier of compensation in the form of a Supplementary Fund was established on 3 March 2005 by means of a Protocol adopted in 2003.

1.6 On 31 August 2006, 113 States had ratified the 1992 Civil Liability Convention, and 98 States had ratified the 1992 Fund Convention. The Supplementary Fund Protocol had been ratified by 19 States.

1.7 The States which are parties to the 1992 Conventions and the Supplementary Fund Protocol are listed in the Annex.

MAIN FEATURES OF THE 1992 CONVENTIONS

1.8 The 1992 Conventions and the Supplementary Fund Protocol apply to pollution damage suffered in the territory (including the territorial sea) and the exclusive

---

* Director, International Oil Pollution Compensation Funds.

3

economic zone (EEZ) or equivalent area of a State party to the respective Conventions. "Pollution damage" is defined as damage caused by contamination and includes the cost of "preventive measures", i.e. measures to prevent or minimise pollution damage.

1.9 The treaties apply to ships which actually carry oil in bulk as cargo, i.e. generally laden tankers, as well as to spills of bunker oil from unladen tankers in certain circumstances.

1.10 The liability rests on the registered owner of the ship from which the oil originated. Shipowners have strict liability for pollution damage (with very limited defences) and are obliged to cover their liability by insurance. Shipowners are normally entitled to limit their liability to an amount which is calculated on the basis of the tonnage of the ship, and which – after increases by some 50% with effect from 1 November 2003 – ranges from 4.51 million SDR (US$6.7 million) for small ships to 89.77 million SDR (US$134 million) for large tankers.[1]

1.11 Shipowners are deprived of the right to limit their liability if it is proved that the pollution damage resulted from the shipowner's personal act or omission, committed with the intent to cause such damage, or recklessly and with knowledge that such damage would probably result.

1.12 Claims for pollution damage under the 1992 Civil Liability Convention can be made only against the registered owner of the ship concerned. This does not preclude victims from claiming compensation outside the Convention from persons other than the owner. However, the Convention prohibits claims against the servants or agents of the owner, the crew, the pilot, the charterer (including a bareboat charterer), manager or operator of the ship, or any person carrying out salvage operations or taking preventive measures.

1.13 The compensation payable by the 1992 Fund in respect of an incident is limited to an aggregate amount which, with effect from 1 November 2003, was increased from 135 million SDR (US$201 million) to 203 million SDR (US$302 million), including the sum actually paid by the shipowner (or the shipowner's insurer) under the 1992 Civil Liability Convention.

1.14 The 1992 Fund is financed by contributions levied on any entity which has received in one calendar year more than 150 000 tonnes of crude or heavy fuel oil (contributing oil) in a State party to the 1992 Fund Convention after sea transport. Member States are obliged to submit annually to the Fund reports on the quantities of contributing oil received.

1.15 The Japanese oil industry is the major contributor to the 1992 Fund, paying 18% of the total contributions. The Italian oil industry is the second largest contributor paying 10%, followed by the oil industries in the Republic of Korea (9%), the Netherlands (8%), France (7%), India (7%), United Kingdom (5%), Singapore (5%) and Spain (5%).

1.16 The Supplementary Fund has available an amount of 547 million SDR (U$814 million), in addition to the amount of 203 million SDR (US$302 million) available under the 1992 Conventions. As a result, the total amount available for

---

1. The unit of currency in the 1992 Conventions and the Supplementary Fund Protocol is the Special Drawing Right (SDR) as defined by the International Monetary Fund. In this document the SDR has been converted into US dollars at the rate applicable on 31 August 2006, i.e. 1 SDR = US$1.48852.

compensation for each incident for pollution damage in the States which are Members of the Supplementary Fund will be 750 million SDR (US$1,116 million).

1.17 The 1992 Fund has an Assembly, which is composed of representatives of all 1992 Fund Member States. The Assembly is the supreme organ governing the 1992 Fund, and it holds regular sessions once a year. The 1992 Fund also has an Executive Committee composed of 15 Member States elected by the Assembly. The main task of the Committee is to approve compensation claims to the extent that the Director has not been given the authority to do so. The Supplementary Fund has its own Assembly composed of representatives of its Member States. During the winding up of the 1971 Fund it is governed by an Administrative Council.

1.18 The 1992 Fund, the 1971 Fund and the Supplementary Fund have a joint Secretariat. The Secretariat is headed by a Director and has at present 27 staff members.

1.19 The Director has been granted extensive authority to approve claims for compensation.

1.20 The IOPC Funds have a trilingual website (*http://www.iopcfund.org*) containing information on the international compensation regime and the activities of the IOPC Funds.

CLAIMS SETTLEMENT

Claims experience

1.21 Since their establishment, the 1971 and 1992 Funds have been involved in approximately 135 incidents and have made compensation payments totalling some US$1,040 million. The Supplementary Fund has so far not been involved in any incidents.

1.22 In the great majority of these incidents, all claims have been settled out of court. To date, court actions against the Funds have been taken in respect of only a handful of incidents.

1.23 The cases involving the largest total payments are as follows:

Incident	Payments to claimants
Antonio Gramsci (Sweden, 1979)	US$18million
Tanio (France, 1986)	US$36million
Haven (Italy, 1991)	US$58million
Aegean Sea (Spain, 1992)	US$65million
Braer (United Kingdom, 1993)	US$87million
Keumdong No. 5 (Republic of Korea, 1993)	US$21million
Sea Prince (Republic of Korea, 1995)	US$40million
Yuil No. 1 (Republic of Korea, 1995)	US$30million
Sea Empress (United Kingdom, 1996)	US$60million
Nakhodka (Japan, 1997)	US$211million
Nissos Amorgos (Venezuela, 1997)	US$21million
Erika (France, 1999) (payments up to 01.09.06)	US$131million
Prestige (Spain, France, Portugal, 2002) (payments up to 01.09.06)	US$153million

1.24 A major oil spill can give rise to a large number of claims. The *Erika* incident resulted in over 6,900 compensation claims, of which over 50% were presented by businesses in the tourism sector and 27% originated from the fishery and mariculture sectors.

Admissibility of claims for compensation

1.25 The 1992 Fund and the Supplementary Fund can pay compensation to a claimant only to the extent that the claim meets the criteria laid down in the 1992 Fund Convention and the 2003 Protocol.

1.26 The Funds have acquired considerable experience with regard to the admissibility of claims. In connection with the settlement of claims they have developed certain principles as regards the meaning of the definition of "pollution damage", which is specified as "damage caused by contamination".

1.27 The 1992 Fund has published a Claims Manual which contains general information on how claims should be presented and sets out the general criteria for the admissibility of various types of claims. A revised version of the Claims Manual has been adopted by the Assembly and was published in May 2005.

1.28 Decisions on the admissibility of claims which are of general interest are reported in the Funds' Annual Report. Some of the main types of claim are dealt with below.

Property damage

1.29 Pollution incidents often result in damage to property: the oil may contaminate fishing boats, fishing gear, yachts, beaches, piers and embankments. The Funds accept costs for cleaning polluted property. If the polluted property (e.g. fishing gear) cannot be cleaned, the Funds compensate the cost of replacement, subject to deduction for wear and tear. Measures taken to combat an oil spill may cause damage to roads, piers and embankments and thus necessitate repair work, and reasonable costs for such repairs are accepted by the Funds.

Clean-up operations on shore and at sea, and preventive measures

1.30 The Funds pay compensation for expenses incurred for clean-up operations at sea or on the shore. Operations at sea may relate to the deployment of vessels, the salaries of crew, the use of booms and the spraying of dispersants. In respect of onshore clean-up, the operations may result in major costs for personnel, equipment, absorbents, etc.

1.31 Measures taken to prevent or minimise pollution damage ("preventive measures") are compensated under the 1992 Conventions and the Supplementary Fund Protocol. Measures may be taken to prevent oil which has escaped from a ship from reaching the coast, e.g. by placing booms along the coast which is threatened. Dispersants may be used at sea to combat the oil. Oil may be removed from a sunken vessel. Costs for such operations are in principle considered as costs of preventive measures. It must be emphasised, however, that the definition only covers costs of reasonable measures.

1.32 The admissibility of claims for preventive measures is decided on the basis of objective criteria. The fact that a government or other public body decides to take certain measures does not in itself mean that the measures are reasonable for the purpose of the Conventions. The technical reasonableness is assessed on the basis of the facts available at the time of the decision to take the measures. However, those in charge of the operations should continually reappraise their decisions in the light of developments and further technical advice.

1.33 Claims for costs are not accepted when it could have been foreseen that the measures taken would be ineffective. On the other hand, the fact that the measures proved to be ineffective is not in itself a reason for rejection of a claim for the costs incurred. The costs incurred, and the relationship between those costs and the benefits derived or expected, should be reasonable. In the assessment, the Funds take account of the particular circumstances of the incident.

1.34 The meaning of the criterion of reasonableness was considered by the 1992 Fund Executive Committee in February/March 2006 in reaction to the *Prestige* incident (November 2002) when considering a claim by the Spanish Government for the costs of the operation to remove the oil from the wreck of the *Prestige*. The *Prestige* broke into two sections and sank at some 3,800 metres depth approximately 260 kilometres off the Spanish Atlantic coast. After extensive studies the Spanish Government decided that the cargo remaining in the wreck should be removed, using aluminium shuttle containers filled by gravity through holes cut in the tanks. The removal was carried out during the period May–September 2004. Some 13,000 tonnes of oil cargo was removed from the forepart of the wreck which was treated with biological agents aimed at accelerating the degradation of the oil. No attempt was made to remove the 700 tonnes of oil in the aft section which was not treated with biological agents.

1.35 In a document presented to the 1992 Fund Executive Committee the Director expressed the view that costs of secondary sealing of oil leaks from the wreck in 2003 were proportionate and therefore admissible in principle. The Director also considered that the costs of a number of studies and surveys carried out were admissible in principle to the extent that the studies and surveys assisted in the assessment of the pollution threat posed by the wreck. The total cost of these potentially admissible items was some €11.3 million (US$14.5 million), although, in the Director's view, a further, more detailed analysis of these claim items would be required in order to identify the extent to which they had a bearing on the risk posed by the oil in the wreck and to assess the admissible quantum. The Director expressed the view that the other costs incurred in 2003, totalling €21.8 million (US$27.9 million), relating to basic engineering studies of the two proposed alternative methods of extracting the oil and pilot-scale and field-scale tests of the shuttle containers, were not admissible, since they were incurred after the very high costs of the operation in relation to the potential economic and environmental effects of leaving the oil in the wreck had been known.

1.36 The Director further expressed the view that the costs incurred in 2004, totalling €76.1 million (US$97.6 million), relating to the actual oil removal operations and the application of nutrients to the tanks in the forepart of the wreck after the bulk oil had been removed, were inadmissible in principle, since these costs were disproportionate to any potential economic and environmental consequences of leaving the oil in the wreck. Although, as a result of European Commission aid payments, the Spanish Government's claim for the costs of the operations in 2004 had been reduced to €19,383,265 (US$24.8 million), the Director was of the view that in considering the admissibility of the claim, the technical reasonableness of the operation and the proportionality between the costs of the operation and the potential economic and environmental consequences, the total costs of the oil removal operation, as opposed to the balance of the costs after deducting the amount granted by the European Commission, should be taken into account. In his view the claim for costs incurred in 2004, even for the reduced amount, was therefore inadmissible.

1.37 Some delegations stated that they did not share the Director's view that the cost of the oil removal operation was disproportionate on the grounds that had the oil not been removed from the wreck, pollution would have continued year on year. The point was made that it had not been possible to predict with any certainty what the outcome of leaving the oil in the wreck would have been and that it would therefore be difficult for any government to resist pressure from the public to ensure that the risk was eliminated. The point was also made that there was a very clear link between the costs incurred in 2003 and 2004 in that the operation could not have proceeded in 2004 without the necessary studies and preparatory work in 2003.

1.38 Some delegations considered that the admissibility of the claim should be assessed on the basis of the revised claim amount and not on the actual cost of the operation to remove the oil. Other delegations disagreed and expressed the view that admissibility should not be assessed on the basis of the reduced claim, since this would encourage the manipulation of claims in the future.

1.39 A number of delegations agreed with the Director's analysis that the cost of removing the oil from the wreck did not fulfil the Funds' objective technical criteria. Those delegations considered that for the claim to be admissible the Fund would need to change its existing policy so as to allow assessments to be made on the basis of a broader analysis including a social dimension.

1.40 Most delegations that intervened expressed the view that, on the basis of the Funds' existing admissibility criteria, and in the interest of applying those criteria in a uniform way, the claim for the costs incurred by the Spanish Government in 2004 for the removal of the oil from the wreck was inadmissible. However, some delegations considered that it was important that the Funds were prepared to deal with similar claims in the future in a more flexible manner. To that end, those delegations stated that the Director should be instructed to examine the existing admissibility criteria in respect of preventive measures and to submit to the Assembly detailed proposals for clarifying the criteria within the framework of the existing Conventions. The Spanish delegation considered that the Funds' criteria should allow greater flexibility as regards the admissibility of such claims.

1.41 The Executive Committee decided, as proposed by the Director, that some of the costs incurred in 2003 in respect of sealing the oil leaking from the wreck and various surveys and studies were admissible in principle, but that the claim for costs incurred in 2004 relating to the removal of oil from the wreck was inadmissible.

1.42 The Committee instructed the Director to carry out an examination of the admissibility criteria relating to claims for costs of preventive measures, in particular for the extraction of oil from sunken vessels, with a view to enabling the 1992 Fund Assembly to discuss at its October 2006 session possible alternatives for the existing criteria for admissibility within the framework of the 1992 Conventions.

Consequential loss and pure economic loss

1.43 The Funds accept in principle claims relating to loss of earnings suffered by the owners or users of property which had been contaminated as a result of a spill (consequential loss). One example of consequential loss is a fisherman's loss of income as a result of his nets becoming polluted.

1.44 An important group of claims comprises those relating to *pure economic loss*, i.e. loss of earnings sustained by persons whose property has not been polluted. A fisherman whose boat and nets have not been contaminated may be prevented from fishing because the area of the sea where he normally fishes is polluted and he cannot fish elsewhere. Similarly, an hotelier or restaurateur whose premises are close to a contaminated public beach may suffer loss of profit because the number of guests falls during the period of pollution.

1.45 Claims for pure economic loss are admissible only if they are for loss or damage caused by contamination. The starting point is the pollution, not the incident itself.

1.46 In order to qualify for compensation the basic criterion is that a sufficiently close link of causation exists between the contamination and the loss or damage sustained by the claimant. A claim is not admissible on the sole criterion that the loss or damage would not have occurred but for the oil spill in question. When considering whether the criterion of a sufficiently close link of causation is fulfilled, the following elements are taken into account:

- the geographic proximity between the claimant's activity and the contamination;
- the degree to which a claimant is economically dependent on an affected resource;
- the extent to which a claimant has alternative sources of supply or business opportunities;
- the extent to which a claimant's business forms an integral part of the economic activity within the area affected by the spill.

Account is also taken of the extent to which a claimant can mitigate his loss.

Environmental damage

1.47 In the 1992 Conventions and the Supplementary Fund Protocol "pollution damage" is defined as damage caused by contamination. The definition contains a proviso to the effect that compensation for impairment of the environment (other than loss of profit from such impairment) should be limited to costs of reasonable measures of reinstatement actually undertaken or to be undertaken.

1.48 The Funds' governing bodies have decided that in order for claims for the cost of measures to reinstate the marine environment to be admissible for compensation, the measures should fulfil the following criteria:

- the measures should be likely to accelerate significantly the natural process of recovery;
- the measures should seek to prevent further damage as a result of the incident;
- the measures should, as far as possible, not result in the degradation of other habitats or in adverse consequences for other natural or economic resources;
- the measures should be technically feasible;
- the costs of the measures should not be out of proportion to the extent and duration of the damage and the benefits likely to be achieved.

The assessment should be made on the basis of the information available when the specific reinstatement measures are to be undertaken.

1.49 Compensation is paid only for reasonable measures of reinstatement actually undertaken or to be undertaken, and if the claimant has sustained an economic loss that can be quantified in monetary terms. The Funds will not entertain claims for environmental damage based on an abstract quantification calculated in accordance with theoretical models. They will also not pay damages of a punitive nature on the basis of the degree of fault of the wrongdoer.

1.50 Studies are sometimes required to establish the precise nature and extent of environmental damage caused by an oil spill and to determine whether or not reinstatement measures are necessary and feasible. Such studies will not be necessary after all spills and will normally be most appropriate in the case of major incidents where there is evidence of significant environmental damage.

1.51 The Funds may contribute to the cost of such studies provided that they concern damage which falls within the definition of *pollution damage* in the Conventions, including reasonable measures to reinstate a damaged environment. In order to be admissible for compensation it is essential that any such post-spill studies are likely to provide reliable and usable information. For this reason the studies must be carried out with professionalism, scientific rigour, objectivity and balance. This is most likely to be achieved if a committee or other mechanism is established within the affected Member State to design and co-ordinate any such studies, as well as reinstatement measures.

1.52 The scale of the studies should be in proportion to the extent of the contamination and the predictable effects. On the other hand, the mere fact that a post-spill study demonstrates that no significant long-term environmental damage has occurred or that no reinstatement measures are necessary, does not by itself exclude compensation for the costs of the study.

1.53 The Funds should be invited at an early stage to participate in the determination of whether or not a particular incident should be subject to a post-spill environmental study. If it is agreed that such a study is justified the Funds should then be given the opportunity of becoming involved in the planning and in establishing the terms of reference for the study. In this context the Funds can play an important role in helping to ensure any post-spill environmental study does not unnecessarily repeat what has been done elsewhere. The Funds can also assist in ensuring that appropriate techniques and experts are employed. It is essential that progress with the studies is monitored, and that the results are clearly and impartially documented. This is not only important for the particular incident but also for the compilation of relevant data by the Funds for future cases.

1.54 It should be emphasised that participation of the Funds in the planning of environmental studies does not necessarily mean that any measures of reinstatement later proposed or undertaken will be considered admissible.

UNIFORM APPLICATION OF THE CONVENTIONS

1.55 The 1971 and 1992 Fund Assemblies have expressed the opinion that a uniform interpretation of the definition of "pollution damage" is essential for the functioning of the regime of compensation established by the Conventions. The IOPC Funds' position in this regard applies not only to questions of principle relating to the admissibility of claims but also to the assessment of the actual loss or damage where the claims do not give rise to any question of principle.

1.56 The importance of uniformity of application is obvious. It is important from the point of view of equity that claimants are treated in the same manner independent of the State where the damage was sustained. In addition, the oil industry in one Member State pays for the cost of clean-up operations incurred and economic losses suffered in other Member States. Unless a reasonably high degree of uniformity and consistency is achieved, there is a risk of great tensions arising between Member States and of the international compensation systems no longer being able to function properly.

1.57 It should be noted that the definition of "pollution damage" is the same in the 1992 Civil Liability Convention and the 1992 Fund Convention. For this reason, the concept of "pollution damage" should be interpreted in the same way independent of whether the claim is against the shipowner/the insurer under the 1992 Civil Liability Convention or against the shipowner/the insurer and the 1992 Fund under both 1992 Conventions. Similarly, the concept should also be interpreted in the same way by the national courts whether the claim under consideration is under only the 1992 Civil Liability Convention or under both 1992 Conventions.

1.58 In May 2003 the 1992 Fund Administrative Council (on behalf of the Assembly) adopted a Resolution on the interpretation and application of the 1992 Civil Liability and Fund Conventions. In the Resolution attention was drawn to the importance for the proper and equitable functioning of the regime established by the 1992 Conventions that these Conventions were applied uniformly in all States Parties and that claimants for oil pollution damage were given equal treatment as regards compensation in all States Parties. The Resolution emphasised the importance that national courts in States Parties gave due consideration to the decisions by the governing bodies of the Funds on such matters.

1.59 As already mentioned, court actions have been taken against the Funds only in a handful of cases. The *Braer* incident (Shetland, 1993) gave rise to a number of court actions and the *Sea Empress* (Wales, 1996) to one court action relating to pure economic loss. The Scottish and English courts upheld the 1971 Fund's rejection of the claims, although the courts did not apply the Fund's criteria but rejected the claims on the basis of common law jurisprudence on the general non-admissibility of claims for pure economic loss.

1.60 In the *Erika* case a large number of legal actions have been brought in the French courts. Some 70 judgments have so far been rendered, and the judgments have, with a few exceptions, been very favourable to the 1992 Fund. In some cases the courts have applied the Fund's admissibility criteria and in other cases they did not apply them, but took them into account. In some cases the courts stated that the Fund's criteria were not binding and that the admissibility should be decided by the application of French law but reached the same results as the Fund on its rejection of the claims by applying the requirement that there must be a link of causation between the event and the damage. The Court of Appeal in Rennes held in one case that whilst the 1992 Fund's admissibility criteria were not binding on national courts, they could nevertheless serve as a point of reference (*"une référence à titre indicatif"*) for the national judge.

REVIEW OF THE ADEQUACY OF THE INTERNATIONAL COMPENSATION REGIME

Increase in the limitation amounts available under the 1992 Conventions

1.61 When the 1992 Civil Liability and Fund Conventions were adopted, it was expected that the total amount available under these Conventions, at that time US$201 million, would be sufficient to compensate all victims in full, even in the most serious incidents. However, it became evident already in relation to the first major incident which occurred after the entry into force of the 1992 Conventions, namely the *Nakhodka* incident in Japan in 1997, that this was not the case. The inadequacy of that amount was demonstrated even more clearly in respect of the *Erika* incident in France in 1999.

1.62 In the light of this experience, a number of States took the view that it was necessary to increase significantly the amount of compensation available. A first step to this effect was taken in 2000 when the Legal Committee of IMO decided under a special procedure provided for in the Conventions (the "tacit amendment" procedure), to increase the limits contained in 1992 Civil Liability Convention and the 1992 Fund Convention by some 50%. The amendment to the 1992 Fund Convention brought the total amount available under the 1992 Conventions to US$302 million. The increases entered into force on 1 November 2003.

1992 Fund Working Group

1.63 Many States took the view, however, that the increase in the maximum compensation amount decided by the IMO Legal Committee was insufficient and the point was made that although the system had worked well in most cases, there were inadequacies in the system and it was therefore necessary to carry out a general revision of the 1992 Conventions. For this reason the 1992 Fund Assembly established in 2000 a Working Group open to all Member States to examine the adequacy of the international compensation regime established by these Conventions.

Supplementary Fund

1.64 During the discussions in the Working Group it was decided to work towards the creation of an optional third tier of compensation and to prepare a draft Protocol providing for such a third tier by means of a Supplementary Fund. A Diplomatic Conference held under the auspices of the IMO in London in May 2003 adopted, after difficult negotiations, a Protocol creating such a Supplementary Compensation Fund. The Protocol entered into force on 3 March 2005.

   1.65 The main elements of the Protocol are as follows:

- The Protocol established a new intergovernmental organisation, the International Oil Pollution Compensation Supplementary Fund 2003.
- Any State which is Party to the 1992 Fund Convention may become Party to the Protocol and thereby become a Member of the Supplementary Fund.
- The Protocol applies to pollution damage in the territory, including the territorial sea, of a State which is a Party to the Protocol and in the exclusive economic zone (EEZ) or equivalent area of such a State.
- The total amount of compensation payable for any one incident is 750 million SDR (US$1,116 million), including the amount payable under the 1992 Civil Liability and Fund Conventions, 203 million SDR (US$302 million).
- Annual contributions to the Supplementary Fund are to be made in respect of each Member State by any person who, in any calendar year, has received total quantities of oil exceeding 150,000 tonnes after sea transport in ports and terminal installations in that State. However, the contribution system for the Supplementary Fund differs from that of the 1992 Fund in that at least 1 million tonnes of contributing oil will be deemed to have been received each year in each Member State for the purpose of paying contributions. That means that the Member State itself will be liable to pay contributions for a quantity of contributing oil corresponding to the difference between 1 million tonnes and the aggregate quantity of actual oil receipts reported in respect of that State.
- The Supplementary Fund only pays compensation for incidents which occur after the Protocol has entered into force for the affected State.

   1.66 Difficulties have arisen in some incidents involving the 1971 and 1992 Funds where the total amount of the claims arising from a given incident exceeded the total amount available for compensation or where there was a risk that this might occur. Under the Fund Conventions and the Supplementary Fund Protocol, the Funds are obliged to ensure that all claimants are given equal treatment. In a number of cases the 1971 and 1992 Funds therefore have had to limit (pro-rate) payments to victims to a percentage of the agreed amount of their claims. In most cases it eventually became possible to increase the level of payments to 100% once it was established that the total amount of admissible claims would not exceed the amount available for compensation, but in many cases the delay in payment of part of the compensation nevertheless caused financial hardship to victims – for example, fishermen and small businesses in the tourism sector. The 2003 Protocol will greatly improve the situation for victims in States becoming parties to it. In view of the very high amount available for compensation of pollution damage in these States, it should in practically all cases be possible to pay all established claims in full from the outset.

Consideration of a revision of the 1992 Conventions

1.67 In October 2005 the 1992 Fund Assembly considered the Working Group's final report on the question of whether the 1992 Conventions should be revised. The Working Group had been divided on the issue and had not been in a position to make a recommendation to the 1992 Fund Assembly. It was therefore for the Assembly to make a decision at this session on whether the revision should go ahead. Discussions that ensued reflected the continued division among Member States with one group supporting limited revision, and the other – holding a slighter majority – being strongly against revision and proposing to terminate the Working Group. The Assembly acknowledged that there was insufficient support to move forward with revision of the Conventions – even if limited – and therefore decided that the Working Group should be disbanded and that the revision of the Conventions should be removed from its agenda.

1.68 The deliberations in the Working Group had, in addition to the adoption of the 2003 Supplementary Fund Protocol, resulted in amendments of the 1992 Fund's Claims Manual in respect of the admissibility of claims for costs of reinstatement of the environment and costs of post-spill studies.

1.69 The Working Group had also considered several proposals for dealing with the substandard transportation of oil. The intention of these proposals was to provide disincentives to shipowners to use substandard ships by imposing higher limits of liability on such ships. Under one proposal, there would also be a liability on the cargo owner for pollution damage caused by such ships. Another proposal would have deprived the shipowners of their right to limit their liability if the incident had resulted from structural defects of the ships (i.e. defects due to decay or lack of maintenance). No decision was taken on any of these proposals. Some States considered, however, that the issue of substandard shipping was not within the field of competence of the 1992 Fund but fell within the exclusive competence of the IMO and should be dealt with in the relevant IMO Conventions (SOLAS and MARPOL).

STOPIA 2006 and TOPIA 2006

1.70 The two-tier international compensation regime created by the 1992 Civil Liability and Fund Conventions was intended to ensure an equitable sharing of the economic consequences of marine oil spills from tankers between the shipping and oil industries. In order to address the imbalance created by the establishment of the Supplementary Fund, which will be financed by the oil industry, the International Group of P&I Clubs (a group of 13 mutual insurers that between them provide liability insurance for about 98% of the world's tanker tonnage) has introduced, on a voluntary basis, a compensation package consisting of two agreements, the Small Tanker Oil Pollution Indemnification Agreement (STOPIA) 2006, and the Tanker Oil Pollution Indemnification Agreement (TOPIA) 2006. These contractually-binding agreements entered into force on 20 February 2006.

1.71 The 1992 Fund and the Supplementary Fund will in respect of incidents covered by STOPIA 2006 and TOPIA 2006 continue to be liable to compensate claimants in accordance with the 1992 Fund Convention and the Supplementary Fund Protocol respectively. The Funds will then be indemnified by the shipowner in accordance with STOPIA 2006 and TOPIA 2006. Under STOPIA 2006 the limitation amount is increased on a voluntary basis to 20 million SDR (US$30 million) for tankers up to 29,548 gross tonnage for damage in 1992 Fund Member States. Under TOPIA 2006, the Supplementary Fund is entitled to indemnification by the shipowner of 50% of the compensation payments it has made to claimants if the incident involved a ship covered by the agreement.

1.72 STOPIA 2006 and TOPIA 2006 also provide that a review should be carried out after 10 years of the experience of pollution damage claims during the period 2006–2016, and thereafter at five-year intervals.

HNS Convention

1.73 The International Convention on Liability and Compensation for Damage in Connection with the Carriage of Hazardous and Noxious Substances by Sea, 1996 (HNS Convention) was adopted by a Diplomatic Conference held in May 1996 under the auspices of the IMO. The Convention aims to ensure adequate, prompt and effective compensation for damage to persons and property, costs of clean-up and reinstatement measures and economic losses caused by the maritime transport of hazardous and noxious substances (HNS). The HNS Convention is to a very large extent modelled on the 1992 Conventions.

1.74 HNS include bulk solids, liquids including oils, liquefied gases such as liquefied natural gases (LNG) and liquefied petroleum gases (LPG), and packaged substances. Some bulk solids such as coal and iron ore are excluded because of the low hazards they present. Loss or damage caused by non-persistent oil is covered as is non-pollution damage caused by persistent oil. Pollution damage caused by persistent oil is excluded since such damage is already covered by the existing regime on liability and compensation for oil pollution from tankers, i.e. the 1992 Civil Liability Convention, the 1992 Fund Convention and the Supplementary Fund Protocol. Loss or damage caused by radioactive materials is also excluded.

1.75 The HNS Convention establishes a "two tier" compensation regime. The first tier is provided by the individual shipowner and the insurer and the second tier by the International Hazardous and Noxious Substances Fund (HNS Fund), contributed to by receivers of HNS after sea transport in all States Parties to the Convention. The shipowner is liable up to the following limits: 10 million SDR (US$14.9 million) for ships up to 2,000 units of gross tonnage (GT), rising to 100 million SDR (US$149 million) for ships of 100,000 GT or over. The HNS Fund will provide additional compensation up to a maximum of 250 million SDR (US$372 million), including the amount paid by the shipowner and the insurer.

1.76 The HNS Convention will enter into force 18 months after ratification by at least 12 States, subject to the following conditions: in the previous calendar year a total of at least 40 million tonnes of cargo consisting of bulk solids and other HNS liable for contributions to the general account was received in States which have ratified the Convention; and four of these States each have ships with a total tonnage of at least 2 million GT.

1.77 As at 31 August 2006, eight States (Angola, Cyprus, Morocco, the Russian Federation, Saint Kitts and Nevis, Samoa, Slovenia and Tonga) had ratified the Convention.

CONCLUDING REMARKS

1.78 The international compensation regimes established under the Civil Liability and Fund Conventions are one of the most successful compensation schemes in existence over the years. Most compensation claims have been settled amicably as a result of negotiations.

1.79 When the 1971 Fund was set up in 1978 it had only 14 Member States. Over the years the number of 1992 Fund Member States has increased to 98. It is expected that a number of States will ratify the 1992 Conventions in the near future. This increase in the number of Member States appears to indicate that the Governments have in general considered the international compensation regime to be working well. This explains why the regime based on the 1992 Conventions has served as a model for the creation of liability and compensation systems in other fields, such as the carriage of hazardous and noxious substances by sea.

1.80 As a result of recent major incidents, the compensation regime based on the 1992 Conventions became subject to criticism for not providing adequate protection to victims of oil pollution. The 1992 Fund's Member States have listened to this criticism and have taken it into account in a constructive way in the review of the adequacy of the regime which began in 2000. Steps to that effect were taken by the increases in the limits of liability and compensation which entered into force on 1 November 2003, by the adoption in May 2003 of the Protocol establishing a Supplementary Fund and by amendments to the Claims Manual in respect of the cost of post-spill studies and the costs of reinstatement of the polluted environment.

APPENDIX

1.81 States parties to both the 1992 Civil Liability Convention and the 1992 Fund Convention
(and therefore Members of the 1992 Fund)
as at 31 August 2006

95 States for which 1992 Fund Convention is in force		
Albania	Germany	Papua New Guinea
Algeria	Ghana	Philippines
Angola	Greece	Poland
Antigua and Barbuda	Grenada	Portugal
Argentina	Guinea	Qatar
Australia	Iceland	Republic of Korea
Bahamas	India	Russian Federation
Bahrain	Ireland	Saint Kitts and Nevis
Barbados	Israel	Saint Lucia
Belgium	Italy	Saint Vincent and the
Belize	Jamaica	Grenadines
Brunei Darussalam	Japan	Samoa
Cambodia	Kenya	Seychelles
Cameroon	Latvia	Sierra Leone
Canada	Liberia	Singapore
Cape Verde	Lithuania	Slovenia
China (Hong Kong Special	Madagascar	South Africa
Administrative Region)	Malaysia	Spain
Colombia	Maldives	Sri Lanka
Comoros	Malta	Sweden
Congo	Marshall Islands	Tonga
Croatia	Mauritius	Trinidad and Tobago
Cyprus	Mexico	Tunisia
Denmark	Monaco	Turkey
Djibouti	Morocco	Tuvalu
Dominica	Mozambique	United Arab Emirates
Dominican Republic	Namibia	United Kingdom
Estonia	Netherlands	United Republic of Tanzania
Fiji	New Zealand	Uruguay
Finland	Nigeria	Vanuatu
France	Norway	Venezuela
Gabon	Oman	
Georgia	Panama	

Three States which have deposited instruments of accession, but for which the 1992 Fund Convention does not enter into force until date indicated	
Switzerland	10 October 2006
Bulgaria	18 November 2006
Luxembourg	21 November 2006

States parties to the Supplementary Fund Protocol
(and therefore Members of the Supplementary Fund)
as at 31 August 2006

18 States for which the 2003 Supplementary Fund Protocol is in force		
Barbados	Germany	Netherlands
Belgium	Ireland	Norway
Croatia	Italy	Portugal
Denmark	Latvia	Slovenia
Finland	Lithuania	Spain
France	Japan	Sweden
One State which has deposited an instrument of accession but for which the Protocol does not enter into force until date indicated		
United Kingdom		8 September 2006

States parties to the 1992 Civil Liability Convention but not to the 1992 Fund Convention
(and therefore not Members of the 1992 Fund)
as at 31 August 2006

14 States for which the 1992 Civil Liability Convention is in force		
Azerbaijan	Indonesia	Saudi Arabia
Chile	Kuwait	Solomon Islands
China	Lebanon	Syrian Arab Republic
Egypt	Pakistan	Viet Nam
El Salvador	Romania	
Two States which have deposited an instrument of accession but for which the 1992 Civil Liability Convention does not enter into force until date indicated		
Peru		1 September 2006
Republic of Moldova		11 October 2006

States parties to the 1969 Civil Liability Convention
as at 31 August 2006

39 States parties to the 1969 Civil Liability Convention		
Azerbaijan	Georgia	Maldives
Benin	Ghana	Mauritania
Brazil	Guatemala	Mongolia
Cambodia	Guyana	Nicaragua
Chile	Honduras	Peru
Costa Rica	Indonesia	Saint Kitts and Nevis
Côte d'Ivoire	Jordan	Sao Tomé and Principe
Dominican Republic	Kazakhstan	Saudi Arabia
Ecuador	Kuwait	Senegal
Egypt	Latvia	Serbia and Montenegro
El Salvador	Lebanon	Syrian Arab Republic
Equatorial Guinea	Libyan Arab Jamahiriya	United Arab Emirates
Gambia	Luxembourg	Yemen
One State which has deposited an instrument of denunciation which will take effect on the date indicated		
Luxembourg		21 November 2006

Note: The 1971 Fund Convention ceased to be in force on 24 May 2002

CHAPTER 2

Pollution from ships: EU Directive on criminal sanctions for ship-source pollution

COLIN DE LA RUE*

2.1 The *Erika* and *Prestige* incidents have been unparalleled by any other oil spills in Europe, and they have stimulated change in the law relating to maritime safety and marine pollution.

2.2 Some of the measures taken have raised issues of fundamental importance in relation both to criminal as well as civil liability regimes. In the criminal sphere debate has been dominated by the EU Directive on Criminal Sanctions for Ship-source Pollution. Although primarily concerned with criminal responsibility, the Directive is a debate that has centred not only on the content of the Directive itself but also on the wider relationship between EU legislation and global regulation of the maritime industry.

2.3 Earlier this summer the High Court in London handed down an important decision in proceedings brought to test the validity of the Directive. Mr Justice Hodge delivered a reserved judgment in which he held that the coalition had well-founded arguments for challenging the legal validity of the Directive. These are based mainly on conflict between the Directive and international law.

2.4 Granting permission for the action to proceed, the judge decided that a number of questions relating to the validity of the Directive should be referred to the European Court of Justice in Luxembourg, which may be expected to hear the matter next year.

2.5 This is of an unusual lawsuit, without direct precedent in the maritime sector, and understandably there have been many questions from the sidelines as to what the proceedings involve.

BACKGROUND

2.6 The background is well known. In November 2002 the single-hull tanker *Prestige* got into difficulties off Spain but was refused access to sheltered waters and sank six days later some 230km west of Portugal. Much of her cargo of heavy fuel oil was released and polluted long stretches of coastline in France as well as on the Iberian peninsula.

2.7 Re-opening wounds in Spain from the *Aegean Sea* major oil spill in 1992 and in France from the *Erika* disaster of 1999, the *Prestige* unleashed great political pressure in Europe for new laws designed, as the Commission put it, to "tighten the net".

---

* Partner, Ince & Co.

Regulation of the maritime industry

2.8 In the international community it has long been agreed that the maritime industry should be governed by uniform international laws and regulations. There are many practical reasons why this is important, and why a plethora of conflicting national regulations would result in commercial distortion whilst compromising ship safety and efficiency of world trade.

2.9 Since 1958 international law in this field has been developed under the auspices of the International Maritime Organisation (IMO), a specialised agency of the UN with its headquarters in London and 166 member states. Some 40 or so IMO conventions and protocols have been adopted, including notably the Safety of Life at Sea Conventions (SOLAS) and the International Convention for the Prevention of Pollution from Ships (MARPOL), and these have been replicated on a uniform basis in the national laws of member states around the world.

2.10 MARPOL is the main international instrument dealing with prevention of pollution from ships. It was adopted in 1973, modified by a Protocol of 1978, and came into force in 1983. MARPOL has been amended many times under the auspices of the IMO, and it is in force in all EU states.

Operational discharges and accidental spills

2.11 MARPOL differentiates between pollution caused by "operational" discharges and spills resulting from maritime accidents. Operational discharges involve deliberate releases of oily wastes in circumstances which may or may not be permissible under international law. MARPOL recognises that ships need to dispose of oily wastes which accumulate on board, and it encourages States to install reception facilities enabling this to be done ashore. It also recognises that there are many ports where reception facilities are not available. It therefore allows oily wastes to be discharged into the sea provided certain stringent conditions are met, relating to such matters as the distance from land, the oil content of the effluent, the rate of discharge, and protection of special areas.

2.12 Operational discharges which contravene these restrictions are violations of international law, and contracting states are required to impose penalties on offenders which are adequate in severity to discourage them.

2.13 Accidental discharges, on the other hand, raise different issues and are treated differently in MARPOL. A discharge does not constitute a breach of international law when it results from damage to a ship or its equipment – e.g. as a result of a collision or grounding. In such a case a violation of MARPOL is committed only if there has been a failure to act reasonably to minimize damage after discovering the discharge, or if the owner or the master acted either with intent to cause damage, or recklessly and with knowledge that damage would probably result.

2.14 Accordingly, on international law as it stands, there should be no criminal implications involved where pollution results from a genuine accident. There may be very significant civil liabilities, but those caught up in the incident would not be branded as criminals.

2.15 So much for the theory. However familiar it may be to those involved in shipping, all over the world the two different types of case are commonly confused.

Regrettably ships' engineers have sometimes succumbed to temptation, with or without the knowledge of their owners and masters, to carry out operational discharges in breach of the applicable controls. The response to rogue operations of this kind is rightly one of outrage, but there has been a tendency for complex accidental incidents to be tarred with the same brush.

2.16 So it came about that the *Prestige*, an accidental spill, brought in its wake powerful demands for new laws in Europe to crack down on what the French President called "gangsters of the seas".

THE EU DIRECTIVE

2.17 In March 2003, less than four months after the *Prestige* sank, a draft was on the table of a directive imposing criminal liability for all "illegal discharges" committed with gross negligence, without distinction between the illicit activities of rogue operators and maritime accidents which may happen to anyone.

2.18 A report of the European Parliament expressed a number of legal objections to the draft: whilst professing to give effect to MARPOL, it in fact conflicted with the Convention by imposing criminal liability for accidental discharges in circumstances where there would be no offence in international law. In particular it would alter the effect of Regulation 11(b) by making it unavailable where the discharge resulted from the defendant's "serious negligence".

2.19 The notion of "serious negligence" is not a legally established concept, but is uncertain and prone to mislead. In the Directive it is unaccompanied by any criteria or guidance as to what it is intended to mean. Experience shows that in a significant oil spill there is a risk of subjective elements impinging on the decision to prosecute, as the seriousness of alleged negligence may all too readily be judged by the consequences of the incident rather than the culpability of the defendant's actions.

2.20 The Parliamentary Report noted that the meaning of this phrase was uncertain, and that there were various respects in which the proposed Directive was unclear.

2.21 These criticisms reflected widespread concerns about the draft Directive which were voiced by several industry bodies, by speakers at international conferences and seminars, and by Governments. However, these objections were substantially overruled in the subsequent political process. Despite opposition from Greece, Malta and Cyprus the EU Directive 2005/35/EC of 7 September 2005 on Ship-source Pollution and on the Introduction of Penalties for Infringements was published on 30 September 2005 and came into effect the following day.

2.22 In its final form the Directive remains controversial for much the same reasons as those expressed ever since the first draft. The essence of the controversy was highlighted at the Eighth Annual Cadwallader Memorial Lecture in London on 4 October 2005 when the eminent jurist Dr Thomas Mensah, a recently retired judge and former presiding judge of the Law of the Sea Tribunal in Hamburg, gave a public lecture expressing the view that the Directive does not conform with international law.

2.23 Member states are required to implement the Directive by 1 March 2007.

INTERTANKO AND OTHERS v SECRETARY OF STATE FOR TRANSPORT

2.24 Legal action to test the validity of the Directive was started on 23 December 2005 when an application for judicial review was filed in the Administrative Court of the High Court of Justice in London. The proceedings named as defendant the Secretary of State for the Department for Transport and were brought by the industry coalition consisting of INTERTANKO, INTERCARGO, the Greek Shipping Co-operation Committee, Lloyd's Register and the International Salvage Union.

2.25 Previous rulings of the ECJ have established that EU legislation cannot validly put Member States in breach of existing treaty obligations. The coalition contends that implementation of the Directive would have this effect as MARPOL imposes a treaty obligation to legislate in accordance with the regulations set out in Annexes I and II to the Convention. All EU member states are parties to MARPOL and must therefore adhere to the provisions of these Annexes.

2.26 For technical reasons the coalition does not have direct access to the ECJ, but the issue could be referred to it for a preliminary ruling in proceedings brought in the courts of a Member State. The High Court in London was chosen as the route to the ECJ partly because the coalition members all have offices in the UK, and partly because there is established precedent for similar cases being referred to the ECJ by the courts in London. Previous cases have established that the High Court is prepared to refer issues to Luxembourg in proceedings for judicial review of EU law without waiting for implementing legislation to be introduced in the UK.

2.27 References to the European Court are not made lightly. The ECJ has a great deal of business on its plate, and significant work is involved in translating the documents for the benefit of Community governments, who are entitled to intervene. Claimants have to show that they have "well founded" arguments, which the court interpreted to mean having "a reasonable prospect of success".

2.28 In a detailed reserved judgment Mr Justice Hodge gave reasons for referring four key issues to the ECJ. These are:

(1) whether it is lawful for the EU to impose criminal liability in respect of discharges from foreign flag ships on the high seas or in the Exclusive Economic Zone, and to limit MARPOL defences in such cases;
(2) whether it is lawful for the EU to exclude MARPOL defences for discharges in the territorial sea;
(3) whether the imposition of criminal liability for discharges caused by "serious negligence" hampers the right of innocent passage;
(4) whether the standard of liability in the Directive of "serious negligence" satisfies the requirement of legal certainty.

2.29 The first of the four questions referred to the ECJ concerns the effect of the Directive outside territorial waters. Under the UN Convention on the Law of the Sea (UNCLOS) a state has jurisdiction over discharges on the high seas only when these come from vessels which are flying its flag or where its legislation implements international rules. Within the Exclusive Economic Zone (EEZ) of a state its competence to legislate is limited to giving effect to general international standards.

2.30 The claimants argued that the relevant international standards are those set out in MARPOL, and that the Directive goes beyond them inasmuch as it imposes liability for discharges in cases of serious negligence by persons other than the owner, master or crew. The judge agreed with the claimants that all persons associated with ships – not only the owner, master and crew – would normally be entitled to rely on provisions in MARPOL Annexes I and II which restrict liability to cases of intent or recklessness. He held that it was clear that the Directive, by limiting the effect of these regulations, changes the position; and he shared the doubts (which had been expressed by the Secretary of State as well as by the claimants) that the EU had power under international law to legislate in this way for foreign flagged ships. The judge therefore referred to the ECJ the question whether it is lawful for the EU to legislate independently of MARPOL for foreign flagged ships on the high seas or in the EEZ.

2.31 Next the judge considered the effect of the Directive in territorial waters, where it imposes criminal liability for all discharges caused by serious negligence, and where it precludes any defendant – even the owner, master or crew – from taking advantage of the MARPOL regulations which restrict liability to cases of intent or recklessness.

2.32 The claimants maintained that MARPOL Annexes I and II provide a uniform set of rules from which contracting states cannot depart without denouncing the Convention unless it is amended. Despite the procedure available for speedy amendment of MARPOL by tacit acceptance, no proposals have been made by any European or other MARPOL states for the relevant regulations to be changed.

2.33 The defendant's stance, in line with that of the Commission, was that Article 9(2) of MARPOL provided that nothing in the Convention was to prejudice the "codification and development of the Law of the Sea by the United Nations Conference", and that under UNCLOS coastal states retain sovereign power to legislate as they see fit for their territorial sea, subject to rights of innocent passage. On this basis it was contended that in the territorial sea MARPOL was only a minimum standards regime, and that it did not preclude states from imposing more stringent requirements.

2.34 The claimants' response was that MARPOL, when read together with UNCLOS, is properly understood as an agreement among states that their sovereign rights in international law should on this subject be exercised in a uniform manner. Article 9(2) of MARPOL was designed simply to avoid any argument that the Convention could be seen as evidence of the views of states as to the full extent of their sovereign rights for the purposes of UNCLOS.

2.35 The judge referred to provisions in MARPOL which stipulate that contracting states are bound by Annexes I and II in their entirety; to the intention of the 1973 Conference, as expressed in the Preamble, to adopt rules of "universal purport"; and to records of the Conference showing that states rejected both a Canadian proposal that the Convention be treated as a minimum standards regime, and a compromise text which would have allowed a degree of departure from the agreed uniform standards.

2.36 The judge held that the claimants had well-founded arguments and decided to refer to the ECJ the question whether it is lawful for the EU to legislate for the territorial sea otherwise than in accordance with MARPOL.

2.37 As a third issue, the claimants contended that the effect of the Directive in territorial seas is not only incompatible with MARPOL but also contravenes UNCLOS on the grounds that it hampers the right of innocent passage. They argued that under UNCLOS only "wilful and serious" pollution should affect this right, and that it is hampered if legislation of the coastal state lowers the threshold of liability to one of serious negligence. In support of this view the claimants cited the analysis contained in a paper given by Dr Thomas Mensah, the former Presiding Judge of the International Tribunal for the Law of the Sea (ITLOS) in Hamburg.

2.38 Mr Justice Hodge held that it is "clearly arguable" that the adoption of the Directive potentially hampers the right of innocent passage. "There are differing obligations", he said, "under the Directive and under the international regimes provided for in MARPOL and UNCLOS. This creates potential difficult legal problems in the relationship between parties to the international instruments who are not member states of the EU and a state which implements the Directive." Here again he held that the coalition's argument had a reasonable prospect of success and that the issue merited a reference to the European Court of Justice.

2.39 The fourth question is whether the standard of liability of "serious negligence" is consistent with the requirement in EU law of legal certainty. The claimants contended that the phrase does not have a clearly-defined meaning and that, in the highly charged context of a serious oil spill, there would be a risk of subjectivity infecting any decision to prosecute. The defendant argued that the phrase was sufficiently precise but the judge did not agree. "There is arguably a need", he said, "for some factors to be set out to guide member states as to when the standard of 'serious negligence' is satisfied. Without such a provision there may be a danger of different states implementing the Directive in a different manner." Accordingly, he found the claimants' contention to be well founded for the purpose of a reference to the European Court.

2.40 The case is therefore now being transferred to the ECJ where a hearing and decision may be expected next year. Only the Luxembourg court can give a decisive ruling, and this must be awaited before it can be said whether the industry's objections to the Directive have been upheld.

2.41 In the meantime this much already is clear. The ECJ will hear the case only because a procedure exists in this instance for a complaint based on international law to be taken to court by industry interests. Often this is not the case.

2.42 The unusual nature of these proceedings does not reflect the growing frequency of concerns that coastal state authorities, in their reaction to serious incidents, or in a commendable resolve to eliminate pollution from ships, have at times resorted to measures perilously close to or beyond the boundaries of international law – whether by forcing single hull tankers 200 miles offshore, by forcing ships into port from outside territorial waters for suspected MARPOL violations, by unfair treatment of seafarers involved in maritime accidents, or by enacting legislation at odds with agreed uniform standards.

2.43 This is not to say that governments routinely flout international law, but that it is often difficult or impossible for reasonable concerns to be raised. Generally only governments have the standing to take other states to court for breach of treaty obligations, but in the maritime sector they have seldom seen any public interest in doing so. Normally the impact is limited to private parties who do not have access to the competent international tribunals.

2.44 This not only means that well-founded grievances may go without remedy; it can also lead to governments taking measures which are guided less by international law than by the precedent of other states acquiescing in departures from it. At best this engenders uncertainty as to where people stand; at worst it undermines respect for international legal order.

2.45 The action taken by the coalition has been brought by responsible organisations for the constructive purpose of clarifying important issues of international law. Underpinning this is the belief that fair and respectful treatment should be accorded to seafarers and as well as others engaged in an industry which is vital to the global economy, and which provides an efficient and environmentally sensitive solution to transportation of goods and raw materials in bulk.

2.46 Whatever their outcome, these proceedings should be welcomed by anyone committed to global regulation of shipping. Hopefully they will serve among other things to encourage governments to review the rules which currently restrict access to ITLOS and other tribunals in the law of the sea, and to facilitate similar well-founded steps to test important issues of international law.

APPENDIX

2.47 DIRECTIVE 2005/35/EC OF THE EUROPEAN PARLIAMENT AND OF THE COUNCIL

of 7 September 2005

on ship-source pollution and on the introduction of penalties for infringements

THE EUROPEAN PARLIAMENT AND THE COUNCIL OF THE EUROPEAN UNION,

Having regard to the Treaty establishing the European Community, and in particular Article 80(2) thereof,

Having regard to the proposal from the Commission,

Having regard to the opinion of the European Economic and Social Committee,[1]

After consulting the Committee of the Regions,

Acting in accordance with the procedure laid down in Article 251 of the Treaty,[2]

Whereas:
(1) The Community's maritime safety policy is aimed at a high level of safety and environmental protection and is based on the understanding that all parties involved in the transport of goods by sea have a responsibility for ensuring that ships used in Community waters comply with applicable rules and standards.
(2) The material standards in all Member States for discharges of polluting substances from ships are based upon the Marpol 73/78 Convention; however these rules are being ignored on a daily basis by a very large number of ships sailing in Community waters, without corrective action being taken.
(3) The implementation of Marpol 73/78 shows discrepancies among Member States and there is thus a need to harmonise its implementation at Community level; in particular

1. OJ C 220, 16.9.2003, p. 72.
2. Opinion of the European Parliament of 13 January 2004 (OJ C 92 E, 16.4.2004, p. 77), Council Common Position of 7 October 2004 (OJ C 25 E, 1.2.2005, p. 29), Position of the European Parliament of 23 February 2005 (not yet published in the Official Journal) and Council Decision of 12 July 2005.

the practices of Member States relating to the imposition of penalties for discharges of polluting substances from ships differ significantly.

(4) Measures of a dissuasive nature form an integral part of the Community's maritime safety policy, as they ensure a link between the responsibility of each of the parties involved in the transport of polluting goods by sea and their exposure to penalties; in order to achieve effective protection of the environment there is therefore a need for effective, dissuasive and proportionate penalties.

(5) To that end it is essential to approximate, by way of the proper legal instruments, existing legal provisions, in particular on the precise definition of the infringement in question, the cases of exemption and minimum rules for penalties, and on liability and jurisdiction.

(6) This Directive is supplemented by detailed rules on criminal offences and penalties as well as other provisions set out in Council Framework Decision 2005/667/JHA of 12 July 2005 to strengthen the criminal law framework for the enforcement of the law against ship-source pollution.[3]

(7) Neither the international regime for the civil liability and compensation of oil pollution nor that relating to pollution by other hazardous or noxious substances provides sufficient dissuasive effects to discourage the parties involved in the transport of hazardous cargoes by sea from engaging in substandard practices; the required dissuasive effects can only be achieved through the introduction of penalties applying to any person who causes or contributes to marine pollution; penalties should be applicable not only to the shipowner or the master of the ship, but also the owner of the cargo, the classification society or any other person involved.

(8) Ship-source discharges of polluting substances should be regarded as infringements if committed with intent, recklessly or by serious negligence. These infringements are regarded as criminal offences by, and in the circumstances provided for in, Framework Decision 2005/667/JHA supplementing this Directive.

(9) Penalties for discharges of polluting substances from ships are not related to the civil liability of the parties concerned and are thus not subject to any rules relating to the limitation or channelling of civil liabilities, nor do they limit the efficient compensation of victims of pollution incidents.

(10) There is a need for further effective cooperation among Member States to ensure that discharges of polluting substances from ships are detected in time and that the offenders are identified. For this reason, the European Maritime Safety Agency set up by Regulation (EC) No. 1406/2002 of the European Parliament and of the Council of 27 June 2002[4] has a key role to play in working with the Member States in developing technical solutions and providing technical assistance relating to the implementation of this Directive and in assisting the Commission in the performance of any task assigned to it for the effective implementation of this Directive.

(11) In order better to prevent and combat marine pollution, synergies should be created between enforcement authorities such as national coastguard services. In this context, the Commission should undertake a feasibility study on a European coastguard dedicated to pollution prevention and response, making clear the costs and benefits. This study should, if appropriate, be followed by a proposal on a European coastguard.

(12) Where there is clear, objective evidence of a discharge causing major damage or a threat of major damage, Member States should submit the matter to their competent authorities with a view to instituting proceedings in accordance with Article 220 of the 1982 United Nations Convention on the Law of the Sea.

(13) The enforcement of Directive 2000/59/EC of the European Parliament and of the Council of 27 November 2000 on port reception facilities for ship-generated waste and cargo residues[5] is, together with this Directive, a key instrument in the set of measures to prevent ship-source pollution.

3. See page 164 of this Official Journal.
4. OJ L 208, 5.8.2002, p. 1. Regulation as last amended by Regulation (EC) No. 724/2004 (OJ L 129, 29.4.2004, p. 1).
5. OJ L 332, 28.12.2000, p. 81. Directive as amended by Directive 2002/84/EC (OJ L 324, 29.11.2002, p. 53).

(14) The measures necessary for the implementation of this Directive should be adopted in accordance with Council Decision 1999/468/EC of 28 June 1999 laying down the procedures for the exercise of implementing powers conferred on the Commission.[6]

(15) Since the objectives of this Directive, namely the incorporation of the international ship-source pollution standards into Community law and the establishment of penalties – criminal or administrative – for violation of them in order to ensure a high level of safety and environmental protection in maritime transport, cannot be sufficiently achieved by the Member States and can therefore be better achieved at Community level, the Community may adopt measures, in accordance with the principle of subsidiarity as set out in Article 5 of the Treaty. In accordance with the principle of proportionality, as set out in that Article, this Directive does not go beyond what is necessary in order to achieve those objectives.

(16) This Directive fully respects the Charter of fundamental rights of the European Union; any person suspected of having committed an infringement must be guaranteed a fair and impartial hearing and the penalties must be proportional,

HAVE ADOPTED THIS DIRECTIVE:

Article 1 – Purpose

1. The purpose of this Directive is to incorporate international standards for ship-source pollution into Community law and to ensure that persons responsible for discharges are subject to adequate penalties as referred to in Article 8, in order to improve maritime safety and to enhance protection of the marine environment from pollution by ships.

2. This Directive does not prevent Member States from taking more stringent measures against ship-source pollution in conformity with international law.

Article 2 – Definitions

For the purpose of this Directive:

1. "Marpol 73/78" shall mean the International Convention for the Prevention of Pollution from Ships, 1973 and its 1978 Protocol, in its up-to-date version;

2. "polluting substances" shall mean substances covered by Annexes I (oil) and II (noxious liquid substances in bulk) to Marpol 73/78;

3. "discharge" shall mean any release howsoever caused from a ship, as referred to in Article 2 of Marpol 73/78;

4. "ship" shall mean a seagoing vessel, irrespective of its flag, of any type whatsoever operating in the marine environment and shall include hydrofoil boats, air-cushion vehicles, submersibles and floating craft.

Article 3 – Scope

1. This Directive shall apply, in accordance with international law, to discharges of polluting substances in:
   (a) the internal waters, including ports, of a Member State, in so far as the Marpol regime is applicable;
   (b) the territorial sea of a Member State;
   (c) straits used for international navigation subject to the regime of transit passage, as laid down in Part III, section 2, of the 1982 United Nations Convention on the Law of the Sea, to the extent that a Member State exercises jurisdiction over such straits;
   (d) the exclusive economic zone or equivalent zone of a Member State, established in accordance with international law; and
   (e) the high seas.

2. This Directive shall apply to discharges of polluting substances from any ship, irrespective of its flag, with the exception of any warship, naval auxiliary or other ship owned or operated by a State and used, for the time being, only on government non-commercial service.

---

6. OJ L 184, 17.7.1999, p. 23.

Article 4 – Infringements

Member States shall ensure that ship-source discharges of polluting substances into any of the areas referred to in Article 3(1) are regarded as infringements if committed with intent, recklessly or by serious negligence. These infringements are regarded as criminal offences by, and in the circumstances provided for in, Framework Decision 2005/667/JHA supplementing this Directive.

Article 5 – Exceptions

1. A discharge of polluting substances into any of the areas referred to in Article 3(1) shall not be regarded as an infringement if it satisfies the conditions set out in Annex I, Regulations 9, 10, 11(a) or 11(c) or in Annex II, Regulations 5, 6(a) or 6(c) of Marpol 73/78.
2. A discharge of polluting substances into the areas referred to in Article 3(1)(c), (d) and (e) shall not be regarded as an infringement for the owner, the master or the crew when acting under the master's responsibility if it satisfies the conditions set out in Annex I, Regulation 11(b) or in Annex II, Regulation 6(b) of Marpol 73/78.

Article 6 – Enforcement measures with respect to ships within a port of a Member State

1. If irregularities or information give rise to a suspicion that a ship which is voluntarily within a port or at an off-shore terminal of a Member State has been engaged in or is engaging in a discharge of polluting substances into any of the areas referred to in Article 3(1), that Member State shall ensure that an appropriate inspection, taking into account the relevant guidelines adopted by the International Maritime Organisation (IMO), is undertaken in accordance with its national law.
2. In so far as the inspection referred to in paragraph 1 reveals facts that could indicate an infringement within the meaning of Article 4, the competent authorities of that Member State and of the flag State shall be informed.

Article 7 – Enforcement measures by coastal States with respect to ships in transit

1. If the suspected discharge of polluting substances takes place in the areas referred to in Article 3(1)(b), (c), (d) or (e) and the ship which is suspected of the discharge does not call at a port of the Member State holding the information relating to the suspected discharge, the following shall apply:
    (a) If the next port of call of the ship is in another Member State, the Member States concerned shall cooperate closely in the inspection referred to in Article 6(1) and in deciding on the appropriate measures in respect of any such discharge;
    (b) If the next port of call of the ship is a port of a State outside the Community, the Member State shall take the necessary measures to ensure that the next port of call of the ship is informed about the suspected discharge and shall request the State of the next port of call to take the appropriate measures in respect of any such discharge.
2. Where there is clear, objective evidence that a ship navigating in the areas referred to in Article 3(1)(b) or (d) has, in the area referred to in Article 3(1)(d), committed an infringement resulting in a discharge causing major damage or a threat of major damage to the coastline or related interests of the Member State concerned, or to any resources of the areas referred to in Article 3(1)(b) or (d), that State shall, subject to Part XII, Section 7 of the 1982 United Nations Convention on the Law of the Sea and provided that the evidence so warrants, submit the matter to its competent authorities with a view to instituting proceedings, including detention of the ship, in accordance with its national law.
3. In any event, the authorities of the flag State shall be informed.

Article 8 – Penalties

1. Member States shall take the necessary measures to ensure that infringements within the meaning of Article 4 are subject to effective, proportionate and dissuasive penalties, which may include criminal or administrative penalties.

2. Each Member State shall take the measures necessary to ensure that the penalties referred to in paragraph 1 apply to any person who is found responsible for an infringement within the meaning of Article 4.

Article 9 – Compliance with international law

Member States shall apply the provisions of this Directive without any discrimination in form or in fact against foreign ships and in accordance with applicable international law, including Section 7 of Part XII of the 1982 United Nations Convention on the Law of the Sea, and they shall promptly notify the flag State of the vessel and any other State concerned of measures taken in accordance with this Directive.

Article 10 – Accompanying measures

1. For the purposes of this Directive, Member States and the Commission shall cooperate, where appropriate, in close collaboration with the European Maritime Safety Agency and taking account of the action programme to respond to accidental or deliberate marine pollution set up by Decision No 2850/2000/EC[7] and if appropriate, of the implementation of Directive 2000/59/EC in order to:
    (a) develop the necessary information systems required for the effective implementation of this Directive;
    (b) establish common practices and guidelines on the basis of those existing at international level, in particular for:
        – the monitoring and early identification of ships discharging polluting substances in violation of this Directive, including, where appropriate, on-board monitoring equipment,
        – reliable methods of tracing polluting substances in the sea to a particular ship, and
        – the effective enforcement of this Directive.
2. In accordance with its tasks as defined in Regulation (EC) No 1406/2002, the European Maritime Safety Agency shall:
    (a) work with the Member States in developing technical solutions and providing technical assistance in relation to the implementation of this Directive, in actions such as tracing discharges by satellite monitoring and surveillance;
    (b) assist the Commission in the implementation of this Directive, including, if appropriate, by means of visits to the Member States, in accordance with Article 3 of Regulation (EC) No 1406/2002.

Article 11 – Feasibility Study

The Commission shall, before the end of 2006, submit to the European Parliament and the Council a feasibility study on a European coastguard dedicated to pollution prevention and response, making clear the costs and benefits.

Article 12 – Reporting

Every three years, Member States shall transmit a report to the Commission on the application of this Directive by the competent authorities. On the basis of these reports, the Commission shall submit a Community report to the European Parliament and the Council. In this report, the Commission shall assess, *inter alia*, the desirability of revising or extending the scope of this Directive. It shall also describe the evolution of relevant case-law in the Member States and shall consider the possibility of creating a public database containing such relevant case-law.

---

7. Decision No 2850/2000/EC of the European Parliament and of the Council of 20 December 2000 setting up a Community framework for cooperation in the field of accidental or deliberate marine pollution (OJ L 332, 28.12.2000, p. 1). Decision as amended by Decision No. 787/2004/EC (OJ L 138, 30.4.2004, p. 12).

Article 13 – Committee procedure

1. The Commission shall be assisted by the Committee on Safe Seas and the Prevention of Pollution from Ships (COSS), established by Article 3 of Regulation (EC) No 2099/2002 of the European Parliament and of the Council, of 5 November 2002.[8]
2. Where reference is made to this Article, Articles 5 and 7 of Decision 1999/468/EC shall apply, having regard to the provisions of Article 8 thereof.

The period laid down in Article 5(6) of Decision 1999/468/EC shall be set at one month.

Article 14 – Provision of information

The Commission shall regularly inform the Committee set up by Article 4 of Decision No 2850/2000/EC of any proposed measures or other relevant activities concerning the response to marine pollution.

Article 15 – Amendment procedure

In accordance with Article 5 of Regulation (EC) No 2099/2002 and following the procedure referred to in Article 13 of this Directive, the COSS may exclude amendments to Marpol 73/78 from the scope of this Directive.

Article 16 – Implementation

Member States shall bring into force the laws, regulations and administrative provisions necessary to comply with this Directive by 1 March 2007 and forthwith inform the Commission thereof.

When Member States adopt those provisions, they shall contain a reference to this Directive or be accompanied by such a reference on the occasion of their official publication. Member States shall determine how such reference is to be made.

Article 17 – Entry into force

This Directive shall enter into force on the day following its publication in the Official Journal of the European Union.

Article 18 – Addressees

This Directive is addressed to the Member States.

Done at Strasbourg, 7 September 2005.

<table>
<tr><td>*For the European Parliament*</td><td>*For the Council*</td></tr>
<tr><td>*The President*</td><td>*The President*</td></tr>
<tr><td>J. BORRELL FONTELLES</td><td>C. CLARKE</td></tr>
</table>

ANNEX

Summary, for reference purposes, of the Marpol 73/78 discharge regulations relating to discharges of oil and noxious liquid substances, as referred to in Article 2.2

Part I: Oil (Marpol 73/78, Annex I)

For the purposes of Marpol 73/78 Annex I, "oil" means petroleum in any form including crude oil, fuel oil, sludge, oil refuse and refined products (other than petrochemicals which are subject to the provisions of Marpol 73/78 Annex II) and "oily mixture" means a mixture with any oil content.

Excerpts of the relevant provisions of Marpol 73/78 Annex I:

8. OJ L 324, 29.11.2002, p. 1. Regulation as amended by Commission Regulation (EC) No. 415/2004 (OJ L 68, 6.3.2004, p. 10).

Regulation 9: Control of discharge of oil

1. Subject to the provisions of Regulations 10 and 11 of this Annex and paragraph 2 of this Regulation, any discharge into the sea of oil or oily mixtures from ships to which this Annex applies shall be prohibited except when all the following conditions are satisfied:
    (a) for an oil tanker, except as provided for in subparagraph (b) of this paragraph:
        (i) the tanker is not within a special area;
        (ii) the tanker is more than 50 nautical miles from the nearest land;
        (iii) the tanker is proceeding en route;
        (iv) the instantaneous rate of discharge of oil content does not exceed 30 litres per nautical mile;
        (v) the total quantity of oil discharged into the sea does not exceed for existing tankers 1/15000 of the total quantity of the particular cargo of which the residue formed a part, and for new tankers 1/30000 of the total quantity of the particular cargo of which the residue formed a part; and
        (vi) the tanker has in operation an oil discharge monitoring and control system and a slop tank arrangement as required by Regulation 15 of this Annex.
    (b) from a ship of 400 tons gross tonnage and above other than an oil tanker and from machinery space bilges excluding cargo pump-room bilges of an oil tanker unless mixed with oil cargo residue:
        (i) the ship is not within a special area;
        (ii) the ship is proceeding en route;
        (iii) the oil content of the effluent without dilution does not exceed 15 parts per million; and
        (iv) the ship has in operation (monitoring, control and filtering equipment) as required by regulation 16 of this Annex.
2. In the case of a ship of less than 400 tons gross tonnage other than an oil tanker whilst outside the special area, the (flag State) Administration shall ensure that it is equipped as far as practicable and reasonable with installations to ensure the storage of oil residues on board and their discharge to reception facilities or into the sea in compliance with the requirements of paragraph (1)(b) of this Regulation.
3. [...].
4. The provisions of paragraph 1 of this Regulation shall not apply to the discharge of clean or segregated ballast or unprocessed oily mixtures which without dilution have an oil content not exceeding 15 parts per million and which do not originate from cargo pump-room bilges and are not mixed with oil cargo residues.
5. No discharge into the sea shall contain chemicals or other substances in quantities or concentrations which are hazardous to the marine environment or chemicals or other substances introduced for the purpose of circumventing the conditions of discharge specified in this regulation.
6. The oil residues which cannot be discharged into the sea in compliance with paragraphs 1, 2 and 4 of this Regulation shall be retained on board or discharged to reception facilities.
7. [...].

Regulation 10: Methods for the prevention of oil pollution from ships while operating in special areas

1. For the purpose of this Annex, the special areas are the Mediterranean Sea area, the Baltic Sea area, the Black Sea area, the Red Sea area, the "Gulfs area", the Gulf of Aden area, the Antarctic area and the North-West European waters, (as further defined and specified).
2. Subject to the provisions of regulation 11 of this Annex:
    (a) Any discharge into the sea of oil or oily mixture from any oil tanker and any ship of 400 tons gross tonnage and above other than an oil tanker shall be prohibited while in a special area. [...];
    (b) [...] Any discharge into the sea of oil or oily mixture from a ship of less than 400 tons gross tonnage, other than an oil tanker, shall be prohibited while in a special

area, except when the oil content of the effluent without dilution does not exceed 15 parts per million.

3. (a) The provisions of paragraph 2 of this Regulation shall not apply to the discharge of clean or segregated ballast.

(b) The provisions of subparagraph (2)(a) of this regulation shall not apply to the discharge of processed bilge water from machinery spaces, provided that all of the following conditions are satisfied:

(i) the bilge water does not originate from cargo pump-room bilges;

(ii) the bilge water is not mixed with oil cargo residues;

(iii) the ship is proceeding en route;

(iv) the oil content of the effluent without dilution does not exceed 15 parts per million;

(v) the ship has in operation oil filtering equipment complying with Regulation 16(5) of this Annex; and

(vi) the filtering system is equipped with a stopping device which will ensure that the discharge is automatically stopped when the oil content of the effluent exceeds 15 parts per million.

4. (a) No discharge into the sea shall contain chemicals or other substances in quantities or concentrations which are hazardous to the marine environment or chemicals or other substances introduced for the purpose of circumventing the conditions of discharge specified in this regulation.

(b) The oil residues which cannot be discharged into the sea in compliance with paragraph 2 or 3 of this Regulation shall be retained on board or discharged to reception facilities.

5. Nothing in this Regulation shall prohibit a ship on a voyage only part of which is in a special area from discharging outside the special area in accordance with Regulation 9 of this Annex.

6. [...].

7. [...].

8. [...].

Regulation 11: Exceptions

Regulations 9 and 10 of this Annex shall not apply to:

(a) the discharge into the sea of oil or oily mixture necessary for the purpose of securing the safety of a ship or saving life at sea; or

(b) the discharge into the sea of oil or oily mixture resulting from damage to a ship or its equipment:

(i) provided that all reasonable precautions have been taken after the occurrence of the damage or discovery of the discharge for the purpose of preventing or minimising the discharge; and

(ii) except if the owner or the master acted either with intent to cause damage, or recklessly and with knowledge that damage would probably result; or

(c) the discharge into the sea of substances containing oil, approved by the (flag State) administration, when being used for the purpose of combating specific pollution incidents in order to minimise the damage from pollution. Any such discharge shall be subject to the approval of any Government in whose jurisdiction it is contemplated the discharge will occur.

Part II: Noxious liquid substances (Marpol 73/78 Annex II)

Excerpts of the relevant provisions of Marpol 73/78 Annex II:

Regulation 3: Categorisation and listing of noxious liquid substances

1. For the purpose of the Regulations of this Annex, noxious liquid substances shall be divided into four categories as follows:

(a) Category A: noxious liquid substances which if discharged into the sea from tank cleaning or deballasting operations would present a major hazard to either marine resources or human health or cause serious harm to amenities or other legitimate uses of the sea and therefore justify the application of stringent anti-pollution measures;

(b) Category B: noxious liquid substances which if discharged into the sea from tank cleaning or deballasting operations would present a hazard to either marine resources or human health or cause harm to amenities or other legitimate uses of the sea and therefore justify the application of special anti-pollution measures;

(c) Category C: noxious liquid substances which if discharged into the sea from tank cleaning or deballasting operations would present a minor hazard to either marine resources or human health or cause minor harm to amenities or other legitimate uses of the sea and therefore require special operational conditions;

(d) Category D: noxious liquid substances which if discharged into the sea from tank cleaning or deballasting operations would present a recognisable hazard to either marine resources or human health or cause minimal harm to amenities or other legitimate uses of the sea and therefore require some attention in operational conditions.

2. [...].
3. [...].
4. [...].

(Further guidelines on the categorisation of substances, including a list of categorised substances are given in Regulation 3(2) to (4) and Regulation 4 and the Appendices to Marpol 73/78 Annex II)

Regulation 5: Discharge of noxious liquid substances

Category A, B and C substances outside special areas and Category D substances in all areas

Subject to the provisions of [...] Regulation 6 of this Annex,

1. The discharge into the sea of substances in Category A as defined in Regulation 3(1)(a) of this Annex or of those provisionally assessed as such or ballast water, tank washings, or other residues or mixtures containing such substances shall be prohibited. If tanks containing such substances or mixtures are to be washed, the resulting residues shall be discharged to a reception facility until the concentration of the substance in the effluent to such facility is at or below 0,1 % by weight and until the tank is empty, with the exception of phosphorus, yellow or white, for which the residual concentration shall be 0,01 % by weight. Any water subsequently added to the tank may be discharged into the sea when all the following conditions are satisfied:
   (a) the ship is proceeding en route at a speed of at least 7 knots in the case of self-propelled ships or at least 4 knots in the case of ships which are not self-propelled;
   (b) the discharge is made below the waterline, taking into account the location of the seawater intakes; and
   (c) the discharge is made at a distance of not less than 12 nautical miles from the nearest land in a depth of water of not less than 25 m.

2. The discharge into the sea of substances in Category B as defined in Regulation 3(1)(b) of this Annex or of those provisionally assessed as such, or ballast water, tank washings, or other residues or mixtures containing such substances shall be prohibited except when all the following conditions are satisfied:
   (a) the ship is proceeding en route at a speed of at least 7 knots in the case of self-propelled ships or at least 4 knots in the case of ships which are not self-propelled;
   (b) the procedures and arrangements for discharge are approved by the (flag State) administration. Such procedures and arrangements shall be based upon standards developed by the (IMO) and shall ensure that the concentration and rate of discharge of the effluent is such that the concentration of the substance in the wake astern of the ship does not exceed 1 part per million;

    (c) the maximum quantity of cargo discharged from each tank and its associated piping system does not exceed the maximum quantity approved in accordance with the procedures referred to in subparagraph (b) of this paragraph, which shall in no case exceed the greater of 1 m^3 or 1/3000 of the tank capacity in m^3;

    (d) the discharge is made below the waterline, taking into account the location of the seawater intakes; and

    (e) the discharge is made at a distance of not less than 12 nautical miles from the nearest land and in a depth of water of not less than 25 m.

3. The discharge into the sea of substances in Category C as defined in Regulation 3(1)(c) of this Annex or of those provisionally assessed as such, or ballast water, tank washings, or other residues or mixtures containing such substances shall be prohibited except when all the following conditions are satisfied:

    (a) the ship is proceeding en route at a speed of at least 7 knots in the case of self-propelled ships or at least 4 knots in the case of ships which are not self-propelled;

    (b) the procedures and arrangements for discharge are approved by the (flag State) administration. Such procedures and arrangements shall be based upon standards developed by the (IMO) and shall ensure that the concentration and rate of discharge of the effluent is such that the concentration of the substance in the wake astern of the ship does not exceed 10 parts per million;

    (c) the maximum quantity of cargo discharged from each tank and its associated piping system does not exceed the maximum quantity approved in accordance with the procedures referred to in subparagraph (b) of this paragraph, which shall in no case exceed the greater of 3 m^3 or 1/1000 of the tank capacity in m^3;

    (d) the discharge is made below the waterline, taking into account the location of the seawater intakes; and

    (e) the discharge is made at a distance of not less than 12 nautical miles from the nearest land and in a depth of water of not less than 25 m.

4. The discharge into the sea of substances in Category D as defined in Regulation 3(1)(d) of this Annex, or of those provisionally assessed as such, or ballast water, tank washings, or other residues or mixtures containing such substances shall be prohibited except when all the following conditions are satisfied:

    (a) the ship is proceeding en route at a speed of at least 7 knots in the case of self-propelled ships or at least 4 knots in the case of ships which are not self-propelled;

    (b) such mixtures are of a concentration not greater than one part of the substance in ten parts of water; and

    (c) the discharge is made at a distance of not less than 12 nautical miles from the nearest land.

5. Ventilation procedures approved by the (flag State) administration may be used to remove cargo residues from a tank. Such procedures shall be based upon standards developed by the (IMO). Any water subsequently introduced into the tank shall be regarded as clean and shall not be subject to paragraphs 1, 2, 3 or 4 of this Regulation.

6. The discharge into the sea of substances which have not been categorised, provisionally assessed, or evaluated as referred to in Regulation 4(1) of this Annex, or of ballast water, tank washings, or other residues or mixtures containing such substances shall be prohibited.

Category A, B and C substances within special areas (as defined in Marpol 73/78 Annex II, Regulation 1, including the Baltic Sea)

Subject to the provisions of [...] Regulation 6 of this Annex,

7. The discharge into the sea of substances in Category A as defined in Regulation 3(1)(a) of this Annex or of those provisionally assessed as such, or ballast water, tank washings, or other residues or mixtures containing such substances shall be prohibited. If tanks containing such substances or mixtures are to be washed, the resulting residues shall be dis-

charged to a reception facility which the States bordering the special area shall provide in accordance with Regulation 7 of this Annex, until the concentration of the substance in the effluent to such facility is at or below 0.05 % by weight and until the tank is empty, with the exception of phosphorus, yellow or white, for which the residual concentration shall be 0.005 % by weight. Any water subsequently added to the tank may be discharged into the sea when all the following conditions are satisfied:

    (a) the ship is proceeding en route at a speed of at least 7 knots in the case of self-propelled ships or at least 4 knots in the case of ships which are not self-propelled;

    (b) the discharge is made below the waterline, taking into account the location of the seawater intakes; and

    (c) the discharge is made at a distance of not less than 12 nautical miles from the nearest land and in a depth of water of not less than 25 m.

8. The discharge into the sea of substances in Category B as defined in Regulation (3)(1)(b) of this Annex or of those provisionally assessed as such, or ballast water, tank washings, or other residues or mixtures containing such substances shall be prohibited except when all the following conditions are satisfied:

    (a) the tank has been prewashed in accordance with the procedure approved by the (flag State) Administration and based on standards developed by the (IMO) and the resulting tank washings have been discharged to a reception facility;

    (b) the ship is proceeding en route at a speed of at least 7 knots in the case of self-propelled ships or at least 4 knots in the case of ships which are not self-propelled;

    (c) the procedures and arrangements for discharge and washings are approved by the (flag State) Administration. Such procedures and arrangements shall be based upon standards developed by the (IMO) and shall ensure that the concentration and rate of discharge of the effluent is such that the concentration of the substance in the wake astern of the ship does not exceed 1 part per million;

    (d) the discharge is made below the waterline, taking into account the location of the seawater intakes; and

    (e) the discharge is made at a distance of not less than 12 nautical miles from the nearest land and in a depth of water of not less than 25 m.

9. The discharge into the sea of substances in Category C as defined in Regulation 3(1)(c) of this Annex or of those provisionally assessed as such, or ballast water, tank washings, or other residues or mixtures containing such substances shall be prohibited except when all the following conditions are satisfied:

    (a) the ship is proceeding en route at a speed of at least 7 knots in the case of self-propelled ships or at least 4 knots in the case of ships which are not self-propelled;

    (b) the procedures and arrangements for discharge are approved by the (flag State) administration. Such procedures and arrangements shall be based upon standards developed by the (IMO) and shall ensure that the concentration and rate of discharge of the effluent is such that the concentration of the substance in the wake astern of the ship does not exceed 1 part per million;

    (c) the maximum quantity of cargo discharged from each tank and its associated piping system does not exceed the maximum quantity approved in accordance with the procedures referred to in subparagraph (b) of this paragraph which shall in no case exceed the greater of 1 m^3 or 1/3000 of the tank capacity in m^3;

    (d) the discharge is made below the waterline, taking into account the location of the seawater intakes; and

    (e) the discharge is made at a distance of not less than 12 nautical miles from the nearest land and in a depth of water of not less than 25 m.

10. Ventilation procedures approved by the (flag State) administration may be used to remove cargo residues from a tank. Such procedures shall be based upon standards developed by the (IMO). Any water subsequently introduced into the tank shall be regarded as clean and shall not be subject to paragraphs 7, 8 or 9 of this Regulation.

11. The discharge into the sea of substances which have not been categorised, provisionally assessed or evaluated as referred to in Regulation 4(1) of this Annex, or of ballast water,

tank washings, or other residues or mixtures containing such substances shall be prohibited.

12. Nothing in this regulation shall prohibit a ship from retaining on board the residues from a Category B or C cargo and discharging such residues into the sea outside a special area in accordance with paragraphs 2 or 3 of this Regulation, respectively.

Regulation 6: Exceptions

Regulation 5 of this Annex shall not apply to:

(a) the discharge into the sea of noxious liquid substances or mixtures containing such substances necessary for the purpose of securing the safety of a ship or saving life at sea; or

(b) the discharge into the sea of noxious liquid substances or mixtures containing such substances resulting from damage to a ship or its equipment:

   (i) provided that all reasonable precautions have been taken after the occurrence of the damage or discovery of the discharge for the purpose of preventing or minimising the discharge; and

   (ii) except if the owner or the master acted either with intent to cause damage, or recklessly and with knowledge that damage would probably result; or

(c) the discharge into the sea of noxious liquid substances or mixtures containing such substances, approved by the (flag State) administration, when being used for the purpose of combating specific pollution incidents in order to minimise the damage from pollution. Any such discharge shall be subject to the approval of any government in whose jurisdiction it is contemplated the discharge will occur.

CHAPTER 3

Marine pollution liabilities under US law

PROFESSOR ROBERT FORCE[*]

INTRODUCTION

3.1 First, pollution is a species of tort having its grounding in trespass and public and private nuisance. Therefore, pollution liability is imposed under the US tort regime. We are not writing on a clean slate here. All of the features of the US tort system, the good, the bad and the ugly will be found in pollution litigation in the US. These include the right of the parties to a jury trial, the respective roles of the judge and the jury, the contingent fee arrangement that is typical in tort cases, and a broader range of damages. Another factor is the role played by the tort system in the protection of the public. The tort system, for better or worse, is used by the plaintiffs bar as a means for bringing public attention to and correcting products and practices that endanger public health and safety.[1] This view holds that the "Government" is unable or in some cases unwilling to police and rein in certain business practices because to do so will have a negative effect on the economy. Anyone who follows product recalls must acknowledge that often those recalls occur only after the defects were exposed in tort litigation against the manufacturer.

3.2 Second, none of the Federal statutes to which I will refer, the Clean Water Act (the Federal Water Pollution Control Act),[2] the Oil Pollution Act of 1990,[3] and the Comprehensive Environmental Response, Compensation, and Liability Act[4] are preemptive of state remedies. This means that a person or governmental entity that incurs costs or sustains damages as a result of pollution has a choice of electing to sue under federal or state law, or, in some cases, to enhance federal remedies by invoking state law provisions.

3.3 I might add that the CWA deals with both oil and hazardous substance pollution, but has been superseded as to oil pollution damages by OPA and as to hazardous substance pollution damages by CERCLA.

3.4 Third, with respect to remedies, US pollution laws are not tied to international conventions, and our marine pollution statutes apply to inland navigable waterways as well as waters that lie off the coast of the US. I will say more about OPA later. I will, however, predict with confidence that the US will not adopt the

* Niels F. Johnsen Professor of Maritime Law and Director Emeritus, Tulane Maritime Law Center. The author wishes to thank Julie Batt, LL.M. in Admiralty, Tulane Law School, 2005, Ph.D. Candidate for her assistance.
1. R. Force, "US Tort Law Problems", in *United States Shipping Policies and the World Market*, pp. 211–214 (edited by Wm. A. Lovett, 1996).
2. 33 U.S.C. §§1251, *et seq.* Hereafter "CWA".
3. 33 U.S.C. §§2701, *et seq.* Hereafter "OPA".
4. 42 U.S.C. §§9601, *et seq.* Hereafter "CERCLA".

HNS convention because we have a statute that comprehensively deals with hazardous substance pollution in navigable waters, non-navigable waters, drinking water, in the soil and in the air.

3.5 Fourth, undoubtedly you all have some knowledge of OPA. Much of what you have heard is bad, for example, that it was a political response to the *Exxon Valdez* incident. Much of the criticism focused on the contention that OPA, in application, will result in unlimited liability. I will address that point later. But OPA, as well as other environmental statutes, is about much more than liability and damages. It is a comprehensive approach to marine pollution. All of these statutes also provide for the imposition of civil[5] and criminal penalties,[6] provisions designed to prevent the discharge of oil or hazardous substances,[7] funding for projects designed to improve safety,[8] etc. The damage remedies are only one part of the picture. Needless to say, to some extent it is a matter of whose ox is being gored. Look at the reaction in France after the *Erika* and the reaction in Spain after the *Prestige*. Consider the actions in the EU toward the imposition of more severe sanctions against dischargers.[9] OPA initially differed from the CLC in that OPA applied to all oil, both cargo and bunkers.[10] Now the international community wants to expand coverage to include liability for discharge of bunker oil.[11] OPA was initially criticized for having limits of liability that were too high. Now the international community has followed suit.[12] But I have not come here to be an apologist for the various US regimes but to discuss some important, and I hope interesting, issues with you.

3.6 Historically, the US response to pollution has evolved from a point where originally either the US or a state government cleaned up the mess to the current OPA which provides not only governments but private citizens with express remedies against polluters. This is not the time or place to retrace that history. The three US statutes to which I have previously referred, the CWA, CERCLA and OPA, have much in common, and, in fact, they have much in common with the CLC. Each imposes strict liability on the transporter of oil or hazardous substances.[13] Very narrow defences are provided.[14] Those liable have a right to limit their liability,[15]

---

5. 33 U.S.C. §1319(b).

6. 33 U.S.C. §1319(c).

7. Pub. L. No. 101–380, 104 Stat. 484 §§4101–18 (including double hull requirements), 33 U.S.C. §§4101–4118.

8. Pub. L. No. 101–380, 104 Stat. 484 §§5001, 5006 and 7001, 33 U.S.C. §§5001, 5006 and 7001.

9. Directive 2005/35/EC of the European Parliament and of the Council of 7 September 2005 on ship-source pollution and on the introduction of penalties for infringements, 2005 O.J. (L 255) 11.

10. 33 U.S.C. §2701(23).

11. International Convention on Civil Liability for Bunker Oil Pollution Damage, 23 March 2001.

12. Article V of the CLC now provides:
   1. The owner of a ship shall be entitled to limit his liability under this Convention in respect of any one incident to an aggregate amount calculated as follows:
       (a) 4,510,000 units of account for a ship not exceeding 5,000 units of tonnage;
       (b) for a ship with a tonnage in excess thereof, for each additional unit of tonnage, 631 units of account in addition to the amount mentioned in sub-paragraph (a);
       provided, however, that this aggregate amount shall not in any event exceed 89,770,000 units of account.

13. 33 U.S.C. §1321(f)(1), 42 U.S.C. §9607(a), 33 U.S.C. §2702(a), Article Ill. 1.

14. 33 U.S.C. §1321(f)(1), 42 U.S.C. §9607(b), 33 U.S.C. §2703, Article III.2.

15. 33 U.S.C. §1321(f)(1), 42 U.S.C. §9607(c)(1), 33 U.S.C. §2704(a), Article V.1.

but the right to limit may be lost under certain circumstances.[16] Finally, the transporter, as a prerequisite to using US waterways, must provide the US government with proof of financial responsibility sufficient to cover its liabilities in case of a worst case scenario discharge.[17] By way of enforcement there is a self-reporting requirement in the US statutes[18] with fairly draconian sanctions for failing to do so including criminal penalties[19] and the loss of the right to present a defence[20] and to limit one's liability.[21] Still, I have seen reports that indicate that probably half the discharges of oil are mystery spills for which the government is unable to identify the discharger.

3.7 Each of the US statutes creates a fund that provides financial remedies in case the discharger cannot be identified and for those situations where, because of limited liability, the remedy against the discharger is insufficient. The Oil Spill Liability Trust Fund which is funded in part by a tax on oil, has recently been reauthorized by Congress.[22] All of the US statutes permit a direct action against the party that provides a financial guarantee such as an insurance company, and generally do not permit an insurance company to invoke policy defences.[23]

3.8 Transporters of oil and hazardous substances may not contract out of liability but the statutes preserve the remedies of indemnity and contribution.[24]

3.9 There are some major differences among the statutes. The CWA and CERCLA do not provide private remedies. They authorise only governmental recovery of clean-up (removal) costs and recovery for damage to natural resources. These statutes do not take away existing remedies for damage to persons or property under the general maritime law or state law. In OPA, however, Congress for the first time provides novel damage actions to state and local governments for financial losses attributed to loss of tax revenue and by way of reimbursement for special expenditures incurred to protect health and safety of the population in an area affected by an oil spill. The statute also provides private parties with the right to sue the discharger for damages, including economic losses about which I will say more later.

3.10 I will focus on the following areas:

1. The third-party defence.
2. The standard for breaking limitation.
3. Removal Costs – Monitoring and base costs.
4. Damages including economic losses.
5. Damages for Injury and Destruction of Natural Resources.

(1) The third party defence

3.11 The US statutes impose liability on owners and operators of vessels and facilities from which oil is discharged into the navigable waters of the US. In the case of

16. 33 U.S.C. §1321(f)(1), 42 U.S.C. §9607(c)(2), 33 U.S.C. §2704(c), Article V.2.
17. 33 U.S.C. §2716, 42 U.S.C. §9608.
18. 33 U.S.C. §1321(b)(5), 42 U.S.C. §9603(a).
19. 33 U.S.C. §1319(c)(4) (False Statement), 42 U.S.C. §9603(b).
20. 33 U.S.C. §2703(c)(1).
21. 33 U.S.C. §2704(c)(2).
22. Pub. L. No. 109–241, 120 Stat. 516, §101.
23. 33 U.S.C. §2716(f), 42 U.S.C. §9608(c).
24. 33 U.S.C. §2710.

vessels, demise charterers are also included. For simplicity, I will use the terminology of OPA and refer to each of them as a "responsible party". All of the US statutes provide a responsible party[25] with a defence where a discharger can prove that a third party was the sole cause of the discharge. The defence, however, is not available if the discharger's conduct contributed to the spill in any degree. The defences are not geared to fault but to causation, and a discharger does not have a defence merely by proving that it was not at fault. Thus, in one case a vessel operated out of the navigational channel that had been charted by the Coast Guard.[26] It did so because the master thought that, under the conditions then present, it was safer to do so. The vessel hit an unmarked wreck. The court held that even though the vessel may not have been negligent, the decision to navigate outside of the channel was a contributing factor in causing the discharge. The defendant's argument that its action was not the proximate cause of the collision was rejected. The court interpreted the word "cause" literally, i.e. cause in fact. There is no reason to believe that Congress intended for the word to have the complicated meaning of proximate cause. It rejected the argument that its decision will deny the third-party defence whenever the discharger is a moving vessel.

3.12 The current OPA provision[27] provides:

"(a) Complete defenses
   A responsible party is not liable for removal costs or damages under section 2702 of this title if the responsible party establishes, by a preponderance of the evidence, that the discharge or substantial threat of a discharge of oil and the resulting damages or removal costs were caused solely by an act or omission of a third party, other than an employee or agent of the responsible party or a third party whose act or omission occurs in connection with any contractual relationship with the responsible party ..., if the responsible party establishes, by a preponderance of the evidence, that the responsible party:
   (A) exercised due care with respect to the oil concerned, taking into consideration the characteristics of the oil and in light of all relevant facts and circumstances; and
   (B) took precautions against foreseeable acts or omissions of any such third party and the foreseeable consequences of those acts or omissions;

...

(c) Limitation on complete defense
   Subsection (a) of this section does not apply with respect to a responsible party who fails or refuses:
   (1) to report the incident as required by law if the responsible party knows or has reason to know of the incident;
   (2) to provide all reasonable cooperation and assistance requested by a responsible official in connection with removal activities; or
   (3) without sufficient cause, to comply with an order issued under subsection (c) or (e) of section 1321 of this title or the Intervention on the High Seas Act (33 U.S.C. 1471 *et seq.*).

..."

3.13 Two matters immediately come to mind. First, there is a major exclusion from the third party defence, that is, a person who has a contractual relationship with the responsible party is not a third party for the purpose of this defence. Clearly contractors who are providing services to a vessel owned or operated by a

---

25. Some refer to the Personally Responsible Party or PRP.
26. *US v West of England Ship Owner's Mut. Protection & Indem. Ass'n*, 872 F.2d 1192 (5th Cir. 1989).
27. 33 U.S.C. §2703.

responsible party are most likely to engage in conduct leading to the discharge of oil. CERCLA has a similar exclusion.[28] The CWA, unlike CERCLA and OPA, does not expressly exclude from the third party defence, those in a contractual relationship with a responsible party, but courts have interpreted the defence as impliedly excluding those in a contractual relationship.[29] The reason is to prevent an owner or operator from avoiding liability under the statute by contracting out all of the functions that must be performed as part of its business.

3.14 A question arises as to whether or not the exclusion applies only to those in a direct contractual relationship with the responsible party or does it apply to any person contractually obligated to perform services for the vessel. At least one court has held that under OPA anyone providing services to a vessel as a result of a contract does not qualify as a third party for purposes of this defence.[30] In this case, the responsible party operated a vessel for the US Navy. The Navy had arranged for the vessel to be supplied with bunkers from a particular supplier. An employee of the supplier was negligent and caused the discharge of oil into the navigable waters of the US. The contractor had no direct contract with the supplier. The court held that the third party defence was not applicable because:

(1) the commercial contacts between IMC [operator] and Terminal [supplier] are sufficient to imply a contractual agreement;
(2) the Declaration of Inspection [signed by an employee of IMC and an employee of Terminal] evidences this contractual relationship;
(3) IMC is an intended third-party beneficiary of the contract between the Navy and the Terminal; and
(4) a maritime contract lien arose ... when the Terminal transferred fuel to IMC.[31]

3.15 The court dismissed IMC's contention that the "Declaration of Inspection" was merely a checklist and not a contract. The court held that the agency's determination[32] that "commercial contacts constitute an OPA contractual relationship" was not unreasonable.[33] In support of its conclusion the court cited numerous CERCLA cases that have limited the third-party defence "to situations where the responsible party has no connection to the third party".[34] In other words, the third-party defence can be invoked only where the third party is a stranger to the responsible party. The court acknowledged that some courts have interpreted the third party defence under CERCLA as excluding only contracts between the responsible party and the third party.[35]

3.16 The second limitation on the third-party defence is that even if there is no contractual relationship between the responsible party and the third party, the

---

28. 42 U.S.C. § 9607(b)(3).
29. *Burgess v MN Tamano*, 564 F.2d 964 (1st Cir. 1977).
30. *Int'l Marine Carriers v Oil Spill Liability Trust Fund*, 903 F. Supp. 1097 (S.D. Tex. 1994).
31. *Ibid.* at 1105.
32. The case was before the court on appeal from the Coast Guard's denial of IMC's request for reimbursement of clean-up costs. IMC claimed that, inasmuch as it had a complete third-party defence, it was entitled to reimbursement from the Oil Spill Liability Trust Fund under 33 U.S.C. §2708 (a)(1).
33. 903 F. Supp. at 1106.
34. *Ibid.* at 1105 (citing *Philadelphia v Stephan Chemical Co.*, 1987 WL 15214 (E.D. Pa. 1987)).
35. *Ibid.* at 1106.

responsible party under §2703 (a)(3)(A–B) must prove it was not negligent and that it "took reasonable precautions against foreseeable acts or omissions of any such third party and the foreseeable consequences of those acts or omissions, ..." In other words, a responsible party must anticipate that there are circumstances where the conduct of a third party might create risks of an oil spill and must take precautions against such conduct.

(2) Limitation of liability and the standard for breaking limitation of liability

3.17 In addition to limits of liability in OPA, which were viewed as high by industry and insurance interests, the most controversial aspects of OPA is its failure to preempt state remedies and the concern that the standard for breaking limitation was too low. The CWA states that limitation is denied where it is proven that "the discharge of oil or hazardous substance ... was the result of wilful negligence or wilful misconduct within the privity and knowledge of the owner(s)."[36] This is not too different from the original CLC which provided that "[i]f the incident occurred as a result of the actual fault or privity of the owner, he shall not be entitled to avail himself of the limitation provided in paragraph 1 of this Article". The CERCLA standard is virtually identical to the CWA, but added two additional bases for denial of limitation. Under CERCLA, limitation will also be denied where the "primary cause of the release was a violation (within the privity and knowledge of such person [owner or operator]) of applicable safety, construction or operating standards or regulations ..."[37] Limitation is also denied where an owner or operator "fails or refuses all reasonable cooperation and assistance requested by a responsible public official in connection with response activities under the National Contingency Plan...."[38] Subsequently, the CLC raised the bar for denial of limitation by adopting the current standard used in other Conventions which is very high, making it unlikely that limitation will be broken except in the most egregious circumstances. Currently the CLC provides: "The owner shall not be able to limit his liability under this Convention if it is proved that the pollution damage resulted from his personal act or omission, committed with the intent to cause such damage, or recklessly and with knowledge that such damage would probably result."[39] These grounds require an owner to engage in, what is to all intents and purposes, criminal conduct.

3.18 The approach to limitation moved in the opposite direction under OPA. First let me call to your attention that Congress in 2006 increased the limits of liability. The new limits provide[40]:

"(a) General rule
Except as otherwise provided in this section, the total of the liability of a responsible party under section 2702 of this title and any removal costs incurred by, or on behalf of, the responsible party, with respect to each incident shall not exceed
    (1) for a tank vessel, the greater of

36. 33 U.S.C. §1321(f)(1).
37. 42 U.S.C. §9607(c)(2).
38. *Ibid.*
39. Article V.2.
40. Pub. L. No. 109–241, 120 Stat. 516, §603, 33 U.S.C. §2703.

(A) with respect to a single-hull vessel, including a single-hull vessel fitted with double sides only or a double bottom only, $3,000 per gross ton;

(B) with respect to a vessel other than a vessel referred to in subparagraph (A), $1,900 per gross ton; or

(C)(1) with respect to a vessel greater than 3,000 gross tons that is
  (i) (I) a vessel described in subparagraph (A), $22,000,000; or (II) a vessel described in subparagraph (B), $16,000,000; or
  (ii) with respect to a vessel of 3,000 gross tons or less that is (I) a vessel described in subparagraph (A), $6,000,000; or (II) a vessel described in subparagraph (B), $4,000,000;

  (2) for any other vessel, $950 per gross ton or $800,000, whichever is greater;

  (3) for an offshore facility except a deepwater port, the total of all removal costs plus $75,000,000; and

  (4) for any onshore facility and a deepwater port, $350,000,000.

...

(c) Exceptions
  (1) Acts of responsible party
  Subsection (a) of this section does not apply if the incident was proximately caused by
    (A) gross negligence or willful misconduct of, or
    (B) the violation of an applicable Federal safety, construction, or operating regulation by, the responsible party, an agent or employee of the responsible party, or a person acting pursuant to a contractual relationship with the responsible party ...
  (2) Failure or refusal of responsible party
  Subsection (a) of this section does not apply if the responsible party fails or refuses
    (A) to report the incident as required by law and the responsible party knows or has reason to know of the incident;
    (B) to provide all reasonable cooperation and assistance requested by a responsible official in connection with removal activities; or
    (C) without sufficient cause, to comply with an order issued under subsection (c) or (e) of section 1321 of this title or the Intervention on the High Seas Act (33 U.S.C. 1471 *et seq.*).
..."

3.19 In OPA the limits provided do not apply "if the incident was proximately caused by 'gross negligence or wilful misconduct', 'by the responsible party, an agent or employee of the responsible party or a person acting pursuant to a contractual relationship'".[41] This represents a dramatic lowering of standard for denial of limitation. It does away with the "privity" and "knowledge" element that requires personal fault of the owner or operator or in the usual case of corporate owner the fault of someone of managerial status. Instead, under OPA, limitation can be lost because of the conduct of a low level employee of a contractor performing services for a vessel. Another change is the use of "gross negligence" as a standard of conduct. It was not clear whether the "wilful negligence" standard required proof of recklessness or gross negligence. Some courts equate the two, but some courts distinguish "recklessness" as requiring a conscious disregard of a known risk as compared with "gross negligence" that is based on a failure to perceive a risk under circumstances where such failure constitutes a gross departure from the standard of reasonable care. Recklessness is considered a more culpable state of mind. It is not clear how courts will apply the "gross negligence" standard in OPA. Will they merely require something more than ordinary negligence or will

41. 33 U.S.C. §2704(c)(1)(A).

they equate gross negligence with recklessness? To the best of my knowledge there are no reported decisions on the point.

3.20 Limitation may also be lost if the discharge results from "the violation of an applicable Federal safety, construction or operating regulation by, the responsible party, an agent or employee of a responsible party, or by a person acting pursuant to contractual relationship with the responsible party...".[42] A literal construction would strip a responsible party of its right to limit if an employee of a contractor providing services to a vessel engages in some unsafe practice thereby violating a safety regulation.

3.21 There is more. Limitation will be denied where a responsible party fails or refuses "to report the incident as required by law" under circumstances where "the responsible party knows or has reason to know of the incident" or where the responsible party fails or refuses to "provide all reasonable cooperation and assistance requested by a responsible official in connection with removal activities, or without sufficient cause, to comply with" various orders issued in the implementation of the duties and powers of the US in removing oil that has been discharged or in preventing a discharge.[43]

3.22 Loss of limitation is significant. Under the US scheme of financial responsibility, the owner needs evidence of financial responsibility only in an amount calculated on a worst case scenario discharge that assumes that the responsible party is entitled to limit its liability. If the responsible party uses insurance as a means of providing that evidence, the insurer agrees to accept responsibility only for that maximum amount. The US can sue the insurer directly but only up to the limitation amount. That leaves the responsible party liable for the actual amount of clean-up costs and damages that exceed the amount of insurance. This is one of the reasons that the P&I Clubs were so opposed to OPA – they did not want to give Uncle Sam a blank cheque.

3.23 A claimant in presenting its claim may resist the responsible party's attempt to limit liability. Also, the responsible party may complete the clean-up expending an amount greater than its limitation amount and then present a claim to the Fund to be indemnified in the excess amount, that is, the difference between the limitation amount and the amount it actually spent. To temper this grim picture of an illusory right to limit, I must add that I am aware of no reported decisions where the right to limit has been contested and defeated, although there are cases that deal with the appropriate formula for limitation. OPA has been in effect for 15 years, yet the number of reported decisions is minimal. Why is that? There are several explanations. For the limitation issue to arise, the amount of the clean-up expenses must exceed the responsible party's limitation amount. Because OPA has very high limits it is unlikely to occur in many cases. Another factor is the unwillingness of a responsible party to abandon the clean-up activity it has undertaken when it has expended an amount equal to its limitation amount. In the latter event, if there was no gross negligence involved, the responsible party or its guarantor may present a claim to the Fund. If the Fund pays the claim, the limitation issue never surfaces. Also by undertaking and completing the clean up, a responsible party is better able

---

42. 33 U.S.C. §2704(c)(1)(B).
43. 33 U.S.C. §2704(c)(2).

to control its costs. It uses its clean-up contractors. There is another point to consider. Oil spills generate negative publicity locally, nationally or even internationally depending on the size of the discharge. Stepping in quickly and getting the discharge cleaned up tempers adverse publicity. There seems to be practical considerations that explain the lack of reported decisions.

3.24 One of the problems in asserting a defence of limitation of liability under environmental statutes is that they are not subject to the procedural provisions of the general Shipowners Limitation of Liability Act and Rule F of the Supplemental Rules of Civil Procedure. Making matters worse there are no procedural rules at all provided in the environmental statutes. Courts that have considered this issue have denied a responsible party's attempts to compel a concursus of claims thereby denying a responsible party an opportunity to compel all claimants to enforce their claims in a single proceeding.[44] These courts have distinguished limitation under environmental statutes and limitation under the general limitation statute on the basis that in the latter proceedings there is truly a limited fund, whereas in environmental litigation, claimants who are not fully compensated may present their unpaid claims to the Fund. These courts view the only reason for concursus is to treat claimants equally and to prevent those who are the first to bring suit from exhausting the fund. As this should not occur when there is a "fund" available to those who cannot be satisfied out of the limitation fund, there will be no unfairness to claimants.

(3) Removal costs – monitoring and base costs

3.25 Each of the three statutes provides the US with the right to recover removal (clean-up) costs. In fact that was the only remedy in the original CWA. That Act was subsequently amended to allow recovery for natural resource damage. CERCLA only provides recovery for removal costs and natural resource damages. Under the statutory schemes, the US is tasked with removing oil and hazardous substances from the navigable waters of the US. The US may, but it is not obligated, to permit a responsible party to undertake the removal activity. Allowing the responsible party to arrange for the clean-up means no initial outlay of government funds and no necessity of initiating a suit against the responsible party to recover clean-up costs. Under this arrangement, the responsible party also benefits from the advantage of being able to select the clean-up contractor and thereby control the cost of the removal.

3.26 If the government permits the responsible party to undertake the removal, and the responsible party is not doing the job properly, the US may "federalise" the removal activity and take over. Therein lies the rub. The US may insist on a Rolls Royce type of clean-up while the responsible party prefers a Kia type of clean-up. Which position prevails in this type of conflict? The various statutes do not limit clean-up expenditures to those that are "necessary" or even "reasonably" required. Where responsible parties have challenged expenditures incurred by the US, usually

---

44. *Metlife Capital Corp. v MN Emily*, 132 F.3d 818 (lst Cir. 1997), *Bouchard Transp. Co. Inc. v Updegraff*, 147 F.3d 1344 (11th Cir. 1998). See also, Robert Force & Jonathan F. Gutoff, "Limitation of Liability in Oil Pollution: in Search of Concursus or Procedural Alternatives to Concursus", in 22 Tul. Mar. L.J. 331 (1998).

the US has prevailed. The US does not have to prove the reasonableness of removal expenditures. As one court has stated: "[T]he OPA does not restrict the recovery of the United States to costs that were prudent, necessary or reasonable."[45] To contest a claim for recovery of an item incurred by the US as a clean-up expense, the responsible party must prove that in incurring the expense, the US acted in "an arbitrary or capricious manner".[46] This is a very difficult standard to satisfy because it requires the responsible party to show that the government decision-maker was acting on what was essentially a "whim". Virtually any reason that makes sense will be enough to sustain the government's position. Of course, the government does not have to allow the responsible party to clean up. If the US has a reason for not allowing the responsible party to undertake the clean-up, perhaps based on past experience, it may decline to do so.

3.27 If the US allows the responsible party to undertake the removal, how does it assure itself that the job is being done properly? The answer is quite simple, the Coast Guard monitors the activities of the responsible party's clean-up contractor. If the Coast Guard believes that the job is not being done properly, it advises the responsible party and requires the responsible party to act accordingly. If the responsible party fails to correct the situation, the Coast Guard steps in and takes over the removal process. The Coast Guard assigns its personnel, vessels, aircraft, etc., to monitor the clean up. Can the Coast Guard recover the costs of monitoring removal activities? CERCLA expressly includes monitoring within the definition of "removal".[47] However, it is not as clear in OPA. The only express provision concerning monitoring costs appears in the section on "Uses of the Fund".[48] But nothing expressly authorises the US Government to recover monitoring costs directly from the responsible party. In the *Hyundai* case, the defendant argued that the monitoring costs were not included in the removal costs recoverable under OPA. Only necessary actions are.[49] The Court of Appeals for the Ninth Circuit rejected the argument. For the court, the definition of "removal costs" under §2702(a) includes monitoring costs by reference to §1321(c)–(e).[50] These subsections of CWA expressly delegate to the President of the United States the responsibility to "ensure effective and immediate removal of a discharge, and mitigation or prevention of a substantial threat of discharge of, oil or a hazardous substance" into US waters[51] and specifically states that the President shall "direct or monitor all Federal, State, and private actions to remove a discharge...."[52] The duty of the President has been delegated to the Coast Guard for discharges into navigable waters and to the Environmental Protection Agency for discharges on land. This duty extends beyond actual physical removal and extends to activities that prevent discharges of oil or hazardous substances.

---

45. *United States v Hyundai Merchant Marine Co. Ltd*, 172 F.3d 1187, 1191 (9th Cir. 1999).
46. *Ibid.* ("the government concedes that the general standard of the Administrative Procedure Act applies to its actions in seeking to prevent or contain oil-spill disaster ...").
47. 42 U.S.C. §9601(23).
48. 33 U.S.C. §2712(a)(1).
49. 33 U.S.C. §2701(30) (definition of "removal").
50. 33 U.S.C. §2701(b)(1).
51. 33 U.S.C. §1321(c)(1)(A).
52. 33 U.S.C. §1321(c)(1)(B)(ii).

3.28 Therefore the court concluded that "these cross-referenced provisions of OPA and [CWA] ... entitle the United States to recover the costs incurred by the Coast Guard in monitoring" the defendant's removal actions.[53]

3.29 One important component of monitoring expenses is the recovery of "base costs". Responsible parties argue that monitoring expenses should be restricted to additional expenses incurred by an administrative agency directly related to the monitoring of removal activities. They reason that because agencies such as the Coast Guard are funded by annual congressional appropriations and have a complement of personnel and equipment such as vessels and aircraft, the salaries and expenses of procuring and maintaining equipment are not directly incurred as a result of any particular discharge. Thus, they should not be included in computation of monitoring expenses. If this approach was accepted by the courts, only additional expenses such as that expended on fuel for a vessel assigned to personnel monitoring a removal activity would be included. This argument has been rejected by the United States Court of Appeals for the Ninth Circuit.[54] The court concluded that personnel and equipment assigned to monitor a clean-up operation are recoverable as proper monitoring costs because, for example, personnel assigned to monitor clean-up activity "could not carry out their other duties such as safety inspections and drug interdiction. Base costs represent real costs to the United States...."[55]

(4) Damages including economic losses

3.30 As stated earlier, the Clean Water Act and CERCLA provide only for governmental entities to recover removal costs and damages for injuries to natural resources. In regard to other damages they essentially maintain the *status quo* by stating the legislation does not repeal any existing remedies for damage to property.[56] Those remedies are based on the general maritime law if the tort satisfies the criteria for admiralty tort jurisdiction and, if not, they are based on state law. OPA changes that in regard to discharges of oil. Section 2702 on damages provides:

"(a) In general
    Notwithstanding any other provision or rule of law, and subject to the provisions of this Act, each responsible party for a vessel or a facility from which oil is discharged, or which poses the substantial threat of a discharge of oil, into or upon the navigable waters or adjoining shorelines or the exclusive economic zone is liable for the removal costs and damages specified in subsection (b) of this section that result from such incident.

(b) Covered removal costs and damages

...

(2) Damages
    The damages referred to in subsection (a) of this section are the following:
    (A) Natural resources
        Damages for injury to, destruction of, loss of, or loss of use of, natural resources, including the reasonable costs of assessing the damage, which shall be recoverable by a United States trustee, a State trustee, an Indian tribe trustee, or a foreign trustee.

---

53. *United States v Hyundai Merchant Marine Co. Ltd*, 172 F.3d 1187, 1190 (9th Cir. 1999).
54. *Ibid.*
55. *Ibid.* at 1192.
56. 33 U.S.C. §1321(0), 42 U.S.C. §9614.

(B) Real or personal property

Damages for injury to, or economic losses resulting from destruction of, real or personal property, which shall be recoverable by a claimant who owns or leases that property.

(C) Subsistence use

Damages for loss of subsistence use of natural resources, which shall be recoverable by any claimant who so uses natural resources which have been injured, destroyed, or lost, without regard to the ownership or management of the resources.

(D) Revenues

Damages equal to the net loss of taxes, royalties, rents, fees, or net profit shares due to the injury, destruction, or loss of real property, personal property, or natural resources, which shall be recoverable by the Government of the United States, a State, or a political subdivision thereof.

(E) Profits and earning capacity

Damages equal to the loss of profits or impairment of earning capacity due to the injury, destruction, or loss of real property, personal property, or natural resources, which shall be recoverable by any claimant.

(F) Public services

Damages for net costs of providing increased or additional public services during or after removal activities, including protection from fire, safety, or health hazards, caused by a discharge of oil, which shall be recoverable by a State, or a political subdivision of a State."

3.31 Subsection (B) requires no explanation. It reflects prior law with these important changes. Recovery in tort under the general maritime law or under state law requires proof of negligence. OPA imposes strict liability. In tort actions limitation of liability is determined under the general limitation of liability statute. Tort actions brought under OPA are subject to the OPA limitation of liability scheme.

3.32 Subsections (D), (E) and (F) represent changes to prior law. These provisions expressly authorise the recovery of economic losses unrelated to property ownership. The general rule in the United States, with some exceptions, is that a person may not recover damages in tort for economic losses sustained as a result of damage to property in which he does not have a proprietary interest. The rule is intended to limit the scope of liability. In the US, the rule is known as the "*Robins Dry Dock*" rule based upon a case decided by the United States Supreme Court bearing that name.[57] That case was an admiralty case but that is a mere coincidence because the rule is a general rule applicable in land-based tort cases as well. A time-chartered vessel was having routine maintenance, and the shipyard negligently damaged its propeller. Therefore, the vessel's return to service was delayed. The shipyard settled with the shipowner, but the charterer sued the shipyard claiming that, although it was relieved of the obligation to pay hire by reason of the off-hire clause in the charter party, it had lost profits by not being able to use the vessel during the period of time it took to replace the damaged propeller. Justice Holmes stated that:

"No authority need be cited to show that as a general rule, at least, a tort to the person or property of one man does not make the tortfeasor liable to another merely because the injured person was under a contract with that other unknown to the doer of the wrong."[58]

57. *Robins Dry Dock v Flint*, 275 U.S. 303, 48 S.Ct. 134, 72 L.Ed. 290 (1927).
58. *Ibid.* at 309 (citing *Elliot Steam Tug Co. Ltd v The Shipping Controller* [1922] 1 K.B. 127, 139).

3.33 Thus, in the US in jurisdictions that follow the *Robins Dry Dock* rule, a person who sustains economic loss because of damage to property may not recover that loss in tort unless he owns or leases the property. If he has no proprietary interest in the property he cannot recover.

3.34 The rule was re-examined in an environmental context by the United States Court of Appeals for the Fifth Circuit in *State of Louisiana, ex rel. Guste v MY Testbank*.[59] There, two vessels collided in the Mississippi Gulf Outlet. Containers of PCP, a hazardous substance, fell into the water. The Coast Guard closed the waterway to navigation and also imposed an embargo on fishing, shrimping and related activities from July 22 until August 10. This was to permit the waters to be cleaned. Suit was brought by commercial fishermen, shipping interests whose vessels had been trapped in port, drydock, marina and boat rental operators, wholesale and retail enterprises not actually engaged in fishing, seafood restaurants, tackle and bait shops, and recreational fishermen. Defendants moved to dismiss all of the claims for purely economic losses under the *Robins Dry Dock* rule. After all, none of the plaintiffs owned the waters that had been damaged or the fish, shrimp and oysters. The trial judge dismissed all of the claims except those of the commercial fishermen, oystermen, crabbers and shrimpers. The trial court analogised these plaintiffs as "deserving a special protection akin to that enjoyed by seamen".[60] The plaintiffs whose cases had been dismissed appealed. The primary issue on appeal was whether or not to affirm the dismissal under the *Robins Dry Dock* rule. A majority of the Court of Appeals affirmed the vitality and application of the rule. A vigorous dissent was written by Judge Wisdom who stated that the case should be resolved by the application of the usual tort rules of foreseeability and proximate cause coupled with the "'particular damage' requirement in public nuisance law as an additional means of limiting claims". The latter requires that a plaintiff show that he has suffered damage that is "different in kind and degree from that of the general public".

3.35 Subsections (D) and (F) expressly authorise governmental entities to recover pure economic loss including lost revenue and for out of pocket expenditures for providing additional public services, including those incurred to protect public health and safety. There is no requirement that the governmental entity show that its property was damaged. More controversial, however, is Subsection (E) that deals with "Profits and Earning Capacity". That subsection provides for the recovery of: "Damages equal to the loss of profits or impairment of earning capacity due to the injury, destruction or loss of real property, personal property or natural resources which shall be recovered by any claimant." By its very terms and considering Subsection (B), it is a clear legislative overruling of the *Robins Dry Dock* rule in the context of oil spills. An indication of what Subsection (E) means is revealed in the House-Senate Conference Report on the Oil Pollution Act of 1990,[61] which states:

"Subsection (b)(2)(E) provides that any claimant may recover for loss of profits or impairment of earning capacity resulting from injury to property or natural resources. The claimant need not be the owner of the damaged property or resources to recover for lost profits or

---

59. 752 F.2d 1019 (5th Cir. 1985).
60. 524 F. Supp. 1170, 1173–74 (E.D.La. 1981).
61. H. Rep. No. 653, 101 Cong., 2d Sess. 103 (1990).

income. For example, a fisherman may recover lost income due to damaged fisheries resources, even though the fisherman does not own those resources."

3.36 There has been virtually no examination of this Subsection in the case law. One Court [62] suggested that it merely states the *Robins Dry Dock* rule, but that cannot be correct because of what use would Subsection (E) be in light of Subsection (B) that provides for the recovery of: "Damages for injury or economic losses resulting from destruction of, real or personal property, which shall be recoverable by a claimant who owns or leases that property." Furthermore, that court's statement is *dictum* because the economic losses in that case were caused by the obstruction of a waterway by a vessel that had exploded, caught fire and then partially sank causing the Coast Guard to close the waterway until it could be removed. The fact that oil leaked into the water had nothing to do with the obstruction.

3.37 Assuming I am correct and *Robins Dry Dock* has been overruled to some extent by OPA, how should a court apply the OPA rule? To use the *Testbank* scenario it is necessary to modify one fact. Because OPA deals with oil and not hazardous substances, OPA would not apply to a PCP spill. Let us assume that OPA does apply either by substituting oil for the PCPs or by amending CERCLA to include the OPA provision. In looking at *Testbank* in this new light, it would be improper not only to apply the *Robins Dry Dock* bright line rule that requires a proprietary interest as a prerequisite to recovery of economic losses but also to reach the same result as the majority did there. Let's look at how would the case have been decided if Judge Wisdom had the votes. He states in his dissenting opinion that recovery should be allowed for all of the commercial fishermen who routinely used those waters and surrounding areas that were closed by the Coast Guard. According to his analysis, it is foreseeable that a ship carrying containers of PCP might lose some of them overboard in a collision and that the waters would be closed to fishing until they had been recovered. The damages suffered by the commercial fishermen are proximately caused by the discharge. Finally, their damages certainly set them apart from the public at large. It is interesting to observe that even before OPA was enacted, the Court of Appeals for the Ninth Circuit had simply created an exception to the *Robins Dry Dock* rule for commercial fishermen. It reasoned that commercial fishermen and merchant vessels share the same resource, the sea, and, in doing so, each must conduct its activities so as not to interfere with the other.

3.38 Judge Wisdom would also allow recovery by ships that incurred additional expenses as a result of being trapped. Land-based businesses, he acknowledges, may present a different situation. In this case, this group includes drydocks, marinas, bait and tackle shops, seafood processors, seafood wholesalers and restaurants. Judge Wisdom states: "The general test for recovery for these claimants is whether their business of supplying a vital commodity or service to those engaged in the maritime industry has been interrupted by the collision, the closure or the embargo." His approach takes into account the ability of a particular type of business to mitigate its damages. Thus, those who supply services directly to the maritime industry such as marinas, drydocks, fishing boat charterers, and bait and tackle shops are not in a position to mitigate. Their situation is different from the general

---

62. *In re Petition of Cleveland Tankers Inc.*, 791 F. Supp. 669 (E.D. Mich. 1992).

public. "The condemnation of a large fishing area damages or destroys the liveli-hood of those shops whose business is exclusively predicated upon supplying direct inputs (bait, fuel) to those whose commercial undertakings have been foreclosed by the quarantine and embargo." Seafood processors and seafood wholesalers should recover. Judge Wisdom draws the line at seafood restaurants because they are not sufficiently closely connected to the industry. This may be another way of saying they can buy fish caught in other areas not affected by the spill. He finds that "[t]heir damage is not sufficiently distinguishable from general economic disloca-tion to allow for recovery. They are too far removed from the tortious act."

3.39 Whether courts will follow Judge Wisdom's approach in the application of Subsection (E) remains to be seen. One conclusion that fairly may be drawn is that this subsection does not seem to include recreational fishermen or boaters who, although they may have lost an opportunity to enjoy themselves and even incurred some expenses, they have not, in the words of the statute, suffered a "loss of profits" or "earning capacity".

(5) Damages for injury and destruction of natural resources

3.40 Section 2706 of OPA provides in pertinent part:

"(d) Measure of damages

    (1) In general

The measure of natural resource damages under section 2702(b)(2)(A) of this title is:

      (A) the cost of restoring, rehabilitating, replacing, or acquiring the equivalent of, the damaged natural resources;

      (B) the diminution in value of those natural resources pending restoration; plus

      (C) the reasonable cost of assessing those damages.

(2) Determine costs with respect to plans

Costs shall be determined under paragraph (1) with respect to plans adopted under sub-section (c) of this section.

(3) No double recovery

There shall be no double recovery under this Act for natural resource damages, including with respect to the costs of damage assessment or restoration, rehabilitation, replacement, or acquisition for the same incident and natural resource.

(e) Damage assessment regulations

(1) Regulations

The President, acting through the Under Secretary of Commerce for Oceans and Atmosphere and in consultation with the Administrator of the Environmental Protection Agency, the Director of the United States Fish and Wildlife Service, and the heads of other affected agencies, not later than 2 years after August 18, 1990, shall promulgate regula-tions for the assessment of natural resource damages under section 2702(b)(2)(A) of this title resulting from a discharge of oil for the purpose of this Act.

(f) Use of recovered sums

Sums recovered under this Act by a Federal, State, Indian, or foreign trustee for natural resource damages under section 2702(b)(2)(A) of this title shall be retained by the trustee in a revolving trust account, without further appropriation, for use only to reimburse or pay costs incurred by the trustee under subsection (c) of this section with respect to the damaged natural resources. Any amounts in excess of those required for these reimburse-ments and costs shall be deposited in the Fund.

3.41 Not every dimension of assessing natural resource damages is difficult. For example, if polluted conditions can be remediated, i.e. restored to their pre-polluted state, for a sum of money that is not exorbitant, then that is a fair sum to award in damages. However, that may not be the full extent of the loss because it may take one year to reach the base line and during that year people have been denied access or full use of that resource. In some cases where remediation is not possible or practical, it may be possible to acquire from the private sector resources that are the equivalent to those that have been lost. That approach too may have the effect, at least in the short term, of denying society or a segment of it full or partial use of the resource.

3.42 Nevertheless, in my opinion, assessing damages for injury to or destruction of natural resources is the most difficult problem in the area of environmental liability. The reason for this is easy to understand. It is simply that the assessment of damages requires that a monetary value be placed on an injury that, in some respects, has no monetary value. There is an imperfect analogy in personal injury litigation. Most of the items of recovery, for example, when a person has been injured in an automobile accident are pecuniary losses including repairs to a car, replacement of damaged clothing, medical bills, loss of wages, etc. Sometimes there is speculation as to future damages. How long will the plaintiff need medical care or how long will the plaintiff be out of work? But all of these damages are about money, therefore, there is no problem in translating these losses into a money award.

3.43 This is not true of all personal injury damages. In the US, one who is injured by the negligence of another is entitled to recover for "pain and suffering". "Pain and suffering" is a broad term that includes embarrassment, humiliation, inability to engage in recreational or sexual activities, etc. These consequences of injury are not monetary losses. Thus, there is no market, hence no objective criteria to arrive at a specific sum of money for a particular type or degree of pain. We know that some people have a high tolerance of pain and some do not. Nevertheless, we leave it to the fact finder, judge or jury as the case may be, to allocate a monetary award for pain and suffering. In part we rely on the common experience of people. The matter is not completely arbitrary or irrational because everyone has experienced pain and suffering of one sort or another. Everyone should be able to distinguish between a sprained ankle that healed in a week and a crushed ankle that required the amputation of a foot. In cases where a jury goes off the deep end, judges who are aware of standards set in appellate decisions in similar cases can bring the verdict within the bounds of reason.

3.44 Awarding damages for injury to the environment is similar in some respects, but it is different and more difficult than awarding damages for pain and suffering. Usually, a personal injury case involves a single plaintiff, and the scale of an award is shaped by the scope of the injury. Compare, however, a typical automobile accident with the *Exxon Valdez*, the *Erika*, and the *Prestige* incidents. Admittedly these are extreme examples, but even small spills can have serious consequences in a sensitive environment. The ramifications of an oil or hazardous substance spill, except the most minor ones, is liable to be substantial when compared to the injury of a single person.

3.45 In the end, it depends on how we define "the injury". Some aspects of damage to natural resources can be quantified using market techniques. If a strand of trees has been destroyed and if that area is used only for commercial logging, then it is possible to put a value on those lost trees by looking at the market. This type of assessment has commercial integrity. The problem arises from the fact that the same strand of trees may have other values as well. The trees may serve as a nesting area for an endangered species of bird. The trees may be 200 years old. The trees may be part of a beautiful landscape utilised by artists and frequented by nature lovers. Should those values be included in the calculation of natural resource damages? If so, how does one put a monetary value on these non-commercial values? How does one put a value on something society or some part of society values but not in a monetary sense? There can be at least two responses to these questions. The easiest response is that you do not calculate in monetary terms values that are non-monetary. If something does not have monetary value then we should not try to put a monetary value on it, because it is too arbitrary. The other approach is that we should do the best that we can. That is the approach used in OPA and CERCLA cases. I am not a scientist or an economist, and the most diffi-cult area for me in my Marine Pollution course is to understand how to translate a non-monetary value of a natural resource into monetary terms.

3.46 Courts have struggled with the problem acknowledging the dilemma. In an early case, one court stated that the state legislature

"… obviously meant to sanction the difficult, but perhaps not impossible task of putting a price tag on resources whose value cannot always be measured by the rules of the market place. Although the diminution [in value] rule is appropriate in most contexts … it does not measure the loss which the statute seeks to redress."

3.47 In this case,[63] the damage was to mangrove forests that had little commer-cial real estate value but were important to the ecology of the area. Later the court said:

"In recent times, mankind has become increasingly aware that the planet's resources are finite and portions of the land and sea which at first glance seem useless, like salt marshes, barrier reefs, and other coastal areas, often contribute in subtle but critical ways to an envi-ronment capable of supporting both human life and other forms of life on which we all depend." [64]

3.48 Under the environmental statutes that have been referred to previously, Congress has delegated to administrative agencies the responsibility for formulating regulations prescribing the methods for calculating damages for injury to or des-truction of natural resources. There are relatively few cases discussing natural resource damages and most of the cases are pre-enforcement challenges to these regulations. One important case [65] challenging the US Department of the Interior's regulations for calculating natural resource damages under CERCLA involved a number of issues. Two of the most important were (1) whether or not "use" values trumped restoration costs whenever use values were lower, and (2) whether in com-puting "use" values market value should be the exclusive determinant wherever market values were available. The court stated:

"The fatal flaw in Interior's approach, however, is that it assumes that natural resources are fungible goods, just like any other, and that the value to society generated by a particular

---

63. *Commonwealth of Puerto Rico v SS Zoe Colocotroni*, 628 F.2d 652, 674 (1st Cir. 1980).
64. *Ibid.*
65. *State of Ohio v US Dept. of the Interior*, 880 F.2d 432, 456–457 (D.C. Cir. 1989).

resource can be accurately measured in every case – assumptions that Congress apparently rejected.... Our reading of CERCLA does not attribute to Congress an irrational dislike of 'efficiency'; rather, it suggests that Congress was skeptical of the ability of human beings to measure the true 'value' of a natural resource.... Congress' refusal to view use value and restoration cost as having equal presumptive legitimacy merely recognises that natural resources have value that is not readily measured by traditional means. Congress delegated to Interior the job of deciding at what point the presumption of restoration falls away, but its repeated emphasis on the primacy of restoration rejected the underlying premise of Interior's rule, which is that restoration is wasteful if its costs exceeds – by even the slightest amount – the diminution in use value of the injured resource."

3.49 In this case the court struck down two important elements in regulations promulgated under CERCLA. The court held the rule that damages for natural resources should always be the lesser of restoration costs or lost use value was contrary to Congressional preference for restoration. The court also invalidated the rule that provided that, in calculating lost use values, market values should be used exclusively when market values are available, because the rule did not include other values that Congress wanted to be taken into account. In this respect the court said:

"While it is not irrational to look at market price as one factor in determining the use value of a resource, it is unreasonable to view market price as the exclusive factor, or even the predominant one. From the bald eagle to the blue whale and snail darter, natural resources have values that are not fully captured by the market system." [66]

3.50 The fallacy in this regulation was the "strong presumption" that Interior wanted accord to market price and appraisal methodologies.

3.51 One problem with Interior's presumption that market values should be used is that it ignores the fact that other "non-consumptive" values are also use values. These are sometimes referred to as passive-use values. One such value is an "option" value which is defined as

"the dollar amount an individual is willing to pay although he or she is not currently using a resource but wishes to reserve the option to use that resource in a certain state of being in the future.... For example, an individual who does not plan to use a beach or visit the Grand Canyon may nevertheless place some value in preservation of the resource in its natural state for personal enjoyment in the event of a later change of mind." [67]

3.52 Another so-called passive use value is "existence" value which is defined as:

"... the dollar amount an individual is willing to pay although he or she does not plan to use the resource, either at present or in the future.... Though lacking any interest in personally enjoying the resource, an individual may attach some value to it because he or she may wish to have the resource available for others to enjoy." [68]

3.53 Some courts have allowed recreational value to be included. As one court explained: "Recreational value of a natural resource is the value the consumer places on the use of that natural resource...." [69] In this case the court allowed an award for the number of fished killed and not available to recreational fishermen. The value was established by using a survey technique called the "travel cost

66. *Ibid.* at 462–463.
67. *Ibid.* at 476, n. 72.
68. *Ibid.* at 476, n. 73.
69. *State of Idaho v Southern Refrigerated Transp. Inc.*, 1991 WL 22479, at para. 20 (D. Idaho 1991).

method" in which it determined the "values" of fishermen by how much they paid to travel to various areas in the state in order to fish. The study was conducted by federal agencies and a university and was not done for the purposes of this litigation. The court, however, rejected a claim for "existence" value that purported to rely on a technique known as contingent valuation. The court did not hold that contingent valuation to be an unacceptable method for proving existence value. Rather, it concluded that the purpose for which the survey had been conducted made it unsuitable for establishing existence value in this case.

3.54 When dealing with values that cannot be measured by true market values or that cannot fully be measured by true market values, on what basis are those values calculated? Admission to a natural resource may be free or for a very small fee in order to encourage and enable people to appreciate the beauty of the site or to learn about nature. In such case, the market price in the case of free admission is zero or a very low value where the admission fees are grossly insufficient to sustain and maintain the site. These are not fair indicators of the use value of the resource. An alternative technique is called "contingent valuation".

"The CV process 'includes all techniques that set up hypothetical markets to elicit an individual's economic valuation of a natural resource'. CV involves a series of interviews with individuals for the purpose of ascertaining the values they respectively attach to particular changes to particular resources. Among the several formats available to an interviewer in developing the hypothetical scenario embodied in a CV survey are direct questioning, by which the interviewer learns how much the interviewee is willing to pay for the resource; bidding formats, for example, the interviewee is asked whether he or she would pay a given amount for a resource and, depending on the response, the bid is set higher or lower until a final price is derived; and a 'take it or leave it' format, in which the interviewee decides whether or not he or she is willing to pay a designated amount of money for the resource. CV methodology thus enables ascertainment of individually-expressed values for different levels of quality of resources and dollar values of individual's changes in well-being." [70]

3.55 CV methodology has been suggested as appropriate for determining option and existence values but it is very controversial. I am not aware of a reported decision that has based damages on this technique. On a final note, to illustrate how difficult and complicated the process for determining natural resource damages can be, I have included an Appendix, part of the current regulations of the Department of the Interior for assessing natural resources damages under CERCLA.

APPENDIX

3.56 43. Code of Federal Regulations Subpart E. Type B Procedures

§11.82 Damage Determination phase-alternatives for restoration, rehabilitation, replacement, and/or acquisition of equivalent resources.

(a) Requirement. The authorised official shall develop a reasonable number of possible alternatives for the restoration, rehabilitation, replacement, and/or acquisition of the equivalent of the injured natural resources and the services those resources provide. For each possible alternative developed, the authorised official will identify an action, or set of actions, to be taken singly or in combination by the trustee agency to achieve the restoration, rehabilitation, replacement, and/or acquisition of equivalent natural resources and the

---

70. 880 F.2d at 475.

services those resources provide to the baseline. The authorised official shall then select from among the possible alternatives the alternative that he determines to be the most appropriate based on the guidance provided in this section.

(b) Steps

(1) The authorised official shall develop a reasonable number of possible alternatives that would restore, rehabilitate, replace, and/or acquire the equivalent of the injured resources. Each of the possible alternatives may, at the discretion of the authorised official, consist of actions, singly or in combination, that would achieve those purposes.

    (i) Restoration or rehabilitation actions are those actions undertaken to return injured resources to their baseline condition, as measured in terms of the physical, chemical, or biological properties that the injured resources would have exhibited or the services that would have been provided by those resources had the discharge of oil or release of the hazardous substance under investigation not occurred. Such actions would be in addition to response actions completed or anticipated pursuant to the National Contingency Plan (NCP).

    (ii) Replacement or acquisition of the equivalent means the substitution for injured resources with resources that provide the same or substantially similar services, when such substitutions are in addition to any substitutions made or anticipated as part of response actions and when such substitutions exceed the level of response actions determined appropriate to the site pursuant to the NCP.

    (iii) Possible alternatives are limited to those actions that restore, rehabilitate, replace, and/or acquire the equivalent of the injured resources and services to no more than their baseline, that is, the condition without a discharge or release as determined in §11.72 of this part.

(2) Services provided by the resources.

    (i) In developing each of the possible alternatives, the authorised official shall list the proposed actions that would restore, rehabilitate, replace, and/or acquire the equivalent of the services provided by the injured natural resources that have been lost, and the period of time over which these services would continue to be lost.

    (ii) The authorised official shall identify services previously provided by the resources in their baseline condition in accordance with §11.72 of this part and compare those services with services now provided by the injured resources, that is, the with-a-discharge-or-release condition. All estimates of the with-a-discharge-or-release condition shall incorporate consideration of the ability of the resources to recover as determined in §11.73 of this part.

(c) Range of possible alternatives.

(1) The possible alternatives considered by the authorised official that return the injured resources and their lost services to baseline level could range from: Intensive action on the part of the authorised official to return the various resources and services provided by those resources to baseline conditions as quickly as possible; to natural recovery with minimal management actions. Possible alternatives within this range could reflect varying rates of recovery, combination of management actions, and needs for resource replacements or acquisitions.

(2) An alternative considering natural recovery with minimal management actions, based upon the "No Action-Natural Recovery" determination made in §11.73(a) (1) of this part, shall be one of the possible alternatives considered.

(d) Factors to consider when selecting the alternative to pursue. When selecting the alternative to pursue, the authorised official shall evaluate each of the possible alternatives based on all relevant considerations, including the following factors:

    (1) Technical feasibility, as that term is used in this part.

    (2) The relationship of the expected costs of the proposed actions to the expected benefits from the restoration, rehabilitation, replacement, and/or acquisition of equivalent resources.

    (3) Cost-effectiveness, as that term is used in this part.

    (4) The results of any actual or planned response actions.

    (5) Potential for additional injury resulting from the proposed actions, including long-term and indirect impacts, to the injured resources or other resources.

    (6) The natural recovery period determined in § 11.73(a)(1) of this part.

    (7) Ability of the resources to recover with or without alternative actions.

    (8) Potential effects of the action on human health and safety.

    (9) Consistency with relevant Federal, State, and tribal policies.

    (10) Compliance with applicable Federal, State, and tribal laws.

(e) A Federal authorised official shall not select an alternative that requires acquisition of land for Federal management unless the Federal authorised official determines that restoration, rehabilitation, and/or other replacement of the injured resources is not possible.

§11.83 Damage Determination phase – cost estimating and valuation methodologies.

(a) General.

(1) This section contains guidance and methodologies for determining: The costs of the selected alternative for restoration, rehabilitation, replacement, and/or acquisition of equivalent resources; and the compensable value of the services lost to the public through the completion of the restoration, rehabilitation, replacement, and/or acquisition of the equivalent of the injured resources and their services to baseline.

(2)   (i) The authorised official shall select among the cost estimating and valuation methodologies set forth in this section, or methodologies that meet the acceptance criterion of either paragraph (b)(3) or (c)(3) of this section.

    (ii) The authorised official shall define the objectives to be achieved by the application of the methodologies.

    (iii) The authorised official shall follow the guidance provided in this section for choosing among the methodologies that will be used in the Damage Determination phase.

    (iv) The authorised official shall describe his selection of methodologies and objectives in the Restoration and Compensation Determination Plan.

(3) The authorised official shall determine that the following criteria have been met when choosing among the cost estimating and valuation methodologies. The authorised official shall document this determination in the Report of the Assessment. Only those methodologies shall be chosen:

    (i) That are feasible and reliable for a particular incident and type of damage to be measured.

    (ii) That can be performed at a reasonable cost, as that term is used in this part.

    (iii) That avoid double counting or that allow any double counting to be estimated and eliminated in the final damage calculation.

    (iv) That are cost-effective, as that term is used in this part.

(b) Costs of restoration, rehabilitation, replacement, and/or acquisition of equivalent resources.

(1) Costs for restoration, rehabilitation, replacement, and/or acquisition of equivalent resources are the amount of money determined by the authorised official as necessary to complete all actions identified in the selected alternative for restoration, rehabilitation, replacement, and/or acquisition of equivalent resources, as selected in the Restoration and Compensation Determination Plan of §11.81 of this part. Such costs shall include direct and indirect costs, consistent with the provisions of this section.

    (i) Direct costs are those that are identified by the authorised official as attributed to the selected alternative. Direct costs are those charged directly to the conduct of the selected alternative including, but not limited to, the compensation of employees for the time and effort devoted to the completion of the selected alternative;

cost of materials acquired, consumed, or expended specifically for the purpose of the action; equipment and other capital expenditures; and other items of expense identified by the authorised official that are expected to be incurred in the performance of the selected alternative.

(ii) Indirect costs are costs of activities or items that support the selected alternative, but that cannot practically be directly accounted for as costs of the selected alternative. The simplest example of indirect costs is traditional overhead, e.g. a portion of the lease costs of the buildings that contain the offices of trustee employees involved in work on the selected alternative may, under some circumstances, be considered as an indirect cost. In referring to costs that cannot practically be directly accounted for, this subpart means to include costs that are not readily assignable to the selected alternative without a level of effort disproportionate to the results achieved.

(iii) An indirect cost rate for overhead costs may, at the discretion of the authorised official, be applied instead of calculating indirect costs where the benefits derived from the estimation of indirect costs do not outweigh the costs of the indirect cost estimation. When an indirect cost rate is used, the authorised official shall document the assumptions from which that rate has been derived.

(2) Cost estimating methodologies. The authorised official may choose among the cost estimating methodologies listed in this section or may choose other methodologies that meet the acceptance criterion in paragraph (b)(3) of this section. Nothing in this section precludes the use of a combination of cost estimating methodologies so long as the authorised official does not double count or uses techniques that allow any double counting to be estimated and eliminated in the final damage calculation.

(i) Comparison methodology. This methodology may be used for unique or difficult design and estimating conditions. This methodology requires the construction of a simple design for which an estimate can be found and applied to the unique or difficult design.

(ii) Unit methodology. This methodology derives an estimate based on the cost per unit of a particular item. Many other names exist for describing the same basic approach, such as order of magnitude, lump sum, module estimating, flat rates, and involve various refinements. Data used by this methodology may be collected from technical literature or previous cost expenditures.

(iii) Probability methodologies. Under these methodologies, the cost estimate represents an "average" value. These methodologies require information which is called certain, or deterministic, to derive the expected value of the cost estimate. Expected value estimates and range estimates represent two types of probability methodologies that may be used.

(iv) Factor methodology. This methodology derives a cost estimate by summing the product of several items or activities. Other terms such as ratio and percentage methodologies describe the same basic approach.

(v) Standard time data methodology. This methodology provides for a cost estimate for labor. Standard time data are a catalogue of standard tasks typically undertaken in performing a given type of work.

(vi) Cost-and time-estimating relationships (CERs and TERs). CERs and TERs are statistical regression models that mathematically describe the cost of an item or activity as a function of one or more independent variables. The regression models provide statistical relationships between cost or time and physical or performance characteristics of past designs.

(3) Other cost estimating methodologies. Other cost estimating methodologies that are based upon standard and accepted cost estimating practices and are cost-effective are acceptable methodologies to determine the costs of restoration, rehabilitation, replacement, and/or acquisition of equivalent resources under this part.

(c) Compensable value.

(1) Compensable value is the amount of money required to compensate the public for the loss in services provided by the injured resources between the time of the discharge or release and the time the resources and the services those resources provided are fully returned to their baseline conditions. The compensable value includes the value of lost public use of the services provided by the injured resources, plus lost nonuse values such as existence and bequest values. Compensable value is measured by changes in consumer surplus, economic rent, and any fees or other payments collectable by a Federal or State agency or an Indian tribe for a private party's use of the natural resources; and any economic rent accruing to a private party because the Federal or State agency or Indian tribe does not charge a fee or price for the use of the resources.

   (i) Use value is the value of the resources to the public attributable to the direct use of the services provided by the natural resources.

   (ii) Nonuse value is the difference between compensable value and use value, as those terms are used in this section.

   (iii) Estimation of option and existence values shall be used only if the authorised official determines that no use values can be determined.

(2) Valuation methodologies. The authorised official may choose among the valuation methodologies listed in this section to estimate willingness to pay (WTP) or may choose other methodologies provided that the methodology can satisfy the acceptance criterion in paragraph(c)(3) of this section. Nothing in this section precludes the use of a combination of valuation methodologies so long as the authorised official does not double count or uses techniques that allow any double counting to be estimated and eliminated in the final damage calculation.

   (i) Market price methodology. This methodology may be used if the natural resources are traded in the market. In using this methodology, the authorised official should make a determination as to whether the market for the resources is reasonably competitive. If the authorised official determines that the market for the resources, or the services provided by the resources, is reasonably competitive, the diminution in the market price of the injured resources, or the lost services, may be used to determine the compensable value of the injured resources.

   (ii) Appraisal methodology. Where sufficient information exists, the appraisal methodology may be used. In using this methodology, compensable value should be measured, to the extent possible, in accordance with the applicable sections of the "Uniform Appraisal Standards for Federal Land Acquisition" (Uniform Appraisal Standards), Interagency Land Acquisition Conference, Washington, DC, 1973 (incorporated by reference, see § 11.18). The measure of compensable value under this appraisal methodology will be the difference between the with- and without-injury appraisal value determined by the comparable sales approach as described in the Uniform Appraisal Standards.

   (iii) Factor income methodology. If the injured resources are inputs to a production process, which has as an output a product with a well-defined market price, the factor income methodology may be used. This methodology may be used to determine the economic rent associated with the use of resources in the production process. This methodology is sometimes referred to as the "reverse value added" methodology. The factor income methodology may be used to measure the in-place value of the resources.

   (iv) Travel cost methodology. The travel cost methodology may be used to determine a value for the use of a specific area. An individual's incremental travel costs to an area are used as a proxy for the price of the services of that area. Compensable value of the area to the traveler is the difference between the value of the area with and without a discharge or release. When regional travel cost models exist, they may be used if appropriate.

   (v) Hedonic pricing methodology. The hedonic pricing methodology may be used to determine the value of nonmarketed resources by an analysis of private market choices. The demand for nonmarketed natural resources is thereby estimated indirectly by an analysis of commodities that are traded in a market.

(vi) Unit value methodology. Unit values are preassigned dollar values for various types of nonmarketed recreational or other experiences by the public. Where feasible, unit values in the region of the affected resources and unit values that closely resemble the recreational or other experience lost with the affected resources may be used.

(vii) Contingent valuation methodology

(A) The contingent valuation methodology includes all techniques that set up hypothetical markets to elicit an individual's economic valuation of a natural resource. This methodology can determine use values and explicitly determine option and existence values. This methodology may be used to determine lost use values of injured natural resources.

(B) The use of the contingent valuation methodology to explicitly estimate option and existence values should be used only if the authorised official determines that no use values can be determined.

(3) Other valuation methodologies. Other valuation methodologies that measure compensable value in accordance with the public's WTP, in a cost-effective manner, are acceptable methodologies to determine compensable value under this part.

PART 2

Port Liabilities

CHAPTER 4

Liabilities of ports in respect of marine pollution and related matters

PROFESSOR PROSHANTO K. MUKHERJEE*

INTRODUCTION

4.1 In the traditional sense, a port is a haven for ships and seafarers. The place from where a ship starts its voyage is a port and the place where it ends its voyage is another port. In the current maritime milieu, a port is variously referred to as a harbour or terminal. It may comprise a complex and technologically sophisticated loading/discharging facility, or simply a jetty, wharf or even a pipeline. As well, a port may be a place of anchorage or a roadstead, without any structure connected to land.[1]

4.2 In legal terms, a port is usually defined by reference to its geographical perimeter or by cartographic depiction in a schedule to relevant legislation. In the modern context, the port is more than simply a haven; it has numerous functions in terms of providing both a public as well as a commercial service. It is part of the transportation infrastructure serving as the gateway to the hinterland. As such, ports as entities exist in various forms. A port may be administered by a government ministry or department, in which case it is part of the domain of public facilities. It may be an autonomous or semi-autonomous parastatal body independent of the government's budget allocation; or it may be entirely owned and operated as a private enterprise. In the two latter cases, it would have legal personality which will allow it to sue and be sued in its own name. It will obviously have its own charter, constitution or statute and be governed by an independent board of directors, but may still be subject to ministerial supervision. At any rate, a port modelled along any of the above lines would incur liabilities for wrongs committed by it either in its own capacity or as a constituent part of government.

4.3 The purpose of this paper is to examine, first, the subject of port liability in general, and its liabilities for wreck removal and marine pollution, in particular. The discussion embraces liability from a common law perspective but also extends to a synoptic examination of the salient features of the draft Wreck Removal Convention (DWRC) of the International Maritime Organization (IMO) currently on the agenda of its Legal Committee. Relevant United Kingdom legislation is referred to as appropriate in connection with the law of wrecks. Port liability in the context of pollution damage is discussed by reference to a novel aspect of the *Tasman Spirit*

---

* ITF Professor of Maritime Safety and Environmental Protection, Director of Doctoral Programmes, World Maritime University, Malmö, Sweden.
1. Port means "Harbour having facilities for ships to moor or load and discharge". See Peter Brodie, *Dictionary of Shipping Terms* (3rd edition) (London: LLP Limited, 1997) at p.148. See also "roadstead" at p. 160.

episode, and in relatively more detail, the *Sea Empress* incident which occurred in the port of Milford Haven in Wales. The relevant case law will be perused in contextual detail. A summary highlighting the principal points of interest is presented in conclusion.

PORT LIABILITY IN GENERAL

The port as an occupier of premises

4.4 In general terms, the liability of a port for loss or damage suffered by a person or property situated in the port stems from its status as an occupier of premises. The legal responsibility of the port for keeping the premises safe may emanate from statute, or by virtue of an express or implied contract.[2] The position at common law is reflected in the United Kingdom Occupiers' Liability Act 1957, s.2(2), which provides that port or harbour authorities are required to keep the port reasonably safe for users who have entered into a contract with the port for the use of it. There are a number of English and Canadian cases that have affirmed this duty.[3] In *Maclenan v Segar*[4] the general rule was stated by McCardie J. in the following words:

"Where the occupier of premises agrees for reward that a person shall have the right to enter and use them for a mutually contemplated purpose, the contract between the parties (unless it provides to the contrary) contains an implied warranty that the premises are as safe for that purpose as reasonable care and skill on the part of anyone can make them."

4.5 The rule includes the duty on the part of the port to give warning if it is unable to keep the port safe.[5] The duty to warn is exemplified in the decision of the House of Lords in *Workington Harbour and Dock Board v Owners of the SS Towerfield*.[6] It extends to the occupier even if no charge is imposed for the use of a wharf on the basis that some benefit is accrued by the wharfinger by the carriage of the cargo discharged there.[7]

4.6 The common law duty to keep the port safe is circumscribed by the exercise of reasonable care on the part of the port. In *The Quercus*[8] the duty in question was inspection of mooring arrangements provided by the port for use by visiting ships. In *The Bearn*,[9] the corresponding duty was to ascertain whether the berth was in a

---

2. Simon Gault, Steven J. Hazelwood and Andrew Tettenborn, *Marsden on Collisions at Sea* (13th edition) (London: Sweet & Maxwell, 2003) at p. 364.

3. See *Williams v Swansea Harbour Trustees* (1863), 14 C.B. (N.S.) 845; *Mersey Docks and Harbour Board v Gibbs* (1866), L.R.1 H.L. 93 and *Bede SS Co. v River Wear Commissioners* [1907] 1 K.B. 310. See P. K. Mukherjee, "The Charting and Safekeeping of Oceans and Waterways: Legal Implications", (1981), 3(6) Dalhousie L.J. 578 for a discussion on the Canadian cases *The Hermes* [1969] 1 Lloyd's Rep. 425 (Can. Exchq. Ct) and *The King v Hochelaga Shipping* [1940] S.C.R. 155 (S.C.C.) in which Tacshereau J. of the Supreme Court of Canada stated that "... captains who bring their ships into port are entitled to expect that the road will be in a safe condition ...".

4. [1917] 2 K.B. 325 at p. 332.

5. *The Moorcock* (1888) 14 P.D. 64; *The Cawood III* [1951] 1 Lloyd's. Rep. 350.

6. [1951] A.C. 112 (H.L.).

7. *The Grit* [1924] P. 246.

8. [1943] P. 96.

9. [1906] P. 48.

proper state for docking. Regardless of whether or not there is a contractual obligation on the part of the port, the ship using the port is a visiting ship, and from a legal point of view, the ship stands in the position of an invitee or licensee. At common law, even a trespassing ship without any contractual rights is entitled to a safe port.[10]

Common law duty codified by statute

4.7 The statutory position is set out in the Occupiers' Liability Acts of 1957[11] and 1984.[12] The 1957 Act has been applied to docks owned privately as well as by public authorities and it contains provisions which in essence reflect codifications of the common law position. The provisions also regulate and prescribe the nature of the obligations of a person in occupation or control of premises due to a visitor or an invitee with regard to, *inter alia*, hazards attributable to the condition of the premises.[13] The 1984 Act enlarges the scope of application of the common law duty to encompass persons not originally covered under the 1957 Act or the common law. The 1957 Act provides in section 2 as follows:

"(1) An occupier of premises owes the same duty, the 'common duty of care', to all his visitors, except in so far as he is free to and does extend, restrict or exclude his duty to any visitor or visitors by agreement or otherwise.

(2) The common duty of care is a duty to take such care as in all the circumstances of the case is reasonable to see that the visitor will be reasonably safe in using the premises for the purposes for which he is invited or permitted by the occupier to be there."

4.8 As the 1957 Act applies to a moveable structure including a vessel, ships using docks or any areas of the port fall under the legislation; and arguably, passengers and crew who suffer injury to their persons or property attributable to negligence of a port authority or owner, or even a wharfinger as occupier, may have a valid cause of action under that Act. However, the wharfinger owes only a duty to take reasonable care consonant with common law principles. As such, he is liable as an occupier only if the premises, i.e. the docks are defective and the damage or injury suffered by the plaintiff is caused by the defect. Furthermore, as an occupier he is vicariously liable for the negligence of his independent contractors only in certain cases, and owes a duty of care only to ships that navigate properly within the waters under his occupation or control. If the plaintiff proves that the defect in the dock was the cause of his loss or damage, or where the wharfinger is held to be a bailee of the ship, the occupier must carry the burden of proof to extricate himself from liability.[14]

---

10. See *supra*, note 2 at p. 374, and in particular note 49 at that page for a comment on the subtleties in the common law with regard the legal status of the invitee and the licensee, and the statutory status of a visitor.

11. 5 & 6 Eliz. 2, c.31.

12. 1984 c.3.

13. *Supra*, note 2 at p. 375.

14. *Ibid.*, at p. 377. See *The Sound Fisher* (1937) 59 Ll.L.R. 123 and *Vancouver Tug Boat Co. v Sooke Forest Products Ltd* [1969] 2 Lloyd's Rep. 634.

Contractual liability of port as occupier

4.9 The port can contract out of liability provided the exemption clause in the contract in question between the port and the visiting ship meets the requirements of any "unfair contract" legislation that may be applicable in the circumstances. Specifically, any contract between the port authority and the shipowner of a visiting ship must be fair and reasonable in light of what were the circumstances which were known or ought to have been known or contemplated by the parties at the time they entered into the contract.[15]

4.10 In *George Mitchell v Finney Lock Seeds Ltd*,[16] a non-maritime case, the House of Lords held that in order for a defendant to successfully exculpate himself from liability to which he would have otherwise been subject, the relevant question for a court should be whether the subject matter of the exemption clause was a risk in respect of which the defendant would be expected to take out insurance, and whether it was normal practice for defendants to invoke such a clause. It would appear that courts in general would uphold an exemption clause in favour of a port authority as reasonable, on the basis that such arrangements are made expressly and clearly by the parties in the interests of business efficacy to apportion risks.[17]

4.11 There are regulatory provisions in the 1957 Act that are relevant in this context. In the absence of an express exemption clause, a visitor entering an occupier's premises under a contract is entitled to a common duty of care on the part of the occupier pursuant to section 5 of the 1957 Act.[18] As indicated earlier, the Act applies to movable structures including vessels. Where there is a contract between a port authority and a shipowner under which third parties such as agents of the shipowner are entitled to enter the premises as visitors, the port authority as an occupier owes the same duty of care to the third parties as it does to the shipowner.[19]

LIABILITY FOR WRECK REMOVAL

Law of wrecks

4.12 The law of wrecks is closely associated with salvage law and practice. Wrecks become a concern of port or harbour authorities when they are situated within the port premises. The legal and practical implications for a port including its potential liability for marine pollution damage, inevitably becomes more serious if the wreck happens to be that of a leaking tanker. In the early part of the 17th century when the rivalry between the common law courts and the admiralty court was probably at its peak, a subject matter as obviously maritime such as wreck was judicially defined in such a manner as to remove it from the Admiralty jurisdiction to that of the common law courts.[20] In *Sir Henry Constable's Case*,[21] a piece of colourful classic in the

---

15. Gault, *ibid.*
16. [1983] 2 A.C. 803.
17. *Supra*, note 2 at pp. 377–378.
18. *Ibid.*, at p. 378.
19. *Ibid.* See also pp. 493–494 for a summarised discussion on the duties and liabilities of harbour authorities.
20. Proshanto K. Mukherjee, *Maritime Legislation* (Malmö, WMU Publications, 2002) at pp. 35–36.
21. *Constable v Gamble* (1601) 5 Co. Rep. 106a, 77 E.R. 218.

annals of English admiralty history, Sir Edward Coke, "the chief antagonist of the Admiralty jurisdiction",[22] defined wreck as "that cast at ebb tide upon the shelf below the flood mark". The significance of this judicial definition is that prior to this decision, the Admiralty had, since its inception, exercised jurisdiction below the high water mark.[23]

4.13 At common law, wreck included jetsam, flotsam, derelicts and deodands.[24] Civil droits were the Admiralty's perquisites or proprietary rights in wrecks at sea in the early 19th century. An owner's sole remedy for wreck found ashore, except for deodands, was in common law, but wreck found at sea and taken ashore was subject to Admiralty jurisdiction. Unclaimed wreck was sold under a court order and the proceeds remaining after payment of salvage became an Admiralty perquisite.[25]

4.14 The contemporary definition of wreck as found in section 255(1) of the United Kingdom Merchant Shipping Act 1995 (MSA 1995) is as follows:

"'wreck' includes jetsam, flotsam, lagan and derelict found in or on the shores of the sea or any tidal water."

4.15 In contrast, the definition of wreck in the Ghana Shipping Act appears to have a much wider scope. In that Act,

"'wreck' includes –
  (a) flotsam, jetsam, lagan and derelict found in the waters of or on the shores of Ghana;
  (b) cargo, stores, tackle and equipment;
  (c) the personal property of shipwrecked persons; and
  (d) any wrecked or any part of wrecked aircraft or any cargo."[26]

4.16 However, on closer examination of section 252 of MSA 1995, it is evident that subsection (3) enlarges the notion of property to include "equipment, cargo, stores or ballast" of the vessel, thus the two above-noted definitions are not substantially different.

4.17 It is interesting to note the contrasting definition of wreck in the DWRC[27] currently being developed by the Legal Committee of the IMO. It reads as follows:

"'wreck' means –
  (a) a sunken or stranded ship; or
  (b) any part of a sunken or stranded ship, including any object that is or has been on board such a ship;
  (c) any object that is lost at sea from a ship and that is stranded, sunken or adrift at sea; or
  (d) a ship that is about, or may reasonably be expected, to sink or to strand, where an act or activity to effectively[28] assist the ship or any property in danger is not already under way."

---

22. F. L. Wiswall, *The Development of Admiralty Jurisdiction and Practice Since 1800* (Cambridge: Cambridge University Press, 1970) at p. 6.
23. *Ibid.*, and *supra*, note 20 at p. 36.
24. Deodands ceased to be maritime property pursuant to the Deodands Act of 1846. See *supra*, note 20 at p. 40.
25. *Ibid.*, at p. 36.
26. Ghana Shipping Act, 2003, s. 481.
27. For the text of the DWRC, see IMO Doc. LEG 90/5 Annex 1. See also IMO Doc. LEG 90/15 at pp. 29–41 containing the report on agenda item 5 (Draft Convention on Wreck Removal) of the Legal Committee's deliberations at its 90th session.
28. The word "effectively" was added pursuant to a proposal made by the Comite Maritime International (CMI) at LEG 90 in May 2006. See IMO Doc. LEG 90/15 at p. 31.

4.18 The law of wrecks consists of three facets. The first is the legal consideration of wreck as property. When a ship becomes a wreck, it remains the property of
the shipowner, except where he has issued a notice of abandonment in tandem with
a claim for constructive total loss. In such case the insurer becomes the owner of
the wreck. Within this scenario, as a matter of public policy the wreck is protected
through the intervention of a public authority. In several common law jurisdictions
it is the office of the receiver of wreck who, for the time being, exercises regulatory
control over the wreck as property. In some jurisdictions, the receiver of wreck is the
port administrator.[29] In others, the receiver of wreck is a public official appointed
specifically for carrying out certain prescribed functions, and there may be more
than one person so appointed with allocated responsibility over wrecks in various
geographical regions within the jurisdiction. In the United Kingdom this scheme is
provided for in sections 248 and 249 of MSA 1995.

4.19 The second facet of wreck law is the regulatory dimension, the purpose of
which is to ensure safety of navigation within the port or harbour areas, and in particular, where the wreck is situated in a fairway or navigation channel. In the latter
case where the wreck poses a navigational hazard or is an obstruction to navigation,
the issue of its removal becomes crucial. In such case the regulatory regime extends
to salvage operations as well as marking of the wreck for purposes of safety until it
is removed and is no longer a hazard or obstruction to navigation.

4.20 The third facet of wreck law consists of public protection given to wrecks
that have a historical significance. In this context there are provisions in the United
Nations Convention on the Law of the Sea, 1982 (UNCLOS) that deal with
archaeological finds.[30] In recent times, the archaeological find that drew the most
international attention was that of the *Titanic* in 1987. In the context of this incident it is important to note that the continental shelf doctrine of the international
law of the sea was not applicable because the wreck was not a natural resource.
Rather, the claims and rights were governed by the law of salvage.[31] Needless to say,
this was not a case that involved a port authority.

Statutory and common law liability for removal of wrecks and other obstacles

4.21 The issue of liability of a port for wreck removal consists of two sub-issues. The
first is the question of whether such a liability exists either by virtue of statute or
under common law.[32] The second is whether the cost of wreck removal by the port
authority can be passed on to the owner of the wreck. As a practical matter, it is
obvious that the port or harbour authority itself must bear the costs in the absence
of a readily identifiable owner.

29. See s.269(1) of the Cayman Islands Merchant Shipping Law (2004 Revision).
30. See UNCLOS Articles 143, 149, 303. It is notable that contrary to international law the United
States applies the notion of "finders-keepers" for wrecks on the high seas. See Minutes of 54th Annual
General Meeting of Canadian Maritime Law Association dated 27 May 2005.
31. Ian Townsend Gault and David Vander Zwaag, "Now that Pandora's Box is Open Could Canada
Assume Responsibility for the Wreck of the Titanic" in *New Directions*, IITOPS Newsletter, Vol. 1, Nos.
2 and 3, 1987, at pp. 6–7.
32. In this discussion first statutory liability and then liability under common law is addressed.

4.22 It appears that historically there was no positive duty imposed by statute upon a harbour or conservancy authority to remove wrecks lying within its geographical perimeter. This is evident from the provision contained in section 530 of the Merchant Shipping Act 1894 which is the predecessor of the current section 252 of MSA 1995.[33] It is important to note that in the current statutory provision the competence of the harbour or conservancy authority is characterised as a series of powers rather than obligations or duties. The powers are exercisable where a vessel is sunk, stranded or abandoned, or in or near any approach to a harbour or tidal water under the control of the relevant authority such that the vessel is or is likely to become an obstruction or navigational danger. In those circumstances the authority can exercise any of the following powers under subsection (2):

"(a) to take possession of, and raise, remove or destroy the whole or any part of the vessel and any other property to which the power extends;
  (b) to light or buoy the vessel or part of the vessel and any such other property until it is raised, removed, or destroyed[34]; and
  (c) subject to subsections (5) and (6) below, to sell, in such manner as the authority think fit, the vessel or part of the vessel so raised or removed and any other property recovered in the exercise of the powers conferred by paragraph (a) or (b) above[35];
  (d) to reimburse themselves, out of the proceeds of the sale, for the expenses incurred by them in relation to the sale."

4.23 Under subsection (4) the surplus, if any, of the sale proceeds are to be held in trust by the authority for the persons entitled to it. Under subsection (7) the market value of the property is to be determined by the agreement between the authority and the owner failing which it is to be determined by a person appointed by the Secretary of State for that purpose.

4.24 It is notable that apart from a harbour or conservancy authority, lighthouse authorities have virtually the same powers pursuant to section 253 of MSA 1995. If there is any question regarding powers in relation to a wreck between a harbour or conservancy authority and a general lighthouse authority, then pursuant to section 254 of MSA 1995 the question must be referred to the Secretary of State whose decision in the matter shall be final.

4.25 It is important to note that neither section 252 nor section 253 of MSA 1995 expressly provide for the relevant authority to recover wreck removal expenses from the owner. Under both these sections a port authority can only seek reimbursement for wreck removal expenses from the proceeds of sale of the wreck. However, section 253 expressly provides a right of recovery from the owner for the shortfall where the proceeds of sale are insufficient to meet the authority's expenses. Section 252 is silent on this point.

---

33. See A. R. M. Fogarty, *Merchant Shipping Legislation* (2d ed.) (London: LLP, 2004), paragraph 8.155 at p. 284 where a number of cases including *The Gregerso* [1971] 1 Lloyd's Rep. 220 are cited in support of this statement.

34. This provision is a codification of the duty of a port authority at common law to mark and light a dangerous wreck. See further discussion on this point below.

35. Subsection (5) provides for a minimum of seven days as the required notice period for the intended sale except in the case of perishable goods. Subsection (6) provides that the owner of the property is entitled, at any time prior to the sale, to have it delivered to him upon payment of its fair market value.

4.26 Apart from MSA 1995, the Harbour, Docks, and Piers Clauses Act 1847 in its section 56 provides for similar powers of wreck removal and recovery of expenses. But in this section there is express provision for recovery of wreck removal expenses from the owner regardless of whether the wreck is sold. This section reads as follows:

"56. The harbour master may remove any wreck or other obstruction to the harbour, dock, or pier, or the approaches to the same, and also floating timber which impedes the navigation thereof, and the expense of removing any such wreck, obstruction or floating timber shall be repaid by the owner of the same; and the harbour master may detain such wreck or floating timber for securing the expenses, and on nonpayment of such expenses, on demand, may sell such wreck or floating timber, and out of the proceeds of such sale pay such expenses, rendering the overplus, if any, to the owner on demand."

4.27 The right of the port authority to recover the wreck removal expenses under the above provision is subject to liabilities and defences provided at common law. In *Greenock Port and Harbour Trustees v British Oil and Cake Mills*,[36] a Scottish case, negligence was alleged on the part of the harbour authorities who sought to recover expenses under the above-noted section.

4.28 It is not entirely clear whether the power of the port authority under section 252 of MSA 1995 to remove a wreck can be viewed as statutory compulsion. At any rate, where a wreck constitutes a danger to navigational safety a port authority is obliged to remove the wreck by virtue of its common law duty as an occupier to ensure that the harbour is safe for navigation.[37] The port authority must, within a reasonable time of determining whether the wreck should be removed, exercise its powers, failure of which may result in the authority being liable in damages.[38]

4.29 The legal position of a port authority as the occupier of port premises has already been discussed in general terms. A more specific question is whether a port that has statutory power to remove a wreck but does not exercise that power can be held liable if a vessel collides with the wreck. Under the Occupiers' Liability Act 1957 discussed previously a port authority would be required to take reasonable steps to remove wrecks or mark or light them in pursuance of its statutory duty of care. Failure to do so can result in liability for foreseeable damage. A port or harbour authority may also be under a common law duty to mark and light a wreck that poses a navigational hazard, and failure to do so may make the authority liable in the event a vessel collides with that wreck.[39]

4.30 It is important to note that the steps that need to be taken by the port authority need only be reasonable in the circumstances. In other words, if the cost of wreck removal was disproportionately high compared to the benefit to be derived, then failure to remove the wreck would not result in liability on the part of the port authority.[40]

4.31 If a vessel sinks within the port premises and the sinking is attributable to the negligence of its owner, vicariously or otherwise; or if the sinking is caused by the negligence of another vessel, the relevant owner is liable for wreck removal

---

36. 1944 S.C. 70 (Scot.).
37. See *The Towerfield* [1951] A.C. 112 and other cases cited in *supra*, note 32.
38. *Jones v Mersey Docks and Harbour Board* (1913) Asp. M.L.C. 335: *Christie v Trinity House Corporation* (1919) 35 T.L.R. 480.
39. *The Manorbier Castle* (1922) 13 Ll.L.R. 549.
40. *Supra*, note 2 at p. 490.

costs.[41] However, after possession, control and management of the wreck passes to a port authority, the owner of the wreck is no longer responsible to third parties for damage caused by failure to mark and light the wreck.[42]

4.32 If a port authority in the exercise of its statutory powers introduces a new danger, such as by failing to properly light a wreck removed to a new position, it appears that the authority will be liable.[43]

IMO Draft Wreck Removal Convention

Background and structure

4.33 The purpose of the draft Wreck Removal Convention (DWRC), currently on the IMO agenda, is to create an international regime to govern wreck removal outside territorial seas globally. The Convention will provide a legal basis for States to remove from their exclusive economic zones (EEZ), wrecks that are hazardous to navigation and the marine and coastal environments. The exercise leading up to the current draft was initiated within the Legal Committee several years ago. It was approved at the Committee's recent 92nd session and will be forwarded for adoption to a Diplomatic Conference, scheduled to be held in May 2007 in Nairobi, Kenya. Its priority ranking in the Legal Committee agenda gave way to other more pressing issues such as the recently adopted Suppression of Unlawful Acts (SUA) Protocol of 2005. Consideration of the DWRC has now resurfaced under a Netherlands-led intercessional working group. The diplomatic conference to adopt the Convention is planned for 2007.

4.34 There are 22 Articles contained in 8 Parts. Parts I to IV consist of, respectively, the Preamble, Definitions (Article 1), Objectives and general principles (Article 2) and Scope of Application (Articles 3 to 5). Part V consisting of Articles 6 to 10 sets out the general obligations which are the substantive safety-related provisions. Articles 11 to 14 contained in Part VI consist of substantive financial liability-related provisions. Part VII (Article 15) and Part VIII (Articles 16 to 22) consist of the Final Provisions. The following are the salient features of the DWRC.

Definitions

4.35 To understand the Convention it is important to note the following definitions set out below in summary form:

"Convention area" – EEZ;
"Maritime Casualty" – "… collision, stranding or other incident of navigation or other occurrence on board or external to it resulting in material damage or imminent threat of material damage to a ship or its cargo";
"Wreck" –
   – a sunken or stranded ship; or
   – any part of a sunken or stranded ship, including any object that is or has been on board such a ship; or

---

41. *Dee Conservancy Board v McConnell* [1928] 2 K.B. 159; *The Ella* [1915] P. 111.
42. *The Utopia* [1893] A.C. 492 (P.C.). Notably, a contrary view was held in *Dee Conservancy Board v McConnell*.
43. See *Kane v New Forest District Council* [2001] 3 All E.R. 914, a non-maritime decision.

– any object that is lost at sea from a ship and that is stranded, sunken or adrift at sea; or

– a ship that is about, or may reasonably be expected, to sink or to strand, where an act or activity to effectively[44] assist the ship or any property in danger is not already underway;

"Hazard" – condition or threat posing danger or impediment to navigation; reasonable expectation of major harmful consequences to marine environment, coastline or related interests;

"Related interests" – coastal state interests directly affected or threatened by a wreck (see examples);

"Removal" – prevention, mitigation, elimination of hazard;

"Registered owner" (RO) includes the owner if the ship is not registered; and for a state-owned ship includes the operating company;

"Operator" includes manager or bareboat charterer who has assumed ISM Code duties and responsibilities;

"The Affected State" (AS) – State in whose Convention area the wreck is located;

"State of ship's registry" – state of registration or if unregistered ship state whose flag she is entitled to fly.

Objectives, General Principles and Scope of Application (Articles 2 to 5)

4.36 The measures to be taken by an AS must be proportionate to the hazard and not beyond reasonable necessity to remove it. No unnecessary interference is allowed; nor is there any sovereignty or sovereign right over the high seas. The application of the Convention is primarily to wrecks in the convention area, and by optional declaration, to wrecks in the territorial sea. The Convention is not applicable to measures described in the Intervention Convention. Wrecks are to be reported to the AS and must include information necessary for the AS to determine whether the wreck in question is hazardous.

General Obligations (Articles 6 to 10)

4.37 The criteria specified in Article 7 are to be used by the AS to determine whether a wreck poses a hazard. Upon obtaining knowledge of a wreck, the AS must urgently warn mariners and coastal states and ensure that all reasonable steps are taken to establish the precise location of the wreck if it is reasonably believed to be hazardous. If it is determined to be hazardous, the AS is to mark the wreck according to the international buoyage system of the area. The AS must immediately inform the flag state and the RO, and must consult the flag state and other affected states regarding measures to be taken. The RO must remove a wreck determined to constitute a hazard. The RO must provide the AS with evidence of insurance or other financial security. The RO may contract with a salvor to remove the wreck. The AS may intervene only to ensure that the removal procedure is safe and environmentally sound, and may lay down certain conditions. The AS must set a reasonable

---

44. The addition of the word "effectively" was proposed by the CMI at LEG 90, May 2006.

deadline for the RO to remove the wreck; and if the RO does not comply or is not contactable, the AS may remove it at the RO's expense.

Financial Liability and Insurance Requirements (Articles 11 to 14)

4.38 The RO is strictly liable for the cost of locating, marking and removal of a wreck subject to the exceptions (defences) set out in Article 11(1). He is entitled to limit liability under the applicable regime but is not liable under this Convention if other Conventions apply (CLC, HNS, Nuclear 1960, Vienna, Nuclear 1963, Bunkers). The RO must maintain insurance or other financial security at least to cover liability as per the limits under the International Convention on Limitation of Liability for Maritime Claims (LLMC), 1976.[45] The flag state must issue a certificate attesting to the required insurance cover and containing specified details. An authorized institution or organisation may issue such a certificate in which case the state party must guarantee its completeness and accuracy. Details of such delegation must be notified to the Secretary General of the IMO. Certificates must be carried on board and copies of the same must be deposited with the ship's registry. Claims for compensation may be brought directly against the insurer who will be entitled to invoke the same defences as those of the assured and will have the same limitation rights. The insurer may allege wilful misconduct on the part of the assured owner as per Article 13, paragraph 11. Actions shall be time-barred by three years from the date of determination of the hazard to a maximum of six years from the date of the maritime casualty.

LIABILITY FOR MARINE POLLUTION

Preliminary remarks

4.39 A port or harbour authority may be held liable for marine pollution damage in relatively few instances. The oil spill from the Liberian tanker *Sea Empress* which took place while the vessel was entering the port of Milford Haven is probably the most significant case in recent times which involved liability of a port authority. Another incident is the *Tasman Spirit* oil spill in the harbour of Karachi in which petitioners including local fishermen's welfare associations entered petitions in the High Court of Sindh at Karachi on constitutional grounds against several respondents including the Karachi Port Trust (KPT). The petitioners alleged on behalf of their constituent members that KPT, by failing to clean up the contaminated waters of the harbour, had deprived fishermen of their fundamental right to earn their traditional income and livelihood as guaranteed by the constitution of Pakistan.[46] The author is not aware of the outcome of the petitions.

4.40 In the following discussion the potential liability of the Milford Haven Port Authority (MHPA) in relation to the *Sea Empress* oil spill is examined. The facts are briefly as follows:

4.41 The Liberian tanker *Sea Empress* laden with over 130,000 tonnes of crude oil ran aground at the entrance to the port of Milford Haven on 15 February 1996.

---

45. It should be noted that the limits under the 1996 Protocol of LLMC are considerably higher.
46. Information gleaned from personal sources.

Approximately 72,000 tonnes of crude oil and 360 tonnes of heavy oil escaped from the grounded tanker which was eventually refloated and brought alongside a jetty in the port where the remainder of the cargo of 58,000 tonnes of crude oil was discharged. The incident led to civil claims by pollution victims against the P&I Club of the registered owners of the vessel as well as the International Oil Pollution Compensation (IOPC) Fund.[47]

4.42 Subsequently, recourse action was taken by the 1971 Fund against MHPA. The Fund alleged that MHPA had failed to take reasonable care to avoid the risk of the tanker grounding and consequently releasing oil. It was alleged in particular that MHPA had failed to consider the serious pollution risk a laden tanker could cause by running aground and had failed to take measures to control or reduce that risk. The action was brought in negligence alleging a breach of duty of care on the part of MHPA. It was alleged, inter alia, that MHPA had failed to have in place effective and fully operational vessel traffic services (VTS) and to mark the entrance to the west channel. Its pilot allocation system was negligent and training for pilots was defective. It was further alleged that the response action of MHPA was *ad hoc*, improvised and negligent as a consequence of which approximately 69,300 tonnes of crude oil entered the waters of the harbour.[48]

4.43 MHPA denied all allegations specifically arguing that it did not owe any duty of care and was not subject to any statutory duty to claimants in respect of any economic losses. It also denied owing any duty of care to the 1971 Fund. It is interesting to note that the MHPA denied liability in respect of a pilot's negligence on the ground that it only authorized pilots to provide pilotage services. The pilots were employees of a separate corporation, mainly the MHPL, for whose acts the MHPA could not be liable. The MHPA also referred to the channelling of liability provisions in the Merchant Shipping (Oil Pollution) Act 1995 and to the Milford Haven Conservancy Act 1993 in relation to salvage operations. The MHPA contended that by virtue of these two acts, it was not liable for any pollution damage resulting from the *Sea Empress* oil spill.[49]

4.44 After the trial date was fixed, the 1971 Fund and MHPA accepted the court's proposal to attempt to settle by mediation. This was eventually achieved and a settlement amount of £20 million was paid by the MHPA to the 1971 Fund in December 2003.[50]

4.45 Recourse action was also initiated by Texaco, the operator of the oil terminal in Milford Haven against MHPA as well as Milford Haven Pilotage Limited (MHPL), the employer of pilots in that port.[51] The allegations were substantially the same as those of the 1971 Fund. In particular, Texaco alleged that both MHPA and MHPL were causing a public nuisance which resulted in the losses in respect of which the claims were advanced. Eventually an out-of-court settlement was reached with regard to the action brought by Texaco.[52]

---

47. IOPC Funds Annual Report, 2003, at p. 58.
48. *Ibid.*, at p. 60.
49. *Ibid.*, at p. 61.
50. *Ibid.*, at p. 62.
51. *Ibid.*, at pp. 60, 62.
52. *Ibid.*, at pp. 62, 63.

4.46 A criminal action was also brought against the MHPA by the Environment Agency in Cardiff Crown Court. Judgment was rendered by Steel J. on 15 January 1999.[53] As mentioned in his judgment, the casualty was attributable to negligent navigation by the pilot. The charge against the port authority was framed under section 85 of the Water Resources Act 1991 which provides in subsection (1) that "[a] person contravenes this section if he causes or knowingly permits any poisonous, noxious or polluting matter or any solid waste matter to enter any controlled waters". The offence is characteristically one of strict liability; the prosecution need only prove the *actus reus* of the offence for the action to succeed. The *actus reus* in this case was "causing" polluted matter to enter the relevant waters, to which the MHPA pleaded guilty. Steel J. made the point that the constituent elements of the offence had been considered by the House of Lords in *Empress Car Co. (Abertillery) Ltd v National Rivers Authority*.[54] In that case Lord Hoffmann held that this provision constituted a strict liability offence independent of intention, negligence, fault or knowledge on the part of the perpetrator.[55] It appears that the word "knowingly" in this provision relates only to permitting the entry of any poisonous, noxious or polluting substance into controlled waters. If a person "causes" this to happen, he is strictly liable regardless of whether he had knowledge of the consequences.[56] Steel J. set out the effect of that decision in summary form in the following words:

"(a) If the charge is 'causing', the prosecution must prove that the pollution was caused by something which the defendants did, rather than merely failed to prevent.

(b) Thus there must have been some positive act by the defendants. But that positive act need not have been the immediate cause of the escape. The only question was whether something which the defendants had done, whether immediately or antecedently, had caused the pollution.

(c) Thus, for instance, simply maintaining a tank of diesel is doing something; if diesel escapes, it solely remains to consider whether the necessary causal connection is established.

(d) The only question which has to be asked for the purposes of s.85(1) is 'did the defendants cause the pollution?' The fact that for different purposes or even for the same purpose one could also say that someone or something else caused the pollution is not inconsistent with the defendants having caused it."[57]

4.47 Steel J. stated that he analysed the scope of the statutory provision to put the guilty plea of MHPA in its proper perspective and reached the conclusion that in fact the port authority did something that caused the pollution. As such, he accepted the plea on the basis of strict liability without any admission of fault on the part of MHPA and disposed of the case.[58] The quantum of the fine was set at £4,000,000 and prosecution costs of £825,000 were imposed on the MHPA.

4.48 An issue that is marginally relevant is the statutory requirement by the owner or master of a ship discharging oil or oily mixture, or where oil is found

---

53. *Environment Agency v Milford Haven Port Authority and Andrews (The Sea Empress)* [1999] 1 Lloyd's Rep. 673.
54. [1998] 1 All E.R. 481.
55. *Ibid.*, at p. 489.
56. See Proshanto K. Mukherjee, "Refuge and Salvage", chapter 10 in Aldo Chircop and Olof Linden (eds), *Places of Refuge for Ships* (Leiden/Boston: Martinus Nijhoff Publishers, 2006), pp. 271, 290–291.
57. *Supra*, note 53 at p. 675.
58. *Ibid.*, at p. 676.

escaping into the waters of a United Kingdom harbour, to report the occurrence. The report is to be made pursuant to section 136 of MSA 1995 to the harbour master or in his absence to the harbour authority. Failure to make such a report can lead to penal liability on summary conviction.

OTHER LIABILITY RELATED ISSUES FOR A PORT OR HARBOUR AUTHORITY

Limitation of liability of a port authority

4.49 The global limitation regime applicable in the United Kingdom is the LLMC 1976 amended by its 1996 Protocol. The Convention provisions are appended to MSA 1995 as Schedule 7, Part I. In Article 2 of the Convention, paragraphs (d), (e) and (f) are of particular relevance as they deal with claims in respect of wrecks and are subject to limitation by virtue of that Article. The provisions of paragraphs (d), (e) and (f) are as follows:

"(d) claims in respect of the raising, removal, destruction or the rendering harmless of a ship which is sunk, wrecked, stranded or abandoned, including anything that is or has been on board such ship;
(e) claims in respect of the removal, destruction or the rendering harmless of the cargo of the ship;
(f) claims of a person other than the person liable in respect of measures taken in order to avert or minimise loss for which the person liable may limit his liability in accordance with this Convention, and further loss caused by such measures."

4.50 It is submitted that allowing shipowners to limit liability in respect of wreck removal is in the interest of the state because limitation provides an incentive and encourages them to remove wrecks that would otherwise constitute a navigational hazard. This, in turn, would result in the port authority being burdened with the obligation to remove them. Be that as it may, it is interesting that the United Kingdom has entered a reservation with regard to these provisions in the Convention.[59]

4.51 The entitlement of a port or harbour authority to limit liability is outside the scope of the Convention. However, under United Kingdom law contained in section 191 of the MSA 1995, a harbour authority, a conservancy authority and the owners of any dock or canal may limit liability for any loss or damage done to any ship, or to cargo or any other property on board in accordance with that section. The limitation as provided in subsection (5) is by reference to the tonnage of the largest United Kingdom ship which has been within the area of responsibility of the relevant authority, at the time of the loss or damage or within the preceding five years. The method of calculation of limitation as per subsection (5), in turn, cross refers to the method set out in Article 6, paragraph 1(b) of the Convention. The provision must be read together with paragraphs 5(1) and (2) of Part II of Schedule 7 to the MSA 1995 which sets out the limits for ships under 300 tons.

---

59. MSA 1995, Sch. 7, Part II, para. 3. See also Christopher Hill, *Maritime Law* (6th edition) (London, Hong Kong: LLP, 2003), p. 404.

The spirit of the Convention is maintained in that section 191 of MSA 1995 does not exclude the liability of an authority or person for loss or damage resulting from any personal act or omission. The limitation regime is also extended to harbour authorities and conservancy authorities under other acts such as the Harbours Act 1964 and Dangerous Vessels Act 1985.[60]

Priority ranking of wreck removal claims

4.52 Expenses incurred for wreck removal by a port or harbour authority enjoy a specific position in the priority ranking structure of the International Convention on Maritime Liens and Mortgages 1993 (L&M Convention 1993). It is not surprising that the United Kingdom is not a party to this Convention, and it is highly unlikely that this will ever happen since it has never been a party to any of the previous Conventions on this subject. However, by virtue of the various statutory provisions referred to above, which entitle a port or harbour authority to claim wreck removal expenses, this claim is afforded a special status when there are other contesting claims in respect of an arrested vessel or one that is the subject of a judicial or forced sale. According to Professor Tetley a claim for wreck removal expenses incurred by a port authority is a special legislative right.[61] Professor D. R. Thomas refers to this as a claim of paramount priority.[62]

4.53 Notable in this context is the position of the receiver of wreck. Under section 243 of the MSA 1995, a receiver is empowered to dispose of an unclaimed wreck by sale, and to deduct from the sale proceeds, the expenses associated with the sale and his fees. Pursuant to section 249(3) of the MSA 1995, a receiver of wreck has the same rights and remedies in respect of fees and expenses as a salvor has in respect of salvage due to him. It means that a receiver claiming wreck removal expenses would enjoy the same rights and remedies as the holder of a salvage lien, including the priority ranking of such a lienholder. While, as indicated earlier, there are no express statutory provisions under MSA 1995 giving a harbour or conservancy authority the right to claim wreck removal expenses, such right exists under section 56 of the Harbours, Docks, and Piers Clauses Act 1847. In situations falling under that Act and otherwise under the common law, the position of the relevant authority may well be that the claim has the status of a salvage lien analogous to the corresponding claim of a receiver of wreck.

4.54 According to Article 12, paragraph 2 of the L&M Convention 1993, the ranking of all costs associated with the arrest and sale of a vessel must be paid out of the sale proceeds first, before any payments are made in respect of other claims subject to the Convention. Paragraph 3 allows state parties to give priority to wreck removal costs *vis-à-vis* other costs referred to in paragraph 2, through national legislation giving effect to the Convention.[63]

---

60. *Supra*, note 33 at pp. 581–583.
61. William Tetley, *Maritime Liens and Claims* (Montreal: International Shipping Publications, 1989), at p. 42.
62. D. R. Thomas, *Maritime Liens*, British Shipping Laws, Vol. 14 (London: Stevens & Sons, 1980), at pp. 231–234.
63. See, e.g., Ghana Shipping Act 2003, s.74(5).

CONCLUSION

4.55 In this paper an attempt has been made to examine port liability largely from an environmental perspective. The emphasis has been on liability issues as they pertain in the common law system, in particular, with regard to English law and United Kingdom legislation, but the laws of other jurisdictions such as Canada and Ghana have also been mentioned as deemed appropriate. The law relating to removal of wrecks and the legal position of a port authority has been discussed in context-ual detail based on the premise that the legal principles involved would apply commensurately, if a wreck was that of a laden or partially laden tanker and the casualty led to serious pollution liability implications. The liability of a port authority as an occupier of premises has been discussed in terms of both common law as well as relevant English statute law. The discussion, needless to say, is centred on the port's obligation to remove a wreck that is a danger to navigation, or is an environ-mental hazard. On the topical issue of wreck removal, a synoptic overview has been presented on the current IMO initiative concerning the development of a wreck removal convention.

4.56 The environmental perspective is undoubtedly the focus of this paper which is consonant with the theme of this session of the colloquium. In acknowl-edging the indisputable importance of that theme, it is instructive to note the statement of Steel J. in *The Sea Empress* case where he recognises the legal status of the MHPA as a public trust established as a statutory body pursuant to the Milford Haven Conservancy Act 1958; and then refers to that which is of paramount con-cern, namely, safety. In his words:

"… whatever may be the laudable interests of the company in promoting the public benefit and providing employment, this cannot be relevant to the standards of efficiency and care that are required in matters of safety." [64]

4.57 This must surely constitute the very essence of the judgment; a grim reminder to all involved in matters maritime that safety and environmental concerns must remain uppermost in the consideration of all law and policy decisions including those made by port and harbour authorities, by virtue of statutory powers or otherwise. It is an admonishment to the international maritime community, lest we forget, to ceaselessly strive to protect the marine environment of this planet from the devastating consequences of pollution.

---

64. *Supra*, note 53 at p. 680.

PART 3

Civil and Pollution Liabilities of Salvors

CHAPTER 5

Liabilities of salvors

PROFESSOR STEPHEN GIRVIN* and TOBY STEPHENS†

INTRODUCTION

5.1 It is in the nature of salvage[1] that salvage contractors very often render services in circumstances of acute danger and considerable difficulty to themselves and their equipment.[2] The task at hand is often arduous and frustrating.[3] In return for performing this rather special type of altruistic service, salvage law, which is of considerable antiquity,[4] willingly remunerates the salvor for his services in respect of recognised subjects of salvage,[5] provided such services are offered voluntarily and rendered when the property is in danger.[6] The salvage services delivered must also be successful, usually represented by the maxim "no cure, no pay",[7] in order to garner a reward.[8] As Justice Story put it in *The Henry Ewbank*:

"Salvage, it is true, is not a question of compensation *pro opera et labore*. It rises to a higher dignity. It takes its source in a deeper policy. It combines with private merit and individual sacrifices larger considerations of the public good, of commercial liberality, and of international justice. It offers a premium, by way of honorary reward, for prompt and ready assistance to human sufferings; for a bold and fearless intrepidity; and for that affecting chivalry, which forgets itself in an anxiety to save property, as well as life." [9]

5.2 Our concern in this chapter is not, however, a reconsideration of the well-established principles, but rather the extent of the reward offered when the salvage

---

* Professor of Maritime Law, School of Law, University of Birmingham.

† Partner, Holman, Fenwick & Willan, London.

1. As to the juridical basis, see, e.g., F. D. Rose "Restitution for the rescuer", in (1989) 9 O.J.L.S. 167–204; Kennedy & Rose, *The Law of Salvage* (6th ed., 2002), para. 21 (hereafter "Kennedy & Rose"). See too J. P. van Niekerk, "Salvage and Negotiorum Gestio: Exploratory Reflections on the Jurisprudential Foundation and Classification of the South African Law of Salvage", in 1992 *Acta Juridica* 148–174.

2. See, e.g., *Tojo Maru (Owners) v NV Bureau Wijsmuller (The Tojo Maru)* [1972] A.C. 242, 294 (Lord Diplock).

3. Graphically illustrated by some of the cases reported by the International Salvage Union (ISU): see *www.marine-salvage.com/* and by the dramatic salvage operation surrounding the *MSC Napoli*. See, e.g., Sandra Speares, "MSC Napoli salvage may cost 'up to $20m' in event of break-up", in *Lloyd's List*, 24 January 2007.

4. See, e.g., F. R. Sanborn, *Origins of the Early Maritime and Commercial Law* (1930), pp. 37, 113, 315–317.

5. I.e. ship and cargo (including freight): see *The Gas Float Whitton (No 2)* [1896] P. 42 (C.A.), 58–59 (Lord Esher MR); *The Fusilier* (1865) Br. 7 Lush 341, 344; 167 E.R. 391, 393 (Dr Lushington). For the contribution of Dr Lushington to salvage law generally, see S. M. Waddams, "Dr Lushington's contribution to the law of maritime salvage (1838–67)", in [1989] L.M.C.L.Q. 59–80.

6. See, e.g., *The Neptune* (1824) 1 Hagg. 227, 236; 166 E.R. 81, 85 (Lord Stowell).

7. Salvage contracts reflect this too: see, e.g., LOF 2000.

8. *The Zephyrus* (1842) 1 W. Rob. 329, 330; 166 E.R. 596 (Dr Lushington); John Reeder, *Brice on Maritime Law of Salvage* (4th ed., 2003), para. 1–01 (hereafter "Brice").

9. (1833) 11 Fed. Cas. 1166, 1170.

service involves some element of liability on the part of the salvor.[10] Our consideration inevitably concentrates on the law as it is today and, for this reason, we consider the position at common law and under the Salvage Convention of 1989 and the interface of the principles with the Limitation Convention of 1976 and its Protocol of 1996.

POLICY: SUPPORT FOR SALVORS

5.3 Public policy arguments have long underlined the importance of the role of the salvor. Thus, in *The Industry*, Sir John Nicholl referred to the important principle of encouraging "enterprise, reward exertion, and to be liberal in all that is due to the general interests of commerce, and the general benefit of owners and underwriters, even though the reward may fall upon an individual owner with some severity".[11] However, though this policy is strongly endorsed in the case law, it was also recognised at an early stage that, independently of any formal salvage agreement,

"when persons undertake to perform a salvage service, they are bound to exercise ordinary skill and ordinary prudence in the execution of the duty which they take upon themselves to perform. I do not mean to say that they must be finished navigators; but they must possess and exercise such a degree of prudence and skill as persons in their condition ordinarily do possess, and may fairly be expected to display."[12]

5.4 A prominent professional salvor once gave credence to why such support was necessary, in outlining the professional salvage business in terms of four elements:

"First, a commitment to hold tugs in readiness for salvage operation for a considerable part of their time; second, a significant proportion of that time will be devoted to being on salvage station, not necessarily at specific places but in strategic areas or sections of trade routes; third, a heavy investment in an easy access to the specialized equipment needed to cope with the wide range of possible salvage operations; and fourth, the employment of crews and specialists with expert skills and wide experience in salvage work."[13]

---

10. See D. Rhidian Thomas, "Aspects of the Impact of Negligence upon Maritime Salvage in United Kingdom Admiralty Law", in (1976–1977) 2 *Maritime Lawyer* 57–90; Kennedy & Rose, ch. 11; Brice, ch. 7. For a US perspective, see Martin J. Norris, "Misconduct of Salvors", in (1951–52) Brooklyn L.R. 247–262; James L. Rudolph, "Negligence Salvage: Reduction of Award, Forfeiture of Award of Damages?", in (1975–1976) J.M.L.C. 419–431; Thomas J. Schoenbaum, *Admiralty Law and Maritime Law* (4th ed., 2004), §16–04. We do not in this chapter consider the question whether there is liability for fault or misconduct leading to the need for salvage services: see *The Beaverford (Owners) v The Kafiristan (Owners)* [1938] A.C. 136; *The Susan V Luckenbach* [1951] P. 197 (C.A.).

11. (1835) 3 Hag. Adm. 203; 166 E.R. 381. See also *The William Beckford* (1800) 3 C. Rob. 355–356; 165 E.R. 492 (Lord Stowell); *The Clifton* (1834) 3 Hag. Adm. 117, 121; 166 ER 349, 351 (Sir John Nicholl); *The Cape Packet* (1848) 3 W. Rob. 122, 123; 166 E.R. 909 (Dr Lushington); *The Fusilier* (1865) Br. & Lush. 341, 347; 167 E.R. 391, 394 (Dr Lushington); *The Glengyle* [1898] P. 97 (C.A.), 102–103 (Gorell Barnes J.); *The St Blane* [1974] 1 Lloyd's Rep 557, 560 (Brandon J.); *Tojo Maru (Owners) v NV Bureau Wijsmuller (The Tojo Maru)* [1972] A.C. 242, 267 (Lord Reid); *Fisher v The Oceanic Grandeur* (1972) 127 C.L.R. 312, 336 (Stephen J.).

12. *The Cape Packet* (1848) 3 W. Rob. 122, 125; 166 E.R. 909–910 (Dr Lushington); *The Perla* (1857) Swab. 230, 231–232; 166 E.R. 1111, 1112 (Dr Lushington).

13. Cited in William L. Neilson, "The 1989 International Convention on Salvage", in (1991–92) Connecticut L.R. 1203–1252, at 1205. See too the websites of leading salvage companies, such as Semco (*www.semco.com.sg/*), Smit (*www.smit.com/*), SvitzerWijsmuller (*www.svitzerwijsmuller.com/*), and Tsavliris (*www.tsavliris.com/*).

5.5 The policy arguments supporting salvage are in our time also reflected in the Preamble to the Salvage Convention 1989 which states that the State Parties to the Convention are:

"Conscious of the major contribution which efficient and timely salvage operations can make to the safety of vessels and other property in danger and to the protection of the environment."

LIABILITY IN ADMIRALTY

5.6 Inevitably, where a salvage situation exists, there will often be a need to act promptly and a degree of danger will be involved which even the best equipment and the most advanced training programme cannot prepare a salvage crew for. It follows that, in the heat of the moment, it should not be unheard of for salvors to make mistakes. As we have seen, there is Admiralty Court[14] authority for the proposition that salvors owe a duty of care toward salvees. At least by the time of *The Cape Packet*,[15] Dr Lushington confirmed that if there was neglect or misconduct which was wilful there could be a forfeiture of the whole claim to salvage remuneration and that if there was gross negligence[16] then the salvage remuneration might be completely debarred.[17] However, he also stated that:

"There is also another kind of negligence, the effect of which is to diminish the amount of salvage reward, not to take it entirely away. The extent of this diminution, I may further state, is not measured by the amount of loss or injury sustained, but is framed upon the principle of proportioning the diminution to the degree of negligence, not to the consequences."[18]

5.7 Later, in *The Atlas*, Sir John Coleridge, stated that:

"no mere mistake or error of judgment in the manner of procuring it, no misconduct short of that which is wilful and may be considered criminal, and that proved beyond a reasonable doubt by the owners resisting the claim, will work an entire forfeiture of the salvage. Mistake or misconduct other than criminal, which diminished the value of the property salved, or occasions expense to the owners, are properly considered in the amount of compensation to be awarded."[19]

The extent to which there should be any diminution in the award to which a salvor might otherwise be entitled obviously sits uneasily with the overwhelming policy arguments which are traditionally cited in favour of granting salvors their reward. As such, salvors earlier enjoyed a certain leniency by the courts for any misconduct,

14. I.e. during the period in which that court prospered, thanks to the sustained efforts of leading judges such as Lord Stowell and Dr Lushington, and before its amalgamation with Probate and Divorce following the Supreme Court of Judicature Act 1873 (36 & 37 Vict., c. 66). See Frank Wiswall, *The Development of Admiralty Jurisdiction and Practice since 1800* (Cambridge, 1970).

15. (1848) 3 W. Rob. 122, 125; 166 E.R. 909.

16. At this time a distinction was drawn between those situations which gave rise to ordinary negligence and others, which saw liability arise for gross negligence (finally rejected in *Grill v The General Iron Screw Collier Co Ltd* (1866) L.R. 1 C.P. 600, 612 (Willes J.)). See David Ibbetson, *A Historical Introduction to the Law of Obligations* (1999), ch. 9.

17. Reiterated by him in *The Lady Worsley* (1855) 2 Sp. Ecc. & Ad. 253, 256; 164 E.R. 417, 419: "It is an established rule of this court, and one I shall never depart from, that however valuable a service may be, salvors may forfeit their just reward if they are guilty of misconduct."

18. (1848) 3 W. Rob. 122, 125; 166 E.R. 909, 910.

19. (1862) Lush. 518, 528; 167 E.R. 235, 241.

particularly where that misconduct was more apparent with the benefit of hind-sight.[20]

COMMON LAW LIABILITY

5.8 In the 20th century, the earlier lenient view adopted towards salvors became subject to greater scrutiny by the courts. Although not always supported when reviewed in later cases,[21] it would not now be safe to assume that the courts will necessarily deal leniently with transgressions by salvors, even if occurring under the pressure of having to find a solution under pressure and in adverse conditions. Reflecting developments to this point in the law of negligence a decade or so before,[22] Atkinson J. in *Anglo-Saxon Petroleum Co Ltd v The Admiralty (The Delphinula)* stated that:

"I do not think any different law applies to people undertaking salvage operations from the law which applies to those rendering any other sort of service. They have to exhibit the skill and care which can be reasonably be expected from persons in their position. There is a different measure of skill expected from a Harley Street specialist from an ordinary country general practitioner; but if one ship comes to the aid of another which is in distress, those in charge are not professing any salvage skill, but they just do their best to help, and it may well be very difficult, if not impossible, to hold them liable for negligence. If through want of skill and care their services turned out to be of less value, all that is dealt with in assessing their salvage award, but it would doubtless be very difficult to establish a case of negligence against them."[23]

NEGLIGENCE AND *THE TOJO MARU*

5.9 The leading case on the question of salvorial negligence is now *The Tojo Maru*.[24] That case arose following a collision between the *Tojo Maru*, a tanker, with another tanker, the *Fina Italia*, in the Persian Gulf. As a result of the extensive damage sustained by the *Tojo Maru*, salvage was offered and accepted on LOF terms. It was necessary as part of the salvage process to cover a large shell plating collision wound of some 30 feet. In order to cover the aperture, it was necessary to bolt the plate to the hull by means of bolts fired from a Cox bolt gun. Notwithstanding orders to the contrary, the salvor's chief diver fired the gun, before an adjoining tank had been made gas free. The resulting explosion caused extensive damage and a fire on board the *Tojo Maru*. She was eventually towed to Singapore and then on to Kobe where repairs were effected.

5.10 In the initial arbitration hearings, the owners denied that the salvors were entitled to any remuneration and counterclaimed for damages. The arbitrator found

20. See, e.g., *The Leon Blum* [1915] P. 90, 102 (Sir Samuel Evans); *Tojo Maru (Owners) v NV Bureau Wijsmuller (The Tojo Maru)* [1972] A.C. 242, 289 (Lord Pearson).

21. See, e.g., *Anglo-Saxon Petroleum Co Ltd v The Admiralty (The Delphinula)* (1947) 80 Ll.L.R. 459 (C.A.), upholding (1946) 79 Ll.L.R. 611.

22. I.e. the seminal decision in *Donoghue v Stevenson* [1932] A.C. 562. For a modern restatement of the requirements, see A. M. Dugdale & M. A. Jones (eds), *Clerk & Lindsell on Torts* (19th ed., 2006), para. 8–04.

23. (1946) 79 Ll.L.R. 611, 634. See too *The Thetis* (1869) L.R. 2 A. & E. 365.

24. *Tojo Maru (Owners) v NV Bureau Wijsmuller (The Tojo Maru)* [1972] A.C. 242.

that the sole cause of the explosion was the negligence of the diver, which was foreseeable. Although allowing the owners counterclaim, he held that there was no fault or privity on the part of the salvors and they were therefore entitled to limit their liability[25] under the Merchant Shipping Act 1894.[26] Willmer L.J.,[27] sitting as an additional judge of the (then) Probate, Divorce, and Admiralty Division, agreed that the owners were entitled to counterclaim for their loss but that the salvors were not entitled to limit their liability.[28] The Court of Appeal disagreed[29] and held that the owners were not entitled to counterclaim for damages caused by the negligence of the salvors. The Court of Appeal also held that, on the basis that the salvors had done more good than harm by effecting a cure, the negligence of their diver went to diminish their salvage award.

5.11 In the House of Lords it was argued strenuously that it was a rule of maritime law that a successful salvor could not be liable in damages to the owner for any negligence on his part. At best, it was argued that such negligence entitled the court or the arbitrator to reduce or forfeit the salvage award.

5.12 All five of their Lordships read speeches on the matter before them.[30] They unanimously agreed that there was no support in principle or in the authorities for the view that the salvors who had negligently caused damage were protected if the salvage operation had been successful or, alternatively, if the harm they had done was to be measured as being the value or the improved value of the ship in respect of which their services had been rendered. Accordingly, they concluded that it was permissible to entertain the owners' counterclaim for damages. While there was a recognition that public policy required that every proper encouragement should be given to salvors, and confirmation that the courts would be "slow to impute negligence to salvors",[31] nevertheless on the facts it was clearly established that the salvors were liable for the negligence of their diver. There was no support as a matter of principle, or in the authorities, for the view that salvors who had negligently caused damage were protected if the salvage operation had been successful or, alternatively, if the harm they had done was counterbalanced by the good they had done. Thus on this first important point in the case, their Lordships dispelled any doubts which may have arisen from the earlier decisions of this particular question.

SALVOR'S CONTRACTUAL DUTIES

5.13 The decision in *The Tojo Maru* was one broadly concerned with the general principle as to the scope of the salvage contractor's potential liability in negligence. However, the salvage rendered in that case was provided on the terms described as the "Standard Form of Salvage Agreement approved and published by the

---

25. Further as to limitation, see the discussion below at para. 5.23.
26. 57 & 58 Vict., c. 60.
27. [1969] 2 W.L.R. 594.
28. We discuss this point further below at para. 5.20.
29. [1970] P. 21 (this Report also incidentally contains the earlier judgment of Willmer L.J.).
30. [1972] A.C. 242.
31. At p. 267 (Lord Reid).

Committee of Lloyd's and known as "no cure – no pay".[32] Lloyd's Open Form (LOF), as it is better known,[33] is the heavily-used industry form.[34] The contract embodied in the form is a contract for work and labour,[35] clause A of which states that the salvage contractors are to use their "best endeavours" to salve the property specified. Clause B of LOF 2000 goes on to provide that while performing such salvage services the salvage contractors are also to use their best endeavours to prevent or minimise damage to the environment.[36] Lord Diplock explained in *The Tojo Maru* that:

"Under the general English law of contracts for work and labour by a person who carries on the business of undertaking services of the kind which he has contracted to provide, he warrants that he will use reasonable skill and care in the provision of the services; and the measure of his liability for breach of that warranty is such a sum by way of damages as will put the other party, so far as money can do so, in the same position as if the contract had been performed without such breach.

Under Lloyd's Standard Form it is expressly provided that "The services shall be rendered and accepted as salvage services upon the principle of 'no cure - no pay' ". This imports into what would otherwise be an ordinary contract for work and labour, certain characteristics which must now be examined to see what modification, if any, these involve to what would otherwise be the liability of the salvage contractor for damage caused by his lack of reasonable skill and care in rendering the contractual services.

These special characteristics of the remuneration payable for salvage services whether rendered under Lloyd's Standard Form of Salvage Agreement with a professional salvage contractor, or volunteered by a passing vessel and accepted without any express contract, would not appear in themselves sufficient to oust the ordinary rule of English law that a person who undertakes for reward to do work and labour upon the property of another owes to the owner of the property a duty to exercise that care which the circumstances demand and, where he holds himself out as carrying on the business or profession of undertaking services of that kind, to use such skill in the performance of them as a person carrying on such a business may reasonably be expected to possess." [37]

5.14 The question might therefore arise as to how a salvage contractor's contractual duties under LOF and his common law obligations interface. It seems to be accepted that where there is a salvage contract, the paradigm case, then as a matter of contract there is a contractual obligation not to perform his duties negligently. Additionally, there is still a common law duty of care, which is not ousted by the existence of the contractual duty. The knock-on effect of these respective duties

32. At p. 245. Presumably the version of the form published in 1953, as the contract was made on 28 February 1965. See Kennedy & Rose (2002), para. 791.

33. For the background, see A. F. Bessemer-Clark, "The Role of Lloyd's Open Form", in [1980] L.M.C.L.Q. 297; Donald R. O'May, "Lloyd's Form and the Montreal Convention", in (1982–83) 57 Tulane L.R. 1412–1438.

34. It is said to form the basis of the majority of salvage claims: Kennedy & Rose (2002), para. 792; Schoenbaum (2004), §16–6. One of the principal reasons for its popularity is undoubtedly the fact that the form provides for arbitration before experienced arbitrators and backed by a tried and tested formula providing for security and payment of an award.

35. *The Tojo Maru* [1972] AC 242, 292 (Lord Diplock).

36. I.e. as defined in the Salvage Convention 1989, *viz.* "substantial physical damage to human health or to marine life or resources in conastal or inland waters or areas adjacent thereto, caused by pollution, contamination, fire, explosion, or similar major incidents" (art. 1(d)). For discussion, see Kennedy & Rose, paras 398–405.

37. *The Tojo Maru* [1972] A.C. 242, 293–294.

is the possibility of suit against the salvage contractor in tort – for negligence – or for breach of contract.[38]

THE SALVAGE CONVENTION 1989

5.15 After a protracted parturition, a new International Salvage Convention was enacted in 1989.[39] That Convention was ratified by the United Kingdom and, as is the practice in this country for implementing international conventions, enacted as part of domestic English law in section 224(1) of the Merchant Shipping Act 1995.[40] That section provides that the Convention has the "force of law"[41] and Part I of Schedule 11 contains the text of the Convention. Part II of Schedule 11 contains various reservations and amplifications of that Convention so far as the United Kingdom is concerned.[42] The obligations of the salvor (and of the owner and master) are set out in some detail in Article 8(1),[43] which provides that:

"The salvor shall owe a duty of care to the owner of the vessel or other property in danger –
   (a) to carry out the salvage operations with due care;
   (b) in performing the duty specified in subparagraph (a), to exercise due care to prevent or minimise damage to the environment;
   (c) whenever circumstances reasonably require, to seek assistance from other salvors ..."

5.16 As stated, these obligations were derived directly from the CMI's Draft Convention on Salvage 1981. It may be noted that this Convention provision obliges that the salvor owes a "duty of care" to the owner of the vessel. This may be contrasted with LOF 2000, clause A, which refers to the requirement to use "best endeavours". The "due care" standard identified in the Convention is generally thought to be one of reasonableness, as opposed to the "best endeavours" in LOF, which requires a somewhat higher standard.[44]

5.17 Article 18 of the Salvage Convention deals specifically with the effect of any misconduct on the part of the salvor. It provides that:

"A salvor may be deprived of the whole or part of the payment due under this Convention to the extent that the salvage operations have become necessary or more difficult because

---

38. See, e.g., Kennedy & Rose, para. 1117.
39. There is impressive periodical literature on the Convention. A good starting point is Michael Kerr, "The International Convention on Salvage 1989 – How it came to be", in (1990) 39 I.C.L.Q. 530–556. See also Barry Sheen, "Conventions on Salvage", in (1983) 57 Tulane L.R. 1387–1411; Edgar Gold, "Marine Salvage: Towards a New Regime", in (1989) 20 J.M.L.C. 487–503; Donald A. Kerr, "The 1989 Salvage Convention: Expediency or Equity?", in (1989) 20 J.M.L.C. 505–520; Catherine Redgwell, "The greening of salvage law", in (1990) 14 *Marine Policy* 142–150; Nicholas Gaskell, "The enactment of the 1989 Salvage Convention in English Law: Policy Issues", in [1990] L.M.C.L.Q. 352–363; James B. Wooder, "The New Salvage Convention: A Shipowner's Perspective", in (1990) 21 J.M.L.C. 81–98; Nicholas Gaskell, "The 1989 Salvage Convention and the Lloyd's Open Form (LOF) Salvage Agreement 1990", in (1991) 16 Tulane Maritime L.J. 1–103; Richard Shaw, "The 1989 Salvage Convention and English law", in [1996] L.M.C.L.Q. 202–231.
40. C. 21.
41. As to the meaning of this concept, as considered under the Hague-Visby Rules, see *The Hollandia* [1982] Q.B. 872 (C.A.), 883.
42. I.e. as permitted under art. 30.
43. Art. 8(2) sets out the corresponding duties of the owner and master of the vessel or the owner of other property in danger.
44. See Nicholas Gaskell, "The 1989 Salvage Convention and the Lloyd's Open Form (LOF) Salvage Agreement 1990", in (1991) 16 Tulane Maritime L.J. 1, 41.

of fault or neglect on his part or if the salvor has been guilty of fraud or other dishonest conduct."

5.18 This provision is in similar terms to an equivalent provision of the 1910 Salvage Convention. It may be observed that Article 18 requires that the fault or neglect of the salvor should be such as to have occasioned the salvage in the first place, or to have made the salvage operation more difficult. If the negligence of the salvor does neither, but perhaps causes other losses to the salved vessels' owners,[45] it is doubtful whether the shipowner would be able to invoke Article 18 to reduce the award. Article 18 also does not indicate whether the salvor might be subject to a counterclaim for the damage done, as is now recognised in English law following *The Tojo Maru*.[46] It has, accordingly, been suggested that this may be a matter for domestic law to decide.[47]

5.19 This issue was not, however, addressed in *The Owners, Masters & Crews of the Tugs Maridive VII, Maridive XIII, Maridive 85 & Maridive 94 v The Owners and Demise Charters of the Oil Rig Key Singapore*.[48] In that case one of the key questions was the extent of any salvage award due to the owners of a series of tugs which had been used to move a jack up rig, the *Key Singapore*. What had started out as a contract for the towage of the jack up rig had deteriorated owing to severe weather. In the earlier arbitration hearing, the arbitrator was asked to determine whether the claimants were entitled to salvage remuneration in respect of the services rendered by the tugs.[49] The arbitrator[50] had found in favour of the claimants, assessing their award under article 13[51] of the Salvage Convention 1989 at US$1.8m, starting from a notional base award of US$3m less $1.2m to reflect the claimants' contributory fault under article 18. The appeal arbitrator[52] reduced this award further to US$1m, starting from a notional base award of US$2m. Both arbitrators found that the claimants and the respondents were jointly at fault in failing to ensure that the flotilla had heaved to in time. At issue in the appeal before Mr Justice David Steel was whether the finding on joint responsibility was contrary to established law.[53] The claimants argued that because the tow was in overall charge of the move,[54] primary responsibility for the decision whether to heave to had lain with the tow. David Steel J. agreed with the arbitrators as to the established law as to the tug and tow and concluded that there was nothing in any of the authorities which supported the proposition that overall command of a towage convoy imported with it an enhanced degree of fault in circumstances where both the tug and tow had fallen short of their mutual duty to take care.[55]

---

45. For example, excessive delay.
46. *The Tojo Maru* [1972] A.C. 242. See the discussion of this point above at para. 5.12.
47. See Gaskell (1991) 16 Tulane Maritime L.J. 1, 63.
48. [2004] E.W.H.C. 2227 (Comm.); [2005] 1 Lloyd's Rep. 91.
49. Generally as to this, see *The Minnehaha* (1861) 15 Moo P.C. 133; 15 E.R. 444; *The White Star* (1866) L.R. 1 A. & E. 68; *The Five Steel Barges* (1890) 15 P.D. 142; *The North Goodwin No. 16* [1980] 1 Lloyd's Rep. 71; Simon Rainey, *The Law of Tug and Tow* (2nd ed., 2002), ch. 6.
50. Mr John Reeder Q.C. (now the Appeals Arbitrator).
51. I.e. the provision of the Convention which lays down the criteria to be used in fixing an award.
52. Mr Nigel Teare Q.C. Mr Teare was appointed to the High Court Bench in 2006.
53. It was on this ground that Gross J. gave leave to appeal.
54. See *The Niobe* (1888) 13 P.D. 55.
55. [2004] E.W.H.C. 2227 (Comm.); [2005] 1 Lloyd's Rep. 91, at [34].

SALVAGE AND LIMITATION OF LIABILITY
UNDER *THE TOJO MARU*

5.20 We have noted earlier that one of the important consequences of *The Tojo Maru*[56] was to settle the question as to whether a counterclaim for damages might be made against the salvor. However, another important point which arose in that case concerned whether the salvor might avail himself of the limitation of liability provisions then contained in section 503 of the Merchant Shipping Act 1894 (as amended).[57] In so far as material, that section provided that:

"The owners of a ship, British or foreign, shall not ... (d) where any loss or damage is caused to any property (other than any property mentioned in paragraph (b) of this subsection) or any rights are infringed through the act or omission of any person (whether on board the ship or not) in the navigation or management of the ship, or in the loading, carriage or discharge of its cargo or in the embarkation, carriage or disembarkation of its passengers, or through any other act or omission of any person on board the ship; be liable in damages beyond the following amounts ..."[58]

5.21 The arbitrator had found that the salvors could limit their liability, but Willmer L.J. reversed this.[59] A majority of the Court of Appeal agreed.[60] The point was further considered by their Lordships in the House of Lords. It was contended by the salvors that, for the purposes of section 503, the explosion took place in the "management" of their tug or alternatively that these took place "on board" the tug. Their Lordships disagreed; the act of firing the bolt gun into the plating of the *Tojo Maru* could not be regarded as an act in the management of the tug.[61] Nor, for that matter, could the negligent act of the diver be described as one which had occurred "on board" the tug; if anything the diver was on board the *Tojo Maru*. Lord Reid was constrained to say that:

"I am bound to say that I have some sympathy with the [salvors] on this issue of limitation of liability. But a court must go by the provisions which have been agreed and enacted. If the special position of salvors was unforeseen, then we must await alteration of those provisions if those concerned see fit to make some alteration. As the law stands I must decide this issue against the [salvors]."[62]

5.22 Perhaps unsurprisingly, the outcome on this part of the case caused considerable consternation among salvors.[63] In the deliberations which ultimately led to the enactment of a new limitation convention,[64] this decision rapidly became a

---

56. [1972] A.C. 242. See the discussion of this point above at para. 5.12.
57. 57 & 58 Vict., c. 60.
58. See Michael Thomas, "British concepts of limitation of liability", in (1978–79) Tulane L.R. 1205–1258.
59. [1969] 2 W.L.R. 594, 613.
60. [1970] P. 21, 67 (Lord Denning M.R.); 76 (Karminski L.J.). *Cf.* the dissenting reasoning of Salmon L.J. (at p. 75).
61. [1972] A.C. 242, 288.
62. At p. 270. See too the speech of Lord Morris of Borth-y-Gest (at p. 282) and *Felda Oil Products Sdn Bhd v Owners of the ship MV Maritime Prudence* [1996] 1 S.L.R. 168.
63. See, e.g., Barry Sheen, "Conventions on Salvage", in (1982–1983) Tulane L.R. 1387, 1403: "The Tojo Maru incident was most unfortunate."
64. Intended to replace the International Convention for the Unification of Certain Rules Relating to the Limitation of the liability of Owners of Sea-going Vessels 1924 (in force 2 June 1931) and the Brussels International Convention relating to the Limitation of the liability of Owners of Sea-going Ships 1957 (in force 31 May 1968).

catalyst for reform, although ultimately just one of a package of provisions which recast the law on limitation of liability.[65]

SALVAGE AND LIMITATION OF LIABILITY UNDER THE LLMC[66]

Background

5.23 Although the underlying basis for limitation of liability in maritime law has sometimes come under attack,[67] the traditional justification that limitation is necessary, as a matter of policy,[68] in order to encourage investment and to serve the needs of commerce[69] has tended to dominate. Lord Denning M.R. once boldly opined that "limitation of liability is not a matter of justice ... [but] a rule of public policy which has its origin in history and its justification in convenience".[70] Indeed, it is not now seriously questioned that limitation of liability has a secure place in maritime conventions generally and in its own right.

5.24 One of the essential features of the LLMC,[71] which entered into force on 1 December 1986,[72] is the availability of a significantly enhanced fund at what was in 1976 perceived to be the maximum insurable level[73] in return for making it more difficult to "break" the limits.[74] The passage of time meant that the limitation amounts adopted became unrealistic and, in 1996, a Protocol to the LLMC was passed.[75] After some years, the requisite number of ratifications[76] were achieved and the Protocol entered into force on 13 May 2004. The Protocol and the Convention are to be read as one instrument[77] and the Protocol applies to claims

65. See, e.g., *Aegean Sea Traders Corporation v Repsol Petroleo SA (The Aegean Sea)* [1998] 2 Lloyd's Rep. 39, 44 (Thomas J.).

66. As the Convention on Limitation of Liability for Maritime Claims 1976 (or the "London" Convention) is sometimes known.

67. See Lord Mustill, "Ships are different – or are they?", in [1993] L.M.C.L.Q. 490–501; Gotthard Gauci, "Limitation of liability in maritime law: an anachronism?", in (1995) 19 *Marine Policy* 65–74.

68. See, for example, *Cail v Papayanni (The Amalia)* (1863) 1 Moo P.C. (N.S.) 471, 473; 15 E.R. 778, 779: "The principle of limited liability is, that full indemnity, the natural right of justice, shall be abridged for political reasons" (Dr Lushington).

69. See, e.g., *Gale v Laurie* (1826) B. & C. 156, 163–164; 108 E.R. 58, 61 (Abbott C.J.); *British Columbia Telephone Co v Marpole Towing Ltd* [1971] S.C.R. 321, 338 (Ritchie J.); *Browner International Ltd v Monarch Shipping Co Ltd (The European Enterprise)* [1989] 2 Lloyd's Rep. 185, 191 (Steyn J.). See too David Steel, "Ships are different: the case for limitation of liability", in [1995] L.M.C.L.Q. 77–87.

70. *Alexandra Towing Co Ltd v Millet and Egret (The Bramley Moore)* [1964] P. 200 (C.A.), 220; *Polish Steam Ship Co v Atlantic Maritime Co (The Garden City (No 2))* [1984] 2 Lloyd's Rep. 37 (C.A.), 44 (Griffiths L.J.).

71. See Erling Selvig, "An Introduction to the 1976 Convention", in Nicholas Gaskell (ed.), *Limitation of Shipowners Liability: The New Law* (1986), ch. 1.

72. For detailed consideration, see Patrick Griggs, Richard Williams, & Jeremy Farr, *Limitation of Liability for Maritime Claims* (4th ed., 2005), ch. 3 (hereafter "Griggs, Williams & Farr"); Nigel Meeson, *Admiralty Jurisdiction and Practice* (3rd ed., 2003), 250–264.

73. See *CMA CGM SA v Classica Shipping Co Ltd* [2003] E.W.H.C. 641 (Comm.); [2003] 2 Lloyd's Rep. 50, at [25].

74. As to which, see Art. 4 of the Convention.

75. Protocol on the Convention on Limitation of Liability for Maritime Claims (LLMC Protocol).

76. Art. 11(1) of the Protocol provided that it should enter into force "ninety days following the date on which ten States have expressed their consent to be bound by it". Malta was that tenth State.

77. See Art. 9(1) of the Protocol.

"arising out of occurrences which take place after the entry into force for each State of this Protocol".[78]

Implementation

5.25 The relevant provisions of the Merchant Shipping Act 1894 were repealed by the Merchant Shipping Act 1979[79] as from 1 December 1986,[80] giving the "force of law"[81] to the 1976 Convention.[82] Following the consolidation of maritime legislation in the Merchant Shipping Act in 1995,[83] the text of the Convention is to be found at Schedule 7.[84] Section 185(1) provides that the Convention is to have the force of law in the United Kingdom, while section 185(2) provides that Part II of Schedule 7 to the Merchant Shipping Act 1995 "shall have effect in connection with the Convention, and subsection (1) above shall have effect subject to the provisions of that Part". In a move signifying early acceptance of the Protocol, section 15 of the Merchant Shipping Maritime and Security Act 1997[85] made changes to the Merchant Shipping Act 1995, such that modifications to the relevant provisions of that Act could be made following the coming into force of the LLMC Protocol. Subsidiary legislation in 1998[86] and 2004[87] effected the relevant changes.

The Convention and salvors

5.26 The LLMC, which was enacted after the *Tojo Maru*,[88] has gone some way to rectifying the outcome of that case that a salvor's negligence was not subject to limitation. This seemingly brought the law back into line with the policy that a volunteer should not be unduly penalised for attempting to save property at sea. Article 1(1) of the Convention therefore entitles both shipowners and salvors to limit their liability under the Convention and Article 1(3) defines "salvor" as "any person rendering services in direct connection with salvage operations".[89] The claims covered by the Convention are listed in Article 2(1), which provides that:

"Subject to Articles 3 and 4 the following claims, whatever the basis of liability may be, shall be subject to limitation of liability:
  (a) claims in respect of loss of life or personal injury or loss of or damage to property (including damage to harbour works, basins and waterways and aids to navigation), occurring on board or in direct connection with the operation of the ship or with salvage operations, and consequential loss resulting therefrom;

78. See Art. 9(3) of the Protocol.
79. C. 39. See Steven Hazelwood, "The United Kingdom and the Limitation Convention", in Gaskell (1986), ch. 19.
80. Merchant Shipping Act 1979 (Commencement No. 10) Order 1986, S.I. 1986 No. 1052.
81. S.17.
82. The LLMC has been ratified by more than 34 states: see *www.imo.org*.
83. C. 21.
84. This contains the text of the LLMC 1976, but with some omissions as the United Kingdom has not ratified all the provisions.
85. C. 28.
86. Merchant Shipping (Convention on Limitation of Liability for Maritime Claims) (Amendment) Order 1998, S.I. 1998 No. 1258.
87. Merchant Shipping (Convention on Limitation of Liability for Maritime Claims) (Amendment) Order 2004, S.I. 2004 No. 1273.
88. [1972] A.C. 242.
89. See Griggs, Williams, & Farr, 12.

(b) claims in respect of loss resulting from delay in the carriage by sea of cargo, passengers or their luggage;

(c) claims in respect of other loss resulting from infringement of rights other than contractual rights, occurring in direct connection with the operation of the ship or salvage operations;

(d) claims in respect of the raising, removal, destruction or the rendering harmless of a ship which is sunk, wrecked, stranded or abandoned, including anything that is or has been on board such ship;

(e) claims in respect of the removal, destruction or the rendering harmless of the cargo of the ship;

(f) claims of a person other than the person liable in respect of measures taken in order to avert or minimise loss for which the person liable may limit his liability in accordance with this Convention, and further loss caused by such measures." [90]

5.27 Particularly important in Article 2 is the wording that the limits of liability are to apply "whatever the basis of liability may be".[91] Article 3 of the Convention excludes from the ambit of the Convention certain claims, such as claims for salvage, including, if applicable, any claim for special compensation under Article 14 of the Salvage Convention 1989[92] or contribution in general average.[93] The exclusion of salvage claims relates solely to claims by a salvor against the owner of the salved property and does not extend to claims between other parties relating to salvage payments, which are subject to limitation. In *The Breydon Merchant* Sheen J. explained that:

"There are good reasons why limitation of liability should not apply to claims for salvage ... First, any limitation upon the amount of the salvage reward would discourage salvors. It is public policy to encourage mariners to go to the assistance of persons and property in peril at sea. Secondly, it would be anomalous if shipowners could limit their liability for salvage, whereas cargo-owners are not afforded that privilege. Such reasons do not have any relevance when considering the question: upon whom does the burden ultimately fall?" [94]

5.28 The heart of the Convention is contained in Article 6, which is the provisions setting out the various limitation levels. The limitation amounts are expressed in Special Drawing Rights (SDR's),[95] the almost universally applied monetary mechanism for determining limitation in international maritime conventions.[96] Although modified quite significantly by the 1996 LLMC Protocol,[97] there is little

---

90. See Griggs, Williams, & Farr, 18–25.

91. I.e. whether the cause of action is tortious, statutory, contractual, or some other basis.

92. I.e. the "special compensation" provision of that Convention. See *Semco Salvage & Marine Pte Ltd v Lancer Navigation Co Ltd (The Nagasaki Spirit)* [1997] A.C. 455 and Stephen Girvin, "Special Compensation under the Salvage Convention 1989: A fair rate? (The Nagasaki Spirit)", in [1997] L.M.C.L.Q. 321–328; Geoffrey Brice, "The Law of Salvage: A Time for Change? 'No Cure No Pay' No Good?", in (1998-1999) 73 Tulane L.R. 1831–1861.

93. Art. 3(a), as amended by art. 2 of the LLMC Protocol.

94. [1992] 1 Lloyd's Rep. 373, 375; *Aegean Sea Traders Corporation v Repsol Petroleo SA (The Aegean Sea)* [1998] 2 Lloyd's Rep. 39, 55 (Thomas J.).

95. See Art. 8 of the LLMC.

96. This is an artificial unit of the International Monetary Fund (IMF) determined by a "basket" of currencies, namely the Euro, the Japanese Yen, Pounds Sterling, and the US dollar. See *www.imf.org* and Les Ward, "The SDR in Transport Liability Conventions: Some clarification", in (1981–1982) 13 J.M.L.C. 1–20.

97. See Griggs, Williams, & Farr (2005), 48–52.

which specifically affects salvors, although we may note a number of points. The first of these is that the tonnage[98] basis for determining limitation consists of a series of bands.[99] The second is Article 6(4) of the Convention, which provides that:

"The limits of liability for any salvor not operating from any ship, or for any salvor operating solely on the ship to, or in respect of which he is rendering salvage services, shall be calculated according to a tonnage of 1,500 tons."

5.29 In effect, this provision provides an alternative system for assessing limitation if the salvor does not come under the earlier provisions. Thus, if loss is caused by someone who is not operating from one of the salvors' vessels, such as a shore-based diver negligently welding, or a team of men put on board a casualty and "solely" operating there, then the Convention requires that the limit of liability for loss be in each case 1,500 tons. This was apparently intended to cover the "loophole" brought about in the *Tojo Maru*. If the salvors are operating from a tug, then the limit of their liability will be based on the tonnage of the tug.

5.30 A further point under Article 6 is that under Article 6(1) of the LLMC 1976, the minimum tonnage provided for in calculating the fund was 500 tons. However, under the LLMC Protocol, the revised minimum tonnage under Article 6(1) is 2,000 tons.[100] The effect of the changes in the LLMC Protocol has meant that the limitation fund for a salvor has risen to 2 million SDR's for personal injury claims and 1 million SDR's for other claims.[101]

5.31 These limitation thresholds must, of course, be set alongside Article 4 of the Convention, which makes it extremely difficult to break limitation. However, to do so, the claimant must prove that the loss or damage resulted from a personal act or omission of the party liable, "committed with the intent to cause such loss or recklessly and with knowledge that such loss would probably result". As will be evident from this standard, the higher limits prescribed under the LLMC and under the LLMC Protocol are balanced out by a test which makes the likelihood of breaking the limits extremely difficult.[102] Not only must the loss result from a personal act or omission of the party liable, but it must be established that the party liable either intended such loss or was reckless as to the consequences of his act or omission in

---

98. Tonnage for these purposes is the gross tonnage calculated in accordance with the tonnage measurement rules contained in the International Convention on Tonnage Measurement of Ships 1969: Art. 6(5).

99. E.g., the limits under Art. 6(1)(a) are 333,333 SDRs for a ship with a tonnage not exceeding 500 tons but for ships over that tonnage an additional 500 SDRs is added (for ships up to 3,000 tonnes). Under the LLMC Protocol the limits under art. 3(1)(a) are 2 million SDRs for a ship with a tonnage not exceeding 2,000 tons. For ships in excess of 2,000 tons, the following additional amounts must be added: (i) for each ton from 2,001 to 30,000 tons, 800 SDRs; (ii) for each ton from 30,001 to 70,000 tons, 600 SDRs; and (iii) for each ton in excess of 70,000 tons, 400 SDRs.

100. Note, however, that under UK law, Sched. 7, Part II of the Merchant Shipping Act 1995, c. 21, provides that, in the case of a ship with a tonnage less than 300 tons, Art. 6 is to have effect as if Art. 6(1)(a)(i) referred to 1 million SDRs and Art 6(1)(b)(i) referred to 500,000 SDRs.

101. But with the further variation in UK law for ships of less than 300 tons.

102. See, for example, *MSC Mediterranean Shipping Co SA v Delumar BVBA (The MSC Rosa M)* [2000] 2 Lloyd's Rep. 399, 401 (David Steel J.); *Schiffahrtsgesellschaft MS Merkur Sky mbH & Co KG v MS Leerort Nth Schiffahrts GmbH & Co KG (The Leerort)* [2001] 2 Lloyd's Rep. 291 (C.A.). But *cf. Margolle v Delta Maritime Co Ltd (The Saint Jacques II & Gudermes)* [2003] 1 Lloyd's Rep. 203.

the sense that he realised that such a loss would probably result.[103] Knowledge means actual, not constructive knowledge[104] and merely "turning a blind eye" would not constitute actual knowledge.[105]

Applying the limits of liability

5.32 Unfortunately for salvors, the LLMC and the LLMC Protocol do not necessarily resolve all the potential difficulties which may be encountered. One particular problem arises when complex salvage operations are undertaken,[106] possibly involving numerous craft, as such services are wont to do. Thus, if loss was caused by salvors' negligence in operating tugs A, and B, but not in operating tugs C and D, though they too were participating in the salvage operations, there is a question whether the limitation fund[107] would be based on the aggregate tonnage of tugs A and B only, or of all four of the tugs. A further issue is concerned with what would happen if a shore-based salvage master was negligent in directing those two tugs. In such circumstances, what would the applicable limit be? Both Articles 6 and 9[108] of the LLMC say that the statutory limit applies to a claim or to the aggregate of all the claims arising on "any distinct occasion", but the LLMC does not identify the relationship between the "ship" or "ships" in calculating that limit. Whilst it is possible that a court would calculate the limit by aggregating the tonnage of all of the tugs in every case, an alternative method would be for the court to follow a similar approach to that which was adopted prior to the LLMC. Similar wording was used in section 503(3) of the Merchant Shipping Act 1894 (as amended). In interpreting that provision, the courts looked to see which ships had been negligently navigated or managed or were involved in the damage, and calculated the limit according to those tonnages alone. In particular, a tug and tow case, *The Bramley Moore*,[109] involved the subject tug which was towing two barges, the *Buckwheat* and the *Millett*. The latter came into collision with another ship, the *MV Egret*, and sunk. In an action by the owners of the *Millett* against the *MV Egret* and the *Bramley Moore*, it was held that, where those on the tug were negligent and those on the tow were not, the owners of the tug could limit their liability according to the tonnage of the tug. The Court of Appeal also decided that the limitation fund should be based on the limit of the tug alone, rather than the aggregate of the tug and two barges (or a

---

103. See, for a case involving Art. 25 of the Warsaw Convention (which uses the same words as Art. 4), *Goldman v Thai Airways International Ltd* [1983] 1 W.L.R. 1186 (C.A.).

104. *Goldman v Thai Airways International Ltd* [1983] 1 W.L.R. 1186 (C.A.), 1194 (Eveleigh L.J.); *MSC Mediterranean Shipping Co SA v Delumar BVBA (The MSC Rosa M)* [2000] 2 Lloyd's Rep. 399.

105. *MSC Mediterranean Shipping Co SA v Delumar BVBA (The MSC Rosa M)* [2000] 2 Lloyd's Rep. 399, at [15].

106. See, e.g., Brice, para 7-109.

107. Art. 11(1) of the LLMC provides that a person liable may constitute a fund with the court or other competent authority in any State Party in which legal proceedings are instituted. The fund may either consist of a deposit of the sum, or by producing a guarantee, subject to the legislation of the State Party where the fund is constituted. In England and Wales the mechanics of constituting the fund is regulated by the Civil Procedure Rules (CPR); see, in particular, CPR Part 61.11(18).

108. Art. 9 is the provision of the LLMC which deals with aggregation of claims. See Griggs, Williams & Farr (2005), 58.

109. *Alexandra Towing Co Ltd v Millett and Egret (The Bramley Moore)* [1964] P. 200 (C.A.).

combination of these) because the damage had been caused by the negligent navigation of the tug and not of the barge. This went against earlier decisions which had been based on the limit of the barge[110] and the aggregated tonnages of the tug and the barges under tow which were at fault.[111]

5.33 On this particular point, neither the LLMC, its Protocol, or the *travaux préparatoires* gives any guidance on this and there have not, to the best of our knowledge, been any cases on point. It is submitted, however, that if there were two separate and successive acts of negligence, there might well be two limitation funds for the losses attributable to each of the two events. Indeed, there is nothing in the LLMC to prevent the salvor paying up to the limit of his liability more than once if there are successive acts of negligence, each causing loss.

To what sums of money do the limits apply?

5.34 If we assume that a salvor can limit his liability, a further question is whether the limit applies to the claims, or to the excess of the claims over the salvage? If we were to assume, for example, that the damage resulting from the negligence was £10m, the salvor's limit of liability was £2m and the salvage award was £7m, would the salvors be paid £7m less £2m, or would the shipowners and cargo-owners recover £2m from the salvors on the basis that after giving credit for the salvage liability, their claim was reduced to £3m (i.e. £10m minus £7m) and it is to that excess that the limit of £2m applies? This may be illustrated as follows:

Example 1:

Salvage Award	£7,000,000
Less Limitation of Negligence Claim	(*£2,000,000*)
Balance due to Salvors	£5,000,000

Example 2:

Negligence Claim	£10,000,000
Less Salvage Award	*£7,000,000*
Balance (in shipowners favour)	£3,000,000
Limitation paid to shipowners	£2,000,000

5.35 Example 1 represents the view taken after the point had been fully argued in *The Tojo Maru* by Willmer L.J. at first instance[112] and by Lord Denning M.R. and Salmon L.J. in the Court of Appeal.[113] In the House of Lords, there was no argument on this point although Lord Reid did say that he was not convinced that the judgments on this point were right, and that the point was open for further consideration should it arise in the future.[114] The other Law Lords did not comment.

Counterclaims under the LLMC

5.36 The LLMC has altered the position just discussed but, as we shall see, not conclusively. Article 5 provides that:

110. See *The Ran; The Graygarth* [1922] P. 80 (C.A.).
111. *The Harlow* [1922] P. 175.
112. [1970] P. 21, 47–49.
113. At pp. 67–68; 75.
114. [1972] A.C. 242, 270.

"Where a person entitled to limitation of liability under the rules of this Convention has a claim against the claimant arising out of the same occurrence, their respective claims shall be set off against each other and the provisions of this Convention shall only apply to the balance, if any."[115]

5.37 At the time of *The Tojo Maru* there was a substantially similar provision in the 1957 Convention (which was not part of UK law),[116] but its effect was apparently not considered by the court in that case. The views in *The Tojo Maru* were *obiter* since Willmer L.J. would have denied the right to limit and in the Court of Appeal it was thought there could be no counterclaim for damages in a successful salvage case. However, this raises an interesting question if *The Tojo Maru* approach were subjected to critical examination in the appellate courts, where Lord Reid has said that it would be open for future consideration. Though these views were, strictly speaking, *obiter dicta*, it must be said that the point was comprehensively argued with much citation of authority in both courts, and the reasoned and firm conclusions reached by three distinguished judges can be relied upon as strong and persuasive support for the view that salvage remuneration will only be reduced to the extent of the salvors' limited liability to the shipowners and cargo owners. There are, as we have seen, powerful arguments for both views. One view is that the origins of salvage do not lie in the common law and that, as a matter of public policy, a salvor who has achieved success and saved that which faced total loss should not have his award taken away on account of a larger claim for damage caused by incidental negligence.[117] The other view is, of course, that a salvor should not profit from his own negligence.[118]

5.38 It is very difficult to see how the ordinary meaning of the words in Article 5 of the LLMC can be consistent with the *Tojo Maru* approach. The salvors are "a person entitled to limitation of liability under the rules of this Convention" and they have "a claim against the claimant".[119] Why then should not the respective "claims be set off against each other", and the "provisions of this Convention" (i.e. the provisions for limitation of liability) be applied to any balance? One suggestion is that because the salvors' claim arises out of the contract of engagement and the claim in negligence arises out of subsequent acts, the two claims do not "arise out of the same occurrence".[120] Although this distinction has been described as "unattractively refined and unconvincing"[121] the obvious "occurrence" is the casualty, or the vessel's situation of danger. If a less broad view were taken, it is difficult to see why the "occurrence" from the salvors' point of view should be the contract and not the salvage operations. Brice has concluded that Article 5 is not relevant because the salvors' claim is not one that is itself subject to limitation. He submits that "the operation of Article 5 is by implication restricted to cases in which there are two claims … both of which fall within Article 2" (i.e. both are subject to

---

115. See Griggs, Williams & Farr, 40–41; Brice, para. 7-128.
116. Art. 1(5).
117. See the discussion above at para. 5.3.
118. I.e. the essence of the decision in *The Tojo Maru* [1972] A.C. 242 and now art. 18 of the Salvage Convention 1989.
119. I.e. the wording of Art. 5.
120. Griggs, Williams & Farr, 40–41.
121. Griggs, Williams & Farr, 42.

limitation).[122] Further, because the salvors' claim against ship and cargo is not subject to limitation he argues that Article 5 does not affect the validity of the *Tojo Maru* approach.[123]

5.39 It is submitted that the construction of Article 5 depends upon the ordinary and natural meaning of the words, express or implied. There is not necessarily any reason, therefore, to imply words that would restrict its application to the case of "limit-able" claim and "limit-able" counterclaim.

The defence of abatement

5.40 Another problem in determining the set-off in the salvors' favour comes from the old, though well-established, rule in the case of *Mondel v Steel*,[124] which has since become somewhat neglected.[125] The defendant in this case pleaded that the claimant's right to be paid was abated because the value of the goods or property at the time of delivery were of no or diminished value. This operates as a true defence and is not dependent on a counterclaim or a plea of set-off. One established exception to this rule is the case of freight claimed under a charter, where there is no right of set-off.[126] In the salvage context, the defence, known as abatement,[127] might mean that the salvors had, in effect, no claim for remuneration, leaving the limit to apply to the counterclaim. Though it is thought the concept of abatement might be limited to cases where the counterclaim is subject to a time limit, it is submitted that it may well also be of importance where there is a question of liability limitation.

CONCLUSIONS

5.41 Salvors are widely recognised as performing an essential service to the various constituencies they serve. We have shown that *The Tojo Maru* case [128] was the seminal decision on salvage law during the latter half of the 20th century.[129] As a result of it, the House of Lords settled a number of points and the case provided the catalyst for including salvors for the first time within the class of persons entitled to limit claims made against them. The case does, however, leave other questions unresolved. Thus, as we have noted, whether Article 5 of the LLMC alters the approach to set-off favoured in *The Tojo Maru*[130] does not yet appear to have been considered. It is thought that Article 5 simply reproduces the same provision from the 1957 Convention and there does not, therefore, appear to be a convincing counter to the

122. Brice, para. 7-130.
123. *Ibid.*
124. (1841) 8 M. & W. 858, 871; 151 E.R. 1288, 1293 (Parke B.).
125. But *cf.* the recent case of *Totsa Total Oil Trading SA v Bharat Petroleum Corp Ltd* [2005] E.W.H.C. 1641.
126. See *Aries Tanker Corp v Total Transport Ltd (The Aries)* [1977] 1 W.L.R. 185 (H.L.), upholding *Henriksens Rederi A/S v THZ Rolimpex (The Brede)* [1974] 1 Q.B. 233 (C.A.). See too J. C. Sheppard, "The rule against deduction from freight reconsidered", in [2006] J.B.L. 1.
127. Known as "recoupment" in the USA.
128. [1972] A.C. 242.
129. With the exception, perhaps, of *Semco Salvage & Marine Pte Ltd v Lancer Navigation Co Ltd (The Nagasaki Spirit)* [1997] A.C. 455.
130. [1972] A.C. 242.

argument that the conventional approach based on *The Tojo Maru dicta* is contrary to the plain and ordinary meaning of Article 5.

5.42 While the present state of the authorities favours the view that salvors can recover their salvage reward, diminished only by the amount to which the claim of ship and cargo is limited by the LLMC, the matter cannot be regarded as finally settled and is open for reconsideration by the courts. It is to be hoped by salvors that the peculiar features of salvage will lead to the courts to conclude that Article 5 was not intended to change the way in which the court in *The Tojo Maru* had treated the impact of limitation in a case where the salvors had completed a successful service.

CHAPTER 6

The liability of salvors for pollution

ARCHIE BISHOP*

6.1 The previous chapter covered the traditional liabilities of salvors. My brief is to deal with their potential liabilities, both civil and criminal, as a result of pollution.

6.2 The modern day blame culture, which insists on finding someone at fault and liable for any incident which attracts public disquiet, is very much alive, and continues to develop rapidly, whenever there is concern for the environment. This is particularly so in the marine industry and the salvor, although a rescuer, is no exception to the trend towards increased civil and criminal liability.

6.3 Whenever a shipping casualty occurs the salvor is at the forefront of events and a highly visible target when retribution is sought by outside parties. This is particularly so in large pollution cases. Angry third party claimants can hit out at anyone who they perceive could be involved – including the rescuer. A few examples will illustrate the point.

6.4 The tanker *Tasman Spirit*, laden with 67,500 tons of crude oil, ran aground in July 2003 in the entrance channel to Karachi Harbour causing substantial pollution. Some 28,000 tons of oil was spilt. To enforce the provision of security for their claim, the local authorities detained seven of the ship's crew and the salvage master who had been engaged to salve the ship and cargo – even though he had not personally arrived on the scene until after the polluting event. All were detained in Pakistan for some nine months, without charge, whilst security for the claim was negotiated. To add weight to the pressure to provide security a transhipping tanker engaged by the salvors to assist in removing the oil from the casualty, was arrested and detained.

6.5 In another case, a tug towed a ship which had broken down, into a west African port under the terms of an ordinary towage contract. Having delivered the ship the towage contract was complete and the tug left to go about its business. Two months later the same tug happened to put into the same port to refuel only to be seized by the Harbour Authorities. The ship she had brought in two months earlier was still in the port and her owners had not paid any bills. The locals had a very pragmatic approach – the tug had brought the ship in so she was responsible. She would not be allowed to leave unless she took the ship with her. The tug had no alternative but to comply but it resulted in her having a dead ship on the end of a tow line for some six weeks before it could finally be disposed of. These are the sort of problems salvors regularly have to face and probably go with the turf. But developing law is aggravating this type of problem.

---

* Consultant, Holman Fenwick and Willan.

CIVIL LIABILITY

6.6 The CLC Convention of 1992 and the HNS Convention of 1996 impose strict liability on the ship owner for damage caused by pollution. However, rescuers, without prejudice to the owners' right of recourse, are given responder immunity from third party claims under both Conventions, unless the damage results from "their personal act or omission, committed with intent to cause such damage, or recklessly and with knowledge that such damage would probably result".

6.7 These provisions are important to the salvor for, although subject to the terms of his contract he remains responsible to the shipowner under normal legal principles, he is protected from claims from third parties which could otherwise be brought in a variety of jurisdictions. Without it, there is a strong chance that he would be one of many defendants sued by a plaintiff with a scattergun approach to litigation. The threat of being sued in itself is discouraging. There may well be a good defence to the claim but the cost and time to personnel involved in preparing that defence, possibly in numerous jurisdictions, will be considerable, and be very disruptive to a salvor's business. A positive disincentive to become involved in future salvage operations.

6.8 The salvors were therefore very disappointed when The Bunker Convention 2001 (which is not yet in force) did not make a similar provision. Notwithstanding the above points, which were strongly made, the Conference which adopted that Convention consciously refused to give the same immunity from suit, though it left open the option for States to grant it should they so wish. As the German delegation put it, if there is damage caused by bunker pollution "We want to be able to sue whoever we feel may be liable". Fortunately for the salvage industry other States, including the UK, have stated they intend to exercise the option and give responder immunity, when enacting the provisions of the Convention.

CRIMINAL LIABILITY

6.9 However, a salvor's potential civil liability is eclipsed by his potential criminal liability.

6.10 The common law of England generally required *mens rea* (actual foresight of the consequences) on the part of the defendant for criminal liability to be established. An exception is gross negligence (or recklessness) in the case of manslaughter. However, negligence, in the sense of culpable inadvertence to the consequences, is generally not sufficient to found criminal liability.

6.11 Statutory law has changed that common law rule substantially in recent times, and all too often we find new laws which establish a criminal liability based on simple negligence or, in some cases, regardless of whether there was any fault at all. The shipping industry which has been beset with an ever-increasing amount of new regulation in recent years, is no exception to this trend.

6.12 The reason for the creation of these new offences and severity of punishment is said to be because the sanction imposed will persuade the potential miscreant from committing the offence. If the stick is big enough you will not want to be beaten. To a limited degree this might be right but there is a very real danger of overdoing it, and by so doing actively discouraging people from doing jobs that carry the risk of such liability or, for reasons of self-protection, encourage them to not do what they would otherwise do in the best interest of all.

6.13 Accompanying the creation of these new criminal offences, is the increasing tendency of authorities in some jurisdictions to seek a scapegoat following any major casualty which involves pollution. Someone always has to be to blame and it should never be the politician or servants of those authorities. This blame culture is even more damaging than the new offence itself for it makes people fearful to even do their job.

6.14 An example of this is perhaps the *Prestige*. In November 2002 the *Prestige* lost part of her shell plating in bad weather in the Bay of Biscay resulting in substantial pollution which threatened and ultimately caused damage to the coast of NW Spain. The facts of the case have yet to be judicially determined but many regard the captain of that ship, Captain Mangouras, to be the scapegoat for the faults of others. Despite ordering his crew to abandon the ship for their safety he remained with her for several days to assist salvors in their efforts to salve ship and cargo. However, as soon as he got ashore he was arrested, held in prison for three months pending the provision of bail in the sum of €3million and, when bail was posted, held in the country, under daily reporting conditions, for three years before being allowed to leave Spain to visit to his home in Greece. To this day he has still to stand trial (some four years later).

6.15 The criminalisation in our workplace affects all seafarers but this paper is focused on salvors and I will concentrate on the statutory criminal offences which directly and indirectly affect the salvage industry, offences which, if hard and unfairly pressed, could result in discouraging salvors from doing the job we want them to do. All relate to the environment and all seem to ignore that a rescuer who goes to the assistance of others, will not be encouraged to do so again if, without *mens rea*, criminal liability falls on his shoulders.

UK WATER RESOURCES ACT

6.16 I begin with an English statute, the Water Resources Act of 1991. Section 85 of that Act imposes strict liability on anyone, whether negligent or not, who causes, or contributes to, pollution in the rivers, estuaries or coastal waters of the United Kingdom. An offence under the Act is punishable by an unlimited fine and up to two years' imprisonment.

6.17 It was under this Act that the Milford Haven Harbour Authority were prosecuted following the grounding of the *Sea Empress* in Milford Haven in 1996. An initial fine of £4million was reduced on appeal to £750,000. The salvage industry were aghast when they realised that rescuers such as themselves were not protected and even in the absence of negligence could be prosecuted under the Act. They realised there were many circumstances in which they could be liable under the provisions of the Act notwithstanding there was no actual fault on their part.

6.18 If for instance a tug put a tow line on a ship which was drifting ashore and that tow line broke through no fault on their part, perhaps because of stress of weather, they could be prosecuted and found liable under the Act, if the ship subsequently grounded and caused pollution; for the breaking of the tow line, whilst not the main cause, would have been a contributing cause to the grounding and the pollution. As another example, if to prevent further pollution salvors were transhipping a cargo of oil from a casualty to another vessel and the pipeline connection were to break because of stress of weather, they would be liable. Further, if a tug were pushing on the side of a ship in an effort to refloat her and the shell plating cracked due to its unknown fragility, again they would be liable.

6.19 Realising the discouraging effect on a potential rescuer the Minister of Shipping at the time quickly undertook, that in the absence of any deliberate pollution for commercial gain, no salvor would be prosecuted under the Act and that amending legislation would be prepared.

6.20 The undertaking has so far been honoured in that no salvor has ever been prosecuted but the amending legislation has not yet materialised. A government departmental review was commenced some time ago and an industry consultation promised before amending legislation was passed. No consultation has yet taken place. However, the salvage industry is concerned, for it has seen a paper prepared by the Environment Agency which it finds very disquieting. The paper makes it clear that whilst the Agency would support the creation of a defence to a salvor who deliberately causes pollution in order to avoid greater environmental damage (perhaps to pump out oil to lighten a ship in order to refloat her before a devastating approaching storm strikes) or to save life, or who followed the instructions of the Secretary of State's Representative (SOSREP), the Agency remains of the view that in all other respects, salvors should continue to have a potential criminal liability. Thus, in any of the events mentioned above, salvors would continue to be criminally liable. As the Agency puts it:

"The Agency sees the role of the criminal law in preventing marine pollution as a significant deterrent against conduct which causes environmental harm and as providing a way in which the proper concern of society against such conduct can be formally marked in a manner in which civil liability could not of itself achieve."

6.21 Aside from the discouraging effect of potential strict criminal liability on salvors who go to the assistance of others – which surely cannot be in the public interest – it is disquieting to note from the paper that the Agency is of the view that no amending legislation is needed "for it will only take action if the Agency feels it is needed and justified"! In short it will act as both judge and jury. Perhaps this is why the review has not officially been completed and that no public consultation has taken place.

6.22 Such a position is very unsatisfactory for if the Agency is to act as judge and jury (and that is in that position now) there is no guarantee it will always do so fairly. Political pressures after a major pollution disaster are enormous and it would be easy for a government department to succumb to such pressure and find a scapegoat. The current situation would allow it to do so.

THE EU SHIP-SOURCE POLLUTION DIRECTIVE

6.23 We have already heard from Colin de la Rue on the EU Directive as to ship-source pollution and the challenge that is being mounted against it by industry, including the International Salvage Union. I will not trespass on his territory, of which he is more than the master, but I will briefly mention the concerns of the salvage industry if this Directive is implemented as planned in March 2008.

6.24 The creation of a criminal offence for pollution, not just within the territorial waters of the EU but also the economic zone, will be very discouraging to salvors if its provisions are ever implemented against them. Many non-EU salvors operate from time to time in the EU economic zone, salving non-EU ships in international waters. Why should EU criminal law apply to them? Surely it cannot be in the interest of the EU to discourage them from salving ships which might otherwise pose a problem to EU States.

6.25 Criminal liability for "serious negligence" is very worrying. The term is a new one which will need judicial definition and that definition may well vary from one EU State to another. Is it something less than gross negligence, or more than just negligence, or does it mean negligence during the course of a serious event? There is a great fear that some countries will interpret it as the latter.

6.26 We are all human and we all make mistakes. It is right that we should be civilly liable for those mistakes but is it right that we should be criminally liable and face bankrupting fines or substantial terms of imprisonment? It should not be forgotten that even if innocent, the defence of a prosecution can be traumatic, time consuming and a very expensive experience. To some the very thought of putting themselves in a position where they might be prosecuted would be a sufficient deterrent to being involved in the first place. Particularly in a country where there is likely to be a politically induced prosecution.

6.27 It remains to be seen how the EU Nations enact the EU Directive. Greece, Cyprus and Malta have already said that they will not enact it but bearing in mind the economic sanctions which the EU has for the non-compliance of a Directive it is likely that these nations will ultimately succumb.

6.28 The shipping industry is alarmed at the effect the Directive will have on the willingness of seafarers to go to sea. The salvage industry is also much alarmed – particularly as to how it may be applied by differing States. They can see their being in the front line of a casualty is likely to result in their being prosecuted if anything goes wrong. Potential scapegoats.

6.29 As rescuers, salvors are often thrust into situations not created by themselves. Situations in which they are called upon to risk their lives – in all sorts of weather. To work under pressure – often without rest – in difficult, strange and dangerous conditions, on complicated and damaged ships – some with hazardous cargoes. In such circumstances it is easy to make an unintentional mistake. To many, it is questionable whether they should even be civilly liable for such errors but certainly they should not be criminally liable. As yet, there is no exemption for the rescuer – no responder immunity. I cannot believe potential criminal liability would make any rescuer perform his or her task any better. It is far more likely to convince him not to get involved in the first place. That cannot be in the public interest.

6.30 The President of the ISU made the following comment on the Directive:

"Salvors could be forced to back away from assisting casualties in EU waters if oil is spilt or an active threat of a spill exists. Hardening attitudes on criminalisation are forcing salvors to consider their positions in relation to potentially hostile jurisdictions. We are drawing ever closer to the position where salvors may be forced to stay their hand until they receive guaranteed immunity from prosecution. Just one prosecution of a salvor 'guilty' only of using his best endeavours would damage the casualty salvage service provided at a global level."

The above are examples of recent legislation or potential legislation which affects the salvor in the EU. Other countries are proceeding along similar lines and imposing criminal liability for pollution resulting from negligence. It is a matter of some concern to the IMO who have placed the matter on the agenda of its Legal Committee who in turn have asked the CMI to carry out a review of the existing position in all member countries. It will be interesting to see the results.

THE HIDDEN EFFECT OF CRIMINALISATION

6.31 Aside from discouraging people from doing their jobs properly, whether it be seafaring or salving, for reasons of self preservation criminalisation also has the effect of dissuading people from doing what they should and would otherwise be doing. This, together with the tendency to find a scapegoat after every casualty, can be particularly damaging. Let us take an example.

6.32 Pollution can cause enormous damage to our environment and result in huge claims for compensation. Three large casualties testify as to this. The *Exxon Valdez*, the *Erika* and *Prestige* have together resulted in damage costing billions of dollars. Salvors cannot prevent the initial pollution but they can prevent further pollution by salving the damaged casualty and keep the remaining oil in the ship. Preventing the remaining oil in the ship from escaping prevents further damage. However, the salving of a cargo of oil usually requires the transhipment of that cargo into another vessel which in turn requires sheltered waters so a ship can lay safely alongside another and avoid further damage. In short, a place of refuge.

6.33 Following the *Erika*, *Castor* and *Prestige* the IMO appreciating the need for a place of refuge for casualties which could be salved, proposed new guidelines for shipmasters, salvors, harbour authorities and governments. The guidelines listed the common sense considerations to be weighed in the balance in making the decision.

6.34 Unfortunately the guidelines were only recommendations and some nations have since developed them making it even more difficult for a ship to be granted a place of refuge.

6.35 Imagine the effect on the port authority or harbour master who has to make the decision as to whether to grant a place of refuge. Whilst there are guidelines they are not binding, and he knows full well that if he grants a place of refuge to a ship, if things go wrong, he will, more than likely, end up in prison. Look what happened to Captain Mangouras, the Master of the *Prestige*: three months in a high security prison, bailed for €3million, three years restrained in Spain where he had to report to the police daily, yet nearly four years later he has still not been brought to trial. Fear of the consequences would make any man think twice before granting a ship a place of refuge. And the result could well be: more damage.

CONCLUSIONS

6.36 Criminal sanctions for negligence have now become the norm in many aspects of our life. When used appropriately they can be of assistance in persuading people to take better care not to do what they ought not to do and to that extent perhaps should be welcomed.

6.37 However, there is a real danger of heavy handed legislation, and the consequent fear of prosecution, being counter-productive by making the lives of seafarers so potentially uncomfortable that people will either cease to be employed in the jobs in which they are at risk (such as seafarers going to sea) or carrying out work that puts them at risk (such as salvaging ships causing, or threatening to cause, pollution) or preventing people, for reasons of self preservation, taking sensible and proper steps beneficial to the prevailing situation.

6.38 Our legislators should be far more circumspect in creating new offences and should look closely at the ramifications and effect on those they target. Unless they do – there could be ramifications well beyond those currently envisaged.

PART 4

Liabilities of Classification Societies under English and US Law

CHAPTER 7

The liabilities of classification societies – more awkward than it looks?

PROFESSOR ANDREW TETTENBORN*

7.1 In the last thirty years or so, the operations and commercial functions of classification societies have changed markedly. Originally they were organisations occupying a modest backwater in the shipping world, set up predominantly in the nineteenth century[1] as honest brokers providing a private-enterprise certification service to shipowners, and with it a means for insurers to have some confidence in the condition of vessels they were being asked to cover.[2] To insurers there were quickly added others with similar interests, such as purchasers, charterers and others; and in due course it became standard practice in (for example) ship purchase contracts to include a "class clause".[3] Today, these functions remain in full force. But in addition, most such societies have mutated into multifunction, multimillion-dollar marine consultancy operations, adding to their traditional business the giving of advice on most aspects of maritime operations. As well as this they have enthusiastically entered the public arena, typically being deputed by governments to certify vessels for a large number of regulatory purposes such as compliance with SOLAS, MARPOL and similar regimes.[4] Moreover, this has also had an effect on their projected public image, and on the way they choose to be regarded by lawyers and others. Once happy to be seen as private organisations existing simply for the mutual benefit of owners, insurers and others in the shipping business, they now stress their public function of ensuring safety at sea for the benefit of society as a whole.

7.2 This process has no doubt had its advantages for societies. But it also has its drawbacks. Rather like the privateers of old, an enterprising maritime plaintiffs' bar has lost little time in noticing that there may be some rich pickings here. This is for at least two reasons. One is that societies are now perceived as big organisations having correspondingly deep pockets. The other, more significant, is that unlike traditional targets such as shipowners, charterers, salvors and the like, class (a) has no right to limit its liability, and (b) is not subject to the multifarious protections

---

* Bracton Professor of Law, University of Exeter.
1. Lloyd's Register was set up in 1760, Bureau Veritas in 1828. Virtually all the other significant classification societies date from the 19th or early 20th century.
2. For some background, see, e.g., Feehan, "Liability of Classification Societies from the British Perspective: 'The Nicholas H' ", in Tul. Mar. L.J. 163, 164 (1997); Hudson & Allen, *The Institute Clauses* (3rd ed., 1999), pp. 95–99; Lay, *The History of Marine Insurance, including the Functions of Lloyd's Register* (1925); Merkin, *Marine Insurance Legislation* (2000), pp. 147–148.
3. See Goldrein & Turner, *Ship Sale and Purchase* (4th ed., 2003), pp. 96–139.
4. Begines, "The EU Law on Classification Societies: Scope and Liability Issues", in (2005) 36 J. Mar. L. & Com. 487.

from liability to be found in, for example, the Hague Rules. Not surprisingly, classification societies are concerned at this, as for that matter are courts faced with the possibility of liabilities being imposed on class that are wildly disproportionate to the fees it charges.[5]

7.3 The object of this chapter is to ask just how far the liability of class can, and ought to, extend today: hence its official title, "the liabilities of classification societies". But a moment's thought will show that this question actually arises in a number of very disparate circumstances, and that correspondingly disparate answers may well be appropriate.

7.4 To begin with, the issue of liability arises in connection with two very different types of claimant. On the one hand there are claims against a classification society by its own shipowner clients (suing, as in any case of professional negligence, in contract and/or tort). On the other, there are potential liabilities to third parties, such as cargo-owners and other potential victims (suing in tort). Very different practical issues are likely to be involved in each of these situations.

7.5 Secondly, it has to be remembered that societies today do a very large number of different jobs, extending well beyond inspection and supervision of ships with a view to classification and preservation of class *tout court*. One such function, of burgeoning contemporary importance, is their *de facto* licensing function as surrogates of the state. Vessels registered in, or visiting, most advanced jurisdictions not only have to conform to regimes such as SOLAS or MARPOL, but also are required to undergo periodic inspections to make sure they do. And, while states can if they wish carry out such inspections themselves through some specialised government agency, in fact they increasingly subcontract the operation to approved classification societies. Yet another function of classification societies is a direct result of diversification: namely, consultancy and advice of a more general sort. If a shipowner needs advice or information on anything from risk management to fuel analysis, or for that matter the paperwork necessary to transit the Suez Canal, the chances are increasingly that it will hire class to provide it. Once again, each of these three areas may well call for substantially different treatment. In short, any coverage of the potential liabilities of classification societies has to be fairly nuanced: any attempt to analyse it just using concepts from the general law is likely to fail.

7.6 Hence the coverage in this paper will be broken up into a number of sections dealing with specific situations in which questions of liability may arise.

NON-STATUTORY SURVEYS AND OTHER SERVICES

Liability to the client

(a) Class surveys and the like

7.7 There is little difficulty here as regards the existence of a duty *of some sort* owed to the client. As a matter of contract, and normally in tort too,[6] class clearly owes a

---

5. For example, see the reservations of Lord Steyn in *The Nicholas H* [1995] 2 Lloyd's Rep. 299, 315, and in the US in *Cargill Inc. v Bureau Veritas*, 902 F. Supp. 49, 52, 1996 A.M.C. 577, 581 (S.D.N.Y. 1995).

6. In England because of *Henderson v Merrett Syndicates Ltd* [1995] 2 A.C. 145, effectively holding that any claim by a client for professional negligence can be cast in either tort or contract. In most US jurisdictions the result is likely to be much the same.

duty of care to the shipowner who engages and pays it. The issue is not so much whether there is a duty, as how far it ought to go and what it covers.

7.8 When we are dealing with classification proper, the answer, it is suggested, is that liability is likely to be fairly constricted. Take the most straightforward scenario: a society fails to spot some defect on survey that, if noticed, would have affected class or at least led to some specific instruction for repair. Later on there is a casualty due to that defect, damaging or delaying the vessel and possibly causing loss or damage to cargo on board her. Assuming negligence and causation can be proved (admittedly quite a big assumption[7]), a claim by owners for the loss caused to the vessel or the amount paid out to cargo, is clearly possible as a matter of law.[8] In practice, however, the omens for claimants in this situation are not good, for a number of reasons.

7.9 First, a claim of this sort, whether in contract or tort, is essentially one for reliance ("had you not given our ship a clean bill of health we would have acted differently"): but in a situation of this sort the owner is unusually vulnerable to a finding that any such reliance is unjustified in the circumstances. A prudent shipowner, after all, is expected to do a good deal more to keep its ship seaworthy than merely commissioning periodic surveys from class and then hoping for the best: from which it follows that to rely on such surveys as a means of maintaining the condition of one's vessel is itself unreasonable.[9] Indeed, in the English context the point can be taken further. In order for a negligent misrepresentation claim to succeed, it must be shown that the statement was intended to be relied on for the purpose for which the claimant relied on it[10]: and, it is suggested, it must always be open to class to argue that class surveys exist more to enhance the marketability and insurability of a vessel than as legally watertight assurances to the owner of its safety.

7.10 Secondly, it should be borne in mind that a class survey is just that: it is limited by its terms of reference to matters going to class, and does not oblige the surveyor to point out everything that might cause danger or otherwise harm the owner's interests. An important point follows: there will be a number of situations where, even if a given defect is not flagged up, there is simply no breach of duty.[11]

---

7. Since (a) the evidence may by then be underwater; (b) some time may well have passed between survey and casualty, letting in the possibility of other causes; and (c) conversely, the casualty may have happened before the deadline fixed for repair by the society and hence the defendant may be able to argue it would have occurred anyhow.

8. There is little English authority: but the possibility is clearly admitted in a number of American cases. See, e.g., *Steamship Mutual Underwriting Ass'n v Bureau Veritas*, 380 F. Supp. 482, 1973 A.M.C. 2184 (E.D. La. 1973); *Great American Insurance Co. v Bureau Veritas*, 338 F. Supp. 999, 1972 A.M.C. 1455 (S.D.N.Y. 1972), aff'd, 478 F.2d 235, 1973 A.M.C. 1755 (2d Cir. 1973); *In re Oil Spill by the Amoco Cadiz*, 1986 A.M.C. 1945; and the unreported *In re Dann Marine Towing LC*, US District Court E.D. La, 2004 U.S. Dist. LEXIS 5857, 7 April 2004. Note, however, a significant point: in none of these did the plaintiff's claim actually succeed on the facts.

9. *Cf.* the American decision in *In re Oil Spill by the Amoco Cadiz*, 1986 A.M.C. 1945, where the fact that it is primarily a shipowner's duty to keep his ship seaworthy was held to prevent the owners of the *Amoco Cadiz* from claiming indemnity from ABS in respect of its liability for the 1978 spill off Brittany, even if the latter had been negligent. Note, however, that that case only concerned total indemnity: it did not close off the route of demanding a partial indemnity by third party proceedings or otherwise.

10. See, e.g., the auditors' case of *Caparo Industries plc v Dickman* [1990] 2 A.C. 605, especially Lord Roskill at p.629.

11. The point arose neatly in a 2002 New York arbitration on the subject, *Ibar Ltd v ABS* (summarised at *http://www.onlinedmc.co.uk/ibar_ltd_v__abs.htm*) (large yacht burnt out and sunk by fire in unmanned engine room, which detector would have prevented: ABS not liable for failing to recommend this in class

Furthermore, it should always be remembered that there are clauses that constrain the scope of any liability that might otherwise arise (typically, by making it clear that class "is not an insurer or guarantor of a vessel's integrity or safety or that of any of its equipment or machinery"[12] or using some similar language). Such provisions are, for obvious reasons, likely to strengthen the hand of class when sued by shipowners for negligently classifying a vessel which should not have been classified.

7.11 Thirdly, it has to be remembered that in most cases where an owner sues class for having classified a ship in fact unsatisfactory, it is actually the owner itself that is largely responsible for its own misfortune: the immediate cause of its loss is its having employed an unsatisfactory ship in the first place. This is a matter which in the influential *Sundance Cruises Corp. v American Bureau of Shipping*[13] led an American court to deny recovery entirely, on the basis that such primary responsibility ought not to be able to be laid off onto third parties. This may be an over-drastic response,[14] but even in England one suspects liability would be drastically reduced for contributory negligence even if not denied entirely on causation grounds.

7.12 Failure to notice defects is not, of course, the only possible source of liability to the client. A society could equally be guilty of over-precaution. Imagine, for example, that it insists on repairs being done to a vessel which are not in fact necessary to maintain class, with the result that she is needlessly taken out of service.[15] Or again, suppose that a prospective sale or charter contains a standard "class clause" making it dependent on the vessel remaining in class, and then a negligent decision to de-class causes the transaction to go off. Losses suffered by owners from events of this sort would be likely to be regarded as foreseeable, at least where class was on notice that a transaction of this sort was on the cards; and on principle there seems no reason why there should not be liability. On the other hand, it is suggested that claimants are likely to face at least two practical difficulties in recovering them. To begin with, since it is in the nature of class surveys that societies should have a fair margin of appreciation when deciding whether repairs are in fact necessary and if so how far they should go, proving fault is likely to be an uphill task.[16] Furthermore, it is suggested that as a matter of judicial psychology courts are likely to keep one eye on the classification societies' stated aim of

---

survey, since only bound to point to clear dangers, not to act as naval architect or look generally to best interests of owner). A similar decision is the cargo case of *Continental Ins. Co. v Daewoo Shipbuilding & Heavy Machinery Ltd*, 707 F. Supp. 123 (1988) (class not liable to cargo for not pointing out defect in manhole cover that, while significant, did not otherwise affect class).

12. This particular example comes from the ABS *Agreement for Classification of Existing Vessels*, Clause 11. The subject of limitation clauses is dealt with further below.

13. 799 F. Supp. 363, 385, 1992 A.M.C. 2946 (S.D.N.Y. 1992), aff'd, 7 F.3d 1077, 1994 A.M.C. 1 (2d Cir. 1993), cert. denied, 114 S. Ct. 1399 (1994). See too *Great American Insurance Co. v Bureau Veritas*, 338 F. Supp. 999, 1972 A.M.C. 1455 (S.D.N.Y. 1972), aff'd, 478 F.2d 235, 1973 A.M.C. 1755 (2d Cir. 1973).

14. See generally Miller, "Liability of classification societies from the perspective of US law", in 22 Tul. Mar. L.J. 75, 94 (1997).

15. A claim of this sort was brought, but failed on the facts, in another New York arbitration, *Shipping Force v ABS* (2004) (summarised at *http://www.onlinedmc.co.uk/shipping_force_v__abs.htm*).

16. One suspects that courts on both sides of the Atlantic would apply a test analogous to that in the English malpractice case of *Bolam v Friern HMC* [1957] 1 W.L.R. 582 and hold the defendant negligent only if no competent surveyor would have reached the same conclusion.

preserving safety and allow a fair deal of leeway to a defendant that erred on the side of caution, even though the result may have been a loss of profit to the owner employing it.

(b) Other services

7.13 Class surveys are, of course, only a relatively small part of a classification society's business, even as regards ships classed by it. After a casualty representatives of class are likely, like seagulls and lawyers, to be among the first on the scene – giving advice as to how to deal with the damage, when and where repairs have to be carried out, what needs to be done with cargo in the meantime, and so on. Furthermore, at particular times class may provide, or arrange the provision of, all sorts of other information and advice of various sorts of use to owners. The potential for negligence is patent. Class may miss particular items of damage that need repair; advocate repairs (or repairers) that are in fact substandard or danger-ous; or otherwise mislead clients by information it provides. Here, unless there is an apt limitation clause, there seems no reason to doubt potential liability. A straight-forward American example, which could equally well have been English, is *Somarelf v ABS*.[17] ABS negligently provided owners with a Suez Canal tonnage certificate which was understated by some 25%.[18] After a number of transits of the Canal under voyage charter where this certificate had been presented and accepted for dues calculation purposes, the Canal Authority discovered the truth and raised a substantial charge for excess fees. The owners had to pay these, but could not pass them on to the charterers. They were nevertheless allowed to recover them from ABS on the basis of negligent misrepresentation.[19]

7.14 However, the accepted scope of a classification society's duty may well qualify this. In so far as advice is outside the scope of the service normally provided by class, then even if the advice is otherwise specific and unequivocal it may be possible to infer that no duty of care arose. For example, while class is very much concerned with deciding what repairs are to be done, advising how to do them is arguably different. Thus in another American case, *Gulf Tampa Drydock Co. v Germanischer Lloyd*,[20] repairers patching up cracked deck plating under classifica-tion society supervision negligently set fire to the vessel they were meant to be repairing. Sued by the owners, the repairers sought contribution from Germanischer Lloyd as concurrently liable to the owners for not overseeing the job properly. In view partly of the fact that class was not to be regarded as providing a surrogate guarantee of vessels' seaworthiness or physical integrity assurance against damage, the Fifth Circuit Court of Appeals was highly sceptical. While not exoner-ating the defendants, it pointedly remitted the matter to the court below to make a proper determination of the duty owed.

---

17. 720 F. Supp. 441 (D.N.J. 1989).
18. Essentially ABS forgot that the Suez Canal way of measuring tonnage was idiosyncratic, in that it included spaces disregarded for other purposes.
19. Strictly speaking the claim was by the owners' agents, who had indemnified the time-charterer who had let the ship on the relevant voyage charters. But nothing turns on this: a claim by owners would equally have succeeded.
20. 634 F.2d 874 (1981).

Liability to others

7.15 As pointed out above, class's liability to its own client is in one sense artificially easy. If he who pays the piper calls the tune, the piper for his part must owe his paymaster at least some obligation to play tunefully. But, to continue the analogy, it is much less clear whether, and if so why, the piper's duty should enure to the benefit of other guests and freeloaders at the same party. This is essentially the problem dealt with in the next two sections – i.e. class's liability to third parties other than the immediate client. Since different issues tend to arise in different types of case, this topic is best split into a number of subtopics.

(a) Buyers and charterers

7.16 Normally a buyer or charterer is interested only in taking a vessel if it is in class: even if he is already bound on principle to buy or charter, that contract will nearly always be subject to a class clause.[21] This leads to an obvious question of potential liability: if, relying on class's actions or comments, a person buys or charters a vessel that is seriously substandard, can he sue class in tort for not noticing the fact?[22]

7.17 One's first instinct, faced in such a case with fault, and assuming no difficulties arise about proving loss and a causal link, might be to say "Why not?" Some systems indeed do this. French law, for example, with its very expansive notion of fault liability and lack of a cohesive duty of care concept, regards the existence of a duty as clear in this situation: the defendant may of course escape responsibility on other grounds, such as unforeseeability and the like, but if he cannot do this will be liable as of course.[23] Elsewhere, however, lawyers have realised that matters are less simple than that. Whatever the situation as between classification society and owner, the moral claim of the buyer or charterer to be allowed to stabilise an otherwise bad investment by reference to a survey it neither commissioned nor paid for is inherently rather weak – especially when the amount of any damages may well be entirely out of proportion to the fee charged for the survey. Furthermore, it is worth bearing in mind that under Anglo-American law the economic loss rule precludes the buyer or user of a ship (or for that matter any other chattel) from using the law of tort to sue builders, repairers or others similarly involved in its production or maintenance in respect of defects in the vessel itself.[24] If this is right, then it seems a little curious not to extend the same protection to class, who did not even introduce the defect but merely failed to spot it.

---

21. See, e.g., Clause 8(c) of the Norwegian Saleform 1993.

22. There is a theoretical possibility of a claim as a third party beneficiary of the contract between the classification society and the owner, a claim recognised both in England (since the Contracts (Rights of Third Parties) Act 1999) and also in virtually every American jurisdiction. But whether a buyer would be regarded as gaining contractual rights is highly doubtful. Further, at least some societies' terms expressly exclude third party contractual rights (see, e.g., the ABS *Application for survey of existing Vessel*, para. 11 ("... nothing in this agreement or in any certificate or report issued under this Agreement shall be deemed to create any interest, right, claim, or benefit in any insurer or other third party").

23. A claim of exactly this kind succeeded against BV in 1992 in France: see *The Elodie II*, Tribunal de Commerce de Nanterre, 26.6.1992, D.M.F. 1994, 19.

24. England: see *Hamble Fisheries Ltd v Gardner* [1999] 2 Lloyd's Rep. 1 and, more generally, *Simaan General Contracting Co v Pilkington Glass Ltd (No. 2)* [1988] Q.B. 758. US: the leading decision is *East River SS Corp. v Transamerica Delaval Inc.*, 476 U.S. 858, 106 S.Ct. 2295, 90 L.Ed.2d 865 (1986).

7.18 In England, which in general takes the economic loss rule fairly seriously, a decidedly negative signal was sent out by *The Morning Watch*.[25] The seller of an 80-foot yacht described her – perfectly correctly – as classed A1 at Lloyd's. The buyer, having got her, found horrendous under-deck corrosion which, had the boat been surveyed properly, would have prevented her being classed without major improvements. Phillips J. nevertheless denied that Lloyd's owed a duty to the buyer. Admittedly this was largely on the basis that at the time of the survey Lloyd's had not known that any particular sale was in the offing, thus theoretically leaving matters open if there had been such knowledge. But in fact at least two other factors have effectively persuaded English-style courts to close the door on negligence liability. One appeared in *The Morning Watch* itself. There Phillips J. also expressed the view that the classification system was aimed not so much at protecting the financial interests of third party buyers as in promoting maritime safety generally, and regarded this as a further strong counterindication to liability.[26] Admittedly this seems a somewhat cavalier take on history, since Lloyd's Register, the oldest classification society, *was* started precisely to protect the financial interests of those dealing with shipowners, as for that matter were most of its later followers. Nevertheless, times no doubt have changed. The safety point was taken up later by the same judge in the Court of Appeal,[27] and apparently regarded as sufficient of itself to deny liability.[28] And, as if this was not enough, an Australian court seised of the same issue later made a further point against liability. This was that direct liability to third parties was undesirable, and should be disallowed, because it would effectively bypass limitation clauses agreed between shipowners and classification societies.[29]

7.19 Both for the reasons in *The Morning Watch* and also for those mentioned above, there is, it is suggested, much to be said for the English view effectively shutting off liability for financial losses to those with an interest in the vessel. It should be noted, however, that this view has not completely triumphed in the US. While the mere fact that a third party may rely on a certificate will not of itself be enough (any more than it is in England),[30] things may be different where the classification society actually knows about the third party and its potential interest. The leading case is the controversial[31] 2003 decision in *Otto Candies LLC v NKK*.[32] American

25. [1990] 1 Lloyd's Rep. 547.

26. See [1990] 1 Lloyd's Rep. 547, 559.

27. In *Reeman v Dept of Transport* [1997] 2 Lloyd's Rep. 648. See too the parallel New Zealand decision in *Att.-Gen. v Carter* [2003] 2 N.Z.L.R. 160, reaching effectively the same result.

28. See [1997] 2 Lloyd's Rep. 648, 680 (Phillips L.J.). In fact the case concerned not the liability of class, but rather that of the Department of Transport (who had allegedly failed to carry out proper stability tests on a fishing-boat which the plaintiffs then bought and found they could not use). But clearly the same reasoning applies to class. See too Tipping J. in *Att.-Gen. v Carter* [2003] 2 N.Z.L.R. 160 at [36] ("The safety focus of the survey regime is another policy reason which ... points away from the imposition of a duty of care to guard against economic loss").

29. See the unreported Queensland decision in *Natcraft Pty Ltd & Henlock Pty Ltd v Det Norske Veritas* [2001] Q.S.C. 348, affirmed [2002] Q.C.A. 284. This point is dealt with further below.

30. See *Otto Candies LLC v NKK*, 346 F.3d 530, 536 (2003) ("mere foreseeability that third parties may rely on such reports or certificates" not enough).

31. See, for example, the trenchant criticism of the decision in O'Halloran, "Note: In a Novel Decision, the Fifth Circuit Recognizes the Tort of Negligent Misrepresentation in Connection with Maritime Classification Societies and Third-Party Plaintiffs", in 78 Tul. L.Rev. 1389 (2004).

32. 346 F.3d 530, 536 (2003).

purchasers agreed to buy a secondhand Japanese ferry then laid up and out of class. The sale contract being conditional on class restoration, NKK duly surveyed the vessel and re-classed her, whereupon the buyers accepted her. Having brought her to Florida and tried to transfer her to ABS, they found that she was in fact suffering from a congeries of problems which ought to have prevented her being classed at all by NKK, and which cost them over $300,000 to put right. The buyers sued NKK for this sum, won, and the Fifth Circuit affirmed. This was on the basis that the *Sundance* case,[33] mentioned above, did not absolutely preclude liability to third parties; that there was already authority making (for example) cargo inspectors liable to buyers for defects they missed[34]; and that the requirements for liability for negligent misstatement were otherwise made out in that (as NKK knew) the report was being prepared with a view to a specific sale.

7.20 While *Otto Candies* clearly shows a more plaintiff-friendly attitude than appears in England, one suspects that is not quite the green light for actions against class that it might appear. It was a rare case, in that the plaintiff there appears – somewhat unusually – to have had no problem in establishing causation or reliance, and also in that the re-classification survey was carried out with the specific sale in mind. Furthermore, there seems no reported successful claim against class based on the holding in it. Nevertheless, one has to draw from it the conclusion that, in the US as against England, buyer claims are not predestined to fail, that it will be more difficult for defendants to get summary judgment, and that this will no doubt have to be reflected in any settlement negotiations.

(b) Cargo owners

7.21 Suppose that some alleged negligence by class – an oversight during a regular survey, a failure to supervise post-collision repairs or check that they have been properly done, or whatever – causes a vessel to sail when unseaworthy. Suppose also that, had the vessel been properly classed, she would not have sailed at all, and that as a result of her sailing a casualty occurs and her cargo is damaged or lost. Can cargo interests, normally cargo underwriters,[35] sue class?

7.22 In one sense, this logically raises the same issue as claims by buyers: if the issue is whether a person contracting to provide services to A can be liable for foreseeable loss caused to B by failure to provide them properly, then it should not matter whether B is a buyer of the vessel or the owner of cargo on it.[36] On the other hand, as soon as one admits – as one must in Anglo-American law – the idea that duties of care can be fairly readily limited by reference to outside factors, then it becomes apparent that this liability has to be dealt with separately.

---

33. *Sundance Cruises Corp. v American Bureau of Shipping*, 799 F. Supp. 363, 385, 1992 A.M.C. 2946 (S.D.N.Y. 1992), aff'd, 7 F.3d 1077, 1994 A.M.C. 1 (2d Cir. 1993), cert. denied, 114 S. Ct. 1399 (1994).

34. This argument is open to the obvious riposte that cargo inspectors tend to produce their reports specifically to allow the cargo to be sold, while classification societies are not necessarily in the same relation with buyers of ships. But this does not seem to have worried anyone.

35. Normally, but not always. It could equally well be P&I interests who, having paid out to cargo, now seek contribution against anyone they can find.

36. Hence a court in Belgium, which follows the French legal tradition, has held class liable to cargo: *The Spero*, Cour d'appel d'Anvers (4e Ch.), 14 February 1995.

7.23 In the specific cargo context of cargo liability, there are arguments both ways. In favour of liability is the fact that the cargo owner, unlike a buyer of the ship, has suffered physical damage, so the economic loss rule has no part to play. But there are also contrary points. In particular, even assuming that class carelessly fails to spot some defect with which it should be concerned, three factors need to be borne in mind. One is that the connection between the defendant's negligence and the damage is not particularly close: the failure of the shipowner to take his own precautions intervenes between the two, while conversely the cargo owner is not directly concerned with reports by class and certainly cannot be said to have relied on any recommendations in the same way as a normal negligent misrepresentation claimant. Secondly, it is worth noting the case for class liability as a matter of policy is not very compelling, since effectively if we do allow a suit by cargo all we are doing is making a sterile shift of burdens between insurance carriers (i.e. cargo underwriters to class's liability insurers[37]). The last, and perhaps the most important, point against liability is that as often as not actions by cargo against class allow the claimant to give the go-by to limitations of liability that would apply in a claim against the carrier itself. Although in a sense a claimant in this situation is simply seeking to profit from a loophole in the relevant limitation regime,[38] it can equally well be argued that this regime represents a decision by the maritime community that certain risks should rest with cargo, and that the law of negligence should not allow this to be displaced by a sidewind.

7.24 The English regime on cargo liability has largely – and, it is suggested, rightly – accepted these points and denied a duty. The leading (in effect, the only) decision is *The Nicholas H*.[39] A ship carrying a cargo of lead developed shell plating cracks. Her classification society, NKK, were told; but following some prodding by her owners, they reluctantly agreed to her completing her voyage after merely temporary repairs. These repairs were not enough, and she sank en route. Despite the fact that negligently-caused physical damage to property tends in practice to give rise to liability as of course in English law, the House of Lords, by a majority of 4–1, struck out cargo's claim against NKK. There had, said Lord Steyn (giving the leading opinion), been no reliance by cargo on NKK's recommendations[40]; classification societies existed not so much to protect the financial interests of goods owners as "to promote safety of life and ships at sea in the public interest"[41]; allowing suit by cargo would "disturb the balance created by the Hague Rules and Hague-Visby Rules as well as by tonnage limitation provisions, by enabling cargo-owners to recover in tort against a peripheral party to the prejudice of the protection of shipowners under the existing system"[42]; and the work of

37. And possibly also P&I Clubs to class's liability insurance carriers. In so far as cargo succeeds against class, the carrier's P&I club is to that extent exonerated: furthermore, even if cargo does not sue class, there is the possibility of a contribution claim by P&I interests against class's insurers.
38. This point was made by the Lord Lloyd, the dissentient in *The Nicholas H*, below: see [1995] 2 Lloyd's Rep. 299, 304–305.
39. [1995] 2 Lloyd's Rep. 299.
40. Lord Steyn said it might be different if, for some reason, there had been direct reliance (p. 314). But it is difficult to envisage any practical situation in which the point would arise. A possible example might, however, be a situation where cargo was involved in negotiations with class and threatened to offload the cargo unless it received satisfactory assurances from class.
41. *Ibid.*, at p. 311.
42. *Ibid.*, at p. 315.

classification societies in the public interest might be prejudiced by the spectre of liability to cargo arising out of mere advice.[43]

7.25 The view in the United States is much the same, though – if one may say so – less well-reasoned. The first decision denying cargo liability was in 1988, but was hardly strong authority because the defect did not go to class anyway.[44] The present leading decision is *Cargill Inc. v Bureau Veritas*.[45] A vessel's engines were in decidedly shaky condition; BV indulgently allowed the necessary repairs to be postponed, whereupon on her next voyage she broke down completely and cargo suffered long delays. Cargo interests sued BV, alleging negligence, but a New York district court denied recovery for two reasons. The first reason was slightly enigmatic: class, it was said, did not guarantee seaworthiness.[46] But the second largely reflected the indirectness point made in *The Nicholas H*, above: that is, that there should not be liability for negligent misrepresentation in the absence of reliance by the plaintiff.[47] It is true that the court accepted in principle that the society might have been liable to cargo for negligent misrepresentation had there been actual reliance by the latter.[48] However, such reliance is likely in practice to be impossible to show, and hence in practice, it is suggested that class is effectively immune to actions by cargo.

(c) Collision and similar claims

7.26 The decided cases on third party liability all seem to concern buyers and the like, or cargo claimants. But there are other possibilities. One involves collisions. Suppose a vessel which has been negligently surveyed and given a clean bill of health by class is involved in a collision with another ship as a result of some defect going to class that ought to have been spotted (for example, defective reversing gear or rudder controls). Imagine that the outcome is damage to that other ship and possibly the loss of cargo on board it. Can the latter ship or cargo choose to sue class? On one level, this seems to involve the same issues as cargo, if not more so: if class is not liable to the owners of property on the ship it surveys, why should it be liable for damage to property elsewhere? On the other hand it could be argued that the case is subtly different, on the basis that even accepting that classification is not aimed at ensuring cargo-worthiness, it emphatically is aimed at the promotion of maritime safety, an aspiration which presumably does include the avoidance of collisions.

---

43. *Ibid.*, at pp. 316–317.

44. *Continental Ins. Co. v Daewoo Shipbuilding & Heavy Mach. Co. Ltd*, 888 F.2d 125 (2d Circuit 1989) (badly sealed manhole cover: no liability merely because surveyor was on board and might have drawn attention to it had he been sharper-eyed).

45. 902 F. Supp. 49 (S.D.N.Y., 1995).

46. See 902 F. Supp. 49, 52 (1995). This derived from a throwaway line in *Sundance Cruises Corp. v American Bureau of Shipping*, 7 F.3d 1077 (2d Cir. 1993), referred to above; a similar statement can be found in *Great Am. Ins. Co. v Bureau Veritas*, 338 F. Supp. 999, 1012 (S.D.N.Y. 1972). But it is hard to see its relevance, since no-one ever said that class did guarantee seaworthiness. The only alleged duty on class is a duty to take care not to miss defects going to class which the classification one ought to spot which might make the vessel unseaworthy.

47. See 902 F. Supp. 49, 53 (1995).

48. *Ibid.*

7.27 In fact, however, apart from this point it is suggested that most of the other arguments against liability to cargo apply equally in collision claims. There is no direct reliance by the plaintiff on anything said by class. Liability, if allowed, will again amount simply to a rearrangement of insurance coverage: and, perhaps most importantly, it would still allow an end-run around the limitation regime.[49] It is respectfully suggested that these arguments ought to prevail, and that class – at least in respect of ordinary surveys – should remain immune from liability if their negligence causes a ship to be in collision.

(d) Personal injury

7.28 So far we have been dealing with commercial losses of one sort or another. But it is of course possible that negligence in allowing a dangerous vessel to sail may cause personal injury: either to someone on board the vessel surveyed or to a person elsewhere (for example, if the unseaworthiness of the vessel leads to its loss, or to a collision or explosion). Oddly enough, however, there is little authority on whether a duty of care will be owed in such a case.

7.29 Logically, claims of this sort share many features of cargo claims, including a number of the arguments against liability there. The primary duty to provide a safe ship is on the shipowner, not class. Mariners, like cargo owners, are not generally the addressees of reports from classification societies, and cannot be said (except in the most exceptional circumstances) to have relied on their contents. Like cargo interests, injured seamen on board the ship concerned and others in the line of fire have the undoubted possibility of a claim against the owner, either under the general law of tort or (especially in the US) under some general legislative scheme.[50] Lastly, it has to be remembered that limitation issues may arise in respect of personal injury,[51] thus engendering a parallel argument to that in *The Nicholas H* that we should not subvert that regime by allowing victims to sue class direct.

7.30 On the other hand, two important points do distinguish injury claims here. One is that the lesion is human rather than material. It is normally regarded as more important generally to compensate personal injury than property damage: people, unlike cargo or ships, are not normally insured against loss or damage, and the argument does not apply that, in allowing suit against class, we are doing nothing more then merely rearranging insurance carriers. The second is that, while classification societies can say with some plausibility that they do not exist to protect cargo owners' commercial interests, they do have as their avowed aim the preservation of safety at sea – including presumably the protection of the bodily integrity of seamen and others. The point is finely balanced: but it is suggested that this feature might well tip the scales, at least in the English context, particularly as in England the context and purpose of the defendant's activity is regarded as extremely important

---

49. And also in England (though not the US) around the rule that cargo on one ship can recover against another vessel only to the extent that the latter is in fault for the collision: Merchant Shipping Act 1995, s.187.

50. Notably under the Jones Act (46 U.S.C. §688); the Death on the High Seas Act (46 U.S.C. §§761–68); and (in the case of shore-based workers) the Longshoremen's and Harbor Workers' Compensation Act (33 U.S.C. §901).

51. See 46 USCA §183; Merchant Shipping Act 1995, Sch. 7, Art. 2(1)(a).

to liability in tort.[52] The leading English case denying liability to purchasers, it will be remembered, stressed this "safety" angle in denying protection to the commercial interest of the buyer.[53] Despite scepticism in a 1997 case as to whether government inspectors of a fishing-boat would owe a duty to crewmen drowned as a result of its unseaworthiness,[54] there is an English decision in 1998[55] and a Canadian one in 1991[56] allowing claims to proceed in the analogous case of the negligent issue of certificates of airworthiness for aircraft. In the English case *The Nicholas H* was specifically discussed, only to be sidelined as depending on its particular context.[57] Whatever the merits or demerits of allowing cargo to sue, to deny the personal injury claim "would leave a gap in the law of tort notwithstanding that a plaintiff has suffered foreseeable personal injury as a result of the unsafety of the aircraft and the unreasonable and careless conduct of the defendant". It would, said Hobhouse L.J., "be remarkable if that were the law".[58] It is therefore suggested that, at least in England, a personal injury claimant can sue.

7.31 American jurisprudence has tended to play less on such "purpose" arguments and rely more on such matters as the lack of specific reliance by plaintiffs. It might thus be thought that personal injury claimants faced a more uphill task. Nevertheless, at least one decided case did give rise to a substantial jury verdict against ABS, when a misguided survey by them returned to class a previously laid-up rust-bucket that promptly sank off Japan with the loss of eight crew[59]; and this decision seems to have gone without serious question.[60] Hence, at least in the present state of the law, it may well be that a duty is likely to be accepted.

Liability to others: two footnotes

(a) Contractual limitation of liability

7.32 A complication we have so far mentioned only in passing arises out of contractual limitations on class's liability. Classification societies invariably act for owners under disclaimers of liability of one sort or another[61]: these clauses on their

---

52. This does leave the limitation point, to which there is no entirely satisfactory answer. On the other hand, objection never seems to have been raised to personal injury plaintiffs on either side of the Atlantic bypassing limitation by using some other theory of recovery, such as the employer's nondelegable duty in England (e.g. *McDermid v Nash Dredging & Reclamation Co. Ltd* [1987] A.C. 906), or – very importantly – products liability in the US.

53. See Phillips J. in *The Morning Watch* [1990] 1 Lloyd's Rep. 547, 559.

54. See *Reeman v Department of Transport* [1997] 2 Lloyd's Rep. 648, 679.

55. See *Perrett v Collins* [1998] 2 Lloyd's Rep. 255.

56. See *Swanson Estate v R.* (1991) 80 D.L.R. (4th) 741.

57. *Perrett v Collins* [1998] 2 Lloyd's Rep. 255, 259 (Hobhouse L.J.).

58. *Ibid.*, pp. 255, 259–260.

59. See *Psarianos v Standard Marine Ltd*, 728 F. Supp. 438 (1989). It should be noted, however, that the reported case was mainly concerned with insurance and arbitration issues.

60. It was mentioned, without comment, in *Sundance Cruises Corp. v American Bureau of Shipping*, 799 F. Supp. 363 (1992), referred to above.

61. Issues could theoretically arise as to whether a given clause was incorporated in the arrangement between class and owner. But there is no space to go into these here. In any case, in practice the matter is unlikely to matter too much since all work is likely to be undertaken against a signed written order incorporating class's standard conditions.

wording have the effect both of limiting what losses the society is liable f
also of imposing a top limit of liability in the event that they are liable at al

7.33 As regards class's liability to owners with whom it is in contractuɛ
the question is at least relatively simple: assuming the limitation to have been
properly incorporated in the contract, does the jurisdiction concerned give effect to
it? In the US, apart from state statutes dealing with exculpatory clauses (whose
relevance depends on which state law governs the contract between class and
owner), it should be remembered that there is a tendency to disallow them as
unconscionable, or if particularly ferocious to excise them as contrary to public
policy.[64] In England such clauses are theoretically subject to a reasonableness test
under the Unfair Contract Terms Act 1977.[65] But one suspects that, except perhaps in the event of an attempt to exclude all liability or limit it to a derisory sum,
in practice such clauses would almost certainly pass muster.

7.34 More awkward is the question how far clauses of this sort can be opposed
to third parties or otherwise cut down the rights of a third party plaintiff suing in
tort. Although it is unlikely to arise very often (in view of the fact that third-party
liability is apt to be difficult to establish anyway), it is worth touching on briefly.

7.35 In cases where (a) the claim is based on actual reliance by the plaintiff on
information from class, as in the *Otto Candies* situation (i.e. the disappointed buyer)
and (b) the report actually contains a disclaimer, then there would seem little
difficulty. The basis of the liability is negligent misrepresentation, and there is little
doubt on either side of the Atlantic that a representor can avoid liability by making
it clear that he does not accept it.[66]

7.36 In other situations, however, the general position seems to be the orthodox
one: a plaintiff suing in tort cannot be affected by a contractual disclaimer to which
it was not a party. This was certainly the view of Lord Steyn in *The Nicholas H*[67]
as regards classification societies, and this was accepted in another Australian case:
indeed, in the latter this factor (i.e. that class would be unable to limit its liability
by contract) was regarded as telling strongly against the recognition of a duty of
care *vis-à-vis* third parties.[68] It is true that against this it might be argued that,
according to a number of authorities in England, the situation may be different
where there is a "web of contracts" between a series of parties. For example, a

---

62. See, for example, Clause 12 of ABS's standard survey conditions: "ABS makes no representations beyond those contained in sections 1 and 11 hereof regarding its reports, statements, plan review, surveys, certificates or other services. Except as set out herein, neither ABS, nor any of its officers, employees or agents shall be liable for any loss, damage or expense of whatever type or kind sustained by any person due to any act, omission or error of any nature caused by ABS, its officers, employees or agents, or due to any inaccuracy of any nature, even if held to amount to a breach of warranty."

63. Thus, BV in Art. 6.2 of its general conditions limits liability for negligence to 1½ times the fee received or €800,000, whichever is the greater.

64. For a topical example see. e.g.. *Great Am. Ins. Co. v Bureau Veritas*, 338 F. Supp. 999 (D.C.N.Y., 1972), in which the term "The Bureau Veritas declines any responsibility for errors of judgment, mistakes or negligence which may be committed by its technical or administrative staff or by its agents" was summarily tossed out as "overbroad".

65. See s.2 (liability in negligence) and s.3 (liability for breach of contract).

66. See in England *Hedley Byrne & Co Ltd v Heller & Partners Ltd* [1964] A.C. 465.

67. See [1995] 2 Lloyd's Rep. 299, 315–316.

68. See the unreported Queensland decision in *Natcraft Pty Ltd & Henlock Pty Ltd v Det Norske Veritas* [2001] Q.S.C. 348, affirmed [2002] Q.C.A. 284.

contract between a construction company and a subcontractor may exclude the latter's liability for some loss on the basis that this is to be covered by insurance elsewhere. If this is common practice in the business, then this factor may militate against then the existence of a duty of care owed by the subcontractor to the building owner and hence give de facto effect to the exemption clause against third parties.[69] However, this principle is fairly narrowly construed, and in *The Nicholas H* Lord Steyn was firmly of the view that it would not apply to the situation of classification society and third party.[70]

(b) Liability other than in negligence

7.37 Hitherto all discussion of class's third party liability has been predicated on the idea that the only plausible cause of action is negligence. However, it is worth making the point that this is not necessarily true. In particular, perhaps surprisingly the question of claims based on deceit, or fraud, cannot be ruled out on either side of the Atlantic. Deceit, it will be remembered, includes not only a deliberately fraudulent statement, but any statement made without belief in its truth[71]: and this latter form of the tort can be surprisingly wide. For example, in a recent English case[72] concerning the closely related field of cargo inspection, inspectors innocently certified as sound a cargo of petrol which was in fact substandard. Doubts having been expressed, the inspectors without further investigation said that they "stood by" the previous report. Although no doubt indolent rather than mendacious, this latter conduct was held to amount to the tort of deceit. The implication for classification societies is obvious. Suppose a contract for sale contains a standard clause requiring "confirmation of class issued within 72 hours prior to delivery"[73] or some such. If the society is aware that doubts have been expressed as to whether the vessel is still fit to be classed, it must now be arguable that its reiteration or repetition of a previous report is potentially deceitful unless the society can produce evidence of a positive belief in its truth. The impact of this point on settlement negotiators could be considerable, since it must always be remembered that as soon as the boundary is crossed from negligence to deceit, then not only are questions of duty of care irrelevant, but also exception clauses are less likely to protect a defendant.[74]

---

69. Typical is *Pacific Associates Inc. v Baxter* [1990] 1 Q.B. 993. An earlier instance is *Norwich City Council v Harvey* [1989] 1 W.L.R. 828.

70. See [1995] 2 Lloyd's Rep. 299, 316.

71. *Derry v Peek* (1889) 14 App. Cas. 337. The rule in the US is generally the same: Prosser & Keeton, *Torts* (5th ed.), 741–742.

72. See *AIC Ltd v ITS Testing Services (UK) Ltd* [2006] 1 Lloyd's Rep. 1. The decision was reversed on the facts by the Court of Appeal (see [2006] E.W.C.A. Civ. 1601): but it is suggested that this does not affect the point in the text.

73. This is the wording in Clause 8(c) of the Norwegian Saleform 1993.

74. As a matter of English law, one cannot disclaim liability for one's own lies; and while it is possible to disclaim it for the deceit of one's employees acting in the course of their employment, very explicit words indeed are required to do this. See generally *HIH Casualty & General Insurance Ltd v Chase Manhattan Bank* [2003] 2 Lloyd's Rep. 61, [2003] U.K.H.L. 6, especially at [76] (Lord Hoffmann) and also at [16] (Lord Bingham). The same is largely true in the US: Farnsworth, *Contracts* (3rd ed.), §5.2.

LIABILITY ARISING OUT OF STATUTORY FUNCTIONS

7.38 So far we have been concentrating on the essentially private law functions of classification societies. As noted above, however, societies increasingly certify ships on behalf of regulatory authorities for what are in effect licensing purposes. For example, it is now largely left up to them to ensure that shipowners comply with SOLAS, MARPOL, the International Load Line certificate, the ISM safety code, and a host of other requirements without which it becomes in effect legally imposs- ible for an owner to operate his ship at all. Typically, a number of classification societies will be licensed to provide these services within a particular jurisdiction: it is then up to the shipowner to select which he will contract with. The potential effect of mistakes in this area is obvious. Improper failure to certify can be disastrous for owners; miscertification for its part can be catastrophic not only for the owner him- self, but also for any number of third parties.

(a) Liability to owners

7.39 Absent some statutory protection from liability, there seems no reason to doubt that a classification society carrying out a statutory inspection owes at the very least some duty to the owner to take care.[75] The question is, once again, how far this goes.

7.40 In so far as the plaintiff's complaint concerns failure to notice defects that ought to have been spotted, and the claim is for with resulting loss or damage to the ship and/or liability to third parties, it is suggested that class will in practice have little to worry about. Indeed, if anything the case for liability to the client is weaker here than with other inspections. One reason is that the object of legislation requir- ing compliance with statutory standards is clearly the promotion of safety and good environmental stewardship at sea: if ordinary class surveys are not ordinarily regarded as aimed at protecting the economic interests of shipowner clients, statutory stan- dards are even less so.[76] Secondly, it has to be remembered that with regimes such as SOLAS and MARPOL, a primary duty is placed on the shipowner, enforced by criminal sanctions, to comply with the provisions of the relevant code before sailing. The requirement for survey and certification is, as it were, simply a prophy- lactic way of enforcing that primary obligation. If so, it lies somewhat ill in the mouth of a shipowner to argue, in effect: "I culpably and criminally took a danger- ous vessel to sea and suffered loss as a result: and I now blame you for negligently allowing me to do it." If it tried to do so, it is suggested that it would be likely to fail on a causation analysis, or possibly even on the basis of illegality.[77]

7.41 More likely to be significant, however, is the converse situation: imagine an over-zealous inspector culpably refuses to certify a ship, with the result that the ship is unnecessarily sterilised for a period, or forced to undergo pointless repairs. No

---

75. For example, it would pretty clearly be liable if the inspector carelessly dropped a spanner into a delicate satnav system, damaging it; or if the inspection was so dilatory as to immobilise the ship for longer than necessary, thus causing loss of charter profits.

76. *Cf.* the decision in *Reeman v Dept of Transport* [1997] 2 Lloyd's Rep. 648.

77. *Cf.* the English decision in *Clunis v Camden & Islington HA* [1998] Q.B. 978.

doubt negligence will be somewhat difficult to prove here[78]: but if it is, is there a duty of care? As a matter of the general law there might be: thus in England the Court of Appeal has held that statutory authorities can be liable for demanding more by way of precaution than is justified, specifically rejecting a contention that liability should be barred as a matter of policy because the defendant is acting for the protection of the public.[79]

7.42 However, in the case of statutory inspections the matter is more doubtful. Under the relevant English regulations[80] there is an appeal to an arbitrator in the event of dissatisfaction with the non-issue of a certificate[81] or of the ship's detention for lack of one[82]; furthermore, the arbitrator has the power, if satisfied that there were in fact no grounds for detention and that there were no reasonable grounds for the inspector to form the opinion that there were, to order compensation from the Secretary of State.[83] It is suggested that this may well be regarded as excluding any collateral right to sue the inspector or the classification society for damages at common law.[84]

7.43 It is suggested, though there seems no authority, that plaintiffs seeking to establish a duty of care against the classification society in the US are also likely to face an uphill struggle. This is for two reasons. First, effectively the same appeal regime applies in the US as in England: analogous provision is made for statutory inspections,[85] and a similar right of appeal given to those dissatisfied with the outcome.[86] Hence the same pre-emption argument might well be applied there. The second reason is that the doctrine of "qualified immunity", which broadly protects governmental authorities acting in good faith from liability,[87] might conceivably apply. This has been held by the Fifth Circuit to be capable of applying equally to private bodies who by arrangement with government "perform a governmental function",[88] a matter that might well serve to protect classification societies acting for government.

7.44 In either case, it also needs to be remembered that, as with liability to the client elsewhere, the limitations on liability which are invariably contained in any contract between an owner and a classification society may well be relevant and limit the effectiveness of any damage remedy.

---

78. For the reasons given above in connection with liability for ordinary surveys.
79. See *Welton v North Cornwall District Council* [1997] 1 W.L.R. 570 (over-zealous food inspector demanding vast, and totally unnecessary, improvements to restaurant premises: appeal against award of damages for negligence dismissed).
80. The Merchant Shipping (Survey and Certification) Regulations 1995 (SI 1995 No. 1210), as amended.
81. SI 1995 No. 1210, Reg. 26.
82. *Ibid.*, Reg. 25.
83. Merchant Shipping Act 1995, s.97(1)(b).
84. So held in Canada in connection with a fairly analogous provision: *Budisukma Puncak Sdn Bhd v The Queen in Right of Canada* (2005) 338 N.R. 75. This case actually concerned the liability of the Crown, the relevant inspector having been a Crown employee: but it is suggested that the reasoning – i.e. that collateral attack should not be allowed – applies equally to others involved in inspections.
85. See 46 U.S.C.A., Subtitle II, Part B.
86. See 46 CFR, §2.01–70.
87. See *Harlow v Fitzgerald*, 457 U.S. 800 (1982).
88. See *De Vargas v Mason & Hanger-Silas Mason Co. Inc.*, 844 F.2d 714, 722 (1988) (though the rule is not universal: *cf. Royal Ins. Co. of Am. v Ru-Val Elec. Corp.*, 918 F. Supp. 647, 654–55 (E.D.N.Y. 1996)).

(b) Liability to others

7.45 We dealt above with societies carrying out ordinary classification or non-statutory surveys, or determining if and when repairs ought to be done to keep a vessel in class. They are, as we have seen, likely on both sides of the Atlantic to escape liability to cargo interests and (probably) collision claimants. They are also reasonably well protected against suits by buyers and others whose interest in the integrity of the vessel is merely financial (though this has of course to be qualified, in the case of the US, by the exception in *Otto Candies LLC v NKK*[89] applying to surveys done with a particular transaction in mind).

7.46 Does it make any difference that the document on which the third-party plaintiff bases its case is not a survey or visa, but a statutorily-required certificate of compliance with (say) SOLAS or MARPOL? It is submitted that in most cases the answer ought logically to be No. Exactly the same arguments against liability apply in the case of cargo claims, claims by buyers and collision claims whatever the origin of the document: the frequent lack of reliance by the plaintiff on the contents of the information received from class, the desirability of protecting the limitation regime (in the case of cargo and collision claims), and the perception that class does not exist to protect business investments made by third parties. Indeed, the latter argument is even stronger here: certificates of compliance are issued against the background of legislation giving effect to such regimes as SOLAS or ISPS, and it seems pretty clear that that legislation is aimed squarely at safety at sea rather than safeguarding the financial interests of third parties. Conversely, when it comes to personal injury claimants, if such claims are to be allowed in the case of ordinary surveys, then the argument for allowing crew members and others to sue on the basis of wrongly given statutory certificates is all the stronger.

7.47 In discussing liability to cargo claimants, collision victims and the like, however, we have left out one vital and very topical issue: pollution, and in particular oil pollution.[90] The question – which is currently being litigated in the US on a grand scale[91] – is simply whether victims of pollution ought to be able to send a possibly catastrophic cleanup or damage bill to a classification society that wrongly certified a vessel as hazard-free.

7.48 At first sight, there seem to be strong reasons in favour of liability. Particularly if a vessel has been certified as satisfying the requirements of MARPOL, the relevant statutory provisions are aimed at protecting precisely the interest in respect of which compensation is being sought. In fact, however, matters are more complex, and there are a number of counter-arguments. First of all, liability in oil pollution cases is likely to be colossal, and this (as pointed out in *The Nicholas H*)

---

89. 346 F.3d 530 (2003).

90. See Gauci, *Oil Pollution at Sea* (1997), pp. 108–109; also Abecassis, *Oil Pollution from Ships* (1985), ch. 21. Though dated, this latter describes the issues well.

91. Most notoriously, the Spanish government is currently pursuing ABS in the US courts for the cost of clearing up after the *Prestige* disaster that decanted some 70,000 tonnes of oil onto the Galician coast in 2002. (Some preliminary skirmishes appear in *Reino de España v American Bureau of Shipping*, 2004 A.M.C. 2050, 2005 A.M.C. 2257.) In addition, ABS as classification society for the *Amoco Cadiz* are known to have paid out very substantial clean-up costs in the face of litigation by French authorities after the massive spill in 1978: see *The Amoco Cadiz*, 1992 A.M.C. 913. Class is correspondingly worried: see *Lloyd's List*, 16 May 2006 ("ABS chief expresses worries over Prestige litigation").

is a reason – though of course not necessarily a knock-out one – for providing protection to subsidiary actors. Secondly, and more importantly, there is in all industrialised nations a limitation regime,[92] which may well affect matters. However, as will appear, this latter argument may apply in different ways according to whether suit is brought in England or the US.

7.49 In England, in fact, liability seems to be precluded by the terms in which the Civil Liability Convention 1969 has been transposed.[93] This convention (which is also is in force in most other advanced nations, with the notable exception of the US) sets up a specific regime that aims to channel liability narrowly through the owner of the ship concerned by way of insurance, and contains a specific provision ousting the liability of any "servant or agent" of the shipowner.[94] Although these words do not seem to cover class,[95] they are reproduced in section 156(2)(b) of the Merchant Shipping Act 1995 in a wider form, namely excluding the liability of "any person ... employed or engaged in any capacity on board the ship or to perform any service for the ship". It is suggested that these words are likely to be widely construed, and that a classification society is indeed a person engaged "to perform any service for the ship" and hence statutorily immune.[96]

7.50 In the US, there is a superficially similar scheme of federal shipowner liability under the Oil Pollution Act 1990[97]; but there is one vital difference. While this legislation requires all claims under it to be made first against the shipowner,[98] it not only has no general bar to claims against others, but on the contrary specifically preserves the right of the individual States to impose requirements over and above the limits set by it,[99] together with any other rights of indemnity.[100] Hence any argument that the specific scheme of liability should be regarded as pre-empting suits against others not covered by it is likely to fail. The possibility therefore remains very much open of a classification society finding itself open to (unlimited) liability claims arising under State law where oil pollution causes damage to property within particular states.

---

92. In England under the CLC Convention, 2002 Protocol, the limit is 133 SDR per registered ton. Under the US Oil Pollution Act 1990 (33 U.S.C.A., §§2701–2720) the limit is set higher, at $1200 per ton, with a floor of $10 million for a ship of over 3000 tons (33 U.S.C.A. §2704).
93. It is enacted into domestic English law by way of Ch. VI of the Merchant Shipping Act 1995.
94. Art. III.4.
95. Class is clearly not a "servant," and it seems doubtful whether it is an "agent" even if an extended interpretation is accepted.
96. It is suggested that the exclusion in s.156(2)(b) is limited to claims brought by the actual victims of the pollution, and does not bar claims by the shipowner against class for an indemnity against his liability under the CLC (*cf. The Aegean Sea* [1998] 2 Lloyd's Rep. 39). But we have already suggested that the prospects of liability of class to owners for misinspection are not good, for other reasons.
97. 33 U.S.C.A., §§2701–2720, providing for strict liability subject to limits as referred to above. For a useful discussion, see Swanson, "The Oil Pollution Act of 1990 after ten years", in 32 J. Mar. L. & Com. 135 (2001).
98. 33 U.S.C.A., §2713(a). There is a possibility of a claim under the statute against a third party wholly responsible (33 U.S.C. §2702(d)(1)(A)), but this does not cover a a third party "whose act or omission occurs in connection with any contractual relationship with the responsible party" – a term that would seem to include a negligent classification society.
99. 33 U.S.C.A., §2718(a)(1). See, e.g., the unreported *Dostie Development, Inc. v Arctic Peace Shipping Co.*, 1996 W.L. 866119 (M.D.Fla.) (common law claim against ship managers for pollution damage allowed to proceed).
100. 33 U.S.C.A., §2710. Nevertheless, US courts have been unsympathetic to claims to indemnity against class for other reasons, as appears above.

7.51 The discussion above has been limited to oil pollution. As regards other forms of pollution there is no international convention involved,[101] and hence it follows that the matter is exclusively governed by national law.

7.52 As far as the US is concerned, the most important source of statutory liability is the federal Comprehensive Environmental Response and Clean-up Act 1980[102] (known as CERCLA), which though not specifically angled towards maritime pollution can have the effect of imposing liability on a shipowner for clean-up costs resulting from noxious discharges other than oil.[103] CERCLA does not cover any losses other than clean-up costs; but it is specifically stated not to pre-empt other forms of state liability for pollution taking place within a state.[104] It follows that where (for instance) noxious discharges from a ship damage property, classification remains at risk, though the difficulties that have arisen elsewhere in holding classification societies liable for negligent damage will no doubt apply here too. However, claims for clean-up costs and other economic losses are likely to be less successful owing to the prevalence of the economic loss rule.

7.53 As regards England, the position is much the same. There is as yet no general legislation concerning liability for discharge (though there is a EU Directive on the matter, which when in force will have a similar effect to CERCLA[105]). As a result, the possibility must remain open of liability of classification societies for negligence, or possibly nuisance[106] where the escape of hazardous or polluting material affects the use or amenity of land.

CONCLUSION

7.54 This chapter has attempted to highlight the most important issues that are likely to arise in connection with claims against class under Anglo-American law. The conclusions that can be drawn from it are perhaps twofold. First, the topic is less simple than it may seem at first sight. The circumstances in which liability could arise are varied and the relevant policy considerations multifarious; hence the simple application of general rules is unlikely to be particularly useful. Secondly, despite certain disconcerting cases where class has been found liable (or has settled to avoid awkward litigation with its attendant publicity), the practical chances of class being held liable in England or the US for negligence in carrying out its core functions remain satisfyingly low. To that extent, class may draw a crumb of comfort from what appears above.

---

101. The HNS (Hazardous and Noxious Substances) Convention of 1996 aims to set up a regime parallel to that of the Civil Liability Convention dealing with liability for discharge of non-oil pollutants. But the Convention has not received enough ratifications to bring it into force, and there is some doubt as to whether it ever will.

102. 42 U.S.C.A., Ch. 103.

103. 42 U.S.C.A. §9607(a). See Anderson & Marinelli, "CERCLA and the Carriage of Dangerous Goods and Hazardous Substances", in 21 Tul Mar L.J. 501, 508 (1997).

104. See 42 U.S.C.A., §§9601, 9614(a).

105. Directive 2004/35/EC.

106. Under *Esso Petroleum Co Ltd v Southport Corp'n* [1956] A.C. 218, there can be liability in nuisance for shipborne pollution; and it is also clear that the person responsible for creating the nuisance is liable for it. See Clerk & Lindsell, *Torts* (19th ed.), §20-51.

CHAPTER 8

Classification society liability in the United States

PROFESSOR MARTIN DAVIES*

INTRODUCTION

8.1 It is difficult to succeed in a claim against a classification society under US law,[1] but a steady stream of plaintiffs continues to try. The reason for such apparently quixotic behavior is not difficult to find. The liability of shipowners for the unseaworthiness of their vessels is often limited in amount by international conventions or by contract or by both. When faced with limited recovery from the shipowner, the plaintiff may pursue the prospect of unlimited recovery from the ship's classification society, however difficult the claim may be to establish. After all, it may be possible for the plaintiff to recover something by way of settlement, even if the claim would have little prospect of success at trial. As well, the shipowner itself may seek to pass on to the classification society any loss that it has sustained or liability that it has incurred to others.

8.2 This chapter sets out the principles governing the liability of classification societies under US law in Section 3. Before reaching that point, however, it considers, in Section 2, the impact that forum selection clauses and choice of law analysis have on claims brought against classification societies in US courts. Transnational litigation increasingly involves disputes about jurisdiction and choice of law,[2] and classification society disputes are no exception. Preliminary battles about forum and governing law often have the effect that a decision on the merits of the case under US law is never reached.

8.3 The most significant piece of litigation about classification society liability in the United States is still in progress. The Kingdom of Spain is seeking US$700,000,000 in damages from the American Bureau of Shipping in the US District Court for the Southern District of New York for losses sustained as a result of the sinking of the *Prestige* off the coast of Spain in 2002. Section 4 of this paper outlines the present position in that litigation and offers some reflections in the light of the principles stated in Sections 2 and 3.

---

* Admiralty Law Institute Professor of Maritime Law, Tulane Law School; Director, Tulane Maritime Law Center.

1. Tort and contract liability are generally governed by state law. Each of the 50 states has its own common law, often modified by statute; with very few exceptions, there is no such thing as federal common law, applicable uniformly in all 50 states. See *Erie Railroad Co. v Tompkins*, 304 U.S. 64, 58 S.Ct. 817 (1938), overruling *Swift v Tyson*, 41 U.S. 1 (1842). Maritime law claims are one of the important exceptions to the *Erie* rule. Maritime tort claims and maritime contract claims are governed by general maritime law, which is federal law that should be applied uniformly in all 50 states.

2. See, e.g., Adrian Briggs, *The Conflict of Laws* (2002): "When the world loses its fascination with jurisdictional issues – something it shows no sign of doing any day soon – it will be time to write a different book; but the broad issue of jurisdiction is where today's litigators focus their attention."

JURISDICTION AND CHOICE OF LAW

Forum selection clauses

8.4 The contract between a shipowner and its classification society often contains a forum selection clause and the class certificates issued by the society typically incorporate the terms of that contract. Obviously, the contracting parties themselves are bound by the forum selection clause, with the result that the plaintiff may be forced to submit its claim to arbitration if that is what the agreement provides.[3] When the forum selection clause provides for arbitration, the classification society may also be able to insist on arbitration of claims brought by persons who are not party to the classification contract. There is a strong federal policy in favour of arbitration,[4] which leads US courts to apply very liberal rules about binding non-parties to arbitration agreements, rules that go far beyond what a believer in the doctrine of privity of contract would expect or find acceptable.

8.5 The leading case is *American Bureau of Shipping v Tencara Shipyard SpA*.[5] A group of investors (the owners) contracted with an Italian shipyard for construction of a racing yacht that was eventually named *Tag Heuer*.[6] The construction contract specified that the yacht would be classed by the Genoa office of the American Bureau of Shipping (ABS). The shipyard contracted with ABS under terms that included an agreement that all disputes would be arbitrated in New York. As is usually the case, the hull insurance coverage obtained by the owners was premised on the existence of valid classification by ABS. A few months after *Tag Heuer* was delivered to the owners, it suffered serious hull damage during an ocean voyage. Surveys indicated that the damage had been caused by defective design and poor construction. The Italian shipyard sued ABS in Italy. Having indemnified the owners, the hull underwriters sued ABS in France, as did the owners themselves. ABS responded by bringing suit in the US District Court for the Southern District of New York, seeking to compel the shipyard, the owners and the underwriters to arbitrate their claims in New York, as provided in the agreement between the shipyard and ABS. The district court held that the shipyard was bound to arbitrate its claim but that the owners and underwriters were not. On appeal, the US Court of Appeals for the Second Circuit held that all three claimants – the shipyard, the owners and the underwriters – were required to arbitrate their claims against ABS in New York.

8.6 The shipyard was bound to arbitrate its claim because it was an original party to the arbitration agreement. The Second Circuit had little difficulty in dis-

---

3. See, e.g., *Shipping Force Co. Ltd v American Bureau of Shipping*, S.M.A. Arbitration No. 3815, 1 December 2003. The shipowner brought an action against the classification society in the U.S. District Court for the Southern District of New York, but then consented to arbitration after the classification society asserted its right to rely on an arbitration clause in the classification certificate.

4. *Mitsubishi Motors Corp. v Soler Chrysler-Plymouth Inc.*, 473 U.S. 614, 631 (1985) ("[the] emphatic federal policy in favor of arbitral dispute resolution ... applies with special force in the field of international commerce"); *Scherk v Alberto-Culver Co.*, 417 U.S. 506, 520 (1974).

5. 170 F.3d 349, 1999 A.M.C. 1858 (2d Cir. 1999).

6. This *Tag Heuer* was designed to compete for the Jules Verne Trophy, which is awarded to yachts circumnavigating the globe in fewer than 80 days. *American Bureau*, 170 F.3d at 351, 1999 A.M.C. at p. 1859. *Tag Heuer* still sponsors ocean yacht racing; it is collaborating with the first-ever Chinese challenge for the America's Cup in 2007: see *http://www.tagheuer.com/the-brand/sport-tag-heuer/americas-cup/index.lbl* (last visited 4 September 2006).

posing of the shipyard's argument that it should not be bound to the arbitration clause because it had been acting solely as agent for the owners when it contracted with ABS; clearly, the shipyard had been acting, at least in part, on its own behalf as well.[7] Although the owners were never in privity with ABS, the Second Circuit held that they were estopped from denying their obligation to arbitrate because they had received direct benefits from the contract containing the arbitration clause.[8] Those direct benefits included their ability to obtain significantly lower insurance rates than they would have if *Tag Heuer* had not been classed by ABS.[9] Because the owners were bound to arbitrate in New York, the federal courts in New York had personal jurisdiction over them.[10] The underwriters were also bound to arbitrate because they were subrogated to the owners' rights against ABS and so stood in their shoes for all purposes, including the obligation to arbitrate.[11]

8.7 Before we move on to consider later applications of the *American Bureau* principles in US courts, it is interesting to note that the French Cour de Cassation also referred the owners of *Tag Heuer* to arbitration, holding that the question of whether the owners were bound by ABS's arbitration clause must be decided by the arbitrators themselves, not by the French courts.[12] The decision of the Cour de Cassation is thus a striking example of the negative *Kompetenz-Kompetenz* doctrine, more strongly applied in France than in the United States: the French courts held that they did not have jurisdiction to consider the arbitrability question that the Second Circuit considered and decided in favor of ABS.[13]

8.8 Estoppel of the kind found in *American Bureau* is not the only basis on which non-parties may be bound to an arbitration agreement. The *American Bureau* court noted that there are five different bases for binding a non-signatory to the terms of an arbitration agreement: (1) incorporation by reference; (2) assumption of the obligation to arbitrate by subsequent conduct; (3) agency; (4) veil-piercing/alter ego, as in the case where a corporate parent dominates and controls its subsidiary;

7. *American Bureau*, 170 F.3d at 353, 1999 A.M.C. at p. 1863.

8. *Ibid*. For the proposition that a party is estopped from denying an obligation to arbitrate if it receives a direct benefit from a contract containing an arbitration agreement, see *Thomson-CSF, S.A. v American Arbitration Association*, 64 F.3d 773, 778-79 (2d Cir. 1995).

9. *American Bureau*, 170 F.3d at 353, 1999 A.M.C. at p. 1862.

10. The Second Circuit rejected the owners' argument for the opposite process of reasoning – i.e. that because the court did not have personal jurisdiction over them (the owners were not resident or doing business in the United States), it could not consider the estoppel argument. *Ibid.*, 170 F.3d at 352, 1999 AMC at p. 1861.

11. *Ibid.*, 170 F.3d at 353, 1999 AMC at p. 1862.

12. *American Bureau of Shipping v Jules Verne*, 17(1) Mealey's Int'l Arb. Rep. 18 (2002), describing Cass. 1e civ., June 26, 2001. The Cour de Cassation reversed the decision of the Paris Court of Appeal, which had held that the owners were not bound by the clause. On remand from the Cour de Cassation, the Court of Appeal referred the owners and ABS to arbitration, holding that under the New York Convention, an arbitrator and not the courts, must decide whether an arbitration agreement is valid: see "Court of Appeal of Paris Enforces Arbitration Agreement", in 18(12) Mealey's Int'l Arb. Rep. 11 (2003).

13. See, e.g., E. Gaillard, "The Negative Effect of Competence-Competence", in 17(1) Mealey's Int'l Arb. Rep. 18 (2002), who writes that the Cour de Cassation's decision in *American Bureau of Shipping* "rank[s] among the most noteworthy judgments of French case law in relation to international arbitration". The positive *Kompetenz-Kompetenz* doctrine holds that arbitrators have authority to decide on their own jurisdiction, by deciding questions of arbitrability. The negative *Kompetenz-Kompetenz* doctrine is the complementary counterpart of the positive doctrine, holding that courts cannot hear litigation relating to the existence, validity or scope of an arbitration agreement, which must be decided by the arbitrators.

and (5) estoppel.[14] Nevertheless, it is the *American Bureau* court's broad-ranging finding of estoppel that seems to hold most significance for cases involving classification societies. There are at least two other examples of courts applying the *American Bureau* approach to estoppel to bind a non-signatory to a forum selection clause in a classification society certificate.

8.9 In *Hellenic Investment Fund, Inc. v Det Norske Veritas*,[15] the classification society Det Norske Veritas (DNV) issued a classification certificate for a bulk carrier named *Marianna*, which was sold to a purchaser on terms that *Marianna*'s class certificates were to be, on delivery, "clean valid and unextended for six months". The classification certificate stated that it was issued under the DNV Rules, which require that any dispute be brought in the Municipal Court in Oslo, pursuant to Norwegian law.[16] After the purchase was completed, the purchaser's P&I Club surveyors discovered numerous defects and deficiencies that materially affected the buyer's ability to get Club cover for its next two voyages, one of which was imminent. On one of those two voyages, the vessel (now named *Tranquility*) was detained in the port of Montreal by port state control authorities. The purchaser sued DNV seeking recovery of the losses it had sustained as a result of the defective condition of *Marianna/Tranquility*, alleging tortious misrepresentation. The district court granted DNV's motion to dismiss the purchaser's claim, and the US Court of Appeals for the Fifth Circuit affirmed on appeal, holding that the purchaser was bound by the forum selection clause in the DNV Rules, even though it was not party to any contract with DNV. Citing and following the Second Circuit's *American Bureau* decision, the Fifth Circuit held that the purchaser was estopped from denying its obligation to arbitrate because it had received a direct benefit from the classification society contract containing the arbitration clause.[17] The court said[18]:

"[T]he *Marianna*'s ability to be flagged and operate in commerce was founded on DNV's classification. It is clear that many benefits flowed directly to Hellenic when DNV performed its contract with [the seller]."

8.10 Similarly, in *Holland America Line Inc. v Wartsila North America Inc.*,[19] the US District Court for the Western District of Washington dismissed a claim brought by Holland America Line Inc. against Bureau Veritas S.A. (BV) in relation to the loss of a Holland America ship by fire, because the contract between Holland America and BV contained an exclusive jurisdiction clause providing that all disputes were to be litigated before the Court of Nanterre in France. The same court later dismissed an action brought by Holland America against Bureau Veritas (Canada) Inc. and Bureau Veritas North America Inc. on the ground that those two entities were entitled to enforce the French forum selection clause in the contract between Holland America and Bureau Veritas S.A., even though neither defendant was party to that contract.[20]

---

14. *American Bureau*, 170 F.3d at 352, 1999 A.M.C. at p. 1861, citing *Thomson-CSF, S.A. v American Arbitration Association*, 64 F.3d 773, 777–779 (2d Cir. 1995).
15. 464 F.3d 514, 2006 A.M.C. 2312 (5th Cir. 2006).
16. *Ibid.*, at p. 517.
17. *Ibid.*, at pp. 519–520.
18. *Ibid.*, at p. 519.
19. 2005 A.M.C. 1769 (W. D. Wash. 2005).
20. 2005 W.L. 1287993 (W. D. Wash. 2005).

8.11 Both *American Bureau* and *Hellenic Investment Fund* bound the purchaser of a vessel to the forum selection clause in the contract between the vendor and its classification society. It is not yet clear whether the *American Bureau* estoppel rationale can be extended beyond purchasers to other plaintiffs not in privity with the classification society, and if so, how far beyond. Many commercial parties benefit, directly or indirectly, from the lower insurance rates that classification society certification helps to secure. However, the Second Circuit in *American Bureau* and the Fifth Circuit in *Hellenic Investment Fund* stressed the need for *direct* benefit as the basis of the estoppel that binds the plaintiff to the forum selection clause.[21] Any benefit obtained by charterers or cargo owners in paying lower freight and hire rates than they would have to pay on a ship without classification society certification would surely be indirect, having been passed on from the shipowner. To that extent, however, it is possible to identify a Catch-22 problem for third-party plaintiffs. As we shall see in Section 3, a third party plaintiff's chance of success in a tort claim is greater the more closely linked it is to the classification society, particularly by reliance on the class certificate. The closer the link between a third party plaintiff and the classification society, the more likely it is that the plaintiff will be bound by any forum selection clause in the classification society's contract with its immediate client, the shipowner. If the plaintiff is sufficiently remote from the relationship between classification society and shipowner to escape the effect of the forum selection clause, it may be unable for that very reason to establish that the classification society owed it a duty of care.

Choice of law

8.12 The traditional choice of law test in tort cases selects the *lex loci delicti*, the law of the place of the tort.[22] A large majority of American states have now abandoned the traditional approach in favour of the "most significant relationship rule" in the Second Restatement (Second) of Conflicts of Law[23] or some other kind of government interest or choice-influencing analysis.[24] Federal courts exercising admiralty jurisdiction apply a very different choice of law approach derived from the decisions of the Supreme Court of the United States in *Lauritzen v Larsen*[25] and *Hellenic Lines Ltd v Rhoditis*.[26] The *Lauritzen/Rhoditis* approach requires the court to consider eight factors, none of which is dispositive in itself: (1) the place of the wrongful act; (2) the law of the ship's flag; (3) the domicile of the injured party; (4) the domicile of the shipowner; (5) the place of the contract; (6) inaccessibility of the foreign forum; (7)

---

21. See *supra*, notes 8, 17.
22. See, e.g., *Dowis v Mud Slingers Inc.*, 621 S.E.2d 413 (Ga. 2005) (reaffirming the *lex loci delicti* approach).
23. Restatement (Second) of Conflicts of Law, §145 (1971).
24. Professor Symeon Symeonides, Dean of the Willamette University College of Law, publishes an annual survey of choice of law in each of the American states. The most recent published survey states that only ten of the 50 states (Alabama, Georgia, Kansas, Maryland, New Mexico, North Carolina, South Carolina, Virginia, West Virginia and Wyoming) continue to follow the traditional *lex loci delicti* rule: see Symeon Symeonides, "Choice of Law in the American Courts in 2005: Nineteenth Annual Survey", in 53 Am. J. Comp. L. 559, 595 (2005).
25. 345 U.S. 571, 73 S.Ct. 921 (1953).
26. 398 U.S. 306, 90 S.Ct. 1731 (1970).

the law of the forum; and (8) the shipowner's base of operations.[27] *Lauritzen* and *Rhoditis* were both actions brought by injured seamen under the Jones Act,[28] but the Supreme Court of the United States later confirmed that these criteria for choice of law are not confined to Jones Act cases but are intended to guide courts in all cases involving maritime claims.[29] Thus, it is the *Lauritzen/Rhoditis* multi-factor test that US courts must apply when considering tort actions against classification societies.

8.13 In *Carbotrade SpA v Bureau Veritas*,[30] the plaintiff, which was charterer of the Gibraltar-flagged ship *Star of Alexandria*, brought an action against Bureau Veritas (BV) in the US District Court for the Southern District of New York, seeking to recover damages it had sustained as a result of the sinking of the ship.[31] The owner of *Star of Alexandria* was a Gibraltar corporation; the plaintiff charterer, Carbotrade, was an Italian corporation; the ship's manager was Greek; the owner of the cargo that went down with the ship was American; the defendant, BV, was French; the BV surveys of which the plaintiff complained were conducted in Greece.

8.14 BV moved for summary judgment, arguing that English law applied to the dispute and so it could not be held liable to a third party such as the plaintiff because it owed no duty according to the principles stated by the House of Lords in *The Nicholas H*.[32] The district court accepted BV's argument that English law applied and ordered summary judgment for BV.[33] On appeal by the plaintiff, the US Court of Appeals for the Second Circuit applied a *Lauritzen/Rhoditis* analysis and concluded that the plaintiff's claim was governed by Greek law.[34]

8.15 The district court chose English law because that was the law of the flag and the other *Lauritzen/Rhoditis* factors pointed "indiscriminately to much of the globe",[35] but the Second Circuit reiterated that none of the *Lauritzen/Rhoditis* factors is dispositive and noted that the Supreme Court had applied US law in *Rhoditis* itself, even though the law of the flag there was Greek law.[36] The Second Circuit also noted that several of the eight *Lauritzen/Rhoditis* factors did not apply to the case at hand.[37] The fifth factor, the place of the contract, was irrelevant because there was no direct contractual relationship between plaintiff and defen-

27. Lauritzen, 345 U.S. at 583–92; Rhoditis, 398 U.S. at 309.

28. 46 app. U.S.C. §688.

29. *Romero v International Terminal Operating Co.*, 358 U.S. 354, 382, 79 S.Ct. 468, 485 (1959).

30. 99 F.3d 86, 1997 A.M.C. 98 (2d Cir. 1996).

31. The plaintiff first instituted arbitration proceedings against the shipowner in London under the arbitration clause in the charterparty. It obtained a default award, which the shipowner did not satisfy because it had no assets. The shipowner's P&I Club refused to satisfy the award because it claimed that the shipowner was in violation of manning requirements imposed by Gibraltar, the flag state. *Carbotrade*, 99 F.3d at 88, 1997 A.M.C. at p. 101.

32. *Marc Rich & Co. v Bishop Rock Marine Co. (The Nicholas H)* [1996] A.C. 211.

33. *Carbotrade S.p.A. v Bureau Veritas*, 901 F.Supp. 737, 1996 A.M.C. 561 (S.D.N.Y. 1995). In fact, the district court held that "British law" applied.

34. The Second Circuit thus reversed the district court's order for summary judgment in favor of BV and remanded the case to the district court. On remand, the district court first denied BV's later motion for summary judgment on the basis of Greek law (*Carbotrade S.p.A. v Bureau Veritas*, 1998 W.L. 397847 (S.D.N.Y. 1998)) then tried the case applying Greek law, concluding that BV had not been negligent and in any event that the alleged negligence was not the cause of the vessel's loss: see *Carbotrade S.p.A. v Bureau Veritas*, 1999 W.L. 714126 (S.D.N.Y. 1999). The plaintiff appealed unsuccessfully. *Carbotrade S.p.A. v. Bureau Veritas*, 216 F.3d 1071 (2d Cir. 2000).

35. *Carbotrade*, 901 F.Supp. at 743, 1996 A.M.C. at 568.

36. *Carbotrade*, 99 F.3d at 90, 1997 A.M.C. at 104.

37. *Ibid.*, 99 F.3d at 91, 1997 A.M.C. at 105.

dant.[38] The sixth and seventh factors – the accessibility of the foreign forum and the law of the forum – were also irrelevant because there was no bar to the district court applying foreign law and none of the possible forums would require the plaintiff to be present there to institute suit, which was what the *Lauritzen* court had been concerned with when including the sixth factor.[39] Academic writers have frequently noted that the fifth, sixth and seventh factors were not emphasized in *Lauritzen* and *Rhoditis* and they serve little useful purpose.[40]

8.16 That left factors one to four and eight. Factors four and eight were concerned with the shipowner's domicile and base of operations, respectively, but their effect had to be adjusted in a case such as the present, where (unlike *Lauritzen* and *Rhoditis* themselves) the shipowner was not a party to the action.[41] The domicile of the plaintiff (factor three) was plainly relevant, as was the domicile of the defendant classification society (a modified version of factor four). Although the shipowner was not a defendant, its domicile continued to be relevant both because it was expressly stated in *Lauritzen* (factor four as originally stated) and because it was the shipowner who was in privity with BV. Similarly, the base of operations of all three parties – plaintiff, defendant and shipowner – should be taken into account, modifying factor eight.

8.17 Taken together, these factors and their modifications favoured application of Greek law. Greece was the place of the wrongful act (factor one). Although the defendant, BV, was domiciled in France (modified factor four), its relevant base of operations was Greece because it was the actions of BV's Greek employees that gave rise to the dispute (modified factor eight). The real domicile and base of operations of the shipowner was Greece (factors four and eight). Although the "paper owner" was a Gibraltar corporation, that was merely a shell corporation; both of its directors were Greek, as was the management company.[42] The plaintiff was domiciled in Italy (factor three). Although the law of the flag was UK law as a result of the ship's Gibraltar registry (factor two), the plaintiff had provided at least some evidence that the ship's owners and managers had selected Gibraltar as a flag of convenience.[43] Even assuming the ship's UK nationality to be genuine, the single factor pointing to UK law was greatly outweighed by the factors pointing towards Greek law. The Second Circuit rejected BV's argument that the law of the flag should be favoured for reasons of certainty, saying there was no reason to apply the law of the flag in preference to that of another jurisdiction with ties more pertinent to the dispute, particularly as neither the ship nor its owner was a party.[44]

---

38. *Ibid.* In a case not involving a classification society, a district court in the Ninth Circuit has declined to fully adopt the *Carbotrade* principle by completely disregarding the place of contract factor, although it did accord that factor less weight. *Trans-Tec Asia* v *M/V Harmony Container*, 435 F.Supp.2d 1015, 1039, 2006 A.M.C. 864, 893 (C.D. Cal. 2005). However, the Second Circuit has reaffirmed its view that this factor is irrelevant, in another case not involving a classification society. *Rationis Enterpises, Inc. of Panama* v *Hyundai Mipo Dockyard Co. Ltd*, 426 F.3d 580, 587, 2005 A.M.C. 2516, 2523 (2d Cir. 2005).

39. *Carbotrade*, 99 F.3d at p. 91, 1997 A.M.C. at p. 105.

40. See, e.g., Jack Allbritton, "Choice of Law in a Maritime Personal Injury Setting", in 43 La. L. Rev. 879, 883 (1983); Michael Boydston, Note, "Cruz v Chesapeake Shipping and the Choice-of-Law Problem in Admiralty Actions", in 27 Tex. Int'l L.J. 419, 439–440 (1992).

41. *Carbotrade*, 99 F.3d at 91, 1997 A.M.C. at p. 105.

42. *Ibid.*, 99 F.3d at 92, 1997 A.M.C. at pp. 106–107.

43. *Ibid.*

44. *Ibid.*

8.18 In *Sealord Marine Co. Ltd v American Bureau of Shipping*,[45] the US District Court for the Southern District of New York applied the *Lauritzen/Rhoditis* test as modified by the US Court of Appeals for the Second Circuit in *Carbotrade* to an action brought by the purchaser of a ship against American Bureau of Shipping (ABS), the classification society that had issued a Survey Status Report prior to the ship's sale. The plaintiff was a Cypriot corporation with its principal place of business in Cyprus, managed by an agent that was a Liberian corporation with its principal place of business in Greece. The vendor was also a Cypriot corporation with its principal place of business in Cyprus, but it, too, conducted its affairs through an agent with its principal place of business in Greece. ABS is organised under New York law but has its principal place of business in Texas. The ship was flagged in Cyprus. Through its Liberian/Greek agent, the plaintiff requested ABS to issue a Ship Survey Report at an early stage of negotiations for purchase of the ship; ABS issued the Ship Survey Report from its office in Piraeus, Greece. After the contract was made but before the sale had been completed, structural problems were discovered that the plaintiff said were inconsistent with ABS's Ship Survey Report. An ABS surveyor inspected the ship in Spain and the sale was eventually completed after ABS had issued a clean Confirmation of Class Certificate to the plaintiff in Piraeus. The plaintiff eventually had to spend considerable sums of money on repairing the ship and it sued both the vendor and ABS. After settling with the vendor, it continued to pursue its action against ABS.

8.19 Applying the *Lauritzen/Rhoditis* factors as modified in *Carbotrade*, the district court concluded that the plaintiff's claim was governed by Greek law. Ignoring the fifth, sixth and seventh factors, the court focused on the place of the wrongful acts (the first factor), the law of the flag (the second factor) and the domicile and base of operations of the plaintiff, defendant and shipowner (the third, fourth and eighth factors and the modified fourth and eighth factors).[46]

8.20 Although ABS had inspected the ship in Greece and Spain, the negligence alleged by the plaintiff consisted principally in the issue of the Survey Status Report and Confirmation of Class Certificate, both of which had been issued in Piraeus. Thus, the place of the wrong (the first factor) indicated Greek law. The law of the flag (the second factor) indicated the law of Cyprus. The domicile and base of operations of the plaintiff (the third factor as modified in *Carbotrade*) also indicated Greek law: although the plaintiff itself had its base of operations in Cyprus, all of its dealings in relation to this purchase had been conducted through its agent based in Greece. The defendant, ABS, was domiciled in the United States but its relevant base of operations was its Greek office, just as BV's was in *Carbotrade* itself, so these factors (the modified fourth and eighth factors) also indicated Greek law. Finally, the vendor, the original shipowner, was domiciled in Cyprus but had its relevant base of operations in Greece through its Greek agent; to the extent that that factor (the modified fifth factor) had any relevance to the dispute between plaintiff and defendant, it, too, indicated Greek law.

8.21 The court rejected ABS's argument that English law should apply because of a choice of English law clause in the sale contract. ABS was not party to that

---

45. 220 F.Supp.2d 260 (S.D.N.Y. 2002).
46. *Ibid.*, at p. 267.

contract and the plaintiff's claims against ABS were not based on the contract of sale.[47] ABS had not produced any evidence that it was intended to be a third party beneficiary of the sale contract, so it could not take the benefit of the choice of law clause therein.[48]

8.22 In both *Carbotrade* and *Sealord Marine*, the *Lauritzen/Rhoditis* choice of law analysis pointed to Greek law, which apparently does conceive of the possibility of classification societies being held liable to non-party plaintiffs in limited circumstances,[49] as does US law.[50] However, because the law in many countries denies the possibility of recovery altogether, as English law does,[51] it should be obvious how the *Lauritzen/Rhoditis/Carbotrade* choice of law analysis can be used by classification societies to ward off any prospect of liability on the merits.

THE US LAW ON LIABILITY OF CLASSIFICATION SOCIETIES

8.23 When considering the potential liability of classification societies, it is important to begin by remembering that classification societies play a dual role in relation to ship structure and seaworthiness.[52] Classification societies perform tasks in a private capacity, such as promulgating rules and performing surveys, but they also often perform tasks in a public capacity, exercising powers delegated to them by national authorities, usually flag state administrations. In exercise of the latter, public role, classification societies conduct surveys in accordance with international conventions such as SOLAS and MARPOL, and they issue safety certificates in that capacity. After the *Erika* and *Prestige* disasters, both the IMO and the European Union have implemented measures to increase scrutiny of the public role of classification societies.[53] Those measures fall beyond the scope of this paper. For present purposes, it is sufficient to note that any question of liability of the classification society for performance of its public functions will often fall to be determined by the law of the relevant flag state. When delegating certification functions to classification societies, many countries also confer on their delegates the immunity that they would themselves have had if they had performed those functions in exercise of their sovereign powers. An American court will not impose liability on a classification society acting as delegate of a foreign flag state if the law of the flag state confers immunity on the society.

8.24 The principal authority in support of that proposition is *Sundance Cruises Corp. v American Bureau of Shipping*,[54] where the luxury cruise ship *Sundancer* sank

---

47. *Ibid.*, at pp. 269–270.
48. *Ibid.*
49. See *supra*, note 34.
50. See *infra*, Section 3.
51. See *supra*, note 32.
52. See, e.g., Hannu Honka, "The Classification System and Its Problems With Special Reference to the Liability of Classification Societies", in 19 Tul. Mar. L.J. 1, 3–5 (1994); Juan L. Pulido Begines, "The E.U. Law on Classification Societies: Scope and Liability Issues", in 36 J. Mar. L. & Com. 487, 487–488 (2005).
53. See Pulido Begines, *supra*, note 52; Malgorzata Nesterowicz, "European Union Legal Measures in Response to the Oil Pollution of the Sea", in 29 Tul. Mar. L.J. 29 (2004).
54. 7 F.3d 1077, 1994 A.M.C. 1 (2d Cir. 1993).

after striking an underwater rock off the coast of Canada. The owners of *Sundancer* sued the American Bureau of Shipping (ABS) alleging that ABS had negligently issued certificates representing that the vessel complied with the SOLAS Convention and the Load Line Convention. ABS had issued those certificates acting on behalf of the Bahamian government, the Bahamas being the flag state.[55] (The owners also alleged negligence in the issue of ABS's own classification certificate, issued in its private capacity. That aspect of the case is considered below.)

8.25 The US District Court for the Southern District of New York gave summary judgment for ABS in relation to its liability for the SOLAS and Load Line certificates, holding that ABS was immune under the law of *Sundancer*'s flag, the law of the Bahamas, for its actions done as agent for the Bahamian government. The US Court of Appeals for the Second Circuit affirmed that part of the district court's decision, agreeing with the district court's conclusion that the question of ABS's liability for issuing the SOLAS and Load Line certificates for the Bahamian government should be governed by the law of the Bahamas. Although the Second Circuit conducted a *Lauritzen/Rhoditis* multi-factor choice-of-law analysis, it concluded, perhaps not surprisingly, that the most important factor in relation to ABS's liability for issuing the SOLAS and Load Line certificates was the law of the flag. The court said[56]:

"The SOLAS and Load Line certificates were necessary for Sundance to register the ship in the Bahamas, and Sundance had freely chosen the Bahamian flag for the *Sundancer* for its own reasons of convenience. The Supreme Court has expressed concern over assertions of flag law when shipowners appear to have selected 'sham' flag countries in order to avoid the more stringent requirements of other countries. See Lauritzen, 345 U.S. at p. 587. Significantly, however, this concern is not present here, as it is Sundance, the shipowner, who seeks to avoid application of the law of the flag and thereby undo the consequence of its own choice of flag. Application of the law of the flag here benefits the classification societies selected by the Bahamian government to perform safety inspections and not shipowners such as Sundance."

8.26 Bahamian law conferred immunity on ABS as one of the six classification societies authorised to perform surveys on behalf of the Bahamian government.[57] Accordingly, the Second Circuit affirmed the district court's order for summary judgment in favour of ABS in relation to the SOLAS and Load Line certificates.[58]

8.27 Rather surprisingly, the original contract between the owners of *Sundancer* and ABS did not contain a choice of law clause.[59] It is interesting to speculate about what law the Second Circuit would have applied to the immunity question if the contract had contained a choice of law clause. Normally, the parties' choice of a governing law would be given precedence but would that necessarily have been the right approach when the contract was for ABS to perform surveys required by the Bahamian authorities? ABS was only able to contract to perform the SOLAS and Load Line surveys because it was authorised to do so by the Bahamian government. ABS's authorisation carried with it immunity by Bahamian law. Could it have lost

55. *Ibid.*, 7 F.3d at 1079; 1994 A.M.C. at p. 2.
56. *Ibid.*, 7 F.3d at 1082; 1994 A.M.C. at p. 8.
57. *Ibid.*, 7 F.3d at 1082; 1994 A.M.C. at p. 9.
58. *Ibid.*, 7 F.3d at 1083; 1994 A.M.C. at p. 10.
59. *Ibid.*, 7 F.3d at 1081; 1994 A.M.C. at p. 6, citing *Sundance Cruises Corp. v American Bureau of Shipping*, 799 F.Supp. 363, 369, 1992 A.M.C. 2946, 2951 (S.D.N.Y. 1992).

that immunity simply by contracting with the owners of *Sundancer* on terms that included choice of a governing law other than Bahamian law? Would the governing law of the contract necessarily be the appropriate law to govern the question of ABS's immunity for its performance as governmental delegate?

8.28 On the one hand, it seems undesirable to allow classification society immunity to be decided on a purely national basis by flag state governments in the context of a convention-based, mandatory, protective safety-at-sea regime.[60] It would be much better if there were some internationally uniform rules about the potential liability of classification societies for performing public functions (as there are now in the European Union). On the other hand, basic principles of the comity of nations suggest that any court should baulk at overriding an immunity provided by a foreign government to its agents, even if that immunity seems inconsistent with the laws that that court would otherwise apply.[61]

8.29 The liability of classification societies for performing the private function of issuing their own rules and certificates raises quite different questions. In *Sundance Cruises*, the Second Circuit held that the immunity conferred on ABS by the Bahamian government did not extend to everything that ABS might do in the course of its business and, in particular, it did not cover ABS in the issuance of its own classification certificate for *Sundancer*.[62] ABS's liability for exercising that private function was governed by the contract between it and the owners of *Sundancer*. The Second Circuit held that ABS was not liable for breach of that contract because the owners of *Sundancer* had failed to show any damage flowing from the issuance of the classification certificate.[63] The court said that a shipowner is not entitled to rely on a classification certificate as a guarantee that the vessel is soundly constructed, principally because it is the shipowner, not the classification society, that is ultimately responsible for and in control of the activities aboard the ship. The classification society (in this case, ABS) did not take over the shipowner's obligations in relation to the repair and maintenance of the vessel by agreeing to inspect and issue its classification certificate.[64]

8.30 Thus, in actions brought by the shipowner under the contract with the classification society for private certification services, the shipowner must show that the classification society caused harm in some way that would not be revealed by the shipowner's discharge of its routine obligations of repair and maintenance of the seaworthiness of the vessel. Without such proof, the shipowner cannot establish a causal connection between the fault of the classification society (even if established) and its own loss.

8.31 The same is true even when a classification society supervises the construction of a new vessel. For example, in a recent arbitration in New York between the American Bureau of Shipping (ABS) and the owner of a newly-built yacht that was lost by fire soon after completion, the arbitrators emphatically rejected the yacht-owner's contention that: "With no supervising engineer or independent marine surveyor present during construction of the [yacht], claimants could only

60. Honka, *supra*, note 52, at p. 19.
61. *Ibid.*
62. Sundance Cruises, supra note 54, 7 F.3d at 1083–84; 1994 AMC at 10–11.
63. *Ibid.*, 7 F.3d at 1084; 1994 AMC at 11.
64. *Ibid.*

rely on ABS to ensure that the fire extinguishing system would be effective in operation."[65] The arbitrators unanimously held that this amounted to a "misapprehension of the role and function of ABS": ABS was not the yacht-owner's supervising engineer or independent marine surveyor and did not become so merely because the yacht-owner did not engage such an engineer or surveyor. The arbitrators said[66]:

"The classification society and its surveyors are not responsible for insisting that all design decisions result in the best choice for this or that purpose ... Nor are classification societies and their surveyors under any duty to recommend additional optional safety features not required by their rules or the regulatory authorities, in the absence of serious, dangerous defects. They are not overall safety/seaworthiness guarantors ... If a classification society fails to advise an owner of a condition not readily apparent to such owner, which it perceives or should perceive creates an unsafe condition and should be corrected, with the result that the vessel is damaged or lost, the classification society should respond in damages. But there needs to be direct evidence connecting that negligence causally to the loss or damage sustained."

8.32 The US District Court for the Southern District of New York confirmed the arbitrators' award in favor of ABS[67] and the US Court of Appeals for the Second Circuit affirmed the district court's decision.[68]

8.33 The position is different when the plaintiff is not the shipowner but a third party affected by loss of or damage to the vessel in question.[69] Unlike the shipowner, a third party plaintiff is not responsible for ensuring the seaworthiness of the vessel and so it cannot be met with the objection that it is attempting to delegate to the classification society responsibilities that it should properly bear itself. Nevertheless, third-party plaintiffs are also affected by the fact that it is the shipowner who is primarily responsible for ensuring the seaworthiness of the vessel. A third-party plaintiff must show that it relied on the classification society, rather than the shipowner, in relation to the seaworthiness of the vessel. That will always be difficult to show.

8.34 For example, in *Cargill Inc. v Bureau Veritas*,[70] the owners of a cargo of vegetable oil carried on the ship *Pacific Dawn* sued the ship's classification society, Bureau Veritas (BV), to recover losses suffered as a result of repeated breakdowns of *Pacific Dawn* on the voyage carrying the plaintiffs' cargo. The plaintiffs argued that BV had been negligent in failing to revoke *Pacific Dawn*'s class after earlier breakdowns, and in postponing the expiration date for the survey of overdue survey items. BV successfully moved for summary judgment. The US District Court for the Southern District of New York was terse in its dismissal of the plaintiffs' claim[71]:

"Where, as here, plaintiffs are third party cargo owners who claim to have been injured by relying upon a ship's classification certificates, a cause of action may exist for negligent misrepresentation. However, plaintiffs cannot recover on a claim of negligent misrepresentation

---

65. *Ibar Ltd v American Bureau of Shipping*, S.M.A. Arbitration No. 3760, 28 October 2002.
66. *Ibid.*
67. *In re Ibar Ltd*, 2003 W.L. 2012400 (S.D.N.Y. 2003).
68. *Ibar Ltd v American Bureau of Shipping*, 92 Fed. Appx. 820 (2d Cir. 2004).
69. See, e.g., *Sundance Cruises, supra*, note 54, 7 F.3d at 1084; 1994 A.M.C. at p. 11 ("This case [i.e. one brought by the shipowner] must be distinguished from a suit brought by an injured third party who relied on the classification or safety certificates").
70. 902 F.Supp. 49, 1996 A.M.C. 577 (S.D.N.Y. 1995).
71. *Ibid.*, 902 F.Supp. at 52, 1996 A.M.C. at p. 582.

unless they establish that they actually and reasonably relied on the certificates issued by Bureau Veritas ... However, plaintiffs cannot establish that they actually relied on Bureau Veritas' classification of the *Pacific Dawn*. The record is devoid of any evidence that plaintiffs even consulted Bureau Veritas' Register classifying the *Pacific Dawn*."

8.35 It is not sufficient for a third party plaintiff such as a cargo-owner to show that it relied generally on the fact that the ship was in class as a representation by the classification society about seaworthiness. Entry of a ship on a classification society's class register only reflects the ship's condition at the time of the most recent survey, which may have taken place some time before the incident causing the plaintiff's loss.[72] It cannot be assumed that the ship's condition has remained static since the most recent survey, so the *Cargill* court held that it is unreasonable to rely on the ship's class status as a representation of its current condition.[73] In order to ascertain the current status of the ship, the plaintiff would have to have requested an attestation of class from the classification society. Only if there had been such a specific representation made to the plaintiff itself would reliance be reasonable. A representation of class status in a charterparty is not sufficient, either, because it is made by the shipowner (or head charterer) not by the classification society.[74]

8.36 The third party plaintiff faces yet another hurdle in relation to causation. Even if the plaintiff can establish that the classification society was negligent in failing to detect defects, or in failing to insist on the repair of defects that it did detect, the plaintiff must still show that those defects were the cause of the incident that caused the loss. In *Great American Insurance Co. v Bureau Veritas*,[75] the ship *Tradeways II* sank in the North Atlantic shortly after leaving Antwerp bound for the United States. The ship's hull underwriters sued the classification society, Bureau Veritas (BV), alleging that BV had surveyed and reported various defects in *Tradeways II* but the vessel had sailed with those defects unrepaired. The US Court of Appeals for the Second Circuit affirmed the district court's conclusion that there was no evidence that the defects in question had caused the sinking of *Tradeways II*. In the absence of such evidence, the requisite causal connection could not be established.

8.37 In summary, a third party plaintiff can only succeed in an action against a classification society if it can show: (1) that it relied on the classification society, not the shipowner, in relation to the seaworthiness of the vessel, (2) that the classification society made a specific representation about the condition of the vessel at the time of the plaintiff's loss, and (3) that the inaccuracy of the representation was the cause of the plaintiff's loss. Examples of such specific, actual reliance are few and far between but some do exist. In *Otto Candies L.L.C. v Nippon Kaiji Kyokai Corp.*,[76] the plaintiff bought from a Japanese seller a high speed coastal ferry named *Speeder* that had been taken out of service after its classification with the defendant, NKK, had lapsed. The sale contract contained a condition requiring the seller to restore

---

72. *Ibid.*
73. *Ibid.*, 902 F.Supp. at 53, 1996 A.M.C. at p. 583.
74. *Ibid.*, 902 F.Supp. at 52 n.6, 1996 A.M.C. at p. 582, n.6.
75. 478 F.2d 235, 1973 A.M.C. 1755 (2d Cir. 1973).
76. 346 F.3d 530, 2003 A.M.C. 2409 (5th Cir. 2003). See also *In re Complaint of Dann Marine Towing, L.C.*, 2004 W.L. 744881 (E.D.La. 2004) (refusing to grant classification society judgment on the pleadings because of triable issues of fact).

and make current *Speeder*'s NKK classification free from any outstanding recommendations. NKK issued the seller a Class Maintenance Certificate showing that *Speeder* was in class with no outstanding deficiencies, knowing that the seller needed this certificate to complete the sale to the plaintiff. After the sale was completed, the plaintiff had *Speeder* surveyed by the American Bureau of Shipping (ABS) so that its classification could be transferred from NKK to ABS. ABS discovered significant deficiencies that needed repair before ABS would classify the vessel. The repairs cost over $300,000, which the plaintiff then sought to recover from NKK. The US Court of Appeals for the Fifth Circuit affirmed the decision of the US District Court for the Eastern District of Louisiana in favour of the plaintiff. The Fifth Circuit held: (1) that NKK had provided false information for the plaintiff's guidance in a business transaction; (2) that NKK had failed to exercise reasonable care in gathering that information; (3) that the plaintiff justifiably relied on the false information in a transaction that NKK intended to influence; (4) that the plaintiff thereby suffered pecuniary loss; and (5) that NKK knew that the Japanese seller intended to provide the class certificate to the plaintiff.[77]

8.38 Although the plaintiff succeeded in *Otto Candies*, the Fifth Circuit took great pains to make it clear that this was a result that arose from the unusually close relationship between the plaintiff and the classification society and that it should not be regarded as lending any support to claims brought by other kinds of third-party plaintiff[78]:

"Although the verdict was appropriate in this case, we emphasise that a claim for negligent misrepresentation in connection with the work of maritime classification societies should be strictly and carefully limited. The societies' surveys and certificate system are essential to maintaining the safety of maritime commerce, yet their activities should not derogate from shipowners' and charters' nondelegable duty to maintain seaworthy vessels. Imposition of undue liability on classification societies could be harmful in several ways. The societies could be deterred by the prospect of liability from performing work on old or damaged vessels that most need their advice. The spreading of liability could diminish owners' sense of responsibility for vessel safety even as it complicates liability determinations. Ultimately, broader imposition of liability upon classification societies would increase their risk management costs and rebound in higher fees charged to the societies' clients throughout the maritime industry. Whether such risk-spreading is cost-efficient in an industry with well-developed legal duties and insurance requirements is doubtful. The distinctions articulated in caselaw to date recognise the care with which claims against classification societies must be studied."

THE *PRESTIGE* LITIGATION

8.39 The Kingdom of Spain and a group of Basque government plaintiffs[79] sued the American Bureau of Shipping (ABS) to recover damages sustained as a result of

---

77. *Otto Candies*, 346 F.3d at 535, 2003 A.M.C. at p. 2414, citing the *Restatement (Second) of Torts*, §552 (1977) for the first four requirements and *Great Plains Trust Co. v Morgan Stanley Dean Witter & Co.*, 313 F.3d 305, 318 (5th Cir. 2002) for the fifth.

78. *Ibid.*, 346 F.3d at 535, 2003 A.M.C. at pp. 2413–2414.

79. The Basque plaintiffs were led by the Basque *comunidad*, known in (Castilian) Spanish as Comunidad Autonoma del Pais Vasco and in the Basque language as Euskal Autonomia Erkidegoa. The *comunidad* was joined by three municipal entities, Diputación Foral de Biskaia, Diputación Foral de Gipuzkoa and Ayuntamiento de Donostia-San Sebastián.

oil pollution of the waters and coastline of Spain after the sinking of the oil tanker *Prestige*. The compensation recoverable from the ship's P&I Club and the IOPC Fund, although large, was limited in amount, about €171.5 million in total, €22.8 million of which came from the London Club, €148.7 million from the 1992 IOPC Fund.[80] Spain claimed damages in the sum of US$700 million from ABS, alleging that ABS should be held responsible for the sinking of the *Prestige* and the subsequent pollution suffered by Spain.

8.40 At the time of writing, the litigation is still far from reaching any conclusion on the merits but it has already wound through several years' worth of interlocutory rulings. The procedural background is rather complicated. The Basque plaintiffs were the first to bring suit against ABS, by filing a Complaint seeking US$50 million in damages in the US District Court for the Southern District of Texas, which is based in Houston, ABS's base of operations.[81] The Basque plaintiffs also began but quickly discontinued an action in Texas state court.[82] ABS responded by filing "nullity actions" in Spain, seeking a ruling from the Spanish courts that the Basque plaintiffs have no standing under Spanish law to bring suit in the United States. In the meantime, the Kingdom of Spain had brought suit against ABS in the US District Court for the Southern District of New York.[83] The Basque plaintiffs moved successfully to have their case transferred from the Southern District of Texas to the Southern District of New York.[84] In September 2005, the Kingdom of Spain and the Basque plaintiffs entered into a compensation agreement, under which Spain agreed to compensate the Basque plaintiffs in the sum of €45,603,721.09 for damages sustained as a result of the *Prestige* casualty, which covered only "direct" damages, not any "indirect" damages such as environmental or economic injury.[85] The Basque plaintiffs then moved to dismiss their action against ABS without prejudice; ABS cross-moved to dismiss with prejudice. On 4 August 2006, the US District Court for the Southern District of New York dismissed the Basque plaintiffs' suit with prejudice.[86] That means that the Basque plaintiffs cannot re-open the case, despite the fact that they had indicated that they might, in the future, wish to pursue their claims for "indirect, economic and environmental damages".[87]

8.41 ABS counter-claimed against Spain, seeking a declaratory judgment that Spain should indemnify ABS and/or contribute to payment of any damages assessed against ABS as a result of the sinking of the *Prestige*, arguing that the ship would not have been lost if the Spanish authorities had not ordered it to be towed away from possible places of refuge near the Spanish coast. ABS's counterclaims were dismissed for lack of subject matter jurisdiction because of Spain's sovereign immunity

---

80. See IOPC Fund, *Prestige*: Spain, 13 November 2002, *http://www.iopcfund.org/prestige.htm* (last visited 4 September 2006).
81. *Comunidad Autonoma del País Vasco v American Bureau of Shipping Inc.*, 2006 W.L. 2254958 at *1 (S.D.N.Y. 2006).
82. *Ibid.*
83. *Reino de España v American Bureau of Shipping Inc., et al.*, No. 03 Civ. 3573, filed on 16 May 2003.
84. *País Vasco, supra*, note 81 at *1.
85. *Ibid.*, at *2.
86. *País Vasco, supra*, note 81.
87. *Ibid.*, at *4.

from suit.[88] The US District Court for the Southern District of New York recently denied ABS's application for reconsideration of that dismissal, repeating its earlier finding that Spain had not lost its sovereign immunity against ABS's counter-claim by bringing suit against ABS, because the "core issues" presented by ABS's counter-claim (Spain's duties, if any to ABS and others in connection with vessels in distress) did not arise from the same "transaction or occurrence" that gave rise to Spain's claim (classification of the *Prestige* by ABS).[89] Thus, the only claim that continues is Spain's original action against ABS.

8.42 It is perhaps to be expected that litigation involving such large sums of money has also involved interlocutory battles about the scope and extent of discovery. ABS recently won a fairly significant victory in the discovery battle, when the US District Court for the Southern District of New York denied Spain's motion that certain judicial and quasi-judicial documents and materials were privileged from production in the proceedings in New York.[90] The Number One Preliminary Investigating Court of Corcubión in the *comunidad* of Galicia is considering criminal charges against the Director General of the Spanish Merchant Marine, the head of the government delegation in the port of La Coruña and the Harbour Master of La Coruña, as well as civil proceedings that have been stayed pending completion of the criminal investigation.[91] The Permanent Commission on the Investigation of Maritime Casualties investigated the *Prestige* casualty and issued a Report containing findings, conclusions and recommendations concerning the cause of, and response to, the casualty, including a description of the documents relied on by the Commission in reaching its conclusions and recommendations. As part of their discovery demands in the proceedings in New York, ABS requested production of the Corcubión Investigating Court file and also the evidence that the Permanent Commission reviewed or generated in preparing its final report. Spain objected to the production of these documents, claiming that they were privileged. Spain's motion was denied by the Magistrate Judge assigned to handle pretrial supervision, who held that comity demanded that Spain, which had chosen to bring suit in the United States, should submit itself to US discovery procedures and make available the documents required by ABS.[92] The Magistrate Judge's order was later confirmed by the judge who will hear the case.[93] More recently, the same Magistrate Judge granted ABS's motion to compel Spain's disclosure of e-mail communications from several Spanish government agencies and departments in the casualty

---

88. *Reino de España v American Bureau of Shipping Inc.*, 328 F.Supp.2d 489, 2004 A.M.C. 2050 (S.D.N.Y. 2004).
89. *Reino de España v American Bureau of Shipping Inc.*, 2006 W.L. 2034632 (S.D.N.Y. 2006). A foreign state does not have immunity under the Foreign States Immunity Act (28 U.S.C. §§1601ff.) with respect to a counterclaim "arising out of the transaction or occurrence that is the subject-matter of the claim of the foreign state". 28 U.S.C. §1607(b).
90. *Reino de España v American Bureau of Shipping Inc.*, 2005 A.M.C. 2257 (S.D.N.Y. 2005).
91. It is expected that the investigatory phase of the Corcubión proceedings will conclude at some time between February 2007 and July 2007. *Reino de España v American Bureau of Shipping Inc.*, 2006 W.L. 2239641 at *1 (S.D.N.Y. 2006). If the Corcubión court orders a criminal trial, the matter will be transferred to a trial court and the testimony and submitted documents in the investigating court's file will remain under seal until the trial phase of the proceeding. *Reino de España v American Bureau of Shipping Inc.*, 2005 A.M.C. 2257, 2259 (S.D.N.Y. 2005).
92. *Reino de España v American Bureau of Shipping Inc.*, 2005 W.L. 1813017 (S.D.N.Y. 2005).
93. *Reino de España v American Bureau of Shipping Inc.*, 2006 W.L. 2239641 (S.D.N.Y. 2006).

period, and also an addendum to the Permanent Commission's report.[94]

8.43 The contents of the Corcubión Investigating Court file and Permanent Commission evidence would obviously have been of considerable assistance to ABS in pursuing its counter-claim against Spain if that had not been dismissed, but the documents will also presumably shed light on the twin issues of reliance and causation, which lie at the heart of any tort claim against a classification society, as noted above in Section 3.

8.44 In other skirmishes about discovery, the Magistrate Judge denied Spain's request to take more than the agreed number of 50 depositions,[95] denied ABS's request for return of supposedly privileged documents that had been produced in error[96] and denied Spain's request for production of ABS's financial records.[97] The Magistrate Judge also refused to permit further discovery to investigate Spain's claims that a former employee of ABS had been pressured not to appear for his scheduled deposition by his present employer, Det Norske Veritas (DNV), at ABS's request.[98]

8.45 As noted above, Spain's claim is still far from reaching the trial stage. Discovery was scheduled to close until 30 September 2006; dispositive motions were due no later than 15 December 2006 and a final pretrial conference was scheduled on 30 March 2007.[99] The original Complaint, which made allegations only against American Bureau of Shipping Inc., was amended to include allegations against other ABS entities, including a consulting subsidiary. Despite all the procedural complexity surrounding the case, it seems likely that the core issues at trial will be (as they usually are): whether Spain can be said to have relied on the classification society certificate issued by ABS and whether ABS's classification certificates and survey reports can be regarded as the proximate cause of the loss of the *Prestige*, which occurred months after those documents were issued.[100] Perhaps anticipating those problems with its claim based upon tortious misrepresentation, Spain has also pleaded a cause of action for strict liability under US law, as well as causes of action based upon Spanish law.

8.46 ABS has not yet raised any arguments based upon an arbitration or forum selection clause in its classification society certificate, as it did in *American Bureau of Shipping v Tencara Shipyard SpA*,[101] presumably because Spain is not sufficiently closely linked to the owner of the *Prestige* to have received any direct benefit from the classification contract that could form the basis of an estoppel. That is the

---

94. *Reino de España v American Bureau of Shipping Inc.*, 2006 W.L. 3208579 (S.D.N.Y. 2006).

95. *Reino de España v American Bureau of Shipping Inc.*, 2005 W.L. 3071551 (S.D.N.Y. 2005); motion to set aside denied, 2006 W.L. 2128789 (S.D.N.Y. 2006) (Swain J.).

96. *Reino de España v American Bureau of Shipping Inc.*, 2005 W.L. 3455782 (S.D.N.Y. 2005).

97. *Ibid.*, 2006 W.L. 1564809 (S.D.N.Y. 2006).

98. *Ibid.*, 2006 W.L. 228826 (S.D.N.Y. 2006).

99. *Comunidad Autonoma del Pais Vasco v American Bureau of Shipping Inc.*, 2006 W.L. 2254958 at *3 (S.D.N.Y. 2006), describing the contents of a Scheduling Order made by the Magistrate Judge on 17 February 2005.

100. The *Prestige* completed its fifth special or renewal survey in Guangzhou on 20 May 2001; the ABS certificate of classification was issued on 24 May 2001 and verified at ABS headquarters in Houston on 14 June 2001. Original Complaint, *Reino de España v American Bureau of Shipping Inc.*, *et al.*, No. 03 Civ. 3573, para. 34. ABS conducted an annual class survey in Dubai from 15–26 May 2002. *Ibid.*, para. 37. The *Prestige* sank on 19 November 2002. *Ibid.*, para. 45.

101. *Supra*, note 5.

Catch-22 described above: because it is not so closely linked to the shipowner as to be bound by the arbitration clause in the classification contract, Spain may be too remote from that contract to be able to show reliance upon ABS's statements. In any event, it would presumably now be too late for ABS to move for dismissal of Spain's claim; having participated in so many stages of the litigation it must surely have waived its right to rely on any arbitration agreement, even if one were to be applicable.[102]

8.47 Perhaps more interesting is Spain's avowed intention to rely on Spanish law. The US District Court for the Southern District of New York will presumably undertake a *Lauritzen/Rhoditis* analysis as modified by the US Court of Appeals for the Second Circuit in *Carbotrade SpA v Bureau Veritas*,[103] not least because the Second Circuit's *Carbotrade* decision will be binding authority on the district court. The first *Lauritzen/Rhoditis/Carbotrade* factor (the place of the wrongful act) points to the law of China or Dubai or possibly the United States, rather than Spain, which was merely the place where ABS's allegedly wrongful acts caused harm.[104] The second factor (the law of the ship's flag) points to the law of the Bahamas. The domicile of the injured party (the third factor) is obviously Spain, if it makes any sense to think of a country having a domicile. The domicile of the defendant (modified factor four) is the United States but its relevant base of operations (modified factor eight) might also be in China or Dubai, where the fifth special survey and the annual survey, respectively, were performed. Although the shipowner is not a party to the proceedings, its domicile and base of operations were considered in both *Carbotrade* and *Sealord Marine*.[105] The owner of the *Prestige* was Mare Shipping Inc., a Liberian corporation, but the ship was managed by Universe Maritime Ltd, a Liberian corporation having its principal place of business in Greece.[106] If the *Prestige* court treats the base of operations of the management company as the shipowner's base of operations for these purposes, as the *Carbotrade* and *Sealord Marine* courts did, the modified eighth factor points to Greek law. The fourth factor (the domicile of the shipowner) points to Liberian law. The fifth, sixth and seventh factors – the place of the contract, the accessibility of the foreign forum and the law of the forum – all seem as irrelevant here as they did in *Carbotrade* and *Sealord Marine*.

8.48 Where, then, does the *Lauritzen/Rhoditis/Carbotrade* choice of law analysis point on the facts of the *Prestige*? To China, Dubai, the Bahamas, the United States, Spain, Greece or Liberia. Neither Spanish law nor US law is particularly strongly indicated unless the court focuses on the *verification* of the classification certificate as the wrongful act, rather than the conduct of the special survey or annual survey. That took place in the United States, which is also where the defendant is domiciled. Two factors pointing to one law may be enough in an analysis that is otherwise so inconclusive.

---

102. Engaging in extensive pre-trial motion litigation has often been held to amount to a waiver of a contractual right to arbitration. See, e.g., *S. & R. Co. of Kingston v Latona Trucking Inc.*, 159 F.3d 80 (2d Cir. 1998).

103. *Supra*, note 30.

104. See *supra*, note 100.

105. *Supra*, note 45.

106. Original Complaint, *Reino de España v American Bureau of Shipping Inc.*, et al., No. 03 Civ. 3573, paras 5–6.

8.49 If Spain's claim does ultimately fall to be determined by US law, it will clearly encounter difficulties in relation to reliance and causation, as has already been noted. Spain has also pleaded a cause of action based on strict liability. The Supreme Court of the United States has held that strict liability for defective products is part of general maritime law,[107] but there is as yet no authority for the proposition that classification societies can be held strictly liable for the consequences of their operations. Such a conclusion would dramatically change the insurance and risk management arrangements emphasised by the *Otto Candies* court,[108] and could surely only be made by a court higher in the judicial hierarchy than the US District Court for the Southern District of New York. Whatever the outcome of Spain's strict liability claim, an appeal seems likely – unless the court concludes that US law is irrelevant.

CONCLUSION

8.50 The US law governing the liability of classification societies is more hospitable to plaintiffs than is English law, but only just. It is possible, but difficult, for a non-party plaintiff to establish liability and very difficult indeed for a shipowner to do so. Any plaintiff seeking out the glimmer of hope that such limited hospitality provides may find itself met with preliminary objections based on jurisdiction and choice of law. The strong federal policy in favour of arbitration and the multi-factor nature of the maritime choice of law test may produce the result that many classification society disputes will not reach determination on the merits under US law.

---

107. *East River Steamship Corp. v Transamerica Delaval Inc.*, 476 U.S. 858, 106 S. Ct. 2295, 1986 A.M.C. 2027 (1986).
108. *Supra*, note 78.

PART 5

The ISM and ISPS Codes and Maritime Liabilities

CHAPTER 9

The ISM and ISPS Codes: Influence on the evolution of liabilities

SIMON KVERNDAL Q.C.*

INTRODUCTION

9.1 The ISM and ISPS Codes were not intended to create new inter party liabilities: both codes were formulated with the clear purpose of improving and extending standards of maritime safety and security. Though in force for six years and more (ISM Code) and two years or so (ISPS Code), no cases have come to the courts which have turned on their implementation; this is not, it may be rightly surmised, evidence suggestive of new liabilities evolving as a result of the Codes. Further, in spite of the regulatory purpose of both Codes, they are not couched as a set of quasi-statutory rules and regulations: instead, those to whom the Codes are directed are required by the Codes to create their own sets of procedures and systems; these tailormade procedures and systems must then be approved by the flag state or substitute. Of course, a ship which is not properly certificated will be unseaworthy and without insurance; but this is no different from a ship which is out of class. It follows, not surprisingly, that with one notable exception (ISM Article 6, discussed below) the Codes do not expressly alter or directly affect the mutual obligations or liabilities of maritime users. There are, nevertheless, a number of ways or potential ways in which the requirement to comply with these Codes may have a considerable indirect impact on the development of liabilities and enforcement of contractual obligations. It is to those indirect consequences of the introduction of these Codes, to the reshaping rather than the creation of liabilities, that this chapter is directed.

9.2 Following a brief introduction to the ISM Code and its key areas of application, this paper will focus on the following:

(1) The effect of the requirement that the Master should be "fully conversant" with the Ship safety management system (Article 6).
(2) The possible legal consequences of the direction that the DPA – designated person ashore – should have access to the highest level of management (Article 4).
(3) The potential for successful claims against Classification Societies who carry out the tasks of certification and auditing on behalf of flag state administrations.
(4) A brief summary of the practical consequences, for litigants, of the introduction of the ISM Code.
(5) The ISPS Code and safe/unsafe ports.

* Barrister at Law, Quadrant Chambers.

THE ISM CODE

The main features of the Code

9.3 The ISM Code is appended to this paper (see Appendix 9). It may nevertheless be helpful to summarise its principal provisions. They are:

- the establishment of a written Safety Management System ("SMS") for every ship owner/manager[1] which should include a wide range of programmes, activities and procedures;
- the creation of a "designated person ashore" ("DPA") who is responsible for the ship's safety and pollution-prevention aspects and ensuring adequate resources and shore-based support and who has direct access to the highest level of management;
- a clearly defined role for the Master with regard to implementing, monitoring and reviewing the SMS;
- the setting up of systems and procedures by the owner/manager to ensure that the Master and crew are properly qualified, competent, trained and familiarised;
- the setting up of procedures by the owner/manager for emergencies, reporting non-conformities, maintenance and document control and the carrying out of internal safety audits to verify, review and evaluate compliance with the SMS;
- certification of the compliant owner/manager by means of a "Document of Compliance" ("DC") issued by the flag state or substitute which is subject to annual verification and may be withdrawn in the event of a "major non-conformity" (or failure to request annual verification);
- certification of each ship by means of a "Safety Management Certificate" ("SMC") issued by the flag state or substitute, to be verified once within its five-year validity (between years two and three), which may be withdrawn in the event of a "major non-conformity" (or failure to request the periodic verification).

9.4 A quick glance through the text of the Code reveals two important features of its structure and language. The first is that the language of the code is not, with one exception,[2] mandatory: the word "should" is used again and again. Thus although *compliance* with the requirements of the Code is mandatory,[3] the Code leaves to the "Administration" (flag state or substitute[4]) the task of ensuring that the SMS and the Company's policies and procedures fully comply with the Code and of verifying compliance by audit. The second feature[5] is that the Code is couched as a general direction to owners/managers to write their own rules (which

---

1. The owner or, if there is a manager which is responsible for the operation of the ship, the manager, is known throughout the ISM Code as the "Company": Article 1.1.2.

2. 3.1: that if the entity which is responsible for operation is not the owner, then the owner must report to the "Administration" (i.e. flag state or substitute). In other words the shipowners must inform flag state whether they or their managers are the actual operator, i.e. "the Company" for the purposes of the Code.

3. In the UK under SI 1998 No. 1561, The Merchant Shipping (ISM Code) Regulations 1998.

4. In practice the Flag States delegate this function to a "Recognised Organisation" ("RO"), usually one of the leading classification societies.

5. To which, as I have noted, there is one important exception: Article 6, discussed below.

then have to be approved by flag state or substitute); as the Preamble to the ISM Code states, it recognises that "no two shipping companies or shipowners are the same, and that ships operate under a wide range of different conditions". Thus in order to "comply" with the Code, it is – apart from the one important exception – merely necessary to have an SMS and other qualifying systems/procedures and to pass the Administration's audits: a breach or failure to comply with the SMS itself is not of itself a breach or non-compliance with the Code. Though it is of course far from straightforward to set up a ship's and ship managers' systems, once they are in place and SMC and DC obtained and maintained, the vessel will be – subject to the one exception – compliant.

9.5 It is important at this point to emphasise the difference between "non-compliance" and "non-conformity". As well as being a statutory requirement *compliance* with the Code is expressly required under contracts of insurance by clause 14.4 of the International Hull Clauses 2003,[6] which provides that the assured has a continuing duty to "comply with all statutory requirements of the vessel's flag state relating to … operation and manning of the vessel". Further, most time charters and contracts of carriage now use or incorporate the standard BIMCO ISM clause – by which owners "shall procure that both the vessel and the owner/managers shall comply with the requirements of the ISM Code" (the full text can be found at the end of this chapter). But as noted above, so long as SMS and related systems are in place and SMC and DC are valid, a vessel will be compliant. It follows that a breach of the standard BIMCO ISM clause is likely to be rare: a chartered vessel may in many respects fail to comply with its SMS and may be found to have numerous non-conformities on a flag state or internal audit, but if it has a valid SMC and its owner/manager has a valid DC, it will (subject to Article 6, see below) be compliant.

9.6 By contrast, the word "*non-conformity*" is used to describe a particular aspect or state of affairs, revealed in an internal or flag state audit, which amounts to a failure to observe the SMS and its underlying requirements. It is defined by the Code as "an observed situation where objective evidence indicated the non-fulfilment of a special requirement", and the Code deals in some detail with the discovery and consequences of "non-conformity" and "major non-conformity"; it is probable that a "non-conformity" will be a failure to comply with the requirements of another code or convention such as SOLAS or MARPOL. Non-conformities are likely to be numerous and common, but unless they are "major" or repeatedly left uncorrected they are unlikely to lead to action by the flag state or substitute and so will have no bearing on a vessel's or her owners'/managers' certification (SMC and DC: see paragraph 9.4 above). Nor, of themselves, will non-conformities amount to non-compliance with ISM.

---

6. "It is the duty of the Assured, Owners and Managers at the inception of and throughout the period of this insurance and any extension thereof to
   14.4.1. comply with all statutory requirements of the vessel's flag state relating to … operation and manning of the vessel.
   …
   In the event of any breach of any of the duties in this Clause 14.4, the Underwriters shall not be liable for any loss, damage, liability or expense attributable to such breach."

Article 6.1/6.2/6.4/6.7 [7]

9.7 In contrast to the other main Articles of the Code, 6.1, 6.2, 6.4 and 6.7 are not satisfied by establishing procedures and policies. It seems unlikely that 6.2, 6.4 and 6.7 will of themselves give rise to disputes: any breach of these provisions is likely to amount also to a breach of an existing statutory or contractual obligation. But Article 6.1 does appear to go further than requiring that the owner/manager sets up an appropriate written policies, systems and procedures.

9.8 First, 6.1.1, that the Master should be "properly qualified for command" goes slightly further than the basic requirement – which goes without saying – of proper certification. It may be construed as a requirement to ensure that a Master is fit for command of his particular vessel, so as to penalise an owner/manager who appoints a Master who knows nothing about the type of vessel to which he is appointed.[8] Linked to this requirement, but of potentially more wide-ranging effect, is the requirement in 6.1.2 for an owner or manager to ensure that a Master is *fully conversant* with a ship's safety management system. If the owner/manager fails to comply with this statutory requirement in relation to "operation and manning of the vessel" he will on the face of it be in breach of his duty under IHC Clause 14.4 and his insurers will not be liable for any loss or damage attributable to this breach; in addition, the owners will be liable to charterers under the BIMCO standard ISM clause. "Ensure" is a very strong word and is undiluted by any due diligence standard. A typical SMS will run to dozens of pages and may cross refer to other manuals and guides: it would take hours of time and study in order to be closely acquainted with the breadth and detail of this body of information, yet even in the best-run companies a Master may have to join a vessel with precious little time to get to grips with the minutiae of its SMS. Further, it is not difficult to envisage an accident which might have been prevented or better controlled had the Master had detailed knowledge of the SMS. Unrealistic though this might be, one can see that the necessary elements of a successful cause of action might well be established.

9.9 Pausing at this point, is this enlargement of a shipowners' liability consistent with the regime of the Hague/Hague-Visby Rules? It is suggested that the short answer is: strictly speaking "no", in practice "maybe". The strict answer is "no" because Article V of the Hague/Hague-Visby Rules permits an increase in the carrier's responsibilities "provided such increase shall be embodied in the bill of lading issued to the shipper"; but Article 6 of the ISM Code is a regime imposed by statute

---

7. 6.1 The Company should ensure that the Master is:
   .1 properly qualified for command;
   .2 fully conversant with the Company's safety management system; and
   .3 given the necessary support so that the master's duties can be safely performed.
   The Company should ensure that each ship is manned with qualified, certificated and medically fit seafarers in accordance with national and international requirements.
   ...
   6.4 The Company should ensure that all personnel involved in the Company's SMS have an adequate understanding of relevant rules, regulations, codes and guidelines.
   ...
   6.7 The Company should ensure that the ship's personnel are able to communicate effectively in the execution of their duties related to the SMS.
8. As in *The Eurasian Dream* [2002] 1 Lloyd's Rep. 719, discussed further below.

and is not "embodied" in the bill of lading. In practice, however, a bill of lading will incorporate charterparty terms which will almost certainly include the BIMCO ISM clause. Does such an incorporation mean that the increase of responsibility is "embodied" in the bill of lading? This is a question which may be worthy of rather fuller consideration, either in court or by an academic commentator.[9]

9.10 It can readily be seen that the impact of the requirement that the owners ensure that the Master is fully conversant with his ship's SMS may be very significant: at the same time as more and more responsibility is being heaped on the modern Master, the consequences of his failing to have a remarkably high degree of knowledge of almost everything about his ship become very much more serious. This is something which is being considered by the IMO; meanwhile, however, whilst it may be right that there should be insurance implications for the owners/managers of a *poorly* managed vessel, the effect of Article 6.1.2 read with clause 14.4 of the IHC may strike at all but the most highly organised and diligent of owners, namely those whose pool of Masters have encyclopaedic knowledge of the ships they habitually command.

9.11 An example from the case law, albeit a fairly extreme one, illustrates how easy it may be for an owner to be not merely liable for unseaworthiness but without insurance for its consequences. In *The Eurasian Dream*[10] a fire broke out during discharge of a cargo of new and second-hand cars as a result of the simultaneous and proximate refuelling and jump-starting of the cars by the local stevedores. The Master, a Captain Villondo, should have been a key figure in a fi-fi operation. The problem here was that this was his first time with these owners and his first time on board a car carrier, let alone command of a car carrier; he had received no oral briefing before taking command, just a standard form briefing letter telling him to read all the literature on the vessel when he arrived on board (when of course, he hardly had plenty of idle time to do so); there had been no period of overlap with the previous Master; no superintendent had been sent out to assist him in taking over his position even though he had never worked for these managers before; and by the time of the incident he had only been in command for three months. He was not, it may be argued, "qualified for command" under Article 6.1.1. His fi-fi training on board had been no more than a tour of the CO_2 room with the Chief Engineer. He had had no instruction or training as to how to deal with the fire – he did not even know that gas-tight doors had to be closed before CO_2 was used. It would have taken the Master several weeks to read all the manuals which were relevant to his command of this vessel, some 150 manuals running to some 75–100 pages each; and even then he would probably have missed the CO_2 manual as it was in the Chief Engineer's cabin. But as there was no guidance in the briefing letter from the ship's superintendent as to which manuals were relevant to him as Master, there was not much chance that he would have tried to read it anyway. He was not conversant, certainly not "fully conversant" with the SMS: if the ISM Code had at that time applied to his vessel then there would have been non-compliance with the Code.

---

9. As to "embodied" see Treitel and Reynolds' *Carver on Bills of Lading* (2nd ed.), at para. 9-300.
10. [2002] 1 Lloyd's Rep. 719. The case was pre-ISM in the sense that the ship and her managers were not yet required to comply; but the vessel already had begun the process leading towards compliance and the judgment contains some passing references to the Code.

The role of the DPA: Article 4

9.12 This topic concerns the role of the "designated person ashore" and the way in which the operation of ISM Article 4 may mean that the "alter ego" or directing mind of a company has actual or imputed knowledge of facts which give rise to legal liability.

9.13 From the perspective of legal liability, the most significant aspect of the role of the DPA is that he should have "direct access to the highest level of management".[11] There are many occasions in English law standard form maritime contracts, statute and convention where a shipowner is excepted from liability save where he is in some way *personally* involved, by act or default or privity. In particular:

(a) Charterparty exceptions:
   (i) Gencon clause 2[12];
   (ii) Baltime clause 12.[13]
(b) Fire exceptions:
   (i) Shelltime cl.27(a)[14];
   (ii) ASBA clause 19, STB form clause 22(a)[15];
   (iii) Hague/Hague-Visby Rules Article IV, rule 2(b).[16]
(c) Marine Insurance: MIA, section 39(5).[17]
(d) 1957 Limitation Convention.

9.14 Dealing first with the exception provisions: in spite of the fact that the burden of proof always lies on the owner who seeks to take advantage of the exception or right to limit, it has never been easy and in the last half century or so increasingly difficult, to fix that owner with personal involvement: it has been rare to find the directing mind of the company to have been in prior possession of an incriminating report or memo, even rarer to find that the person actually in default could be regarded as being the directing mind of the company. In English law we have now lost the "actual fault or privity" test for limiting a shipowner's liability under the 1957 Convention, but the words remain in broadly similar form or effect in the

---

11. A less important aspect is that the owner/manager is responsible for ensuring that he has adequate resources and shore-based support to carry out his functions [Art. 3.3] – that would seem to be too nebulous a requirement to give rise to legal liability save in a case where the owner will be liable on other grounds anyway.

12. "Owners are to be responsible for loss or of damage to the goods or for delay in delivery of the goods only in case the loss, damage or delay has been caused by ... or by personal want of due diligence on the part of the Owners or their Manager to make the vessel in all respects seaworthy and to secure that she is properly manned, equipped and supplied or by the personal act or default of the Owners or their Manager."

13. "The Owners only shall be responsible for delay in delivery of the Vessel or for delay during the currency of the Charter and for loss or damage to goods on board, if such delay or loss has been caused by want of due diligence on the part of the Owner or their Manager in making the Vessel seaworthy and fitted for the voyage or any other personal act or omission or default of the Owners or their Manager."

14. "The vessel her master and Owners shall not, unless otherwise in this charter expressly provided, be liable for any loss or damage or delay or failure arising or resulting from ... fire, unless caused by the actual fault or privity of Owners."

15. " ... fire, unless caused by the personal design or neglect of the Owner."

16. "Fire, unless caused by the actual fault or privity of the carrier."

17. " ... but where, with the privity of the assured, the ship is sent to sea in an unseaworthy state, the insurer is not liable for any loss attributable to unseaworthiness."

fire exceptions, under Gencon clause 2 and Baltime clause 12. In contrast to the non-delegable duties of the Hague Rules, the shipowner seeking to avoid liability under Gencon or recover under his insurance policy where his ship has sailed in unseaworthy condition has been able to hide behind and dissociate himself from the faults of his servants.

9.15 This is where the creation of the role of the DPA, with his "direct access to the highest level of management", becomes important in a liabilities context. What does "direct access" mean? It could be argued that it simply means that there should be an open and readily available line of communication – a director who says 'my door is always open'. It is suggested that the better view is that it contemplates a two-way channel, for reporting and for reacting to reports, between the DPA and a senior director. Unless the owner is a small company (see, for a rare example, *The Ert Stefanie*,[18] where the technical superintendent was a director), the marine superintendent or technical manager is most unlikely to be regarded as "the directing mind and will of the company". Though there has been some debate as to whether the DPA himself may be so regarded this is just as improbable as the marine superintendent being the "alter ego". But the DPA's duty to report to what must surely be the "alter ego" or directing mind of "the Company" bridges the gap between the inadequacies on board ship and the knowledge or privity of the owner/manager. It was this that Lord Donaldson[19] described as "the errant shipowners' Achilles' heel". He went on to observe this:

"The 'blind eye' shipowner is faced with a 'Catch 22' situation. If he hears nothing from the designated person, he will be bound to call for reports, for it is inconceivable there will be nothing to report. If the report is to the effect that all is well in a perfect world, the shipowners would be bound to enquire how that could be, as the safety management system is clearly intended to be a dynamic system which is subject to continuous change in the light not only of the experience of the individual ship, and of the company as a whole, but also of the experience of others in the industry."

9.16 Of course, it must be recognised that fire cases which have not been caused by unseaworthiness are comparatively rare, that the Baltime form, or at least Baltime with clause 12, is not seen so often, whilst English lawyers today will rarely be involved in a case under the 1957 Limitation Convention. Having said that it does seem likely that there will be cases particularly where Gencon clause 2 is relied upon, which are decided differently because of the "errant Owners' Achilles heel". In such cases requests for extensive disclosure of owners/managers may be expected, in order to discover evidence that the highest level of management knew or ought to have known of technical or structural or operational defects in their vessel.

9.17 So to cases under section 39(5)[20] of the Marine Insurance Act: at first sight it might appear that the forging of a link between the DPA, who is likely to know his ship's darkest secrets, and the "highest level of management", means that the shipowner may be privy to those dark secrets which in due course amount to causative unseaworthiness. After all, the director cannot escape from being privy to that unseaworthiness by blindly or blandly ignoring those facts which amount to

18. [1989] 1 Lloyd's Rep. 349 (C.A.).
19. "The ISM Code: the road to discovery?", in [1998] L.M.C.L.Q. 526.
20. See footnote 16 to para. 9.15 above.

unseaworthiness or by refraining from asking relevant questions in relation to them in the hope that by his lack of inquiry he will not know for certain that which any inquiry must have made plain beyond possibility of doubt.[21] And Lord Donaldson expressly referred to this "blind eye knowledge" when identifying the errant shipowners' Achilles heel.

9.18 In practice, however, as *The Star Sea*[22] has made clear, it will be a tough task for the zealous insurer to escape liability on the basis of section 39(5), essentially for two reasons. First, the burden is on the underwriters not simply to show that the relevant individual or individuals had the information or glaring lack of information in front of them, but also that this must have created a suspicion or realisation in the mind of that individual or individuals that the vessel was unseaworthy and that he had decided not to check for fear of having certain knowledge of it. It is not enough that the director was lazy or grossly negligent in failing to make further inquiry: the underwriter must have subjective proof both that the assured's suspicion was aroused and then that he decided to take no steps to confirm the existence of the facts giving rise to unseaworthiness. Secondly, the person who must be "privy" for the purpose of section 39(5) is not the person who had ultimate responsibility for the seaworthiness of the vessel but the person who was involved in the decision-making processes required for sending the vessel to sea.[23] Two very different persons may be involved; but it is the one responsible for sending the vessel to sea who must be shown to have had the blind-eye knowledge of the facts amounting to unseaworthiness. That, given the separation of commercial and technical management even at the very highest level, seems a most unlikely burden to discharge.

9.19 But there is another way in which the ISM Code and the role of the DPA and his access to the highest level of management may give rise to a defence to a claim under the hull policy – under the proviso to the "Inchmaree Clause". Up until the 1995 amendments to the Institute Hull Clauses this read:

" ... provided that such loss or damage has not resulted from want of due diligence by the Assured, Owners or Managers."

The 1995 Institute Clauses added the words "*or Superintendents or any of their onshore management*". It appears that these words were not popular in the market and were often deleted, and they were taken out again in the new International Hull Clauses in 2003. Obviously under the 1995 clauses the DPA would have qualified as a "superintendent or part of onshore management", and want of due diligence by him would have provided insurers with a defence to a claim. Under the 2003 clauses we are back to the old system where insurers must prove want of due diligence on the part of the "alter ego".

9.20 The difference now is that Article 4 of the ISM Code bridges the gap between the DPA and the alter ego, where a DPA may have passed to "the highest level of management" a report or memorandum which has not been acted upon.

---

21. The standard definition of "blind eye knowledge" formulated by Roskill L.J. in *The Eurysthenes* [1976] 2 Lloyd's Rep. 171 at p. 184.
22. [1997] 1 Lloyd's Rep. 360 at p. 371 (C.A.), [2001] 1 Lloyd's Rep. 389 (H.L.).
23. *The Star Sea* at p. 375 of the C.A. judgment.

Moreover, although some might draw a parallel between the Inchmaree proviso and section 39(5), this approach may be doubted. First, and most obviously, the wording is different, "want of due diligence" is not the same as "with the privity of". The wording "want of due diligence" has a clear, well-established meaning in a maritime context: it is founded on an *objective* test of what the ordinarily competent and reasonable owner, or master, or superintendent, or whomever, would have done. Why, it may be asked, should the narrow, subjective, test expounded in *The Star Sea*, that the underwriter must have subjective proof both that the assured's suspicion was aroused and then that he decided to take no steps to confirm the existence of the facts giving rise to unseaworthiness, be applied in this different context? There may of course be good policy reasons for doing so, but that is hardly the point when the words used are so clear: the draftsmen of the Institute clauses could have, but did not, use the section 39(5) phraseology.

9.21 If it is right to apply the wider, objective test – would, on the basis of the material provided to him by his DPA, a reasonable director have taken steps to rectify reported defects? – then the potential for a successful defence by insurers to a claim under the policy is significantly increased. Even more so if the court were to hold that the proviso should extend to causative want of due diligence during the voyage (a moot point given the wording of the proviso).

9.22 Finally, on this topic of the DPA's knowledge imparted to the highest level of management, some mention ought to be made of the possible impact on the assured's duty of disclosure under section 18 of the Marine Insurance Act. The assured is, of course, deemed to know of every circumstance which, in the ordinary course of business, ought to be known by him. This must surely include the reports which the DPA will be expected to submit as part of his access to the highest level of management. Suffice to say, it does not seem unlikely that the courts may be tested by an insurer who seeks to avoid a policy on the basis that the highest level of management of the Assured had or ought to have had knowledge of facts relating to the condition of the vessel which should have been disclosed on placing.

Liability of the "RO"

9.23 The scheme and purpose of the ISM Code is dependent on the proper execution of its certification and auditing functions by the Flag State Administration. It has already been noted that the Flag State Administration, which is entrusted with ISM certification and audit, is permitted to, and in practice generally does, delegate its functions to a Recognised Organisation or "RO"; these, in practice, are the leading classification societies. It should be noted that there is an important parallel here with EU Directive 94/57/EC of November 1994 and subordinate legislation concerned with "recognised organisations": Member States of the EU delegate their responsibility to approved classification societies pursuant to this directive.

9.24 It is well established in English Law, if not entirely uncontroversially, that Classification Societies do not owe a duty of care to cargo owners and those with similar interests: *The Nicholas H*.[24] The rationale for the majority decision of the

---

24. [1995] 2 Lloyd's Rep. 299. The dissenting judgment of Lord Lloyd is, however, a *tour de force*.

House of Lords was that it was not fair, just and reasonable to impose such a duty, being at variance with the bargain between shipowners and cargo-owners and unfair to classification societies who act for the collective welfare and have no benefit of limitation provisions. The decision has been distinguished in cases of personal injury.[25]

9.25 Does the authority of *The Nicholas H* apply when Classification Societies are acting as ROs? In relation to personal injury claims, no: thus where a vessel suffers a casualty involving loss of life which would have been prevented by a proper audit, Class may well be liable. What about in cases involving property damage or economic loss? Given the snowballing development of the law of tort during the 1990s, *The Nicholas H* must in any event be applied with some care, the correct approach today having been reviewed (yet again) in *Commissioners for Customs and Excise v Barclays Bank*[26]: one should apply "the threefold test" (foreseeability, proximity, fairness) and the "assumption of responsibility test" and the "incremental approach" (but this last was regarded by Lord Bingham as of little value as a test in itself[27]).

9.26 The incremental approach was applied by Phillips L.J. in *Reeman v DOT*, in which the buyers of a fishing vessel which had been wrongly and negligently certificated by the Department failed in their claim for the economic loss suffered since the boat was virtually worthless without the certificate. Phillips L.J. made a number of observations which would no doubt be relied upon by a Classification Society defending a claim brought against it as RO acting on behalf of a Flag State:

"The statutory framework in the present case is one designed to promote safety at sea. The scheme adopted to achieve this is to impose duties as to seaworthiness on the owners of vessels and then to provide for the department to check and certify that these duties have been complied with. The purpose of issuing certificates is not really to encourage skippers or others to rely upon them by putting to sea, or in any other manner. Somewhat paradoxically, the purpose of issuing certificates is to help to prevent fishing vessels which are uncertified, and which may be unseaworthy, from putting to sea. More broadly, one can say that the purpose of issuing certificates is the promotion of safety at sea." (At p. 680.)

"In [*The Morning Watch*[28] and *The Nicholas H*] ... the Court attached importance to the fact that classification societies are non-profit-making organisations which exist for the

---

25. *Perrett v Collins* [1998] 2 Lloyd's Rep. 255.

26. [2006] 2 Lloyd's Rep. 327 (H.L.). But as Gibson L.J. observed in the Court of Appeal, [2005] 1 Lloyd's Rep. 165: "It is impossible to reconcile all the judicial statements on the correct methodology to be applied to novel situations in which a person is alleged to owe a duty of care to another. It is clear that the courts take a more cautious approach to imposing that duty where economic loss is claimed than in relation to physical damage. Throughout this area considerations of legal policy predominate in the determination of whether the law recognises a duty of care. Whilst eminent judges have from time to time suggested that the adoption of one test precludes the need to apply another test, I respectfully agree with the pragmatic suggestion of the editors of *Clerk & Lindsell on Torts* (18th ed., 2000) at para. 7-95, that the most helpful approach is that taken by Sir Brian Neill in *BCCI (Overseas) Ltd v Price Waterhouse (No. 2)* [1998] B.C.C. 617 at p. 634 to use in turn the threefold test (stated by Lord Griffiths in *Smith v Bush* [1990] 1 A.C. 831 at p. 862), the assumption of responsibility test (expounded by Lord Goff in *Henderson v Merrett Syndicates Ltd* [1995] 2 A.C. 145) and the incremental approach (explained by Lord Justice Phillips in *Reeman v Department of Transport* [1997] P.N.L.R. 618 at p. 625)." "If the facts are properly analysed and the policy considerations are correctly evaluated the several approaches will yield the same result": see *Bank of Credit and Commerce International (Overseas) Ltd v Price Waterhouse (No. 2)* [1998] B.C.C. 617, 634, *per* Sir Brian Neill.

27. *Op. cit.*, p. 332.

28. [1990] 1 Lloyd's Rep. 547.

purpose of furthering safety at sea rather than for the protection of commercial interests. Mr Aikens submitted that the Department of Transport, when performing its regulatory functions under the Merchant Shipping Acts, performs a very similar role and, indeed, often delegates to classification societies the performance of some of its duties. In my judgment this point has force. It reinforces my conclusion that, for the reasons that I have given, to impose on the Department of Transport the duty for which Mr Ullstein contends would be neither fair, just nor reasonable." (At p. 683.)

It is, however, submitted that there are good grounds for distinguishing both *Reeman* and *The Nicholas H* in the case of an RO carrying out the duties of a Flag State in relation to ISM certification and auditing.

9.27 First, the "collective welfare" argument which held sway[29] in *The Nicholas H* does not apply, or at least with nowhere near the same force: the RO is charging a fee for carrying out a function which the Flag State has agreed to perform and for which it remains ultimately responsible. The Classification Societies have taken on the job of acting as RO for essentially commercial reasons: they are paid for carrying out their tasks and one may fairly ask why they should not be liable for their negligent execution; they can, no doubt, obtain insurance[30] and can, no doubt, recover this cost from the fee paid to them by the Flag State Administration. If the consequence is that Flag State tonnage dues increase no one should complain as the end result should be higher standards of certification and auditing and thus of maritime safety. And it is surely wrong to say that to impose a duty in these circumstances "outflanks the bargain between shipowners and cargo-owners"[31]: part of the rationale behind the ISM Code is for Flag State Administrations to ensure that safety standards are set and maintained and thereby to protect powerless cargo interests.

9.28 Secondly, by approving an SMS and maintaining a SMC, the RO *is* doing more than simply "promoting safety at sea". By approving the ship's systems the RO declares, in these respects at least, that the ship is seaworthy. It is most unlikely that others involved in the maritime adventure – cargo owners, charterers, insurers – will have an equivalent opportunity to survey and check the ship's systems: why then should it not be fair, just and reasonable that the RO should be held to account where that declaration has been given negligently? Will the RO's attention be drawn from its prime function to save life and ships at sea? – no: it should simply devote more resources to this associated task. In his paper, Dr Philip Anderson has noted that Audits are being carried out in less and less time: that cannot be right and can be corrected by making ROs liable for seriously deficient audits.

9.29 Thirdly, it seems that the essential ingredient of *reliance* can be established: one need look no further than the fact that charterers are so concerned with ISM compliance – as a standard to which the vessel must conform – that they demand the inclusion of the BIMCO ISM clause in their charterparties. Is the clause included because charterers merely wish to be satisfied that the certificates are in place? One would think not. Just as important as the certificate itself is that the certificate means what it says: that the vessel is in fact compliant. The RO must surely know

29. Notwithstanding the vigorous dissent of Lord Lloyd, pellucidly analysed by Peter Cane in [1995] L.M.C.L.Q. 433.
30. Lord Mance regarded this as a relevant consideration: *CCE v Barclays Bank, op. cit.*, at para. 102.
31. Lord Steyn in *The Nicholas H*.

that that approval will be relied upon by all those involved in the marine adventure; equally the RO will know who they are – cargo owners, charterers, insurers.

9.30 The most serious objection to the proposition that the RO may be liable for negligently given ISM approval is that it, unlike the carrier, cannot limit liability. Leaving aside the fact that the carrier can limit, why should it be unfair for the RO to have unlimited liability when his negligence has caused loss to innocent cargo interests? Classification societies are substantial major international organisations, run (certainly with regard to their ISM functions) for profit: the argument that they should be treated differently from other service or survey organisations has become less easy to justify. True, one would approach with great concern the possibility that a Classification Society might be liable for the full consequences of a catastrophe, but it is difficult to envisage this happening in practice: one ought to expect the court to find that the RO does not "assume responsibility" to (say) governments faced with clean-up costs or fishermen whose livelihoods are ruined, nor would it be fair and reasonable for the court to hold that a duty was owed to such parties. But the same, it is submitted, does not apply to cargo interests whose property is carried on board a ship audited by an RO. It may not be too long before a case emerges where a cargo-owner with a claim against a worthless one-ship company turns his attention to the RO who has negligently approved an SMS or maintained an SMC which should have been withdrawn on any proper audit.

Ship management

9.31 Under the standard SHIPMAN form clause 3.2/4.2 provides that the provision of technical management includes ISM compliance and also that managers are the "Company" for ISM purposes. The BIMCO drafting sub-committee reported that the Code was perceived to have no significant bearing on the balance of liabilities between the two parties, but that it was important to clarify which of the two – the managers – should assume direct responsibilities under the Code.

9.32 There is one respect in which legal liabilities between owners and managers will be affected. The situation may be envisaged of a vessel which is herself fully compliant with the Code, with SMC in place, which is under the management of a company which for reasons unconnected with that vessel loses its DC. How does that impact on the owners' liabilities? First, of course, the absence of a DC means that the vessel is no longer ISM compliant and insurance will be withdrawn; there is, in truth, very little that the Owner can do about this. Secondly, whilst he will have legal recourse against the managers under clause 4 of SHIPMAN, the managers' liabilities (assuming they have assets or insurance to meet them) are limited to 10 times the annual management fee (SHIPMAN, clause 11). Perhaps the withdrawal of a DC from a manager is an unlikely event, but if it happens it will certainly have serious consequences for all owners who have put their vessels under this management.

Unseaworthiness claims

9.33 I have left to the later part of my chapter discussion of perhaps the most significant consequences of the introduction of the ISM Code for English maritime lawyers, namely the practical effect on the conduct of litigation as opposed to the Code's influence on legal liabilities. Even though it is slightly outside the strict confines of the title of this chapter, I think that it is nevertheless appropriate at least to draw attention to some of those consequences and the areas of maritime litigation which are affected.

9.34 The first important consequence is that the ISM Code sets a practical rather than legal standard of what the reasonable and prudent shipowner ought to do and it requires the shipowner to set up his own standard practices, systems and procedures which must be approved and subjected to audit to check that they are being followed and complied with. In general terms this means that it may no longer be necessary, across a wide range of areas of potential issue, to call expert evidence on what is the standard of a reasonable and prudent shipowner: that standard will be writ large in the shipmanager's SMS. There will probably be no need to call an expert to say that an ordinary and careful owner would have carried out such and such an inspection, or training, or drill: that requirement may be found in the SMS. Thus in *The Eurasian Dream* (a pre-ISM Code case), the parties called experts on "proper system". The claimants' systems expert was from Wallenius and it was common ground that the Wallenius yardstick or standard of operation was higher than that which was generally adopted in the car carrier industry. But the Code itself now sets a standard, a minimum acceptable standard; it may be difficult to see how a shipowner who does less than this or who fails to conform to the standard can be said to be exercising due diligence. Had the Code applied to *The Eurasian Dream* a checklist of the numerous respects in which the Managers Univan failed to comply with the Code would have led very quickly to a finding that there was a failure to exercise due diligence.

9.35 Secondly, the provisions of the ISM Code mean that it will be harder for shipowners to escape liability for accidents caused by ship's personnel, the "act in the navigation or management of the ship". A helpful distinction may be drawn[32] between *equipment failures* – where the ship's structure or equipment has failed – and *system failures* – where accidents have occurred through operational errors or omissions. Examples of the first category, where the ISM Code is likely to have little impact on issues of seaworthiness and unseaworthiness, are engine room breakdowns, loss of integrity in cargo custody and transfer, and deficient or defective navigational aids; true, there may be a more detailed document trail than before which in a few rare cases may tip the balance, but otherwise claims litigation will be little changed. Examples of the second category, where the ISM Code may have a significant impact, are the broad range of human error accidents – fire and explosion; collision, grounding and other navigational accidents. In this context the deliberations of UNCITRAL on the proposed abolition of the "act in the navigation or management of the vessel" exception take on fresh interest.

9.36 Thirdly, introduction of the ISM Code has significantly impacted on documentary disclosure in cargo actions. Prior to the introduction of the Code, Lord

---

32. But it is not all embracing: thus bad cargo stowage – which means that the ship is unstable and thus unseaworthy or that the cargo will damage other cargo – fits into either category. One would not rule out the influence of ISM Code procedures in such a case.

Donaldson gave a paper entitled *The ISM Code: the road to discovery?*[33] The title indicates that he foresaw a sea change in documentary disclosure arising from the written systems and procedures and record keeping and reporting, which would have a decisive impact on the prosecution of claims by cargo interests. Of course, identifying, through the ISM reporting procedures, a litany of defects is not necessarily indicative of a sloppy system. Defects will always arise in any ship, however new or old, and the ISM Code requires that they be reported and acted upon. One must always remember the test for unseaworthiness: is the defect one which *a prudent owner would have required to be made good before sending his ship to sea, had he known of it?* Or, supplemented by the Code, is it one which the SMS requires the shipowner to make good before sending his ship to sea? If the answer is "yes", and the defect is not remedied and an accident results, then the litigator may be handed a smoking gun. More likely, it seems, is that the reported defects are in fact remedied.

THE ISPS CODE

9.37 The ISPS (International Ship and Port Facility Security) Code came into force on 1 July 2004; though the need for such a code had been highlighted by the events of 9/11, its gestation was already well advanced by 2001. Unlike the ISM Code it is a very detailed and extensive code, couched in mandatory language. In contrast to the ISM Code, the Chief Safety Officer who must be appointed under the ISPS Code is not someone who has to have "direct access to the highest level of management". The shipowner/manager must formulate a ship security plan conforming to the extensive requirements of the Code and approved by the Flag State Administration or substitute.[34] Compliance is, of course, obligatory for ships and shipowners; wisely, owners, charterers, brokers and their insurers have taken on board the legal ramifications[35] and dealt with them by making compliance a standard contractual[36] as well as statutory requirement. Thus, for example, the BIMCO voyage charter clause provides that a vessel may give NOR even though she has not received formal ISPS port clearance; in addition, the terms allocate risk in respect of delay attributable to ISPS related matters. Even without formal clauses, it seems probable that under both time and voyage charters an owner warrants that he is ISPS compliant: under a time charter, because he warrants that the vessel is "in every way fitted for the service", under a voyage charter, because the warranty of seaworthiness

33. *Op. cit.*, note 19 above.
34. Contracting governments may delegate the task of approval and certification to a "recognised security organisation" (Articles 4.3, 9.2). Part B of the Code sets out guidelines at 4.3–4.5 for considering the competency of such an organisation. It may be suggested that such an organisation may be liable on the same grounds as those acting as Flag State Administration substitutes for ISM Code compliance purposes; see above.
35. There has been much helpful guidance from representative organisations and academics; see in particular, Baris Soyer and Richard Williams in [2005] L.M.C.L.Q. 515.
36. BIMCO have drafted standard clauses which are now routinely incorporated into both time and voyage charters. FONASBA have also drafted a standard clause for ship's agents and brokers to incorporate into their contracts to protect the agent who innocently lodges inaccurate information provided to him by his principal.

probably extends to possessing standard certification. Non-compliance has obvious legal consequences, in terms of breach of seaworthiness obligations and liability for delay: a clear extension of a shipowner's legal liabilities, yes, but in such a clearcut way as to provide little scope for legal analysis and debate.

9.38 At this relatively early stage of the implementation of the Code, the main areas of legal interest would seem to derive first, from the need for *ports* to be ISPS Code compliant and from the consequences of visiting a non-compliant port or loading a cargo which has originated from a non-compliant port; secondly, in relation to the consequences of a vessel being ordered to a port which is operating at a security level 2 (medium risk) or 3 (high risk). Both situations will, on the facts of a given case, give rise to issues as to whether a port is "unsafe", but it seems unlikely that the legal principles relating to unsafe ports will be reshaped by the requirements of the Code.

9.39 At the time of writing it is understood that many ports are not ISPS Code compliant; yet ships may be ordered to such ports or may load cargoes which originate from them. Because a ship's ISPS log must be declared to the next 10 ports to which she is entered, a visit to a non-compliant port means that the ship's "card is marked"; she may thereafter be refused entry to some ports and delayed at others; the effect of the call at the non-compliant port will be to restrict her trading capability and marketability and lead to damages for delay. Who is to pay for this? Is such a port "unsafe"?

9.40 Somewhat surprisingly, the standard BIMCO clauses do not address this problem. A distinction, of course, must be drawn between time and voyage charters. Under a standard voyage charter to a named port Owners will have had the opportunity to check the compliance of that named port and will bear the risk of non-compliance. Under a voyage charter to a range of ports warranted as safe by the Charterers, is a non-compliant port "unsafe" so as to give rise to a right to damages if the ship proceeds there and/or to a right to refuse to proceed there on the grounds of that non-compliance (rather than any perceived security risk)? Albeit that owners probably have a right to be indemnified in respect of their losses under the indemnity to be implied into clause 8 of NYPE (or equivalent in other standard form charters), a similar point arises under time charters: will a non-compliant port be "unsafe" because of the probable consequences of trading there? My personal view is that the answer to all these questions must be "no": "unsafe" in this context means not free from physical dangers, "safe" means free from physical dangers. True, a cargo may be "dangerous" even when it causes no physical damage to other cargo or to the carrying vessel,[37] but there is neither reason nor logic for applying this analogy to ports. True, unsafety includes political risks of seizure or of risks to personnel at the port to which the vessel has been ordered or has visited; but it would be wrong to extend this to future non-physical consequences (detention, black-listing, delay).[38] Unless the non-compliance is symptomatic of an actual security risk, a vessel which goes to a non-compliant port is not "exposed to danger"

---

37. *The Giannis NK* [1998] 1 Lloyd's Rep. 337.

38. A different view is expressed by the editors of *Cooke on Voyage Charters* (2nd ed.) at p. 113, para. 5.68, though that passage appears to be dealing with non-physical consequences of physical unsafety (fever, disease, etc.).

and the port cannot be said to be unsafe. Owners who wish to protect themselves from the consequences of being ordered to non-compliant ports need only to incorporate express terms to this effect (as they have, for many years, in respect of trading to Israeli or Libyan ports, for example).

9.41 Potentially more interesting, but only from a factual perspective and case by case, are the possible consequences of the ISPS classification of the level of security risk. Is, for example, a shipowner entitled to say: "the port to which my ship has been ordered has just been reclassified level 3 (high risk[39]); the ISPS code provides a clear standard classification for all maritime users; I need no further evidence that this port is prospectively unsafe for my ship and I refuse the order to go there"? It would indeed be convenient for a shipowner simply to have to point to classified level risk and avoid the dilemma for any owner ordered to a danger zone (see, for example, *The Kanchenjunga*[40]). Convenient and practical, yes; but (in my view) fair and realistic, no: the level of security risk is in truth just one of several factors to be taken into account when assessing whether a port, and not just the port but the particular berth or mooring, is prospectively safe for the chartered vessel. It seems to me that there may well be occasions when an Owner would be in breach of charter for refusing to proceed to a security level 3 port, where the security risk in question is – though probable or imminent – one which can be fully addressed by the protective security measures taken, or is not one which puts ships at risk, or is not one which is likely to impact on that part of the port to which the vessel is ordered.

9.42 It remains to be seen whether the introduction of the ISPS Code has any significant impact on the liabilities of and allocation of risk between shipowners, charterers and cargo owners. Full of interest and importance for the maritime user it may be, but to the litigator it seems unlikely to be an area of ground-breaking changes.

---

39. Defined as "the level for which further specific protective security measures shall be maintained for a limited period of time when a security incident is probable or imminent, although it may not be possible to identify the specific target".
40. [1990] 1 Lloyd's Rep. 391.

APPENDIX

9.43 BIMCO STANDARD ISM CLAUSE FOR VOYAGE AND TIME CHARTERPARTIES

From the date of coming into force of the International Safety Management (ISM) Code in relation to the Vessel and thereafter during the currency of this Charterparty, the Owners shall procure that both the Vessel and "the Company" (as defined by the ISM Code) shall comply with the requirements of the ISM Code. Upon request the Owners shall provide a copy of the relevant Document of Compliance (DOC) and Safety Management Certificate (SMC) to the Charterers.

Except as otherwise provided in this Charterparty, loss, damage, expense or delay caused by failure on the part of the Owners or "the Company" to comply with the ISM Code shall be for the Owners' account.

9.44 ISPS/MTSA CLAUSE FOR TIME CHARTERPARTIES 2005

(a)(i) The Owners shall comply with the requirements of the International Code for the Security of Ships and of Port Facilities and the relevant amendments to Chapter XI of SOLAS (ISPS Code) relating to the Vessel and "the Company" (as defined by the ISPS Code). If trading to or from the United States or passing through United States waters, the Owners shall also comply with the requirements of the US Maritime Transportation Security Act 2002 (MTSA) relating to the Vessel and the "Owner" (as defined by the MTSA).

(ii) Upon request the Owners shall provide the Charterers with a copy of the relevant International Ship Security Certificate (or the Interim International Ship Security Certificate) and the full style contact details of the Company Security Officer (CSO).

(iii) Loss, damages, expense or delay (excluding consequential loss, damages, expense or delay) caused by failure on the part of the Owners or "the Company"/"Owner" to comply with the requirements of the ISPS Code/MTSA or this Clause shall be for the Owners' account, except as otherwise provided in this Charter Party.

(b)(i) The Charterers shall provide the Owners and the Master with their full style contact details and, upon request, any other information the Owners require to comply with the ISPS Code/MTSA. Where sub-letting is permitted under the terms of this Charter Party, the Charterers shall ensure that the contact details of all sub-charterers are likewise provided to the Owners and the Master. Furthermore, the Charterers shall ensure that all sub-charter parties they enter into during the period of this Charter Party contain the following provision:

> "The Charterers shall provide the Owners with their full style contact details and, where sub-letting is permitted under the terms of the charter party, shall ensure that the contact details of all sub-charterers are likewise provided to the Owners."

(ii) Loss, damages, expense or delay (excluding consequential loss, damages, expense or delay) caused by failure on the part of the Charterers to comply with this Clause shall be for the Charterers' account, except as otherwise provided in this Charter Party.

(c) Notwithstanding anything else contained in this Charter Party all delay, costs or expenses whatsoever arising out of or related to security regulations or measures required by the port facility or any relevant authority in accordance with the ISPS Code/MTSA including, but not limited to, security guards, launch services, vessel escorts, security fees or taxes and inspections, shall be for the Charterers' account, unless such costs or expenses result solely from the negligence of the Owners, Master or crew. All measures required by the Owners to comply with the Ship Security Plan shall be for the Owners' account.

(d) If either party makes any payment which is for the other party's account according to this Clause, the other party shall indemnify the paying party.

9.45 ISPS/MTSA CLAUSE FOR VOYAGE CHARTER PARTIES 2005

(a)(i) The Owners shall comply with the requirements of the International Code for the Security of Ships and of Port Facilities and the relevant amendments to Chapter XI of SOLAS (ISPS Code) relating to the Vessel and "the Company" (as defined by the ISPS Code). If trading to or from the United States or passing through United States waters, the Owners shall also comply with the requirements of the US Maritime Transportation Security Act 2002 (MTSA) relating to the Vessel and the "Owner" (as defined by the MTSA).

(ii) Upon request the Owners shall provide the Charterers with a copy of the relevant International Ship Security Certificate (or the Interim International Ship Security Certificate) and the full style contact details of the Company Security Officer (CSO).

(iii) Loss, damages, expense or delay (excluding consequential loss, damages, expense or delay) caused by failure on the part of the Owners or "the Company"/"Owner" to comply with the requirements of the ISPS Code/MTSA or this Clause shall be for the Owners' account, except as otherwise provided in this Charter Party.

(b)(i) The Charterers shall provide the Owners and the Master with their full style contact details and, upon request, any other information the Owners require to comply with the ISPS Code/MTSA.

(ii) Loss, damages or expense (excluding consequential loss, damages or expense) caused by failure on the part of the Charterers to comply with this Clause shall be for the Charterers' account, except as otherwise provided in this Charter Party, and any delay caused by such failure shall count as laytime or time on demurrage.

(c) Provided that the delay is not caused by the Owners' failure to comply with their obligations under the ISPS Code/MTSA, the following shall apply:

(i) Notwithstanding anything to the contrary provided in this Charter Party, the Vessel shall be entitled to tender Notice of Readiness even if not cleared due to applicable security regulations or measures imposed by a port facility or any relevant authority under the ISPS Code/MTSA.

(ii) Any delay resulting from measures imposed by a port facility or by any relevant authority under the ISPS Code/MTSA shall count as laytime or time on demurrage, unless such measures result solely from the negligence of the Owners, Master or crew or the previous trading of the Vessel, the nationality of the crew or the identity of the Owners' managers.

(d) Notwithstanding anything to the contrary provided in this Charter Party, any costs or expenses whatsoever solely arising out of or related to security regulations or measures required by the port facility or any relevant authority in accordance with the ISPS Code/MTSA including, but not limited to, security guards, launch services, vessel escorts, security fees or taxes and inspections, shall be for the Charterers' account, unless such costs or expenses result solely from the negligence of the Owners, Master or crew or the previous trading of the Vessel, the nationality of the crew or the identity of the Owners' managers. All measures required by the Owners to comply with the Ship Security Plan shall be for the Owners' account.

(e) If either party makes any payment which is for the other party's account according to this Clause, the other party shall indemnify the paying party.

CHAPTER 10

The ISM and ISPS Codes: A Critical Analysis of Content, Philosophy and Legal Implications

DR PHIL ANDERSON*

10.1 The ISM Code was not developed, and was never intended to be a tool for lawyers and the courts to determine issues of liability. Nor was it developed to make the lives of ship operators and seafarers unbearably difficult or to down load their ships with mountains of paper. These are by-products! The ISM Code was intended to make ships safer and seas cleaner. In our deliberations we must never lose sight of that goal.

10.2 I fully concur with my colleague, Mr Simon Kverndal Q.C., when he reflects that: "… the first important consequence is that the ISM Code sets a practical rather than legal standard of what the reasonable and prudent shipowner ought to do …" Whilst I fully respect the nature of this book I will, with your permission, address more that "practical" standard rather than the strictly "legal" issues of ISM – which have of course been dealt with so admirably by Mr Kverndal in the previous chapter.

10.3 It is well established that standards can and do change. In 1926 Lord Sumner said, in *Bradley & Sons v Federal Steam Navigation Co.*, "… in the law of carriage of goods by sea neither seaworthiness nor due diligence is absolute. Both are relative, among other things, to the state of knowledge and standards prevailing at the time…"[1] and in a more recent case, to which Mr Kverndal has already referred, *The Eurasian Dream*, Mr Justice Cresswell echoed the words of Lord Sumner: "… Seaworthiness must be judged by the standards and practices of the industry at the relevant time, at least so long as those standards and practices are reasonable…."[2] It is, I believe, through understanding the full nature and significance of that practical standard that we will gain an insight into the influence – past, present and future – on the Evolution of Liabilities both with regard to the ISM Code and the ISPS Code.

THE THREE FOLD MANTRA

10.4 I think the place to start is by reminding ourselves of a very simple, but yet profound, *Three Fold Mantra* in which is set out a full explanation of how the ISM Code

---

* BA(Hons.), D.Prof., FNI, MEWI, AMAE, Master Mariner; Managing Director – ConsultISM Ltd; Immediate Past President, The Nautical Institute.
1. Lord Sumner, *Bradley & Sons Ltd v Federal Steam Navigation Co.* (1926) 24 Ll.L.Rep. 446, (1927) 27 Ll.L.Rep. 395.
2. Mr Justice Cresswell, *Papera Traders Co. Ltd & others v Hyundai Merchant Marine Co. Ltd & Another (The "Eurasian Dream")* [2002] 1 Lloyd's Rep. 719.

is intended to work – and the link to issues involving legal liabilities. The Mantra states:

- Say what you do;
- Do what you say that you do;
- Show that you do what you say that you do!

10.5 The Company will "say what it does" through its various Safety Management and Procedures Manuals, checklists, instruction books, circulars and whatever else it decides to use to set out its documented Safety Management System. This is the first part of the Mantra.

10.6 The second part of the Mantra involves bringing those written and documented procedures alive – to make them part of the way in which the Company, its ships and its people, both on shore and on board ship, live, work and breath!

10.7 From a purely practical point of view – if you have achieved the second stage of the Mantra then you are flying! (Or rather sailing!) However, it is crucial that not only does the Company have good procedures in place and has fully implemented those procedures in a living, dynamic system but it must be able to demonstrate, to prove, that the system is working as it was intended. This will be achieved, mainly, through the creation of objective evidence. This is the third level of the Three Fold Mantra – to show that you do what you say that you do.

10.8 Interestingly though, the reason for creating this "objective evidence" is not, primarily, to provide lawyers and the courts with information to consider in liability cases – it is created to allow the Company, and those involved in running the management system to measure and assess their success with their implementation efforts such that they can make properly considered decisions when it comes to implementing corrective action and in their activities of continually improving their system. The possible use by lawyers and the courts is coincidental. That, in itself though, does create a potential dilemma – because the "risk" or "fear" that this objective evidence may be used against the ship operator, or its employees personally, in some future legal action may have the propensity to inhibit the willingness of those involved in its production to actually generate the hard evidence. If it is not produced then it is very unlikely that the safety management system could function – as a "management system" – and we may as well go back to the position which existed previously of a prescriptive system of complying with sets of rules and regulations produced by government bureaucrats. Of course, if the objective evidence is deliberately not created the Company would also be non-compliant with the requirements of the ISM Code.

10.9 A problem which arises, however, at a practical level, is the interpretation of the requirements of the ISM Code; this has become a very subjective matter. Consequently, what is required to satisfy the first level of the Mantra is not at all universally agreed – which clearly will have a knock-on effect with regard to the second and third levels. The introduction of the ISM Code carried with it at least two quite major presuppositions:

(i) it presupposed a level of understanding by the shipping industry of the "systems approach" to management – which, in some cases, I fear was an unwarranted assumption to make;

(ii) it presupposed that the shipping industry, to a large extent, was capable of regulating and policing itself – which, in some cases, I fear was an unwarranted assumption to make!

AN ILL-DEFINED STANDARD

10.10 IMO Resolution A.741(18) of 1993, as amended in December 2000 by Resolution MSC.104(73) – or, as it is otherwise known, The International Management Code for the Safe Operation of Ships and for Pollution Prevention (the International Safety Management (ISM) Code) – or simply The ISM Code – comprises 16 very short Sections – set out on 10 sides of a small A5 booklet. At one level it provides great latitude – recognising that there are many different types and sizes of commercial ship-operating companies which will operate in quite different ways – but, at another level, it requires each Company to achieve certain common objectives or goals through the development of its safety management system. Those objectives are loosely defined within the ISM Code but the details were left to each individual ship-operating company to work out and develop.

10.11 This latitude, I would say, has been one of the greatest strengths and also the greatest weaknesses of the ISM Code. Not only has it been left to each ship-operating company to decide what it needs to do to satisfy those objectives – but it has also been left to individual Flag State Administrations, and Recognised Organisations (R/O's) acting on their behalf, to apply their own interpretation on what is required – although they did receive a little more help by way of IMO Resolution A.788(19) – Guidelines on Implementation of the International Safety Management (ISM) Code by Administrations – which were replaced with Revised Guidelines which were adopted by Resolution A.913(22) in November 2001. Still there were, and to some extent still are, widely differing interpretations, and consequently different standards adopted, by different Administrations and R/O's – although the International Association of Classification Societies (IACS) and the International Chamber of Shipping (ICS)/International Shipping Federation (ISF) have also done their bit to try and introduce a common approach.[3] The policing of the Code, however, has been left very much to Port State Control and similar bodies – who also apply their own interpretation of what is required to comply. Although they have been helped with some guidance from IMO and from their MOU's.

10.12 What I have seen and experienced in practice is that not only are there differences in interpretation between ship-operating companies, between Flag State Administrations, between Recognised Organisations/Classification Societies, between different Port State Controls/Coast Guards and their MOU's – but also between individuals within the same organisations. Although that situation is improving as individuals and organisations progress up the learning curve with the passage of time, it would be a mistake however to believe that there exists, at this time, one universal standard which would define "ISM Compliance" – although each Company will have its Document of Compliance (DOC) proudly displayed in a nice frame in its office ashore and each ship will have its Safety Management Certificate (SMC) neatly filed away ready for inspection.

3. For example: *IACS Recommendation No 41 – Guidance for IACS Auditors to the ISM Code* and *ICS/ISF – Guidelines on the application of the IMO International Safety Management (ISM) Code.*

10.13 It must also be remembered that the verification audits which led to the issue of the DOC to the Company and the SMC to the ship were a snapshot of the SMS in operation by specific individuals who happened to be there at that particular point in time. As those individuals change (as they invariably will, particularly on board ship) then there is every possibility that the operation of the SMS could be influenced and consequently changed. At a practical level therefore the possession of a DOC and SMC may not necessarily be coincidental with "compliance" with the ISM Code – although it may be *prima facie* evidence of compliance.

10.14 From an evidential point of view, in the event of an incident which may give rise to legal liabilities, it will not only be necessary to take another "snapshot" of the SMS at the time of the incident but, more importantly, it will be necessary to produce a "movie" of what had been happening in the weeks and months prior to the incident. From a review of the movie we will gain an impression of the level to which compliance was being achieved.

10.15 One thing I would mention, within the context of reviewing that movie – or indeed of any other review of the SMS – is that we should not expect to find perfection. Things can and do go wrong: we should be looking for a management system which is working such that mistakes, omissions, problems are spotted, analysed and corrective action is implemented to learn lessons and avoid recurrence, within a cycle of continual improvement. Of course we should also be looking for an active regime of proactive accident prevention and risk management. Those types of activities should be interpreted as being much more indicative of a working SMS than the occasional mistake which might be made by an individual.

HAS ISM CHANGED ANYTHING?

10.16 This is an interesting question – and one which I believe requires more attention than has been given to it since ISM first came on the scene.

10.17 We could interpret the question to be asking whether ships have indeed become safer and seas cleaner since ISM implementation, but I think that question is for another venue and event. For the purpose of this book, I think the question is alluding to legal liabilities and at that level it can be stated quite clearly that there has been very little or no change in the law with regard to the raft of marine-related liabilities as a consequence of the introduction of the ISM Code.

10.18 It is important to remember that the ISM Code is concerned with a "systems" approach to management – a Safety Management System. It is that management system which should ensure compliance with MARPOL, SOLAS, IMDG Code, STCW and all the other conventions, statutes, rules and regulations – as they may be adopted into the domestic legislation of the Flag State and as they may apply to visiting ships within a Port State situation. If the Oil Record Book has not been properly completed then, in the first instance, that is likely to be a violation under the relevant section of the MARPOL Convention. If the navigation charts have not been corrected then that will be a violation under the relevant section of SOLAS. The obligations, responsibilities and potential consequences under the relevant national legislation will be the same after ISM implementation as they would have been before. What is new is the requirement to have a management system in place which will ensure compliance with those various rules and regulations. It is quite likely that the incident has arisen because of some failure in the Management System – but that, in itself, is not the breach which incurred the liability. Let us remind ourselves of the requirement of Section 1.2.3 of the ISM Code:

"**1.2.3** The safety management system should ensure:
  .1 compliance with mandatory rules and regulations; and
  .2 that applicable codes, guidelines and standards recommended by the Organisation, Administrations, classification societies and maritime industry organisations are taken into account."

10.19 Although it may be a long list, it should be realistically possible to identify and define all the "mandatory rules and regulations" which apply to ships flying the flag of a particular Flag State administration, and presumably it would be at least theoretically possible to identify and define all the rules and regulations which might apply to all the different countries to which each of the vessels within a ship operator's fleet might visit; however, can we realistically identify the boundaries for compliance with Section 1.2.3.2? That is difficult and, I suspect, will become an evidential issue in some case in the future.

10.20 There are three aspects which I think can be considered as "new" and which have changed the situation with regard to the way in which companies operate post-ISM Implementation and which I think will have a significant bearing upon the evolution of marine liabilities:

(1) Audit trails.
(2) The Designated Person.
(3) The Company Verification, Review and Evaluation.

10.21 The changes are at the evidential level – because of "new" expectations which have been created through the ISM Code. This evidence, and the expectation of the existence of that evidence, does have the propensity to affect the outcome of liability cases. It may be sufficient to tip the "balance of probability", or maybe even, in a criminal case, to "prove beyond reasonable doubt" a state of affairs; it may make the difference between distinguishing simple "negligence" of an individual from the more significant status of "incompetence".

10.22 I would like to consider each of these in a little more detail to explore what I see as their potential significance.

AUDIT TRAILS

10.23 This takes us back to our Three Fold Mantra. It should be possible to identify in the Procedures Manual(s) how a particular procedure or process should be carried out – it should "say what you should do". By following the process through, by observing objective evidence – by following an audit trail – it should be possible to verify whether or not what was supposed to be done was actually done, on that occasion.

10.24 However, neither audit trails nor objective evidence are particularly new – and they certainly were not an invention coming out of the ISM Code. What is new is the expectation of actually finding the objective evidence and being able to follow a meaningful audit trail. There will be an expectation of the existence of a procedure and there will be a realistic expectation that there will have been records maintained to confirm that certain things were done to confirm that the correct procedures had been followed – for example, a checklist completed, an entry made in a log book, etc. In theory, therefore, it should be a relatively easy task to verify whether those on board were doing what they were supposed to be doing. Unfortunately there is a rather large practical problem here which has significant potential consequences when considering the legal tests which might be used to establish legal liability – for example, due diligence.

10.25 How many individual jobs or tasks exist, or can be envisaged, on board a commercial ship – let us say a large Passenger Cruise Vessel, or maybe a Product Tanker? A few hundred? A few thousand maybe? Maybe more! It would depend at what depth you might want to draw the line. Let us consider just two of the relevant requirements of the ISM Code, in order to put this matter into some sort of perspective and thus start to appreciate the scale of the potential problem:

"1.2.2 Safety management objectives of the Company should, *inter alia*:
  .... 2 establish safeguards against all identified risks ..."

That is quite a tall order if we are to read the requirement literally and if we interpret the requirement to mean that we should document all the safeguards we may have identified.

"7 DEVELOPMENT OF PLANS FOR SHIPBOARD OPERATIONS
The Company should establish procedures for the preparation of plans and instructions, including checklists as appropriate, for key shipboard operations concerning the safety of the ship and the prevention of pollution. The various tasks involved should be defined and assigned to qualified personnel."

10.26 There is something of a limit provided in that we are only here dealing with "key" shipboard operations; but if we assume that what was intended by "key" shipboard operations are those operations which might impact upon, or involve the management of safety – then there would be few operations on board which would not fall into that criteria.

10.27 It seems to have become expected, by some, that the SMS must have a procedure for every single task imaginable. I have certainly seen systems running to 20, even 30 and more Lever Arch files in size – in which the Company has tried to include everything. I was on board a ship quite recently, a very small ship, and counted 65 manuals stacked upon the shelves of a specially constructed bookcase in the wheelhouse. The reality is that those volumes gather dust and the system, whilst it may look impressive to an outside observer, is of very little practical value. In fact such a system can easily become counter-productive. Many companies have realised that they need to reduce the size of their manuals and cut down on the paperwork generally. Indeed at the May 2006 session of the IMO Maritime Safety Committee meeting a report was presented which set out the result of some extensive research carried out by a team of industry experts looking into the success, or otherwise, of ISM implementation.[4] One of the recommendations coming out of

---

4. IMO Maritime Safety Committee MSC 81/17/1 (21 December 2005): *Role of the Human Element – Assessment of the impact and effectiveness of the ISM Code.*

that report was to cut down on the size of the manuals and the paperwork generally. That is all well and good, but what is the potential end result when it comes to such things as paper trails and objective evidence? What would be the consequences in the event of an incident which may give rise to liability action when it turns out that there was no clear written procedure for that very thing which was causative of the accident?

10.28 The reduction of paperwork and the production of objective evidence are not necessarily compatible goals!

10.29 I suspect there are many Safety Management Systems out there which are intentionally voluminous because by doing so the Company believes that it can shield itself from blame by saying that it had provided its Masters and sea staff with all the procedures they could ever need for the safe operation of their vessel, and the incident occurred because the Master or other member of the sea staff did not follow the correct procedure. My own belief is that any ship-operating company which harbours such ideas is seriously misguided and is likely to receive a shock if an incident does occur, since an investigation would almost certainly reveal a non-functioning SMS and, through one means or another, find itself back on the boardroom table.

THE DESIGNATED PERSON

10.30 Mr Kverndal has already described, in some detail, the role of the Designated Person (D.P.), some of the potential issues and problems which might arise out of the role and, I think, dispelled a myth that had developed in some quarters that the D.P. would be considered as being synonymous with the alter-ego of the Company.

10.31 I do not intend repeating what Mr Kverndal has already stated so well – along with the profound insight which had been provided by Lord Donaldson – other than to reiterate the important requirement, set out in Section 4 of the Code, that the D.P. should have "… direct access to the highest levels of management …" What use the D.P. makes of this is not made clear in the Code – but it can be safely implied, I believe, that it would be used to communicate issues relating to the management of safety within the Company and particularly where there may be problems encountered. This is the "Achilles heel" to which Lord Donaldson had referred.

10.32 However, there is one further, related, issue which should be considered alongside the requirement of the D.P. as set out in Section 4 – particularly relating to the "… monitoring of the safety and pollution prevention aspects of the operation of each ship …" and that is the obligation and responsibility upon the Company under Section 3.3 to ensure that "… adequate resources and shore-based support are provided to enable the designated person or persons to carry out their functions …"

10.33 The role of the D.P. should be a very active and participatory role and it will be an expectation, no doubt, that evidence will exist to demonstrate that the D.P. was keeping his/her eye on the safety ball, was ensuring that safety-related problems were resolved and was communicating safety-related matters to the highest levels of management. The unresolved "question" is how much information should be communicated?

THE COMPANY VERIFICATION, REVIEW AND EVALUATION

10.34 Section 12 of the ISM Code is headed "Company Verification, Review and Evaluation". This Section of the Code has not, in my view, received the attention it really deserves. In my view it is within this Section of the Code that issues of "due diligence", privity and possibly even more extreme levels of the Company implications will be established.

10.35 I think it will be helpful to remind ourselves of the requirements of Section 12 of the Code:

"12.1 The Company should carry out internal safety audits to verify whether safety and pollution-prevention activities comply with the safety management system.

12.2 The Company should periodically evaluate the efficiency of and, when needed, review the safety management system in accordance with procedures established by the Company.

12.3 The audits and possible corrective actions should be carried out in accordance with documented procedures.

12.4 Personnel carrying out audits should be independent of the areas being audited unless this is impracticable due to the size and the nature of the Company.

12.5 The results of the audits and reviews should be brought to the attention of all personnel having responsibility in the area involved.

12.6 The management personnel responsible for the area involved should take timely corrective action on deficiencies found."

10.36 In a way this can be considered as an extra dimension beyond the Three Fold Mantra. In fact it is merely part of "closing the loop" in the cycle of continual improvement of any Management System. Section 12, however, brings the Company management on centre-stage to monitor and check how they are performing with their management of safety. They will then be in a position whereby they can improve their System.

10.37 Under the ISM Code the Company, with a capital "C", has an enormous range of responsibilities and obligations. It is one thing to set out the procedures and guidance with the Company directions on what those on board should be doing – but that is not enough. The required training and familiarisation of the Master, officers and crew must be given – but that is not enough. The emergency drills and exercises can be carried out and safety committee meetings can be held, and much more – but that is not enough. In addition to all that, there is a clear obligation upon the Company to check that what they are supposed to be doing they are indeed doing and they are doing it properly! This is where the Company will have an opportunity to demonstrate the level of due diligence it is exercising.

10.38 The responsibility for managing safety is, in my view, back on the board-room table, irrespective of what we may interpret the role of the Designated Person to be. There must be a very clear expectation that the Company will not only do the things required of it under Section 12 but these things will be reviewed and fully considered by those in the Company capable of making high level decisions and, consequently, that must equate to the highest levels of management.

10.39 The Flag State Administration/Recognised Organisation will carry out external, verification, audits – and these are important with regard to maintaining the DOC's and SMC's. However, the most important checks on the system are those conducted by the Company to check that its own systems are working as they are supposed to be working. Of course those with most to gain from a properly functioning SMS are the Company and its people. The Internal Audits of the Company therefore should receive close attention – it is here that the Company is checking that those on board are doing what they are supposed to be doing. It is a learning opportunity and an opportunity to self improve.

10.40 There is no clear guidance from IMO as to the frequency of Internal Audits – however, industry practice seems to have settled on a standard of at least one Internal Audit per year. I would suggest this is a minimum. Personally, I would prefer an ongoing, rolling audit, involving not only an auditor from head office but also auditing by individuals on board who have received training in auditing techniques.

10.41 In any event neither the External Audit nor the Internal Audit can be anything more than a "sample" audit. I understand that, typically, External Audits by R/O's (invariably Classification Societies) are "allowed" just one day to review the entire SMS (although I have been told on good authority that at least one leading Classification Society has bowed to pressure from its "clients" to reduce its attendance for an intermediate verification audit to half a day). So, as far as the SMC is concerned, we are talking about a time period of between a half and one working day every two and a half years or so for the Administration to satisfy itself that those on board the ship really are doing what they are supposed to be doing. I would suggest that the system of external audits, as it presently exists, is seriously flawed.

10.42 To come back to the Internal Audits then I would have to say that "annual" audits on board each vessel really should be considered a minimum. Exactly how long such an Internal Audit of the SMS would take would depend upon a number of factors. The size, type and complexity of the ship are certainly factors which must be taken into account, as well as the number of people on board, and whether those people are "Company" people and are well familiar with the SMS.

10.43 Ideally the whole of the system should be audited annually – but that is usually perceived to be impractical within the time scale available. Consequently, a range of different areas of the SMS will be identified, and a sample of procedures within those areas will be subjected to thorough audit. If that sample audit is satisfactory then an assumption will tend to be made that it will be safe to believe that the rest of the procedures and systems will be adequate and working satisfactorily.

10.44 There will be an expectation that at least an annual internal audit will have taken place and that a report will have been prepared following such an audit.

10.45 However, what might be the consequences if an incident does happen and it transpires that the most relevant procedure, closely linked to causation of the incident, had not been the subject of an Internal Audit?

10.46 In partial satisfaction of the requirements of Section 12.2, it has become common practice for the Company to hold at least one annual formal, minuted meeting involving the highest levels of management where the entire meeting, or at least a major agenda item, involves those senior managers formally reviewing the working of the SMS. An expectation will exist that such a meeting will have been held and that a set of minutes will exist. From my own experience there are considerable variations between companies in the way in which they discharge this requirement, and a clear insight can be gleaned from reviewing the minutes of those Management Review Meetings into the attitudes, beliefs and values of that Company when it comes to the importance they place on the management of safety.

THE ISPS CODE

10.47 I have not discussed in any detail the implications or influence of the ISPS Code on the Evolution of Liabilities. This is not because I consider the ISPS Code to be in any way less important but rather because the principle of many of the evidential issues involved will be similar to those arising under the ISM Code.

10.48 Both ISM and ISPS are based upon a systems approach to management – which includes a cycle of continual improvement. There is, though, one major difference between ISM and ISPS in that, to a large extent, the documented procedures of the Security Management System (specifically the Ship Security Plan (SSP) and the Company Security Plan (CSP)) will, because of their very nature, be "confidential" with very restricted access, limited to a small number of identified individuals.

10.49 Mr Kverndal has identified a number of possible scenarios where legal liabilities may follow from some security breach and which may in turn require an examination of evidence to establish how and why the security management system may have failed which possibly resulted in the security breach. However, such an investigation and disclosure of evidence may, potentially, compromise the security of the vessel.

10.50 I again believe that the ISPS Code, like the ISM Code, sets a practical rather than a legal standard of what is required of the reasonable and prudent shipowner.

CONCLUSION

10.51 The range of liabilities to which ship operators and others involved in related maritime and insurance sectors are exposed has not changed as a consequence of the ISM and ISPS Codes. What has changed, and what will, in my opinion, influence the evolution of marine liability claims and disputes is the expectation, by potential claimants and the Courts, of the existence of specific "objective evidence". Prior to ISM implementation deadlines it may well have been "hoped" that such evidence would exist – it can now be presumed that it will exist or, if it does not, then the ship operator may need a very good explanation as to why it does not exist!

10.52 In another pre-ISM case, *The Torepo*,[5] a number of important and relevant principles were explored. The product tanker *Torepo* did have an embryonic ISM Safety Management System on board but had not gone through the full verification process and consequently did not have a Safety Management Certificate at the time of the incident, the incident having occurred some months before the implementation deadline. However, it would appear, from reading the judgment, that the

---

5. *The Torepo* [2002] 2 Lloyd's Rep. 535, David Steel J.

Admiralty judge was aware of the existence and purpose of those procedures in the management of the vessel. Despite efforts of the claimants to undertake something of a "fishing expedition" around the safety management system to uncover incriminating, or at least embarrassing, evidence, the investigation remained focused upon the navigational procedures and whether any failure to follow those navigational procedures was causative in the vessel grounding and having to be subsequently salvaged. Mr Justice Steel seemed to be satisfied with the adequacy of the procedures and satisfied that they were being followed. The cause of the grounding was a result of a series of almost simultaneous mistakes by the Pilot, Chief Officer and Lookout – he allowed the shipowners to rely upon the "error in navigation" defence.[6]

10.53 It is possible, and logically probable, that the frequency of marine liability claims and disputes coming to Arbitration or the Courts will decrease, since they should be capable of being better and more easily evaluated, based upon the objective evidence, by the respective parties prior to ever reaching the steps of the court. However, I believe there are a number of important issues which do require clarification and guidance to be provided to the industry before that situation can be reached, including:

- What is the significance of the role of the Designated Person and, specifically, what use should be made of that right of access to the highest levels of management?
- What level of documentation, by way of written procedures, guidelines and records, really will be expected?
- Will the creation of documentation which is brought into existence to improve safety, maybe following an incident, but which may be self incriminating in nature be allowed some sort of "privileged" status?

10.54 In some cases ship operators, and their management and staff, both ashore and onboard, do need to overcome a barrier which seems to exist which is inhibiting a full embracing of the ISM Code. A belief which seems to be held by some that the documentation which will be generated from a full and proper implementation of the Code will be used as a big stick to beat them with.

10.55 Maybe one way of overcoming such a barrier is for ship operators to understand that a properly implemented ISM system will work in their favour. That the ISM Code will be the greatest friend a ship operator could ever wish for – or the worst enemy it could ever imagine. It will all depend upon how well they have developed and implemented their SMS – and whether they can prove that they really were doing what they say that they do.

---

6. Carriage of Goods by Sea Act 1971 (1971, c. 190)/Hague Visby Rules, Article IV, Rule 2:
  "(a) ... Neither the carrier nor ship shall be responsible for loss or damage arising or resulting from:– Act, neglect, or default of the master, mariner, pilot, or the servants of the carrier in the navigation or in the management of the ship ..."

PART 6

Passenger Liabilities and Insurance

CHAPTER 11

Boundaries of the Athens Convention: What you see is not always what you get!

Dr BARIS SOYER*

INTRODUCTION

11.1 The idea of establishing an international framework to provide a minimum degree of legal protection for passengers carried by sea has been on the agenda of the international community for a considerable amount of time.[1] Following a number of unsuccessful attempts,[2] the Athens Convention 1974[3] became the first international agreement to receive a reasonable degree of international recognition.[4] That said, it has to be stated that the Athens Convention 1974 is not amongst the most successful international conventions in terms of achieving worldwide support.[5] Many hold the financial limits of liability set by the Convention responsible for this outcome.[6]

11.2 In an attempt to improve the rights of passengers under the Athens Convention 1974 and make the regime a more attractive proposition for the ratification of more states, the Protocol of 2002 to the Athens Convention[7] was adopted in a diplomatic conference in London. Apart from introducing a compulsory insurance

---

* Reader in Commercial and Maritime Law, University of Wales, Swansea, School of Law, Member of the Institute of International Trade and Shipping Law.

1. Other modes of transport have witnessed similar attempts over the years. For example, an international liability regime in relation to air passengers was established as early as 1929 by the Convention for the Unification of Certain Rules relating to International Transportation by Air (Warsaw Convention). The Warsaw regime underwent substantial modifications in the years to follow, most notably in 1955 and 1961, and the entire web of instruments was codified into one instrument in 1999 known also as the Convention for the Unification of Certain Rules Relating to International Carriage by Air (Montreal Convention).

2. See the International Convention for the Unification of Certain Rules relating to the Carriage of Passengers by Sea 1961 and International Convention for the Unification of Certain Rules relating to Carriage of Passenger Luggage at Sea 1967.

3. The full name of the convention is the Convention Relating to the Carriage of Passengers and their Luggage by Sea 1974.

4. As of December 2006, the member states are: Albania, Argentina, Bahamas, Barbados, Belgium, China, Croatia, Dominica, Egypt, Equatorial Guinea, Estonia, Georgia, Greece, Guyana, Ireland, Jordan, Latvia, Liberia, Luxembourg, Malawi, Marshall Islands, Nigeria, Poland, Russian Federation, Saint Kitts and Nevis, Spain, Switzerland, Tonga, Ukraine, United Kingdom, Vanuatu, Yemen and Hong Kong-China and Macau-China (as associated members). The Athens Convention regime has been incorporated into the national laws of some states, such as Denmark, Finland, France, Germany, Norway, Slovenia, Sweden and Vietnam even though these states have not officially ratified the Convention.

5. The level of ratification represents less than 40% of the world's tonnage. There are still huge gaps; significant omissions include Canada, Australia, India and the United States. Also, the Convention has not achieved wide-spread recognition in Africa and Latin America.

6. The limits set by the original Athens Convention 1974 (i.e. 46,666 SDR for death or personal injury) were regarded as too low by most European states, Australia and Canada. To the contrary, some states, particularly in East Asia, have eschewed the Athens Convention 1974 on the basis that the limits were too high.

7. Hereinafter referred to as the Athens Convention 2002.

regime and allowing a direct action against the insurers,[8] the Athens Convention 2002 has also introduced fundamental changes in the liability regime.[9] In the new regime, there are two tiers to the liability of a carrier for loss from a passenger's death or personal injury caused by shipwreck, capsizing, collision or stranding of the ship, explosion or fire in the ship or defect in the ship. In the first tier, the carrier is strictly liable up to 250,000 SDR,[10] unless the carrier were to prove that the accident was caused solely by an act of war; hostilities, civil war, insurrection or an exceptional natural phenomenon. Similarly, the carrier would be exempted from liability were he to prove that the incident was wholly caused by a third party whose act or omission occurred with the intent to cause the incident.[11] In the second tier, that is, above the strict liability limit, the carrier is liable unless he can prove that the incident causing the loss occurred without his fault or neglect. Therefore, a reverse burden of proof is imposed on the carrier for losses between the strict liability limit, which is 250,000 SDR, and the maximum liability expressed in Article 7 of the Athens Convention, as amended by the protocol, which is 400,000 SDR.[12]

11.3 Despite its shortcomings,[13] the Athens Convention 2002 has been regarded as satisfactory in many respects at the EU level. On 23 November 2005, the Commission presented a proposal for a Regulation of the European Parliament and of the Council on the liability of carriers of passengers by sea and inland waterways in the event of accidents.[14] The proposed Regulation intends to provide a uniform liability regime within the European Community by incorporating the Athens Convention into the EC law but it also extends the scope of application of the Convention to domestic carriage and inland waterways.[15]

11.4 Without doubt, the proposed Regulation goes a long way towards achieving a uniform liability regime within the European Union and one gets the impression that it will be made an integral part of the EC law regime especially considering that a compromise has now been reached to address the concerns of insurers and

---

8. See Art. 4 *bis* of the Athens Convention 2002.

9. See new Article 3 of the Athens Convention 2002.

10. The carrier is required to obtain compulsory insurance in respect of the death of and personal injury to passengers up to this figure, see Article 4 *bis* of the Athens Convention 2002.

11. See Article 4 of the Athens Convention 2002. Similar exceptions appear in other conventions adopting a strict liability regime, see for example, Article III, paragraph 2 of the International Convention on Civil Liability for Oil Pollution Damage 1992 and Article 7, para. 2, of the International Convention on Liability and Compensation for Damage in Connection with the Carriage of Hazardous and Noxious Substances by Sea 1996 (not yet in force).

12. The other main changes, which have been brought about by the protocol, are: an increase of 25% on luggage claims; allowing the court seized to suspend the operation or interrupt the running of the 2-year time limit and the possibility for regional integration organisations, such as the EU, to sign the new Convention with the same rights and obligations as a nation state.

13. See B. Soyer, "Sundry Considerations on the Draft Protocol to the Athens Convention Relating to the Carriage of Passengers and Their Luggage by Sea 1974", in (2002) *Journal of Maritime Law and Commerce* 519.

14. COM(2005) 592.

15. The Regulation also makes the following major changes in this area:
   – removal of the possibility for Member States under the Athens Convention 2002 in fixing limits of liability higher than those provided for in the Convention (Article 4);
   – making advance payment in the event of the death of, or personal injury to, a passenger (Article 5); and
   – providing detailed pre-journey information to passengers (Article 6).

governments in relation to compulsory insurance and level of liability.[16] However, one should bear in mind that incorporation of the Athens Convention into Community legislation will mean that there will always be a correlation between provisions of the Athens Convention which define its scope and the desired uniformity. Put another way, any obscurity inherent in the meaning of provisions defining the scope of the Athens Convention will hinder the uniformity of the passenger liability regime within the European Union.

11.5 The author is of the opinion that some provisions in the Athens Convention, which are designed to specify its scope, are vague and open to misinterpretation. One might, at this stage, argue that this is not a problem unique to the Athens Convention but is one often arising in the context of international conventions.[17] This is, undoubtedly, an accurate observation. However, the mission of mapping the scope of the Athens Convention becomes a serious consideration in the light of the fact that the EU is seriously considering its implementation into the Community's legal system. If obscurities surrounding certain provisions of Athens Convention are identified accurately, there is a possibility that certain modifications are made in the proposed Regulation with a view to clarifying the scope of the new liability regime proposed for passengers carried by sea within the EU. It is, therefore, the main objective of this chapter to demonstrate potential ambiguities inherent in certain provisions of the Athens Convention designed to define its scope. The author also intends to make recommendations as to how these ambiguities can be addressed.

11.6 The second theme which the author intends to develop throughout this chapter is to attract attention to a possible conflict between the Athens Convention and a particular domestic legislation. Recent case law has demonstrated that certain provisions of the Package Travel, Package Holidays and Package Tours Regulations 1992[18] might be, in fact, in conflict with the Athens Convention and if this proves to be the case the Package Regulations might act as an indirect limit to the Athens regime. Admittedly, this potential conflict will be precluded if the Athens Convention is implemented into the legal system of the Community by the proposed Regulation,[19] but until that day comes any clash between two legal regimes has the potential of creating uncertainty as to the scope of the Athens Convention. Bearing

---

16. The Legal Committee of the International Maritime Organisation at its 92nd session in Paris in October 2006 adopted Guidelines for the implementation of the Athens Convention 2002. The Guidelines recommend that states which ratify, approve or accede to the Athens Convention 2002 include a reservation or declaration to the same effect concerning a limitation of liability for carriers and a limitation for compulsory insurance for acts of terrorism, taking into account the current stage of the insurance market. It has to be mentioned that in reaching this compromise the work of the IMO Correspondence Group led by Professor Erik Røsæg has been instrumental. An official version of the Guidelines can be found at the web-site of the Correspondence Group, *http://folk.uio.no/erikro/WWW/corrgr/index.html#NYHET* (last tested on 31 December 2006).

17. See Griggs, P. J. S., "Obstacles to Uniformity of Maritime Law", in (2003) *Journal of Maritime Law and Commerce* 191 at p. 207.

18. SI 1992/3288, as amended by SI 1995/1648 and SI 1998/1208, hereinafter referred to as the Package Regulations 1992.

19. It is an established principle of the EC law that national courts are required to give immediate effect to the provisions of directly effective EC law, i.e. regulations, in cases which arise before them, and to ignore or to set aside any national law (of whatever rank) which could impede the application of EC law. See, for example, *Factortame Ltd v Secretary of State for Transport (No. 2)* [1991] 1 A.C. 603.

in mind that the Package Regulations are designed to implement an EC Directive, it is possible that similar interpretation difficulties might also arise in the other EU jurisdictions. The author is of the opinion that the legal position between the Athens regime and the Package Regulations 1992 requires a thorough scrutiny and this will form the subject-matter of the debate in the second part of this chapter.

THE ATHENS CONVENTION 2002 – A MAJOR STEP TOWARDS UNIFORMITY WITHIN THE EU?

11.7 The main provision of the Athens Convention 2002 designed to determine in which instances the Athens regime will apply is Article 2(1), which reads:

"This Convention shall apply to any international carriage if:
  (a) the ship is flying the flag of or is registered in a State Party to this Convention, or
  (b) the contract of carriage has been made in a State Party to this Convention, or
  (c) the place of departure or destination, according to the contract of carriage, is in a State Party to this Convention." [20]

Obviously, the meaning of terms such as "ship" and "contract of carriage" will play a crucial role in identifying the scope of the Athens regime. The Convention itself attempts to define these terms.[21] It is, however, the view of the author that a certain degree of controversy and ambiguity surround the definitions provided in the Convention which might lead to inconsistent interpretations in various jurisdictions. It is intended to illustrate the shortcomings of relevant provisions in this chapter.

11.8 The task of ascertaining the scope of the Athens Convention cannot be complete without considering provisions of the Athens Convention which deal with types of loss recoverable once the liability of the carrier is established.[22] Two provisions call for special mention in this context. Article 1(7) indicates that "loss of or damage to luggage" includes pecuniary loss resulting from the luggage not having been redelivered to the passenger within a reasonable time after the arrival of the ship on which the luggage has been or should have been carried, but does not include delays resulting from labour disputes. It will be appreciated by the reader that the definition provided leaves a lot to be desired in terms of clarity and precision. In similar fashion, Article 3 allows passengers to recover the loss suffered as a result of death or personal injury, but offers very little in terms of defining the meaning of "personal injury" apart from indicating that for the purposes of this Article loss shall not include punitive or exemplary damages.[23] Possible meanings

---

20. The proposed Regulation incorporates Article 2(1) of the Athens Convention 2002, but extends the scope of application to domestic carriage. Article 2 of the proposed Regulation reads:
  "The Regulation shall apply to any international or domestic carriage, by sea or inland waterway, if:
    (a) the ship is flying the flag of a Member State;
    (b) the contract of carriage has been made in a Member State; or
    (c) the place of departure or destination, according to the contract of carriage, is in a Member State."
21. See Article 1 of the Athens Convention 2002.
22. Even though the Athens Convention is, *prima facie*, applicable to a particular carriage contract, the claimant passenger will not be able to recover unless he can demonstrate that the type of loss is one which is recoverable under the Athens regime.
23. See Article 3(5)(d) of the Athens Convention 2002.

which can reasonably be attributed by courts to these provisions of the Convention will also be explored in this chapter.

(a) Ship

11.9 One of the pre-conditions for the application of the Athens regime is that the carriage of passengers and their luggage is performed on a ship. Article 1(3) defines the ship for the purposes of the Athens Convention as a "sea-going vessel, excluding an air-cushion vehicle". The definition clearly excludes air-cushion vessels, such as hovercraft, from the scope of the Athens Convention[24] and indicates that only sea-going vessels will come under the scope of the Athens regime. At common law, the region in which the ship operates is the main factor in determining whether a vessel is sea-going or not. In *Salt Union Ltd v Wood*,[25] a steamer used to carry salt upon the rivers Weaver and Mersey from Windsor to Liverpool was held to be a non sea-going vessel as the steamer never set out to go anywhere other than inland waters.[26] It looks, therefore, that the question whether a ship is sea-going or not depends wholly on the geographical area in which she is operated and not her capability of proceeding to sea. It naturally follows that a vessel operated within a harbour to provide sight-seeing tours for tourists will possibly not be regarded as sea-going. It is, on the other hand, possible that courts in another jurisdiction might attribute a more liberal meaning to the term "sea-going" and bring a ship used for harbour trips under the scope of the Convention. The distinction between sea-going and non sea-going vessels will not be one of much utility within the EU considering that the proposed Regulation intends to extend the scope of the Athens Convention to cover carriage in inland waterways as well.[27] However, in other states which have incorporated the Athens regime into their legal system, valuable court time might be required to determine the meaning of sea-going, which has not been clarified in the Convention itself.

11.10 No further guidance has been provided in the Convention as to the physical attributes a craft should carry to be considered as a "ship".[28] Therefore, one must turn to general maritime law in search of an appropriate definition of the term "ship". As far as English maritime law is concerned, the most general definition of the term can be found in section 313 of the Merchant Shipping Act (MSA) 1995, which indicates that the term "ship" includes every description of vessel used in navigation. A close reading of this section reveals that when assessing whether a craft/object falls under the definition of the "ship" under the MSA 1995, three

---

24. In the UK, the rights of hovercraft passengers and their baggage are covered by the Carriage by Air Act 1961 as modified by Schedule 1 to the Hovercraft (Civil Liability) Order 1986 (SI 1986/1305), as amended by the Hovercraft (Civil Liability) (Amendment) Order 1987 (SI 1987/1835).

25. [1893] 1 Q.B. 370.

26. See also *Union Steamship Co. of New Zealand Ltd v Commonwealth* (1925) 37 C.L.R. 130 and *Kirmani v Captain Cook Cruises Pty Ltd (No. 1)* (1985) 159 C.L.R. 351.

27. The extension of the Athens regime to inland waterways would impliedly repeal the requirement that a ship must be sea-going.

28. The position is different under some other international conventions. For example, in the International Regulations for Preventing Collisions at Sea 1972 a vessel is defined (Rule 3(a)) as including every description of "water craft … used or capable of being used as a means of transportation on water".

factors must be borne in mind. First, the use of the word "includes" is a clear indication that the definition is not exhaustive and can be flexible to accommodate new types of craft. Second, factors such as the shape, construction of the craft/object in question are not decisive in defining what a "ship" is. Last but not least, the definition of ship under this section is restricted to vessels which are "used in navigation". Over the years, British judges have equated navigation with controlled/planned travel over the water[29] and set their face against classifying crafts used purely for pleasure purposes, i.e. messing about in boats, as vessels capable of navigation.[30]

11.11 Against this background, it is debateable whether a British court would classify a sailing dinghy as a ship as these crafts are essentially used for pleasure purposes. In similar vein, it was held in *McEwan v Bingham (t/a StudlandWatersports)*[31] that a 17ft inflatable banana raft which was towed in a bay by a marine assault craft was not a vessel for the same reason.[32] No doubt the outcome in these cases is in line with the legal precedent set, but one cannot help thinking about the position of members of public who purchase tickets from operators of this kind of crafts especially at holiday resorts. It looks like, at least in Britain, their carriage contract will not come under the Athens Convention, even though the regime is extended to apply to carriage in inland waterways due to the fact that these craft will not be regarded as ship from the point of view of English maritime law. That said, the outcome might be different in other European jurisdictions depending on the definition afforded to the term "ship".[33] Even in certain common law jurisdictions courts have been more liberal in their approach when defining the term "ship". For instance, New Zealand courts found a kayak[34] and a dinghy[35] to be ships.[36] In Canada, ships include a jet boat used on a lake 3½ miles long[37] and a 32-foot pleasure craft.[38]

11.12 Therefore, there is a genuine possibility that in case of an accident, passengers who purchase a ticket for a ride on an inflatable raft in Britain will be treated differently compared to those who decide to enjoy their ride say in the Mediterranean coast of France. One way of addressing this anomaly is to provide a comprehensive definition of the term "ship" in the proposed Regulation indicating physical attributes a ship should carry. The author sees no difficulty in treating passengers having a ride on various crafts for pleasure purposes similar to passengers using vessels for transportation purposes. Whether it is for pleasure purposes or not, any passenger on board of a ship/craft is exposed to maritime perils, which are rather distinct from any peril encountered on land.

---

29. *Steedman v Schofield* [1992] 2 Lloyd's Rep. 163 and *R. v Goodwin* [2005] E.W.C.A. Crim. 3184; [2006] 1 Lloyd's Rep. 432.
30. *Curtis v Wild* [1991] 4 All E.R. 172.
31. Unreported, decided by the County Court (Hove) on 28 July 2000.
32. Whether the raft could be considered as part of a ship is also an interesting question, which was not debated thoroughly in the case.
33. See, for example, the decisions of the French Cour de Cassation, 6 December 1976 D.M.F. 1978, 514 where a fishing canoe was held to be a "boat".
34. *Thompson v Police*, H.C. W.N. AP250/92 21 December 1992, judgment by Gallen J.
35. *Wilson v Nightingale Trading Ltd*, High Court of New Zealand, Wellington Registry C.P. No. 88/99, August 1999, judgment by Durie J.
36. More recently, a rigid inflatable boat was held to be a ship for the purposes of limitation of liability by the Supreme Court of New Zealand in *Bikenfield v Yachting New Zealand Inc.* [2006] N.Z.S.C. 93.
37. *Chamberland v Fleming* (1984) 12 D.L.R. (4th) 688.
38. *Whitbread v Walley* (1990) 77 D.L.R. (4th) 25.

(b) Contract of carriage

11.13 The existence of a contract of carriage is vital for the application of the Athens Convention. It has been stated in Article 1(2) of the Convention that a contract of carriage is "a contract made by or on behalf of a carrier for the carriage by sea of a passenger or of a passenger and his luggage, as the case may be". It emerges from this definition that the meaning of the terms "carrier", "passenger" and "luggage" need to be identified to be able to determine whether there is a contract or carriage within the scope of the Athens Convention.

11.14 The term "luggage" has been defined in Article 1(5) of the Convention[39] and the definition seems to be straightforward and free from any controversy. The definition of the term "carrier" is, on the other hand, a bit more loosely worded and its meaning is open to deliberation. The contracting carrier is defined in the Convention as "a person by or on behalf of whom a contract of carriage has been concluded, whether the carriage is actually performed by him or by a performing carrier".[40] A performing carrier within the meaning of the Convention is "a person other than the carrier, being the owner, charterer or operator of a ship, who actually performs the whole or part of the carriage".[41] While the extent of the term "performing carrier" is reasonably clear, the question is how far the definition of the term "contracting carrier" goes. The author will turn to this question later in this chapter when the relationship between the Athens regime and Package Regulations 1992 is evaluated.

11.15 It is submitted that the definition of the term "passenger" is potentially capable of causing a reasonable degree of uncertainty. Article 1(4) of the Athens Convention 2002 defines a passenger as any person carried on a ship: (a) either under a contract of carriage, or (b) one who is with the consent of the carrier accompanying a vehicle or live animals which are carried under a contract for the carriage of goods not governed by the Convention. Bus drivers and drivers accompanying commercial vehicles are likely to come under (b). However, when it comes to identifying the meaning of "contract of carriage" under (a), practical problems may arise. Is there, for example, a contract of carriage if a passenger obtains a free ticket from the operators of the ship as a result of an advertising promotion?[42] In similar fashion, what will be the position of a passenger holding a gratuitous pass issued by reason of him being a relative of the master?

11.16 One would expect that the answer to this question will be different in common law jurisdictions compared to jurisdictions which follow the civil law tradition. In English law, it is a requirement that both parties provide consideration for the contract.[43] It is, therefore, debateable whether there will be a contract in the

---

39. Article 1(5) reads:
    "luggage means any article or vehicle carried by the carrier under a contract of carriage, excluding:
      (a) articles and vehicles carried under a charter party, bill of lading or other contract primarily concerned with the carriage of goods; and
      (b) live animals; ..."
40. See Article 1(1)(a) of the Athens Convention 2002.
41. See Article 1(1)(b) of the Athens Convention 2002.
42. Conversely, under Article 1(1) of the Convention on the Contract for the International Carriage of Passengers and Luggage by Road 1973 a passenger has been described as "any person who, in the performance of a contract of carriage made by him or on his behalf, is carried either for reward or gratuitously by a carrier".
43. *Thomas v Thomas* (1842) 2 Q.B. 851.

first instance if a person simply accepts a free ticket offered to him by the carrier or if he is carried on a gratuitous basis. That is the reason why paragraph 9 of Part II of Schedule 6 to the MSA 1995 provides that in any contract for the carriage of passengers to which the law of the United Kingdom applies, "any reference in the Convention to a contract of carriage excludes a contract of carriage which is not for reward". Despite the express wording of paragraph 9 of Part II of Schedule 6 to the MSA 1995, it is not beyond the bounds of possibility to envisage problematic cases arising in this context. For example, what happens if a ticket holder who has been given the ticket on a gratuitous basis decides later on to sell the ticket to another person?[44] Is there a contract of carriage for reward in this case on the basis that the second person has made a payment? It is possible to argue in that case that the assignment takes effect subject to equities[45] and on that basis the assignee cannot acquire a legal position which the assignor does not himself hold.

11.17 Although a carriage contract comes under the scope of the Convention under the MSA 1995 only if it is for reward, the application of this principle in practice is not entirely unproblematic. First, there is the question whether the value of the reward must reflect the costs incurred by the carrier in carrying the passenger. What springs to mind in this context is tickets purchased through certain newspapers for a nominal fare of £1–2.[46] It is trite law that while the existence of consideration is vital in English law, it does not need to be adequate.[47] On this basis, it is presumably safe to assume that there is a contract of carriage if a ticket is purchased for a nominal fee.[48] Second, it is debateable whether there is a contract of carriage in cases where remuneration does not come directly from the passenger. For example, is there a contract of carriage if ticket fares for the players of a football team are paid by one of the sponsors of the team? In this case, it is undisputable that consideration moves to the promisor (carrier), but it might be difficult to show that any consideration moves from the promisee (football players). While it might be possible to overcome this problem by arguing that the sponsor has acted as the agent of the players (passengers) in making a contract with the carrier, the legal analysis is not free of criticism. A similar problem could arise if a vessel is chartered by an individual for his guests. In fact, an arrangement of this nature was made in the case of the *Marchioness* disaster.[49] There, the boat was hired by an individual for the purpose of celebrating his birthday, but none of those whom he invited to attend the party had purchased or been issued with tickets.[50]

---

44. It should be remembered that most passenger tickets are issued on the basis that they are not transferable.

45. *Stoddart v Union-Trust* [1912] K.B. 181.

46. Some passengers who were on board the *Herald of Free Enterprise*, the cross-Channel roll on-roll off ferry which capsized near Zeebrugge on 6 March 1987, had purchased tickets through the *Sun* newspaper for a nominal fare of £1.

47. *Haigh v Brooks* (1840) 10 A. & E. 309; *Wild v Tucker* [1914] 3 K.B. 36 and *Brady v Brady* [1989] A.C. 755.

48. Service providers, i.e. entertainers or masseurs, who might be given a reduced price for the cruise are likely to be in a similar position.

49. On 20 August 1989, a dredger, the *Bowbelle*, crashed into the *Marchioness*, a pleasure cruiser on the Thames. The much bigger, heavier dredger forced the *Marchioness* under the water claiming the lives of over 50 people.

50. For a similar analysis, see Gaskell, N., "The Zeebrugge Disaster; Application of the Athens Convention 1974", in (1987) *New Law Journal* pp. 285–288.

11.18 To make matters more complicated, it transpires that even in jurisdictions which follow continental law tradition, different interpretations have been adopted as to what "a person carried on a ship under a contract of carriage" means.[51] For example, in Greece and Ireland, which are parties to the Athens Convention 1974, the Convention does not apply to a contract which is not for reward. Conversely, in another Athens Convention 1974 state, namely Croatia, the Athens regime applies even though no reward is involved in the carriage.

11.19 By considering practical problems that can arise when attempting to identify the meaning of the term "passenger", one gets the feeling that achieving uniformity within the EU in the realm of passenger liabilities might not be as straightforward as initially contemplated. The first step will be that the proposed Regulation clarifies the term "contract of carriage" with more precision taking into account the problems that have been illustrated earlier in this part.

(c) The position of passengers falling outside the Athens Regime

11.20 It is vital at this stage to point out briefly the legal position of passengers carried on board but not under a contract of carriage. The liability of a carrier towards such passengers will be decided under general principles of the relevant legal system. In England and Wales, for example, a passenger coming under this category can only succeed against a carrier by proving negligence pursuant to common law principles.

11.21 With respect to personal safety, at common law the duty owed by the carrier is to exercise due care to carry a passenger safely. This means "exercising all vigilance to see that whatever is required for the safety of passengers is in fit and proper order". There is, however, no absolute warranty of seaworthiness that is found in contracts for the carriage of goods.[52] The position is the same with respect to goods which are in the passenger's personal custody such as clothing or jewellery.[53] By way of contrast, the carrier undertakes full liability of a common carrier with respect to personal luggage of the passenger which is not in the passenger's custody. The liability of the carrier is absolute and can only be modified by contract or by the passenger's interference or assumption of control.[54]

(d) Damages recoverable

(a) Damage/loss to the luggage

11.22 Article 1(7) of the Athens Convention 2002 provides that "loss of or damage to luggage includes pecuniary loss resulting from the luggage not having been re-delivered to the passenger within a reasonable time after the arrival of the ship on which the luggage has been or should have been carried, but does not include delays resulting from labour disputes". At common law, pecuniary loss arising out of breach

---

51. See the Synopsis of the Replies to the Questionnaire sent by the CMI on Carriage of Passengers and their Luggage by Sea (The Athens Convention 1974 and its Protocols). This can be found on the website of the British Maritime Law Association: *http://www.bmla.org.uk/* (last tested on 31 December 2006).
52. *Kopitoff v Wilson* (1876) 1 Q.B.D. 377 and *Bank of Australasia v Clan Line* [1916] 1 K.B. 39.
53. *Smitton v Orient S. N. Co.* (1907) 12 Com. Cas. 270.
54. *Brooke v Pickwick* (1827) 4 Bing. 218 and *Macrow v G. W. Ry* (1871) L.R. 6 Q.B. 612.

of contract takes two main forms. First, there is what is called normal pecuniary loss, that is loss that any claimant would be likely to suffer because of the breach. Essentially, this is the difference between the value of the performance as contracted for and its value as in fact tendered. In cases where the luggage is lost this will be the value of the luggage and in cases of damage to the luggage this will be the diminution in its value. Secondly, there is consequential loss which is the expenditure or loss of profit over and above the loss of or diminution in the value of the immediate subject-matter of the contract.

11.23 Article 1(7) seems to concentrate on pecuniary loss resulting from delay in the delivery of the luggage or failure in delivery. Late delivery or non-delivery of the subject-matter of the contract would normally give rise to consequential loss as both types of breach might prevent the innocent party from acquiring a potential gain. Assuming that this analysis is correct, it follows that passengers should be able to claim consequential loss under the Athens regime in addition to normal pecuniary loss in cases where the carrier fails to re-deliver the luggage within a reasonable time[55] after the arrival of the ship on which the luggage has been or should have been carried.[56]

11.24 It should not, however, be assumed that because consequential loss forms a permissible head of damage under the Athens regime, there is no limit to types of consequential loss claims under English law. For example, if a passenger claims that delay in the delivery of his luggage has prevented him from obtaining a lucrative business contract as his luggage contained vital documents required for a tender, he needs to demonstrate that the loss is not too remote. The test of remoteness in contract cases has been formulated in *Hadley v Baxendale*[57] where it has been stated that damages are not too remote if "they are reasonably in the contemplation of both parties at the time they made the contract as the probable result of the breach".[58]

11.25 The first difficulty Article 1(7) possesses is that no attempt has been made to address the questions of causation/remoteness. Therefore, this issue has been left to the relevant national law. Bearing in mind that remoteness/causation might be addressed in a different manner in civil law countries compared to the common law countries,[59] lack of clear guidance on this point in the Convention has the potential of hindering uniformity within the EU. This is a serious consideration to take into account as the objective of the proposed Regulation is to uniform the law in

55. Naturally what is reasonable is a question of fact. It should also be noted that delay caused by labour disputes does not give rise to a pecuniary loss claim for consequential loss.

56. Such a claim will, of course, be subject to the financial limits set in the Convention. By virtue of Article 8(3) of the Athens Convention 2002 the liability of the carrier for the loss of or damage to luggage, other than the cabin luggage, shall not exceed 3375 SDR per passenger, per carriage.

57. (1854) 9 Exch. 341.

58. A higher degree of probability is required to satisfy the remoteness in contract than in tort. See Treitel, G. H., *The Law of Contract* (London: Sweet & Maxwell, 11th ed., 2003), pp. 965–968. See also *The Heron II* [1969] 1 A.C. 350.

59. For example, under the German Civil Code (*Bürgerliches Gesetzbuch*) any damage which objectively and naturally follows the breach is recoverable from the party in breach of the contract. Section 280(1) provides: "*Verletzt der Schuldner eine Pflicht aus dem Schuldverhältnis, so kann der Gläubiger Ersatz des hierdurch entstehenden Schadens verlangen.*" (If the obligor fails to comply with a duty arising under the obligation, the obligee may claim compensation for the loss resulting from this breach –author's translation.)

relation to the treatment of passengers within the EU and not simply achieving a degree of harmonisation.

11.26 The second difficulty associated with Article 1(7) is that it is debateable, to say the least, whether its scope can be extended to cover cabin luggage. The scenario which comes to mind is a passenger who claims that failure of the carrier to deliver his laptop computer kept in his cabin has cost him a very lucrative business deal as very valuable information was kept on the machine. Do consequential loss claims form a permissible head of damage as far as cabin luggage is concerned? Cabin luggage has been described under Article 1(6) as luggage which the passenger has kept in his cabin or is otherwise in his possession, custody or control. As terms "luggage" and "cabin luggage" have been described separately under the Convention and Article 1(7) makes specifically reference to loss of or damage to luggage one gets the impression that the intention of the draftsman was to exclude cabin luggage from this provision.[60]

(b) Personal injury to a passenger

11.27 Article 3 of the Athens Convention regulates under which circumstances a carrier is obliged to compensate a passenger for loss suffered as a result of the death of the passenger or personal injury suffered by him.[61] The relevant provision makes no attempt to define the meaning of "personal injury" other than stating that "loss shall not include punitive or exemplary damages".[62] An interesting question in this context is whether the term can be extended to cover a mental (psychiatric) injury sustained by a passenger in an accident in addition to a physical injury. A negative answer to this question has emerged when the issue was deliberated in the context of the Warsaw Convention 1929[63] both in the United Kingdom[64] and the United States of America.[65] However, the author wishes to attract the attention of the reader to a fundamental difference in the wording between the Warsaw and Athens Conventions. When identifying types of claims recoverable, the former one makes reference to "bodily injury", while the term "personal injury" has been chosen in the latter one. Regardless of the manner these terms are prescribed in domestic law,[66]

---

60. It should be noted that the liability regime for cabin luggage is also different than the liability regime for other luggage. See Art. 3(3) and (4) of the Athens Convention.

61. The liability regime varies depending on whether the incident is caused by a shipping incident or not. By virtue of Article 3(5)(a) shipping incident means shipwreck, capsizing, collision or stranding of the ship, explosion or fire in the ship or defect in the ship.

62. Article 3(5)(d) of the Athens Convention 2002.

63. The relevant provision, which is now expressed in Article 17 of the Montreal Convention 1999, reads:

> "The carrier is liable for damage sustained in case of death or bodily injury of a passenger upon condition only that the accident which caused the death or injury took place on board the aircraft or in the course of any of the operations of embarking or disembarking."

64. *King v Bristow Helicopters Ltd, Morris v KLM Royal Dutch Airlines* [2002] U.K.H.L. 7; [2002] 2 A.C. 628; [2002] 2 Lloyd's Rep. 745.

65. It was held by the Supreme Court in *Eastern Airlines Inc. v Floyd* (1991) 499 U.S. 530 that Article 17 of the Warsaw Convention did not permit recovery for mental injury unaccompanied by physical injury. It should be borne in mind that at the Montreal Convention diplomatic conference in 1999, Sweden's proposal that there should be a separate head of claim for mental injury was withdrawn as a result of strong resistance coming from the airline and insurance lobby.

66. See, for example, *Godley v Perry* [1960] 1 W.L.R. 9.

there is evidence to the effect that when drafting international conventions the term "bodily injury" is regarded distinct from mental injury. For example, Article 11(1) of the Convention on the Contracts for International Carriage of Passengers and Luggage by Road 1973 reads:

"The carrier shall be liable for loss or damage resulting from the death or wounding of or from any other bodily or mental injury caused to a passenger as a result of an accident connected with the carriage and occurring while the passenger is inside the vehicle or is entering or alighting from the vehicle, or occurring in connexion with the loading or unloading of luggage."

11.28 However, as the draftsman in the Athens Convention preferred the term "personal injury" to "bodily injury", there is room to argue that the drafting enables the courts to interpret this provision under Athens Convention in the widest possible way so that it would be possible in pursuance thereof to award compensation for pure mental anguish in addition to physical injury. Perhaps, the difference between the Warsaw Convention and other international conventions regulating liability of carrier in other modes of transport could be explained with the fact that at the time when the former one was formulated most states had not recognised mental anguish as a cause of action or because the possibility of mental anguish which was not accompanied by physical injury had not been contemplated scientifically.[67] The position was, of course, very different in the 1970s when the Athens Convention 1974 and the Convention on the Contracts for International Carriage of Passengers and Luggage by Road 1973 were promulgated. By that time, the jurisdiction on mental injury had been developed in most states and mental anguish had claimed a predominant place in scientific studies. It is, therefore, understandable that the international community was more accommodating in recognising mental injury as a separate and permissible head of damage.

11.29 Taking the current debate one step forward, the next question is whether a passenger could recover damages for distress or vexation following breach of the contract of carriage. As far as the English law is concerned, it has recently been confirmed by the House of Lords that this kind of damages can be awarded in a group of cases in which at least one of the "major and important" objects of the contract was to provide "pleasure, relaxation, and peace of mind".[68] It is hardly an overstatement to suggest that one of the major and important objects of a contract for a cruise in the Caribbean is pleasure and relaxation.[69] Whether the same is true for other carriage of passengers by sea contracts remains debateable. Also, there is a fine distinction between mental illness and distress caused by annoyance or irritation. It is, therefore, interesting to see how influential domestic law will prove in

67. At the start of the 20th century there were only a dozen recognized mental illnesses. By 1952 there were 192 and the 4th edition of the *Diagnostic and Statistical Manual of Mental Disorders*, published by the American Psychiatric Association in 2000, lists 374.
68. *Farley v Skinner* [2001] U.K.H.L. 49; [2002] 2 A.C. 737 at [24], *per* Lord Steyn. This principle was also followed in Canada (*Vorvis v Insurance Commissioner of British Columbia* (1989) 58 D.L.R. (4th) 193 (Canadian Supreme Court)) and also in New Zealand (*Vyrne v Auckland Irish Society Inc.* [1979] 1 N.Z.L.R. 351).
69. In *Jarvis v Swans Tours Ltd* [1973] Q.B. 233, award for damage caused by distress was made against a package-tour operator who provided accommodation falling short of the standard promised and so spoilt his client's holiday.

interpreting whether "personal injury" can be extended to cover damages for distress or vexation under the Athens Convention 2002.[70] It emerges from this debate that the term "personal injury" is capable of being given different interpretations in different EU jurisdictions which is a cause of concern for uniformity. The author feels that the proposed Regulation should take further steps in clarifying types of losses recoverable under this heading.

APPLICATION OF THE ATHENS CONVENTION TO TOUR OPERATORS

(a) The Package Regulations 1992: background and main provisions

11.30 Even though it did not form an essential part of the initial economic integration process,[71] consumer protection[72] is a phenomenon which has gained momentum within the EC since the mid-1970s.[73] An area which attracted the attention of the policy makers within the Community was package travel, holidays and tours where the relevant industry enjoyed a considerable growth in most Member States. Despite the expansion in business, differences were noted between Member States in relation to operating practices and regulations in respect of package travel, holidays and tours which required intervention of the Community not only for the purposes of consumer protection, but also to eliminate distortions of competition amongst operators established in different Member States. To this end, the Council of the European Communities adopted a Directive, the Package Travel, Package Holidays and Package Tours Directive.[74] Member States were required to implement the Directive by 31 December 1992. To this end, the UK Parliament passed the Package Regulations 1992.

11.31 The Package Regulations 1992 apply to a package contract which includes the five features expressed in Regulation 2:

(a) the contract must be sold or offered for sale in the United Kingdom;

---

70. The Supreme Court of New South Wales Court of Appeal (Australia) in *Dillon and Others v Baltic Shipping Co. (The Mikhail Lermontov)* [1991] 2 Lloyd's Rep. 155 allowed a cruise passenger to recover compensation for disappointment following sinking of her vessel due to negligent navigation. It should, however, be noted that the case did not come under the Athens Convention 1974 and so it cannot be suggested that these type of damages are recoverable under the head of "personal injury".

71. The Treaty of Rome, which was agreed in 1957, contains only five explicit references to the consumer: Article 39, 40, 85(3), 86 and 92(2)(a).

72. For a comprehensive analysis of this area of law, see Weatherill, S., *EU Consumer Law and Policy* (Cheltenham, Edward Elgar, 2nd ed., 2005).

73. The Council Resolution of 14 April 1975 (Official Journal (O.J.) 1975 C92/1) supported a preliminary programme of the European Economic Community for a consumer protection and information policy. The 1975 Resolution on the preliminary programme was followed in 1981 by the Council Resolution of 19 May (O.J. 1981 C1333/1) on a second programme of the European Economic Community for consumer protection and information policy. In December 1986, the Council adopted a Resolution (O.J. 1987 C3/1) on the integration of consumer policy in the other common policies. This was followed by the Council Resolution of November 1989 (O.J. 1989 C294/1) on future priorities for relaunching consumer protection policy. It was in the Maastricht Treaty 1992, which entered into force in 1993, that the EC was granted an explicit legislative competence in the field of consumer protection by Article 129a (now Article 153 EC).

74. 90/314/EEC.

(b) it must include at least two of the following components:
   - transport;
   - accommodation;
   - other tourist services not ancillary to transport or accommodation and accounting for a significant proportion of the package;
(c) the combination of components must be pre-arranged;
(d) the combination must be sold or offered for sale at an inclusive price; and
(e) each service must cover a period of more than 24 hours or include overnight accommodation.[75]

11.32 The purpose of the Package Regulations 1992 is to set out minimum standards concerning the information provided to the consumer,[76] formal requirements for package travel contracts,[77] to provide compulsory rules applicable to the contractual obligations, such as cancellation by organiser and withdrawal by consumer,[78] modification,[79] liability of package tour organiser and retailers,[80] and to achieve an effective protection for consumers in case of insolvency of the tour organiser.[81]

11.33 Regulation 15 is the main provision in the Package Regulations 1992 dealing with the liability of tour operators and retailers and it is this provision which might potentially be in conflict with the Athens Convention 1974. Before embarking on an analysis of the relationship between these two legal instruments, it is essential to set out the scope of Regulation 15 in clear terms. Regulation 15 reads:

"(1) The other party to the contract is liable to the consumer for the proper performance of the obligations under the contract, irrespective of whether such obligations are to be performed by that other party or by other suppliers of services but this shall not affect any remedy or right of action which that other party may have against those other suppliers of services.

(2) The other party to the contract is liable to the consumer for any damage caused to him by the failure to perform the contract or the improper performance of the contract unless the failure or the improper performance is due neither to any fault of that other party nor to that of another supplier of services, because–
   (a) the failures which occur in the performance of the contract are attributable to the consumer;
   (b) such failures are attributable to a third party unconnected with the provision of the services contracted for, and are unforeseeable or unavoidable; or

---

75. For a detailed analysis on the scope of Regulations see, Grant, D., & Mason, M., *Holiday Law* (London: Sweet and Maxwell, 3rd ed., 2003), pp. 33–53.

76. Regulation 5 sets out the minimum information to be contained in brochures and Regulation 7 identifies minimum information to be given to the consumer, such as visa requirements and health formalities, before the contract is concluded. Regulation 8, on the other hand, deals with the information that has to be provided after the formation of the contract but before the commencement of the journey.

77. See Regulation 9 of the Package Regulations 1992.

78. See Regulation 13 of the Package Regulations 1992.

79. See Regulations 10 and 14 of the Package Regulations 1992.

80. Regulation 4 of the Package Regulations 1992 provides:

"(1) No organiser or retailer shall supply to a consumer any descriptive matter concerning a package, the price of package or any other conditions applying to the contract which contains any misleading information.

(2) If an organiser or retailer is in breach of paragraph (1) he shall be liable to compensate the consumer for any loss which the consumer suffers in consequence."

Regulation 15 is another provision setting out the civil liability regime for tour organisers and retailers.

81. Regulation 16 of the Package Regulations 1992 dictates that the tour operator must provide evidence of security for the refund of money paid over and for the repatriation of the consumer in the event of insolvency.

(c) such failures are due to–

    (i) unusual and unforeseeable circumstances beyond the control of the party by whom this exception is pleaded, the consequences of which could not have been avoided even if all due care had been exercised; or

    (ii) an event which the other party to the contract or the supplier of services, even with all due care, could not foresee or forestall.

(3) In the case of damage arising from the non-performance or improper performance of the services involved in the package, the contract may provide for compensation to be limited in accordance with the international conventions which govern such services.

(4) In the case of damage other than personal injury resulting from the non-performance or improper performance of the services involved in the package, the contract may include a term limiting the amount of compensation which will be paid to the consumer, provided that the limitation is not unreasonable.

(5) Without prejudice to paragraph (3) and paragraph (4) above, liability under paragraphs (1) and (2) above cannot be excluded by any contractual term."

11.34 The provision indicates that the other party to the contract (usually the tour operator)[82] is liable to the consumer if there has been failure or improper performance of the contract. It has been argued before the Court of Appeal in *Hone v Going Places Leisure Travel Ltd*[83] that Regulation 15 creates an absolute liability on the part of the tour operator who is liable unless he can show that the cause of loss is attributable to factors expressed in Regulation 15(2)(a), (b) and (c). However, the Court of Appeal rejected this argument by holding that terms of the contract need to be looked at in order to assess whether there has been a failure in the performance of the contract or improper performance. Put another way, the consumer still needs to prove non-performance or improper performance of the contract so as to hold the tour operator liable under Regulation 15.[84] The exceptions expressed in Regulation 15(2)(a), (b) and (c) come into play if the tour operator assumes obligations under the contract which are themselves not fault-based.[85] Last, but not least, it should be noted that Regulation 15(3) to (5) regulate under which circumstances a tour operator can exclude his liability.

(b) The legal position of a tour operator/carrier under the Athens Convention?

11.35 From the perspective of contract law, identifying the legal position of a tour operator might not be as straightforward as it initially seems. In most cases, the role of a tour operator is to arrange services to be provided by others, i.e. carrier and

---

82. By virtue of Regulation 2(1) the other party to the contract means the party, other than the consumer, to the contract, that is, the organiser or the retailer, or both, as the case may be. It is not entirely clear when liability should attach solely to the organiser and when to the retailer as well. One possibility is that the liability could vary depending on the facts of the case. See, Grant, D., & Mason, M., *Holiday Law* (London: Sweet & Maxwell) (3rd ed., 2003) p. 59. In *Hone v Going Places Leisure Travel* [2001] E.W.C.A. Civ. 947, a travel agent which led the consumer to believe that it was in fact the organiser for the package, was held out as an organiser under Regulation 15.

83. [2001] E.W.C.A. Civ. 917.

84. In the absence of any contrary intention, the normal implication will be that the services contracted for will be rendered with reasonable care and skill. It is trite law that in the absence of any express clause standards are judged against the standards available in the country in which the accident happened at that time: *Wilson v Best Travel* [1993] 1 All E.R. 353; *Singh v Libra Holidays Ltd* [2003] E.W.H.C. 276 and *Healy v Cosmoair plc* [2005] E.W.H.C. 1657.

85. *Hone v Going Places Leisure Travel Ltd* [2001] E.W.C.A. Civ. 917, at [15–20], *per* Longmore, L.J.

holiday resort. It can, therefore, be concluded that a tour operator normally acts as the agent of other service providers.[86] This was certainly the case before the introduction of the Package Regulations 1992 and if things went wrong during transit or while a consumer's stay at a holiday resort, a tour operator could only be sued by consumers on the basis that he failed to exercise reasonable care and skill in selecting the relevant service provider(s) in question. Of course, there was always the possibility that a consumer could directly sue the carrier or holiday resort under the relevant contract. As one would appreciate, bringing an action directly against the relevant carrier or holiday resort can generate practical problems for the consumer in addition to legal difficulties that can arise in terms of jurisdiction and choice of law.

11.36 Regulation 15 of the Package Regulations is designed with a view to assisting consumers in this regard and it makes tour operators (and in some cases the travel agents) liable to consumers for failure or improper performance of the package contract.[87] Therefore the Package Regulations 1992 enables consumers to bring an action in the UK against a tour operator, say for defective performance of an air carrier. However, a consumer might decide to sue the carrier or owner of the holiday resort in addition to the tour operator. In that case, the consumer's case against the carrier would not normally come under the Package Regulations 1992 but instead it might be subject to an international regime, such as the Warsaw Convention 1929. *Akehurst & Ors v Thomson Holidays Ltd & Britannia Airways Ltd (The Gerona Air Crash Group Litigation)*[88] provides a good illustration on this point. There, Mr Akehurst purchased a package holiday from Thomson Holidays Ltd (the tour operator). The package included a flight from Cardiff to Gerona in Spain. The flight was performed by Britannia Airways Ltd (the carrier). The plane suffered a crash at the time of landing and ran off the runway following a missed approach in poor weather conditions. Mr Akehurst and other claimants sued the carrier and tour operator for physical and/or psychological injury and loss suffered by them as a result of the way in which the aircraft landed. The same injury, loss and damage were claimed against each defendant. Following the consolidation of two actions, a group litigation order was made. The trial judge dealt with the carrier's liability first. There was no doubt that the carriage contract was subject to the Warsaw Convention 1929 as amended at the Hague in 1955 and as incorporated into the law of England and Wales, which was in force at the time of the litigation. The carrier admitted that the crash was an "accident" for which it was liable to the claimant under Article 17; however, it was argued that the carrier was not liable to pay for psychological injuries as the scope of "bodily injury" in Article 17 could not be extended to cover this type of loss in the light of the decision of the House of Lords in *King v Bristow Helicopters Ltd* and *Morris v KLM Royal Dutch Airlines*.[89] Agreeing with the contention of the

---

86. There have been instances in which a tour operator has been held out to be contracting as the principal who undertakes to supply the services. In each case, it is a matter of construction to determine into which category the contract falls. It emerges from the case law that the impression a tour operator gives to the other part of the contract by his actions is an important element in identifying his legal position: see, for example, *Wong Mee Wan v Kwan Kin Travel Services Ltd and Ors* [1996] 1 W.L.R. 38.

87. It should be noted that the Regulation 15 does not affect any remedy or right of action which the tour operator may have against those other suppliers of services.

88. Unreported, decided by the County Court (Cardiff) on 6 May 2003.

89. [2002] U.K.H.L. 7; [2002] 2 Lloyd's Rep. 745.

carrier, the judge considered whether the tour operator could be liable to pay compensation for such injuries. The tour operator decided to fight the case on the ground that its contract with the claimants incorporated Article 17 of the Warsaw Convention which acted as a bar to any claim for psychological injuries. The construction point went against the tour operator and it was held that the Warsaw regime had not been incorporated into the contract.

11.37 One interesting point emerging from the *Akehurst* litigation is that the tour operator did not go down the route of arguing that it was the "carrier" within the meaning of the Warsaw Convention 1929. This was possibly a sensible litigation strategy on the part of the tour operator bearing in mind that the definition of the term "carrier" which appears in the Warsaw Convention 1929[90] is not a broad one. This can be regarded as an attempt on the part of the draftsmen to restrict the ability to issue tickets to passengers solely to air carriers. It follows that under the Warsaw regime, it is unlikely that a tour operator will carry the status of the carrier.

11.38 At this juncture, the fundamental question is whether this analysis can be extended to sea carriage or would the position of a tour operator be different under the Athens regime? If, for example, the package contract included a cruise to the Bahamas and the consumer suffered from food poisoning as a result of the food he was served during the cruise, identifying the liability regime which will form the legal basis for the consumer's claim might be a challenging task. Naturally, one would expect a claim of this nature to be subject to the Package Regulations 1992. However, assuming that the ticket was purchased in the UK and the cruise included an international voyage, it is arguable that the rights of a passenger should be determined by the Athens Convention 1974, which applies in the UK by force of law. The controversy arises as a result of the manner in which the term "carrier" has been described in the Athens Convention 1974.

11.39 Article 1 of the Athens Convention provides:

"(a) 'carrier' means a person by or on behalf of whom a contract of carriage has been concluded, whether the carriage is actually performed by that person or by a performing carrier;

(b) 'performing carrier' means a person other than the carrier, being the owner, charterer or operator of a ship, who actually performs the whole or a part of the carriage."

The performing carrier is the party who, by virtue of authority from the carrier, performs the whole or part of the carriage,[91] and it is obvious that a tour operator is unlikely to find himself wearing the shoes of the performing carrier. This, however, leaves the question wide open whether a tour operator could come under the definition of the term "contracting carrier". The *travaux préparatoires* do not provide any assistance on this point indicating the possibility that the issue did not occupy the minds of draftsmen perhaps because at the time the Athens Convention 1974 was drafted the package travel industry was in still its infancy. There is also no guidance in the text of the Convention in this regard. It must be, however, noted that the definition of the term "carrier" in the Convention is very wide which suggests that

---

90. See Article 3 of the Warsaw Convention 1929.

91. By virtue of Article 4, if the performance of the carriage or part thereof has been entrusted to a performing carrier, the carrier and performing carrier are liable jointly and severally for the part of the carriage performed by the performing carrier.

anybody who has been involved in the process of establishing a contractual relationship with the passenger could possibly, regardless of his status, be regarded as the contractual carrier.[92] Considered from this angle, it is possible that the definition of the term "carrier" might include tour operators under the Athens regime.[93] Also, one should not lose sight of the fact that the rationale behind the liberal definition of the term "carrier" in the Convention was to enable passengers to find a contracting party with ease to bring their claims against without going through the difficulty of tracing the performing carrier who might be based in a foreign jurisdiction. Therefore, it is likely that tour operators were intended to be drawn into the equation by the draftsmen of the Convention.

11.40 Recent judicial view concurs with this analysis. In *Lee and Another v Airtours Holidays Ltd and Another*, His Honour Judge Hallgarten Q.C. made the following observation[94]:

"... I do not consider that the [Athens] Convention is concerned with status at all: there is nothing which confines its application to concerns in the nature of shipping lines. Basically what emerge from the Convention are two categories:

(1) the carrier – being the person by or on whose behalf a contract of carriage has been concluded; and

(2) the performing carrier – being the person to whom such carriage is entrusted.

As I see it, the essential question is whether, as between the claimants and the [tour operators] there was a contract of carriage by sea: if so then the [tour operators] assumed responsibilities as carriers, with the word carrier being used in a non-technical sense... The matter is very largely one of impression, but for my part I see no difficulty in saying that the [tour operators] were carriers, in that the agreement with the claimants included obligations pertaining to carriage by sea and to that extent, it represented a contract for the carriage by sea of the claimants by the [tour operators] ..."

11.41 In similar vein, in *Norfolk v My Travel Group plc*[95] the judgment of the court seems to be based on the assumption that the tour operator was the carrier within the meaning of the Athens Convention 1974 and this point was not contested by any of the parties.

(c) Athens Convention or Package Regulations 1992?

11.42 Ascertaining the nature of the relationship between the Athens Convention 1974 and Package Regulations 1992 poses a genuine challenge especially if a tour operator can be viewed as the contracting carrier from the perspective of the Athens Convention 1974. Which regime will be the legal basis when identifying rights and liabilities of a tour operator? On one hand, there is an international regime, which has been given the force of law in the UK (and no doubt in several other EU jurisdictions), and, on the other hand there is a domestic legislation, which is designed to give effect to an EC Directive and focuses its concentration on tour operators (and retailers). Regulation 15(3) of the Package Regulations 1992 makes matters more mystifying by stating:

92. See Article 1(1) of the United Nations Convention on the Carriage of Goods by Sea (Hamburg Rules) 1978 which provides a similar definition of the term "carrier".
93. See Griggs, P., Williams, R., & Farr, J., *Limitation of Liability for Maritime Claims* (London: Informa Professional, 4th ed., 2005), p. 97.
94. [2004] 1 Lloyd's Rep. 683 at [32].
95. [2004] 1 Lloyd's Rep. 106.

"In the case of damage arising from the non-performance or improper performance of the services involved in the package, the contract may provide for compensation to be limited in accordance with the international conventions which govern such services." [96]

In this part, it is intended to analyse various approaches which can be taken to address a potential conflict between these two legal regimes.

(a) Supremacy of the Package Regulations 1992?

11.43 Recognizing the supremacy of the Package Regulations 1992 over the Athens Convention 1974 is a possible way of avoiding any conflict between these two regimes. In fact, this view was advocated in *Lee and Another v Airtours Holidays Ltd and Another* by His Honour Judge Hallgarten Q.C.[97] and is based on the understanding that in so far as a domestic legislation is in conflict with a regulation made under section 2(2) of the European Communities Act 1972, the latter should prevail.[98] This approach can also be supported by the Latin maxim of *"lex specialis derogat lex generalis"*[99]: the Package Regulations 1992 being the legislation designed particularly to regulate the liability of tour operators should take precedence over the provisions of the Athens Convention 1974 which are more general in character as far as the position of tour operators are concerned.

11.44 Adopting this approach will mean that the liability regime of the Athens Convention 1974 should be disregarded and Regulation 15(1) and (2) of the Package Regulations 1992 will determine the liability of a tour operator. An interesting question which arises in this context is what happens to other ancillary provisions of the Athens Convention, i.e. limitation provisions and provisions dealing with valuables, once the liability provisions of the Convention are overridden by the Package Regulations 1992. His Honour Judge Hallgarten Q.C. is convinced that once the liability regime of the Convention is set aside, other provisions of the Convention dealing with limitation and valuables should also be disregarded. This is, in fact, a rational standpoint considering that the main objective of the Athens Convention is to provide a liability regime for passengers and ancillary provisions take colour from this context. If the underlying context is overridden, there should certainly be no role to play for the ancillary provisions. Taking this approach to its natural conclusion, the only role the Athens Convention 1974 could play is to give the tour operator the opportunity to incorporate one particular aspect of the Athens Convention – that in relation to limitation of liability – which, absent Regulation 15(3) of the Package Regulations 1992, would be wholly inapplicable.

11.45 The author is of the opinion that the approach advocated in *Lee v Airtours* is open to criticism on several grounds.

---

96. The Regulations do not actually specify which international conventions are being referred to. However, the Preamble to the Directive 90/314/EEC does refer to the Warsaw Convention on Carriage by Air, the Berne Convention on Carriage by Rail, the Athens Convention and the Paris Convention on the Liability of Hotelkeepers.

97. [2004] 1 Lloyd's Rep. 683 at [20].

98. It was held in *Hunt v London Borough of Hackney and other cases* [2002] E.W.H.C. 195 (Admin.); [2002] 3 W.L.R. 247 that regulations made under s.2(2) of the European Communities Act 1972 could lawfully amend an Act of Parliament. The Act in question was the Weights and Measures Act 1985.

99. When two or more laws contradict, the more specific law has precedence over the general law.

(i) Article 14 of the Athens Convention 1974 stipulates that no action for damages for the death of or personal injury to a passenger, or damage to luggage, can be brought against a carrier or performing carrier otherwise than in accordance with this Convention. Giving priority to the Package Regulations 1992 over the Athens Convention 1974 will be inconsistent with this provision, which has the force of law in the UK. Hobhouse J. in *R. G. Mayor (t/a Granville Coaches) v P & O Ferries Ltd and Others (The Lion)* [100] seems to reinforce the predominance of the Athens regime by indicating that it is a scheme which imposes its provisions as a matter of law upon the parties. [101]

(ii) There is no provision in the Package Regulations 1992 suggesting that the Regulations intend to restrict the application of any international regime. To the contrary, Regulation 15(3) intends to regulate the extent tour operators could make use of limitation provisions available in various international conventions which govern the services performed by other parties, e.g. carriage of passengers.

(iii) The current liability regime under the Athens Convention 1974 is more claimant friendly in the sense that for personal injury and death claims arising from or in connection with the shipwreck, collision, stranding, explosion or fire or defect in the ship, the fault or neglect of the carrier is presumed. [102] On the other hand, under the Package Regulations 1992, if the liability is contested, the claimant (consumer) is expected to prove that personal injury or death has arisen as a consequence of "improper performance" of the contract in accordance with Regulation 15(2). Similarly, the Athens Convention 2002 will introduce not only a strict liability regime up to 250,000 SDR for personal injury and death claims caused by a shipping incident, [103] but also will give the claimant an option to bring a direct claim against the insurer of the carrier. [104] It is, therefore, clear that the legal position of consumers will be sacrificed to a large extent if the Package Regulations 1992 are given priority over the Athens Convention 1974. It is submitted that this is against the spirit of the EC Directive, which has been designed to be a consumer protection measure. In this context, it is worth remembering that Article 8 of the relevant Directive enables Member States to adopt more stringent provisions in the field to protect the consumer. One could argue that liability provisions of the Athens Convention, which provide a more consumer-friendly regime, should be regarded as the kind of measures alluded to by Article 8 of the Directive.

(b) Partial qualification of the Athens Convention?

11.46 Another method of reconciling these two regimes is to proceed on the basis that the liability of a tour operator is regulated by the Athens Convention 1974 as long as there is no conflict between the Athens regime and the Package Regulations

---

100. [1990] 2 Lloyd's Rep. 144.
101. *Ibid.*, 153.
102. See Article 3(3) of the Athens Convention 1974.
103. See Article 3(1) of the Athens Convention 2002.
104. See Article 3(10) of the Athens Convention 2002.

1992. The only provision in the Package Regulations 1992 which is seemingly in conflict with the Athens Convention is Regulation 15(3). This provision allows a tour operator to incorporate damage-capping provisions of any international convention into his contract with the consumer. Therefore, provisions of the Athens Convention should apply to a tour operator by force of law, apart from damage capping provisions, i.e. Articles 7 and 8 of the Convention. The tour operator can, on the other hand, benefit from the limits set by Articles 7 and 8 provided an express reference to the Athens Convention is made in the contract.

11.47 It is obvious that His Honour Judge Overend proceeded on this basis in *Norfolk v My Travel Group plc*.[105] There, Mr Norfolk entered into a contract with My Travel, where the latter agreed to organise and retail a package holiday to Mr Norfolk and his wife. The package holiday included flights to and from Bristol, and a sea cruise on the motor vessel *Carousel* starting at Palma. The vessel sailed on 18 September 1999 and on 30 September 1999. Mrs Norfolk slipped on water on the floor of a lift and, as a result, suffered personal injuries. She claimed in her claim form consequential losses including losses for pain and suffering and loss of amenity, and also loss of enjoyment of the rest of her holiday. The claim form was issued on 25 September 2002 against the defendant under the Package Regulations 1992. The claimant made an admission to the effect that the defendant tour operator was the carrier within the meaning of Article 1(1) of the Athens Convention 1974.

11.48 In the light of this admission, the main contention of the defendant was that the Athens Convention 1974 applied in this case by force of law and accordingly Mrs Norfolk's claim was caught by the two-year time bar expressed in Article 16 of the Athens Convention 1974.[106] The claimants argued that the effect of Regulation 15(3) was that the Athens Convention 1974 and other international regimes should continue to apply only if they are brought to the notice of the consumer and no such notice was given in the contract. His Honour Judge Overend, however, attributing a much narrower meaning to Regulation 15(3) indicated that this provision made reference only to damage-capping provisions of the Athens Convention 1974, i.e. Articles 7 and 8, and, therefore, there was no conflict in the present case between these two regimes on the issue of time bar and accordingly the time bar provisions of the Athens Convention 1974 applied without the need for any express reference. On that basis, Mrs Norfolk's claim was held to be time-barred under the Athens Convention 1974.

(c) Supremacy of the Athens Convention in areas which it regulates

11.49 The common feature of the approaches developed in *Lee v Air Tours* and *Norfolk v My Travel* is that both introduce a degree of limitation on the scope of the Athens Convention 1974 in cases where the tour operator is also regarded as the carrier under the Convention. *Lee v Air Tours* indicates that the tour operator is

---

105. [2004] 1 Lloyd's Rep. 106.
106. The relevant provision reads:
    "(1) Any action for damages arising out of death or personal injury to a passenger or for the loss of or damage to luggage shall be time-barred after the period of two years.
    (2) The limitation period shall be calculated as follows:
        (a) in case of personal injury, from the date of disembarkation of the passenger; ..."

subject to the liability regime set out in the Package Regulations 1992 and he can benefit from the limitation provisions of an international convention provided that the relevant convention is expressly incorporated into the contract. It has been, on the other hand, suggested in *Norfolk v My Travel* that a tour operator's liability is determined by the relevant international liability regime save for the limitation provisions of that regime, which a tour operator can take advantage of only if the relevant regime is expressly incorporated into the contract.

11.50 The author finds both of these approaches unpersuasive. The Package Regulations 1992 has been designed to afford protection to consumers in their dealings with tour operators (retailers). At the time the relevant EC Directive was formulated, it was possibly not contemplated by the draftsman that a tour operator could be regarded as carrier under any of the relevant conventions. And it has to be stated that a tour operator is unlikely to be regarded as carrier under most international carriage regimes. The rationale of Regulation 15(3) is, therefore, to restore the balance between a tour operator and his supplier (e.g. air carrier) by allowing the former to limit his liability to the extent his supplier could under the relevant international regime. The situation could conceivably arise where the tour operator was held liable under the Regulations for the fault of his supplier, i.e. air carrier, and would have to pay full compensation whereas the supplier himself would be able to limit his liability under the Warsaw or Montreal regime even though he was at fault. Regulation 15(3) gives the opportunity to the tour operator to take advantage of the limitation provisions in the relevant carriage contract by expressly incorporating the Convention into his contract.

11.51 If, however, it is the case that the tour operator could be regarded as the contracting carrier under the Athens Convention,[107] it seems that we face a situation which was certainly not foreseen by policy makers. If this possibility was not on the minds of those who were responsible for the drafting of the Directive, it is difficult to suggest that their intention was to give priority to the Package Regulations 1992 over the Athens regime. There is certainly no provision in the Package Regulations 1992 to support the view that the Regulations should be treated superior to any international liability regime. By the same token, it is irrational to argue that the same draftsmen, who could not foresee any conflict between these two regimes, nevertheless took the conscious decision of repealing international liability regimes partially by introducing Regulation 15(3). Undoubtedly, the credibility and significance of international law principles will be undermined if such a role is attributed to Regulation 15(3) through interpretation.

11.52 The author suggests that the conflict between these two legal regimes should be avoided in the following manner:

(i) In cases where the tour operator under the Package Regulations 1992 is also the contracting carrier within an international convention, such as the Athens Convention 1974, the convention regime, in areas which it regulates, should prevail. This means that liability and limitation provisions of the international regime, i.e. Athens regime, should apply regardless of the fact whether the

---

107. It should be noted that there is a possibility that two County Court decisions to this effect could be challenged at a later date.

international regime has been incorporated into the package contract or not. This course of action is in line with Article 14 of the Athens Convention 1974, which excludes other causes of action in cases where the Convention applies. It follows that any provision of the Package Regulations 1992, which is in direct conflict with the Athens Convention, e.g. Regulation 15(1), (2), (3) and (4) (as they introduce a different liability and limitation regime), is made redundant. However, other provisions of the Package Regulations 1992 remain intact. The tour operator is, for example, still under an obligation to find appropriate solutions if the consumer complains about a defect in the performance of the contract under Regulation 15(8).

(ii) On the other hand, in cases where the tour operator is not attributed the carrier status under an international convention regime, the liability regime for a tour operator is regulated entirely by the Package Regulations 1992. In that case, however, the tour operator is provided with the option of limiting his exposure to pay damages for the same limits as would have applied if he had been a carrier by Regulation 15(3) of the Package Regulations 1992.

CONCLUSION

11.53 When contract terms that derive from international regimes come under consideration in various jurisdictions, it is desirable in the interest of uniformity that their interpretation should not be rigidly controlled by domestic precedents of antecedent date, but rather that the language of the rules should be construed on broad principles of general acceptance.[108] However, over the decades it has been observed that national courts in most instances pay more attention to the views and decisions of their predecessors rather than attempting to find relevant principles of general acceptance.[109] It has been demonstrated in this chapter that the Athens Convention 2002 contains several provisions that can give rise to interpretation problems in relation to its scope.

11.54 This is not a desirable outcome, particularly in the light of the fact that the EU is currently considering to implement the Convention into the legal system of the Community through a Regulation. It is the feeling of the author that potentially 27 different interpretations can be attributed to the blurred provisions of the Convention by the courts of Member States, seriously harming uniformity in this field within the EU. Of course, it is possible that the European Court of Justice might be called in to determine the accurate legal position once the proposed Regulation has been implemented. However, surely there is sufficient time to make changes in the proposed Regulation with a view to clarifying the scope of the Athens Con-

---

108. *Stag Line v Foscolo Mango and Co. Ltd* [1932] A.C. 328, 350, *per* Lord Macmillan. See also *J. I. Macwilliam Co. Inc. v Mediterranean Shipping Co. SA* [2005] U.K.H.L. 11; [2005] 2 A.C. 423; [2005] 1 Lloyd's Rep. 347 at [44], *per* Lord Steyn.

109. Recently, for instance, the House of Lords in *Jindal Iron and Steel Co. Ltd and Others v Islamic Solidarity Shipping Co. Jordan Inc. (The Jordan II)* [2004] U.K.H.L. 49; [2005] 1 W.L.R. 1363; [2005] 1 Lloyd's Rep. 57, disregarding foreign decisions to the contrary on the meaning of Article III rule 2 of the Hague-Visby Rules, decided to follow the established common law rule that the duty to load, stow and discharge the cargo can be transferred from the shipowner to cargo interests by agreement.

vention. Taking measures to prevent complexities that might arise in the years to come is certainly a better course of action than expecting solutions to come from expensive and time-consuming litigation. It is, therefore, submitted that relevant institutions within the EU should consider the points made in this paper and make necessary clarifications in the draft Regulation with a view to achieving a real not an illusory uniformity as far as rights of passengers travelling by sea in the EU are concerned. Otherwise, one of the main achievements of the proposed Regulation will be transferring the ambiguities inherent in the Athens regime into the legal system of the Community!

11.55 Turning to the relationship between the Package Regulations 1992 and the Athens Convention, at first sight it seems that the former is capable of imposing serious limitations on the scope of the latter, especially if a tour operator is considered to be the carrier under the Athens regime. This was certainly the view of two English judges who had an opportunity to comment on the issue in the last few years. The author, however, believes that when considering an appropriate solution to the potential conflict between these two regimes it should be appreciated that any conflict was neither intended nor foreseen at the time when the Package Regulations 1992 were brought into life. The intention of the EC Directive, the driving force behind the Package Regulations, was to introduce protection for consumers who purchase package contracts from tour operators and retailers. The author, therefore, argues that any solution to this problem should take this into account and make the interest of the consumers its paramount consideration. It is clear that this will be achieved if the Athens Convention is given priority over the Package Regulations 1992 on liability matters. This will not mean that other provisions of the Package Regulations should be made redundant. In areas not regulated by the Athens Convention, provisions of the Package Regulations should still be the yardstick in determining rights and obligations of parties.

CHAPTER 12

Passenger liabilities and insurance: Terrorism and war risks

PROFESSOR ERIK RØSÆG*

INTRODUCTION

12.1 This presentation was originally given on 15 September 2006.[1] This was the day the documents[2] were submitted to IMO that would later form the basis of the compromise[3] on war and terrorism insurance under the Athens Convention on passenger liability[4] in the IMO. Albeit I was quite strongly involved in this process (the "Athens implementation negotiations"), I shall try to keep an academic distance. My purpose is primarily not to tell the news from the IMO or to describe the political process leading up to the compromise. I would rather reflect on and structure different solutions with a particular view to the further implementation of the Athens Convention.

12.2 A basis for such reflections is, of course, the study of law in relevant jurisdictions. But even more important are analysis *de lege ferenda* and the study of insurance clauses and practice. These kinds of analysis have perhaps been underestimated in legal writing.

12.3 My starting point is *not* that the more liability or the more insurance, the better. This may be the political goals of some governments. But there are limits to how much liability and how much insurance there should be, simply because there is a cost to it. And even if the cost in the first place is borne by the ship and the benefit is received by the passenger, the repercussions on the cost of the carriage may not be desirable. I will, however, not venture to analyze when insurance or liability would be desirable, but rather look upon the rules of liability and compulsory insurance set by the governments in the Athens Conventions as the target.

12.4 I will limit the discussions below to claims for death and personal injuries.

ATHENS OVERVIEW

12.5 The Athens Convention 1974 was amended by a Protocol in 2002.[5] The amended Convention is called the Athens Convention 2002; there is indeed a provi-

---

* Scandinavian Institute of Maritime Law, University of Oslo.
1. All URLs accessed 20 December 2006.
2. IMO documents LEG 92/5/2 and LEG 92/5/3.
3. The compromise, "the Athens Guidelines", is annexed to this chapter.
4. Athens Convention Relating to the Carriage of Passengers and Their Luggage by Sea 2002, hereinafter "the Athens Convention". I have collected some materials relating to the Convention and the debate leading up to it at *http://folk.uio.no/erikro/WWW/corrgr/index.html*.
5. Protocol of 2002 to the Athens Convention Relating to the Carriage of Passengers and Their Luggage by Sea 1974, hereinafter "the Athens Protocol".

sion to this effect in the Protocol.[6] In the following, the 2002 amendments will be surveyed with the view to later analyse their effects specifically on liability and insurance in respect of war and terrorism.

12.6 The most salient innovation in 2002 was the enhancement of liabilities. While the Athens Convention 1974 had a maximum liability *per capita* of SDR 46,666, the maximum under the 2002 Convention is SDR 400,000.[7] In both cases, the limits are subject to global limitation.[8] The global limits have, however, been drastically enhanced, the SDR 25 million ceiling in the 1976 LLMC has been abolished,[9] and even a State Party for passenger claims party to the 1996 LLMC can now dispense with the global limits in respect of passenger claims.[10]

12.7 This increase is a lot more than inflation. Just before the 2002 diplomatic Conference, I made the following table of the real value equivalents at that time of the nominal values of the 1974 Athens Convention and the enhanced limits in its 1990 Protocol, which never entered into force[11]:

	Nominal value (A)	Real value equivalent (B)	B in % of A
1974 Convention	46,666 SDR	World 1,322,534 SDR Developed Countries 171,369 SDR Developing Countries 38,896,111 SDR	2,834% 367% 83,350%
1990 Protocol	175,000 SDR	World 539,583 SDR Developed Countries 222,912 SDR Developing Countries 1,736,458 SDR	308% 127% 992%

12.8 The table demonstrates that the enhancement that was actually agreed at the Diplomatic Conference far exceeds an adjustment for inflation in developed countries. In developing countries, the inflation exceeds the 2002 increase, but in these countries most of the personal injury claims, unfortunately, are unlikely to reach the limits anyway.

12.9 Currency fluctuations may enhance or eliminate the effect of inflation. What matters for the liable person is, for example, how much he must use of the currency he possesses to satisfy the claims. Such fluctuations, however, vary a lot from country to country.[12]

12.10 The enhancement of the limitation amount means that the overall exposure per ship can be rather high. For a 3,000 passenger ship, the exposure is more

6. Article 15(3) of the Athens Protocol.

7. Article 7 of both Conventions. The nominal values of the 1976 Protocol to the 1974 Convention, where SDRs were introduced, are used.

8. Article 19 of both Conventions.

9. Convention on Limitation of Liability for Maritime Claims (LLMC), Article 7 in its original version and as amended by Protocol of 1996 to Amend the Convention on Limitation of Liability for Maritime Claims, 1976. In the following, I will refer to the two versions of the Convention as the 1976 LLMC and the 1996 LLMC, respectively.

10. LLMC 1996 Article 15(*3bis*). Indeed, even the Athens limits can be dispensed with under a similar rule in the Athens Convention 2002 Article 7. Together, the use of these two rules could make the liability unlimited.

11. IMO document LEG/CONF.13/8. Consumer price indices are from International Monetary Fund: *International Financial Statistic Yearbook 2001*, pp. 128–129.

12. See an example I made in respect of Norway in *http://folk.uio.no/erikro/WWW/corrgr/insurance/inflation.doc*.

than US$1.8 billion, and for a future 5,000 passenger ship the exposure would be more than US$3 billion. In comparison, the maximum liability for the very largest ULCCs[13] under the civil liability Convention for oil pollution damage,[14] including the TOPIA[15] contributions, would be less than US$550 million.[16] Even the cargo financed compensation funds under the international systems do not exceed USD 1.2 billion, and the legitimate claims after oil catastrophes like *Erika* and *Prestige* are expected to be coverable under a limit at this level. Graphically, the comparison would look like this in billion US$:

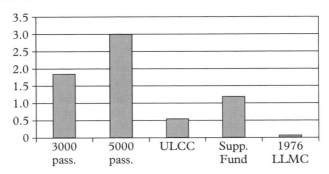

12.11 These increases in liability are so formidable that we may talk about the start of a new generation of liability conventions.

12.12 The other salient feature of the 2002 protocol is strict liability, limited to SDR 250,000 per passenger per incident.[17] Liability is made strict in situations where the burden of proof previously was reversed; that is in typical shipping incidents like stranding and collision, as opposed to hotel incidents like food poisoning. There are exceptions to the strict liability, similar to those of the CLC,[18] which are relevant to war and terrorism liability. I will therefore refer to those later on.

12.13 The third innovation in the 2002 amendments was the compulsory insurance. Carriers are required to insure passengers in so far as the carriers are liable, but not exceeding SDR 250,000 per passenger.[19] For a 3,000 passenger ship, this would mean insurance of almost US$1.2 billion, and for a 5,000 passenger ship US$1.9 billion. This far exceeds the compulsory insurance requirements under the CLC, even if one includes the TOPIA contributions (US$550 million, as above on

13. An ULCC is an Ultra Large Crude Carrier, see further *http://en.wikipedia.org/wiki/ULCC*.
14. International Convention on Civil Liability for Oil Pollution Damage, 1992; hereinafter "CLC".
15. TOPIA stands for Tanker Oil Pollution Indemnification Agreement 2006, see *http://www.ukpandi. com/ukpandi/resource.nsf/Files/STOPIATOPIA2006/$FILE/STOPIATOPIA2006.pdf*. It is a voluntary agreement whereby shipowners/P&I clubs contribute towards what would otherwise be cargo financed compensation funds for oil pollution damage.
16. The maximum amount under CLC Article V is SDR 89,770, 000. In addition there is the contribution under TOPIA Article XVI on 50% of the difference between the maximum liability under the International Convention on the Establishment of an International Fund for Compensation for Oil Pollution Damage 1992 (the Fund Convention), Article 4(4)(b) (SDR 203 million) and the maximum liability under the Protocol of 2003 to the International Convention on the Establishment of an International Fund for Compensation for Oil Pollution Damage 1992 (the Supplementary Fund Protocol), Article 4 (SDR 750 million), that is 50% of SDR 547 million = SDR 273.5 million.
17. Athens Convention, Article 3.
18. CLC, Article III (2)(a) and (b).
19. Athens Convention, Article 4*bis*.

liability). They challenge the reinsurance of the P&I pool of US$2.05 billion.[20] It is well below the maximum of the P&I policies of, say, US$5 billion,[21] but this "overspill" facility is not set up for normal use, and has in fact not been used. It is likely that the Clubs will limit the exposure for passenger claims to US$2 billion in response to the Athens Convention, increases in passenger reinsurance costs and increased awareness of passenger risks. In any event, the new insurance requirements are significant:

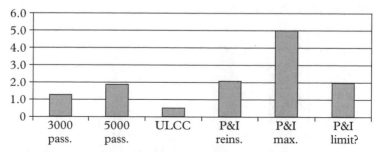

12.14 Apart from the compulsory insurance, the carrier obviously wishes to insure his additional liabilities. This far exceeds the current P&I reinsurance. But, as we shall see, the problems concerning the general P&I cover are small compared to those relating to war and terrorism insurance.

TERRORISM AND WAR EXPOSURE

12.15 The increases in liability, the strict liability and the compulsory insurance levels are themselves generally difficult to handle for the industry. But in relation to terrorism and war risks, the problem is even greater. This is my main focus in this chapter.

12.16 Somewhat surprisingly, the exposure under the 2002 Athens Convention includes some war and terrorism risks. The relevant wording has been copied from the 1969 CLC, when one certainly did not have terrorism problems like the current ones in mind. The issue was highlighted by the P&I Clubs at the Diplomatic Conference.[22] But the issue was perhaps brought to the attention of the delegates too late, and the strategy of the Clubs and shipowners was perhaps not clearly developed at this stage. Also, at this time, just a little more than a year after the attack on the World Trade Center on 11 September 2001, the governments felt a need for insurance, and it was not clear how the insurance marked would recover and develop. Anyway, the CLC wording was adopted by a large majority. Norway was one of the few states that supported the P&I Clubs.

12.17 The more important war and terrorism exposure arises when the carrier or his servants or agents do not exercise due diligence in preventing their passen-

---

20. For an overview for the pooling agreement, see James Brewer: "Extra $1bn on the cards for P&I cover," Lloyd's List 19 December 2006 *http://folk.uio.no/erikro/WWW/corrgr/presseklipp/Lloyd's%20 List_%2019dec06.pdf.*
21. *Ibid.*
22. IMO documents LEG/CONF.13/11 and LEG/CONF.13/18.

gers from being exposed to war and terrorism. In these cases, the carrier will be liable both under the strict rule and under the negligence rule.[23]

12.18 Typically, liability would arise in these cases when the carrier unnecessarily sails into or fails to leave a war zone,[24] or when the passenger control is inadequate, so that terrorists are allowed on board. In particular in the last context, there is a problem in that the obligations of the carrier are not clearly defined. The ISPS Code[25] and security arrangements made under it may set out the minimum requirements and define due diligence, but a carrier could never be sure that this will be accepted in a liability action. An attempt in the Athens implementation negotiations to define the carrier's obligations to prevent terrorism failed.[26]

12.19 In these cases, the damage is not caused by war or terrorism, but by negligence. If there is no negligence, liability for war damage is excluded; there is no strict liability.[27] However, the carrier is only exempted from terrorism-related damage if it is "wholly caused" by terrorism. This leaves room for strict liability, and means that the carrier may be liable for a security failure that is not due to his servants or agents, but, for example, to negligence of the port. He may also be liable for acts that have contributed to the failure to prevent the terrorism even when these acts do not amount to negligence. However, this could also be viewed as an extended rule of *respondeat superior*. Such strict liability is limited by the general rules on strict liability in the Convention to SDR 250,000 per person per incident.[28]

12.20 The liability for terrorism-related acts may have been somewhat extended in this way by the strict basis of liability introduced in the 2002 amendments. In particular this is so because the carrier in such cases may be considered jointly and severally liable with the terrorists in some jurisdictions – as joint tortfeasors.

12.21 At one stage of the negotiations on the implementation of the Athens Convention, the idea was introduced from government quarters that States Parties should make sure that there would be no joint and several liability between terrorists and carriers who had failed to prevent terrorism. The idea was rejected by carriers on the basis of principle. For my part, I think this option would have been better for carriers than the one finally arrived at.

12.22 The limited war and terrorism liability exposure in the Athens Convention that is outlined above is further limited by a special rule on nuclear liability.[29] If

23. Athens Convention, Article 3. The lack of due diligence makes the exemption in Article (3)(1)(b) inapplicable.

24. In these cases, the damage is arguably caused by this failure, and not by war, so that the exemption in Article (3)(1)(a) does not come into play.

25. ISPS stands for International Ship and Port Facility Security Code, 2002.

26. See, e.g., the very clear statement from the Swedish government to the IMO Correspondence Group 2 July 2004, *http://folk.uio.no/erikro/WWW/corrgr/insurance/Sweden2jul.pdf*.

27. Article (3)(1)(a).

28. Article 3(1).

29. Athens Convention, Article 20, as amended by the 2002 Protocol (see the *travail préparatoire* in IMO document LEG 80/3/4). The channelling of liability to the operator of the nuclear facility is well in line with the conventions on nuclear liability (Vienna Convention on Civil Liability for Nuclear Damage, 1963 ("the Vienna Convention"), Article II(5) and the Paris Convention on Third Party Liability in the Field of Nuclear Energy 1960, as amended by the Additional Protocol 1964 ("the Paris Convention"), Article 6(2) as well as the special convention on channelling for maritime cases, Convention relating to Civil Liability in the Field of Maritime Carriage of Nuclear Material 1971. The principle of channelling in the 1971 Convention had to be repeated in the Athens Convention in order not to be superseded by the newer rules in the new convention.

the operator of a nuclear facility is liable under rules corresponding to the nuclear liability conventions, then the carrier is not liable. This means that if nuclear material is used in a terrorism attack, the carrier would not be liable even if the damage has not been wholly caused by the attack, so that the general terrorism exemption[30] does not apply. However, the operator of a nuclear facility has no liability for war damage,[31] so the nuclear clause would not help the carrier in the very limited cases where he would have liability for not keeping passengers out of a war situation. And if the damage has been caused by mere threats of using or releasing nuclear energy, or by the use of nuclear materials with obscure or military origin, there would be no liability for an operator under the nuclear Conventions, and therefore no exemption for the carrier.

12.23 The P&I Clubs have traditionally not covered such liabilities relating to war and terrorism. In addition, it is also noteworthy that the Convention does not include some exemption clauses that are included in most, but not all, policies on liability for death and personal injuries. These clauses are certainly triggered by the fear of terrorism, but they are not limited to terrorist-related damage. These clauses are the Radioactive Contamination, Chemical, Biological, Bio-chemical and Electromagnetic Weapons Exclusion Clause and the Cyber Attack Exclusion Clause.[32]

12.24 Still, the Convention requires insurance cover also for this terrorism-related exposure. How could one go about obtaining such cover, so that the Convention could enter into force?

THE 2006 FORMAL FRAMEWORK

12.25 In the spring of 2005, it became clear for key governments that there would be a problem for carriers finding insurance for their exposure under the Athens Convention, even for the limited amounts for which insurance were required under the Convention. In particular this was a problem in respect of the war and terrorism insurance.

12.26 The IMO then, quite unprecedentedly,[33] recommended that States should ratify the Athens Convention with the reservations necessary to make the insurance requirements workable.[34] Which reservations were considered necessary will be discussed below. In this section, the formal techniques utilised will be discussed.

12.27 The reason why a reservation was preferred over renegotiation and a new Diplomatic Conference was presumably to save time, money and the compromises agreed on.

12.28 It is quite common that a State Party to a Convention makes a reservation. The international law in this respect is codified in the Vienna Convention.[35] In this

30. Athens Convention Article 3(1)(b).
31. Paris Convention, Article 9, and Vienna Convention, Article IV(3), as amended by the Protocol to Amend the Vienna Convention on Civil Liability for Nuclear Damage 1977, Article 6.
32. These clauses are reproduced in Appendix A to the Athens Guidelines, which are annexed to this chapter.
33. Groups of states have on many occasions coordinated their reservations. However, I do not know of any instance in which the international organisation under whose auspices the Convention has been agreed has recommended a reservation.
34. IMO Resolution A.988(24): *http://folk.uio.no/erikro/WWW/corrgr/insurance/988.pdf.*
35. Vienna Convention on the Law of Treaties 1969, Articles 19 *et seq.*

case, the IMO made a model Reservation, so that uniformity could be preserved despite the Reservations.

12.29 Despite the recommendation for a model Reservation, one could imagine that States Parties made their own Reservation. The Legal Committee of the IMO has instructed the IMO Secretariat, as the depositary of the Convention, to raise the issue with the State in such a case.[36] Furthermore, insurance would not be available to cover liabilities in states with separate solutions.[37] Because of this, uniformity will most likely be preserved also under the Reservations.

12.30 The model Reservation is but a model.[38] Therefore, variations of the text to achieve the same substantive ends would be allowed. This was necessary in order to accommodate traditions of different states for the drafting of reservations that apparently were quite disparate. The model even opens the way for calling the reservation a declaration[39]; a term usually used only for statements that do not purport to depart from the text to which the declaration relates – quite unlike the situation here. The French delegation explained that a "declaration" as opposed to a mere "reservation" would make implementation easier.

12.31 Prior to the drafting of the model Reservation in the Legal Committee, the IMO Assembly passed a resolution to the effect that this was the way forward.[40] For the rights of states to make a Reservation – and even a coordinated Reservation – the Resolution does not matter. I can hardly see that it provides the Legal Committee with any authority it did not already have, namely the authority to express opinions on legal matters. However, the Assembly Resolution clearly adds legitimacy to the model Reservation.

12.32 The model Reservation refers to some guidelines, and forms indeed Article 1 of these Guidelines. The idea of the Guidelines is to avoid having too much detail in the Reservation itself. However, during the negotiations more and more were moved to the Reservation to be on the safe side, often without removing it from the Guidelines and so the same point was repeated several times in the Reservation/Guidelines. This is no problem if the text is read in light of the drafting history.[41]

12.33 One advantage of the Guidelines is that they can be amended. This means that if the insurance market improves or deteriorates, the Athens Convention will not necessarily have to be amended. Such flexibility is new in liability conventions. It makes it possible to set the targets high, because one does not have to take into account possible adverse future developments of the insurance market.

12.34 It is not altogether clear exactly how the amendment procedure will work. If there is a sudden breakdown in the insurance market, governments will most likely issue insurance certificates on the basis of the best available insurance, even if the IMO Guidelines have not yet been amended. This would be contrary to the explicit undertaking in the model Reservation to adhere to the specific limits set out therein. However, the catch-all provision in the Guidelines[42] may provide the

---

36. Athens Guidelines, Article 5.
37. Athens Guidelines, Article 2.1.4.
38. See the *chapeau* of Athens Guidelines, paragraph 1.
39. *Ibid.*
40. IMO Resolution A.988(24): *http://folk.uio.no/erikro/WWW/corrgr/insurance/988.pdf.*
41. For a reading guide, see *http://folk.uio.no/erikro/WWW/corrgr/insurance/nor12oct06.html.*
42. Athens Guidelines, Article 1.10.

necessary basis. The reason why the Guidelines were drafted in this way is that there was a lot of ambivalence in respect of how flexible the Guidelines ought to be.

12.35 If the insurance market offers more insurance, it can hardly be argued that the insurance market "necessitate"[43] enhanced insurance requirements. Governments would then have to issue certificates on the basis of the existing Guidelines until they are amended, or withdraw the Reservation altogether.

12.36 When the Guidelines are revised, there is an explicit clause in the Guidelines that the Legal Committee shall determine when the amendments shall enter into force.[44] In the debate, it was suggested that the new Guidelines could apply retroactively. However, for a government that must decide whether or not to issue an insurance certificate in February, there is little help that there is a chance that the Legal Committee may amend the Guidelines with retroactive effect the following April.

12.37 If the Guidelines are amended, the states clearly are expected to implement the amendments. But they are not committed to do so, and there is no absolute undertaking to this effect in the model Reservation.[45] However, if they do not follow suit, the necessary insurance would most likely not be offered.[46]

12.38 Altogether, the model Reservation and Guidelines create a useful formal framework for modifying the requirements of the convention to realistic levels without amending it.

THE COMPROMISE – SUBSTANTIVE FRAMEWORK

12.39 Having established the formal vehicle (see the previous section), the legal Committee had to determine what to recommend in respect of Reservations in order to make the Athens Convention workable. It is likely that the priority was to make as few changes as possible. Still, one would have to be absolutely sure that the Convention would be workable, and preferably so acceptable to the industry that one would not meet major problems in the implementation phase.

12.40 The insurance market is flexible, and can arguably cover whatever risks there is demand for.[47] When legislation requires insurance, it also creates a demand, and in this sense one could always expect that compulsory insurance could be obtained. But there is a limit to how fast the insurance market should be required to reorganise to meet new demands, and what price carriers should be required to pay for compulsory insurance. Therefore, it was perhaps wise that the demands were not set too high.

12.41 All modifications recommended in the Athens Guidelines relate to war and terrorism risks in one way or another. This was perhaps easier to justify than modifications in the core parts of the passenger liability provisions. Also, the P&I Clubs that insure the non-war market are more flexible than the war insurers, partially because their maximum exposure traditionally has been higher and partially because there is no direct link between the insured amounts on the premiums, the clubs being truly mutual.

43. *Ibid.*
44. Athens Guidelines, Article 1.13.
45. *Ibid.*
46. Athens Guidelines, Article 2.1.4.
47. See IMO document LEG 92/5/2.

12.42 In the Guidelines, one has envisaged that there is a war insurer in addition to a P&I club (non-war insurer) that shall provide the basis (the "Blue Card") for the government's issue of an insurance certificate under the Convention.[48] This is strictly speaking not a part of the compromise; one could have had two insurers without the Reservation,[49] and one insurer may undertake both the role of the war insurer and the non-war insurer under the compromise.

12.43 While the issue of Blue Cards by P&I Clubs is well known to governments from the CLC, there were some questions as to who should issue the Blue Card in respect of war insurers. The idea – not expressed in the Guidelines – is that a company or similar entity made for the purpose should do it.[50] This entity will be backed by existing war/terrorism insurance, and in addition a "difference in conditions" insurance that will cover the difference between the existing insurances and the requirements under the Convention as modified by the Reservation. This is a construction well known from the practice under the US oil pollution liability legislation.[51] Also, as the Convention does not require the insurer to be a P&I Club or another well-established financial institution, this organisation of the insurance does not require regulatory intervention.

12.44 The purpose-made entity would have to purchase capacity to handle claims, and also to enter into cooperation agreements with the different insurers in the package. These are details not dealt with in the Guidelines.

INSURANCE EXCEPTIONS APPLICABLE ALL OVER

12.45 There are two exceptions relating to war and terrorism that are generally applied, and which therefore are also allowed in the Athens compulsory insurance.[52] These are:

- BioChem/ RACE clause
  Institute Radioactive Contamination, Chemical, Biological, Bio-chemical and Electromagnetic Weapons Exclusion Clause
- Cyber clause
  Institute Cyber Attack Exclusion Clause

12.46 The clauses will apply even if there is no terrorist intent, and indeed even if there is a liability arising from a nautical problem with a carriage of chemical weapons for a government. And there may be situations that are just as dangerous as the exempted risks that are not exempted – e.g. liabilities arising out of biological substances that are to be used in weapons, but are not yet incorporated in a weapon.

12.47 An alternative strategy to the one chosen in the Guidelines could have been to negotiate for less far-reaching clauses or perhaps for the dispensation of them

---

48. Athens Guidelines, Article 2, the *chapeau*.
49. This is presupposed in Athens Convention, Annex, Explanatory note 2.
50. See IMO document LEG 92/5/2.
51. See the (somewhat dated) overview in the UK P&I Club Circular 4/98: *http://www.ukpandi. com/ukpandi/Infopool.nsf/HTML/ClubCircular0498.*
52. Athens Guidelines, Articles 1.8 and 2.1.

altogether. The reason why this avenue was not chosen was perhaps that the clauses seemed to have a quite strong position in the market, and that these kinds of risks are marginal for passengers after all.

12.48 There was, however, some cover of this kind available. The P&I Clubs offered, at the time the Guidelines were adopted, a BioChem cover of US$30 million, with some exceptions.[53] This cover was, I was told, not reinsured, and it is far below the Athens limits. Also some war clubs offered insurance of these kinds of risks – but not for passenger ships.[54] Finally, a limited Dutch scheme exists without such exemptions,[55] probably because it is a limited, national scheme[56] with government involvement.[57] In the Athens context, however, one chose not to press this issue.

DIVISION WAR – NON-WAR

12.49 For the exemption clauses that are not going to apply across the board – but only in respect of war insurance – the dividing line between the two groups of risks is of paramount importance. The idea has been to follow as closely as possible the dividing line between P&I and war/terrorism insurance as established in practice. Indeed, the division not only determines the applicability of the special war/terrorism risk exemptions, but also the distinction between P&I (non-war) and war insurance.

12.50 The general P&I practice yields a clear picture:

- The exclusion of war/terrorism damage from P&I cover is commonplace, even if the carrier has contributed to it by his negligence.[58] This leaves a bit to be insured by the war/terrorism insurers under the Athens Convention.
- The wording of the terrorism exclusions from P&I cover varies, but the intention is always to exclude terrorism-related damage, even if the insured has contributed to it.[59] Again, there is part of the Athens liability that falls outside the P&I cover.

P&I clubs leave the final decision on whether the terrorism exemption shall apply to a particular damage to the club itself.[60] Obviously, such mechanism would not work

---

53. See, e.g., Assuranceforeningen Gard Appendix 2 to Circular No. 8/2005: *http://www.gard.no/portal/page/portal/GardNO/DivCommon/PrinterFriendly? v=43626*

54. Email from Mr Svein Ringbakken of the Den Norske Krigsforsikring for Skib (DNK), 4 May 2005.

55. The Dutch Terrorism Risk Reinsurance Company (NHT) *http://www.terrorismeverzekerd.nl/talen. php?page=english* offers terrorism insurance with a common limit for all claimants of €1 billion per year (US$1.3 billion; that is not quite sufficient for Athens purposes), and there are also other monetary limits (Articles 2.2 and 2.3 of the conditions). But it does cover malevolent contamination, such as "the spreading of germs of a disease and/or substances which as a result of their (in)direct physical, biological, radioactive or chemical effect may cause injury and/or impairment of health" (Articles 1.2 and 2.1 of the Conditions).

56. *Lc*, Article 1.5.

57. See the analysis of the insurance market and the government role in Brief van de Minister van Financiën an de Voorzitter van de Tweede Kamer der Staten-Generaal, Den Haag, 6 November 2002, *http://www.terrorismeverzekerd.nl/pdf/brief%20tweede%20kamer.pdf*. The Dutch government covers the upper tranche of the annual amount, €300 million (US$395 million), as a reinsurer.

58. See, e.g., Assuranceforeningen Gard: P&I and Defence cover for ships and other floating structures Rule 58(1)(a) *http://www.gard.no/iknowbase/Content/43663/Statutes%20and%20Rules%202006.pdf*.

59. *Ibid*. Some common non-war reinsurance clauses concerning terrorism are collected at *http://folk. uio.no/erikro/WWW/corrgr/insurance/terror.pdf*.

60. See, e.g., Assuranceforeningen Gard *lc* Rule 58(1)(a).

when the point is to determine the borderline between the responsibilities of two insurers.

12.51 The following definition of war/terrorism risks was agreed in the Guidelines for the purpose of distinguishing between war and non-war insurance[61]:

"War insurance shall cover liability, if any, for the loss suffered as a result of death or personal injury to a passenger caused by:
- *war, civil war, revolution, rebellion, insurrection, or civil strife arising therefrom, or any hostile act by or against a belligerent power*;
- capture, seizure, arrest, restraint or detainment, and the consequences thereof or any attempt thereat;
- derelict mines, torpedoes, bombs or other derelict weapons of war;
- *act of any terrorist or any person acting maliciously or from a political motive and any action taken to prevent or counter any such risk*;
- confiscation and expropriation;"

12.52 In order that the war insurance shall kick in, and the P&I insurers be exempted, it suffices that the damage has been "caused by" any of the listed events. Thus, even if the carrier or anyone for whom he is responsible has contributed to the incident by failing to adequately protect the passengers, this will be a matter for the war insurance.

12.53 I have added emphasis to two central clauses. The non-emphasised risks could perhaps have been covered by P&I if they were not in the traditional domain of war insurance. It is questionable whether it is really warranted to apply the special war risk exceptions (see the next section) to these risks.

12.54 The terrorism clause here only applies if the terrorists act with a political motive. The intentional damage to passengers by a madman will therefore be a P&I matter – again only if the carrier is not fully exempted because the damage was "wholly caused"[62] by the madman.

12.55 The alternatives "confiscation and expropriation" of the vessel are unlikely to cause death or personal injuries to passengers. The same may be said about "capture, seizure, arrest, restraint or detainment" of the vessel. But it is not entirely clear that the clause does not refer to capture, seizure, arrest, restraint or detainment of passengers. In many cases "capture, seizure", etc, of passengers would amount to an act of terrorism, which would be exempted from P&I coverage by the fourth point above anyway. However, if the passengers are seized in piracy or barratry, the construction of the "capture, seizure ..." clause becomes crucial.

12.56 In my view, "capture, seizure", etc, of passengers is not a war risk in this context. Piracy and barratry is not exempted from P&I cover,[63] and then there is no reason to let the special war exemptions apply. In line with this, English war insurers do not cover piracy and barratry, albeit war insurers in other markets may cover these risks.[64]

---

61. Athens Guidelines, Article 2.2; emphasis added.
62. Athens Convention, Article 3(1)(b).
63. See, e.g., Assuranceforeningen Gard *lc* Rule 58(1)(b).
64. See Peter Rogan, "Insuring the Risk of Terrorist Damage and Other Hostile Deliberate Damage to Property Involved in the Marine Adventure: An English law Perspective", in (2003) 77 Tul.L.R. 1295–1331 at p. 1303 and the Norwegian Insurance Plan §2-9 *http://www.norwegianplan.no/eng/books/plan/pch2s2.htm* with official comments *http://www.norwegianplan.no/eng/books/comm/cch2s2.htm*.

WAR/TERRORISM INSURANCE

Common arrangements

12.57 In order to determine the extent of the war/terrorism insurance under the Athens Convention, one must first analyse the insurance arrangements that are commonplace for war/terrorism liability in shipping. It can safely be assumed that risks covered by such insurance can also be covered for the purpose of the Athens Convention. Even if war/terrorism insurers usually do not issue Blue Cards or accept being sued directly by a third party, this aspect of the insurance requirement under the Athens Convention will be taken care of by the special facility established to act as the war/terrorism insurer under the scheme (see paragraphs 12.39–12.44 above).

12.58 One should bear in mind that the war/terrorism risks under the Athens convention are very marginal. The carrier has no liability for war or terrorism, only for failures to protect the passengers (see paragraphs 12.15–12.24 above).

12.59 Quite confusingly, an essential part of the war/terrorism insurance is provided via the P&I Clubs.[65] Thus, the clubs provide both war and non-war insurance relevant to the Athens Convention. However, the P&I war cover is not a part of the mutual system, and is subject to special conditions. It is, however, a part of the P&I package, and claims handling is, if what I am told is correct, carried out by the clubs.

12.60 The P&I war cover is limited to US$500 million, and presupposes that the shipowner has taken out a standard war insurance for at least the value of the vessel or US$100 million, whichever is the lower.[66] As cruise ships can be worth several hundred millions, the latter limit is highly relevant in this context.

12.61 War insurance is traditionally combined hull and liability insurance, perhaps with the same insurance amount for hull and P&I.[67] This could explain the reference to the value of the hull in the P&I cover.

12.62 There is also another connection between the hull and the liability insurance: mortgagees and others with interest in the value hull will insist that there is appropriate liability insurance in place to avoid the hull value available to them being undermined by maritime liens for liability claims.[68] However, it does not really matter whether this insurance is combined with the hull insurance or is taken out separately from the hull insurance. Indeed, the mortgagees may insist on a separate insurance to cover their indirect liability exposure via the maritime liens. This is common if the value of the hull is high.

12.63 The first tranche and the P&I tranche may together add up to US$600 million. Over and above these tranches it is not uncommon to purchase additional insurance, often in mutual war clubs.[69] For 2006, the war/terrorism P&I cover for

---

65. See, e.g., UK P&I Club Circular 5/06 *http://www.ukpandi.com/ukpandi/Infopool.nsf/HTML/Club Circular0506.*

66. *Ibid.*

67. There are exceptions. See, e.g., the Norwegian insurance Plan §15-3: *http://www.norwegianplan.no/eng/books/plan/pch15s1.htm.*

68. International Convention for the Unification of Certain Rules Relating to Maritime Liens and Mortgages 1926, Article 2 (No. 4); International Convention for the Unification of Certain Rules Relating to Maritime Liens and Mortgages 1967, Article 4(1)(iii); International Convention on Maritime Liens and Mortgages 1993, Article 4(1)(b).

69. There are links to some war clubs at *http://folk.uio.no/erikro/WWW/corrgr/index.html#ins.*

Den Norske Krigsforsikring for Skib (DNK) was US$200 million, while The Hellenic Mutual War Risks Association (Bermuda) Limited offered double that amount.[70] Apparently, the more cruse vessels there is in the portfolio, the more difficult to get high levels of reinsurance.[71] The passenger ship with the largest war/terrorist cover I have been able to verify is a major cruise ship with a cover of US$750 million.

12.64 In other cases, there are government schemes that can provide quite a lot of war/terrorism liability insurance. In the Dutch scheme, up to US$1.3 billion is covered by a combination of market insurance and government guarantees.[72] Government schemes are naturally limited to national shipping in one way or another.

12.65 At least for some shipowners, then, there is quite a lot of war/terrorism insurance available. The insurance is, however, in no event sufficient to cover the potential Athens liability for the larger vessels, and it is not generally available.

12.66 The conditions for the different kinds of war insurance contain remarkably few exceptions. Perhaps the idea is that the nature of war risks are such that there is little one can do about them anyway. Of the remaining restrictive clauses, many can be waived for an additional premium.

12.67 In the following, I will discuss the limits and restrictive clauses that one would expect to remain to be allowed in the Athens Convention in addition to the defences under the Convention itself. These would be the risks that neither the insurance that was discussed just above nor the difference in condition insurance that supplements it (discussed in paragraphs 12.39–12.44 above) would have to cover.

12.68 The idea of what the market can cover is mainly due to the research of one broker, Mr Nicholas Taylor of Marsh Ltd.[73] Other brokers were invited to participate in the development of the scheme, but decided to withdraw. Presumably, the same sources will be available to them if they wish to arrange competing schemes for Athens war insurance. But by not participating, they lost the possibility of influencing the framework until the next time the scheme is revised.

Geographic scope

12.69 A standard clause in all war insurance restricts the geographical coverage. The war insurance is not valid in areas where there is war or war is imminent, at least not unless an additional premium is paid. The policy typically refers to war zones that may change during the policy period pursuant to decision of the insurer.[74]

12.70 The Athens Convention does not allow such clauses and, apparently, because of this, the potential difference in conditions insurers did not insist on them. Presumably, one felt that as the war risks of the Athens Convention are mainly terrorism-related risks, the risks are not significantly higher in war areas than in

70. Email from Mr Svein Ringbakken of the Den Norske Krigsforsikring for Skib (DNK), 14 August 2006.
71. *Ibid.*
72. See paragraphs 12.45–12.48 above.
73. See IMO document LEG 92/5/2.
74. See, e.g., the information from Den Norske Krigsforsikring for Skib (DNK) at *http://www.wrisk. no/oslo/dnk_eng.nsf/id/8090307AEC42728A41256CEE00325CBF?OpenDocument.*

other areas. On the contrary, a terrorist would only get the maximum attention for his act if it is committed in an otherwise peaceful area. In addition, one may have considered that the States Party to the Convention mainly will be western European states, and that not many passenger ships with such a connection to these states that the Convention will apply will trade in war zones.

12.71 If necessary, the insurance under the Athens Convention could be limited to certain geographical areas if only the ship's sailing area would be restricted accordingly. Even though this issue is not addressed in the Convention, it would not make sense to insist that a vessel whose sailing certificates were restricted to the Baltic Sea should have insurance that also covers the Arabian Gulf. In this way, geographic scope clauses could in theory apply also under the compulsory Athens insurance.

Cancellation

12.72 Another standard clause in war insurance is a cancellation clause. Typically, there is a general seven days' notice clause and an automatic termination of cover in case there is a war between defined superpowers.[75] Damage caused by superpower wars is also excluded altogether.

12.73 The automatic termination of cover in the event of a war between superpowers and the corresponding exclusion are allowed by the Athens Guidelines.[76] The clause is not particularly relevant. Indeed, terrorism attacks at the outbreak of a superpower war would be extremely bad timing, and it is in connection with terrorism attacks that the Athens carrier is most likely to incur liability covered by war insurance. However irrelevant, it is a standard clause that it would be quite costly to get rid of. And from a government point of view, the focus would certainly be on issues other than passenger liability insurance in such an event.

12.74 The standard seven days' notice clause has, however, been dispensed with by insurers for the purposes of the Athens Convention. A more general 30 days' notice clause has been included instead.[77] This would give the insurers the possibility to cancel also for other reasons than risk increases, e.g. default of premium payments, which arguably would not be possible under the standard seven days' notice clause. It would, however, leave the insurers exposed in case of rapid changes in the insurance market or, more importantly, the perception of risk.

12.75 More recent versions of the seven days' notice clause include an undertaking from the insurer to reinstate the insurance against a new premium[78]:

"Cover hereunder in respect of the risks of war, etc. may be cancelled by either the Underwriters or the Assured giving seven days' notice (such cancellation becoming effective on the expiry of seven days from midnight of the day on which notice of cancellation is issued by or to the Underwriters). The Underwriters agree however to reinstate cover subject to agreement between the Underwriters and the Assured prior to the expiry of such notice of cancellation as to new rate of premium and/or conditions and/or warranties."

---

75. The clause is reproduced in IMO document LEG 92/5.
76. Athens Guidelines, Article 2.2.1.
77. Athens Guidelines, Article 2.2.3.
78. From IMO document LEG 92/5.

12.76 Such a clause would most likely be unenforceable due to the uncertainty of the essential term – the premium; it is in fact nothing but a contract to agree. In any event, such an undertaking is not required under the Athens Guidelines – probably because reinstatement is unlikely after a superpower war. But if the insurance is reinstated, the new insurance will count as compulsory insurance cover as if the premium had been adjusted without notice.

12.77 The 30 days' notice clause is considerably shorter than the three months minimum duration of the insurance certificates under the Convention, or the one year duration that is common under the CLC. I expect that the practice of issuing one year certificates will continue even if the Blue Card that forms the basis for it includes a 30 day notice clause. The Convention[79] does not prevent that, because the Reservation expressly allows a 30 days' notice clause.

12.78 In the unlikely event that the war insurance notice clause should be used to effectively terminate the war insurance, the validity of the insurance certificate may endure while there is no effective war insurance under it. The situation then would be as if a general war/terrorism exception clause had been accepted in the first place; but the main part of the insurance – the non-war insurance – will still be available. There is no formal reason to withdraw the certificate in such cases; the certificate is still correct in that there is war/terrorism insurance subject to a notice clause.

12.79 In effect, however, the insurance certificate will be valueless as far as war insurance is concerned in such rare cases. But passengers are unlikely to check the details of the compulsory insurance cover, or to check it and get it wrong, so it is unlikely that there will be any reliance loss. And albeit not a perfect solution, war insurance coverage subject to a notice clause is far better than no war/terrorism insurance at all.

Special limit

12.80 With or without the above clauses, the war market is rather limited. The insurance obligation of the Athens convention was capped at SDR 340 million (US$500 million).[80] The figure is somewhat arbitrary. It has nothing to do with the current limit of the P&I war insurance (see paragraphs 12.57–12.68 above), in particular because that is US$500 million in addition to the first tranche. It has been suggested as a sustainable figure by brokers and that is, of course, convenient, but it is not of paramount importance that it is sustainable over time as long as the Guidelines can be revised if needed (see paragraphs 12.25–12.38 above).

12.81 From a government point of view, there were several arguments for moderation. There is only one terrorist incident known at a passenger ferry in international trade, with only one life being lost.[81] And a huge, new demand for war insurance triggered by the Athens Convention would cause premiums to soar, with negative effects not only on the passenger trade, but also on shipping generally and, most likely, other insureds as well. A high level of war insurance, albeit not quite at the level of the non-war insurance under the Athens Conventions, seemed feasible.

---

79. E.g., Athens Convention, Article 4*bis*(2)(f).
80. Athens Guidelines, Articles 1.6 and 2.2.2.
81. The *Achille Lauro* hijacking in 1985; see Keith Michel, *War, Terror and Carriage by Sea* (London: LLP, 2004), para. 1.22. See also *lc* paras 1.23 *et seq.* on the *City of Poros* in domestic Greek traffic.

The level arrived at is much higher than the compensation paid for oil pollution damage, the supplementary fund exempted.[82]

12.82 The war insurance generally taken out by shipowners (paragraphs 12.57–12.68 above) does not only cover passenger liabilities. This means that claims for damage to property could reduce the passenger claims if there should be an incident with both types of liabilities. From a government point of view, it was important to make sure that passengers got the priority. Therefore, the SDR 340 million is designated to passenger claims only under the Convention.[83]

12.83 This limit applies also to claims paid by the carriers or others, and not by the insurer, if they are paid as settlement under the Convention.[84] However, if claims are paid by the government as support to the victims of an incident, this is not intended to settle claims under the Convention, and does not reduce the liability of the insurer.

12.84 After this, the SDR 340 million limit for war risks available only for passenger claims under the Convention seemed to make sense when it was suggested by brokers. Such per-incident limits are quite common in insurance, e.g. in the general war cover discussed above at paragraphs 12.57–12.68. It may, however, be difficult to distribute this amount when there is direct action for claimants.[85] Should the one who claims first get his claim in full, or should there be some kind of pro rata distribution?

12.85 In English law, the rule is that the first to claim is entitled to get his claim in full, even if the amount may not be sufficient for later claimants.[86] The Guidelines expressly set aside this rule, and favour a *pro rata* distribution.[87]

12.86 It was not possible to add detailed rules of procedure to the Guidelines in respect of the *pro rata* distribution. Hopefully, the more pressing issues of principle are dealt with by the clause that allows distribution before the end of the limitation period, and the clause that designates one jurisdiction – which could be where a LLMC limitation find has been constituted[88] – to resolve conflicts on the distribution of the limited amount.[89]

WAR/TERRORISM LIABILITY

12.87 In principle, there is no problem that liability exceeds the levels of compulsory insurance. This is the rule in the Athens Convention[90] and the Bunkers Convention,[91] and indeed in most compulsory insurance schemes, when the liability is not limited at all. The exceptions are the CLC and the HNSC.[92]

---

82. See paragraphs 12.5–12.14.
83. Athens Convention, Article 4*bis*(11).
84. Athens Guidelines, Article 2.1.5.
85. Athens Convention, Article 4*bis*(10).
86. *Cox v Bankside* [1995] 2 Lloyd's Rep. 437.
87. Athens Guidelines, Article 2.2.2.
88. LLMC, Article 11.
89. *Ibid.*
90. Compare Athens Convention, Articles 7 and 4*bis*.
91. In the International Convention on Civil Liability for Bunker Oil Pollution Damage 2001, only Article 7 on insurance, but not Articles 3 and 6 on liability, includes an obligation for States Parties to respect international limitation rules.
92. See CLC Article VII(1) and International Convention on Liability and Compensation for Damage in Connection with the Carriage of Hazardous and Noxious Substances by Sea 1996, Article 12(1).

12.88 Despite this, the model Reservation invites States Parties to make a Reservation so that war liability is capped at the same levels as the compulsory insurance, and states must implement this capping to benefit from the insurance scheme.[93] This concession was not necessary to arrange for war insurance; the additional liability of carriers would make no difference for market insurers. However, the concession was necessary for the non-passenger carrier majority of the P&I clubs. By this cap, some of the pressure on the war insurance market was relieved, and then these carriers got less premium increase and were perhaps more willing to accept P&I responsibility for the war part of the Athens insurance. In this way, one may say that the capping of Athens war liability contributed towards the insurability of the non-war Athens risks. This risk is, as one will recall, quite substantial (see paragraphs 12.5–12.14 above).

12.89 In the discussions on this capping, the point was raised whether a capping of liability per incident did not amount to a sort of global limitation. If so, that would be a problem, because the capping may be on another level than the limits of the LLMC. A State Party to the LLMC cannot both agree that the global limits shall be on the LLMC level and on the level of the Athens Guidelines.

12.90 If the capping is at a higher level than the LLMC, the LLMC would prevail,[94] and there would be no problem. If the capping is at a lower level than the LLMC, one could have a problem. Under LLMC 1996, that would be the case if the number of injured passengers exceeds 1942,[95] and the State Party has not utilised the opportunity to enhance liability.[96]

12.91 It is quite clear that the LLMC does not prohibit other limitation rules – the Athens Convention itself is the best proof of that. And it is also clear that the States Parties are not free to set other limits for all claims arising out of an incident; that would render the LLMC meaningless. But can the States Parties – as in the Guidelines – set a per incident limit for a certain fraction of the claims, i.e. the war/terrorism related claims?

12.92 There is nothing in the wording to prevent this.[97] And I cannot see that it would be more disloyal to set a sub-limit per incident for certain claims rather than the well accepted *per capita* sub-limits or a per voyage limit. And now, when the Legal Committee of the IMO implicitly has approved of this understanding of the LLMC by adopting the Guidelines, there should in any event be not be much room for doubt that the LLMC does not prevent per incident sub-limits.[98]

12.93 In addition to capping, the Guidelines also relieve the carrier for liability for biochemical risks.[99] This corresponds with one of the insurance exceptions, but not all of them. Again, the idea is to make life easier in the P&I system, which would come under pressure to indemnify shipowners for bio-chemical damage despite the

---

93. Athens Guidelines, Articles 1.2 and 2.1.4.
94. Athens Convention, Article 19.
95. The cap of SDR 340 million divided by the per capita LLMC limit of SDR 175,000.
96. LLMC 1996, Article 15(*3bis*).
97. The limitation rule on LLMC Article 7 relates to "claims arising on any distinct occasion ..." but does not say anything on how these claims shall be calculated.
98. There are also other examples in state practice of per incident limits that may also affect ships subject to LLMC limitation, such as Council Directive 85/374/EEC on product liability, Article 16(1).
99. Athens Guidelines, Article 1.3; by its reference to Article 2.1.1.

exemption clauses in the compulsory and, partially,[100] in the non-compulsory insurance. For governments, biochemical damage perhaps seemed to be a rather marginal risk, which shipowners in any event hardly could protect passengers against, and therefore not easily would be liable for in any event.[101]

CONCLUDING REMARKS

12.94 The Athens Guidelines are only a compromise, and not an ideal solution for any involved. But it is a solution that hopefully can make it possible for the 2002 Athens Convention to enter into force soon.

12.95 The cost of the extra war insurance is far from prohibitive. It has been estimated to be less than US$0.10 per passenger per day or voyage.[102]

12.96 In the implementation negotiations, it has been important for the P&I Clubs to stand firm on the point that they shall have nothing to do with war/terrorism insurance. This tactic has yielded results, in that the war insurance requirements are capped. Later on, however, it is likely that this marginal war/terrorism cover will be integrated in the P&I system. When reinsurance is available, it is unlikely that others in the long run can organise it and issue Blue Cards more efficiently than the Clubs can.

12.97

APPENDIX A

E

INTERNATIONAL MARITIME
   ORGANIZATION
4 ALBERT EMBANKMENT
LONDON SE1 7SR

Telephone: 020 7735 7611
Fax: 020 7587 3210

IMO

Ref. A1/P/5.01

Circular letter No. 2758
20 November 2006

To: All IMO Member States
       United Nations and specialised agencies
       Intergovernmental organisations
       Non-governmental organisations in consultative status
       Liberation movements

Subject: **Guidelines for the implementation of the Athens Convention relating to the Carriage of Passengers and their Luggage by Sea 2002**

The Legal Committee, at its ninety-second session in October 2006, adopted guidelines for the implementation of the Protocol of 2002 to the Athens Convention relating to the Carriage of Passengers and their Luggage by Sea 1974. The guidelines recommend that States which ratify, approve or accede to the 2002 Protocol to the 1974 Athens Convention (the Athens Convention relating to the Carriage of Passengers and their Luggage by Sea 2002) should

---

100. See paragraphs 12.45–12.48 above.
101. See paragraphs 12.15–12.24 above.
102. See IMO document LEG 92/5/2.

include a reservation or declaration to the same effect concerning a limitation of liability for carriers and a limitation for compulsory insurance for acts of terrorism, taking into account the current state of the insurance market. The guidelines provide wording for the recommended reservation.

Member governments are invited to take these Guidelines into account when considering ratification, approval or accession to the Protocol of 2002 to the Athens Convention relating to the Carriage of Passengers and their Luggage by Sea 1974.

★ ★ ★

ANNEX

IMO RESERVATION AND GUIDELINES FOR IMPLEMENTATION
OF THE ATHENS CONVENTION

Reservation

1 The Athens Convention should be ratified with the following reservation or a declaration to the same effect:

"[1.1] ***Reservation in connection with the ratification by the Government of ... of the Athens Convention relating to the Carriage of Passengers and their Luggage by Sea 2002 ("the Convention")***

Limitation of liability of carriers, etc.

[1.2] The Government of ... reserves the right to and undertakes to limit liability under paragraph 1 or 2 of Article 3 of the Convention, if any, in respect of death of or personal injury to a passenger caused by any of the risks referred to in paragraph 2.2 of the IMO Guidelines for Implementation of the Athens Convention to the lower of the following amounts:

  – 250,000 units of account in respect of each passenger on each distinct occasion;

  or

  – 340 million units of account overall per ship on each distinct occasion.

[1.3] Furthermore, the Government of ... reserves the right to and undertakes to apply the IMO Guidelines for Implementation of the Athens Convention paragraphs 2.1.1 and 2.2.2 *mutatis mutandis*, to such liabilities.

[1.4] The liability of the performing carrier pursuant to Article 4 of the Convention, the liability of the servants and agents of the carrier or the performing carrier pursuant to Article 11 of the Convention and the limit of the aggregate of the amounts recoverable pursuant to Article 12 of the Convention shall be limited in the same way.

[1.5] The reservation and undertaking in paragraph 1.2 will apply regardless of the basis of liability under paragraph 1 or 2 of Article 3 and notwithstanding anything to the contrary in Article 4 or 7 of the Convention; but this reservation and undertaking do not affect the operation of Articles 10 and 13.

Compulsory insurance and limitation of liability of insurers

[1.6] The Government of ... reserves the right to and undertakes to limit the requirement under paragraph 1 of Article 4*bis* to maintain insurance or other financial security for death or personal injury to a passenger caused by any of the risks referred to in paragraph 2.2 of the IMO Guidelines for Implementation of the Athens Convention to the lower of the following amounts:

  – 250,000 units of account in respect of each passenger on each distinct occasion;

  or

  – 340 million units of account overall per ship on each distinct occasion.

[1.7] The Government of ... reserves the right to and undertakes to limit the liability of the insurer or other person providing financial security under paragraph 10 of Article 4*bis*, for death or personal injury to a passenger caused by any of the risks referred to in paragraph 2.2 of the IMO Guidelines for Implementation of the Athens Convention, to a maximum limit of the amount of insurance or other financial security which the carrier is required to maintain under paragraph 1.6 of this reservation.

[1.8] The Government of ... also reserves the right to and undertakes to apply the IMO Guidelines for Implementation of the Athens Convention including the application of the clauses referred to in paragraphs 2.1 and 2.2 in the Guidelines in all compulsory insurance under the Convention.

[1.9] The Government of ... reserves the right to and undertakes to exempt the provider of insurance or other financial security under paragraph 1 of Article 4*bis* from any liability for which he has not undertaken to be liable.

Certification

[1.10] The Government of ... reserves the right to and undertakes to issue insurance certificates under paragraph 2 of Article 4*bis* of the Convention so as:
  - to reflect the limitations of liability and the requirements for insurance cover referred to in paragraphs 1.2, 1.6, 1.7 and 1.9; and
  - to include such other limitations, requirements and exemptions as it finds that the insurance market conditions at the time of the issue of the certificate necessitate.

[1.11] The Government of ... reserves the right to and undertakes to accept insurance certificates issued by other States Parties issued pursuant to a similar reservation.

[1.12] All such limitations, requirements and exemptions will be clearly reflected in the Certificate issued or certified under paragraph 2 of Article 4*bis* of the Convention.

Relationship between this Reservation and the IMO Guidelines for Implementation of the Athens Convention

[1.13] The rights retained by this reservation will be exercised with due regard to the IMO Guidelines for Implementation of the Athens Convention, or to any amendments thereto, with an aim to ensure uniformity. If a proposal to amend the IMO Guidelines for Implementation of the Athens Convention, including the limits, has been approved by the Legal Committee of the International Maritime Organization, those amendments will apply as from the time determined by the Committee. This is without prejudice to the rules of international law regarding the right of a State to withdraw or amend its reservation."

Guidelines

2 In the current state of the insurance market, States Parties should issue insurance certificates on the basis of one undertaking from an insurer covering war risks, and another insurer covering non-war risks. Each insurer should only be liable for its part. The following rules should apply (the clauses referred to are set out in Appendix A):

2.1 Both war and non-war insurance may be subject to the following clauses:
  2.1.1 *Institute Radioactive Contamination, Chemical, Biological, Bio-chemical and Electromagnetic Weapons Exclusion Clause* (Institute clause no. 370);
  2.1.2 *Institute Cyber Attack Exclusion Clause* (Institute clause no. 380);
  2.1.3 The defences and limitations of a provider of compulsory financial security under the Convention as modified by these guidelines, in particular the limit of 250,000 units of account per passenger on each distinct occasion;
  2.1.4 The proviso that the insurance shall only cover liabilities subject to the Convention as modified by these guidelines; and
  2.1.5 The proviso that any amounts settled under the Convention shall serve to reduce the outstanding liability of the carrier and/or its insurer under

Article 4*bis* of the Convention even if they are not paid by or claimed from the respective war or non-war insurers.

2.2 War insurance shall cover liability, if any, for the loss suffered as a result of death or personal injury to a passenger caused by:

- war, civil war, revolution, rebellion, insurrection, or civil strife arising therefrom, or any hostile act by or against a belligerent power;
- capture, seizure, arrest, restraint or detainment, and the consequences thereof or any attempt thereat;
- derelict mines, torpedoes, bombs or other derelict weapons of war;
- act of any terrorist or any person acting maliciously or from a political motive and any action taken to prevent or counter any such risk;
- confiscation and expropriation;

and may be subject to the following exemptions, limitations and requirements:

2.2.1 *War Automatic Termination and Exclusion Clause*

2.2.2 In the event the claims of individual passengers exceed in the aggregate the sum of 340 million units of account overall per ship on any distinct occasion, the carrier shall be entitled to invoke limitation of his liability in the amount of 340 million units of account, always provided that:

- this amount should be distributed amongst claimants in proportion to their established claims;
- the distribution of this amount may be made in one or more portions to claimants known at the time of the distribution; and
- the distribution of this amount may be made by the insurer, or by the Court or other competent authority seized by the insurer in any State Party in which legal proceedings are instituted in respect of claims allegedly covered by the insurance.

2.2.3 30 days' notice clause in cases not covered by 2.2.1.

2.3 Non-war insurance should cover all perils subject to compulsory insurance other than those risks listed in 2.2, whether or not they are subject to exemptions, limitations or requirements in 2.1 and 2.2.

3 An example of a set of insurance undertakings (Blue Cards) and an insurance certificate, all reflecting these guidelines, are included in Appendix B.

4 A State Party should not issue certificates on another basis than set out in paragraph 2 unless the matter first has been considered by the Legal Committee of the International Maritime Organization.

5 The Legal Committee encourages the Depositary of the Convention – if necessary – to make these guidelines known to a State that is about to deposit an instrument of signature, ratification, acceptance, approval or accession.

$\star \star \star$

APPENDIX A

Insurance clauses referred to in guidelines 2.1.1, 2.1.2 and 2.2.1

Institute Radioactive Contamination, Chemical, Biological, Bio-chemical and Electromagnetic Exclusion Clause (Cl. 370, 10/11/2003)

This clause shall be paramount and shall override anything contained in this insurance inconsistent therewith

1 In no case shall this insurance cover loss, damage liability, or expense directly or indirectly caused by or contributed to by or arising from:

1.1 ionizing radiations from or contamination by radioactivity from any nuclear fuel or from any nuclear waste or from the combustion of nuclear fuel;

1.2 the radioactive, toxic, explosive or other hazardous or contaminating properties of any nuclear installation, reactor or other nuclear assembly or nuclear component thereof;

1.3 any weapon or device employing atomic or nuclear fission and/or fusion or other like reaction or radioactive force or matter;

1.4 the radioactive, toxic, explosive or other hazardous or contaminating properties of any radioactive matter. The exclusion in this sub-clause does not extend to radioactive isotopes, other than nuclear fuel, when such isotopes are being prepared, carried, stored, or used for commercial, agricultural, medical, scientific or other similar peaceful purposes;

1.5 any chemical, biological, bio-chemical, or electromagnetic weapon.

Institute Cyber Attack Exclusion Clause (Cl. 380, 10/11/03)

1 Subject only to clause 10.2 below, in no case shall this insurance cover loss damage liability or expense directly or indirectly caused by or contributed to by or arising from the use or operation, as a means for inflicting harm, of any computer, computer system, computer software programme, malicious code, computer virus or process or any other electronic system.

2 Where this clause is endorsed on policies covering risks of war, civil war, revolution, rebellion, insurrection, or civil strife arising therefrom, or any hostile act by or against a belligerent power, or terrorism or any person acting from a political motive, Clause 10.1 shall not operate to exclude losses (which would otherwise be covered) arising from the use of any computer, computer system or computer software programme or any other electronic system in the launch and/or guidance system and/or firing mechanism of any weapon or missile.

War Automatic Termination and Exclusion

1.1 Automatic Termination of Cover
Whether or not such notice of cancellation has been given cover hereunder shall TERMINATE AUTOMATICALLY
  1.1.1 upon the outbreak of war (whether there be a declaration of war or not) between any of the following:
  United Kingdom, United States of America, France, the Russian Federation, the People's Republic of China;
  1.1.2 in respect of any vessel, in connection with which cover is granted hereunder, in the event of such vessel being requisitioned either for title or use.

1.2 Five Powers War
This insurance excludes
  1.2.1 loss damage liability or expense arising from:
  the outbreak of war (whether there be a declaration of war or not) between any of the following:
  United Kingdom, United States of America, France, the Russian Federation, the People's Republic of China; and
  1.2.2 requisition either for title or use.

★ ★ ★

APPENDIX B

I. Examples of insurance undertakings (Blue Cards) referred to in guideline 3

Blue Card issued by War Insurer

Certificate furnished as evidence of insurance pursuant to Article 4*bis* of the Athens Convention relating to the Carriage of Passengers and their Luggage by Sea 2002.

Name of Ship:
IMO Ship Identification Number:
Port of registry:
Name and Address of owner:

This is to certify that there is in force in respect of the above named ship while in the above ownership a policy of insurance satisfying the requirements of Article 4*bis* of the Athens

Convention relating to the Carriage of Passengers and their Luggage by Sea 2002, *subject to all exceptions and limitations allowed for compulsory war insurance under the Convention and the implementation guidelines adopted by the Legal Committee of the International Maritime Organization in October 2006, including in particular the following clauses: [Here the text of the Convention and the guidelines with appendices can be inserted to the extent desirable]*.

Period of insurance from: 20 February 2007
                       to: 20 February 2008

Provided always that the insurer may cancel this certificate by giving 30 days' written notice to the above Authority whereupon the liability of the insurer hereunder shall cease as from the date of the expiry of the said period of notice but only as regards incidents arising thereafter.

Date:

This certificate has been issued by: **War Risks, Inc.**
                                            [Address]

....   As agent only for **War Risks, Inc.**
Signature of insurer

Blue Card issued by Non-War Insurer

Certificate furnished as evidence of insurance pursuant to Article 4*bis* of the Athens Convention relating to the Carriage of Passengers and their Luggage by Sea 2002

Name of Ship:
IMO Ship Identification Number:
Port of registry:
Name and Address of owner:

This is to certify that there is in force in respect of the above named ship while in the above ownership a policy of insurance satisfying the requirements of Article 4*bis* of the Athens Convention relating to the Carriage of Passengers and their Luggage by Sea 2002, *subject to all exceptions and limitations allowed for non-war insurers under the Convention and the implementation guidelines adopted by the Legal Committee of the International Maritime Organization in October 2006, including in particular the following clauses: [Here the text of the Convention and the Guidelines with appendices can be inserted to the extent desirable]*.

Period of insurance from: 20 February 2007
                       to: 20 February 2008

Provided always that the insurer may cancel this certificate by giving three months' written notice to the above Authority whereupon the liability of the insurer hereunder shall cease as from the date of the expiry of the said period of notice but only as regards incidents arising thereafter.

Date:

This certificate has been issued by: **PANDI P&I**
                                            [Address]

....   As agent only for **PANDI P&I**
Signature of insurer

* * *

II. Model of certificate of insurance referred to in guideline 3

CERTIFICATE OF INSURANCE OR OTHER FINANCIAL SECURITY IN RESPECT OF LIABILITY FOR THE DEATH OF AND PERSONAL INJURY TO PASSENGERS

Issued in accordance with the provisions of Article 4*bis* of the Athens Convention relating to the Carriage of Passengers and their Luggage by Sea 2002

Name of Ship	Distinctive number or letters	IMO Ship Identification Number	Port of Registry	Name and full address of the principal place of business of the carrier who actually performs the carriage

This is to certify that there is in force in respect of the above-named ship a policy of insurance or other financial security satisfying the requirements of Article 4*bis* of the Athens Convention relating to the Carriage of Passengers and their Luggage by Sea, 2002.

Type of Security ....

Duration of Security ....

Name and address of the insurer(s) and/or guarantor(s)

The insurance cover hereby certified is split in one war insurance part and one non-war insurance part, pursuant to the implementation guidelines adopted by the Legal Committee of the International Maritime Organization in October 2006. Each of these parts of the insurance cover is subject to all exceptions and limitations allowed under the Convention and the implementation guidelines. The insurers are not jointly and severally liable. The insurers are:

For war risks: War Risks, Inc., [address]

For non-war risks: Pandi P&I, [address]

    This certificate is valid until ....

    Issued or certified by the Government of ....

(Full designation of the State)
OR
The following text should be used when a State Party avails itself of Article 4*bis*, paragraph 3:

The present certificate is issued under the authority of the Government of ....
(full designation of the State) by .... (name of institution or organisation)

At .... On ....
      (Place)   (Date)

                  ....
                 (Signature and title of issuing or certifying official)

EXPLANATORY NOTES:

1 If desired, the designation of the State may include a reference to the competent public authority of the country where the certificate is issued.
2 If the total amount of security has been furnished by more than one source, the amount of each of them should be indicated.
3 If security is furnished in several forms, these should be enumerated.
4 The entry "Duration of Security" must stipulate the date on which such security takes effect.
5 The entry "Address" of the insurer(s) and/or guarantor(s) must indicate the principal place of business of the insurer(s) and/or guarantor(s). If appropriate, the place of business where the insurance or other security is established shall be indicated.

PART 7

Liabilities for Wrongful Arrest of Ships under Common Law and Civil Law

CHAPTER 13

Damages for wrongful arrest of ships in the English Admiralty jurisdiction

PROFESSOR D. RHIDIAN THOMAS*

INTRODUCTION

13.1 It is a premiss of the common law that wrongful interference with the personal property of another is a tort. In appropriate circumstances it may also amount to breach of a non-tortious duty, such as breach of trust or contract. Any lawyer of longevity will be familiar with the torts of conversion (also known as trover), detinue and trespass to personal property, an area of tort law now re-fashioned, but not fundamentally changed, by the Torts (Interference with Goods Act) 1977.[1]

13.2 The focus of this chapter is to examine the extent, if at all, the law of tort, or, at least, the values of the law of tort under some other guise, have permeated the practice of arresting ships under the English Admiralty jurisdiction, thereby giving owners the compensatory remedy of damages and/or indemnity when an arrest may be condemned as being, in some sense, wrongful.

13.3 The most prominent feature of the Admiralty Court is the *in rem* jurisdiction and the action *in rem* by which it is invoked. The action *in rem* procedure is a process against maritime property which involves (but not inevitably in practice[2]) the arrest of a ship or other arrestable maritime property.[3] The procedure involves the judicial seizure and restraint of personal property (including on occasions choses in action[4]) which is, in any way defined at law, connected or associated with the claim or disputed question brought before the Admiralty Court.[5]

13.4 It is a procedure which offers claimants many advantages; it is an effective means of establishing jurisdiction, it establishes a pre-judgment security and a claimant with a power to arrest is a category of secured claimant who will, invariably, also enjoy some degree of priority.[6] But the procedure also carries the threat of detriment to defendant owners and demise charterers, for the impact of an actual

---

* Professor of Maritime Law, Director of the Institute of International Shipping and Trade Law, School of Law, University of Wales, Swansea.
1. *Clerk & Lindsell on Torts* (19th ed., 2006) (London: Sweet & Maxwell), chap.17 (Professor Andrew Tettenborn).
2. An actual arrest may be avoided by providing security in advance.
3. In addition to ships, cargo, freight, wreck and on occasions aircraft may be arrested. The reference to ships includes hovercraft; see Supreme Court Act 1981, s.24(1), for the definition of "ship".
4. An allusion to the fact that on occasions freight may be arrested, which is effected by an action *in rem* against either (a) the cargo in respect of which the freight was earned, or (b) the ship on which the cargo was carried: C.P.R., Admiralty Practice Direction (Suppl.), section 3.6(1)(b).
5. Meeson, *Admiralty Jurisdiction and Practice* (2nd ed., 2000) (London, LLP), 4-026–4-080; Jackson, *Enforcement of Maritime Claims* (4th ed., 2005) (London, LLP), chap. 15.
6. The claim of a claimant *in rem* will be capable of being characterised as either a maritime lien or a statutory lien, which are security interests.

arrest which is thereafter maintained is to disable the vessel and to prevent her from continuing to perform her commercial operations, resulting, potentially, in financial loss and contractual liabilities. During the arrest it will continue to be necessary to incur costs associated with the maintenance of the vessel and any commercial operations the vessel is capable of continuing to perform. The financial implications of an arrest may be significant and, therefore, when an arrest is established to be wrongful, the question may readily arise as to the allocation of the financial risks as between claimant and defendant owner or demise charterer.[7]

13.5 Before proceeding to respond to and examine this question it is probably beneficial to make a few general observations about the arrest of ships in the English Admiralty jurisdiction.

SHIP ARREST UNDER THE ENGLISH ADMIRALTY JURISDICTION

13.6 The basis of the contemporary English Admiralty jurisdiction is statutory, with the essential law found in the Supreme Court Act 1981, sections 20 to 24 (as amended). In subsections (2)–(5) of section 21 the powers of arrest are segregated into four categories. Each category relates to a designated list of maritime claims drawn from the global list set out in section 20, which establishes the basis of the substantive Admiralty jurisdiction, and provides rights of arrest against specified classes of maritime property. The cumulative effect of the statutory provisions is to establish an extensive range of powers of arrest; a power of arrest exists virtually for every substantive claim that falls within the Admiralty jurisdiction.[8] The different categories do not lend themselves readily to generic labelling, but may conveniently be titled as embracing: proprietary, possessory, security and confiscation claims; maritime liens; statutory rights *in rem* against ships and sister ships; and claims against aircraft.

13.7 The different categories of arrest powers are not uniform; there are significant differences between them. The pre-conditions to a valid arrest and the property capable of being arrested may vary; as also may the legal effect of an arrest.[9]

---

7. Hereafter all references to "owner" include a reference to "demise charterer". A demise charterer is nowadays better known as a bareboat charterer.

8. An exception exists where a claim arises for damage done to a ship by property other than a ship; see Supreme Court Act 1981, s.20(2)(d) "any claim for damage received by a ship".

9. Supreme Court Act 1981, s.21(2)–(5) provides –

"(2) In the case of any such claim as is mentioned in section 20(2)(a)(c) or (s) or any such question as is mentioned in section 20(2)(b), an action *in rem* may be brought in the High Court against the ship or property in connection with which the claim or question arises.

(3) In any case in which there is a maritime lien or other charge on any ship, aircraft or other property for the amount claimed, an action *in rem* may be brought in the High Court against that ship, aircraft or property.

(4) In the case of any such claim as is mentioned in section 20(2)(e) to (r), where—
    (a) the claim arises in connection with a ship; and
    (b) the person who would be liable on the claim in an action *in personam* ('the relevant person') was, when the cause of action arose, the owner or charterer of, or in possession or in control of the ship,
an action *in rem* may (whether or not the claim gives rise to a maritime lien on that ship) be brought in the High Court against –
    (i) that ship, if at the time when the action is brought the relevant person is either the beneficial owner of that ship as respects all the shares in it or the charterer of it under a charter by demise; or

13.8 This is because each category is founded on a distinct *raison d'etre*; in other words, the policy and purpose of the arrest procedure may vary depending on the nature of the claim or question in dispute. The arrest procedure is not uniform in purpose, it serves a variety of objectives.

13.9 The English Admiralty jurisdiction and procedural powers of arrest have been in some regards materially influenced by the International Ship Arrest Convention 1952.[10] The definition of "maritime claim" in Article 1(1) of the Convention has been adopted as the basis of the substantive jurisdiction of the Admiralty Court set out in section 20 of the Supreme Court Act 1981, though this did not introduce any significant change to the historical position. The powers of ship arrest embodied in Article 3 of the 1952 Convention (a notoriously ambiguous provision) are given legislative effect to by section 21(2) to (4) of the Supreme Court Act 1981, though possibly imperfectly and certainly not fully. It is significant that Article 3 was not incorporated as drafted in the Convention into English law. A particularly significant impact of the 1952 Arrest Convention was the introduction into English law of the power to arrest, in certain circumstances, an alternative ship, meaning a ship other than the particular ship in connection with which the claim arises. This is frequently described as an extended power to arrest a sistership, which, although a convenient mode of reference, is in strictness an inaccurate and misleading description. The enlarged power of arrest can operate more widely than a right to arrest a sistership, strictly construed.[11]

13.10 The procedure for ship arrest is governed by the Civil Procedure Rules, Admiralty Practice Direction, Part 6.[12] The primary conditions of the procedure are governed by sections 3 and 5 of the Admiralty Practice Direction, which provide that an arrest is effected by service of a claim form *in rem* (formerly the writ *in rem*) and the execution of a warrant of arrest on the vessel by the Admiralty Marshal or his substitute.

13.11 The claim form *in rem* (Doc ADM 1[13]) indicates the maritime property (predominantly a ship) against which the claim *in rem* is brought; the identity of the claimant and defendant; and sets out brief details and particulars of claim, though the latter may be attached to the form or set out in a separate following document. At the end of the document there is a statement of truth to the effect that "the facts stated in these particulars are true" which may be signed by the claimant or litigation friend or claimant's solicitor. Invariably it will be the latter, but in all cases the statement of truth relates to the belief of the claimant.

13.12 In general, therefore, the claim form does nothing more than record the claim of the claimant and such particulars as the claimant chooses to set out in the

---

(ii) any other ship of which, at the time when the action is brought, the relevant person is the beneficial owner as respects all the shares in it.

(5) In the case of a claim in the nature of towage or pilotage in respect of an aircraft, an action *in rem* may be brought in the High Court against that aircraft if, at the time when the action is brought, it is beneficially owned by the person who would be liable on the claim in an action *in personam*."

10. See below.

11. This is because an "other" ship may be arrested notwithstanding that there does not exist a "particular" ship in connection with which the claim arose, as where the liability is that of a charterer; see, *The Span Terza* [1982] 1 Lloyd's Rep. 225 (C.A.), *The Tychy* [1999] 2 Lloyd's Rep. 11 (C.A.).

12. Civil Procedure (The White Book Service), Sweet & Maxwell, London.

13. See below, Appendix 1 to this chapter.

form. It is wholly under the control of the claimant and does not contain or allude to any supporting evidence. It also records the issue date of the form, which is a vital piece of information for a claimant seeking to establish a statutory lien.[14] It is clear that the court exercises little or no supervisory jurisdiction over the issue of the claim form; if it is properly completed and the statement of truth signed the form will be issued. The statement of truth will only bring the law of contempt of court into play in the face of subjective dishonesty (without honest belief), which will be difficult to prove. Proof of negligence or inaccuracy or the making of a false statement will not of itself suffice. The claimant must (a) know that the claim form included false information, and (b) that its false statement(s) were likely to interfere with the course of justice.[15] But even when these preconditions prevail contempt proceedings may only be brought with the consent of the Attorney General or the court.[16]

13.13 To obtain a warrant of arrest the claimant must complete two forms: First, a *Declaration in support of application for warrant of arrest* (ADM5[17]), which is a document in the nature of an affidavit, though not described as such. It contains information relating to the claim and the failure to satisfy the claim, it identifies the ship to be arrested and the amount of security required (if known), and also confirms if any pre-arrest notices, required by law, have been given. In relation to a claim under section 21(4) of the Supreme Court Act 1981, which is not in the nature of a maritime lien, it also provides information which on its face shows that the claimant has a valid right to arrest the ship under the subsection. There again follows a statement of truth signed by the claimant or claimant's solicitor (predominantly the latter) declaring that "I believe (or the claimant believes) that the facts stated in this declaration form are true".

13.14 Provided the *Declaration* has been properly completed a *Warrant of Arrest* (ADM9[18]) is issued. The Warrant is issued in the name of the Queen and is a command to the Admiralty Marshal "to arrest the ship [named] and to keep the same under arrest until you should receive further orders from Us".

13.15 The execution of the Warrant of Arrest is dependent on the claimant making an *Application and undertaking for arrest and custody* on form ADM4,[19] which is a request addressed to the Admiralty Marshal to execute the warrant of arrest against the ship named and a statement of the ship's present or expected location, coupled with an undertaking to pay on demand the fees and expenses, existing and future, incurred by the Admiralty Marshal or on his behalf in connection with the arrest, care and custody, and release of the ship. This form is signed by the claimant's solicitor, and therefore it is the solicitor (or the legal firm) who undertakes the personal obligation to pay the Marshal's fees and expenses. The *Application* also contains a request (probably, again made to the Admiralty Marshal) that

---

14. A statutory lien comes into existence at the time the claim form *in rem* is issued; see Thomas, *Maritime Liens* (London, Stevens & Co., 1980) chap. 1, paras 45–51.

15. *Sony Computer Entertainment Inc. v Ball* [2004] E.W.H.C. 1984 (Ch.), [23]–[24].

16. CPR 32.14. See also *Zuckerman on Civil Procedure (Principles and Practice)* (2nd ed., 2006) (London, Sweet & Maxwell), paras 6.69–6.70.

17. See below, Appendix 2 to this chapter.

18. See below, Appendix 3 to this chapter.

19. See below, Appendix 4 to this chapter.

before a warrant is issued a search be made in the Admiralty registry to determine whether there is a caution against arrest in respect of the property named.

13.16 Again, it is noteworthy that there is little or no scrutiny of the application for and the execution of an arrest by the Admiralty Marshal. The application is wholly in the hands of the applicant, with the integrity of the process protected only by the declaration of a statement of truth. The only protection offered is to the Admiralty Court, with the solicitor acting for the claimant giving a personal undertaking in relation to the fees and expenses of the Admiralty Marshal.

13.17 One important feature of an arrest is that it provides security for the claim and, therefore, also any future judgment that may be entered for the claimant. The disadvantage the process causes the defendant may be avoided by an agreement to provide and accept an adequate substitute security in return for the release of the arrested ship. A substitute security may also be provided to avoid the necessity of effecting an arrest. The practice protects the commercial position of defendants without prejudicing the position of claimants. The defendant is able to recover his ship from arrest and continue to trade her, with the claimant retaining the benefit of an alternative security which is equivalent to the security represented by the arrested ship.[20] In contemporary practice the main kind of substitute security provided is a letter of undertaking given by a P&I Club.[21]

13.18 Under English law the power to arrest ships arises as an incident of the action *in rem* invoking the *in rem* jurisdiction of the Admiralty Court. The *in rem* jurisdiction is founded on service of process (the *in rem* claim form) on or against property. An actual arrest is not strictly required, though it represents the usual method by which the *in rem* jurisdiction is invoked.[22] In contrast, the *in personam* jurisdiction of the Admiralty Court is founded on service of process on the person of a defendant or by any other acceptable mode of service.[23]

13.19 It is interesting to note that the word "arrest" is not actually adopted in the Supreme Court Act 1981, but it does appear in other associated legislation[24] and it is the operative word in legal systems outside the common law. This observation is not simply a linguistic comment of trifling significance; there is a conceptual difference between ship arrest under common law Admiralty jurisdictions and ship arrest under civilian and other foreign jurisdictions. With regard to the latter the process is an incident of ordinary civil litigation, the primary object of which is to obtain pre-judgment security. Ship arrest was consequently a much more widely available procedure under these foreign legal traditions than the common law, and the principal underlying objective of the International Ship Arrest Convention 1952 was to unify ship arrest procedures internationally. This necessarily involved extending its availability in the common law Admiralty jurisdictions and restricting its availability in civilian and other non-common law jurisdictions.[25] The Ship Arrest Convention 1952 is geared in its language and philosophy towards the civilian concept of ship arrest and this has been the cause of some difficulty and uncertainty in association

---

20. *Meeson*, above, chap. 4, paras 4-066–4-080.
21. Hazelwood, *P&I Clubs: Law and Practice* (3rd ed., 2000) London, LLP), chap.11 and Appendix VI.
22. *The Dictator* [1892] P. 304; *The Nautik* [1895] P. 121.
23. *Cf.* Supreme Court Act 1981, s.21(1).
24. See, for example, Civil Jurisdiction and Judgments Act 1982, s.26.
25. See, generally, *Berlingieri on Arrest of Ships* (4th ed., 2006) (London, Informa).

with its incorporation into English law, with its very different historical and jurisprudential background.

WHEN MIGHT AN ARREST BE REGARDED AS WRONGFUL?

13.20 Precisely when an arrest is to be characterised as wrongful is a question that attracts considerable discussion and disagreement. There is no common approach to be found in the laws of nations and, as it will be seen later in the text, it is also a subject which has been approached cautiously by the international arrest conventions, with a refusal to lay down any mandatory international rule. Why this should be in relation to such a significant area of the law is itself an interesting question, and the attempt at an answer is deferred until later in the text.

13.21 Setting to one side for the moment the legal position under national and international law, as an initial step in the present enquiry it is proposed to address the question as one of abstract theory and to identify the various circumstances when an arrest might be characterised as wrongful. What follows, therefore, is an attempt to categorise the circumstances when an arrest *might* be regarded as wrongful. The identified categories are not necessarily mutually exclusive and represent a position or positions that might be adopted by any system of national or international law:

(a) when the necessary legal pre-conditions to a valid arrest have not been satisfied and the arrest may therefore be characterised as unlawful;

(b) when the arrest is unlawful, as in paragraph (a), with the circumstances aggravated by the fact that the claimant has acted culpably, in the sense of having acted intentionally, recklessly or grossly negligently;

(c) when the arrest is unlawful, as in paragraph (a), and the claimant has acted negligently;

(d) when the arrest is unlawful (as in paragraph (a)) and the associated claim in connection with which the arrest has been effected is defeated or is withdrawn or abandoned;

(e) when the arrest is lawful but the associated claim in connection with which the arrest has been effected is defeated, withdrawn or abandoned;

(f) when the arrest is lawful and the associated claim in connection with which the arrest is effected is arguable, but for procedural reasons the court strikes out the claim or stays proceedings or surrenders jurisdiction in favour of another judicial forum or arbitration tribunal;

(g) when the arrest is lawful but the claimant acted unreasonably or unjustifiably in effecting the arrest or in subsequently maintaining the arrest or in refusing to consent to the release from arrest of the arrested ship;

(h) when the arrest is lawful but the claimant was motivated by considerations other than the quest for justice and therefore abused the process of the court.

13.22 Each of the identified circumstances represents a situation when a defendant owner might suffer loss resulting from the arrest of his ship and when consequently an entitlement to compensation might be advocated. Each, therefore, could be characterised as exemplifying a wrongful arrest. It is highly improbable that any system of law would embrace all the circumstances identified above; more probable is the adoption of one or a small number. Cutting across the entire range of identified circumstances is a debate whether wrongful arrest should be confined to unlawful arrests, and even then whether wrongful arrest should be further limited to culpable conduct. In responding to this debate national jurisdictions manifest both conservative and liberal leanings, and consequently fall to be crudely characterised as pro- or anti-arrest jurisdictions.[26]

13.23 The liberal approach refuses to restrict the concept of wrongful arrest to unlawful arrests, emphasising considerations beyond unlawfulness which find expression in supplementary words such as "unjustified" and "unreasonable" arrests. The debate is therefore one of substance and language, and for advocates of the liberal cause the word "wrongful" used in isolation is both inadequate and a misrepresentation. The essence of the present debate crystallises about the use of the word "wrongful". What does it mean in the present context? In its traditional usage it tends to possess a narrow and restrictive meaning. It follows that the word may assert a similar influence on the concept of wrongful arrest and steer the law towards a very narrow conception. Any attempt to expand the concept of wrongful arrest must consequently confront the infelicity of the word "wrongful" and supplement it by more expansive words such as "unjustified" and/or "unreasonable" arrests.

WRONGFUL ARREST IN THE ENGLISH ADMIRALTY JURISDICTION

13.24 Under the English Admiralty law a very narrow and conservative view is taken of wrongful arrest, and accordingly the jurisdiction is rightly regarded as pro-arrest. In relation to the preceding characterisation of circumstances that might be regarded as wrongful, the English position is confined to paragraph (b).

13.25 That a concept of wrongful arrest and a derivative right to damages exists in English Admiralty law has been articulated since the early jurisprudence of the Admiralty Court,[27] but the modern law is founded on two decisions of the Privy Council in the latter half of the nineteenth century, which represent the keystone to this branch of the law. In *The Evangelismos*[28] a vessel mistakenly believed to have been involved in a collision with a vessel at anchor was arrested and detained for a little under three months. When the mistake was revealed the vessel was released and her owners claimed damages for wrongful arrest. At first instance Dr Lushington awarded costs but rejected the claim for damages, being of the opinion that the vessel had been arrested in the *bona fide* belief that she was the vessel involved in the collision; there had been no *mala fides*.[29] The decision was affirmed by the Privy

---

26. See *Smeele*, chap. 14.
27. Most significantly in *The Kate* (1864) Br. & L. 218, 221, *per* Dr Lushington, "it must be admitted to be right and just that a defendant whose property has been wrongfully arrested and detained should recover costs and damages. As a fact it has always been considered within the power and practice of this court to award costs and damages ... which does justice in the simplest and most direct way...."
28. (1858) 12 Moo. P.C. 352.
29. *Ibid.*, p.352.

Council. The Right Hon. T. Pemberton Leigh, who delivered the judgment of the court, expressed the opinion that to justify damages there must be established "either *mala fides*, or that *crassa negligentia*, which implies malice"[30] and indicated that the real question in issue could be formulated in the following way – "is there or is there not, reason to say, that the action was so unwarrantably brought, or brought with so little colour, or so little foundation, that it rather implies malice on the part of the plaintiff, or that gross negligence which is equivalent to it?"[31] On the facts of the case the claimants had been mistaken but it could not be said that they had acted maliciously or with so little justification as to amount to gross negligence. Although the wrong ship had been arrested, "there were circumstances which afforded ground for believing that this ship was the one that had been in collision with the barge".[32]

13.26 Eleven years later in *The Strathnaver*,[33] the Privy Council, in a case on appeal from the Vice Admiralty Court of New Zealand, approved the decision in *The Evangelismos*. The effect of that decision was summarised by Sir Robert Phillimore, giving the judgment of the court, in the following terms – "in the absence of proof of *mala fides* or malicious negligence, [the court] ought not to give damages against the parties arresting the ship".[34] On the facts of the case the plaintiffs had made an error of judgement in bringing the suit, but nonetheless had acted in the *bona fide* belief that they were entitled to arrest the ship. In these circumstances damages were not recoverable.

13.27 In the period between these two decisions Dr Lushington in *The Volent*[35] stated without equivocation that: "It is a well-established rule in this court that damages for arresting a ship are not given, except in cases where the arrest has been made in bad faith, or with crass negligence."[36] The case also made it clear that the remedy was available to owners and part owners. Other decisions made it clear that the power to award damages existed even if the court did not have jurisdiction over the substantive claim[37]; that the remedy of damages was available in respect of any category of property capable of being proceeded against in an action *in rem*[38]; and that the wrongfulness of an arrest might relate to the initial arrest[39] and to the subsequent maintenance of an arrest,[40] including keeping a vessel under arrest pending an appeal.[41]

13.28 In more recent times, in *The Kommunar (No. 3)*,[42] Colman J., referring back to and affirming the earlier authorities, analysed the law as envisaging two categories of case:

30. *Ibid.*, p. 359.
31. *Ibid.*, p. 359.
32. *Ibid.*, p. 360.
33. (1875) 1 App. Cas. 58.
34. *Ibid.*, p. 67.
35. (1864) Br. & L. 321.
36. *Ibid.*, p. 323.
37. *The Kate* (1864) Br. & L. 218.
38. *The Victor* (1860) Lush. 72.
39. *The Nautilus* (1856) Swab. 105; *The Gloria de Maria* (1856) Swab. 106; *The Glasgow* (1856) Swab. 145.
40. *The Margaret Jane* (1869) L.R. 2 A. & E. 345.
41. *The Cheshire Witch* (1864) Br. & L. 362.
42. 1997] 1 Lloyd's Rep. 22. See also *Astro Vencedor Compania Naviera S.A. v Mabanaft G.m.b.H.* [1971] 1 Lloyd's Rep. 502.

"First, there are cases of *mala fides*, which must be taken to mean those cases where on the primary evidence the arresting party has no honest belief in his entitlement to arrest the vessel. Secondly, there are those cases in which objectively there is so little basis for the arrest that it may be inferred that the arresting party did not believe in his entitlement to arrest the vessel or acted without any serious regard to whether there were adequate grounds for the arrest of the vessel. It is ... in the latter sense that such phrases as '*crassa negligentia*' and 'gross negligence' are used and are described as implying malice or being equivalent to it."[43]

13.29 The case concerned the arrest of a Russian fish processing factory ship. The central question in the case was whether the arrested ship was at the time the writ was issued owned by a person who was personally liable on the underlying claim. Only if it were so owned was the arrest lawful. The answer to this question turned on the issue of legal continuity as between an original and successor Russian organisation, the successor organisation having been created in connection with the privatisation programme initiated following the establishment of the Russian Federation. The issue was complex and raised difficult questions of Russian law.[44] The court ultimately decided that there had been no continuity of legal personality. The consequence of this determination was that the arrest was unlawful but Colman J. rejected the claim for damages. In the light of the legal complexities which surrounded the case the judge considered that the assumption that the vessel could be arrested within English jurisdiction was not "so obviously groundless as to amount to *crassa negligentia*".[45] *Mala fides* was not in issue and was not argued, but on the wider question the judge was satisfied that the position that the claimant had taken and maintained throughout the proceedings was understandable and arguable. The claimants had relied on the advice of a City law firm, on the advice of experts on Russian law and also on a precedent from a Commonwealth jurisdiction.[46] It could not be said that either the claimants or those advising them had acted unreasonably. In the final analysis the claimants had got the law wrong, but it could not be said that they had been negligent.

13.30 The concept of wrongful arrest sounding in damages is therefore a very narrow and restricted concept in English Admiralty law. It is confined to the circumstances set out in paragraph (b) of the categories of possible wrongful arrests identified earlier.[47] To establish that an arrest was unlawful is not enough. Additionally, express or implied malice must be established. The claimant must either know that he had no right to effect the arrest (the subjective test) or otherwise be recklessly indifferent to the question whether or not such a right existed (the objective test); mere negligence or error will not suffice. As a matter of evidence this will be very difficult for a defendant owner to establish. In English Admiralty law there is no wider recognition of the possibility of a lawful arrest being unjustified or unreasonable.

13.31 The ambiguity which survives in English law concerns the precise definition of the label *crassa negligentia*, and alternative labels such as gross negligence and malicious negligence. The one attribute these labels do not possess is precise mean-

---

43. *Ibid.*, p. 30.
44. *Cf.* Thomas, "State reconstruction and ship arrest", [1998] I.J.O.S.L. 236.
45. *Ibid.*, p. 31.
46. *Sovrybfloy v The Ship Efin Gorbenko* (2.4.1996, High Court of New Zealand).
47. See above, "When might an arrest be regarded as wrongful?"

ing and therefore they have very properly fallen out of fashion in legal analysis.[48] There might be a temptation to define them in terms consistent with the contemporary concept of subjective recklessness, alluding to blind eye knowledge[49] or the assumption of a risk of which the claimant is subjectively aware,[50] but this might represent marginally too narrow an approach. The definition of *crassa negligentia* favoured by Mr Justice Colman suggests that the label might be interpreted to bear a slightly wider meaning, embracing the problematic concepts of gross negligence and objective recklessness.

13.32 The narrow approach to wrongful arrest adopted in the English Admiralty jurisdiction is followed in the Admiralty law of the United States[51] and in many other common law jurisdictions.[52] It is also true to comment that some common law jurisdictions have moved away from the position in English Admiralty and formulated new statutory positions on wrongful arrest of ships.[53] These developments will be discussed later in the text.

THE BASIS OF LIABILITY FOR DAMAGES ARISING FROM WRONGFUL ARREST

13.33 This is an aspect of the law which has not been greatly analysed. Only very infrequently have the courts paused to consider the question of the basis of the liability for damages for wrongful arrest and then inconclusively. The question has never been directly isolated for concerted consideration by the judiciary, and consequently there is presently no definitive answer.

13.34 It might be thought at first blush that the remedy is procedural in its derivation, an incident of the inherent jurisdiction of the Admiralty Court. It can be reasoned that a wrongful arrest is an abuse of the process of the Admiralty Court, which has the procedural jurisdiction to respond not only by setting aside the claim form *in rem* and warrant of arrest but also, on proof of causative loss, by awarding damages to compensate the owner who has been wronged. The more narrowly the concept of wrongful arrest is defined, the more firmly it is possible to press the association between the remedy and procedural misconduct, and the greater becomes the analytical claim that the remedy is procedural in character. The idea of wrongful arrest being a procedural abuse sounding in damages cannot be declared to be contrary principle and the Admiralty authorities dating from the Victorian era appear to feed the broadly prevailing presumption that the remedy is procedural.[54] If this is an accurate analysis, it will continue to be necessary to derive the remedy

---

48. The adjective "gross" has frequently been castigated as vituperative; see *The Ohm Marina ex Peony* [1992] 2 S.L.R. 623 (Sing. H.C.); *The Arden* [1997] 2 Lloyd's Rep. 647.

49. Also alluded to as Nelsonian knowledge.

50. *Three Rivers District Council v Governor and Company of the Bank of England (No. 3)* [2003] 2 A.C. 1, 193, *per* Lord Steyn (H.L.).

51. *Fontera Fruit Co. v Dowling*, 91 F.2d 293 (5th Cir. 1937) 297.

52. For example, in Canada *(Armada Lines Ltd v Chaleur Fertilizers Ltd* [1997] 2 S.C.R. 617; noted Margolis [1998] L.M.C.L.Q. 11); Hong Kong *(The Maule* [1995] 2 H.K.C. 769); Singapore *(The Kiku Pacific* [1999] 2 S.L.R. 595 (C.A.), *The Inai Selasih* (Singapore Court of Appeal, 23 February 2006).

53. Woodford, "Damages for Wrongful Arrest: Section 34 of the Admiralty Act 1988" (2005) 19 M.L.A.A.N.Z. 115.

54. *The Nautilus* (1856) Swab. 105; *The Gloria de Maria* (1856) Swab. 106; *The Eleonore* (1863) Br. & L. 185; *The Flora* (1866) L.R. 1 A. & E. 45; *The Analtje Willemina* (1866) L.R. 1 A. & E. 107; *The Margaret Jane* (1869) 2 A. & E. 345; *The Eudora* (1879) 4 P.D. 208; *The Keroula* (1886) 11 P.D. 92.

from the inherent jurisdiction because the Admiralty Practice in the Civil Procedure Rules does not address the subject of wrongful arrest.

13.35 Nonetheless, the law is not free from uncertainty because there is a far from insignificant body of judicial dicta which associates, albeit vaguely and imprecisely, wrongful arrest with the tort of malicious prosecution. This association drives deep into the law. It is witnessed in the judgment of Dr Lushington in *The Kate*,[55] where the parallel with the common law tort is made. It appears again, with the language of the common law tort frequently adopted, in both distant[56] and contemporary authorities.[57]

13.36 Of particular significance is the dictum of the Right Hon T. Pemberton Leigh in *The Evangelismos*,[58] who observed: "Undoubtedly there may be cases in which there is either *mala fides* or that *crassa negligentia* which implies malice, which would justify a Court of Admiralty giving damages, as in an action brought at common law, damages may be obtained."[59] This dictum was cited with approval by the Privy Council in *The Strathnaver*.[60]

13.37 The association appears to have received its most pronounced judicial recognition in the judgment of Sir Francis Jeune P. in *The Walter D. Wallet*,[61] where the learned judge considered that a wrongful arrest in Admiralty was also capable of founding an action at common law for malicious prosecution, without modification of the elements of the tort, save possibly with regards to matters of language, and, further, that in principle a common law court had jurisdiction to entertain such an action.

13.38 The basis of the tort of malicious prosecution was enunciated by Lord Campbell in the early case *Churchill v Siggers*,[62] in the following terms:

"To put into force the process of law maliciously and without any reasonable or probable cause is wrongful; and if thereby another is prejudiced in property or person, there is that conjunction of injury and loss which is the foundation of an action on the case."

13.39 This dictum has been much cited and developed in subsequent authorities, with the result that its constituent words and phrases have developed important technical meanings,[63] an examination of which is beyond the parameters of the present discussion. Nonetheless, it is appropriate to make the comment that the tort applies to civil and criminal process, and that the precise ambit of the tort is uncertain. It also appears to be the case that the language of the law and the manner of its application may display varying degrees of vigour according to the area of its operation. In applying the tort to the arrest process in the Admiralty Court it would, therefore, be open to a common law court to clothe the tort in the language of the

---

55. (1864) Br. & L. 218, 221.
56. *Wilson v R* (1866) L.R. 1 P.C. 405.
57. *The Kommunar (No. 3)* [1997] 1 Lloyd's Rep. 22, 33, where Colman J. uses the phrase "without reasonable and probable cause". See also *The Maule* [1995] 2 H.K.C. (Hong Kong); *The Kiku Pacific* [1999] 2 S.L.R. 595 (Singapore).
58. (1858) 12 Moo. P.C. 352.
59. *Ibid.*, p. 359.
60. (1875) 1 App. Cas. 58, 67.
61. [1893] P. 202.
62. (1854) 3 E. & B. 929, 937.
63. *Clerk & Lindsell on Torts* (19th ed., 2006) (London, Sweet & Maxwell), chap. 16 (Professor M. A. Jones).

Admiralty Court and to apply it in the context of the circumstances appertaining to the Admiralty jurisdiction.[64]

13.40 Sir Francis Jeune P. reasoned that the principle enunciated by Lord Campbell would have applied in the days when Admiralty suits were commenced by the arrest of the person, and since the tort applied equally to persons and property, there was no reason why it should not extend to the malicious arrest of property by Admiralty process.[65] The President also accepted that the basic elements of the tort, as they had evolved at common law, were equally applicable to a claim founded on wrongful arrest in Admiralty, though the language of the law might be different. Speaking of the conduct of the defendant in the case before him, the President observed: "the action of the defendant was, I think, clearly, in [the] common law phrase, without reasonable and probable cause; or, in equivalent Admiralty language, the result of *crassa negligentia*, and in a sufficient sense *mala fides....*"[66] The common law tort also requires proof of actual damage, but with damage presumed when an action is based on the unlawful arrest of a person. The President was of the opinion that the same rule applied in respect of a claim founded on wrongful arrest in Admiralty proceedings, with loss presumed to result from the arrest of the ship.[67] On the facts of the case the ship had been wrongfully arrested when in port and loading cargo. The arrest neither detained the vessel nor interfered with the loading. Nonetheless the ship had been wrongfully seized and damages were fixed at one pound sterling, without condemnation in costs. The same parity doubtlessly exists in relation to the measure and quantification of damages and to matters relating to causation and remoteness, though the presence of fraud in the Admiralty process might render it uncertain whether the "reasonable foreseeable" or "direct consequence" rule of remoteness applies.[68]

13.41 An interesting implication of the case, which was accepted by the President, is that a common law court has jurisdiction to adjudicate on a claim for damages for malicious prosecution based on the wrongful arrest of a ship in Admiralty proceedings.[69] There appears to be no precedent for such a proceeding at common law and it is hardly credible that a common law court would allow such a situation to exist. It is clearly fair, just and appropriate that compensation for wrongful arrest should be determined by the Admiralty Court, which is the court in which the claim was brought, the arrest executed, and which has made the order releasing the ship from the wrongful arrest. The greater appropriateness of the Admiralty Court has also been acknowledged by those courts which have recognised the extended reach of the tort of malicious prosecution to the process of Admiralty.[70]

13.42 What then is the significance of this strand in the law? Does it mean that the jurisdiction of the Admiralty Court to award damages for wrongful arrest is founded on the tort of malicious prosecution, suitably modified to accommodate

---

64. *Ibid.*
65. *Supra*, pp. 205–206.
66. *Supra*, p. 208.
67. *Supra*, pp. 207–208.
68. *Re Polemis and Furniss Withy & Co.* [1921] 3 K.B. 560; *The Wagon Mound* [1961] A.C. 388.
69. *Supra*, pp. 205–206.
70. *The Evangelismos* (1858) 12 Moo. P.C. 352, 359; *The Strathnaver* (1875) 1 App. Cas. 58, 67.

the language and circumstances of Admiralty proceedings? The answer to this question must be an emphatic "no". No authority goes this far. It must also be significant that in more recent times Colman J. in *The Kommunar (No. 3)*[71] did no more than note the connection made by Sir Francis Jeune P.[72] The impact of the authorities is to draw an analogy between the Admiralty jurisdiction to award damages for wrongful arrest and the common law tort of malicious prosecution. The parallel between the two is quite clear, particularly when the Admiralty remedy for wrongful arrest is as narrowly defined as it is at present. Also, the fact that wrongful arrest in Admiralty may in principle found an action for malicious prosecution at common law, does not logically lead to the conclusion that the remedy in Admiralty and the tort of malicious prosecution are one and the same concept. Both logic and common sense suggest that the remedy in Admiralty is a product of the inherent jurisdiction, based on the concept of abuse of process. This analysis is not disturbed by the fact that a wrongful arrest in Admiralty may also fall within the ambit of the common law tort of malicious prosecution.

13.43 A significant disadvantage which would be associated with founding the Admiralty remedy on the tort of malicious prosecution is that the destiny of the concept of wrongful arrest would be assigned to and governed by the manner in which the tort was developed by the common law courts. This in principle would be unacceptable; the remedy properly belongs to the Admiralty jurisdiction. It would also have the consequence of inhibiting any reassessment of the remedy by the Admiralty Court resulting in a possible broadening of the basis on which the remedy is granted and thereby creating a divide between the underpinning principles governing the remedy in Admiralty and those relating to the common law tort of malicious prosecution.

COSTS AS A PARTIAL OR COMPLETE REMEDY

13.44 An owner who establishes wrongful arrest will be entitled to recover costs connected with the application for setting aside process and release of the vessel, although the distinction between costs and damages may not always be crystal clear.[73] The award of costs may fully or partially compensate the owner for expenses and losses suffered as a consequence of the wrongful arrest. In many instances, consequently, the owner will not have cause to seek any further redress beyond costs and this fact may explain the paucity of actions for wrongful arrest.

13.45 Costs fall within the discretion of the Admiralty court,[74] but only in exceptional circumstances would an owner who has suffered adversely as a consequence of a wrongful arrest be denied costs or awarded only a partial recovery.[75] An order for costs will normally cover, in addition to legal expenses, the owner's expenditure in maintaining the vessel while under arrest (in other words in keeping the vessel alive), any special expenditure relating to the vessel made necessary by

---

71. [1997] 1 Lloyd's Rep. 22.
72. *Ibid.*, p. 31.
73. *The Collingrave* (1885) 10 P.D. 158.
74. Supreme Court Act 1981, s.51(1) and CPR Part 44.
75. *Cf. Poulson v The Village Belle* (1896) 12 T.L.R. 630; *The Walter D. Wallet* [1898] P. 202.

the arrest, and also compensate for damage suffered during the period of and by virtue of the arrest.[76] In general terms an owner may recover any ordinary or special expenditure made necessary by the arrest, as distinct from expenditure arising independently of the fact of the arrest.

13.46 The limits of recoverable costs are, however, uncertain and may fall short of the potential compensation recoverable by way of damages. Costs, for example, cannot provide compensation for loss of the commercial use of the vessel for the period of the arrest or loss of a future fixture caused by the arrest.[77] When these circumstances prevail, in order to recover his losses in full it will be necessary for an owner to consider a claim for damages.

13.47 Many of the costs and expenditure associated with an arrest will have been incurred in the first instance by the Admiralty Marshal and recovered from the claimant, through his lawyers, by virtue of the undertaking given in form ADM4[78] to pay on demand the existing and future fees and expenses of the Admiralty Marshal. It will in each case be a question of discretion whether an order for costs should be discounted by the costs incurred by the arresting claimant under the undertaking as to costs given to the Admiralty Marshal.

13.48 This question was discussed in some detail by Colman J. in *The Kommunar (No. 3)*,[79] although the case did not concern wrongful arrest but an order for release from arrest. The case has previously been commented upon in sufficient detail as to suggest that it was a very unusual case. The vessel was maintained under arrest for over six months and for the greater part of that period was operated as a fish factory ship. The cargo of fish was also owned by the owners of the ship. There was, however, a period of about five weeks when the vessel was commercially inoperable because of the arrest. Whilst under arrest the Admiralty Marshal had purchased bunkers for the vessel which the claimants had been required to pay for under the undertaking given to the Admiralty Marshal in what is now form ADM4. The vessel consumed 4mts of bunkers per day, 1mt to keep the vessel alive and 3mts to operate the refrigeration units. The refrigeration units had been worked for 30 days when the fish was on board and during that period 90mts of bunkers with a value of £15,642.00 were consumed. On the release of the vessel from arrest there remained on board 52mts of bunkers with a value of £4,197.00. The application before the court was that the costs order should be made subject to a direction to the Taxing Master that the order for costs should be reduced by an amount equivalent to the value of the bunkers consumed for the purpose of refrigerating the cargo and which remained on board at the time of the release of the vessel from arrest. The essential argument of the claimants was that the benefit conferred on the defendants in the form of bunkers paid for by the claimants should be discounted from the costs of the hearing of the successful motion to release.

13.49 Colman J considered the application as turning on the exercise of his discretion, with it for the claimants to establish that it was just and equitable that the costs of the bunkers should be borne by way of a discount.[80] The claimants

76. *The Kommunar (No. 3)* [1997] 1 Lloyd's Rep. 22.
77. *Ibid.*
78. *Supra*, n. 19.
79. [1997] 1 Lloyd's Rep. 22.
80. *Ibid.*, p. 33.

failed on the application relating to the bunkers used for refrigerating the cargo because the factual basis for a discount had not been established. It had not been established that the defendants would have had to bear the cost of refrigerating the fish for the same period had there not been an arrest and therefore derived benefit from the arrest by avoiding expenditure which they would otherwise have incurred. Nor on the facts of the case could an answer to this question be inferred; it remained entirely speculative. But even if the necessary factual evidence had existed Colman J. expressed the opinion that he would have been reluctant to exercise his discretion in favour of ordering a discount to the full amount claimed, because the interests of justice did not require it. The reason given is of significant interest in the context of the main thesis of this chapter. The arrest had been unlawful and loss of use had resulted from the arrest, but in the absence of *mala fides* or *crassa negligentia* (which had not been established) the owners were not entitled to compensation. A mere unlawful arrest gave no right to compensation and this feature of the Admiralty jurisdiction gave rise to potential injustice. This in turn was a fact which could legitimately be taken into account in the exercise of the discretion whether to order a discount. It would be inappropriate for any such order to be made unless the court was satisfied that no injustice would be suffered by directing a discount, notwithstanding that the owners had suffered irrecoverable loss. Where there has been a loss of use of a vessel whilst under arrest the evidentiary burden is on the claimant seeking a discount to establish that despite the loss of use it is nonetheless equitable that the owners' costs should be reduced to give credit for the benefit of the bunkers paid for by the claimants.[81]

13.50 Colman J. took the same approach to the bunkers remaining on board at the time of release from arrest. Compared with the loss of use of the vessel the value of the bunkers remaining on board was trivial, and taking into account the interests of justice there was no justification for directing a deduction from the recoverable costs of the owners.[82]

WRONGFUL ARREST UNDER THE INTERNATIONAL CONVENTIONS ON SHIP ARREST[83]

International Convention for the Unification of Certain Rules Relating to the Arrest of Sea-Going Ships 1952, Article 6[84]

13.51 The Convention shirks the issue of wrongful arrest and fails to lay down a unifying international rule, with the issue left to individual Contracting States and the *lex fori*.

13.52 Article 6 provides:

"All questions whether in any case the claimant is liable in damages for the arrest of a ship ... shall be determined by the law of the Contracting State in whose jurisdiction the arrest was made or applied for."

81. *Ibid.*, p. 33.
82. *Ibid.*, p. 34.
83. See, generally, *Berlingieri on Arrest of Ships* (4th ed., 2006) (London and Hong Kong, LLP).
84. Brussels, 10 May 1952. See Appendix N to this book.

13.53 Contracting States may or may not have rules relating to wrongful arrest; and when they do, the concept of wrongful arrest and the remedy available is a matter governed by the national law of the relevant Contracting State. Consequently, within the regime of the Convention, whether, and to what extent, owners have legal protection against wrongful arrest will depend on the jurisdiction in which the arrest is made.

International Convention on Arrest of Ships 1999 [85]

13.54 This Convention continues in the same vein as the 1952 Convention, but it is also more expansive for it tentatively signposts a new way forward and also addresses the question of jurisdiction.

13.55 Article 6, which is sub-titled "Protection of owners and demise charterers of arrested ships", provides, to the extent that it is relevant:

"1. The Court may as a condition of the arrest of a ship, or of permitting an arrest already effected to be maintained, impose upon the claimant who seeks to arrest or who has procured the arrest of the ship the obligation to provide security of a kind and for an amount, and upon such terms, as may be determined by that court for any loss which may be incurred by the defendant as a result of the arrest, and for which the claimant may be found liable, including but not restricted to such loss or damage as may be incurred by that defendant in consequence of:
   (a) the arrest having been wrongful or unjustified; or
   (b) ...
2. The Courts of the State in which an arrest has been effected shall have jurisdiction to determine the extent of the liability, if any, of the claimant for loss or damage caused by the arrest of a ship, including but not restricted to such loss or damage as may be caused in consequence of:
   (a) the arrest having been wrongful or unjustified, or
   (b) ...
3. The liability, if any, of the claimant in accordance with paragraph 2 of this article shall be determined by application of the law of the State where the arrest was effected.
4. If a Court in another State or an arbitral tribunal is to determine the merits of the case in accordance with the provisions or article 7, then proceedings relating to the liability of the claimant in accordance with paragraph 2 of this article may be stayed pending that decision.
5. Where pursuant to paragraph 1 of this article security has been provided, the person providing such security may at any time apply to the Court to have that security reduced, modified or cancelled."

13.56 The Convention again recoils from laying down a unifying international rule of wrongful arrest, leaving the matter to the national law of Contracting States. Jurisdiction in respect to what is alluded to in the Convention as wrongful or unjustified arrest claims is vested in the courts of the Contracting State where the arrest was effected. When the arresting court does not have merits jurisdiction it is given a discretionary power to stay the wrongful or unjustified arrest proceedings until the merits have been determined by the foreign court or in arbitration.

13.57 Further, the Article embodies a number of interesting concepts. In addition to wrongful arrest it acknowledges the potential existence of an "unjustified

---

85. The Convention has been acceded to or ratified by only seven States to date and has yet to come into force. There is no immediate indication that the UK will ratify the Convention. See Appendix O to this book.

arrest", though it does not define this concept. This is again a matter for Contracting States. It also recognises that a power of arrest may be granted conditionally on the applicant providing security for any loss that might be caused in the event of the arrest subsequently being established to be wrongful or unjustified. These ideas are very much in conformity with the way the arrest procedure is administered in many civil jurisdictions but are alien to the common law tradition.[86] They will be revisited in the reflection that follows.

13.58 The failure by either of the international conventions to come to a firm determination on the question of wrongful arrest must be an indication of the absence of any existing common national approach and also of an inability to arrive at an international consensus on the issue. The issue is quite clearly controversial and consequently it has been adroitly sidestepped by the international conventions.

REFLECTION AND PROPOSALS FOR REFORM

13.59 The preceding survey undertaken of the English Admiralty law of ship arrest reveals it to be firmly in the pro-arrest camp of national jurisdictions. Procedurally an arrest is relatively easy to obtain and execute; it involves little cost and with barely any judicial review. It almost amounts to a bare administrative process, save that the applicant or his solicitor acting on his behalf beyond setting out the essential facts in the claim form also swears a statement of truth. However, this is of limited value for it is no more than a statement of the subjective belief of the claimant in the truth of the particulars. Only the truly malicious claimant, a rare animal, will be guilty of swearing a dishonest declaration. The declaration is the equivalent of an affidavit and places the claimant in contempt of court if a false declaration is made. This may result in the claimant being punished but it does not provide compensation for the defendant owner.

13.60 The concept of wrongful arrest, as recognised in the English Admiralty jurisdiction, is exceptionally narrow; indeed, it is so narrow that as a question of fact and practice it is virtually non-existent. In the present state of the law it is close to being impossible to establish a wrongful arrest. Only when a claimant knows that he has no right to execute an arrest or is recklessly indifferent or grossly negligent in relation to the question whether such a right exists will the arrest be condemned as wrongful. There is not recognised any wider concept of an unjustified or unreasonable arrest. This reveals the adoption of a particularly tolerant position, and one which is at odds with the position which prevails in other equivalent areas of the law. It, of course, serves to encourage claimants to arrest ships in the Admiralty jurisdiction, but it otherwise leaves owners unfairly exposed and with only limited protection.

13.61 Beyond an order for costs, no protection is provided to owners for pecuniary loss arising from the arrest and detention of their ships. Further, no condition is attached to the application for an arrest to protect the interests of a prejudiced owner. The only protection provided is to the Admiralty Court. In applying for an arrest the solicitor acting for the claimant must undertake a personal obligation to

---

86. Smith (ed.), *Ship Arrest Handbook* (London, LLP, 1997); Verstrepen, "Arrest and judicial sale of ships in Belgium", in [1995] L.M.C.L.Q. 131. See also *Smeele*, chap. 14.

pay on demand the fees of the Admiralty Marshal and all expenses incurred in connection with the arrest. The expenses of the court also represent a first claim on the proceeds in court following the sale of an arrested ship.[87]

13.62 The historical evolution towards the current position appears to have been influenced by two considerations, each of which is now unconvincing. The first takes into account the fact that arrest is the means by which the jurisdiction *in rem* of the Admiralty Court is established. The second, that an arrested ship may be released by giving substitute security, such as bail or security.[88] As for the first, there would appear to be in principle no reason why "wrongful" interference with the property of another should be excused by the law just because it was associated with a legal process invoking jurisdiction. The reasoning emerged at a time when arrest represented the sole procedure by which the Admiralty jurisdiction *in rem* could be invoked, but in the contemporary law there is the additional procedure by service of the claim form *in rem* (formerly the writ *in rem*), and service of the claim form alone is sufficient to invoke the *in rem* jurisdiction.[89] Arrest, therefore, is no longer essential, and contemporary practice reflects this fact. As for the second consideration, it is, of course, true that an arrested ship may be released by making available substitute security, and this route is invariably adopted by owners, which also serves to mitigate the commercial prejudice resulting from an arrest. But owners will not always have the means to provide security, and those who are able to obtain security from their P&I Club or elsewhere will in some way have to bear the cost of the provision. The law should protect owners who are not in a position to obtain the early release of their vessel by providing substitute security and who are therefore exposed to the full pecuniary impact of the arrest.

13.63 In conclusion, it must be doubted if the current law maintains a fair and just balance between claimants and owners. The pecuniary risks incident to ship arrest are unfairly allocated; the law favours claimants and shields them from liability for wrongful or unjustified arrest beyond the order for costs, while owners are left to absorb the brunt of any wider prejudicial pecuniary impact arising from the arrest. The law appears not to fully appreciate the essential nature of ship arrest; it is a pre-judgment seizure of an asset of the defendant, and, therefore, necessarily before the question of liability has been resolved. In this situation justice requires not that claimants should be unreasonably baulked but that defendants should be properly protected in the event that the arrest is shown to be wrongful or unjustified. Under the present law claimants bear little risk if they get matters wrong or fail to substantiate their claims.

13.64 Against this critical assessment of the current law it is suggested that the following proposals for reform should receive consideration.

(i) The introduction of the concept of "unjustified" arrest

13.65 It is suggested that the concept of wrongful arrest should be extended beyond the current position occupied under English law to include an arrest which on the

---

87. Thomas, *Maritime Liens* (London, Stevens & Co., 1980) chap. 9, para. 456.
88. *The Evangelismos* (1858) 12 Moo. P.C. 352, 359; *The Volant* (1864) Br. & L. 321, 323. The giving of bail to the Admiralty Court appears to have ceased to be part of the practice of the court and it is noticeable that the Admiralty Practice, CPR, no longer makes provision for the giving of bail.
89. *The Nautik* [1895] P. 121.

facts is shown to be unjustified. The concept of an "unjustified" arrest is acknowledged in the International Ship Arrest Convention 1999 but not defined, with it left to Contracting States to come to their own definition of the concept. It is quite clear that the question of definition is troublesome but this is not a compelling reason for summarily rejecting the concept. In general terms an unjustified arrest may be defined as meaning an invalid arrest or a valid arrest which on the facts of any particular case can be shown to be unnecessary or unreasonable or without merit. Whether an arrest is valid raises a question of law; and whether a valid arrest is unnecessary or unreasonable or unmerited will in each case be a question of fact.

13.66 If adopted the precise definition of an unjustified arrest would demand careful consideration, taking into account the purpose underlying the extension of the law and the exigencies of contemporary practice. The following comments address some of the issues.

13.67 The primary purpose, or at least a necessary incident, of ship arrest is to obtain security for the claim. If, for example, a satisfactory and sufficient security has already been provided or promised by a reliable source, such as a P&I Club which is a member of the International Group, but, nonetheless, the claimant proceeds to arrest the ship, it may fairly be said that the arrest was unjustified. The same conclusion would be arrived at if the claimant is holding assets of the defendant which have in a legitimate way been charged as security for the claim; it may again be fairly said, in the absence of any subsequent change in the circumstances, that the arrest was unjustified.

13.68 Beyond matters relating to substitute security, the concept of an unjustified arrest must be capable of extending to include matters of evidence and motive. A claimant who abuses the process of the Admiralty Court must be in danger of being condemned for effecting an unjustified arrest. If the underlying claim is wholly without foundation or wildly speculative or the underlying motive of the claimant is unconnected with an attempt to obtain justice the associated arrest may be said to be unjustified. And more widely still, if the claim fails at trial, it is again possible to assert that the arrest was unjustified. This latter example gives the widest possible meaning to unjustified arrest.

13.69 In developing the concept of unjustified arrest it will also be important to bear in mind the realities of Admiralty litigation. Claimants are often compelled to act speedily when arresting ships; there may not have existed the time or opportunity to consider seeking security or to assess the form and sufficiency of any security offered by the defendant or other source. In the circumstances of a particular arrest the nature of the dispute and the precise character of the claim that might result may not yet be clearly understood and formulated. These are matters that may have to be left until later when further and more precise information will be available. It is, therefore, crucial that the prevailing factual circumstances attending on the arrest be taken into account in any later factual enquiry into the question whether the arrest was unjustified. The quest to provide greater protection to owners is not to be obtained at the cost of unfairly baulking procedurally bona fide claimants. A fair and just balance has to be maintained between claimants and owners, with the balance of any doubt given to the benefit of claimants. But the same level of toleration would not survive to any later enquiry into an allegation that an arrest was being unjustifiably maintained.

13.70 Even if the law were extended in the way proposed it is unlikely to have a significant impact on the practice of arresting ships. When ships are arrested they are in the vast majority of instances subsequently quickly released against a substitute security being provided to protect the position of the claimant. The disruption to the owner is either non-existent or minimal and any loss can generally be compensated through an order for costs. It is only when an owner is unable to provide substitute security and the arrest is maintained that the economic impact may be substantial. In this circumstance it would appear to be just that the court should be able to enquire not only into the validity of the arrest and its maintenance, but also its justification.[90]

(ii) The introduction of a discretionary jurisdiction to make the grant of a warrant of arrest conditional on the claimant providing security for the protection of the owner in the event of the arrest being wrongful or unjustified

13.71 That such a discretionary jurisdiction may exist is recognised in Article 6(1) of the International Ship Arrest Convention 1999, but again the sub-paragraph does not establish a mandatory rule. Such a jurisdiction does not currently exist under English Admiralty law, but strong arguments may be marshalled to support its introduction. It would help to secure the position of defendant owners in the event of an arrest being wrongful or unjustified, and more fairly adjust the balance of risk between claimants and owners. It would also encourage a responsible approach to the arrest of ships.

13.72 The security should be in a convenient form, such as an undertaking to pay damages, buttressed by collateral where the court considered this necessary. Although in practice it might be anticipated that the undertaking to pay damages would become a standard feature of the procedure, nonetheless the jurisdiction would be discretionary and this would mean that the order could be dispensed with when it would be unfair to demand security. It is anticipated that the discretion would be exercised in this way where a plaintiff of limited means and with a legitimate and arguable claim sought to invoke the arrest process. Claims by seamen (now rare) would in this way be protected. There is no reason why the existence of such a discretionary jurisdiction should unfairly deny claimants access to the Admiralty jurisdiction. On the other hand, the fact that a claimant was obliged to act speedily when deciding to arrest a ship would not of itself and without more appear to amount to a special circumstance.

13.73 The wider effect of this proposal is to recommend that the practice relating to the arrest of ships should follow closely that adopted in relation to freezing injunctions (formerly Mareva injunctions). The two procedures are, of course, quite different in nature, but outwardly they work in similar ways and share the same objective. The grant of a freezing injunction is discretionary but it has become standard practice for injunctions to be granted conditionally on the applicant undertaking to give a cross-undertaking in damages, supported by a security if

90. *The Kommunar (No. 3)* [1997] 1 Lloyd's Rep. 22, 33, *per* Colman J.

considered necessary. Only in exceptional circumstances is the condition dispensed with. The approach in equity to interlocutory freezing injunctions provides a model that may be beneficially followed by the practice of the Admiralty Court.[91]

CONCLUSION

13.74 Although there are grave doubts about the broad acceptability of the International Ship Arrest Convention 1999, nonetheless Article 7 of the Convention establishes a scheme for the protection of owners and demise charterers that should receive serious consideration. It reflects the position that prevails in many foreign jurisdictions and, ostensibly, without detriment to the interests of claimants. It also represents the law which now prevails in some common law jurisdictions by virtue of legislative reforms.[92] It is impossible to be blind to the fact that the proposals for reform advocated in this chapter are unlikely to attract universal national appeal. They will be perceived by many practitioners in Admiralty in England and Wales as detrimental to the interests of claimants within a national jurisdiction which has a diminishing association with shipowning. Nonetheless, an objective and neutral assessment of the present legal position, which has remained unchanged over the course of the modern history of the Admiralty jurisdiction, generates a distinct sense of unease. In relation to actions *in rem* where an arrest is effected the balance between claimants and owners is not fairly struck, with insufficient consideration given to the potential adverse impact which pre-judgment arrests may have on the pecuniary interests of defendant owners.

---

91. Hoyle, *The Mareva Injunction and Related Orders* (4th ed., 2006) (London and Hong Kong, LLP) chap. 4; Gee, *Commercial Injunctions* (5th ed., 2006) (London, Sweet & Maxwell).
92. Admiralty Jurisdiction Regulation Act 105 of 1983, s.5(4) (South Africa); Admiralty Act 1988 (Cth.), s.31 (Australia); Admiralty Jurisdiction Decree No. 51 of 1991 (Nigeria), s.31. Noted Ojukwu (2004) Tul. Mar. L.J. 264–266.

APPENDIX 1

13.75   Claim Form – Admiralty claim in rem (ADM 1)

	In the **High Court of Justice**
Claim Form **(Admiralty claim in rem)**	**Queen's Bench Division** **Admiralty Court**

Click here to reset form

	for court use only
Claim No.	
Issue date	

Admiralty claim in rem against

SEAL

of the Port of

Claimant

Defendant

Brief details of claim

The Admiralty Registry within the Royal Courts of Justice, Strand, London WC2A 2LL is open between 10am and 4.30pm Monday to Friday.
Please address all correspondence to the Admiralty Registry and quote the claim number.

ADM1 Claim form (Admiralty claim in rem) (03.02)

254

Claim Form – Admiralty claim in rem (ADM 1) – *continued*

	Claim No.	

Particulars of Claim (attached)(to follow)

Statement of Truth
*(I believe)(The Claimant believes) that the facts stated in these particulars of claim are true.
* I am duly authorised by the claimant to sign this statement

Full name

Name of claimant's solicitor's firm

signed   position or office held

*(Claimant)(Claimant's solicitor)   (if signing on behalf of firm or company)

*delete as appropriate

Claimant's or claimant's solicitor's address to which documents or payments should be sent if different from overleaf including (if appropriate) details of DX, fax or e-mail.

APPENDIX 2

13.76 Outline form of declaration in support of application
for warrant of arrest

Declaration in support of application
for warrant of arrest

Click here to reset form

'The claimant's claim is *(state nature of claim)*

I am informed by *(name and occupation of informant)*
that the claimant's claim has not been satisfied.

The property to be arrested is the ship *(name)*
of the port of *(port of registry)*   .

The amount of security for the claim sought by the claimant is *(state amount if known)*

The relevant notice (if required)(exhibit no.   ) has been sent to the consular office
of *(name of country or State)*   ',.

*If the claim falls under section 21(4) of the Supreme Court Act 1981 and it does **not** carry a maritime lien or
other charge the declaration should further include:-*

'The ship *(name of ship to be arrested)*   is the ship (or is one of the
ships) against which the claim is brought and is (is not) the ship in connection with which the claim arose.

The person who would be liable on the claim in an action in personam ("the relevant person")
is *(name)*   .

When the right to bring the claim arose *(name of relevant person)*   was (the owner or charterer)(in
possession or in control) *(as the case may be)*
of the ship *(name of the ship in connection with which the claim arose)*   .

(name of relevant person)   was
on the *(date claim form was issued)*   the beneficial owner of all the shares
in the ship *(name of ship in connection with which the claim arose and is the ship to be arrested)*
or was the charterer of it under a charter by demise.

ADM5 Declaration in support of application for warrant of arrest (03.02)

Outline form of declaration in support of application
for warrant of arrest – *continued*

*(**OR**, if the ship to be arrested is not the one in connection with which the claim arose)*

(name of relevant person)   was

on the *(date claim form was issued)*   the beneficial owner as respects all the

shares in the ship *(name of ship to be arrested)*.

In establishing that the court is not prevented from considering the claim by reason of section 166(2) of the Merchant Shipping Act 1995, the facts relied on are:

Statement of Truth

*(I believe)(The claimant believes) that the facts stated in this declaration form are true.

*I am duly authorised by the claimant to sign this statement.

Full Name

Name of claimant's solicitor's firm

signed   position or office held
        (Claimant)(Claimant's solicitor)   (If signing on behalf of a firm or company)

*delete as appropriate

APPENDIX 3
13.77 Warrant of arrest

Warrant of Arrest

Click here to reset form

| In the High Court of Justice |
| Queen's Bench Division |
| Admiralty Court |

| Claim No. | |

Admiralty claim in rem against:

Claimant(s)

Defendant(s)

ELIZABETH THE SECOND, by the Grace of God, of the United Kingdom of Great Britain and Northern Ireland and of Our other realms and territories Queen, Head of the Commonwealth, Defender of the Faith:

To the Admiralty Marshal of Our High Court of Justice, and to all singular his substitutes, Greeting.

We hereby command you to arrest the ship

of the port of   and to keep same under arrest until you should receive further orders from Us.

WITNESS   , Lord High Chancellor of Great Britain,

the   day of

The Claimant's claim is for [copy from Claim Form]

Taken out by

Solicitors for the

ADM9 Warrant of arrest (03.02)

Warrant of arrest – *continued*

Certificate as to Service

On the   day of

the within-named ship

lying at

was arrested by virtue of

for a short time on*

of the said ship, and on taking off the process, by leaving a copy thereof fixed in its place.

Signed _____   Date _____

*State on
which part of
the outside
of the ship's
superstructure

APPENDIX 4
13.78 Application and undertaking for arrest and custody

Application and undertaking for arrest and custody

Click here to reset form

In the	High Court of Justice
	Queen's Bench Division
	Admiralty Court
Claim No.	

Admiralty claim in rem against:

The Admiralty Marshal is requested to execute the Warrant in the above claim lodged herewith by the arrest

of *(give details)*

lying/expected to arrive at *(give details)*

I (we) undertake personally to pay on demand the fees of the Marshal and all expenses incurred, or to be incurred, by him or on his behalf in respect of

    1.   the arrest, or endeavours to arrest, the property; and

    2.   the care and custody of it while under arrest; and

    3.   the release, or endeavours to release it.

I (we) request that a search be made in the Register before the warrant is issued to determine whether there is a caution against arrest in force in respect of the above property.

Date

Signed...

              To be signed by the Solicitor

Office use only:

I confirm that at: on:

no cautions have been filed or entered against the arrest of the above property.

Signed..

ADM4 Application and undertaking for arrest and custody (03.02)

CHAPTER 14

Liability for wrongful arrest of ships from a civil law perspective

PROFESSOR DR FRANK G. M. SMEELE*

INTRODUCTION

14.1 Pursuant to the 1952 Brussels Arrest Convention[1] all questions relating to liability for wrongful arrest are governed by the law of the place where the arrest was made or applied for (*lex loci arresti*).[2] This implies that one must be familiar with the laws of France, The Netherlands or Germany in order to know if and when a ship's arrest made in Le Havre, Rotterdam or Hamburg may give rise to an action for damages for the shipowner.

14.2 As will be shown below, there exists no unified approach to wrongful arrest among civil law countries in Europe. In fact there appears to be a "North-South"-divide on the European continent about the basic question whether the mere fact that the claim in support of which the arrest was made fails on the merits, is sufficient to base a liability for wrongful arrest. A group of "northerly countries" including The Netherlands, Germany, Poland, Denmark, Norway, Sweden and Finland answer this question decidedly in the affirmative and holds the applicant for arrest strictly liable if his claim fails on the merits, irrespective of fault or good faith.[3] By contrast and similar to English law, the "southerly countries" including Belgium, France, Italy and Greece, answer the above question in the negative and require instead that various degrees of "fault" ("abuse of rights", "gross negligence" or "bad

---

* Professor of Maritime Law at Erasmus University at Rotterdam and partner at Van Traa Advocaten, Rotterdam.
1. International Convention for the unification of certain rules relating to the arrest of sea-going ships, Brussels, 10 May 1952; J. E. de Boer (ed.), *International Transport Treaties (ITT)*, pp. 1–65 *et seq.*
2. Article 6-1 of the 1952 Arrest Convention provides:
   "1. All questions whether in any case the claimant is liable in damages for the arrest of a ship or for the costs of the bail or other security furnished to release or prevent the arrest of a ship, shall be determined by the law of the Contracting State in whose jurisdiction the arrest was made or applied for."
The International Convention on arrest of ships, Geneva 12 March 1999, *ITT*, pp. 1–639 *et seq.*, which has not yet entered into force, provides a more detailed rule to the same effect in subsections (2) and (3) of Article 6, *Protection of owners and demise charterers of arrested ships*:
   "2. The Courts of the State in which an arrest has been affected shall have jurisdiction to determine the extent of the liability, if any, of the claimant for loss or damage caused by the arrest of a ship, including but not restricted to such loss or damage as may be caused in consequence of: (a) the arrest having been wrongful or unjustified, or (b) excessive security having been demanded and provided.
   "3. The liability, if any, of the claimant in accordance with paragraph 2 of this article shall be determined by application of the law of the State where the arrest was effected."
3. For a brief overview of the position in various countries, see *Berlingieri on Arrest of Ships* (3rd ed., 2000) (London), pp. 195 *et seq.*, pp. 266 *et seq.*, and Christian Breitzke/Jonathan Lux/Philomène Verlaan (eds.), *Maritime Law Handbook*, The Hague (looseleaf).

faith") must be proven on the part of the applicant for arrest before a liability for wrongful arrest may arise.

14.3 Needless to say, the above distinction is of an arbitrary nature and boundaries are on closer inspection rarely as neat and sharp. This is illustrated by the fact that the kinds and degrees of fault which give rise to a liability for wrongful arrest in the southerly countries, may do so equally in the northerly countries irrespective of whether the claim for which arrest was made succeeds on the merits. Similarly, where in the northerly countries the mere fact that the claim fails on the merits suffices to create a liability for wrongful arrest, this same fact may be relevant, if not sufficient, to a claim for wrongful arrest in the southerly countries as well.

SCOPE OF THE COMPARATIVE STUDY

14.4 In this chapter, I will examine and describe how liability for wrongful (ship's) arrest is construed in three European legal systems, two of the northerly group, i.e. Germany and The Netherlands, and one of the southerly group, i.e. France. The aim is to understand how each of the three countries deals conceptually with this problem in its legal system, the practical results to which this leads in its case law and (express or hidden) considerations of public policy which (may) lie behind this approach. Because of insurmountable language barriers and restricted access to foreign law reports and legal literature, I had to exclude other interesting legal systems such as the Scandinavian, Mediterranean and eastern European countries from the scope of this study in comparative law from the beginning. Although originally included within the scope of this study, Belgian law had to be excluded unfortunately due to time constraints.[4] The inclusion of French and German law in this study is justified by the highly developed legal doctrine and case law in these countries and by the considerable influence that they have traditionally exerted on other civil law countries on the European Continent. Dutch law was not only included because of my personal knowledge and experience with this legal system, but also in view of the great practical importance of the generous facility to arrest ships in The Netherlands.

SOME STATISTICS

14.5 The importance for the international commercial and maritime practice of ship's arrest in The Netherlands is illustrated by the findings of a fairly recent (2002) statistical study into the relative frequency of ship's arrests in the major ports of England, France, Germany, Belgium and the Netherlands between 1995 and 2000.[5] This study was commissioned by the Dutch Ministry of Justice for policy purposes. The table below originates from this report (which is in Dutch) and shows in the second and third column for each port the average number of visiting sea-going

---

4. English language readers interested in Belgian law may be referred to Walter P. Verstrepen, "Arrest and judicial sale of ships in Belgium", in [1995] L.M.C.L.Q. pp. 131–153; J. Theunis, *Arrest of Ships – Belgium* (London, 1986), pp. 5–29 and *Berlingieri on Arrest of Ships* (3rd ed., 2000) (London, LLP).

5. E.C. van Ginkel, *Telling beslag op zeeschepen in Nederland en omringende landen*, Wetenschappelijk Onderzoek- en Documentatiecentrum, The Hague, 2002.

vessels per day and per year. In the fourth column the average number of ships arrested each year is shown and finally the fifth column contains the number of ships arrested per 10,000 visiting sea-going vessels for each port.

Port	Number of visiting sea-going vessels Per day	Per year	Average number of arrested sea-going vessels per year	Relative number of ships' arrests per 10,000 visiting sea-going vessels
Rotterdam	80	29,200	300 (of which 132 long-term)	102 (of which 45 long-term)
Antwerp	43	15,695	105	67
Gand	8	2,920	14	48
Amsterdam	14	5,110	23	45
Le Havre	20	7,300	12	16
Marseille	25	9,125	13	14
London (incl. Medway ports)	46	16,790	7.5	5
Felixstowe	21	7,665	3	4
Hamburg	33	12,000	1	0.8
Bremen	24	8,760	0	0

(*Source*: E.C. van Ginkel, *Telling beslag op zeeschepen in Nederland en omringende landen*, 2002. p. 7, Table 2.)

14.6 It is obvious from these results that in absolute terms the ports of Rotterdam and Antwerp account for far more ships' arrests each year than the other major ports in the region combined. In relative terms, the same applies for the Dutch and Belgian ports in comparison to the ports in England, France and Germany. Furthermore it is striking that both in absolute and relative terms the number of ships' arrests in England and (especially) Germany is so small.

GERMAN LAW[6]

Introduction

14.7 It is well known that German law is generally rather restrictive in allowing conservatory and provisional measures.[7] The general principle is that a debtor's property may only be attached if and when the creditor has obtained a legal title to that effect, whether a court judgment[8] (or an arbitral award declared enforceable by the court) or a deed from a public notary.[9] It is only as an exception to this rule, that §917 of the Zivilprozeßordnung (ZPO or German Code of Civil Procedure), permits the creditor to seek an arrest order without prior judgment in the following – limited – circumstances (in free translation):

6. For publications in English about the German law of ships' arrest see: J. Trappe, "The Law of a Ship's arrest in Germany", in *European Transport Law* (hereafter *E.T.L.*), 1991, p. 329; K. Soehring, *Arrest of Ships-Germany* (London, 1985), p. 51, V. Looks, "Federal Republic of Germany", in *Maritime Law Handbook*, A. Kirchner, *Maritime Arrest, Legal Reflections on the International Arrest Conventions and on Domestic Law in Germany and Sweden* (Stockholm University, 2001), pp. 14 *et seq.*
7. See Trappe, *E.T.L.*, 1991, p. 329.
8. §704, ZPO.
9. §794, ZPO.

"(1) The arrest of a movable or immovable thing takes place if one has to assume that without it the enforcement of a judgment would be rendered impossible or substantially more difficult.

(2) No further justification for an arrest need be proven if the judgment has to be enforced abroad and the reciprocity (of recognition of judgments) is not guaranteed."

14.8 German law construes the exception of §917 of the ZPO and therefore the grounds for arrest contained herein rather narrowly. This is illustrated by the fact that the rule in §917(1) of the ZPO, permitting arrest if without it the enforcement of the judgment would be rendered impossible or substantially more difficult, is understood not to protect the creditor against possible or imminent deterioration of the financial situation of his debtor (a mere commercial risk), but to be aimed only at situations where the debtor has no assets within the jurisdiction or where he is hiding or selling off his assets, or moving his assets abroad.

14.9 Furthermore, it has long been controversial among German Courts and legal scholars whether the old wording of §917 of the ZPO[10] permitted a conservatory arrest in Germany in support of court or arbitral proceedings to the merits abroad.[11] This matter seems to have been clarified with the above new wording of §917(2) of the ZPO, which entered into force on 1 April 2004. It had already been decided by the European Court of Justice in *Mund & Fester/Hatrex*,[12] that the arrest ground in §917(2) of the ZPO (old wording) did not apply if a (German) judgment was to be enforced abroad in a EU Member State. This excluded 24 European countries from the application of this – already quite restricted – ground for arrest. The reason is that otherwise §917 of the ZPO would violate the *EJJC and EJR* and the non-discrimination rule of Article 6 of the EC Treaty.[13]

14.10 Finally, German law in §920 of the ZPO requires that the claimant provides together with the arrest petition *prima facie* evidence ("*Glaubhaftmachung*") in support of his claim, that he is the holder of this claim and in respect of the grounds for arrest. Mere allegations are insufficient.[14]

14.11 It is probably no coincidence that this general restrictiveness with regard to conservatory arrests in German law, places the interest of the owner to be protected against interference with his property above the interest of the creditor to secure his claim through an arrest whilst he can. After all, this rule fits in nicely with the fact that Germany has even included the right of property in its list of basic rights enshrined in the German Constitution (*Grundgesetz*), thus making it possible to challenge even the constitutionality of an Act of parliament if this impedes upon this fundamental right.

---

10. The old wording of §917(2) of the ZPO was (in free translation): "No further justification for an arrest need be proven if the judgment has to be enforced abroad."

11. The leading opinion was in the negative, see Trappe, *E.T.L.*, 1991, p. 330 referring to Looks, *Transportrecht* (hereafter *TranspR*),1989, p. 345, and *The Mavro Vetranic* decision of the Hamburg Court of Appeal (Hanseatisches Oberlandesgericht Hamburg), 11 December 1989, *TranspR*, 1990, p. 112. *Cf.* Silke Nieschulz, *Der Arrest in Seeschiffe, Eine rechtsvergleichende Untersuchung des deutschen, niederländischen und englischen Rechts*, diss. Hamburg, 1997, pp. 32 *et seq.*

12. ECJ, 10 February 1994, C-398/92, [1994] E.C.R. I-467 [*Mund & Fester/Hatrex*].

13. Now replaced by the European Judgments and Jurisdiction Regulation (E.J.J.R.) 44/2001.

14. See Nieschulz, *Der Arrest in Seeschiffe*, 1997, pp. 65 *et seq.*, and the answer of the German MLA to the questionnaire in *Berlingieri on Arrest of Ships* (3rd ed., 2000) (London), p. 236.

Wrongful arrest

14.12 It is against this general background of "arrest-unfriendliness", that also the German law with regard to liability for wrongful arrest must be seen. The German Code of Civil Procedure, i.e. §945 of the Zivilprozeßordnung (ZPO), contains a special provision for liability for wrongful arrest. In free translation, this provision[15] reads as follows:

"If it appears that an arrest order or an injunction was unjustified from the beginning or the measure that was ordered is subsequently lifted on the grounds of §926(2) of the ZPO or §942(3) of the ZPO, then the party who applied for the order is obliged to compensate the other party its damage resulting from the enforcement of the measure which was ordered or from any security provided in order to avoid the enforcement or to ensure the lifting of the measure."

14.13 As follows from the wording of §945 of the ZPO, German law imposes a liability for wrongful arrest upon an applicant for arrest if: (1) it appears that the arrest order was unjustified from the beginning, or (2) the arrest is subsequently lifted by the court because of failure to commence main proceedings (the ground of §926(2) of the ZPO)[16] or for non-observance of a time-bar set by the court (§942(3) of the ZPO).[17] An arrest is unjustified from the beginning if the claim for which arrest was made fails on the merits or if there was no valid ground for arrest.[18]

14.14 Although there is some debate among German scholars about the proper dogmatic underpinning of the rule,[19] it is common ground that the liability for wrongful arrest pursuant to §945 of the ZPO is a strict liability which arises irrespective of illegality or fault on the part of the applicant for arrest. It is sufficient if by objective standards at the time the arrest was ordered, the preconditions for an arrest were missing.[20] Therefore, even an applicant acting in good faith, who could reasonably assume that the arrest was in support of a valid claim and that the grounds for arrest pursuant to §917 of the ZPO had been fulfilled, is nevertheless liable if the arrest was subsequently lifted because of lack of ground for arrest in summary proceedings pursuant to §927 of the ZPO[21] or if his claim fails on the

---

15. §945, ZPO: "Erweist sich die Anordnung eines Arrestes oder einer einstweiligen Verfügung als von Anfang an ungerechtfertigt oder wird die angeordnete Maßregel auf Grund des §926 Abs. 2 oder des §942 Abs. 3 aufgehoben, so ist die Partei, welche die Anordnung erwirkt hat, verpflichtet, dem Gegner den Schaden zu ersetzen, der ihm aus der Vollziehung der angeordneten Maßregel oder dadurch entsteht, daß er Sicherheit leistet, um die Vollziehung abzuwenden oder die Aufhebung der Maßregel zu erwirken."

16. The ground of §942(3), ZPO, relates to the lifting of an injunction for failure to observe the time fixed by the court for notifying the defendant party, and is of no relevance here. See Nieschulz, *Die Arrest in Seeschiffe*, diss. Hamburg, 1997, pp. 101 *et seq.*

17. Nieschulz, *Die Arrest in Seeschiffe*, diss. Hamburg, 1997, pp. 102 *et seq.*

18. German Federal Supreme Court (*Bundesgerichtshof*) (hereafter B.G.H.), 7 June 1988, N.J.W. 1988, p. 3269, B.G.H. 19 March 1992, N.J.W.-R.R. 1992, p. 736.

19. See Stein/Jonas, *Kommentar zur Zivilprozessordnung*, 21. Aufl., Tübingen, 1996, §945, Rdnr. 2 (Grunsky) and §717 Rdnr. 9 *et seq.* and name amongst others the concepts of vicarious liability (*Gefährdungshaftung*), Risk liability (*Risikohaftung*) and liability for illegal act in a wider sense (*Haftung aus unerlaubte Handlung im weiterer Sinne*).

20. B.G.H. 28 November 1991, N.J.W.-R.R., 1992, p. 1001.

21. *Münchener Kommentar zur Zivilprozessordnung*, 2. Aufl., 2001, §94, Rdnr. 19 (Heinze).

merits,[22] e.g. due to lack of proof.[23] The severity of this view is illustrated by the opinion defended in leading German Commentaries, that even if the applicant relied on a long and widely held interpretation of the law by the courts, which suddenly changed to his detriment in his particular case, he will nevertheless be liable for wrongful arrest.[24]

14.15 However, if the factual circumstances changed after the arrest was made, e.g. because of assignment or settlement of the claim, then this does not invalidate an otherwise validly ordered arrest. Neither will a change in the legal position with retroactive effect (e.g. because a legal act on which the claim was founded is declared null and void ab initio) create a liability pursuant to §945 of the ZPO.[25] In such cases, the other party can seek the lifting of the arrest in summary proceedings pursuant to §927 of the ZPO,[26] but no liability arises.

14.16 Repeatedly, the German Federal Court of Justice has explained and clarified the policy reasons behind the strict liability rule of §945 of the ZPO.[27] These reasons can be summarised as follows.[28] The liability of §945 of the ZPO places on the creditor and applicant the risk, which results from his own decision to take – inherently dangerous – conservatory and provisional measures against his debtor at a time that the legal position is still undecided in view of pending or future legal proceedings to the merits. It is the creditor who wishes to secure his legal position and the future enforcement of his claim without the justification of a prior judgment to the merits and he does so by interfering severely in the legal sphere of his alleged debtor. If this interference causes damage and the claim – in relation to which the arrest is instrumental – fails on the merits, then §945 of the ZPO consistently places the liability on the creditor irrespective of illegality or fault. Needless to say, the same reasoning and policy considerations equally apply if the arrest is lifted because the applicant failed to commence the main proceedings altogether.

14.17 Finally, the measure of damages that applies to the liability for wrongful arrest pursuant to §945 of the ZPO is the general measure applicable to tort liability in §249(1) of the German Civil Code (*Bürgerliches Gesetzbuch* or *B.G.B.*),[29] which provides that anybody liable in damages must restore the situation that would exist, if the circumstance obliging him to pay damages had not occurred. If it appears that the damage caused by the arrest was (partly) the result of own fault of the party whose property was arrested, this may mitigate the liability to compensate the damage.[30]

---

22. See Stein/Jonas, §945, Rdnr. 1–2, 4, 19 (Grunsky); MünchKomm ZPO-Heinze §94, Rdnr. 21, Rosenberg/Gaul/Schilken, *Zwangsvollstreckungsrecht*, 11. Aufl., München, 1997, §80, p. 1056.
23. B.G.H. 7 June 1988, N.J.W.-R.R., 1988, p. 3269. See Thomas/Putzo, *Zivilprozessordnung*, 27. Aufl., 2005, §945, Rdnr. 7 (Reichold).
24. See Stein/Jonas, §945, Rdnr. 19, MünchKomm ZPO-Heinze, §945, Rdnr. 21.
25. See Stein/Jonas, §945, Rdnr. 19a, MünchKomm ZPO-Heinze, §945, Rdnr. 21
26. Nieschulz, *Die Arrest in Seeschiffe*, diss. Hamburg, 1997, p. 96.
27. See B.G.H. 22.3.1990, N.J.W. 1990, p. 2689 referring to B.G.H., B.G.H.Z., 54, p. 80; N.J.W. 1970, p. 1459; B.G.H. 4.12.1973, B.G.H.Z., 62, p. 9, N.J.W. 1974, 642; B.G.H. 23.5.1985, B.G.H.Z., 95, p. 14, N.J.W. 1985, p. 1959.
28. See MünchKomm ZPO-Heinze, §945, Rdnr. 4. *Cf.* Rosenberg/Gaul/Schilken, §80, p. 1054.
29. §249 BGB (1) "Wer zum Schadenersatz verpflichtet ist, hat den Zustand herzustellen, der bestehen wurde, wenn der zum Ersatz verpflichtenden Umstand nicht eingetreten wäre."
30. B.G.H. 22.3.1990, N.J.W. 1990, p. 2690.

FRENCH LAW [31]

Introduction

14.18 French law is fairly liberal in allowing conservatory arrests of ships. In the words of Rodière, conservatory arrest (of a ship) is equally frequent and even commonplace, as enforcement through a public auction is rare.[32] A French Commentary writes: "that strictly speaking, conservatory arrest is not an enforcement measure. Its principal aim is to exercise pressure upon an unwilling debtor to induce him to pay. This explains why under French general law and maritime law it is not required for a conservatory arrest that the claim is certain, of a determined quantity and payable."[33] Neither is it required that the claim for which leave for conservatory arrest is requested, is endangered or urgent.[34]

14.19 In *The African Star*,[35] the French Supreme Court, la Cour de Cassation, has stressed that the 1952 Arrest Convention does not require a "maritime claim" to be certain and sound, the allegation of a maritime claim is sufficient.[36] This rule applies not only to the decision on the arrest petition but also to summary proceedings (even in appeal) to lift the arrest ("*Référé*").[37] Similarly, it was held in *The Friday Star* by the Aix-en-Provence Court of Appeal that the arrest court should not assess the certainty, soundness or possible prescription of the alleged claim, provided it is a maritime claim.[38] This interpretation of the 1952 Arrest Conven-

---

31. For publications in English about the French law of ship's arrest, see J.-S. Rohart, "France", in *Maritime Law Handbook,* and *Berlingieri on arrest of ships* (3rd ed., 2000).

32. R. Rodière, *Traité Général de droit maritime, Le navire,* Dalloz, 1980, p. 231: "la saisie conservatoire est aussi fréquente et même banale que la saisie-exécution est rare". *Cf.* A. Vialard, *Droit Maritime,* 1997, p. 311, no. 364.

33. See J.-B. Racine, "Navire (Saisie et vente publique)" (2001), in L. Vogel (ed.), *Répertoire de Droit Commercial Dalloz (Rép. com. Dalloz),* Tome IV (Looseleaf), p. 6, no. 34 and p. 10, no. 66: "La saisie conservatoire n'est pas une voie d'exécution au sens strict. Elle a principalement pour but d'exercer une pression sur le débiteur récalcitrant pour l'inciter à payer. C'est pourquoi, aussi bien en droit commun qu'en droit maritime, il n'est pas nécessaire pour exercer une saisie conservatoire de se prévaloir d'une créance certaine, liquide et exigible." *Cf.* C. Navarre-Laroche, *La saisie conservatoire des navires en droit français,* Moreux, 2001, p. 61.

34. See Cour de Cassation civ. 18.11.1986, *Droit Maritime Français* (hereafter D.M.F.), 1987, p. 697, Cour d'Appel (CA) Aix-en-Provence 26.1.1990, D.M.F. 1992, p. 354 [*Mont-Blanc Maru*], C.A. Aix-en-Provence 24.9. 1992, *Revue de droit français commercial, maritime et fiscal,* 1992, p. 89 [*Hassi R'Mel*]. Earlier differently, C.A. Aix-en-Provence 28.11.1985, D.M.F. 1986, p. 694 [*Shangri-La*]. See also Navarre-Laroche, *La saisie conservatoire des navires en droit français,* 2001, p. 61 and Racine, "Navire", in *Rép. Com. Dalloz,* 2001, p. 11, no. 67.

35. Cour de Cassation Com 26.5.1987, D.M.F. 1987, p. 645 [*African Star*]: "la convention de Bruxelles n'exige pas que la créance alléguée ait une caractère et sérieux". *Cf.* Cour de Cassation Com. 12.1.1988, DMF 1992, p. 134 [*Nora*], Tribunal (Trib.) Nouméa 17.11.1979, D.M.F. 1980, p. 223 [*La-Bonita*]. See also the corrected decisions of C.A. Poitiers 13.11.1985, D.M.F. 1987, p. 646 [*African Star*] and C.A. Rouen 1.7.1985, D.M.F. 1986, p. 421 [*Nora*]. Critical about this approach is Vialard, *Droit Maritime,* 1997, p. 313, no. 367.

36. See in this respect also *Berlingieri on arrest of ships* (3rd ed., 2000), p. 156, no. I.598 *et seq.,* p. 160, no. I.612.

37. See, e.g., C.A. Aix-en-Provence 26.1.1990, D.M.F. 1992, p. 354 [*Mont-Blanc-Maru*].

38. C.A. Aix-en-Provence 6.12.1995, D.M.F. 1997, p. 591 [*Friday Star*] (comments by Y. Tassel): "(…) constatation qui confère un caractère maritime à la créance alléguée dont le Juge n'a pas à apprécier ni la certitude, ni le sérieux, ni l'éventuelle prescription.". *Cf.* Cour de Cassation Com. 26.1.1990 (unpublished), cited by: Navarre-Laroche, *La saisie conservatoire des navires en droit français,* 2001, p. 60, R. Rodière/ E. du Pontavice, *Droit Maritime* (12th ed., Dalloz, 1997), p. 169, no. 178, note 4. Critical: Vialard, "La saisie conservatoire des navires affrétés", in D.M.F. 1994, p. 305 *et seq.*

tion departs from French domestic law, which requires for a conservatory arrest that the claim[39] must appear to be grounded in principle,[40] allowing the court to verify and determine the strength of the claim.[41] The arrest-friendliness of the French courts is illustrated further by the fact that an applicant for arrest is rarely ordered to provide counter-security by the court.[42]

Wrongful arrest

14.20 Pursuant to French law, creditors may in principle enforce their claims on all assets of their debtors and it is up to the creditor to choose the proper measures to conserve and secure the (future) enforcement of his claim.[43] Article 22, Act No. 91-650 of 9 July 1991, which states (in free translation):

"The creditor has the choice of the proper measures to ensure the enforcement or conservation of his claim. The exercise of these measures may not exceed what will prove necessary to obtain payment of the obligation. The Enforcement Judge has the power to order the lifting of each useless or abusive measure and to condemn the creditor to compensate damages in case of abusive arrest."

14.21 French law conceives the effecting of an arrest as a – in itself legitimate – way of exercising the claimant's basic civic liberty to seek recourse to justice (*voie de droit*).[44] In this approach, it is considered excessive if the mere defeat in court

39. This may be any kind of claim, i.e. not necessarily a maritime claim. See: Rodière/Du Pontavice, *Droit Maritime* (12th ed., 1997), p. 166, no. 176, Vialard, *Droit Maritime*, 1997, p. 314, no. 367.

40. See: Art. 29, §2 Decree no. 67-967 of 27.10.1967 as changed by the Decree no. 161 of 24.2.1971: "l'autorisation peut être accordée dès lors qu'il est justifié d'une créance paraissant fondée en son principe." Previously, the Decree of 27.10.1967 had required: "la saisie conservatoire (...) ne peut (...) être (autorisée) que si le requérant justifie d'une créance certaine". See: Navarre-Laroche, *op. cit.*, 2001, p. 58 *et seq.*, Racine, "Navire", in *Rép. Com. Dalloz*, 2001, p. 10, no. 66, Rodière/Du Pontavice, *Droit Maritime* (12th ed., 1997), p. 166, no. 176, and *Berlingieri on arrest of ships* (3rd ed., 2000), p. 160, no. I.612.

41. *Cf.* Vialard, *Droit Maritime*, 1997, p. 314, no. 367.

42. E.g. C.A. Rouen 30.7.1980, D.M.F. 1980, 668 [*Georgios-K*]. See Racine, "Navire", in *Rép. Com. Dalloz*, 2001, p. 19, no. 120. Some writers would favour it if French courts imposed counter-security more often: Rodière, *Le Navire*, 1980, p. 248, no. 199, Navarre-Laroche, *op. cit.*, p. 219. See also the critical comment of R. Achard below: C.A. Aix-en-Provence 26.1.1990, D.M.F. 1992, p. 354 [*Mont-Blanc-Maru*].

43. See Article 22, Act no. 91-650 of 9 July 1991, which states (in original and free translation): "Le créancier a le choix des mesures propres à assurer l'exécution ou la conservation de sa créance. L'exécution de ces mesures ne peut excéder ce qui se révèle nécessaire pour obtenir le paiement de l'obligation. – Le juge de l'exécution a le pouvoir d'ordonner la mainlevée de toute mesure inutile ou abusive et de condamner le créancier à des dommages-intérêts en cas d'abus de saisie." (The creditor has the choice of the proper measures to ensure the enforcement or conservation of his claim. The exercise of these measures may not exceed what will prove necessary to obtain payment of the obligation. The Enforcement Judge has the power to order the lifting of each useless or abusive measure and to condemn the creditor to compensate damages in case of abusive arrest.). *Cf.* Racine, "Navire", in *Rép. Com. Dalloz*, 2001, p. 12, no. 77.

44. *Cf.* L. Cadiet/Ph. le Tourneau, "Abus de droit", *Répertoire de Droit Civil Dalloz (Rep. Civ. Dalloz)*, Tome I, V°, 2002, p. 23, no. 113 with references, Navarre-Laroche, *op. cit.*, 2001, p. 215 and Racine, "Navire", in *Rép. Com. Dalloz*, 2001, p. 19, no. 121: "Est-il possible de demander au saisissant la réparation de ce préjudice? La réponse est normalement négative. En effet, le fait de pratiquer une saisie est en lui-même légitime car il constitue l'exercice d'une voie de droit. On voit ici le conflit d'intérêts présent dans toute saisie. D'une côté, les intérêts du créancier qui, en garantie de sa créance, doit pouvoir sans entrave saisir les biens de son débiteur. De l'autre, les intérêts du débiteur qui subit un préjudice du fait de la saisie."

proceedings already constituted a *"faute"* (fault), obliging the defeated party to compensate the damage. It does not follow, however, that the claimant is entirely free in the exercise of his (procedural) rights. The public interest of a proper and efficient administration of justice and the legitimate interests of the defendant dictate that limits are set to procedural transgressions. Thus, where the exercise of a right, such as a conservatory arrest, becomes abusive (*abus de droit*),[45] the courts may intervene and condemn the guilty party to pay a civil fine to the state[46] and to compensate the damage[47] of the innocent party pursuant to Article 1382 of the Code Civil.[48] It is interesting and perhaps revealing that the interest of the owner who must bear that his property is being arrested is not mentioned here as ground for an *abus de droit*. It seems that French law does not require the court to balance the interest of the creditor in seeking an arrest, against the interest of the debtor not to suffer an arrest of his property.

14.22 As stated above, pursuant to French law an arrest will become wrongful if it meets the standard of an *abus de droit*, in which case the guilty party will be liable in tort.[49] It goes without saying that not each and every mistake on the part of the applicant for arrest will qualify as an *abus de droit*. Repeatedly, the French courts have rejected liability for applicants for arrest, who had acted under the influence of a mistake with regard to the law or the facts.[50] As stated above, the fact that the claim for which arrest was made failed on the merits, is insufficient as such to base a liability for wrongful arrest.[51]

14.23 There is no general definition of *abus de droit* in French law nor a specific one for abusive arrests.[52] *Abus de droit* has developed and still develops in case law and legal doctrine. Although over time various theories explaining and analysing *abus de droit* have been proposed, the French courts have never formally chosen for any of these interpretations and are far from united.

14.24 In theories about *abus de droit* two extreme poles can be distinguished. On the one hand, there is a narrow, subjective, interpretation, according to which there is only *abus de droit* if a right is exercised with the intent to cause harm to others, e.g. if a person insists upon the use or enforcement of a legal right although this is

---

45. See: J. Ghestin/G. Goubeaux, *Traité de droit civil*, Introduction générale, LGDJ, 4° ed., n° 761 *et seq.*, especially n° 777 *et seq.*

46. See: Art. 32-1 (Décr. n°78-62 du 20.1.1978) of the New French Code of Civil Procedure, which reads as follows: "Celui qui agit en justice de manière dilatoire ou abusive peut être condamné à une amende civile de 15 € à 1 500 €, sans préjudice des dommages-intérêts qui seraient réclamés."

47. Reputation damage due to the ship's arrest was rejected in: Trib. Nouméa 17.11.1979, D.M.F. 1980, p. 223 [*La-Bonita*] and Cour de Cassation com. 29.11.1983, D.M.F. 1984, p. 552 [*La-Bonita*].

48. See also Art. 22, Act no. 91-650 of 9 July 1991, see note 43 above, which general provision however does not apply to arrest of ships directly.

49. *Cf.* Ph. le Tourneau, *Droit de la responsabilité et des contrats*, Dalloz, 2004, p. 1089, no. 6865, Navarre-Laroche, *La saisie conservatoire des navires en droit français*, 2001, p. 215.

50. See Le Tourneau, *Droit de la responsabilité et des contrats*, 2004, p. 1101, no. 6950 *et seq.* and Cadiet/Le Tourneau, *Rep. Civ. Dalloz*, Tome I, V°, 2002, p. 23 *et seq.*, no. 113 *et seq.*

51. See Cadiet/Le Tourneau, *Rep. Civ. Dalloz*, Tome I, V°, 2002, p. 24, no. 123, p. 26, no. 135. See, e.g., C.A. Rouen 20.12.1995, D.M.F. 1997, p. 30 [*Cléo D*] in which the bunkers were released from arrest because it had not been proven that the bunkers were the property of the debtor or that the claim was endangered. Nevertheless, the Court of Appeal Rouen held that arrest being without ground, did not make the arrest abusive. *Cf.* C.A. Rouen 3.11.1998, D.M.F. 1999, p. 123 [*Pom Thule*].

52. See Cadiet/Le Tourneau, *Rep. Civ. Dalloz*, Tome I, V°, 2002, p. 3, no. 4, Vialard, *Droit Maritime*, 1997, p. 322, no. 378, Navarre-Laroche, *op. cit.*, 2001, p. 215.

entirely useless to himself, yet harmful to another.[53] On the other hand, there is a wider, more objective approach, which defines *abus de droit* as an act which contradicts the purpose, spirit and objective of the legal or contractual right at stake.[54] Such conduct constitutes a "fault", because a careful, prudent and reasonable person, the famous *bon père de famille* (a good family father) would not act in this way.[55]

14.25 This raises the question as to what may constitute an *abus de droit* in the exercise of procedural rights such as a conservatory arrest. Traditionally, the question was whether any mistake in the exercise of procedural rights suffices for *abus de droit* or whether intent or gross negligence equivalent to intent must be proven for this.[56] In the past, the Cour de Cassation has held on many occasions that the losing claimant is not liable, except if he commenced proceedings in *"mauvaise foi"* (bad faith),[57] with a "malicious attitude" or at least committing a "gross mistake equivalent to intent".[58] A striking example offers the case of *The Tipasa*,[59] in which on a Friday at the end of the morning, the claimant intentionally and without necessity arrested a ferry loaded with passengers and vehicles and ready to depart in an hour, although another vessel owned by the same debtor was present at the quay.

14.26 More recently, the Cour de Cassation tends to accept a lesser degree of fault, described as *"légèreté blâmable"* (reproachable lightheartedness),[60] *"imprudence grave"* (serious carelessness) or *"témérité fautive"* (recklessness), as sufficient for *abus de droit*.[61] Other decisions illustrate these conflicting tendencies further. In *La-Bonita* the Cour de Cassation reasoned "that the Court of Appeal after having ... decided that bad faith on the part of the claimant had not been shown, ... and after finding that the claim was partially grounded on the merits, could conclude that the claimant had not abused his right by exercising a conservatory arrest in order to obtain security for his claim".[62]

---

53. Cadiet/Le Tourneau, *Rep. Civ. Dalloz*, Tome I, V°, 2002, p. 8, nr. 24: "Dans cette thèse, l'abus n'existera que si le droit a été exercé avec l'intention de nuire, que lorsque le droit légal or contractuel, à l'application ou à l'exécution duquel le demandeur vient prétendre, apparaît tout à la fois inutile pour lui-même et préjudiciable au défendeur, cette conjonction révélant l'intention de nuire."

54. Cadiet/Le Tourneau, *Rep. Civ. Dalloz*, Tome I, V°, 2002, p. 8, no. 25 : "A l'opposé de cette conception individualiste, Josserand définissait l'abus de droit comme 'l'acte contraire au but de l'institution, à son esprit et à sa finalité' ".

55. Le Tourneau, *Droit de la responsabilité et des contrats*, 2004, p. 1089, no. 6865.

56. Cadiet/Le Tourneau, *Rep. Civ. Dalloz*, Tome I, V°, 2002, p. 23, no. 115.

57. See Cour de Cassation 29.11.1983, D.M.F. 1984, p. 552 [*La-Bonita*].

58. See Cadiet/Le Tourneau, *Rep. Civ. Dalloz*, Tome I, V°, 2002, p. 25, no. 128 and 129 and p. 26, no. 136 with further references.

59. C.A. Aix-en-Provence 10.3. 1987, D.M.F. 1988, p. 545 and p. 549 [*Tipasa*].

60. See also C.A. Montpellier 28.6.1984, D.M.F. 1985, p. 625 [*Hadj-Abdul-Satar-Issa*].

61. Cour de Cassation ass. plén, 25.3.1999, cited by P. Bonassies, *Le droit positif en 1999, D.M.F. [hors série]*, 2000, no 42 did not concern a ship's arrest, but an arrest by customs officials. See also Racine, "Navire", in *Rép. Com. Dalloz*, 2001, p. 20, no. 124, Cadiet/Le Tourneau, *Rep. Civ. Dalloz*, Tome I, V°, 2002, p. 25, no. 131, p. 26, no. 137.

62. In free translation of Cour de Cassation com 29.11.1983, D.M.F. 1984, p. 552 [*La-Bonita*]: "La Cour d'appel, après avoir souverainement considéré que la mauvaise foi du sous-affréteur n'était pas établie, et avoir retenu, par une disposition motivée dont la cassation a été écartée par le rejet du premier moyen, que le sous-affréteur était partiellement fondé en son action au fond, a pu décider qu'il n'avait pas commis d'abus de droit en exerçant une saisie-conservatoire pour obtenir garantie de sa créance." In the same sense: C.A. Rouen 9.5.1978, D.M.F. 1979, p. 211 [*Ushgorod*]. See also Navarre-Laroche, *op. cit.*, p. 219.

14.27 The outcome may, however, be different if it appears afterwards that from the beginning the legal basis for the claim was entirely missing. In 1996 in *The Alexander III* the Cour de Cassation criticised the C.A. Aix-en-Provence for not explaining why the conservatory arrest by Zaatari of Lemphy's ship in order to secure a claim against Klides – Lemphy and Klides being separate legal entities – did not involve the liability for wrongful arrest of Zaatari towards Lemphy.[63] In the same decision, the Cour de Cassation chastised the Court of Appeal even further for not responding to the allegation that applicant for arrest Zaatari had also committed an *abus de droit* by considerably exaggerating the claim amount and by demanding a guarantee for a disproportional amount.[64]

14.28 *The Alexander III* decision has been criticised[65] for introducing "lack of proportionality" as an indication of *abus de droit*. In defence of that decision it can be argued that an excessively overstated claim and a demand for disproportional security can be indications of *mauvaise foi* (bad faith) on the part of the claimant and are therefore relevant in establishing an *abus de droit*. If, however, the Cour de Cassation considers lack of proportionality by itself as proof of *abus de droit*, then in my view the above-mentioned criticism is well-deserved, because it will not always be possible for a creditor to know the exact quantum of his claim early on, e.g. shortly after a maritime casualty has occurred. Nevertheless, in such a case he has a legitimate interest in obtaining security for his estimated claim through a ship's arrest, even if afterwards the claim proves to be much lower than earlier expected or feared.[66]

14.29 Furthermore, it is submitted that (lack of) proportionality as such is not a good criterion for *abus de droit*, because there will almost inevitably be a considerable disproportion between the claim amount and the usually much higher value of the ship.[67] For obvious reasons, however, that is not the whole story. First, even in the event of a forced sale, a creditor has no certainty whether he will be able to recover his claim from the sale proceeds because there may well be higher ranking claims of other creditors such as salvors or mortgage banks. But to deny him on that ground the possibility to seek security for his claim by way of a conservatory arrest, seems grotesque. Second, claims against the ship or its owners will often, if not always be covered by P&I insurance, which offers a widely available, efficient and relatively cheap instrument to the debtor to deal with ship's arrests, i.e. the offer of a letter of undertaking from the P&I Club or from a local bank as arranged by the P&I Club.

63. Cour de Cassation com 19.3.1996, DMF 1996, p. 503, 505 [*Alexander III*]: "Attendu qu'en statuant ainsi, sans dire en quoi le fait de saisir un navire de la société Lemphy pour garantir le recouvrement d'une créance sur la société Klides ne serait pas de nature à engager la responsabilité des saississants à l'égard de la société Lemphy, dès lors que ces deux personnes morales sont distinctes, la Cour d'appel a violé susvisé."

64. Earlier C.A. Aix-en-Provence had already held in a decision of 24.5.1985, D.M.F. 1986, p. 681 [*Eva Danielsen*] that to use a conservatory arrest to obtain a bank guarantee for an excessive amount constituted *abus de droit*. In the same sense C.A. Aix-en-Provence 28.11.1985, D.M.F. 1986, p. 694 [*Shangri-La*].

65. See Vialard, "Personnalité morale des sociétés d'armement et apparentement abusif des navires saisis", in D.M.F. 1996, pp. 467, 472.

66. In this sense also Vialard, D.M.F. 1996, p. 473, Navarre-Laroche, "Navire saisi, saisie levée, saisie abusive?", in D.M.F. 2003, p. 775, C.A. Rouen 24.10.2002, D.M.F. 2003, p. 770 [*Tanabata*].

67. In this sense also Racine, "Navire", in *Rép. Com. Dalloz*, 2001, p. 20, no. 126; Vialard, D.M.F. 1996, p. 472; Navarre-Laroche, *La saisie conservatoire des navires en droit français*, 2001, p. 222.

DUTCH LAW[68]

Introduction

14.30 Similar to French law, Dutch law is fairly generous in allowing ship's arrests. A claimant who wishes to arrest a ship within the Dutch jurisdiction must apply to the court to obtain leave for arrest. In the *ex parte* arrest petition, the claimant must briefly explain: (1) the kind of arrest asked, (2) the factual and legal background of the claim, (3) its legal nature, (4) why it is a maritime claim, (5) the claim amount, (6) the court's jurisdiction, and (7) whether the main proceedings for the claim are already pending.[69] Unlike German arrest law, it is not required in case of a ship's arrest that there is a grounded fear that the debtor will embezzle his assets.[70] Neither is it required or customary to attach documentary evidence as *prima facie* proof to the arrest petition.

14.31 After a summary review of the arrest petition, the injunction judge[71] of the court will decide whether or not to grant leave for arrest.[72] Although the injunction judge has discretionary powers to make the leave for arrest conditional upon the claimant putting up counter-security first,[73] in practice this is seldom required. Once leave for arrest has been given, it is up to the claimant to instruct the court bailiff to effect the ship's arrest. After the ship's arrest is made, it will usually be the P&I Club of the shipowner who decides whether to offer alternative security for the claim[74] or to challenge the ship's arrest in summary relief proceedings.

14.32 Pursuant to Article 705 of the CCP, the injunction judge has discretionary powers to lift the arrest, but in some cases he is obliged to do so. Article 705 of the CCP reads in free translation as follows:

"1. The Injunction Judge who granted leave for arrest may, acting in summary relief proceedings, lift the arrest at the request of any interested party, without prejudice to the jurisdiction of the regular court.
2. The release shall be ordered amongst others in case of non-compliance with procedural requirements prescribed at the penalty of annulment, if the invalidity of the grounds relied on by the arrestor or the lack of necessity of the arrest is concisely shown, or, if the arrest is effected for a monetary claim, if sufficient security is put up for this claim.
3. (...)." [75]

---

68. For publications in English about the Dutch law of ship's arrest, see *Berlingieri on arrest of ships* (3rd ed., 2000) and W. Verhoeven/W. Jarigsma, "The Netherlands", in *Maritime Law Handbook*.
69. The general requirements of an arrest petition are stated in art. 700-2 Wetboek van Burgerlijke Rechtsvordering (Code of Civil Procedure or CCP), which in free translation reads as follows: "The leave shall be requested by means of a petition in which are stated the nature of the arrest to be effected and the grounds relied on by the petitioner and, if it is a monetary claim, the amount or, if the amount is not established, the maximum amount of the claim, without prejudice to the special requirements under the law in respect of the specific type of arrest concerned."See also *Berlingieri on arrest of ships* (3rd ed., 2000), p. 238.
70. This follows from Art. 728-1 CCP.
71. In Dutch "*Voorzieningenrechter*".
72. Art. 700-2 CCP.
73. Art. 701-1 CCP.
74. In the Netherlands it is customary to offer alternative security in the form of a letter of undertaking on the basis of the latest version (2000) of the standard Rotterdam Guarantee Form, of which a Dutch and English language version are widely available. See for an English language commentary on the wording of the Rotterdam Form, H. van der Wiel, "The Rotterdam Guarantee Form", in *E. T.L.*, 1999, p. 315 *et seq.*
75. The original wording in Dutch of Art. 705 CCP is as follows:"1. De voorzieningenrechter die verlof tot het beslag heeft gegeven kan, rechtdoende in kort geding, het beslag op vordering van elke belanghebbende opheffen, onverminderd de bevoegdheid van de gewone rechter. 2. De opheffing wordt

14.33 In contrast to French law, the Dutch injunction judge will try to reach an informed, but inevitably *provisional* judgment at the summary hearing about the likely outcome of the main proceedings with regard to the merits of the claim for which the ship's arrest was made.[76] In doing so, he will try to restore the "procedural balance" between the parties, which had been tilted in favour of the arrestor by the *ex parte* decision to grant leave for arrest, by paying special attention to what the shipowner has to say in his defence.

14.34 This helps to explain why it is usually quite fatal to a ship's arrest, if it appears at the summary hearing that the initial arrest petition was incomplete or inaccurate as to the material facts and legal grounds and therefore misleading to the court. It follows also that in Dutch summary relief proceedings, contrary to French law, the mere allegation of a maritime claim will not be enough to defend the ship's arrest. Instead, the arrestor must substantiate his claim, provide *prima facie* evidence in support of it to the extent possible and respond as good as he can to the defences and arguments raised by the shipowner.

14.35 Although summary relief proceedings by their nature do not allow for the hearing of witnesses, the injunction judge will normally base his provisional judgment on all the evidence brought to his attention, including legal opinions on foreign law, but only to the extent that he considers it relevant or persuasive. The same applies *mutatis mutandis* to the shipowner, who will have to come up with quite a strong defence against the claim or with good other arguments in order to persuade the injunction judge to order the lifting of the arrest.

14.36 The result is that Dutch law – different from German law – allows conservatory ship's arrests on a much greater scale. But on the other hand, in case of summary relief proceedings to have the arrest lifted it is – unlike French law – not only the interest of the creditor that counts, the court will also take into consideration the interests of the owner whose ship is arrested. Only if the arguments exchanged and the interests at stake cancel each other out – i.e. all other things being equal at the summary relief hearing – the injunction judge will give the benefit of the doubt to the creditor who wishes to secure his claim through arrest and the shipowner must make do with the strict liability for wrongful arrest of the creditor.

Wrongful arrest

14.37 Dutch law combines an arrest-friendliness similar to French law with a strict liability rule in case of wrongful arrest, which is close to German law. If the claim in support of which an arrest was made, fails in court proceedings on the merits, then the arrestor is liable in tort for wrongful arrest, irrespective of good faith or absence

---

onder meer uitgesproken bij verzuim van op straffe van nietigheid voorgeschreven vormen, indien summierlijk van de ondeugdelijkheid van het door de beslaglegger ingeroepen recht of van het onnodige van het beslag blijkt, of, zo het beslag is gelegd voor een geldvordering, indien voor deze vordering voldoende zekerheid is gesteld. 3. (...)"

76. It is settled case law in the Netherlands that a provisional judgment of the injunction judge in summary relief proceedings is not binding upon the parties or upon the court in main proceedings. See Dutch Supreme Court (*Hoge Raad*) (hereafter *H.R.*) 16.12.1994, *Nederlandse Jurisprudentie* (hereafter *N.J.*), 1995, no. 213.

of fault on his part.[77] Unlike German law, this strict-liability rule under Dutch law is not contained in a specific provision. Instead it is an application of the general rule on "*aansprakelijkheid uit onrechtmatige daad*" (liability for unlawful acts), which until 1992 was governed by Article 1401 of the Burgerlijk Wetboek (Dutch Civil Code or DCC),[78] and since then by Article 6:162 of the DCC. In translation, this latter provision reads as follows:

"1. A person who commits an unlawful act toward another which can be imputed to him, must repair the damage which the other person suffers as a consequence thereof.

2. *Except where there is a ground of justification, the following acts are deemed to be unlawful: the violation of a right*, an act or omission violating a statutory duty or a rule of unwritten law pertaining to proper social conduct.

3. An unlawful act can be imputed to its author if it results from his fault or from a cause for which he is answerable according to law or common opinion." [With added stress.][79]

14.38 Pursuant to Article 6:162 of the DCC the liability for wrongful arrest is construed as follows. By effecting an arrest, the claimant has (willingly) violated the (property) right of the owner, which according to subsection (3) of Article 6:162 of the DCC is imputable to him. Pursuant to subsection (2) of Article 6:162 of the DCC the violation of the property right of the owner is deemed to be unlawful except where there is a ground of justification. A provisional ground of justification results from the court's leave for arrest. The real justification, however, can only be that the claimant has a valid claim against the owner, for which he is entitled to seek recourse on all assets of his debtor.[80] If the claim fails on the merits, it becomes clear that there was no ground of justification after all, and the arrest must be deemed an unlawful act.

14.39 The origin of this rule can be traced to the beginning of last century, when the Dutch courts and legal scholars construed[81] conservatory arrest as an intentional violation by the claimant of the right of property of the owner. This intrusion may be justified if the pretended claim against the owner succeeds, but if it appears afterwards that the claim fails on the merits, then the claimant is liable. That he did or could believe to have a valid claim is irrelevant, because what counted was the intentional violation of the owner's right of property for which in the end there was no justification.

14.40 With regard to the question whether the unlawful arrest is imputable to the creditor, the Dutch courts and legal scholars in later years have – similar to

77. See *Onrechtmatige Daad* (Van Maanen), Art. 162 lid 2, aant. 14 *et seq.* and 43 *et seq.* (looseleaf), and for the law prior to 1992 *Onrechtmatige Daad* (old), I Onrechtmatigheid enz., nr. 277 (looseleaf).

78. A translation of the French art. 1382 of the Code Civil.

79. The original wording in Dutch of Art. 6:162 of the DCC is as follows: "1. Hij die jegens een ander een onrechtmatige daad pleegt, welke hem kan worden toegerekend, is verplicht de schade die de ander dientengevolge lijdt, te vergoeden. 2. Als onrechtmatige daad worden aangemerkt een inbreuk op een recht en een doen of nalaten in strijd met een wettelijke plicht of met hetgeen volgens ongeschreven recht in het maatschappelijk verkeer betaamt, een en ander behoudens de aanwezigheid van een rechtvaardigingsgrond. 3. Een onrechtmatige daad kan aan de dader worden toegerekend, indien zij te wijten is aan zijn schuld of aan een oorzaak welke krachtens de wet of de in het verkeer geldende opvattingen voor zijn rekening komt."

80. This follows from Art. 3:276 of the DCC which in translation reads as follows: "Unless the law or an agreement provide otherwise, the creditor can seek recourse for his claim on all assets of his debtor."

81. See H.R. 4.4.1912, Weekblad van 't Recht (W.), 9358, p. 1 [*Biesing/Weissenbruch*], H.R. 27.12.1929, N.J. 1930, p. 1433 [*Het Hoekhuis/Broeks*], P. Scholten, "De 'schuld' in de leer van de onrechtmatige daad", in W.P.N.R. 2310 (1914), p. 165 *et seq.*

German law – construed the liability for wrongful arrest less in terms of fault and more in terms of the claimant acting for his own risk when effecting and maintaining a conservatory arrest.[82] This is illustrated by a decision of the Hoge Raad regarding the liability for wrongful arrest of two insolvency liquidators. It was held (in my free translation):

"He who effects and maintains an arrest, acts for his own risk and must, but for exceptional circumstances, compensate the damage suffered due to the arrest, if it appears that the arrest was unlawful, even in the case that he was convinced of his claim on defensible grounds and did not act rashly."[83]

14.41 In two recent decisions of 2003, the Hoge Raad has made it clear that the strict liability-rule in case of wrongful arrest applies only if the claim for which arrest was made, is entirely unfounded on the merits.[84] If the claim for which an arrest was made only partially succeeds, then it does not follow that the arrest was wrongful. The question whether an arrestor may be liable for the consequences of an arrest, because the arrest was made for a too high claim amount, or was effected rashly, or was maintained without necessity, must be determined by the standards, which apply to "*misbruik van recht*" (abuse of rights) pursuant to Dutch law.[85]

14.42 Under the general Dutch patrimonial law in Book 3 of the Dutch Civil Code, "abuse of rights" (*abus de droit*) is defined in Article 3:13 of the DCC, which provides as follows (in free translation):

"1. He who is entitled to exercise a right, may not invoke it, to the extent that he abuses it.
2. A right may amongst others be abused by exercising it with no other purpose than to cause harm to another person or with a different purpose than for which it was given or in case, taking into consideration the discrepancy between the interest in exercising it and the interest that will be harmed by it, one may not reasonably decide to the exercise of this right.
3. It may follow from the nature of the power that it cannot be abused."[86]

---

82. H.R. 15.4.1965, N.J. 1965, 331 [*Snel/Ter Steege*], C.A. 's Hertogenbosch 28.2.1984 incl. in H.R. 20.12. 1985, NJ 1986, 231 [*Doodkorte/Dane*], C.A. The Hague 21.1.1992, *Schip & Schade (S&S)* 1993, 61 [*Oranje 12*]; H.R. 21.2.1992, N.J. 1992, 321 [*Van Gastel q.q./Elink-Schuurman q.q.*], Court Rotterdam 9.7.1993, *S&S* 1994, 4 [*Yukon*]; H.R. 13.1.1995, N.J. 1997, 366 [*Ontvanger/Bos*]; H.R. 7.4.1995, N.J. 1996, 486; Court Rotterdam 26.6.1997, *S&S* 1998, 86 [*Yukon*]; H.R. 11.4.2003, N.J. 2003/440 [*Hoda/Mondi Foods*]; H.R. 5.12. 2003, N.J. 2004/150. For a description of this development in Dutch case law and legal doctrine, see Van Rossum, *Aansprakelijkheid voor de tenuitvoerlegging van vernietigde of terzijdegestelde rechterlijke beslissingen*, diss. 1990, p. 27 *et seq.* and p. 21 *et seq.*
83. H.R. 21.2.1992, N.J. 1992, 321 [*Van Gastel q.q./Elink-Schuurman q.q.*]: "dat degene die een beslag legt en handhaaft op eigen risico handelt en, bijzondere omstandigheden daargelaten, de door het beslag geleden schade dient te vergoeden, indien het beslag ten onrechte blijkt te zijn gelegd, zulks ook in het geval dat hij – in de bewoordingen van het eerste onderdeel van het middel – op verdedigbare gronden van zijn vordering overtuigd is en niet lichtvaardig heeft gehandeld."
84. See H.R. 11.4.2003, N.J. 2003/440 [*Hoda/Mondi Foods*]; H.R. 5.12.2003, N.J. 2004/150; Court Arnhem 20. 10.2004, N.J.F. 2005, 57.
85. H.R. 11.4.2003, N.J. 2003/440 [*Hoda/Mondi Foods*].
86. The original wording in Dutch of Art. 3:13 of the DCC is as follows: "1. Degene aan wie een bevoegdheid toekomt, kan haar niet inroepen, voor zover hij haar misbruikt. 2. Een bevoegdheid kan onder meer worden misbruikt door haar uit te oefenen met geen ander doel dan een ander te schaden of met een ander doel dan waarvoor zij is verleend of in geval men, in aanmerking nemende de onevenredigheid tussen het belang bij de uitoefening en het belang dat daardoor wordt geschaad, naar redelijkheid niet tot die uitoefening had kunnen komen. 3. Uit de aard van een bevoegdheid kan voortvloeien dat zij niet kan worden misbruikt."

14.43 As follows from the words "amongst others" in subsection (2) of Article 3:13 of the DCC, the three examples of "abuse of rights" listed there, i.e. the exercise of a right: (1) with the sole purpose to cause harm, or (2) with a different purpose than for which it was given, or (3) in case of an unreasonable discrepancy between the interest in exercising the right and the interest to be harmed by it,[87] are meant to be illustrative and not exhaustive.[88] The Dutch legislator has therefore not excluded the possibility of other examples of "abuse of rights" developing in Dutch case law and legal doctrine.[89]

SOME COMPARATIVE OBSERVATIONS

14.44 Considering the above findings, what comparative conclusions can be drawn? Firstly, it is clear that the civil law approach to liability for wrongful arrest does not exist. Each of the countries examined solves the questions connected to wrongful arrest differently against the background of the fundamental values it holds dearly. Whereas in France the claimant's "sacred" right to arrest is seen as part of the fundamental civic right to seek recourse to justice, in Germany and The Netherlands the protection of the property rights of the defendant is valued more. And whereas German law goes to the other extreme in discouraging conservatory measures as far as possible, Dutch law attempts a balancing act between the conflicting interests of creditors and debtors, by on the one hand allowing arrestors free rein, but on the other hand by imposing a strict liability upon them if their claim fails on the merits.

14.45 Finally, a conclusion which may be of particular interest to an English audience at a time that voices are becoming louder to change the law with regard to liability for wrongful arrest, is that apparently there is no correlation between the strict liability rule and a decrease of the number of ship's arrests in a jurisdiction. The continued attractiveness of ship's arrest in The Netherlands speaks for itself.

---

87. *Cf.* H.R. 17.4.1970, N.J. 1971, 89 [*Kuipers/De Jongh*].
88. *Cf.* Asser-Hartkamp 4-III, (2006), p. 81, no. 57; *Vermogensrecht (Den Tonkelaar)*, art. 3:13, Aant. 34 *et seq.* (looseleaf), P. Rodenburg, *Misbruik van bevoegdheid*, Monografieën Nieuw BW, A-4, 1985, p. 37 *et seq.*
89. See, in greater depth, D. J. van der Kwaak, *Het rechtskarakter van het beslagrecht*, diss. Groningen, 1990, p. 149 *et seq.*, and B. T. M. van der Wiel, *De rechtsverhouding tussen procespartijen*, diss. Leyden, 2004, p. 79 *et seq.*, who compares Dutch law with French and Belgian law.

PART 8

Substantive and Jurisdictional Issues Relating to Limitation of Liability

CHAPTER 15

Problematical areas in the current global limitation regime

PROFESSOR RICHARD WILLIAMS*

15.1 For public policy reasons the limitation of liability has been a major feature of transportation systems particularly transportation by sea for some centuries.[1] Limitation applies in two ways. The liability of carriers for individual claims brought by passengers and by cargo owners may be limited under the provisions of the Athens Convention[2] and the Hague,[3] Hague-Visby[4] and Hamburg Rules[5] respectively. However, the limitation of liability for all qualifying claims occurring on any distinct occasion (usually referred to as global or tonnage limitation) is also available under the provisions of international conventions and municipal statutes. Provided that the person seeking to limit liability is not guilty of the conduct which will debar the right to limit under the various conventions and other laws there is nothing to prevent that person from firstly limiting his liability to each individual claim and then limiting his liability further under the relevant global or tonnage conventions or statutes.

15.2 This chapter will consider issues arising under the 1976 Limitation Convention[6] and the 1996 Protocol thereto which is the global or tonnage regime currently in force in the United Kingdom and a rapidly growing number of countries worldwide.[7]

15.3 There is a current impression that the 1976 Limitation Convention has put to rest all issues relating to the right to limit liability and that the right to limit is available in practically all of the common ship trading scenarios. However, this is a misconception and the thrust of this chapter is to examine some (but by no means all) of those situations which are common but where the right to limit is, perhaps

---

* Visiting Professor of Law, University of Wales, Swansea. Member of the Institute of International Shipping and Trade Law.

1. For a critical analysis see Lord Mustill, "Ships are different – or are they?", in (1993) L.M.C.L.Q. 490; Dr. Gotthard Gauci, "Limitation of Liability in Maritime Law: an anachronism", in *Marine Policy*, Vol. 19, No.1, 65–74 (Elsevier Science Ltd), and D. Steel Q.C., "Ships are Different: the case for Limitation of Liability", in (1995) L.M.C.L.Q. 77.

2. The Convention Relating to the Carriage of Passengers and their Luggage by Sea 1974.

3. The International Convention for the Unification of certain Rules of law relating to Bills of Lading signed at Brussels on 25 August 1924.

4. The International Convention for the Unification of certain Rules of law relating to Bills of Lading signed at Brussels on 25 August 1924 as amended by the Protocol signed at Brussels on 23 February 1968.

5. The United Nations Convention on the Carriage of Goods by Sea 1978.

6. The Convention on Limitation of Liability for Maritime Claims 1976.

7. For a list of which countries give effect to which global limitation convention see Griggs, Williams and Farr, *Limitation of Liability of Maritime Claims* (4th ed., 2005) (London, LLP), Appendix V.

surprisingly, unavailable, uncertain or restricted. Some of these lacunae derive from the wording of the Convention itself whereas others derive from the way in which the Convention has been incorporated into the law of the United Kingdom or applied by the courts in this country.

15.4 The author will also make suggestions where appropriate as to any remedial steps which may be taken.

ISSUES ARISING OUT OF THE CONVENTION ITSELF

(a) The right of "charterers" to limit

15.5 Articles 1(1) and (2) of the 1976 Limitation Convention extend the privilege of limitation to "the charterer ... of a seagoing ship" in respect of the claims which are "subject to limitation" in Article 2. However, there is no definition of "charterer" in the Convention and there is some doubt as to exactly who falls within the definition of "charterer" for the purposes of the Convention. Three questions arise:

(1) do the articles apply to every type of charterer?;
(2) do they apply to a charterer of less than the whole ship?; and
(3) do they extend the right to limit to all claims?

Who is a charterer?

15.6 Historically, the right to limit liability was originally restricted to shipowners but was gradually extended to include demise charterers[8] and to a "charterer, manager or operator ... as they apply to an owner himself" by Article 6(2) of the 1957 Limitation Convention. This was done, *inter alia*, in order to avoid the problem encountered in *The Himalaya*[9] when the claimant chose not to sue the shipowner (who could limit) but against another party (the master) who could not limit. Fears were expressed that charterers acting as carriers under bills of lading would be liable in full in respect of claims which, had they been brought against the shipowner, would be subject to limitation. Accordingly, there has historically been little doubt that demise charterers and time charterers have had the right to limit since both act regularly as carriers under bills of lading. The right of a voyage charterer to limit has not been quite so clear presumably since it is rare for voyage charterers to act as carriers in the same way.[10] However, there seems little doubt that voyage charterers have been treated as persons entitled to limit, and in their report submitted in the discussions leading to the 1976 Convention, the CMI indicated that the 1957 Convention had extended the right to limit to "all charterers (time and voyage charterers)".[11]

15.7 Against that background it is perhaps not surprising that the 1976 Convention does not purport to extend the right to limit to non-charterers such as

8. In the UK by s.7 of the Merchant Shipping Act 1906.
9. *Adler v Dickson* [1955] 1 Q.B. 158.
10. See *Voyage Charters* (2nd ed., 2001) (London, LLP), p. 3.
11. Note 19, page 4, of the CMI Introductory report on the Revision of the (1957 Convention) – attached to IMO Doc. LEG XXIII/2/1, 17 May 1974.

shippers since the line appeared to have been drawn hitherto between those who could be categorised as "ship" (who were allowed the right to limit) and those who could be categorised as "cargo" who were not given such right. This appears to have influenced Thomas J. in *The Aegean Sea*[12] and Steel J. in the *CMA Djakarta*[13] to the extent that both were of the view that the only charterer who could limit liability under the Convention was one which was acting "*qua* shipowner" in relation to the particular claim.

15.8 However, this approach was rejected by the Court of Appeal in *CMA Djakarta*.[14] Longmore L.J. stated at p. 465 that:

"To my mind the ordinary meaning of the word "charterer" connotes a charterer acting in his capacity as such, not a charterer acting in some other capacity."

15.9 Accordingly, it appears that any party who can fairly be described as a charterer is afforded the right to limit whether he is a demise charterer, time charterer or voyage charterer and such right is not restricted to where such charterer is acting "*qua* shipowner". Therefore, now that the requirement to act "*qua* shipowner" has been abandoned two other questions arise for consideration:

(i) is there a logical reason why other "cargo" interests should not also be afforded the right to limit?; and

(ii) what exactly constitutes a "charterer"?

15.10 (i) There is no doubt that the nature of a conventional charterer differs from that of a shipper. A charterer is a party to a contract *for* the carriage of goods which gives the charterer to a greater or lesser extent control over the operation of the ship whereas the shipper is a party to a contract *of* carriage of goods which gives him little control over the operation of the ship. An analogy can perhaps be drawn between the contract between a passenger in a taxi who has the right to control the carrying capacity of the taxi and who has the right to give instructions to the taxi driver (a charterparty) and the contract between a passenger in a bus who has the right to be transported but who has no control over the carrying capacity of the bus and who cannot give instructions to the bus driver (a bill of lading).

15.11 The distinction was explained in legal terms by Hobhouse J. in *The Torrenia*[15] as follows:

"The contract here is a contract in a bill of lading: it is a contract of carriage – that is to say, a species of contract of bailment. It is not, as Mr Pollock for the defendants at one stage argued, a mere contract for the carriage of goods. Charterparties are typically contracts for the carriage of goods. They are executory. They are intended to give rise to bailments (not necessarily) between the parties to the charterparty. They may include terms of an intended bailment but they are not normally the contract of bailment itself. They cover other matters besides the bailor/bailee relationship."

15.12 Accordingly, the line as currently drawn appears to be between those who do have the right to exercise control over the employees of the shipowner in relation to the operation of the ship to some degree by the ability to give commercial or

12. [1998] 2 Lloyd's Rep. 39.
13. [2003] 2 Lloyd's Rep. 50.
14. [2004] 1 Lloyd's Rep. 460.
15. [1983] 2 Lloyd's Rep. at 216.

employment orders and those who do not have such right. Therefore, it can be said that a charterer is "acting in his capacity as such, not a charterer acting in some other capacity" (e.g. as a cargo owner) when he is exercising such control.

15.13 However, in many instances such distinction is illusory. Longmore L.J. concluded in *CMA Djakarta* that a failure to prevent cargo being damaged by bad stowage was an act which could be done by a charterer acting in his capacity as such.[16] However, by agreeing FIOST terms that responsibility can be transferred from a carrier to a shipper/consignee under a bill of lading. Nevertheless, such shipper/consignee could not limit.[17]

15.14 Furthermore, Thomas J. held in *The Aegean Sea* that the phrase "in the operation of the ship" encompasses all that goes to the operation of the ship including the selection of a port and the ascertainment of its safety and suitability for the vessel.[18] Whilst this is clearly a common duty under a charterparty it is also a duty which arises under a bill of lading where the bill is originally made out to a range of ports and the duty arises in due course on the part of the shipper or consignee to nominate a safe port out of the range.

15.15 By way of contrast it can be said that many voyage charterparties give the charterer little control in fact over the operation of the vessel since all the relevant matters will already have been settled in the charter and the charterer merely has the right to demand that the ship should proceed as agreed.

15.16 Lastly, the current demarcation between charterer and shipper/consignee leads to illogicality. If "A" sells goods on a CIF basis to "B", and charters a ship in order to carry the goods, the governing contract of carriage between the shipowner and "A" will be the charterparty whereas the governing contract of carriage between the shipowner and "B" will be the bill of lading.[19] Therefore, "A" will in principle have the right to limit in respect of claims relating to the carriage of the goods, whereas "B" will not have the same advantage albeit that it is the same carriage and the same goods.

15.17 It may be for these reasons that the Nordic countries have extended the right to limit to general charterers and shippers under the statute which incorporated the Convention into the law of those countries.[20]

15.18 (ii) Even if it is right to draw the line between charterparties on the one hand and non-charterparties on the other hand it is frequently difficult to ascertain whether a contract is a charterparty or something else (e.g. a Booking Note or a Contract of Affreightment) as there is no clear definition of what amounts to a charterparty under the common law.

15.19 Much debate has already taken place between the CMI and UNCITRAL in regard to the difference between charterparties and other documents in relation

16. See the discussion at [2004] 1 Lloyd's Rep. 465, para. 14.

17. Clearly, if it was the shipper/consignee's own cargo which had been damaged by bad stowage then the question of limitation would probably not arise since the shipper/consignee would bear their own loss. However, the question would become material if the ship was carrying more than one cargo and a claim was brought in tort by the owners of the damaged cargo against the "other" shippers/consignees whose failure to properly stow their cargo had caused the damage to the other cargo.

18. [1998] 2 Lloyd's Rep. at pp. 51–52.

19. See *The "Island Archon"* [1994] 2 Lloyd's Rep. at 232.

20. See *Betaenkning af Solovsudvalget* (Report of the Danish Maritime Law Committee) No. 924, 1981, p. 29.

to the proposed new rules for carriage by sea but there are no clear demarcation lines and I can do no better than to restate the frustration obviously felt by Julian Cooke Q.C. in a paper given by him at a similar colloquium in 2001[21]:

"So, at the risk of being ridiculed as a person who calls himself a shipping lawyer but who doesn't know what a charterparty is, I maintain that the distinction between a charterparty and these other kinds of contracts will, as a matter of legal analysis, be very difficult to draw, and a source of much dispute. Moreover, I suspect that the distinction will become more rather than less blurred in the future, as we see the multiplication of different types of contract for bulk shipments besides what might be called 'conventional charterparties'."

15.20 A classic example of the difficulty arose in *The Happy Ranger*.[22] The court considered a claim under a contract which was headed "Contract of Carriage" and which regulated the shipment of heavy lift equipment.[23] Tuckey L.J. held that:

"As to Mr Teare's alternative submission I do not think it is possible to characterise the contract in this case as a voyage charter. It was obviously a carefully drawn document and although it does contain certain terms which are to be found in voyage charters, it emphatically calls itself a contract of carriage and that is what I think it is. The fact that the goods to be carried were a part cargo supports this conclusion although I accept that this factor is not conclusive."

15.21 If one tries to apply the distinction made by Hobhouse J. in *The Torrenia* then it would appear that this contract had the basic attributes of a charterparty which would give the "charterer" the right to limit. However, the court appears to have decided that it was not a charterparty to a large extent because the title of the document suggested something else, with the result that, if the need arose, there was no right to limit.

15.22 The document used in *The Happy Ranger* appears to have been a type of Booking Note commonly used in the heavy lift trade and it is, indeed, common to refer to such documents as charterparties. For example, in the 4th edition of *Chartering Documents* Harvey Williams states, on page 2, that:

"In liner trades the shipper is also the charterer. In such cases the charter party may be called a booking note (i.e. a booking of space on board the vessel) but differences of principle are not great."

15.23 This statement may not be true in all circumstances but it is illustrative of the uncertainty of classification of certain documents. In many instances Booking Notes are used as an alternative to part charters and are charter parties in the sense described by Hobhouse J. in *The Torrenia*. However, in other instances, the booking note is merely the contract which is drawn up to record an agreement for the future shipment of goods which is superseded in due course by a bill of lading. Indeed, in some instances, a contract which is clearly a charterparty and describes itself as such provides that it will be superseded by a bill of lading. A classic case is the Baltimore Berth Grain Charter Party 1976,[24] which contains the following clause:

---

21. "Charter Parties – Is there a Need for Mandatory Legislation?" – IX Hasselby Colloquium, reproduced in *Modern Law of Charterparties* (2002) (Axel Axelson Institute of Maritime and Transport Law, University of Stockholm), at p. 12.
22. [2002] 2 Lloyd's Rep. 362.
23. A copy of the document appears at [2001] 2 Lloyd's Rep. at p. 541.
24. See *Voyage Charters*, pp. 1107–1111.

"Bills of Lading
It is also mutually agreed that this contract shall be completed and superseded by the sign-
ing of bills of lading in the form customary for such voyages for grain cargoes, which Bills of
Lading shall contain the following clauses: ..."

15.24 In such cases there is a risk that a party who is initially a charterer, and
who has the right to limit, will cease to be a charterer and therefore lose the right
to limit once the cargo has been loaded and the bills of lading issued!

15.25 It is also noteworthy that as the nature of shipping changes, the nature of
the contracts used to regulate the use of ships is also changing. Accordingly, it is
common in the container and liner trade for parties to enter into Consortia in order
to share space on each other's ships. In some instances these complicated arrangements are regulated by documents which are not described as slot charterparties
but as "Space Sharing Agreements" and the question arises whether they can truly
be considered to be charterparties in the strict sense. Given the current propensity
of charterers of container ships to incur substantial liabilities arising as a result of
mis-stowed or mis-declared containers the question is important.

Does a part charterer have the right to limit?

15.26 An equally difficult question is whether a part charterer has the right to limit.
Historically, part charters have been common in the dry cargo trade but the question
has gained greater impetus with the development of slot charters in the container
trade. It has been recognised that there is no difference in principle between a part
charter and a slot charter.[25]

15.27 However, a particular problem arises in relation to the right of a part charterer to limit under the 1976 Convention since the right is granted to a "charterer
of a seagoing ship". Therefore, it has been argued that a part charterer is not such
a "charterer" since he is merely a charterer of part (and not all) of a ship. In the
context of the Arrest Convention as adopted in the UK by section 21(4) of the
Supreme Court Act 1981 it has been held by the Court of Appeal in *The Tychy*[26]
that a slot charterer is a "charterer" for the purposes of the Act. Subsequently, in
CMA Djakarta, Longmore L.J. held that as the Court of Appeal did not have to
grapple with the problem in that case they would not do so and merely observed
obiter that the Court of Appeal had already considered a slot charterer to be a
"charterer" in the "not dissimilar" context of the Arrest Convention.

15.28 However, different considerations may arise in relation to the 1976
Convention since the question has a practical as well as a theoretical significance in
that context. There is nothing in the Convention which states that the limit of
a "charterer" or indeed, of anyone else, is to be calculated in accordance with the
degree of interest which that person has in the ship. The only available limit is the
tonnage of the ship as a whole and the rationale behind Article 11 which allows a
fund constituted by one of the persons identified in Article 9(2) "to be deemed
constituted by all persons mentioned" in such article is workable only if the fund is
calculated with reference to the ship's total tonnage. Accordingly, if a part charterer
is to be allowed the right to limit that limit can only be calculated in relation to the

25. See *The Tychy* [1999] 2 Lloyd's Rep. 11 at p. 21, *per* Clarke L.J.
26. [1999] 2 Lloyd's Rep. 11.

ship's total tonnage and not in accordance with that proportion of the total tonnage which he has chartered. That raises an issue of principle to which Steel J. referred in *CMA Djakarta* in the lower court. Speaking *obiter*, he said that[27]:

"There seems to me to be two difficulties: (a) by definition, the slot charterer is only charter of part of the vessel. Why is he exposed to a higher limit than a time charterer, i.e. a fund based on the entire tonnage and not the tonnage he has chartered? (b) *per contra*, the slot charter is at least on this basis given a right to limit (albeit disproportionately high) but the shipper of the balance of the cargo is not. Does this make commercial sense?"

15.29 That logic appears to have a certain resonance. However, if the argument is well-founded the part charterer should not have the right to limit and that would leave a substantial and unfortunate lacuna in modern trading arrangements particularly in relation to the container or liner trades where the slot charter plays a major role.

Does the right of a charterer to limit apply to all claims?

15.30 For a claim to be of the type in respect of which the right to limit is given by the 1976 Convention it must be one which is (a) not excluded by Article 3, and which is (b) within the meaning of Article 2.

15.31 The most difficulty arises in relation to whether a claim falls within the meaning of Article 2. There are likely to be three principal types of claim in respect of which a "person entitled to limit" will wish to limit his liability:

  (i)   direct claims by third parties;
  (ii) claims brought by "persons entitled to limit" *inter se* by way of indemnity for claims brought against such persons by third parties;
  (iii) direct claims by one "person entitled to limit" against another.

15.32 The majority of direct claims which are likely to be brought by third parties are likely to be claims for cargo damage, loss or delay or for personal injury or passenger delay and there seems little doubt that the right to limit in respect of such claims is given by Articles 2(1)(a) or (b) of the Convention. Similarly, claims brought for damage or loss to other property such as hotels or private houses or for loss of fishing rights are probably subject to limitation under Article 2(1)(a), (b) or (c).

15.33 To the extent that such claims are first brought by third parties against one "person entitled to limit" who then seeks an indemnity in that regard from another such person the right is given to the second person to limit under Article 2(1) and (2) since the latter sub-paragraph emphasises that the claims itemised in Article 2(1) are subject to limitation "even if brought by way of recourse or indemnity".

15.34 However, not all claims arising as a result of common shipping incidents are subject to limitation. For example, if a ship is damaged or lost as a result of the default of the charterers in shipping undeclared dangerous goods or in sending the vessel to an unsafe port the type of claim which can be expected to be made against the charterer will include the following: personal injury to and/or death of those on board or in the vicinity; damage to or loss of the ship, her cargo, bunkers and containers carried on the ship; and damage to or loss of other property in the vicinity.

---

27. [2003] 2 Lloyd's Rep. 50 at p. 55.

Most of these claims are likely to be subject to limitation under Article 2. However, it was held by the English Court of Appeal in *CMA Djakarta*[28] that the charterers were not able to limit their liability for damage to or loss of the chartered ship since the ship by reference to which the charterers would calculate the relevant limitation tonnage for the purposes of the limitation fund was not "property" for the purposes of Article 2(1)(a).

15.35 The same difficulty arises in relation to other claims which are considered consequential to the loss or damage of the chartered ship for the purpose of Article 2(1)(a). Accordingly, it was held by Thomas J. in *The Aegean Sea*[29] that the shipowner's claim for unearned freight was not a claim in respect of which the charterers could limit their liability and, presumably, the same applies to a claim brought by the shipowner against the charterer for ship's proportion of a salvage award or for Article 14 special compensation or for loss of or damage to the shipowner's own containers.

15.36 The result, therefore, is that a shipowner will normally be able to limit his liability for the majority of claims which may be brought against him by a charterer whereas a charterer will not have a similar advantage in relation to many of the claims which may be brought against him by a shipowner. Apart from questions of equity, if the right to limit is indeed to be granted to a "charterer *acting in his capacity as such* and not as a charterer acting in some other capacity" as stated by the Court of Appeal in *CMA Djakarta*, this is an illogical and, to some extent, unfortunate result. Since the development of consortia, it is often a matter of complete chance whether a company acts as an owner or a charterer on any particular occasion. As a result the right to limit should not depend on the happenstance of what role is played on any occasion.

15.37 The issue is also important in insurance terms. One of the stated aims of the 1976 Convention is not only to encourage charterers and operators to engage in the business of the carriage of goods as well as owners but also to fix liability limits at the maximum figures which can be supported by the available sources of liability insurance cover. Therefore, there can not be much "fat" left in the insurance market to support unlimited claims. Liability insurers must either reduce the levels of insurance cover which they are able to provide to support high levels of liability limits in order to have the assets which will be necessary to cover any unlimited claims which will be made against charterers or, if they are to continue to support the high levels of liability limits which have been fixed, they must refuse cover for any claims against charterers which do not qualify for limitation. Liability insurers will also be aware of the fact that their own right to limit under Article 1(6) of the Convention is available only "to the same extent as the assured himself".

Submission

15.38 The right given in the 1976 Convention to a "charterer" to limit in relation to claims arising "in direct connection with the operation of the ship" has given greater scope for the limitation of a charterer's liability than the more limited words

---

28. [2004] 1 Lloyd's Rep. 460.
29. [1988] 2 Lloyd's Rep. 39.

in the 1957 Convention.[30] If a charterer is to be granted the right to limit as a "charterer acting in his capacity as such and not as a charterer acting in some other capacity" it makes little sense that one of the most important claims which a charterer can expect to meet, i.e. damage to the chartered ship, should be excluded from the list of claims which qualify for the privilege of limitation. Furthermore, if the definition of "charterer" for the purposes of the 1976 Convention extends the right to limit generally to voyage charterers (who, for the most part do not act as carriers) then the historic demarcation between "ship" and "cargo" has been breached and there is no longer any logical reason why the right to limit should not be extended to shippers as it has in the Nordic countries. Therefore, the time has come to re-evaluate the justification for the grant of the privilege of limitation.

15.39 Historically, it appears that one of the primary justifications for the privilege was the desire to encourage entrepreneurs to act as carriers of goods for the benefit of exporting countries.[31] However, it is arguable that in the modern world it is for the benefit of the world community as a whole that all those engaged in the carriage of goods by sea should be encouraged to do so since the world as we know it today could not exist without the international sale and carriage of goods. Therefore, one option would be to extend the privilege of limitation to all who play a part in the business of the carriage of goods by sea including charterers and shippers. However, notwithstanding the view taken by the Nordic countries in this respect, that might be considered too radical a development at this stage.

15.40 An alternative option would be to deprive voyage charterers of the right to limit on the basis that in the majority of cases voyage charterers act as, and can be classified as, "cargo" rather than as "ship". However, that flies in the face of developments since 1957 and would probably be viewed as a retrograde and unjustifiable step.

15.41 A further option might be to re-evaluate in the modern world the concept of "ship" in the context of the traditional divergence between "ship" and "cargo". Originally, carriers of goods were predominantly shipowners, hence the right given to shipowners to limit their liability. However, in the modern world the somewhat simplistic concept of "ship" and "cargo" no longer applies as goods are carried pursuant to a complex mesh of contracts in which the charterer often plays as important a role as carrier as does the shipowner. Therefore, an alternative option might be to preserve the right of all types of charterers to limit but to restrict it to when they are acting "*qua* carriers" (or "*qua* transporter") not simply "*qua* shipowners". This would preserve the historic demarcation between "ship" and "cargo" whilst at the same time enabling a tribunal to consider whether in the context of the particular voyage, incident and mesh of contracts (not merely in the context of the particular contract under which a claim was brought against the charterer) the charterer was acting primarily as carrier (or as transporter) or as goods owner. This might in turn enable the list of claims which are subject to limitation to be extended

---

30. *Viz.*, acts or omissions done by a person on board or in direct connection with the navigation or management of the ship or in the loading, carriage or discharge of cargo or in the embarkation, carriage or disembarkation of passengers.

31. See Lord Mustill, "Ships are different – or are they?", in (1993) L.M.C.L.Q. 490 and *"CMA Djakarta"* [2004] 1 Lloyd's Rep. 460 at p. 464.

to include damage to the chartered ship since such extension would be protected by the safety net of the requirement that only a charterer acting "*qua* carrier" (or "*qua* transporter") would be able to make use of this extended right. It is appreciated that, if this approach is adopted, this would inevitably mean that in many cases a voyage charterer would lose the right to limit. Furthermore, it would make the process of limitation more complicated in that a court would have to engage in the evaluation process discussed above. However, it is submitted that, in the absence of granting the right to limit to all parties who engage in the carriage of goods, it would seem to be the best option.

(b) The right to limit liability resulting from the delivery of cargo other than against surrender of an original bill of lading

15.42 A shipowner is frequently asked to deliver cargo without surrender of original bills of lading despite the oft-repeated warning that:

"... a shipowner who delivers without production of a bill of lading does so at his peril."[32]

The peril lies in the fact that such a delivery amounts to a conversion of the goods and the shipowner is liable to the true owner of the cargo for the full value of the misdelivered goods. Accordingly, very large claims can arise but, traditionally, courts have been loathe to allow shipowners any protection in such circumstances and have consistently construed exception clauses in the relevant contract of carriage as being inapplicable thereby leaving the shipowner without the benefit of any defence. For example, in a recent case[33] it was held that a misdelivery of goods was not within the words "any loss or damage to the goods while in the carrier's actual or constructive possession ... after discharge over the ship's rail" in a bill of lading exception clause.

15.43 In such circumstances a shipowner will wish to claim the benefit of limitation unless it is proved for the purposes of Article 4 of the Convention that the loss resulted from the personal act or omission of the shipowner "committed with the intent to cause such loss or recklessly and with knowledge that such loss would probably occur". Given the regularity with which cargoes are delivered without surrender of the original bills of lading (particularly in the tanker trade) and given the fact that the usual reason why the original bills are not available is the benign one that they are stuck in the banking chain, it can by no means be guaranteed that such conduct can be proved on the part of the shipowner.

15.44 To succeed, the shipowner will need to prove that the claim is either:

(a) one for "loss of or damage to property ... occurring ... in direct connection with the operation of the ship" for the purposes of Article 2(1)(a); or
(b) one for "loss resulting from infringement of rights other than contractual rights occurring in direct connection with the operation of the ship" for the purposes of Article 2(1)(c).

The requirement that the claim arises "in direct connection with the operation of the ship" is common to both heads and it is necessary to consider what the words mean.

---

32. *Sze Hai Tong Bank v Rambler Cycle Co.* [1959] 2 Lloyd's Rep. 121, *per* Lord Denning.
33. See *Motis v Dampskibskelskabet* [2000] 1 Lloyd's Rep. 211.

The relevant words in the 1957 Convention were "in the management of the ship" and the English court came to the conclusion[34] that a distinction should be drawn between the "management of the cargo-carrying venture" and "the management of the ship itself" and that the right to limit under that convention as incorporated into English law by the MSA 1958 did not extend to the first type of "management". However, the words "in the management of the ship" have been replaced in the 1976 Convention by the words "in the operation of the ship" and the court in the *Caspian Basin* case held that:

"'In direct connection with the operation of the ship' is the way in which the Convention expresses the necessary linkage between the loss of or damage to property on the one hand and the ship in respect of which the claim to limit is made on the other."[35]

15.45 This suggests that it is no longer necessary in the context of the 1976 Convention to consider the nature of the activity which resulted in the claim. However, if it is necessary to look further, it is noteworthy that Thomas J. in *The Aegean Sea* agreed with the comments of the court in the *Caspian Basin* case and went to say:

"I do not accept owners' argument that the giving of the orders was not an activity that was part of the operation of the ship; the phrase 'operation of the ship' is not in my judgment confined to action occurring on the ship; it encompasses all that goes to the operation of the ship; the operation of the ship, in my view, includes the selection of a port and the ascertainment of its safety and suitability for the vessel and the provision of what might be necessary for the vessel to use it safely – charts, tugs and the like. To confine the phrase to the narrow scope suggested by the owners in this case would significantly limit the protection that should be available in respect of claims that can reasonably be brought within the scope of the Convention and be contrary to the broad policy of construction that should be applied."

15.46 It is submitted that the phrase "the operation of the ship" is indeed a broader concept than the "management of the ship" and that the delivery of cargo without surrender of an original bill of lading is an act as to the "operation of the ship". The fact that it can be classified as a "commercial order" should not detract from that conclusion. Thomas J.'s comments in the *"Aegean Sea"* as to the scope which is to be given to the phrase "in the operation of the ship" were given in the context of charterers' commercial employment orders under the charter party.

15.47 It is further submitted that a claim for the financial loss resulting from a misdelivery of the cargo is a claim "in respect of ... loss of property" for the purposes of Article 2(1)(a) of the 1976 Convention. It was emphasised by the Court of Appeal in the *Caspian Basin* case[36] that it is the nature of the claim for financial relief that is important in the context of limitation not the way in which the claim is pleaded. Furthermore, although the Court of Appeal held in the *Motis* case that the wording of the particular exemption clause in that case was not wide enough to give protection against loss resulting from the misdelivery it did not seem to disagree with the shipowners' submission that there was in reality a loss of goods. Mance L.J. observed that:

34. *The Tojo Maru* [1972] 1 Lloyd's Rep. 341.
35. *Caspian v. Bouygues (No. 4)* [1997] 2 Lloyd's Rep. 507 at p. 522, *per* Rix J.
36. [1997] 2 Lloyd's Rep. at p. 522 and [1998] 2 Lloyd's Rep. 461.

"Looking at the matter as at the date when the present claimants presented the original bills which they held, Mr Dunning submits that the prior misdelivery which had occurred against forged bills of lading was no different in principle from any loss or damage in the carrier's custody after discharge. This submission has some force, looking at the position at that moment, when it is discovered that the goods are gone, having been abstracted by fraud."

Accordingly, it is submitted that a misdelivery of goods resulting from an order to deliver cargo without surrender of an original bill of lading is a claim in respect of which limitation is available in principle.

15.48 However, it is doubtful whether limitation is also available under sub-paragraph (c) since although it can be argued that the claimant's rights to possession of the cargo have been infringed by the misdelivery or conversion of the cargo it is undeniable that the rights of the claimant to the possession of the goods arise primarily out of and as a result of the bill of lading contract, i.e. out of "contractual rights" which are excluded by Article 2(1)(c).

(c) Protection of assets

15.49 There are a number of the provisions of the 1976 Convention which are problematic in relation to jurisdiction, particularly when considered in the light of the EU jurisdiction rules.[37] However, since jurisdiction will be the subject of the next chapter (by Nigel Meeson Q.C.) I will restrict comment in this paper to an associated problem.

15.50 Article 13 of the Convention gives persons seeking to limit protection against subsequent arrest or attachment of their other ships or property in the jurisdiction of any other State Party "After a limitation fund has been constituted *in accordance with Article 11....*" Article 11 provides that:

"Any person alleged to be liable may constitute a fund with a court or other competent authority in any *State in which legal proceedings are instituted in respect of claims subject to limitation.*" [Author's emphasis.]

15.51 The English court has drawn a distinction between the commencement of a limitation action on the one hand and the constitution of a limitation fund on the other hand. Consistent with historical practise, the English Court of Appeal has held that a shipowner has the right to choose where to bring a limitation action under the 1976 Convention and to make a "pre-emptive strike" in that regard by commencing a limitation action under Article 10 of the Convention (which, as incorporated into the law of the United Kingdom, does not require that a fund be constituted[38]) in the United Kingdom even before a claimant has commenced proceedings on the merits against him.[39] However, it was recognised by the Court of

---

37. See Griggs, Williams and Farr, *Limitation of Liability for Maritime Claims* (4th ed., 2005), pp. 80–86.

38. Since the Convention as incorporated into the law of the UK in Schedule 7, Part 1 to the Merchant Shipping Act 1995 does not include the following provision which appears in the second sentence of Article 10 (1):

"However, a State Party may provide in its national law that, where an action is brought in its courts to enforce a claim subject to limitation, a person liable may only invoke the right to limit liability if a limitation fund has been constituted in accordance with the provisions of this Convention or is constituted when the right to limit is invoked."

39. *"Western Regent"* [2005] 2 Lloyd's Rep. 359. See also the decision to the same effect of Steel J. in *The "Denise"* [2004] E.W.H.C. 3305 (unreported, 3 December 2004).

Appeal in *The Western Regent* that Article 13 gives protection against subsequent arrests only after a limitation fund has been constituted.[40] In this regard the words underlined in Article 11 create a difficulty and there is currently an unresolved debate[41] as to whether such words refer merely to proceedings on the merits brought against the person seeking to limit or whether they include limitation proceedings commenced by the person seeking to limit. If they apply merely to the former situation then it follows that a "pre-emptive strike" of the sort described above will not give the person seeking the right to limit the protection afforded by the provisions of Article 13 (even if after such proceedings have been commenced the person seeking limitation establishes a limitation fund) if those who have claims against the person seeking to limit choose not to bring such claims in that jurisdiction. A subsequent arrest in another State Party may then give rise to complex forum shopping arguments the outcome of which may well be uncertain and may also depend on whether or not the State Party in question is in the EU.

15.52 In *The ICL Vikraman* Colman J. appears to favour the view that the "legal proceedings" to which Article 11(1) refers are proceedings brought *against* the person seeking to limit. He said that:

"Article 11 ties the entitlement to constitute a limitation fund to the commencement of legal proceedings in order to provide certainty as to the venue of the fund, rather than leaving it to the shipowner to constitute the fund in a jurisdiction chosen by him. He is to be confined to a State Party in which such proceedings have already been commenced."[42]

15.53 It is submitted that the natural meaning of the words used in Articles 11 and 13 and the intended overall symmetry of the Convention leads to the conclusion that Article 11 is intended to refer only to proceedings brought *against, and not by,* the person seeking to limit. Such a conclusion also appears to have been accepted by Clarke L.J. in *The Western Regent*,[43] albeit that the same judge also saw the force of the argument that "legal proceedings" in this context could include proceedings to commence a limitation action.[44]

15.54 It is uncertain whether the same result would arise in countries which have made use of the liberty given in the second sentence of Article 10.[45] On one view, the second sentence imposes the obligation to constitute a fund only when limitation is invoked after a claim has been brought in that jurisdiction *against* the person seeking to limit and that there is, accordingly, nothing to prevent a person who has not yet been sued commencing a limitation action under the first sentence of Article 10 as is possible in the UK. In this case the result would be the same as in *The Western Regent*. On the other hand, it is arguable that the effect of such provision is that a limitation action cannot be commenced in such countries *unless* "an action is (*first*) brought in its courts to enforce a claim subject to limitation". This means that the 1976 Limitation Convention is to be construed as though it

---

40. [2005] 2 Lloyd's Rep. at p. 364, para. 14.
41. See *The Western Regent* [2005] 2 Lloyd's Rep. at p. 364, *per* Clarke L.J.
42. [2004] 1 Lloyd's Rep. at p. 31, para. 49.
43. A similar approach appears to have been adopted by the courts of other countries. See Limitation of Griggs, Williams and Farr, *Liability for Maritime Claims* (4th ed., 2005) at pp. 322 (The Netherlands), 349 (Norway) and 412 (Spain).
44. [2005] 2 Lloyd's Rep. at p. 364.
45. [2005] 2 Lloyd's Rep. at p. 364, para. 14.

were a jurisdictional convention to some degree. However, the writer is aware that, albeit in the context of the Convention as incorporated into the United Kingdom, the latter view did not find favour with the Court of Appeal in *The Western Regent*.[46]

15.55 A person seeking to limit by a pre-emptive strike of this nature therefore needs to think carefully before embarking on a journey, which once started, cannot easily be stopped.

(d) The salvor's limit

15.56 Another stated aim of the 1976 Convention was to encourage salvors. Therefore, the right to limit in respect of claims by salvors for salvage was expressly excluded under Article 3. Furthermore, recognising that claims could be made *against* salvors for damage caused by salvors' negligence,[47] salvors were expressly included as persons entitled to limit in Article 1(1). However, the amount to which a salvor can limit his liability depends on a number of factors:

(a) Article 6 of the 1976 Convention provides that the liability of the person entitled to limit is to be calculated by reference to the tonnage of the ship. Therefore, the liability of a salvor operating *from* a salvage vessel will be calculated in accordance with the tonnage of that vessel subject to a minimum tonnage of 500 tons.

(b) However, where a salvor is operating from a number of different salvage vessels difficult questions may arise as to which tonnage is appropriate for the purposes of limitation. If it is possible to specify exactly which ship caused the loss or damage then the tonnage of that ship would appear to be appropriate. However, if this is not possible then the approach traditionally adopted by the English court would be to aggregate the tonnages of the vessels in question.[48]

(c) Where a salvor is "*not* operating from any ship or ... operating solely on the ship to, or in respect of which he is rendering salvage services" Article 6(4) provides that the liability of that salvor "shall be calculated according to a tonnage of 1,500 tons".

(d) The minimum tonnage specified in Article 6 of the 1976 Convention has been increased by the 1996 Protocol from 500 tons to 2,000 tons. However, there is nothing in the 1996 Protocol to amend Article 6(4) of the 1976 Convention. Accordingly, under the Convention as amended by the 1996 Protocol a salvor operating from a small salvage vessel of less than 2,000 tons is exposed to a higher level of liability than a salvor not operating from a salvage vessel since the latter can still take advantage of the "deemed tonnage" of 1,500 tons under the 1976 Convention. This is perhaps an inadvertent additional means of encouraging salvors!

This is an area where a probably unintended anomaly needs to be remedied in a future limitation instrument.

---

46. *Ibid.*, at para. 15.
47. See *The Tojo Maru* [1971] 1 Lloyd's Rep. 341.
48. See *The Bramley Moore* [1964] P. 211 and *The Sir Joseph Rawlinson* [1973] Q.B. 285.

(e) Costs

15.57 Albeit that the element of costs is likely to be a major constituent of any claim arising as a result of a major incident, the 1976 Convention is silent on the question of costs. Two different types of costs arise:

(a) the costs of establishing the claim which is subsequently subject to limitation; and

(b) the costs of contesting the right to limit.

(a) The costs of establishing the claim which is subsequently subject to limitation

15.58 The Nordic countries[49] have added a specific provision to Article 3 ("Claims excepted from limitation") making it clear that claims for interest and costs are not subject to limitation. However, in other countries the position is not so clear since there is nothing in Article 3 itself to indicate that claims for costs are not subject to limitation. Equally, the list of claims which are subject to limitation in Article 2 do not expressly include costs as an item which is subject to limitation. It is arguable that costs might be considered as "consequential loss" for the purposes of Article 2(1)(a) or "further loss" for the purposes of Article 2(1)(f). However, such a conclusion is unlikely since costs are an inevitable result of all claims and it would make no sense for the Convention to allow limitation in respect of costs resulting from some types of qualifying claims but not resulting from other types of qualifying claims.

15.59 Accordingly, recourse needs to be had pursuant to Article 14 to the law of the state where limitation is administered. The traditional rule in England and Wales and other common law jurisdictions is that costs do not form part of the claim but are recoverable in addition to the claim by the discretion of the court having regard to all the relevant circumstances.[50] Accordingly, it would seem to follow that the limitation fund cannot be dissipated by the payment of costs and this is to the benefit of claimants since they are not thereby subsidising the litigation costs of other claimants against the fund.

15.60 It is submitted that the reasonable costs which a claimant could expect to recover in England and Wales from the person seeking to limit in addition to his claim would appear to include the costs of establishing liability, the size of the fund and the amount of his claim against the fund.

(b) The costs of contesting the right to limit

15.61 Under the 1957 Limitation Convention as incorporated into the law of the UK by the MSA 1958 the onus was on the person seeking to limit to prove his right to do so, and in the event of a challenge to that right, the risk of costs was on the person seeking to limit. The position under the 1976 Convention is very different since the burden of proof has to a large extent been completely reversed. In *The Capitan San Luis* Clarke J. held that:

49. Denmark, Finland, Norway and Sweden.

50. *The Dundee* [1830] 2 Hag. Adm 137: *Marsden* (13th ed.), Collisions, paras 16–19. Under CPR costs no longer automatically follow the event and the court's order may take account of, and be influenced by, a party's conduct in the litigation.

"The 1976 Convention … conferred upon the shipowner a right to limit his liability which can only be defeated if certain facts are proved … the right to limit under the 1976 Convention is a legal right, exercisable in circumstances which can readily be established and which can only be defeated if the claimant discharges what Sheen J described as a 'heavy burden'."[51]

It follows that if the person challenging the right to limit cannot prove the conduct necessary to debar the right to limit, he must bear his own costs of the challenge and the costs of the person seeking to limit in defeating the challenge.

15.62 The approach adopted by most countries is to exclude the question of costs from the ambit of the Convention and it is submitted that there are strong issues of principle why this should be so. However, it is to be hoped that most State Parties adopt the same approach when dealing with the associated issue of costs to ensure consistency of approach by all Convention countries.

ISSUES ARISING OUT OF THE LEGISLATIVE INSTRUMENTS GIVING EFFECT TO THE CONVENTION IN THE UNITED KINGDOM

(a) Indemnity claims for wreck removal

15.63 The public policy behind successive statutes and conventions relating to the limitation of liability from the 18th century to the present day has been to extend the privilege of limitation in order to keep pace with developing trends in the industry. Thus, the right to limit has been extended from shipowners to charterers, managers, salvors, etc., and from claims for physical damage to claims for infringement of rights, delay, etc. Therefore, steps have generally been in the forward direction and arguments about limitation have generally been centred on whether, at any particular moment in time, the right to limit has progressed sufficiently quickly to keep pace with developments in the industry and whether evolving public policy considerations require a further step forwards.

15.64 Nevertheless, it is of course true that the justification for the very existence of the right to limit has periodically been questioned.[52] However, there have been few, if, indeed, any, occasions in the past when an existing right to limit has been withdrawn or restricted by a country which professes to believe in the advantages of limitation. It is, therefore, surprising to note that the United Kingdom may have taken such a regressive step, albeit almost certainly unintentionally, by section 185 of the Merchant Shipping Act (MSA) 1995 (formerly section 17 of the MSA 1979).

15.65 The UK has traditionally refused to extend the right of limitation to the owner of a wreck in respect of claims for wreck removal expenses brought by a harbour authority pursuant to its statutory powers.[53] Therefore, although Article 1(1)(c) of the 1957 Limitation Convention purported to extend the right of limitation to "liability imposed by any law relating to the removal of wreck", the UK

---

51. [1994] 1 All E.R. 1016.
52. See Lord Mustill, "Ships are different – or are they?", in (1993) L.M.C.L.Q. 490 and Gotthard Gauci, "Limitation of Liability in Maritime Law – an anachronism", in (1995) L.M.C.L.Q. 77.
53. See *Stonedale No. 1* [1956] A.C. 1.

government refused to change its traditional position. Whilst section 2(2)(a) of the Merchant Shipping (Liability of Shipowners and Others) Act 1958 purported to incorporate Article 1(1)(c) of the 1957 Limitation Convention into UK law, section 2(5) of the Act went on to provide that this section would not come into effect in the UK until such day as the Secretary of State might appoint by statutory instrument. No such day was ever appointed with the result that the right to limit liability for wreck removal expenses brought by a harbour authority under its statutory powers was never a part of the law of the UK under the 1958 Act.

15.66 However, the exclusion under the 1958 Act was limited to where the harbour authority brought a claim pursuant to its statutory powers. Therefore, it did not extend to other situations, e.g. where a claim for wreck removal expenses was brought by a harbour authority or other body at common law.[54] In particular, it did not extend to the situation in which the owner of a wreck ("A") sought to recover wreck removal expenses which it had paid to a harbour authority pursuant to the latter's statutory powers as damages from the owners of another ship ("B"), a collision with which had caused the "A" to become a wreck. The House of Lords confirmed in *The Arabert*[55] that the owner of "B" was entitled to limit its liability to the claim brought by "A" since the public policy considerations underpinning the exclusion in the 1958 Act were designed to protect the rights of harbour authorities and were not intended to protect the rights of other parties pursuing indemnity claims for such expenses. The distinction between the two types of claim was succinctly explained by Macrossan J. (a judge of the Australian Supreme Court) as follows:

"When the innocent shipowner seeks to recover from the wrongdoer the expenses of wreck removal which he has been forced to pay at the behest of the Harbour Authority, he is making a claim arising from the loss of his ship and so the limitation applies. He is seeking to recover what is, in effect, just one more item of special damage flowing from the loss of his ship. On the other hand, at the earlier stage, when the Harbour Authority demands against the innocent shipowner, removal of wreck or seeks to recover the expense of removal, it is not making a claim arising from the loss of a ship (which would pre-eminently be a claim in tort) but is making a claim (a statutory demand in debt) simply arising out of an owner's failure to remove an obstruction which *de facto* exists. For this reason, while the innocent shipowner is not given protection against the Harbour Authority's demand, the wrongdoing owner is permitted to limit his liability against the innocent owner's consequential claim for compensation against him."[56]

15.67 So the situation remained until 1986 when, by section 17 of the MSA the UK adopted the 1976 Limitation Convention "*en bloc*" into the law of the UK "subject to the provisions of" Part II of Schedule 7 to the MSA 1979.[57] Article 2 (1)(d) of the 1976 Convention also allowed the right to limit liability in relation to wreck removal expenses, but, consistent with its traditional public policy considerations, the UK government specified in Paragraph 3 of Schedule 7 to the MSA 1979[58] that:

"Paragraph 1 (d) of Article 2 shall not apply unless provision has been made by an order of the Secretary of State...."

54. *Dee Conservancy v McConnell* [1928] 2 K.B. 159.
55. [1961] 1 Lloyd's Rep. 363.
56. *The Tiruna* [1987] 2 Lloyd's Rep. 666 at pp. 677–678.
57. S.17 of the MSA 1979 is now s.185 of the MSA 1995.
58. Now Schedule 7 to the MSA 1995.

15.68 No such order has yet been made and, therefore, there is no right to limit liability under UK law in respect of wreck removal expenses under Article 2(1)(d) of the 1976 Convention.

15.69 The ability to limit liability in respect of a claim for an indemnity for a claim which is not itself the subject of limitation has been recognised under the 1976 Convention in the context of salvage (direct claims for which are excepted from liability under Article 3).[59] However, there is a danger that the UK government has inadvertently "thrown the baby out with the bath water" in relation to indemnity claims for wreck removal expenses by the form of legislative machinery which it has adopted to give effect to the terms of the 1976 Convention as part of the law of the UK. Whilst the exclusion in section 2(5) of the 1958 Act merely withheld the right to limit to direct claims brought by harbour authorities under statutory powers, the words "paragraph 1(d) of Article 2 shall not apply" in paragraph 3 of Part II of Schedule 7 to the MSA 1979 (now MSA 1995) appears to exclude all the various types of claim which were intended by the drafters of the 1976 Convention to be within paragraph 1(d) of the Convention. In this connection it is important to appreciate that Article 2(1) and (2) of the 1976 Convention (to which Article 2(1)(d) is subject) makes it clear that the wreck removal claims in Article 2(1)(d) are intended to be subject to limitation "whatever the basis of liability may be", "even if brought by way of recourse or indemnity". Therefore, it appears that indemnity claims for wreck removal expenses such as that brought by "A" against "B" in the collision scenario described above may also have been inadvertently excluded from the limitation regime. Put another way, it may be that the authority of the House of Lords in *The Arabert* has been overruled by the slip of a civil servant's pen. If this is, indeed, the case, it is an expensive slip given the cost of wreck removal in the modern world.

15.70 It is not an uncommon occurrence that the wording of statutes purporting to incorporate international conventions into municipal law have had far reaching effect on the wording of the convention which is to be incorporated. Much depends on the words of the particular statute and the truth of this statement has been recognised not only in the UK in relation to the problematical wording of the 1958 Act but also in Australia[60] and also, very recently in Singapore.[61] In most of these cases the exclusion of the right to limit has been the result of deliberate policy on the part of the legislation. However, it is doubtful whether the same state of mind can be imputed to the UK government in relation to the exclusion of indemnity claims for wreck removal expenses. There is no evidence that the UK government gave any conscious thought to the extension of the exclusion under the 1958 Act. Furthermore, there does not seem to be any pressing public policy reason why the exclusion should be extended to indemnity claims for wreck removal expenses.

15.71 The decision of the Australian Supreme Court in *The Tiruna* lends support to the conclusion that the "general exclusion" legislative technique adopted

---

59. See *The Breydon Merchant* [1992] 1 Lloyd's Rep. 373 and *obiter* by Longmore L.J. in *CMA Djakarta* [2004] 1 Lloyd's Rep. 460.
60. See *The Tiruna* (1987) 2 Lloyd's Rep. 666.
61. See *The Seaway* (2004) S.G.C.A. 57.

by the UK government in relation to Article 2(1)(d) of the 1976 Convention may have far-reaching, albeit unintended, consequences. However, it remains to be seen to what extent the "legislative myopia" of the UK government will excuse what would otherwise seem to be the objective construction of the relevant statute.

15.72 If this proves to be a difficulty it may, nevertheless, be possible on the face of it, to argue that since Article 2(2) allows limitation for indemnity claims arising as a result of any of the claims itemised in Article 2(1) there is nothing to prevent "B" from relying on any of the other provisions of Article 2(1) (which have not been excluded by the MSA 1979) if they provide an alternative source of protection against an indemnity claim of this nature. In this regard, Longmore L.J. recently recognised in *CMA Djakarta*[62] that claims resulting from collisions fell within the words "loss of or damage to property … occurring … in connection with the operation of the ship" in Article 2(1)(a) with the result that the cost of removing the wreck of a vessel caused by a collision could be subject to limitation either under these words or the following words, *viz.* "and consequential loss resulting therefrom". Similarly, it was recognised by Lord Denning in *The Putbus*[63] that the blocking of a waterway is an "infringement of rights", in which case a right to limit may also be available under Article 2(1)(c). However, the difficult question which arises is whether it is permissible to allow the right to limit under "general" heads such as those found in paragraphs 1(a) or (c) when the legislature has taken a clear step to exclude the right to limit in respect of the specific claim which is being advanced. Such a question arose for consideration in the Australian case of *The Tiruna*. Two judges of the Australian Supreme Court (Kelly and McPherson JJ.) clearly thought that such an approach was not permissible since, if it were allowed, it would "defeat the obvious intention of Parliament", whereas the third judge (Macrossan J.) had no such inhibitions and believed such an approach to be perfectly permissible.

15.73 It is submitted that this lacuna is the result of an unintended oversight on the part of the legislature of the United Kingdom and that it requires remedial action on its part. The Draft Wreck Removal Convention is now at its final stage and a Diplomatic Conference will convene in 2007 to consider its adoption. Thereafter, the UK legislature might have the opportunity to put right this apparent wrong.

(b) The carriage of passengers on seagoing and non-seagoing ships

15.74 It has always been a source of confusion that the Athens Convention and the 1976 Limitation Convention both contain provisions whereby a shipowner may limit his liability for passenger claims. Under Article 7 of the Athens Convention the limit is expressed as 46,666 SDR[64] "per carriage", i.e. per passenger voyage. Under Article 7 of the 1976 Convention the shipowner may limit to a global fund calculated by multiplying 46,666 SDR by the number of passengers which the ship is authorised to carry but subject to any upper limit of 25 million SDR "on any distinct occasion" (i.e. per separate incident). Reconciling these two rather different approaches

---

62. [2004] 1 Lloyd's Rep. 460 at p. 467.
63. [1969] 1 Lloyd's Rep. 253.
64. Since 1987 this has been increased to approximately £80,000 for UK operators under the Carriage of Passengers and their Luggage by Sea (United Kingdom Carriers) Order 1998 (S.I. 1998/2917).

to limitation for passenger claims has been the subject of much debate. The better view seems to be that by reason of the terms of Articles 14 and 19 of the Athens Convention all passenger claims will be treated as primarily subject to the Athens Convention and its limitation regime. However, if the total amount payable to all claimants under the Athens Convention exceeds the global fund calculated in accordance with Article 7 of the 1976 Convention then the shipowner can rely on the provisions of that Convention to limit further thereby scaling claims down pro-rata.

15.75 The right to limit liability under the provisions of the Athens Convention and the 1976 Limitation Convention (both of which grant the right to limit in respect of passenger claims) is given effect in the United Kingdom by section 185(1) of the Merchant Shipping Act 1995 and by Schedules 6 and 7 respectively of Parts I and II thereof.

15.76 This situation is further complicated in the UK by another apparent inconsistency in the implementation of the 1976 and Athens Conventions. Article 1(3) of the Athens Convention provides that for purposes of that Convention "ship" means only a "seagoing ship". Article 1(2) of the 1976 Convention contains a similar provision. However, paragraph 2 of Part II of Schedule 7 provides that the right of limitation under the 1976 Convention in the UK is accorded to the owners of ships "whether seagoing or not". By way of contrast, there is no similar extension in Part II of Schedule 6 in relation to the Athens Convention.

15.77 This had an unexpected result in the case of the 1989 Thames collision between the *Marchioness* and the *Bowbelle* as the result of which 51 people were killed and several injured. Because the *Marchioness* was not a seagoing ship the Athens Convention did not apply but Article 7 of the 1976 Convention did. Passenger claims were thus to be set against a global limitation fund calculated by reference to the number of passengers which the *Marchioness* was authorised to carry. In the event there was enough money in the global fund to satisfy all claims. However, had the per-passenger limits of the Athens Convention applied many of the bigger claims would have been caught by the per-passenger limits of the Athens Convention and left unsatisfied. An anomalous outcome.

15.78 The UK has now adopted the 1996 Protocol to the London Convention and the legislature has taken the opportunity of the implementation of this Protocol to try to "tidy up" the previous inconsistencies between the two conventions. As from 13 May 2004 the provisions of Article 7 of the 1976 Convention will cease to be applicable to passenger claims on seagoing ships (which will henceforth be subject only to the Athens Convention limits) whereas passenger claims on non-seagoing ships will be regulated by Article 7 of the 1976 Convention as amended by the 1996 Protocol.[65] Since Article 7 of the 1976 Convention (as amended) provides a limit of 175,000 SDR per passenger "in respect of claims arising on any distinct occasion" whereas Article 7(1) of the Athens Convention provides a limit of 46,666 SDR per passenger "per carriage" this will still give a passenger on a non-seagoing ship an advantage over a passenger on a seagoing ship firstly, since the number of SDR per passenger is higher and secondly, since the 1976 Convention limit applies on each separate occasion which gives rise to a claim whereas

65. See paragraph 7(e) of the Merchant Shipping (Convention on Limitation of Liability for Maritime Claims) (Amendment) Order 1998 (S.I 1998/1258).

the Athens Convention limit applies to each carriage irrespective of the number of incidents which occur during that carriage. The advantage is diluted only in the case of a carrier whose ordinary place of business is in the UK since his Athens Convention limit is increased to 300,000 SDR "per carriage".[66] However, when the Athens Protocol of 2002 comes into effect the advantage may well disappear since under that Protocol the limit of a carrier of a seagoing ship will be increased to 400,000 SDR "per carriage".

15.79 Therefore, it is doubtful if the attempt to "tidy up" has been totally successful. Furthermore, an interesting conundrum for the UK is appearing on the horizon since in November 2005 the EU Commission presented a proposal intended to make the Athens Protocol 2002 binding throughout the EU both in relation to sea traffic and inland waters, i.e. to seagoing and non-seagoing ships![67] It is submitted that this may be the catalyst necessary to bring some well-needed consistency to this area of limitation.

CONCLUSION

15.80 The history of limitation has generally been to extend the right of limitation in tandem with developments in the industry. This is logical if it is felt that the right to limit still has a part to play in modern business. Therefore, it follows that where lacunae are spotted in the existing regime these need to be plugged. It is submitted that there are such lacunae in the current regime in relation to the matters considered above and that remedial action is required in that regard.

15.81 To date, extensions to the right to limit have tended to be reactive in nature to specific requirements such as the extension of the right to limit to salvors under the 1976 Convention as a result of the *Tojo Maru* incident. This is understandable but the process has thereby suffered from an element of rigidity which has tended to restrict the ability of courts and tribunals to apply the spirit of limitation to developing systems and scenarios. This, in turn, has resulted in a dilution of the ability to encourage "those who go down to the sea in ships" which, rightly or wrongly depending on one's point of view, has always been considered to be the *raison d'etre* behind the grant of the privilege of limitation. Therefore, it is to be hoped that henceforth, any proposed amendments to the limitation regime should be more "elastic" in nature and terminology to allow the regime to grow organically in tandem with developments in shipping.

---

66. Carriage of Passengers and their Luggage by Sea (United Kingdom Carriers) Order 1998 (S.I. 1998/2917).
67. COM (2005) 592.

CHAPTER 16

Jurisdictional aspects of limitation of liability for maritime claims

NIGEL MEESON Q.C.*

INTRODUCTION

16.1 The purpose of this chapter is to consider three potentially difficult issues of jurisdiction which arise in connection with limitation of liability under the 1976 Convention. These are:

(i) the extent to which the limitation of liability can be used as a sword rather than a shield by a shipowner;
(ii) the extent to which the courts of a state party to the 1996 Protocol are bound to recognise a limitation fund established in a 1976 Contracting State which is not party to the 1996 protocol;
(iii) European jurisdiction in relation to limitation claims.

THE PRE-EMPTIVE USE OF A LIMITATION ACTION

16.2 It is a feature of the Limitation of Liability for Maritime Claims Convention 1976 (LLC) that it has no express provisions concerning jurisdiction. In this respect it is no different to the 1957 Convention which was equally silent on the question of jurisdiction. There are logical reasons why a convention on limitation of liability may not deal explicitly with jurisdiction: The purpose of such a convention is after all to provide a uniform regime whereby the overall liability of a shipowner in respect of a particular maritime accident is capped at a certain level and the claimants in respect of that accident are paid out rateably in accordance with the proportion which their claim bears to the total amount of claims. Given that there is a uniform regime and the main provisions of the Convention are concerned with mechanical or administrative matters one can see why it could be seen as a matter of indifference in which Contracting State limitation of liability is determined. However, this view assumes the utopian dream of a universally applicable limitation convention, which in practice is not going to happen. In the real world there will be contracting states and non-contracting states and it is this divide which will inevitably lead to the potential for forum shopping in relation to limitation of liability. As was said by the Court of Appeal in *The Herceg Novi*[1]:

"The 1976 Convention has not received universal acceptance, or anything like it. It is not 'an internationally sanctioned and objective view of where substantial justice is now viewed as lying'. It is simply the view of some 30 states."

---

* Barrister, Quadrant Chambers.
1. [1998] 2 Lloyd's Rep. 454.

16.3 There is also another potential reason why jurisdiction is not addressed in the Convention, namely that limitation of liability should not be considered as a free standing right, but rather should be seen as ancillary or subsidiary to liability proceedings – absent actual legal proceedings against the shipowner the right to limit liability does not arise. Limitation of liability is a shield and not a sword. However, in common law jurisdictions a shipowner has historically been able to use limitation proceedings pre-emptively as a sword in order to try to force claimants into a jurisdiction with a limitation regime favourable to the shipowner. In *Caspian Basin v Bouygues (No. 4)* Rix J. said this[2]:

"There can be nothing surprising or inappropriate about a limitation action being commenced in the same forum as a claimant's action to establish liability; but equally there is nothing unusual about a limitation action taking place in a different forum from that in which liability is being litigated ... Moreover, the choice of forum for a limitation action belongs in principle to the party seeking to limit, not to the claimant."

16.4 The underlying premise is that it is for the shipowner to choose where to limit his liability and to establish a limitation fund in that jurisdiction against which claims may be enforced.[3]

16.5 The 1976 Convention introduced an express connection between a liability claim and a limitation fund by providing that the establishment of a limitation fund is to be responsive to a claim being made in a Contracting State. Article 11.1 provides:

"Any person alleged to be liable may constitute a fund with the Court or other competent authority in any State Party in which legal proceedings are instituted in respect of the claims subject to limitation."

16.6 Although the intention of this provision is to regulate in which of the contracting states to the 1976 Convention a fund may be established, it also has the necessary consequence that a fund cannot be established in any contracting state absent a claim being brought in a contracting state. This has two related consequences: First a shipowner cannot pre-emptively set up a limitation fund where no claims have yet been made. Secondly, a shipowner cannot set up a limitation fund in a 1976 Contracting State where a claim has been brought against him in a non-contracting state.

16.7 However, the establishment of a limitation fund is not a pre-requisite to limitation as the Convention makes clear in Article 10.1:

"Limitation of liability may be invoked notwithstanding that a limitation fund as mentioned in Article 11 has not been constituted. However, a State Party may provide in its national law that, where an action is brought in its courts to enforce a claim subject to limitation, a person liable may only invoke the right to limit liability if a limitation fund has been constituted in accordance with the provisions of this Convention or is constituted when the right to limit liability is invoked."

16.8 The question which arises from this provision is whether a shipowner is entitled to invoke Article 10 pre-emptively in circumstances where he could not set up a limitation fund under Article 11 because no claim has yet been brought against

2. [1997] 2 Lloyd's Rep. 507 at p. 525.
3. See also *The Volvox Hollandia* [1988] 2 Lloyd's Rep. 361.

him? In England the Court of Appeal has given an affirmative answer to this question in *The Western Regent*.[4]

16.9 The first claimant was the registered owner of the vessel *Western Regent*, a purpose built seismic survey vessel. The second claimant was the demise charterer of the vessel. On 2 October 2004 the vessel was operating in the North Sea towing six streamers. At about 0130 two of the streamers contacted the Ellon Grant marker buoy, which was positioned at a well head in the Total Dunbar oilfield, located about 70 miles east of the Shetlands in the Scottish sector of the North Sea oilfields. The collision was alleged to have dragged the buoy from its position and damaged the well head installation. The defendant was an English registered company and was operator of the Dunbar field and owner of the installation. The claimants accepted that the collision and resulting damage was caused by the negligence of the second claimants, and admitted liability to the defendant. On 5 November 2004 the claimants brought a claim against the defendant with a view to limiting their liability to the defendant under the Convention for Limitation of Liability for Maritime Claims 1976 (the 1976 Convention) set out in Schedule 7 to the Merchant Shipping Act 1995. On 24 January 2005, the defendant filed an original complaint in the United States District Court for the Southern District of Texas, Galveston Division against the claimants, among others. In the complaint, the defendant claimed damages arising out of the collision including damage to property, lost production and business interruption losses of US$9.9 million. In Texas, limitation would be based on the value of the vessel post-collision, and not on the 1976 Convention limits. That value was likely to be in excess of the defendant's entire claim.

16.10 The defendant accepted that the court had personal jurisdiction over it because it was an English registered company. However, it argued that personal jurisdiction was not in itself a sufficient basis for jurisdiction because the court had no "subject matter" jurisdiction. The essence of that submission was that under the Convention for Limitation of Liability for Maritime Claims 1976 ("the Limitation Convention") which, by reason of section 185 of the MSA 1995, has the force of law in the UK, a person seeking to limit liability can only do so where legal proceedings have already been instituted against him in respect of claims subject to limitation. In other words it was argued that the Limitation Convention does not entitle a shipowner to issue pre-emptive limitation proceedings in the absence of any substantive underlying proceedings by a claimant against the shipowner. The scheme of the limitation regime prescribed by the Limitation Convention is responsive and does not entitle an owner to "forum shop".

16.11 This argument was rejected by the Court of Appeal. At paragraph 15 of his judgment Clarke L.J. said:

"There is no general jurisdiction provision in the Convention stating where the right of limitation must be invoked. It therefore appears to me that in principle the Convention permits a party to seek to limit its liability in any contracting state which has personal jurisdiction over the defendant. Since there is no express restriction in the Convention restricting the invocation of the right to limit in any way, if there is such a restriction it must be implied in the Convention. To my mind there is nothing in the Convention to lead to the implication of such a restriction."

4. [2005] 2 Lloyd's Rep. 359.

16.12 The defendants had argued that there was precisely such an implication to be derived from the overall scheme of the Convention, which required a common approach to be taken to Article 10 and 11, and more particularly from the language of Article 10 itself which, they said, showed that the requirement of prior legal proceedings against the shipowner was equally a pre-requisite to invoking limitation under Article 10 as Article 11.

16.13 It was argued that the clear prohibition on forum shopping contained in Article 11 ought not to be undermined or evaded by allowing Article 10 to be invoked pre-emptively because there ought to be no difference between the case where a shipowner sets up a limitation fund and a case where he does not (e.g. because it is a single claim case). The court rejected this argument primarily on the basis that the Convention treats limitation under Article 10 and Article 11 differently: It is only in the latter case, where a fund has been constituted under Article 11 that the protective provisions of Article 13 are applicable. If a shipowner chooses to invoke limitation under Article 10 without constituting a fund, then he runs the risk that his vessel may be arrested in another Contracting State.

16.14 The defendants also raised an argument based upon the wording of Article 10. The full text of Article 10 is as follows:

"Article 10:
1. Limitation of liability may be invoked notwithstanding that a limitation fund as mentioned in Article 11 has not been constituted. *However, a State Party may provide in its national law that, where an action is brought in its courts to enforce a claim subject to limitation, a person liable may only invoke the right to limit liability if a limitation fund has been constituted in accordance with the provisions of this Convention or is constituted when the right to limit liability is invoked.*[5] [Author's emphasis.]
2. If limitation of liability is invoked without the constitution of a limitation fund, the provisions of Article 12 shall apply, correspondingly.
3. Questions of procedure arising out of the rules of this Article shall be decided in accordance with the national law of the State Party in which action is brought."

16.15 The argument was that the phrase "action is brought" in Article 10.3 should be read as "such action is brought" referring back to the phrase "action is brought … to enforce a claim subject to limitation" which appears in the second sentence of Article 10.1. Although the second sentence of Article 10.1 does not form part of English law (being omitted from Schedule 7 to the MSA 1995), it was suggested by the defendant that this was irrelevant because in order to understand the meaning of Article 10.3 it was necessary to have regard to the full Convention text of Article 10.1.

16.16 The Court of Appeal rejected this argument and instead accepted the counter-argument that the option given to Contracting States in the second sentence to require a limitation fund to be established "where an action is brought to enforce a claim subject to limitation" was "entirely consistent with the express provision in the first sentence that limitation may be invoked without the constitution of a fund and with the conclusion that a limitation action may be brought in such a case in the absence of an action to enforce a claim subject to limitation".[6]

---

5. This second sentence highlighted in italic is in the text of the Convention but is not in the text to be found in Schedule 7 to the MSA 1995.
6. Clarke L.J., para. 17.

16.17 Although permission to appeal to the House of Lords was granted to the Defendant, the case settled prior to being heard by the House of Lords.

16.18 Although it may be possible to bring a limitation action in England by way of a pre-emptive strike under Article 10 of the 1976 Convention, unless the English court has jurisdiction under European Regulation (EC) 44/2001[7] then it always has the power to stay the limitation action on the ground of *forum non conveniens*. It will not ordinarily[8] be a relevant factor to prevent a stay being granted that the competing forum will apply a different limitation regime.[9]

16.19 Furthermore, unless recognition or enforcement of the judgment in the limitation action is sought in another Member State of the European Union (or Switzerland, Norway or Iceland), then whether or not the judgment will be recognised or enforced will be a matter for the relevant foreign court. The English court will not grant an anti-suit injunction to prevent liability proceedings taking place elsewhere even in a single claim case.[10]

RECOGNITION OF 1976 LIMITS IN 1996 PROTOCOL CONTRACTING STATES

16.20 An interesting situation can now arise because of the difference in limits under the 1996 Protocol and the 1976 Convention. Not all Contracting States to the 1976 Convention have accepted the 1996 Protocol. This gives rise to the possibility that a shipowner can engage in forum shopping essentially within the 1976 regime by seeking to establish a fund in a 1976 Contracting State which has not implemented the 1996 Protocol and then seeking the protection afforded by Article 13 in a state or states which are party to the 1996 Protocol.

16.21 Whether this will be possible would seem to depend upon whether the State in question remains party to the 1976 Convention or whether it has denounced the 1976 Convention.

16.22 The position in the United Kingdom is that the 1976 Convention was denounced with effect from the entry into force of the 1996 Protocol. The text of the 1976 Convention as amended by the 1996 Protocol is set out in the Schedule to the Merchant Shipping (Convention on Limitation of Liability for Maritime Claims) (Amendment) Order 1998 (S.I. 1998/1258) (being an amended version of Schedule 7 to the 1995 Act). In summary this increases the limits of liability under Article 6 and 7 in accordance with the limits provided by the Protocol. The wording of Articles 11 and 13 are unchanged. Thus Article 13.2 continues to provide in summary that where a limitation fund has been constituted "in accordance with Article 11" any security given may be released by order of the court and shall be released if the fund has been constituted at the specified places. However, Article 11 provides that the fund shall be constituted in the sum of such of the

---

7. See further, below.
8. In *Domansa v Derin Shipping* [2001] 1 Lloyd's Rep. 369 the question was raised whether the position might be different if the limitation regime to be applied was under the English 1894 Act as an historic legacy in the competing jurisdiction, but it was not decided.
9. See *The Herceg Novi* (1957 Convention) and *The Western Regent* (USA value based system).
10. *The Western Regent* [2005] 2 Lloyd's Rep. 54.

amounts set out in Articles 6 and 7 as are applicable for the claims for which the shipowner may be liable. In other words Article 11 now requires a fund to be constituted in accordance with the 1996 Protocol, because of the amendment of Articles 6 and 7. Any limitation fund established in a 1976 State will not be in the amount required by the 1996 Protocol and therefore on an ordinary reading of the amended version of Schedule 7 to the 1995 Act will not be a fund constituted in accordance with Article 11. Accordingly because such a fund is not a fund constituted in accordance with Article 11, then the English Court is not obliged to stay under the mandatory provisions of Article 13.2 nor is the discretionary power under Article 13.2 applicable.

16.23 On the other hand in States which remain parties to the 1976 Convention it was expressly provided by Article 9.4 of the Protocol:

"Nothing in this Protocol shall affect the obligations of a State which is a Party both to the Convention and to this Protocol with respect to a State which is a Party to the Convention but not a Party to this Protocol."

The Vienna Convention on the International Law of Treaties provides by Article 40.4:

"The amending agreement does not bind any State already a party to the treaty which does not become a party to the amending agreement; article 30, paragraph 4(b), applies in relation to such State."

Article 30.4(b) provides:

"When the parties to the later treaty do not include all the parties to the earlier one: (b) as between a State party to both treaties and a State party to only one of the treaties, the treaty to which both States are parties governs their mutual rights and obligations."

16.24 Thus, in accordance with its international obligations arising out of the unamended Convention, such a State would be bound to recognise a limitation fund set up in a 1976 State in accordance with the 1976 Convention and is therefore bound to apply Article 13.2 with respect to such a fund.

EUROPEAN JURISDICTIONAL ISSUES RELATING TO LIMITATION OF LIABILITY

16.25 Council Regulation (EC) No. 44/2001 Article 7 (which replaces Article 6A of the Brussels Convention) provides:

"Where by virtue of this Regulation a court of a Member State has jurisdiction in actions relating to liability from the use or operation of a ship, that court, ... shall have jurisdiction over claims for the limitation of such liability."

The Schlosser report on the Accession Convention 1978 (*Official Journal*, C59, Vol. 22), paragraph 128, explains the purpose of the forerunner, Article 6A:

"The actual or potential limitation of the liability of a shipowner can, however, in all legal systems of the Community be used otherwise than as a defence. If a shipowner anticipates a liability claim, it may be in his interests to take the initiative by asking for a declaration that he has only limited or potentially limited liability for the claim. In that case he can choose from one of the jurisdictions which are competent by virtue of Articles 2 to 6. According to these provisions, he cannot bring an action in the courts of his domicile. Since, however, he could be sued in those courts, it would be desirable also to allow him to have recourse to this jurisdiction. It is the purpose of Article 6A to provide for this. Moreover … this is the only jurisdiction where the shipowner could reasonably concentrate all actions affecting limitation of his liability. The result for English law … is that the fund can be set up and allocated by that same court. In addition, Article 6A makes it clear that proceedings for limitation of liability can also be brought by the shipowner in any other court which has jurisdiction over the claim …"

16.26 This provision does limit the shipowner to a jurisdiction in which he could be sued, but does not require the shipowner actually to have had proceedings commenced against him in order to commence a limitation action. In this respect it is wider than Article 11 of the 1976 Convention which requires an action to have been brought against the shipowner. It is also an unusual provision in that it essentially reverses the normal defendant's domicile rule under Article 2 in favour of a claimant's domicile rule for limitation actions under Article 7.

16.27 In *The Western Regent*[11] the relevant parties were both domiciled in England, being English registered companies.[12] The English court therefore had personal jurisdiction over the defendant in respect of the limitation action under Article 2 of the Regulation and also had jurisdiction under Article 2 of the Regulation over claims against the demise charterer and consequently had jurisdiction in respect of the limitation action under Article 7. If the Defendant had been domiciled in a different Member State, then although *prima facie* it could require any limitation action to be brought against it in the courts of its country of domicile under Article 2 of the Regulation, the shipowner being domiciled in a Member State, he will be able to invoke limitation under Article 10 of the 1976 Convention in the courts of his own country pursuant to Article 7 of the Regulation.

16.28 Once the shipowner has obtained a judgment limiting his liability, then that judgment will be enforceable in any Member State under Article 33 of the Regulation[13] (and in Switzerland, Norway and Iceland under the equivalent provision in the Lugano Convention), so that he has protection throughout Europe irrespective of whether he has established a limitation fund under Article 11.

16.29 Thus a European domiciled shipowner will always be entitled to commence a limitation action in the courts of its country of domicile relying on Article 10 of the Limitation Convention and Article 7 of the Regulation. The only potential obstacle which he may face is where a claim has already been brought against him in the courts of another Member State. Although it has been held by the European Court[14] that a limitation action and a liability action do not have the same subject matter and so that there was no *lis pendens* within Article 27 of the Regulation,[15] it

---

11. *Ibid.*
12. The demise charterer was responsible for the operation of the vessel and was registered in England although the registered owner was a BVI company.
13. *Maersk Olie and Gas A/S v Firma M de Haan and W de Boer* [2005] 1 Lloyd's Rep. 210.
14. *Ibid.*
15. Which provides:
   "1. Where proceedings involving the same cause of action and between the same parties are brought in the courts of different Member States, any court other than the court first seised shall of its own motion stay its proceedings until such time as the jurisdiction of the court first seised is established.
   2. Where the jurisdiction of the court first seised is established, any court other than the court first seised shall decline jurisdiction in favour of that court."

has been held by the Court of Appeal[16] that a limitation action and a liability action are "related actions" within Article 28 of the Regulation.[17] Accordingly, the limitation action could be stayed. There is, however, no power in the English Court to stay on the ground of *forum non conveniens* when it has jurisdiction under the Regulation.[18]

16. *The Happy Fellow* [1997] 1 Lloyd's Rep. 130.
17. Which provides:
   "1. Where related actions are pending in the courts of different Member States, any court other than the court first seised may stay its proceedings.
   2. Where these actions are pending at first instance, any court other than the court first seised may also, on the application of one of the parties, decline jurisdiction if the court first seised has jurisdiction over the actions in question and its law permits consolidation thereof.
   3. For the purposes of this Article, actions are deemed to be related where they are so closely connected that it is expedient to hear and determine them together to avoid the risk of irreconcilable judgments resulting from separate proceedings."
18. *Owusu v Jackson* [2005] 1 Lloyd's Rep. 452 (E.C.J.).

APPENDICES

International Convention on Civil Liability for Oil Pollution Damage, 1992

The States Parties to the present Convention,

CONSCIOUS of the dangers of pollution posed by the worldwide maritime carriage of oil in bulk,

CONVINCED of the need to ensure that adequate compensation is available to persons who suffer damage caused by pollution resulting from the escape or discharge of oil from ships,

DESIRING to adopt uniform international rules and procedures for determining questions of liability and providing adequate compensation in such cases,

HAVE AGREED as follows:

Article I

For the purposes of this Convention:

1. "Ship" means any sea-going vessel and seaborne craft of any type whatsoever constructed or adapted for the carriage of oil in bulk as cargo, provided that a ship capable of carrying oil and other cargoes shall be regarded as a ship only when it is actually carrying oil in bulk as cargo and during any voyage following such carriage unless it is proved that it has no residues of such carriage of oil in bulk aboard.

2. "Person" means any individual or partnership or any public or private body, whether corporate or not, including a State or any of its constituent subdivisions.

3. "Owner" means the person or persons registered as the owner of the ship or, in the absence of registration, the person or persons owning the ship. However in the case of a ship owned by a State and operated by a company which in that State is registered as the ship's operator, "owner" shall mean such company.

4. "State of the ship's registry" means in relation to registered ships the State of registration of the ship, and in relation to unregistered ships the State whose flag the ship is flying.

5. "Oil" means any persistent hydrocarbon mineral oil such as crude oil, fuel oil, heavy diesel oil and lubricating oil, whether carried on board a ship as cargo or in the bunkers of such a ship.

6. "Pollution damage" means:
   (a) loss or damage caused outside the ship by contamination resulting from the escape or discharge of oil from the ship, wherever such escape or discharge may occur, provided that compensation for impairment of the environment other than loss of profit from such impairment shall be limited to costs of reasonable measures of reinstatement actually undertaken or to be undertaken;
   (b) the costs of preventive measures and further loss or damage caused by preventive measures.

7. "Preventive measures" means any reasonable measures taken by any person after an incident has occurred to prevent or minimise pollution damage.

8. "Incident" means any occurrence, or series of occurrences having the same origin, which causes pollution damage or creates a grave and imminent threat of causing such damage.

9. "Organisation" means the International Maritime Organization.

10. "1969 Liability Convention" means the International Convention on Civil Liability for Oil Pollution Damage, 1969. For States Parties to the Protocol of 1976 to that Convention, the term shall be deemed to include the 1969 Liability Convention as amended by that Protocol.

Article II

This Convention shall apply exclusively:

  (a) to pollution damage caused:

    (i) in the territory, including the territorial sea, of a Contracting State, and

    (ii) in the exclusive economic zone of a Contracting State, established in accordance with international law, or, if a Contracting State has not established such a zone, in an area beyond and adjacent to the territorial sea of that State determined by that State in accordance with international law and extending not more than 200 nautical miles from the baselines from which the breadth of its territorial sea is measured;

  (b) to preventive measures, wherever taken, to prevent or minimise such damage.

Article III

1. Except as provided in paragraphs 2 and 3 of this Article, the owner of a ship at the time of an incident, or, where the incident consists of a series of occurrences, at the time of the first such occurrence, shall be liable for any pollution damage caused by the ship as a result of the incident.

2. No liability for pollution damage shall attach to the owner if he proves that the damage:

  (a) resulted from an act of war, hostilities, civil war, insurrection or a natural phenomenon of an exceptional, inevitable and irresistible character, or

  (b) was wholly caused by an act or omission done with intent to cause damage by a third party, or

  (c) was wholly caused by the negligence or other wrongful act of any Government or other authority responsible for the maintenance of lights or other navigational aids in the exercise of that function.

3. If the owner proves that the pollution damage resulted wholly or partially either from an act or omission done with intent to cause damage by the person who suffered the damage or from the negligence of that person, the owner may be exonerated wholly or partially from his liability to such person.

4. No claim for compensation for pollution damage may be made against the owner otherwise than in accordance with this Convention. Subject to paragraph 5 of this Article, no claim for compensation for pollution damage under this Convention or otherwise may be made against:

  (a) the servants or agents of the owner or the members of the crew;

  (b) the pilot or any other person who, without being a member of the crew, performs services for the ship;

  (c) any charterer (howsoever described, including a bareboat charterer), manager or operator of the ship;

  (d) any person performing salvage operations with the consent of the owner or on the instructions of a competent public authority;

  (e) any person taking preventive measures;

  (f) all servants or agents of persons mentioned in subparagraphs (c), (d) and (e); unless the damage resulted from their personal act or omission, committed with the intent to cause such damage, or recklessly and with knowledge that such damage would probably result.

5. Nothing in this Convention shall prejudice any right of recourse of the owner against third parties.

Article IV

When an incident involving two or more ships occurs and pollution damage results therefrom, the owners of all the ships concerned, unless exonerated under Article III, shall be jointly and severally liable for all such damage which is not reasonably separable.

Article V

1. The owner of a ship shall be entitled to limit his liability under this Convention in respect of any one incident to an aggregate amount calculated as follows:
   (a) 4,510,000 units of account for a ship not exceeding 5,000 units of tonnage;
   (b) for a ship with a tonnage in excess thereof, for each additional unit of tonnage, 631 units of account in addition to the amount mentioned in sub-paragraph (a);
provided, however, that this aggregate amount shall not in any event exceed 89,770,000 units of account.

2. The owner shall not be entitled to limit his liability under this Convention if it is proved that the pollution damage resulted from his personal act or omission, committed with the intent to cause such damage, or recklessly and with knowledge that such damage would probably result.

3. For the purpose of availing himself of the benefit of limitation provided for in paragraph 1 of this Article the owner shall constitute a fund for the total sum representing the limit of his liability with the Court or other competent authority of any one of the Contracting States in which action is brought under Article IX or, if no action is brought, with any Court or other competent authority in any one of the Contracting States in which an action can be brought under Article IX. The fund can be constituted either by depositing the sum or by producing a bank guarantee or other guarantee, acceptable under the legislation of the Contracting State where the fund is constituted, and considered to be adequate by the Court or other competent authority.

4. The fund shall be distributed among the claimants in proportion to the amounts of their established claims.

5. If before the fund is distributed the owner or any of his servants or agents or any person providing him insurance or other financial security has as a result of the incident in question, paid compensation for pollution damage, such person shall, up to the amount he has paid, acquire by subrogation the rights which the person so compensated would have enjoyed under this Convention.

6. The right of subrogation provided for in paragraph 5 of this Article may also be exercised by a person other than those mentioned therein in respect of any amount of compensation for pollution damage which he may have paid but only to the extent that such subrogation is permitted under the applicable national law.

7. Where the owner or any other person establishes that he may be compelled to pay at a later date in whole or in part any such amount of compensation, with regard to which such person would have enjoyed a right of subrogation under paragraphs 5 or 6 of this Article, had the compensation been paid before the fund was distributed, the Court or other competent authority of the State where the fund has been constituted may order that a sufficient sum shall be provisionally set aside to enable such person at such later date to enforce his claim against the fund.

8. Claims in respect of expenses reasonably incurred or sacrifices reasonably made by the owner voluntarily to prevent or minimise pollution damage shall rank equally with other claims against the fund.

9.(a) The "unit of account" referred to in paragraph 1 of this Article is the Special Drawing Right as defined by the International Monetary Fund. The amounts mentioned in paragraph 1 shall be converted into national currency on the basis of the value of that currency by reference to the Special Drawing Right on the date of the constitution of the fund referred to in paragraph 3. The value of the national currency, in terms of the Special Drawing Right, of a Contracting State which is a member of the International Monetary Fund shall be calculated in accordance with the method of valuation applied by the International Monetary Fund in effect on the date in question for its operations and transactions. The value of the national currency, in terms of the Special Drawing Right, of a Contracting State which is not a member of the International Monetary Fund shall be calculated in a manner determined by that State.

(b) Nevertheless, a Contracting State which is not a member of the International Monetary Fund and whose law does not permit the application of the provisions of paragraph 9(a) may, at the time of ratification, acceptance, approval of or accession to this Convention or at any time thereafter, declare that the unit of account referred to in paragraph 9(a) shall be equal to 15 gold francs. The gold franc referred to in this paragraph corresponds to sixty-five and a half milligrammes of gold of millesimal fineness nine hundred. The conversion of the gold franc into the national currency shall be made according to the law of the State concerned.

(c) The calculation mentioned in the last sentence of paragraph 9(a) and the conversion mentioned in paragraph 9(b) shall be made in such manner as to express in the national currency of the Contracting State as far as possible the same real value for the amounts in paragraph 1 as would result from the application of the first three sentences of paragraph 9(a). Contracting States shall communicate to the depositary the manner of calculation pursuant to paragraph 9(a), or the result of the conversion in paragraph 9(b) as the case may be, when depositing an instrument of ratification, acceptance, approval of or accession to this Convention and whenever there is a change in either.

10. For the purpose of this Article the ship's tonnage shall be the gross tonnage calculated in accordance with the tonnage measurement regulations contained in Annex I of the International Convention on Tonnage Measurement of Ships, 1969.

11. The insurer or other person providing financial security shall be entitled to constitute a fund in accordance with this Article on the same conditions and having the same effect as if it were constituted by the owner. Such a fund may be constituted even if, under the provisions of paragraph 2, the owner is not entitled to limit his liability, but its constitution shall in that case not prejudice the rights of any claimant against the owner.

Article VI

1. Where the owner, after an incident, has constituted a fund in accordance with Article V, and is entitled to limit his liability,
   (a) no person having a claim for pollution damage arising out of that incident shall be entitled to exercise any right against any other assets of the owner in respect of such claim;
   (b) the Court or other competent authority of any Contracting State shall order the release of any ship or other property belonging to the owner which has been arrested in respect of a claim for pollution damage arising out of that incident, and shall similarly release any bail or other security furnished to avoid such arrest.

2. The foregoing shall, however, only apply if the claimant has access to the Court administering the fund and the fund is actually available in respect of his claim.

Article VII

1. The owner of a ship registered in a Contracting State and carrying more than 2,000 tons of oil in bulk as cargo shall be required to maintain insurance or other financial security, such as the guarantee of a bank or a certificate delivered by an international compensation fund, in the sums fixed by applying the limits of liability prescribed in Article V, paragraph 1 to cover his liability for pollution damage under this Convention.

2. A certificate attesting that insurance or other financial security is in force in accordance with the provisions of this Convention shall be issued to each ship after the appropriate authority of a Contracting State has determined that the requirements of paragraph 1 have

been complied with. With respect to a ship registered in a Contracting State such certificate shall be issued or certified by the appropriate authority of the State of the ship's registry; with respect to a ship not registered in a Contracting State it may be issued or certified by the appropriate authority of any Contracting State. This certificate shall be in the form of the annexed model and shall contain the following particulars:

    (a) name of ship and port of registration;

    (b) name and principal place of business of owner;

    (c) type of security;

    (d) name and principal place of business of insurer or other person giving security and, where appropriate, place of business where the insurance or security is established;

    (e) period of validity of certificate which shall not be longer than the period of validity of the insurance or other security.

3. The certificate shall be in the official language or languages of the issuing State. If the language used is neither English nor French, the text shall include a translation into one of these languages.

4. The certificate shall be carried on board the ship and a copy shall be deposited with the authorities who keep the record of the ship's registry or, if the ship is not registered in a Contracting State, with the authorities of the State issuing or certifying the certificate.

5. An insurance or other financial security shall not satisfy the requirements of this Article if it can cease, for reasons other than the expiry of the period of validity of the insurance or security specified in the certificate under paragraph 2 of this Article, before three months have elapsed from the date on which notice of its termination is given to the authorities referred to in paragraph 4 of this Article, unless the certificate has been surrendered to these authorities or a new certificate has been issued within the said period. The foregoing provisions shall similarly apply to any modification which results in the insurance or security no longer satisfying the requirements of this Article.

6. The State of registry shall, subject to the provisions of this Article, determine the conditions of issue and validity of the certificate.

7. Certificates issued or certified under the authority of a Contracting State in accordance with paragraph 2 shall be accepted by other Contracting States for the purposes of this Convention and shall be regarded by other Contracting States as having the same force as certificates issued or certified by them even if issued or certified in respect of a ship not registered in a Contracting State. A Contracting State may at any time request consultation with the issuing or certifying State should it believe that the insurer or guarantor named in the certificate is not financially capable of meeting the obligations imposed by this Convention.

8. Any claim for compensation for pollution damage may be brought directly against the insurer or other person providing financial security for the owner's liability for pollution damage. In such case the defendant may, even if the owner is not entitled to limit his liability according to Article V, paragraph 2, avail himself of the limits of liability prescribed in Article V, paragraph 1. He may further avail himself of the defences (other than the bankruptcy or winding up of the owner) which the owner himself would have been entitled to invoke. Furthermore, the defendant may avail himself of the defence that the pollution damage resulted from the wilful misconduct of the owner himself, but the defendant shall not avail himself of any other defence which he might have been entitled to invoke in proceedings brought by the owner against him. The defendant shall in any event have the right to require the owner to be joined in the proceedings.

9. Any sums provided by insurance or by other financial security maintained in accordance with paragraph 1 of this Article shall be available exclusively for the satisfaction of claims under this Convention.

10. A Contracting State shall not permit a ship under its flag to which this Article applies to trade unless a certificate has been issued under paragraph 2 or 12 of this Article.

11. Subject to the provisions of this Article, each Contracting State shall ensure, under its national legislation, that insurance or other security to the extent specified in paragraph 1 of this Article is in force in respect of any ship, wherever registered, entering or leaving a port

in its territory, or arriving at or leaving an off-shore terminal in its territorial sea, if the ship actually carries more than 2,000 tons of oil in bulk as cargo.

12. If insurance or other financial security is not maintained in respect of a ship owned by a Contracting State, the provisions of this Article relating thereto shall not be applicable to such ship, but the ship shall carry a certificate issued by the appropriate authorities of the State of the ship's registry stating that the ship is owned by that State and that the ship's liability is covered within the limits prescribed by Article V, paragraph 1. Such a certificate shall follow as closely as practicable the model prescribed by paragraph 2 of this Article.

Article VIII

Rights of compensation under this Convention shall be extinguished unless an action is brought thereunder within three years from the date when the damage occurred. However, in no case shall an action be brought after six years from the date of the incident which caused the damage. Where this incident consists of a series of occurrences, the six years' period shall run from the date of the first such occurrence.

Article IX

1. Where an incident has caused pollution damage in the territory, including the territorial sea or an area referred to in Article II, of one or more Contracting States or preventive measures have been taken to prevent or minimise pollution damage in such territory including the territorial sea or area, actions for compensation may only be brought in the Courts of any such Contracting State or States. Reasonable notice of any such action shall be given to the defendant.

2. Each Contracting State shall ensure that its Courts possess the necessary jurisdiction to entertain such actions for compensation.

3. After the fund has been constituted in accordance with Article V the Courts of the State in which the fund is constituted shall be exclusively competent to determine all matters relating to the apportionment and distribution of the fund.

Article X

1. Any judgment given by a Court with jurisdiction in accordance with Article IX which is enforceable in the State of origin where it is no longer subject to ordinary forms of review, shall be recognised in any Contracting State, except:
   (a) where the judgment was obtained by fraud; or
   (b) where the defendant was not given reasonable notice and a fair opportunity to present his case.

2. A judgment recognised under paragraph 1 of this Article shall be enforceable in each Contracting State as soon as the formalities required in that State have been complied with. The formalities shall not permit the merits of the case to be re-opened.

Article XI

1. The provisions of this Convention shall not apply to warships or other ships owned or operated by a State and used, for the time being, only on government non-commercial service.

2. With respect to ships owned by a Contracting State and used for commercial purposes, each State shall be subject to suit in the jurisdictions set forth in Article IX and shall waive all defences based on its status as a sovereign State.

Article XII

This Convention shall supersede any International Conventions in force or open for signature, ratification or accession at the date on which the Convention is opened for signature, but only to the extent that such Conventions would be in conflict with it; however, nothing in this Article shall affect the obligations of Contracting States to non-Contracting States arising under such International Conventions.

Article XII bis

Transitional provisions

The following transitional provisions shall apply in the case of a State which at the time of an incident is a Party both to this Convention and to the 1969 Liability Convention:
  (a) where an incident has caused pollution damage within the scope of this Convention, liability under this Convention shall be deemed to be discharged if, and to the extent that, it also arises under the 1969 Liability Convention;
  (b) where an incident has caused pollution damage within the scope of this Convention, and the State is a Party both to this Convention and to the International Convention on the Establishment of an International Fund for Compensation for Oil Pollution Damage, 1971, liability remaining to be discharged after the application of subparagraph (a) of this Article shall arise under this Convention only to the extent that pollution damage remains uncompensated after application of the said 1971 Convention;
  (c) in the application of Article III, paragraph 4, of this Convention the expression "this Convention" shall be interpreted as referring to this Convention or the 1969 Liability Convention, as appropriate;
  (d) in the application of Article V, paragraph 3, of this Convention the total sum of the fund to be constituted shall be reduced by the amount by which liability has been deemed to be discharged in accordance with sub-paragraph (a) of this Article.

Article XII ter

Final clauses

The final clauses of this Convention shall be Articles 12 to 18 of the Protocol of 1992 to amend the 1969 Liability Convention. References in this Convention to Contracting States shall be taken to mean references to the Contracting States of that Protocol.

Final Clauses of the Protocol of 1992 to amend the 1969 Civil Liability Convention Article 12

Signature, ratification, acceptance, approval and accession

1. This Protocol shall be open for signature at London from 15 January 1993 to 14 January 1994 by all States.
2. Subject to paragraph 4, any State may become a Party to this Protocol by:
  (a) signature subject to ratification, acceptance or approval followed by ratification, acceptance or approval; or
  (b) accession.

1992 Civil Liability Convention

3. Ratification, acceptance, approval or accession shall be effected by the deposit of a formal instrument to that effect with the Secretary-General of the Organization.
4. Any Contracting State to the International Convention on the Establishment of an International Fund for Compensation for Oil Pollution Damage, 1971, hereinafter referred to as the 1971 Fund Convention, may ratify, accept, approve or accede to this Protocol only if it ratifies, accepts, approves or accedes to the Protocol of 1992 to amend that Convention at the same time, unless it denounces the 1971 Fund Convention to take effect on the date when this Protocol enters into force for that State.

317

5. A State which is a Party to this Protocol but not a Party to the 1969 Liability Convention shall be bound by the provisions of the 1969 Liability Convention as amended by this Protocol in relation to other States Parties hereto, but shall not be bound by the provisions of the 1969 Liability Convention in relation to States Parties thereto.

6. Any instrument of ratification, acceptance, approval or accession deposited after the entry into force of an amendment to the 1969 Liability Convention as amended by this Protocol shall be deemed to apply to the Convention so amended, as modified by such amendment.

Article 13

Entry into force

1. This Protocol shall enter into force twelve months following the date on which ten States including four States each with not less than one million units of gross tanker tonnage have deposited instruments of ratification, acceptance, approval or accession with the Secretary-General of the Organization.

2. However, any Contracting State to the 1971 Fund Convention may, at the time of the deposit of its instrument of ratification, acceptance, approval or accession in respect of this Protocol, declare that such instrument shall be deemed not to be effective for the purposes of this Article until the end of the six-month period in Article 31 of the Protocol of 1992 to amend the 1971 Fund Convention. A State which is not a Contracting State to the 1971 Fund Convention but which deposits an instrument of ratification, acceptance, approval or accession in respect of the Protocol of 1992 to amend the 1971 Fund Convention may also make a declaration in accordance with this paragraph at the same time.

3. Any State which has made a declaration in accordance with the preceding paragraph may withdraw it at any time by means of a notification addressed to the Secretary-General of the Organization. Any such withdrawal shall take effect on the date the notification is received, provided that such State shall be deemed to have deposited its instrument of ratification, acceptance, approval or accession in respect of this Protocol on that date.

4. For any State which ratifies, accepts, approves or accedes to it after the conditions in paragraph 1 for entry into force have been met, this Protocol shall enter into force twelve months following the date of deposit by such State of the appropriate instrument.

Article 14

Revision and amendment

1. A Conference for the purpose of revising or amending the 1992 Liability Convention may be convened by the Organization.

2. The Organization shall convene a Conference of Contracting States for the purpose of revising or amending the 1992 Liability Convention at the request of not less than one third of the Contracting States.

Article 15

Amendments of limitation amounts

1. Upon the request of at least one quarter of the Contracting States any proposal to amend the limits of liability laid down in Article V, paragraph 1, of the 1969 Liability Convention as amended by this Protocol shall be circulated by the Secretary-General to all Members of the Organization and to all Contracting States.

2. Any amendment proposed and circulated as above shall be submitted to the Legal Committee of the Organization for consideration at a date at least six months after the date of its circulation.

3. All Contracting States to the 1969 Liability Convention as amended by this Protocol, whether or not Members of the Organization, shall be entitled to participate in the proceed-

ings of the Legal Committee for the consideration and adoption of amendments.

4. Amendments shall be adopted by a two-thirds majority of the Contracting States present and voting in the Legal Committee, expanded as provided for in paragraph 3, on condition that at least one half of the Contracting States shall be present at the time of voting.

5. When acting on a proposal to amend the limits, the Legal Committee shall take into account the experience of incidents and in particular the amount of damage resulting therefrom, changes in the monetary values and the effect of the proposed amendment on the cost of insurance. It shall also take into account the relationship between the limits in Article V, paragraph 1, of the 1969 Liability Convention as amended by this Protocol and those in Article 4, paragraph 4, of the International Convention on the Establishment of an International Fund for Compensation for Oil Pollution Damage, 1992.

6. (a) No amendment of the limits of liability under this Article may be considered before 15 January 1998 nor less than five years from the date of entry into force of a previous amendment under this Article. No amendment under this Article shall be considered before this Protocol has entered into force.

(b) No limit may be increased so as to exceed an amount which corresponds to the limit laid down in the 1969 Liability Convention as amended by this Protocol increased by 6 per cent per year calculated on a compound basis from 15 January 1993.

(c) No limit may be increased so as to exceed an amount which corresponds to the limit laid down in the 1969 Liability Convention as amended by this Protocol multiplied by 3.

7. Any amendment adopted in accordance with paragraph 4 shall be notified by the Organization to all Contracting States. The amendment shall be deemed to have been accepted at the end of a period of eighteen months after the date of notification, unless within that period not less than one quarter of the States that were Contracting States at the time of the adoption of the amendment by the Legal Committee have communicated to the Organization that they do not accept the amendment in which case the amendment is rejected and shall have no effect.

8. An amendment deemed to have been accepted in accordance with paragraph 7 shall enter into force eighteen months after its acceptance.

9. All Contracting States shall be bound by the amendment, unless they denounce this Protocol in accordance with Article 16, paragraphs 1 and 2, at least six months before the amendment enters into force. Such denunciation shall take effect when the amendment enters into force.

10. When an amendment has been adopted by the Legal Committee but the eighteen-month period for its acceptance has not yet expired, a State which becomes a Contracting State during that period shall be bound by the amendment if it enters into force. A State which becomes a Contracting State after that period shall be bound by an amendment which has been accepted in accordance with paragraph 7. In the cases referred to in this paragraph, a State becomes bound by an amendment when that amendment enters into force, or when this Protocol enters into force for that State, if later.

Article 16

Denunciation

1. This Protocol may be denounced by any Party at any time after the date on which it enters into force for that Party.

2. Denunciation shall be effected by the deposit of an instrument with the Secretary-General of the Organization.

3. A denunciation shall take effect twelve months, or such longer period as may be specified in the instrument of denunciation, after its deposit with the Secretary-General of the Organization.

4. As between the Parties to this Protocol, denunciation by any of them of the 1969 Liability Convention in accordance with Article XVI thereof shall not be construed in any

way as a denunciation of the 1969 Liability Convention as amended by this Protocol.

5. Denunciation of the Protocol of 1992 to amend the 1971 Fund Convention by a State which remains a Party to the 1971 Fund Convention shall be deemed to be a denunciation of this Protocol. Such denunciation shall take effect on the date on which denunciation of the Protocol of 1992 to amend the 1971 Fund Convention takes effect according to Article 34 of that Protocol.

Article 17

Depositary

1. This Protocol and any amendments accepted under Article 15 shall be deposited with the Secretary- General of the Organization.

2. The Secretary-General of the Organization shall:

(a) inform all States which have signed or acceded to this Protocol of:

   (i) each new signature or deposit of an instrument together with the date thereof;

   (ii) each declaration and notification under Article 13 and each declaration and communication under Article V, paragraph 9, of the 1992 Liability Convention;

   (iii) the date of entry into force of this Protocol;

   (iv) any proposal to amend limits of liability which has been made in accordance with Article 15, paragraph 1;

   (v) any amendment which has been adopted in accordance with Article 15, paragraph 4;

   (vi) any amendment deemed to have been accepted under Article 15, paragraph 7, together with the date on which that amendment shall enter into force in accordance with paragraphs 8 and 9 of that Article;

   (vii) the deposit of any instrument of denunciation of this Protocol together with the date of the deposit and the date on which it takes effect;

   (viii) any denunciation deemed to have been made under Article 16, paragraph 5;

   (ix) any communication called for by any Article of this Protocol;

(b) transmit certified true copies of this Protocol to all Signatory States and to all States which accede to this Protocol.

3. As soon as this Protocol enters into force, the text shall be transmitted by the Secretary-General of the Organization to the Secretariat of the United Nations for registration and publication in accordance with Article 102 of the Charter of the United Nations.

Article 18

Languages

This Protocol is established in a single original in the Arabic, Chinese, English, French, Russian and Spanishlanguages, each text being equally authentic.

DONE AT LONDON this twenty-seventh day of November one thousand nine hundred and ninety-two. IN WITNESS WHEREOF the undersigned, being duly authorised by their respective Governments for that purpose, have signed this Protocol.

International Convention on the Establishment of an International Fund for Compensation for Oil Pollution Damage, 1992

The States Parties to the present Convention,

BEING PARTIES to the International Convention on Civil Liability for Oil Pollution Damage, adopted at Brussels on 29 November 1969,

CONSCIOUS of the dangers of pollution posed by the world-wide maritime carriage of oil in bulk,

CONVINCED of the need to ensure that adequate compensation is available to persons who suffer damage caused by pollution resulting from the escape or discharge of oil from ships,

CONSIDERING that the International Convention of 29 November 1969, on Civil Liability for Oil Pollution Damage, by providing a régime for compensation for pollution damage in Contracting States and for the costs of measures, wherever taken, to prevent or minimise such damage, represents a considerable progress towards the achievement of this aim,

CONSIDERING HOWEVER that this régime does not afford full compensation for victims of oil pollution damage in all cases while it imposes an additional financial burden on shipowners,

CONSIDERING FURTHER that the economic consequences of oil pollution damage resulting from the escape or discharge of oil carried in bulk at sea by ships should not exclusively be borne by the shipping industry but should in part be borne by the oil cargo interests,

CONVINCED of the need to elaborate a compensation and indemnification system supplementary to the International Convention on Civil Liability for Oil Pollution Damage with a view to ensuring that full compensation will be available to victims of oil pollution incidents and that the shipowners are at the same time given relief in respect of the additional financial burdens imposed on them by the said Convention,

TAKING NOTE of the Resolution on the Establishment of an International Compensation Fund for Oil Pollution Damage which was adopted on 29 November 1969 by the International Legal Conference on Marine Pollution Damage,

HAVE AGREED as follows:

General Provisions

Article 1

For the purposes of this Convention:

1. "1992 Liability Convention" means the International Convention on Civil Liability for Oil Pollution Damage, 1992. 1bis. "1971 Fund Convention" means the International Convention on the Establishment of an International Fund for Compensation for Oil Pollution Damage, 1971. For States Parties to the Protocol of 1976 to that Convention, the term shall be deemed to include the 1971 Fund Convention as amended by that Protocol.

2. "Ship", "Person", "Owner", "Oil", "Pollution Damage", "Preventive Measures", "Incident", and "Organisation" have the same meaning as in Article I of the 1992 Liability Convention.

3. "Contributing Oil" means crude oil and fuel oil as defined in sub-paragraphs (a) and (b) below:

(a) "Crude Oil" means any liquid hydrocarbon mixture occurring naturally in the earth whether or not treated to render it suitable for transportation. It also includes crude oils from which certain distillate fractions have been removed (sometimes referred to as "topped crudes") or to which certain distillate fractions have been added (sometimes referred to as "spiked" or "reconstituted" crudes).

(b) "Fuel Oil" means heavy distillates or residues from crude oil or blends of such materials intended for use as a fuel for the production of heat or power of a quality equivalent to the "American Society for Testing and Materials' Specification for Number Four Fuel Oil (Designation D 396-69)", or heavier.

4. "Unit of account" has the same meaning as in Article V, paragraph 9, of the 1992 Liability Convention.

5. "Ship's tonnage" has the same meaning as in Article V, paragraph 10, of the 1992 Liability Convention.

6. "Ton", in relation to oil, means a metric ton.

7. "Guarantor" means any person providing insurance or other financial security to cover an owner's liability in pursuance of Article VII, paragraph 1, of the 1992 Liability Convention.

8. "Terminal installation" means any site for the storage of oil in bulk which is capable of receiving oil from waterborne transportation, including any facility situated off-shore and linked to such site.

9. Where an incident consists of a series of occurrences, it shall be treated as having occurred on the date of the first such occurrence.

Article 2

1. An International Fund for compensation for pollution damage, to be named "The International Oil Pollution Compensation Fund 1992" and hereinafter referred to as "the Fund", is hereby established with the following aims:

(a) to provide compensation for pollution damage to the extent that the protection afforded by the 1992 Liability Convention is inadequate;

(b) to give effect to the related purposes set out in this Convention.

2. The Fund shall in each Contracting State be recognised as a legal person capable under the laws of that State of assuming rights and obligations and of being a party in legal proceedings before the courts of that State. Each Contracting State shall recognise the Director of the Fund (hereinafter referred to as "The Director") as the legal representative of the Fund.

Article 3

This Convention shall apply exclusively:

(a) to pollution damage caused:
  (i) in the territory, including the territorial sea, of a Contracting State, and
  (ii) in the exclusive economic zone of a Contracting State, established in accordance with international law, or, if a Contracting State has not established such a zone, in an area beyond and adjacent to the territorial sea of that State determined by that State in accordance with international law and extending not more than 200 nautical miles from the baselines from which the breadth of its territorial sea is measured;

(b) to preventive measures, wherever taken, to prevent or minimise such damage.

Compensation

Article 4

1. For the purpose of fulfilling its function under Article 2, paragraph 1(a), the Fund shall pay compensation to any person suffering pollution damage if such person has been unable

to obtain full and adequate compensation for the damage under the terms of the 1992 Liability Convention,

(a) because no liability for the damage arises under the 1992 Liability Convention;

(b) because the owner liable for the damage under the 1992 Liability Convention is financially incapable of meeting his obligations in full and any financial security that may be provided under Article VII of that Convention does not cover or is insufficient to satisfy the claims for compensation for the damage; an owner being treated as financially incapable of meeting his obligations and a financial security being treated as insufficient if the person suffering the damage has been unable to obtain full satisfaction of the amount of compensation due under the 1992 Liability Convention after having taken all reasonable steps to pursue the legal remedies available to him;

(c) because the damage exceeds the owner's liability under the 1992 Liability Convention as limited pursuant to Article V, paragraph 1, of that Convention or under the terms of any other international Convention in force or open for signature, ratification or accession at the date of this Convention. Expenses reasonably incurred or sacrifices reasonably made by the owner voluntarily to prevent or minimise pollution damage shall be treated as pollution damage for the purposes of this Article.

2. The Fund shall incur no obligation under the preceding paragraph if:

(a) it proves that the pollution damage resulted from an act of war, hostilities, civil war or insurrection or was caused by oil which has escaped or been discharged from a warship or other ship owned or operated by a State and used, at the time of the incident, only on Government non-commercial service; or

(b) the claimant cannot prove that the damage resulted from an incident involving one or more ships.

3. If the Fund proves that the pollution damage resulted wholly or partially either from an act or omission done with the intent to cause damage by the person who suffered the damage or from the negligence of that person, the Fund may be exonerated wholly or partially from its obligation to pay compensation to such person. The Fund shall in any event be exonerated to the extent that the shipowner may have been exonerated under Article III, paragraph 3, of the 1992 Liability Convention. However, there shall be no such exoneration of the Fund with regard to preventive measures.

4. (a) Except as otherwise provided in sub-paragraphs (b) and (c) of this paragraph, the aggregate amount of compensation payable by the Fund under this Article shall in respect of any one incident be limited, so that the total sum of that amount and the amount of compensation actually paid under the 1992 Liability Convention for pollution damage within the scope of application of this Convention as defined in Article 3 shall not exceed 203,000,000 units of account.

(b) Except as otherwise provided in sub-paragraph (c), the aggregate amount of compensation payable by the Fund under this Article for pollution damage resulting from a natural phenomenon of an exceptional, inevitable and irresistible character shall not exceed 203,000,000 units of account.

(c) The maximum amount of compensation referred to in sub-paragraphs (a) and (b) shall be 300,740,000 units of account5 with respect to any incident occurring during any period when there are three Parties to this Convention in respect of which the combined relevant quantity of contributing oil received by persons in the territories of such Parties, during the preceding calendar year, equalled or exceeded 600 million tons.

(d) Interest accrued on a fund constituted in accordance with Article V, paragraph 3, of the 1992 Liability Convention, if any, shall not be taken into account for the computation of the maximum compensation payable by the Fund under this Article.

(e) The amounts mentioned in this Article shall be converted into national currency on the basis of the value of that currency by reference to the Special Drawing Right on the date of the decision of the Assembly of the Fund as to the first date of payment of compensation.

5. Where the amount of established claims against the Fund exceeds the aggregate amount of compensation payable under paragraph 4, the amount available shall be distrib-

uted in such a manner that the proportion between any established claim and the amount of compensation actually recovered by the claimant under this Convention shall be the same for all claimants.

6. The Assembly of the Fund may decide that, in exceptional cases, compensation in accordance with this Convention can be paid even if the owner of the ship has not constituted a fund in accordance with Article V, paragraph 3, of the 1992 Liability Convention. In such case paragraph 4(e) of this Article applies accordingly.

7. The Fund shall, at the request of a Contracting State, use its good offices as necessary to assist that State to secure promptly such personnel, material and services as are necessary to enable the State to take measures to prevent or mitigate pollution damage arising from an incident in respect of which the Fund may be called upon to pay compensation under this Convention.

8. The Fund may on conditions to be laid down in the Internal Regulations provide credit facilities with a view to the taking of preventive measures against pollution damage arising from a particular incident in respect of which the Fund may be called upon to pay compensation under this Convention.

Article 5

(deleted)

Article 6

Rights to compensation under Article 4 shall be extinguished unless an action is brought thereunder or a notification has been made pursuant to Article 7, paragraph 6, within three years from the date when the damage occurred. However, in no case shall an action be brought after six years from the date of the incident which caused the damage.

Article 7

1. Subject to the subsequent provisions of this Article, any action against the Fund for compensation under Article 4 of this Convention shall be brought only before a court competent under Article IX of the 1992 Liability Convention in respect of actions against the owner who is or who would, but for the provisions of Article III, paragraph 2, of that Convention, have been liable for pollution damage caused by the relevant incident.

2. Each Contracting State shall ensure that its courts possess the necessary jurisdiction to entertain such actions against the Fund as are referred to in paragraph 1.

3. Where an action for compensation for pollution damage has been brought before a court competent under Article IX of the 1992 Liability Convention against the owner of a ship or his guarantor, such court shall have exclusive jurisdictional competence over any action against the Fund for compensation under the provisions of Article 4 of this Convention in respect of the same damage. However, where an action for compensation for pollution damage under the 1992 Liability Convention has been brought before a court in a State Party to the 1992 Liability Convention but not to this Convention, any action against the Fund under Article 4 of this Convention shall at the option of the claimant be brought either before a court of the State where the Fund has its headquarters or before any court of a State Party to this Convention competent under Article IX of the 1992 Liability Convention.

4. Each Contracting State shall ensure that the Fund shall have the right to intervene as a party to any legal proceedings instituted in accordance with Article IX of the 1992 Liability Convention before a competent court of that State against the owner of a ship or his guarantor.

5. Except as otherwise provided in paragraph 6, the Fund shall not be bound by any judgment or decision in proceedings to which it has not been a party or by any settlement to which it is not a party.

6. Without prejudice to the provisions of paragraph 4, where an action under the 1992 Liability Convention for compensation for pollution damage has been brought against an

owner or his guarantor before a competent court in a Contracting State, each party to the proceedings shall be entitled under the national law of that State to notify the Fund of the proceedings. Where such notification has been made in accordance with the formalities required by the law of the court seized and in such time and in such a manner that the Fund has in fact been in a position effectively to intervene as a party to the proceedings, any judgment rendered by the court in such proceedings shall, after it has become final and enforceable in the State where the judgment was given, become binding upon the Fund in the sense that the facts and findings in that judgment may not be disputed by the Fund even if the Fund has not actually intervened in the proceedings.

Article 8

Subject to any decision concerning the distribution referred to in Article 4, paragraph 5, any judgment given against the Fund by a court having jurisdiction in accordance with Article 7, paragraphs 1 and 3, shall, when it has become enforceable in the State of origin and is in that State no longer subject to ordinary forms of review, be recognised and enforceable in each Contracting State on the same conditions as are prescribed in Article X of the 1992 Liability Convention.

Article 9

1. The Fund shall, in respect of any amount of compensation for pollution damage paid by the Fund in accordance with Article 4, paragraph 1, of this Convention, acquire by subrogation the rights that the person so compensated may enjoy under the 1992 Liability Convention against the owner or his guarantor.

2. Nothing in this Convention shall prejudice any right of recourse or subrogation of the Fund against persons other than those referred to in the preceding paragraph. In any event the right of the Fund to subrogation against such person shall not be less favourable than that of an insurer of the person to whom compensation has been paid.

3. Without prejudice to any other rights of subrogation or recourse against the Fund which may exist, a Contracting State or agency thereof which has paid compensation for pollution damage in accordance with provisions of national law shall acquire by subrogation the rights which the person so compensated would have enjoyed under this Convention.

Contributions

Article 10

1. Annual contributions to the Fund shall be made in respect of each Contracting State by any person who, in the calendar year referred to in Article 12, paragraph 2(a) or (b), has received in total quantities exceeding 150,000 tons:
   (a) in the ports or terminal installations in the territory of that State contributing oil carried by sea to such ports or terminal installations; and
   (b) in any installations situated in the territory of that Contracting State contributing oil which has been carried by sea and discharged in a port or terminal installation of a non- Contracting State, provided that contributing oil shall only be taken into account by virtue of this sub-paragraph on first receipt in a Contracting State after its discharge in that non-Contracting State.

2. (a) For the purposes of paragraph 1, where the quantity of contributing oil received in the territory of a Contracting State by any person in a calendar year when aggregated with the quantity of contributing oil received in the same Contracting State in that year by any associated person or persons exceeds 150,000 tons, such person shall pay contributions in respect of the actual quantity received by him notwithstanding that that quantity did not exceed 150,000 tons.
   (b) "Associated person" means any subsidiary or commonly controlled entity. The question whether a person comes within this definition shall be determined by the national law of the State concerned.

Article 11

(deleted)

Article 12

1. With a view to assessing the amount of annual contributions due, if any, and taking account of the necessity to maintain sufficient liquid funds, the Assembly shall for each calendar year make an estimate in the form of a budget of:

(i) **Expenditure**

(a) costs and expenses of the administration of the Fund in the relevant year and any deficit from operations in preceding years;

(b) payments to be made by the Fund in the relevant year for the satisfaction of claims against the Fund due under Article 4, including repayment on loans previously taken by the Fund for the satisfaction of such claims, to the extent that the aggregate amount of such claims in respect of any one incident does not exceed four million units of account;

(c) payments to be made by the Fund in the relevant year for the satisfaction of claims against the Fund due under Article 4, including repayments on loans previously taken by the Fund for the satisfaction of such claims, to the extent that the aggregate amount of such claims in respect of any one incident is in excess of four million units of account;

(ii) **Income**

(a) surplus funds from operations in preceding years, including any interest;

(b) annual contributions, if required to balance the budget;

(c) any other income.

2. The Assembly shall decide the total amount of contributions to be levied. On the basis of that decision, the Director shall, in respect of each Contracting State, calculate for each person referred to in Article 10 the amount of his annual contribution:

(a) in so far as the contribution is for the satisfaction of payments referred to in paragraph 1(i)(a) and (b) on the basis of a fixed sum for each ton of contributing oil received in the relevant State by such persons during the preceding calendar year; and

(b) in so far as the contribution is for the satisfaction of payments referred to in aragraph 1(i)(c) of this Article on the basis of a fixed sum for each ton of contributing il received by such person during the calendar year preceding that in which the incident in question occurred, provided that State was a Party to this Convention at the date of the incident.

3. The sums referred to in paragraph 2 above shall be arrived at by dividing the relevant total amount of contributions required by the total amount of contributing oil received in all Contracting States in the relevant year.

4. The annual contribution shall be due on the date to be laid down in the Internal Regulations of the Fund. The Assembly may decide on a different date of payment.

5. The Assembly may decide, under conditions to be laid down in the Financial Regulations of the Fund, to make transfers between funds received in accordance with Article 12.2(a) and funds received in accordance with Article 12.2(b).

Article 13

1. The amount of any contribution due under Article 12 and which is in arrears shall bear interest at a rate which shall be determined in accordance with the Internal Regulations of the Fund, provided that different rates may be fixed for different circumstances.

2. Each Contracting State shall ensure that any obligation to contribute to the Fund arising under this Convention in respect of oil received within the territory of that State is fulfilled and shall take any appropriate measures under its law, including the imposing of such sanctions as it may deem necessary, with a view to the effective execution of any such

obligation; provided, however, that such measures shall only be directed against those persons who are under an obligation to contribute to the Fund.

3. Where a person who is liable in accordance with the provisions of Articles 10 and 12 to make contributions to the Fund does not fulfil his obligations in respect of any such contribution or any part thereof and is in arrear, the Director shall take all appropriate action against such person on behalf of the Fund with a view to the recovery of the amount due. However, where the defaulting contributor is manifestly insolvent or the circumstances otherwise so warrant, the Assembly may, upon recommendation of the Director, decide that no action shall be taken or continued against the contributor.

Article 14

1. Each Contracting State may at the time when it deposits its instrument of ratification or accession or at any time thereafter declare that it assumes itself obligations that are incumbent under this Convention on any person who is liable to contribute to the Fund in accordance with Article 10, paragraph 1, in respect of oil received within the territory of that State. Such declaration shall be made in writing and shall specify which obligations are assumed.

2. Where a declaration under paragraph 1 is made prior to the entry into force of this Convention in accordance with Article 40, it shall be deposited with the Secretary-General of the Organization who shall after the entry into force of the Convention communicate the declaration to the Director.

3. A declaration under paragraph 1 which is made after the entry into force of this Convention shall be deposited with the Director.

4. A declaration made in accordance with this Article may be withdrawn by the relevant State giving notice thereof in writing to the Director. Such notification shall take effect three months after the Director's receipt thereof.

5. Any State which is bound by a declaration made under this Article shall, in any proceedings brought against it before a competent court in respect of any obligation specified in the declaration, waive any immunity that it would otherwise be entitled to invoke.

Article 15

1. Each Contracting State shall ensure that any person who receives contributing oil within its territory in such quantities that he is liable to contribute to the Fund appears on a list to be established and kept up to date by the Director in accordance with the subsequent provisions of this Article.

2. For the purposes set out in paragraph 1, each Contracting State shall communicate, at a time and in the manner to be prescribed in the Internal Regulations, to the Director the name and address of any person who in respect of that State is liable to contribute to the Fund pursuant to Article 10, as well as data on the relevant quantities of contributing oil received by any such person during the preceding calendar year.

3. For the purposes of ascertaining who are, at any given time, the persons liable to contribute to the Fund in accordance with Article 10, paragraph 1, and of establishing, where applicable, the quantities of oil to be taken into account for any such person when determining the amount of his contribution, the list shall be prima facie evidence of the facts stated therein.

4. Where a Contracting State does not fulfil its obligations to submit to the Director the communication referred to in paragraph 2 and this results in a financial loss for the Fund, that Contracting State shall be liable to compensate the Fund for such loss. The Assembly shall, on the recommendation of the Director, decide whether such compensation shall be payable by that Contracting State.

Organisation and Administration

Article 16

The Fund shall have an Assembly and a Secretariat headed by a Director.

Assembly

Article 17

The Assembly shall consist of all Contracting States to this Convention.

Article 18

The functions of the Assembly shall be:

1. to elect at each regular session its Chairman and two Vice-Chairmen who shall hold office until the next regular session;

2. to determine its own rules of procedure, subject to the provisions of this Convention;

3. to adopt Internal Regulations necessary for the proper functioning of the Fund;

4. to appoint the Director and make provisions for the appointment of such other personnel as may be necessary and determine the terms and conditions of service of the Director and other personnel;

5. to adopt the annual budget and fix the annual contributions;

6. to appoint auditors and approve the accounts of the Fund;

7. to approve settlements of claims against the Fund, to take decisions in respect of the distribution among claimants of the available amount of compensation in accordance with Article 4, paragraph 5, and to determine the terms and conditions according to which provisional payments in respect of claims shall be made with a view to ensuring that victims of pollution damage are compensated as promptly as possible;

8. (deleted).

9. to establish any temporary or permanent subsidiary body it may consider to be necessary, to define its terms of reference and to give it the authority needed to perform the functions entrusted to it; when appointing the members of such body, the Assembly shall endeavour to secure an equitable geographical distribution of members and to ensure that the Contracting States, in respect of which the largest quantities of contributing oil are being received, are appropriately represented; the Rules of Procedure of the Assembly may be applied, mutatis mutandis, for the work of such subsidiary body;

10. to determine which non-Contracting States and which inter-governmental and international non-governmental organisations shall be admitted to take part, without voting rights, in meetings of the Assembly and subsidiary bodies;

11. to give instructions concerning the administration of the Fund to the Director and subsidiary bodies;

12. (deleted);

13. to supervise the proper execution of the Convention and of its own decisions;

14. to perform such other functions as are allocated to it under the Convention or are otherwise necessary for the proper operation of the Fund.

Article 19

1. Regular sessions of the Assembly shall take place once every calendar year upon convocation by the Director.

2. Extraordinary sessions of the Assembly shall be convened by the Director at the request of at least one third of the members of the Assembly and may be convened on the Director's own initiative after consultation with the Chairman of the Assembly. The Director shall give members at least thirty days' notice of such sessions.

Article 20

A majority of the members of the Assembly shall constitute a quorum for its meetings. (heading deleted)

Articles 21–27

(deleted)

Secretariat

Article 28

1. The Secretariat shall comprise the Director and such staff as the administration of the Fund may require.

2. The Director shall be the legal representative of the Fund.

Article 29

1. The Director shall be the chief administrative officer of the Fund. Subject to the instructions given to him by the Assembly, he shall perform those functions which are assigned to him by this Convention, the Internal Regulations of the Fund and the Assembly.

2. The Director shall in particular:

(a) appoint the personnel required for the administration of the Fund;

(b) take all appropriate measures with a view to the proper administration of the Fund's assets;

(c) collect the contributions due under this Convention while observing in particular the provisions of Article 13, paragraph 3;

(d) to the extent necessary to deal with claims against the Fund and carry out the other functions of the Fund, employ the services of legal, financial and other experts;

(e) take all appropriate measures for dealing with claims against the Fund within the limits and on conditions to be laid down in the Internal Regulations, including the final settlement of claims without the prior approval of the Assembly where these Regulations so provide;

(f) prepare and submit to the Assembly the financial statements and budget estimates for each calendar year;

(g) prepare, in consultation with the Chairman of the Assembly, and publish a report of the activities of the Fund during the previous calendar year;

(h) prepare, collect and circulate the papers, documents, agenda, minutes and information that may be required for the work of the Assembly and subsidiary bodies.

Article 30

In the performance of their duties the Director and the staff and experts appointed by him shall not seek or receive instructions from any Government or from any authority external to the Fund. They shall refrain from any action which might reflect on their position as international officials. Each Contracting State on its part undertakes to respect the exclusively international character of the responsibilities of the Director and the staff and experts appointed by him, and not to seek to influence them in the discharge of their duties.

Finances

Article 31

1. Each Contracting State shall bear the salary, travel and other expenses of its own delegation to the Assembly and of its representatives on subsidiary bodies.

2. Any other expenses incurred in the operation of the Fund shall be borne by the Fund.

Voting

Article 32

The following provisions shall apply to voting in the Assembly:

(a) each member shall have one vote;

(b) except as otherwise provided in Article 33, decisions of the Assembly shall be by a majority vote of the members present and voting;

(c) decisions where a three-fourths or a two-thirds majority is required shall be by a three-fourths or two-thirds majority vote, as the case may be, of those present;

(d) for the purpose of this Article the phrase "members present" means "members present at the meeting at the time of the vote", and the phrase "members present and voting" means "members present and casting an affirmative or negative vote". Members who abstain from voting shall be considered as not voting.

Article 33

The following decisions of the Assembly shall require a two-thirds majority:
(a) a decision under Article 13, paragraph 3, not to take or continue action against a contributor;
(b) the appointment of the Director under Article 18, paragraph 4;
(c) the establishment of subsidiary bodies, under Article 18, paragraph 9, and matters relating to such establishment.

Article 34

1. The Fund, its assets, income, including contributions, and other property shall enjoy in all Contracting States exemption from all direct taxation.

2. When the Fund makes substantial purchases of movable or immovable property, or has important work carried out which is necessary for the exercise of its official activities and the cost of which includes indirect taxes or sales taxes, the Governments of Member States shall take, whenever possible, appropriate measures for the remission or refund of the amount of such duties and taxes.

3. No exemption shall be accorded in the case of duties, taxes or dues which merely constitute payment for public utility services.

4. The Fund shall enjoy exemption from all customs duties, taxes and other related taxes on articles imported or exported by it or on its behalf for its official use. Articles thus imported shall not be transferred either for consideration or gratis on the territory of the country into which they have been imported except on conditions agreed by the Government of that country.

5. Persons contributing to the Fund and victims and owners of ships receiving compensation from the Fund shall be subject to the fiscal legislation of the State where they are taxable, no special exemption or other benefit being conferred on them in this respect.

6. Information relating to individual contributors supplied for the purpose of this Convention shall not be divulged outside the Fund except in so far as it may be strictly necessary to enable the Fund to carry out its functions including the bringing and defending of legal proceedings.

7. Independently of existing or future regulations concerning currency or transfers, Contracting States shall authorise the transfer and payment of any contribution to the Fund and of any compensation paid by the Fund without any restriction.

Transitional Provisions

Article 35

Claims for compensation under Article 4 arising from incidents occurring after the date of entry into force of this Convention may not be brought against the Fund earlier than the one hundred and twentieth day after that date.

Article 36

The Secretary-General of the Organization shall convene the first session of the Assembly. This session shall take place as soon as possible after entry into force of this Convention and, in any case, not more than thirty days after such entry into force.

Article 36 bis

The following transitional provisions shall apply in the period, hereinafter referred to as the transitional period, commencing with the date of entry into force of this Convention and ending with the date on which the denunciations provided for in Article 31 of the 1992 Protocol to amend the 1971 Fund Convention take effect:

(a) In the application of paragraph 1(a) of Article 2 of this Convention, the reference to the 1992 Liability Convention shall include reference to the International Convention on Civil Liability for Oil Pollution Damage, 1969, either in its original version or as amended by the Protocol thereto of 1976 (referred to in this Article as "the 1969 Liability Convention"), and also the 1971 Fund Convention.

(b) Where an incident has caused pollution damage within the scope of this Convention, the Fund shall pay compensation to any person suffering pollution damage only if, and to the extent that, such person has been unable to obtain full and adequate compensation for the damage under the terms of the 1969 Liability Convention, the 1971 Fund Convention and the 1992 Liability Convention, provided that, in respect of pollution damage within the scope of this Convention in respect of a Party to this Convention but not a Party to the 1971 Fund Convention, the Fund shall pay compensation to any person suffering pollution damage only if, and to the extent that, such person would have been unable to obtain full and adequate compensation had that State been party to each of the above-mentioned Conventions.

(c) In the application of Article 4 of this Convention, the amount to be taken into account in determining the aggregate amount of compensation payable by the Fund shall also include the amount of compensation actually paid under the 1969 Liability Convention, if any, and the amount of compensation actually paid or deemed to have been paid under the 1971 Fund Convention.

(d) Paragraph 1 of Article 9 of this Convention shall also apply to the rights enjoyed under the 1969 Liability Convention.

Article 36 ter

1. Subject to paragraph 4 of this Article, the aggregate amount of the annual contributions payable in respect of contributing oil received in a single Contracting State during a calendar year shall not exceed 27.5% of the total amount of annual contributions pursuant to the 1992 Protocol to amend the 1971 Fund Convention, in respect of that calendar year.

2. If the application of the provisions in paragraphs 2 and 3 of Article 12 would result in the aggregate amount of the contributions payable by contributors in a single Contracting State in respect of a given calendar year exceeding 27.5% of the total annual contributions, the contributions payable by all contributors in that State shall be reduced pro rata so that their aggregate contributions equal 27.5% of the total annual contributions to the Fund in respect of that year.

3. If the contributions payable by persons in a given Contracting State shall be reduced pursuant to paragraph 2 of this Article, the contributions payable by persons in all other Contracting States shall be increased pro rata so as to ensure that the total amount of contributions payable by all persons liable to contribute to the Fund in respect of the calendar year in question will reach the total amount of contributions decided by the Assembly.

4. The provisions in paragraphs 1 to 3 of this Article shall operate until the total quantity of contributing oil received in all Contracting States in a calendar year has reached 750 million tons or until a period of 5 years after the date of entry into force of the said 1992 Protocol has elapsed, whichever occurs earlier.

Article 36 quater

Notwithstanding the provisions of this Convention, the following provisions shall apply to the administration of the Fund during the period in which both the 1971 Fund Convention and this Convention are in force:

(a) The Secretariat of the Fund, established by the 1971 Fund Convention (hereinafter referred to as "the 1971 Fund"), headed by the Director, may also function as the Secretariat and the Director of the Fund.

(b) If, in accordance with sub-paragraph (a), the Secretariat and the Director of the 1971 Fund also perform the function of Secretariat and Director of the Fund, the Fund shall be represented, in cases of conflict of interests between the 1971 Fund and the Fund, by the Chairman of the Assembly of the Fund.

(c) The Director and the staff and experts appointed by him, performing their duties under this Convention and the 1971 Fund Convention, shall not be regarded as contravening the provisions of Article 30 of this Convention in so far as they discharge their duties in accordance with this Article.

(d) The Assembly of the Fund shall endeavour not to take decisions which are incompatible with decisions taken by the Assembly of the 1971 Fund. If differences of opinion with respect to common administrative issues arise, the Assembly of the Fund shall try to reach a consensus with the Assembly of the 1971 Fund, in a spirit of mutual co-operation and with the common aims of both organisations in mind.

(e) The Fund may succeed to the rights, obligations and assets of the 1971 Fund if the Assembly of the 1971 Fund so decides, in accordance with Article 44, paragraph 2, of the 1971 Fund Convention.

(f) The Fund shall reimburse to the 1971 Fund all costs and expenses arising from administrative services performed by the 1971 Fund on behalf of the Fund.

Article 36 quinquies

Final clauses

The final clauses of this Convention shall be Articles 28 to 39 of the Protocol of 1992 to amend the 1971 Fund Convention. References in this Convention to Contracting States shall be taken to mean references to the Contracting States of that Protocol.

Final Clauses of the Protocol of 1992 to amend the 1971 Fund Convention

Article 28

Signature, ratification, acceptance, approval and accession

1. This Protocol shall be open for signature at London from 15 January 1993 to 14 January 1994 by any State which has signed the 1992 Liability Convention.

2. Subject to paragraph 4, this Protocol shall be ratified, accepted or approved by States which have signed it.

3. Subject to paragraph 4, this Protocol is open for accession by States which did not sign it.

4. This Protocol may be ratified, accepted, approved or acceded to only by States which have ratified, accepted, approved or acceded to the 1992 Liability Convention.

5. Ratification, acceptance, approval or accession shall be effected by the deposit of a formal instrument to that effect with the Secretary-General of the Organization.

6. A State which is a Party to this Protocol but is not a Party to the 1971 Fund Convention shall be bound by the provisions of the 1971 Fund Convention as amended by this Protocol in relation to other Parties hereto, but shall not be bound by the provisions of the 1971 Fund Convention in relation to Parties thereto.

7. Any instrument of ratification, acceptance, approval or accession deposited after the entry into force of an amendment to the 1971 Fund Convention as amended by this Protocol shall be deemed to apply to the Convention so amended, as modified by such amendment.

Article 29

Information on contributing oil

1. Before this Protocol comes into force for a State, that State shall, when depositing an instrument referred to in Article 28, paragraph 5, and annually thereafter at a date to be determined by the Secretary-General of the Organization, communicate to him the name and address of any person who in respect of that State would be liable to contribute to the Fund pursuant to Article 10 of the 1971 Fund Convention as amended by this Protocol as

well as data on the relevant quantities of contributing oil received by any such person in the territory of that State during the preceding calendar year.

2. During the transitional period, the Director shall, for Parties, communicate annually to the Secretary General of the Organization data on quantities of contributing oil received by persons liable to contribute to the Fund pursuant to Article 10 of the 1971 Fund Convention as amended by this Protocol.

Article 30

Entry into force

1. This Protocol shall enter into force twelve months following the date on which the following requirements are fulfilled:
   (a) at least eight States have deposited instruments of ratification, acceptance, approval or accession with the Secretary-General of the Organization; and
   (b) the Secretary-General of the Organization has received information in accordance with Article 29 that those persons who would be liable to contribute pursuant to Article 10 of the 1971 Fund Convention as amended by this Protocol have received during the preceding calendar year a total quantity of at least 450 million tons of contributing oil.

2. However, this Protocol shall not enter into force before the 1992 Liability Convention has entered into force.

3. For each State which ratifies, accepts, approves or accedes to this Protocol after the conditions in paragraph 1 for entry into force have been met, the Protocol shall enter into force twelve months following the date of the deposit by such State of the appropriate instrument.

4. Any State may, at the time of the deposit of its instrument of ratification, acceptance, approval or accession in respect of this Protocol declare that such instrument shall not take effect for the purpose of this Article until the end of the six-month period in Article 31.

5. Any State which has made a declaration in accordance with the preceding paragraph may withdraw it at any time by means of a notification addressed to the Secretary-General of the Organization. Any such withdrawal shall take effect on the date the notification is received, and any State making such a withdrawal shall be deemed to have deposited its instrument of ratification, acceptance, approval or accession in respect of this Protocol on that date.

6. Any State which has made a declaration under Article 13, paragraph 2, of the Protocol of 1992 to amend the 1969 Liability Convention shall be deemed to have also made a declaration under paragraph 4 of this Article. Withdrawal of a declaration under the said Article 13, paragraph 2, shall be deemed to constitute withdrawal also under paragraph 5 of this Article.

Article 31

Denunciation of the 1969 and 1971 Conventions

Subject to Article 30, within six months following the date on which the following requirements are fulfilled:
   (a) at least eight States have become Parties to this Protocol or have deposited instruments of ratification, acceptance, approval or accession with the Secretary-General of the Organization, whether or not subject to Article 30, paragraph 4, and
   (b) the Secretary-General of the Organization has received information in accordance with Article 29 that those persons who are or would be liable to contribute pursuant to Article 10 of the 1971 Fund Convention as amended by this Protocol have received during the preceding calendar year a total quantity of at least 750 million tons of contributing oil; each Party to this Protocol and each State which has deposited an instrument of ratification, acceptance, approval or accession, whether or not subject to Article 30, paragraph 4, shall, if party thereto, denounce the 1971 Fund Convention

333

and the 1969 Liability Convention with effect twelve months after the expiry of the above-mentioned six-month period.

Article 32

Revision and amendment

1. A conference for the purpose of revising or amending the 1992 Fund Convention may be convened by the Organization.

2. The Organization shall convene a Conference of Contracting States for the purpose of revising or amending the 1992 Fund Convention at the request of not less than one third of all Contracting States.

Article 33

Amendment of compensation limits

1. Upon the request of at least one quarter of the Contracting States, any proposal to amend the limits of amounts of compensation laid down in Article 4, paragraph 4, of the 1971 Fund Convention as amended by this Protocol shall be circulated by the Secretary-General to all Members of the Organization and to all Contracting States.

2. Any amendment proposed and circulated as above shall be submitted to the Legal Committee of the Organization for consideration at a date at least six months after the date of its circulation.

3. All Contracting States to the 1971 Fund Convention as amended by this Protocol, whether or not Members of the Organization, shall be entitled to participate in the proceedings of the Legal Committee for the consideration and adoption of amendments.

4. Amendments shall be adopted by a two-thirds majority of the Contracting States present and voting in the Legal Committee, expanded as provided for in paragraph 3, on condition that at least one half of the Contracting States shall be present at the time of voting.

5. When acting on a proposal to amend the limits, the Legal Committee shall take into account the experience of incidents and in particular the amount of damage resulting therefrom and changes in the monetary values. It shall also take into account the relationship between the limits in Article 4, paragraph 4, of the 1971 Fund Convention as amended by this Protocol and those in Article V, paragraph 1 of the International Convention on Civil Liability for Oil Pollution Damage, 1992.

6. (a) No amendment of the limits under this Article may be considered before 15 January 1998 nor less than five years from the date of entry into force of a previous amendment under this Article. No amendment under this Article shall be considered before this Protocol has entered into force.

(b) No limit may be increased so as to exceed an amount which corresponds to the limit laid down in the 1971 Fund Convention as amended by this Protocol increased by six per cent per year calculated on a compound basis from 15 January 1993.

(c) No limit may be increased so as to exceed an amount which corresponds to the limit laid down in the 1971 Fund Convention as amended by this Protocol multiplied by three.

7. Any amendment adopted in accordance with paragraph 4 shall be notified by the Organization to all Contracting States. The amendment shall be deemed to have been accepted at the end of a period of eighteen months after the date of notification unless within that period not less than one quarter of the States that were Contracting States at the time of the adoption of the amendment by the Legal Committee have communicated to the Organization that they do not accept the amendment in which case the amendment is rejected and shall have no effect.

8. An amendment deemed to have been accepted in accordance with paragraph 7 shall enter into force eighteen months after its acceptance.

9. All Contracting States shall be bound by the amendment, unless they denounce this Protocol in accordance with Article 34, paragraphs 1 and 2, at least six months before the amendment enters into force. Such denunciation shall take effect when the amendment enters into force.

10. When an amendment has been adopted by the Legal Committee but the eighteen-month period for its acceptance has not yet expired, a State which becomes a Contracting State during that period shall be bound by the amendment if it enters into force. A State which becomes a Contracting State after that period shall be bound by an amendment which has been accepted in accordance with paragraph 7. In the cases referred to in this paragraph, a State becomes bound by an amendment when that amendment enters into force, or when this Protocol enters into force for that State, if later.

Article 34

Denunciation

1. This Protocol may be denounced by any Party at any time after the date on which it enters into force for that Party.

2. Denunciation shall be effected by the deposit of an instrument with the Secretary-General of the Organization.

3. A denunciation shall take effect twelve months, or such longer period as may be specified in the instrument of denunciation, after its deposit with the Secretary-General of the Organization.

4. Denunciation of the 1992 Liability Convention shall be deemed to be a denunciation of this Protocol. Such denunciation shall take effect on the date on which denunciation of the Protocol of 1992 to amend the 1969 Liability Convention takes effect according to Article 16 of that Protocol.

5. Any Contracting State to this Protocol which has not denounced the 1971 Fund Convention and the 1969 Liability Convention as required by Article 31 shall be deemed to have denounced this Protocol with effect twelve months after the expiry of the six-month period mentioned in that Article. As from the date on which the denunciations provided for in Article 31 take effect, any Party to this Protocol which deposits an instrument of ratification, acceptance, approval or accession to the 1969 Liability Convention shall be deemed to have denounced this Protocol with effect from the date on which such instrument takes effect.

6. As between the Parties to this Protocol, denunciation by any of them of the 1971 Fund Convention in accordance with Article 41 thereof shall not be construed in any way as a denunciation of the 1971 Fund Convention as amended by this Protocol.

7. Notwithstanding a denunciation of this Protocol by a Party pursuant to this Article, any provisions of this Protocol relating to the obligations to make contributions under Article 10 of the 1971 Fund Convention as amended by this Protocol with respect to an incident referred to in Article 12, paragraph 2(b), of that amended Convention and occurring before the denunciation takes effect shall continue to apply.

Article 35

Extraordinary sessions of the Assembly

1. Any Contracting State may, within ninety days after the deposit of an instrument of denunciation the result of which it considers will significantly increase the level of contributions for the remaining Contracting States, request the Director to convene an extraordinary session of the Assembly. The Director shall convene the Assembly to meet not later than sixty days after receipt of the request.

2. The Director may convene, on his own initiative, an extraordinary session of the Assembly to meet within sixty days after the deposit of any instrument of denunciation, if he considers that such denunciation will result in a significant increase in the level of contributions of the remaining Contracting States.

3. If the Assembly at an extraordinary session convened in accordance with paragraph 1 or 2 decides that the denunciation will result in a significant increase in the level of contributions for the remaining Contracting States, any such State may, not later than one hundred and twenty days before the date on which the denunciation takes effect, denounce this Protocol with effect from the same date.

Article 36

Termination

1. This Protocol shall cease to be in force on the date when the number of Contracting States falls below three.

2. States which are bound by this Protocol on the day before the date it ceases to be in force shall enable the Fund to exercise its functions as described under Article 37 of this Protocol and shall, for that purpose only, remain bound by this Protocol.

Article 37

Winding up of the Fund

1. If this Protocol ceases to be in force, the Fund shall nevertheless:
   (a) meet its obligations in respect of any incident occurring before the Protocol ceased to be in force;
   (b) be entitled to exercise its rights to contributions to the extent that these contributions are necessary to meet the obligations under sub-paragraph (a), including expenses for the administration of the Fund necessary for this purpose.

2. The Assembly shall take all appropriate measures to complete the winding up of the Fund including the distribution in an equitable manner of any remaining assets among those persons who have contributed to the Fund.

3. For the purposes of this Article the Fund shall remain a legal person.

Article 38

Depositary

1. This Protocol and any amendments accepted under Article 33 shall be deposited with the Secretary-General of the Organization.

2. The Secretary-General of the Organization shall:
   (a) inform all States which have signed or acceded to this Protocol of:
      (i) each new signature or deposit of an instrument together with the date thereof;
      (ii) each declaration and notification under Article 30 including declarations and withdrawals deemed to have been made in accordance with that Article;
      (iii) the date of entry into force of this Protocol;
      (iv) the date by which denunciations provided for in Article 31 are required to be made;
      (v) any proposal to amend limits of amounts of compensation which has been made in accordance with Article 33, paragraph 1;
      (vi) any amendment which has been adopted in accordance with Article 33, paragraph 4;
      (vii) any amendment deemed to have been accepted under Article 33, paragraph 7, together with the date on which that amendment shall enter into force in accordance with paragraphs 8 and 9 of that Article;
      (viii) the deposit of an instrument of denunciation of this Protocol together with the date of the deposit and the date on which it takes effect;
      (ix) any denunciation deemed to have been made under Article 34, paragraph 5;
      (x) any communication called for by any Article in this Protocol;
   (b) transmit certified true copies of this Protocol to all Signatory States and to all States which accede to the Protocol.

3. As soon as this Protocol enters into force, the text shall be transmitted by the Secretary-General of the Organization to the Secretariat of the United Nations for registration and publication in accordance with Article 102 of the Charter of the United Nations.

Article 39

Languages

This Protocol is established in a single original in the Arabic, Chinese, English, French, Russian and Spanish languages, each text being equally authentic.

DONE AT LONDON this twenty-seventh day of November one thousand nine hundred and ninety-two.

IN WITNESS WHEREOF the undersigned, being duly authorised by their respective Governments for that purpose, have signed this Protocol.

Protocol of 2003 to the International Convention on the Establishment of an International Fund for Compensation for Oil Pollution Damage, 1992

THE CONTRACTING STATES TO THE PRESENT PROTOCOL,

BEARING IN MIND the International Convention on Civil Liability for Oil Pollution Damage, 1992 (hereinafter "the 1992 Liability Convention"),

HAVING CONSIDERED the International Convention on the Establishment of an International Fund for Compensation for Oil Pollution Damage, 1992 (hereinafter "the 1992 Fund Convention"),

AFFIRMING the importance of maintaining the viability of the international oil pollution liability and compensation system,

NOTING that the maximum compensation afforded by the 1992 Fund Convention might be insufficient to meet compensation needs in certain circumstances in some Contracting States to that Convention,

RECOGNIZING that a number of Contracting States to the 1992 Liability and 1992 Fund Conventions consider it necessary as a matter of urgency to make available additional funds for compensation through the creation of a supplementary scheme to which States may accede if they so wish,

BELIEVING that the supplementary scheme should seek to ensure that victims of oil pollution damage are compensated in full for their loss or damage and should also alleviate the difficulties faced by victims in cases where there is a risk that the amount of compensation available under the 1992 Liability and 1992 Fund Conventions will be insufficient to pay established claims in full and that as a consequence the International Oil Pollution Compensation Fund, 1992, has decided provisionally that it will pay only a proportion of any established claim,

CONSIDERING that accession to the supplementary scheme will be open only to Contracting States to the 1992 Fund Convention,

Have agreed as follows:

General provisions

Article 1

For the purposes of this Protocol:

1. "1992 Liability Convention" means the International Convention on Civil Liability for Oil Pollution Damage, 1992;

2. "1992 Fund Convention" means the International Convention on the Establishment of an International Fund for Compensation for Oil Pollution Damage, 1992;

3. "1992 Fund" means the International Oil Pollution Compensation Fund, 1992, established under the 1992 Fund Convention;

4. "Contracting State" means a Contracting State to this Protocol, unless stated otherwise;

5. When provisions of the 1992 Fund Convention are incorporated by reference into this Protocol, "Fund" in that Convention means "Supplementary Fund", unless stated otherwise;

6. "Ship", "Person", "Owner", "Oil", "Pollution Damage", "Preventive Measures" and "Incident" have the same meaning as in article I of the 1992 Liability Convention;

7. "Contributing Oil", "Unit of Account", "Ton", "Guarantor" and "Terminal installation" have the same meaning as in article 1 of the 1992 Fund Convention, unless stated otherwise;

8. "Established claim" means a claim which has been recognised by the 1992 Fund or been accepted as admissible by decision of a competent court binding upon the 1992 Fund not subject to ordinary forms of review and which would have been fully compensated if the limit set out in article 4, paragraph 4, of the 1992 Fund Convention had not been applied to that incident;

9. "Assembly" means the Assembly of the International Oil Pollution Compensation Supplementary Fund, 2003, unless otherwise indicated;

10. "Organization" means the International Maritime Organization;

11. "Secretary-General" means the Secretary-General of the Organization.

Article 2

1. An International Supplementary Fund for compensation for pollution damage, to be named "The International Oil Pollution Compensation Supplementary Fund, 2003" (hereinafter "the Supplementary Fund"), is hereby established.

2. The Supplementary Fund shall in each Contracting State be recognized as a legal person capable under the laws of that State of assuming rights and obligations and of being a party in legal proceedings before the courts of that State. Each Contracting State shall recognize the Director of the Supplementary Fund as the legal representative of the Supplementary Fund.

Article 3

This Protocol shall apply exclusively:

(a) to pollution damage caused:
   (i) in the territory, including the territorial sea, of a Contracting State, and
   (ii) in the exclusive economic zone of a Contracting State, established in accordance with international law, or, if a Contracting State has not established such a zone, in an area beyond and adjacent to the territorial sea of that State determined by that State in accordance with international law and extending not more than 200 nautical miles from the baselines from which the breadth of its territorial sea is measured;
(b) to preventive measures, wherever taken, to prevent or minimise such damage.

Supplementary Compensation

Article 4

1. The Supplementary Fund shall pay compensation to any person suffering pollution damage if such person has been unable to obtain full and adequate compensation for an established claim for such damage under the terms of the 1992 Fund Convention, because the total damage exceeds, or there is a risk that it will exceed, the applicable limit of compensation laid down in article 4, paragraph 4, of the 1992 Fund Convention in respect of any one incident.

2. (a) The aggregate amount of compensation payable by the Supplementary Fund under this article shall in respect of any one incident be limited, so that the total sum of that amount together with the amount of compensation actually paid under the 1992 Liability Convention and the 1992 Fund Convention within the scope of application of this Protocol shall not exceed 750 million units of account.

(b) The amount of 750 million units of account mentioned in paragraph 2(a) shall be converted into national currency on the basis of the value of that currency by reference to the Special Drawing Right on the date determined by the Assembly of the 1992 Fund for conversion of the maximum amount payable under the 1992 Liability and 1992 Fund Conventions.

3. Where the amount of established claims against the Supplementary Fund exceeds the aggregate amount of compensation payable under paragraph 2, the amount available shall be distributed in such a manner that the proportion between any established claim and the amount of compensation actually recovered by the claimant under this Protocol shall be the same for all claimants.

4. The Supplementary Fund shall pay compensation in respect of established claims as defined in article 1, paragraph 8, and only in respect of such claims.

Article 5

The Supplementary Fund shall pay compensation when the Assembly of the 1992 Fund has considered that the total amount of the established claims exceeds, or there is a risk that the total amount of established claims will exceed the aggregate amount of compensation available under article 4, paragraph 4, of the 1992 Fund Convention and that as a consequence the Assembly of the 1992 Fund has decided provisionally or finally that payments will only be made for a proportion of any established claim. The Assembly of the Supplementary Fund shall then decide whether and to what extent the Supplementary Fund shall pay the proportion of any established claim not paid under the 1992 Liability Convention and the 1992 Fund Convention.

Article 6

1. Subject to article 15, paragraphs 2 and 3, rights to compensation against the Supplementary Fund shall be extinguished only if they are extinguished against the 1992 Fund under article 6 of the 1992 Fund Convention.

2. A claim made against the 1992 Fund shall be regarded as a claim made by the same claimant against the Supplementary Fund.

Article 7

1. The provisions of article 7, paragraphs 1, 2, 4, 5 and 6, of the 1992 Fund Convention shall apply to actions for compensation brought against the Supplementary Fund in accordance with article 4, paragraph 1, of this Protocol.

2. Where an action for compensation for pollution damage has been brought before a court competent under article IX of the 1992 Liability Convention against the owner of a ship or his guarantor, such court shall have exclusive jurisdictional competence over any action against the Supplementary Fund for compensation under the provisions of article 4 of this Protocol in respect of the same damage. However, where an action for compensation for pollution damage under the 1992 Liability Convention has been brought before a court in a Contracting State to the 1992 Liability Convention but not to this Protocol, any action against the Supplementary Fund under article 4 of this Protocol shall at the option of the claimant be brought either before a court of the State where the Supplementary Fund has its headquarters or before any court of a Contracting State to this Protocol competent under article IX of the 1992 Liability Convention.

3. Notwithstanding paragraph 1, where an action for compensation for pollution damage against the 1992 Fund has been brought before a court in a Contracting State to the 1992 Fund Convention but not to this Protocol, any related action against the Supplementary Fund shall, at the option of the claimant, be brought either before a court of the State where the Supplementary Fund has its headquarters or before any court of a Contracting State competent under paragraph 1.

Article 8

1. Subject to any decision concerning the distribution referred to in article 4, paragraph 3 of this Protocol, any judgment given against the Supplementary Fund by a court having jurisdiction in accordance with article 7 of this Protocol, shall, when it has become enforce-

able in the State of origin and is in that State no longer subject to ordinary forms of review, be recognised and enforceable in each Contracting State on the same conditions as are prescribed in article X of the 1992 Liability Convention.

2. A Contracting State may apply other rules for the recognition and enforcement of judgments, provided that their effect is to ensure that judgments are recognised and enforced at least to the same extent as under paragraph 1.

Article 9

1. The Supplementary Fund shall, in respect of any amount of compensation for pollution damage paid by the Supplementary Fund in accordance with article 4, paragraph 1, of this Protocol, acquire by subrogation the rights that the person so compensated may enjoy under the 1992 Liability Convention against the owner or his guarantor.

2. The Supplementary Fund shall acquire by subrogation the rights that the person compensated by it may enjoy under the 1992 Fund Convention against the 1992 Fund.

3. Nothing in this Protocol shall prejudice any right of recourse or subrogation of the Supplementary Fund against persons other than those referred to in the preceding paragraphs. In any event the right of the Supplementary Fund to subrogation against such person shall not be less favourable than that of an insurer of the person to whom compensation has been paid.

4. Without prejudice to any other rights of subrogation or recourse against the Supplementary Fund which may exist, a Contracting State or agency thereof which has paid compensation for pollution damage in accordance with provisions of national law shall acquire by subrogation the rights which the person so compensated would have enjoyed under this Protocol.

Contributions

Article 10

1. Annual contributions to the Supplementary Fund shall be made in respect of each Contracting State by any person who, in the calendar year referred to in article 11, paragraph 2(a) or (b), has received in total quantities exceeding 150,000 tons:

(a) in the ports or terminal installations in the territory of that State contributing oil carried by sea to such ports or terminal installations; and

(b) in any installations situated in the territory of that Contracting State contributing oil which has been carried by sea and discharged in a port or terminal installation of a non- Contracting State, provided that contributing oil shall only be taken into account by virtue of this sub-paragraph on first receipt in a Contracting State after its discharge in that non-Contracting State.

2. The provisions of article 10, paragraph 2, of the 1992 Fund Convention shall apply in respect of the obligation to pay contributions to the Supplementary Fund.

Article 11

1. With a view to assessing the amount of annual contributions due, if any, and taking account of the necessity to maintain sufficient liquid funds, the Assembly shall for each calendar year make an estimate in the form of a budget of:

(i) Expenditure

(a) costs and expenses of the administration of the Supplementary Fund in the relevant year and any deficit from operations in preceding years;

(b) payments to be made by the Supplementary Fund in the relevant year for the satisfaction of claims against the Supplementary Fund due under article 4, including repayments on loans previously taken by the Supplementary Fund for the satisfaction of such claims;

(ii) **Income**

    (a) surplus funds from operations in preceding years, including any interest;

    (b) annual contributions, if required to balance the budget;

    (c) any other income.

2. The Assembly shall decide the total amount of contributions to be levied. On the basis of that decision, the Director of the Supplementary Fund shall, in respect of each Contracting State, calculate for each person referred to in article 10, the amount of that person's annual contribution:

    (a) in so far as the contribution is for the satisfaction of payments referred to in paragraph 1(i)(a) on the basis of a fixed sum for each ton of contributing oil received in the relevant State by such person during the preceding calendar year; and

    (b) in so far as the contribution is for the satisfaction of payments referred to in paragraph 1(i)(b) on the basis of a fixed sum for each ton of contributing oil received by such person during the calendar year preceding that in which the incident in question occurred, provided that State was a Contracting State to this Protocol at the date of the incident.

3. The sums referred to in paragraph 2 shall be arrived at by dividing the relevant total amount of contributions required by the total amount of contributing oil received in all Contracting States in the relevant year.

4. The annual contribution shall be due on the date to be laid down in the Internal Regulations of the Supplementary Fund. The Assembly may decide on a different date of payment.

5. The Assembly may decide, under conditions to be laid down in the Financial Regulations of the Supplementary Fund, to make transfers between funds received in accordance with paragraph 2(a) and funds received in accordance with paragraph 2(b)

Article 12

1. The provisions of article 13 of the 1992 Fund Convention shall apply to contributions to the Supplementary Fund.

2. A Contracting State itself may assume the obligation to pay contributions to the Supplementary Fund in accordance with the procedure set out in article 14 of the 1992 Fund Convention.

Article 13

1. Contracting States shall communicate to the Director of the Supplementary Fund information on oil receipts in accordance with article 15 of the 1992 Fund Convention provided, however, that communications made to the Director of the 1992 Fund under article 15, paragraph 2, of the 1992 Fund Convention shall be deemed to have been made also under this Protocol.

2. Where a Contracting State does not fulfil its obligations to submit the communication referred to in paragraph 1 and this results in a financial loss for the Supplementary Fund, that Contracting State shall be liable to compensate the Supplementary Fund for such loss. The Assembly shall, on the recommendation of the Director of the Supplementary Fund, decide whether such compensation shall be payable by that Contracting State.

Article 14

1. Notwithstanding article 10, for the purposes of this Protocol there shall be deemed to be a minimum receipt of 1 million tons of contributing oil in each Contracting State.

2. When the aggregate quantity of contributing oil received in a Contracting State is less than 1 million tons, the Contracting State shall assume the obligations that would be incumbent under this Protocol on any person who would be liable to contribute to the Supplementary Fund in respect of oil received within the territory of that State in so far as no liable person exists for the aggregated quantity of oil received.

Article 15

1. If in a Contracting State there is no person meeting the conditions of article 10, that Contracting State shall for the purposes of this Protocol inform the Director of the Supplementary Fund thereof.

2. No compensation shall be paid by the Supplementary Fund for pollution damage in the territory, territorial sea or exclusive economic zone or area determined in accordance with article 3(a)(ii), of this Protocol, of a Contracting State in respect of a given incident or for preventive measures, wherever taken, to prevent or minimise such damage, until the obligations to communicate to the Director of the Supplementary Fund according to article 13, paragraph 1 and paragraph 1 of this article have been complied with in respect of that Contracting State for all years prior to the occurrence of that incident. The Assembly shall determine in the Internal Regulations the circumstances under which a Contracting State shall be considered as having failed to comply with its obligations.

3. Where compensation has been denied temporarily in accordance with paragraph 2, compensation shall be denied permanently in respect of that incident if the obligations to communicate to the Director of the Supplementary Fund under article 13, paragraph 1 and paragraph 1 of this article, have not been complied with within one year after the Director of the Supplementary Fund has notified the Contracting State of its failure to report.

4. Any payments of contributions due to the Supplementary Fund shall be set off against compensation due to the debtor, or the debtor's agents.

Organisation and administration

Article 16

1. The Supplementary Fund shall have an Assembly and a Secretariat headed by a Director.

2. Articles 17 to 20 and 28 to 33 of the 1992 Fund Convention shall apply to the Assembly, Secretariat and Director of the Supplementary Fund.

3. Article 34 of the 1992 Fund Convention shall apply to the Supplementary Fund.

Article 17

1. The Secretariat of the 1992 Fund, headed by the Director of the 1992 Fund, may also function as the Secretariat and the Director of the Supplementary Fund.

2. If, in accordance with paragraph 1, the Secretariat and the Director of the 1992 Fund also perform the function of Secretariat and Director of the Supplementary Fund, the Supplementary Fund shall be represented, in cases of conflict of interests between the 1992 Fund and the Supplementary Fund, by the Chairman of the Assembly.

3. The Director of the Supplementary Fund, and the staff and experts appointed by the Director of the Supplementary Fund, performing their duties under this Protocol and the 1992 Fund Convention, shall not be regarded as contravening the provisions of article 30 of the 1992 Fund Convention as applied by article 16, paragraph 2, of this Protocol in so far as they discharge their duties in accordance with this article.

4. The Assembly shall endeavour not to take decisions which are incompatible with decisions taken by the Assembly of the 1992 Fund. If differences of opinion with respect to common administrative issues arise, the Assembly shall try to reach a consensus with the Assembly of the 1992 Fund, in a spirit of mutual co-operation and with the common aims of both organisations in mind.

5. The Supplementary Fund shall reimburse the 1992 Fund all costs and expenses arising from administrative services performed by the 1992 Fund on behalf of the Supplementary Fund.

Article 18

Transitional provisions

1. Subject to paragraph 4, the aggregate amount of the annual contributions payable in respect of contributing oil received in a single Contracting State during a calendar year shall

not exceed 20% of the total amount of annual contributions pursuant to this Protocol in respect of that calendar year.

2. If the application of the provisions in article 11, paragraphs 2 and 3, would result in the aggregate amount of the contributions payable by contributors in a single Contracting State in respect of a given calendar year exceeding 20% of the total annual contributions, the contributions payable by all contributors in that State shall be reduced pro rata so that their aggregate contributions equal 20% of the total annual contributions to the Supplementary Fund in respect of that year.

3. If the contributions payable by persons in a given Contracting State shall be reduced pursuant to paragraph 2, the contributions payable by persons in all other Contracting States shall be increased pro rata so as to ensure that the total amount of contributions payable by all persons liable to contribute to the Supplementary Fund in respect of the calendar year in question will reach the total amount of contributions decided by the Assembly.

4. The provisions in paragraphs 1 to 3 shall operate until the total quantity of contributing oil received in all Contracting States in a calendar year, including the quantities referred to in article 14, paragraph 1, has reached 1,000 million tons or until a period of 10 years after the date of entry into force of this Protocol has elapsed, whichever occurs earlier.

Final clauses

Article 19

Signature, ratification, acceptance, approval and accession

1. This Protocol shall be open for signature at London from 31 July 2003 to 30 July 2004.
2. States may express their consent to be bound by this Protocol by:
(a) signature without reservation as to ratification, acceptance or approval; or
(b) signature subject to ratification, acceptance or approval followed by ratification, acceptance or approval; or
(c) accession.
3. Only Contracting States to the 1992 Fund Convention may become Contracting States to this Protocol.
4. Ratification, acceptance, approval or accession shall be effected by the deposit of a formal instrument to that effect with the Secretary-General.

Article 20

Information on contributing oil

Before this Protocol comes into force for a State, that State shall, when signing this Protocol in accordance with article 19, paragraph 2(a), or when depositing an instrument referred to in article 19, paragraph 4 of this Protocol, and annually thereafter at a date to be determined by the Secretary-General, communicate to the Secretary-General the name and address of any person who in respect of that State would be liable to contribute to the Supplementary Fund pursuant to article 10 as well as data on the relevant quantities of contributing oil received by any such person in the territory of that State during the preceding calendar year.

Article 21

Entry into force

1. This Protocol shall enter into force three months following the date on which the following requirements are fulfilled:
(a) at least eight States have signed the Protocol without reservation as to ratification, acceptance or approval, or have deposited instruments of ratification, acceptance, approval or accession with the Secretary-General; and
(b) the Secretary-General has received information from the Director of the 1992 Fund that those persons who would be liable to contribute pursuant to article 10 have received during the preceding calendar year a total quantity of at least 450 million tons of contributing oil, including the quantities referred to in article 14, paragraph 1.

2. For each State which signs this Protocol without reservation as to ratification, acceptance or approval, or which ratifies, accepts, approves or accedes to this Protocol, after the conditions in paragraph 1 for entry into force have been met, the Protocol shall enter into force three months following the date of the deposit by such State of the appropriate instrument.

3. Notwithstanding paragraphs 1 and 2, this Protocol shall not enter into force in respect of any State until the 1992 Fund Convention enters into force for that State.

Article 22

First session of the Assembly

The Secretary-General shall convene the first session of the Assembly. This session shall take place as soon as possible after the entry into force of this Protocol and, in any case, not more than thirty days after such entry into force.

Article 23

Revision and amendment

1. A conference for the purpose of revising or amending this Protocol may be convened by the Organization.

2. The Organization shall convene a Conference of Contracting States for the purpose of revising or amending this Protocol at the request of not less than one third of all Contracting States.

Article 24

Amendment of compensation limit

1. Upon the request of at least one quarter of the Contracting States, any proposal to amend the limit of the amount of compensation laid down in article 4, paragraph 2 (a), shall be circulated by the Secretary-General to all Members of the Organization and to all Contracting States.

2. Any amendment proposed and circulated as above shall be submitted to the Legal Committee of the Organization for consideration at a date at least six months after the date of its circulation.

3. All Contracting States to this Protocol, whether or not Members of the Organization, shall be entitled to participate in the proceedings of the Legal Committee for the consideration and adoption of amendments.

4. Amendments shall be adopted by a two-thirds majority of the Contracting States present and voting in the Legal Committee, expanded as provided for in paragraph 3, on condition that at least one half of the Contracting States shall be present at the time of voting.

5. When acting on a proposal to amend the limit, the Legal Committee shall take into account the experience of incidents and in particular the amount of damage resulting therefrom and changes in the monetary values.

6 (a) No amendments of the limit under this article may be considered before the date of entry into force of this Protocol nor less than three years from the date of entry into force of a previous amendment under this article.

(b) The limit may not be increased so as to exceed an amount which corresponds to the limit laid down in this Protocol increased by six per cent per year calculated on a compound basis from the date when this Protocol is opened for signature to the date on which the Legal Committee's decision comes into force.

(c) The limit may not be increased so as to exceed an amount which corresponds to the limit laid down in this Protocol multiplied by three.

7. Any amendment adopted in accordance with paragraph 4 shall be notified by the Organization to all Contracting States. The amendment shall be deemed to have been accepted at the end of a period of twelve months after the date of notification, unless within

that period not less than one quarter of the States that were Contracting States at the time of the adoption of the amendment by the Legal Committee have communicated to the Organization that they do not accept the amendment, in which case the amendment is rejected and shall have no effect.

8. An amendment deemed to have been accepted in accordance with paragraph 7 shall enter into force twelve months after its acceptance.

9. All Contracting States shall be bound by the amendment, unless they denounce this Protocol in accordance with article 26, paragraphs 1 and 2, at least six months before the amendment enters into force. Such denunciation shall take effect when the amendment enters into force.

10. When an amendment has been adopted by the Legal Committee but the twelve-month period for its acceptance has not yet expired, a State which becomes a Contracting State during that period shall be bound by the amendment if it enters into force. A State which becomes a Contracting State after that period shall be bound by an amendment which has been accepted in accordance with paragraph 7 . In the cases referred to in this paragraph, a State becomes bound by an amendment when that amendment enters into force, or when this Protocol enters into force for that State, if later.

Article 25

Protocols to the 1992 Fund Convention

1. If the limits laid down in the 1992 Fund Convention have been increased by a Protocol thereto, the limit laid down in article 4, paragraph 2(a), may be increased by the same amount by means of the procedure set out in article 24. The provisions of article 24, paragraph 6, shall not apply in such cases.

2. If the procedure referred to in paragraph 1 has been applied, any subsequent amendment of the limit laid down in article 4, paragraph 2, by application of the procedure in article 24 shall, for the purpose of article 24, paragraphs 6(b) and (c), be calculated on the basis of the new limit as increased in accordance with paragraph 1.

Article 26

Denunciation

1. This Protocol may be denounced by any Contracting State at any time after the date on which it enters into force for that Contracting State.

2. Denunciation shall be effected by the deposit of an instrument with the Secretary-General.

3. A denunciation shall take effect twelve months, or such longer period as may be specified in the instrument of denunciation, after its deposit with the Secretary-General.

4. Denunciation of the 1992 Fund Convention shall be deemed to be a denunciation of this Protocol. Such denunciation shall take effect on the date on which denunciation of the Protocol of 1992 to amend the 1971 Fund Convention takes effect according to article 34 of that Protocol.

5. Notwithstanding a denunciation of the present Protocol by a Contracting State pursuant to this article, any provisions of this Protocol relating to the obligations to make contributions to the Supplementary Fund with respect to an incident referred to in article 11,paragraph 2(b), and occurring before the denunciation takes effect, shall continue to apply.

Article 27

Extraordinary sessions of the Assembly

1. Any Contracting State may, within ninety days after the deposit of an instrument of denunciation the result of which it considers will significantly increase the level of contributions for the remaining Contracting States, request the Director of the Supplementary Fund

to convene an extraordinary session of the Assembly. The Director of the Supplementary Fund shall convene the Assembly to meet not later than sixty days after receipt of the request.

2. The Director of the Supplementary Fund may take the initiative to convene an extraordinary session of the Assembly to meet within sixty days after the deposit of any instrument of denunciation, if the Director of the Supplementary Fund considers that such denunciation will result in a significant increase in the level of contributions of the remaining Contracting States.

3. If the Assembly at an extraordinary session convened in accordance with paragraph 1 or 2 decides that the denunciation will result in a significant increase in the level of contributions for the remaining Contracting States, any such State may, not later than one hundred and twenty days before the date on which the denunciation takes effect, denounce this Protocol with effect from the same date.

Article 28

Termination

1. This Protocol shall cease to be in force on the date when the number of Contracting States falls below seven or the total quantity of contributing oil received in the remaining Contracting States, including the quantities referred to in article 14, paragraph 1, falls below 350 million tons, whichever occurs earlier.

2. States which are bound by this Protocol on the day before the date it ceases to be in force shall enable the Supplementary Fund to exercise its functions as described in article 29 and shall, for that purpose only, remain bound by this Protocol.

Article 29

Winding up of the Supplementary Fund

1. If this Protocol ceases to be in force, the Supplementary Fund shall nevertheless:
   (a) meet its obligations in respect of any incident occurring before the Protocol ceased to be in force;
   (b) be entitled to exercise its rights to contributions to the extent that these contributions are necessary to meet the obligations under paragraph 1(a), including expenses for the administration of the Supplementary Fund necessary for this purpose.

2. The Assembly shall take all appropriate measures to complete the winding up of the Supplementary Fund, including the distribution in an equitable manner of any remaining assets among those persons who have contributed to the Supplementary Fund.

3. For the purposes of this article the Supplementary Fund shall remain a legal person.

Article 30

Depositary

1. This Protocol and any amendments accepted under article 24 shall be deposited with the Secretary-General.

2. The Secretary-General shall:
   (a) inform all States which have signed or acceded to this Protocol of:
      (i) each new signature or deposit of an instrument together with the date thereof;
      (ii) the date of entry into force of this Protocol;
      (iii) any proposal to amend the limit of the amount of compensation which has been made in accordance with article 24, paragraph 1;
      (iv) any amendment which has been adopted in accordance with article 24, paragraph 4;
      (v) any amendment deemed to have been accepted under article 24, paragraph 7, together with the date on which that amendment shall enter into force in accordance with paragraphs 8 and 9 of that article;

    (vi) the deposit of an instrument of denunciation of this Protocol together with the date of the deposit and the date on which it takes effect;

    (vii) any communication called for by any article in this Protocol;

(b) transmit certified true copies of this Protocol to all Signatory States and to all States which accede to the Protocol.

3. As soon as this Protocol enters into force, the text shall be transmitted by the Secretary-General to the Secretariat of the United Nations for registration and publication in accordance with Article 102 of the Charter of the United Nations.

Article 31

Languages

This Protocol is established in a single original in the Arabic, Chinese, English, French, Russian and Spanish languages, each text being equally authentic.

DONE AT LONDON this sixteenth day of May two thousand and three.

IN WITNESS WHEREOF the undersigned, being duly authorised by their respective Governments for that purpose, have signed this Protocol.

Small Tanker Oil Pollution Indemnification Agreement (STOPIA 2006)

Explanatory Note

This Note explains the purpose behind the Small Tanker Oil Pollution Indemnification Agreement (STOPIA) 2006 and gives a short summary of its main features. It does not form part of the Agreement but is intended to serve as an informal guide for those interested in understanding how it is intended to operate.

The Agreement establishes STOPIA 2006, the object of which is to provide a mechanism for shipowners to pay an increased contribution to the funding of the international system of compensation for oil pollution from ships, as established by the 1992 Civil Liability Convention (CLC 92), the 1992 Fund Convention and the 2003 Supplementary Fund Protocol.

An earlier version of STOPIA came into force on 3 March 2005 but has since been amended. The text set out in this document is a revised version which applies to Incidents which occur on or after 20 February 2006. The original version continues to apply in respect of any Incidents prior to that date.

The Scheme reflects the desire of shipowners to support efforts to ensure the continuing success of this international system. It also reflects the commitment they gave to the Assembly of the International Oil Pollution Compensation Fund 1992 (the 1992 Fund), at its 10th Session in October 2005, to put in place binding contractual schemes to ensure that the overall costs of claims falling within this system are shared approximately equally with oil receivers. STOPIA 2006, together with the Tanker Oil Pollution Indemnification Agreement (TOPIA) 2006, is designed to achieve this. It is also intended to encourage widest possible ratification of the Supplementary Fund Protocol, and has been drawn up in recognition of the potential additional burden imposed by the Protocol on receivers of oil.

STOPIA 2006 provides for shipowners to make payments to the 1992 Fund which are designed to adjust the financial effect of the limitation of liability provisions in CLC 92. The Scheme reflects the fact that CLC 92 provides for the liability limit of the shipowner to be calculated by reference to the tonnage of the ship, subject to a minimum limit of SDR 4.51 million for ships of 5,000 gross tons or less. Given that the 1992 Fund pays compensation where claims exceed the CLC 92 limit, incidents involving small tankers may result in the 1992 Fund bearing a relatively high proportion of the compensation payable, and paying compensation in a larger number of incidents than would be the case if the minimum limit under CLC 92 were higher. Against this background the Scheme provides for the owner of a ship involved in an oil pollution incident to reimburse the 1992 Fund for any compensation it pays as a result of the ship's liability limit under CLC 92 being less than SDR 20 million. That amount is equivalent to the liability limit under CLC 92 for a ship of 29,548 gross tons. STOPIA 2006 therefore re-apportions the ultimate cost of oil spills involving ships up to that size.

The Scheme is established by a legally binding Agreement between the owners of ships in this category which are insured against oil pollution risks by P&I Clubs in the International Group. In all but rare cases, ships of this description will automatically be entered in the Scheme as a condition of Club cover. Their owners will be parties to the Agreement and are referred to as "Participating Owners".

As the Scheme is contractual it does not affect the legal position under the 1992 Conventions, and the victims of oil spills continue to enjoy their existing rights against the 1992 Fund. For this reason the Scheme provides for the owner of the ship involved in an incident to pay Indemnification to the 1992 Fund, rather than to pay extra sums directly to claimants.

Although the 1992 Fund is not a party to STOPIA 2006 the Agreement is intended to confer legally enforceable rights on the 1992 Fund, and it expressly provides that the 1992 Fund may bring proceedings in its own name in respect of any claim under the Scheme. The Scheme is governed by English law, and English legislation enables legally enforceable rights to be conferred in this manner.

Insurers are not parties to the Agreement, but all Clubs in the International Group have amended their Rules to provide shipowners with cover against liability to pay Indemnification under STOPIA 2006. The Clubs are also authorised under the Scheme to enter into ancillary arrangements enabling the 1992 Fund to enjoy a right of direct action against the relevant Club in respect of any claim under the Scheme. It is envisaged that these and other terms supporting the operation of the Scheme will be agreed between the 1992 Fund and the International Group of P&I Clubs.

Whilst the above are the main features of the Scheme, its twelve clauses address numerous matters of detail. Clause I sets out various definitions, most of which are intended to dovetail with the terminology and provisions of the relevant international conventions. Clauses II and III contain general provisions relating to the Scheme and provide for it to apply to "Relevant Ships". Apart from a relatively small category of ships mentioned below, all tankers will be Relevant Ships if they are of 29,548 tons or less and are insured by an International Group Club. The Scheme provides that the owner of any such ship shall become a party to the Agreement when made a party by his Club in accordance with its Rules, and normally this will result in him automatically becoming a party as a condition of cover against oil pollution risks. The Agreement also provides for any Relevant Ship which he owns to be entered automatically in the Scheme.

An exception to these arrangements relates to ships which are insured by an International Group Club but are not reinsured through the Group's Pooling arrangements. A ship in this category is not automatically entered in the Scheme, but may nonetheless be deemed to be a Relevant Ship (and be entered in the Scheme) by written agreement between the owner and his Club. Certain Japanese coastal tankers are insured outside the International Group Pooling arrangements, but it appears that fewer than 200 of these exceed 200 gross tons. By contrast, some 6,000 tankers are expected to be entered in STOPIA 2006.

Clause IV sets out the precise circumstances in which the Participating Owner of a Relevant Ship is liable to pay Indemnification to the 1992 Fund, and it includes detailed provisions affecting the calculation of the precise amount payable. The clause also contains provisions to prevent any recourse claim being prejudiced by a technical argument that Indemnification has reduced the loss for which the 1992 Fund may claim recovery. For these reasons it is stipulated that Indemnification does not accrue until notice is given that no recourse (or further recourse) proceedings are contemplated, and in the meantime the 1992 Fund is entitled to receive payment or payments on account equal to the amount of Indemnification which it expects to fall due. Such payments are to be made at the same time as payment of the levies on contributors to the 1992 Fund.

Clause V deals in more detail with recourse against third parties. Credit is to be given to the Participating Owner for any sums recovered, but the 1992 Fund retains an absolute discretion as to the commencement, conduct and any settlement of such proceedings. Any recoveries made from third parties are to be apportioned "top down", i.e. the shipowner benefits from them only after the 1992 Fund has recouped amounts for which it is liable in excess of the Indemnification.

Clause VI contains time bar provisions designed to dovetail with the 1992 Conventions (and to allow the 1992 Fund a further 12 months in which to claim Indemnification after the expiry of the time period for claims against it under the 1992 Fund Convention).

Clause VII deals with amendment of the Scheme and enables changes to be made by the International Group acting as agent for all Participating Owners. No amendment is to have retrospective effect, and the Clubs have agreed to consult with the 1992 Fund in good time prior to any decision to amend the Scheme.

Clause VIII provides for a review to be carried out after ten years, and thereafter at five year intervals, in consultation with the 1992 Fund, the Supplementary Fund and representatives of oil receivers, to establish the approximate proportions in which the overall cost of oil pollution claims under the international compensation system has been borne respectively by shipowners and by oil receivers, and provides for measures which may be taken (including possible amendments of STOPIA 2006) for the purpose of maintaining an approximately equal apportionment.

Clause IX deals with the duration of the Scheme, which is to apply to any Incident occurring after noon GMT on 20 February 2006, and is to continue until the current international compensation system is materially and significantly changed. The Clause also provides for termination of the Agreement in certain circumstances which may be expected to make the Agreement no longer workable. The Clubs have agreed to consult with the 1992 Fund prior to any decision to terminate STOPIA 2006.

Under Clause X a Participating Owner may withdraw from the Scheme, and the terms on which he may do so are set out. However, it is anticipated that the owner of a Relevant Ship will not normally be able to withdraw from STOPIA 2006 without prejudicing his Club cover in respect of oil pollution risks.

Clause XI sets out the legal rights of the 1992 Fund under the Scheme, and the authority of the International Group to agree ancillary arrangements with the 1992 Fund in respect of direct actions. The Clubs have agreed to bear direct liability on a similar basis to that prescribed by CLC 92.

Finally the Agreement provides by Clause XII that it is to be governed by English law and that the English High Court of Justice shall have exclusive jurisdiction in relation to any disputes thereunder.

Small Tanker Oil Pollution Indemnification Agreement (STOPIA) 2006

Introduction

The Parties to this Agreement are the Participating Owners as defined herein.

The Participating Owners recognize the success of the international system of compensation for oil pollution from ships established by the 1992 Civil Liability and Fund Conventions, and they are aware that it may need to be revised or supplemented from time to time in order to ensure that it continues to meet the needs of society.

A Protocol has been adopted to supplement the 1992 Fund Convention by providing for additional compensation to be available from a Supplementary Fund for Pollution Damage in States which opt to accede to the Protocol. The Parties wish to encourage the widest possible ratification of the Protocol, with a view to facilitating the continuance of the existing compensation system in its current form (but as supplemented by the Protocol).

In consideration of the potential additional burden imposed by the Protocol on receivers of oil, the Participating Owners have agreed to establish the scheme set out herein, whereby the Participating Owners of tankers below a specified tonnage will indemnify the International Oil Pollution Compensation Fund 1992 ("the 1992 Fund") for a portion of its liability to pay compensation under the 1992 Fund Convention for Pollution Damage caused by such tankers.

This Agreement is intended to create legal relations and in consideration of their mutual promises Participating Owners of each Entered Ship have agreed with one another and do agree as follows ?

I. Definitions

(A) The following terms shall have the same meaning as in Article I of the Liability Convention:

"Incident", "Oil", "Owner", "Person", "Pollution Damage", "Preventive Measures", "Ship".

(B) "1992 Fund" means the International Oil Pollution Compensation Fund 1992 as established by the 1992 Fund Convention.

(C) "1992 Fund Convention" means the International Convention on the Establishment of an International Fund for Compensation for Oil Pollution Damage, 1992, as amended and/or supplemented from time to time, and any domestic legislation giving effect thereto.

(D) "Club" means a Protection and Indemnity (P&I) Association in the International Group; "the Owner's Club" means the Club by which a Relevant Ship owned by him is insured, or to which he is applying for Insurance; "his Club", "Club Party" and similar expressions shall be construed accordingly.

(E) "Entered Ship" means a Ship to which the Scheme applies, and "Entry" shall be construed accordingly.

(F) "Indemnification" means the indemnity payable under Clause IV of this Agreement.

(G) "Insurance", "insured" and related expressions refer to protection and indemnity cover against oil pollution risks.

(H) "International Group" means the International Group of P&I Clubs.

(I) "Liability Convention" means the International Convention on Civil Liability for Oil Pollution Damage, 1992, as amended from time to time, and any domestic legislation giving effect thereto, and "CLC 92 State" means a State in respect of which the said Convention is in force.

(J) "Participating Owner" means the Owner of an Entered Ship who is a Party.

(K) "Party" means a party to this Agreement.

(L) "Protocol" means the Protocol of 2003 to supplement the 1992 Fund Convention, and any domestic legislation giving effect thereto.

(M) "Recourse Conclusion Notice" has the meaning set out in Clause V(C).

(N) "Relevant Ship" has the meaning set out in Clause III(B).

(O) "Scheme" means the Small Tanker Oil Pollution Indemnification Agreement (STOPIA) 2006 as established by this Agreement.

(P) "Supplementary Fund" means the Fund established by the Protocol.

(Q) "Tons" means the gross tonnage calculated in accordance with the tonnage measurement regulations contained in Annex I of the International Convention on Tonnage Measurement of Ships, 1969; the word "tonnage" shall be construed accordingly.

(R) "Unit of account" shall have the same meaning as that set out in Article V, paragraph 9 of the Liability Convention.

II. General

(A) This Agreement shall be known as the Small Tanker Oil Pollution Indemnification Agreement (STOPIA) 2006.

(B) The Owner of any Relevant Ship shall be eligible to become a Party and shall do so when made a Party by the Club insuring that Ship as the Rules of that Club may provide.

III. The STOPIA 2006 Scheme

(A) This Agreement is made to establish STOPIA 2006 for payment of Indemnification to the 1992 Fund on the terms set out herein.

(B) A Ship shall be eligible for Entry in the scheme if:

(1) it is of not more than 29,548 Tons;

(2) it is insured by a Club; and

(3) it is reinsured through the Pooling arrangements of the International Group.

Such a ship is referred to herein as a "Relevant Ship".

(C) Any Relevant Ship owned by a Participating Owner shall automatically be entered in the Scheme upon his becoming a Party to this Agreement in accordance with Clause II(B) above.

(D) A Ship which is not a Relevant Ship by reason of the fact that it is reinsured independently of the said Pooling arrangements may nonetheless be deemed to be a Relevant Ship by written agreement between the Owner and his Club.

(E) Once a Relevant Ship has been entered in the Scheme it shall remain so entered until
  (1) it ceases to be a Relevant Ship (as a result of tonnage re-measurement and/or of ceasing to be insured and reinsured as stated in Clause III(B) above); or
  (2) it ceases to be owned by a Participating Owner; or
  (3) the Participating Owner has withdrawn from this Agreement in accordance with Clause X.

IV. Indemnification of the 1992 Fund

(A) Where, as a result of an Incident, an Entered Ship causes Pollution Damage in respect of which (i) liability is incurred under the Liability Convention by the Participating Owner of that Ship and (ii) the 1992 Fund has paid or expects to pay compensation under the 1992 Fund Convention, the said Owner shall indemnify the 1992 Fund in an amount calculated in accordance with this Clause.

(B) Indemnification shall not be payable for:
  (1) the costs of any Preventive Measures to the extent that the Participating Owner is exonerated from liability under Article III, paragraph 3 of the Liability Convention, and for which the 1992 Fund is liable by virtue of Article 4, paragraph 3 of the 1992 Fund Convention;
  (2) any other Pollution Damage to the extent that liability is incurred by the 1992 Fund but not by the Participating Owner.

(C) The amount for which Indemnification is payable by the Participating Owner to the 1992 Fund shall be the amount of compensation which the 1992 Fund has paid or expects to pay for Pollution Damage, provided always that:
  (1) Indemnification shall not exceed in respect of any one Incident an amount equivalent to 20 million units of account less the amount of the Owner's liability under the Liability Convention as limited by Article V, paragraph 1 thereof; and
  (2) the deduction referred to in Clause IV(C)(1) above shall be made irrespective of whether the Participating Owner is entitled to avail himself of limitation.

(D) Liability to pay Indemnification hereunder shall not affect any rights which the Participating Owner or his Club may have to recover from the 1992 Fund any amounts in respect of the Incident, whether in their own right, by subrogation, assignment or otherwise. For the avoidance of doubt, any such amounts shall be included in the amount of compensation referred to in Clause IV(C) above.

(E) Unless otherwise agreed with the 1992 Fund –
  (1) the entitlement of the 1992 Fund to receive Indemnification from the Participating Owner accrues when it gives a Recourse Conclusion Notice as defined in Clause V(C) below;
  (2) prior to that time the 1992 Fund shall be entitled to receive from the Participating Owner such payment or payments on account of Indemnification as the 1992 Fund considers to be equal to the anticipated amount of Indemnification;
  (3) payment of any amounts which the 1992 Fund is entitled to receive under this Agreement shall be made concurrent with payment of the levies on contributors for the Incident concerned in accordance with Articles 10 and 12 of the 1992 Fund Convention.

(F)(1) Any payment on account under Clause IV(E) above is made on the conditions that –
  (i) it is credited by the 1992 Fund to a special account relating solely to Indemnification in respect of the Incident concerned;
  (ii) any surplus of the amount(s) paid by the Participating Owner remaining after all compensation payments by the 1992 Fund have been made shall be refunded to the Participating Owner; and

(iii) in so far as a surplus consists of amounts recovered by way of recourse from third parties it shall be credited to the Participating Owner in accordance with Clause V below.

(2) Nothing in this Clause IV(F) shall prevent the 1992 Fund from making use of any sums paid to it under this Agreement in the payment of claims for compensation arising from the Incident concerned; nor shall it require the 1992 Fund to hold such sums (or any balance thereof) in a separate bank account or to invest them separately from other assets of the 1992 Fund.

(3) Save where the 1992 Fund has been notified to the contrary, the Club insuring the Participating Owner shall be deemed to be authorised to act on his behalf in receiving any refund under this Clause.

(G) For the purposes of this Agreement the conversion of units of account into national currency shall be made in accordance with Article V, paragraph 9 of the Liability Convention.

V. Recourse against third parties

(A) Any decisions as to whether the 1992 Fund is to take recourse action against any third parties, and as to the conduct of any such action, including any out-of-court settlement, are in the absolute discretion of the 1992 Fund.

(B) Without prejudice to Clause V(A) above –

(1) payment by the Participating Owner under this Agreement is made on the condition that he shall, in respect of any amount paid as Indemnification (or as payment on account thereof), acquire by subrogation any rights of recourse that the 1992 Fund may enjoy against third parties, to the extent of the Participating Owner's interest in the benefit of any recoveries from such parties in accordance with this Agreement;

(2) the 1992 Fund may consult with the Participating Owner and/or his Club in relation to any recourse action in which they are actual or potential claimants;

(3) nothing in this Agreement shall prevent the 1992 Fund, the Owner and the Club from agreeing on any arrangements relating to such action as may be considered appropriate in the particular case, including any terms as to the apportionment of costs of funding such action, or as to the allocation of any recoveries made.

(C) For the purposes of this Agreement, a Recourse Conclusion Notice is notice to the Participating Owner that a final conclusion has been reached in relation to all and any recourse action taken or contemplated by the 1992 Fund against any third parties in respect of the Incident. Such a conclusion may include a decision by the 1992 Fund not to take a recourse action, or to discontinue any such action already commenced.

(D) Payment by the Participating Owner under this Agreement is made on the conditions that –

(1) if the 1992 Fund decides to take recourse action against any third party it will, unless otherwise agreed, either (a) seek recovery of compensation it has paid or expects to pay without deduction of any sums paid under this Agreement by the Participating Owner, or (b) on request, execute documentation as described in Clause V(D)(2) below;

(2) if the 1992 Fund decides not to take a recourse action (or to discontinue any such action already commenced) against any third party in respect of the incident, the 1992 Fund will, on request, execute such reasonable documentation as may be required to transfer (or affirm the transfer) to the Participating Owner and/or his Club, by subrogation, assignment or otherwise, any rights of recourse which the 1992 Fund may have against that third party, to the extent of any interest which the Participating Owner and/or his Club may have in recovering from that party any amounts paid under this Agreement;

(3) if, after it has been paid, the 1992 Fund for any reason recovers any sums from any third party, the 1992 Fund will account to the Participating Owner for such sums after deduction of –

      (i) any costs incurred by the 1992 Fund in recovering the said sums; and

     (ii) an amount equal to the compensation which the 1992 Fund has paid or expects to pay for Pollution Damage in respect of the Incident, insofar as this exceeds the amount paid under this Agreement by the Participating Owner.

(E) Save where the 1992 Fund has been notified to the contrary, the Club insuring the Participating Owner shall be deemed to be authorised to act on his behalf in receiving notice under Clause V(C) above; in receiving any sums payable to the Participating Owner under Clause V(D) above; and in agreeing all and any other matters relating to the operation of this Clause V.

VI. Procedure and miscellaneous

Any rights of the 1992 Fund to Indemnification under this Agreement shall be extinguished unless an action is brought hereunder within four years from the date when the Pollution Damage occurred. However, in no case shall an action be brought after seven years from the date of the Incident which caused the damage. Where this Incident consists of a series of occurrences, the seven year period shall run from the date of the first such occurrence.

VII. Amendment

(A) This Agreement may be amended at any time by the International Group acting as agent for all Participating Owners.

Any such amendment to this Agreement will take effect three months from the date on which written notice is given by the International Group to the 1992 Fund.

(B) Each Participating Owner agrees that the International Group shall be authorised to agree on his behalf to an amendment of this Agreement if ?

    (1) it is so authorised by his Club, and

    (2) his Club has approved of the amendment by the same procedure as that required for alteration of its Rules.

(C) Subject to Clause IX(A) below, any amendment of this Agreement shall not affect rights and obligations in respect of any Incident which occurred prior to the date when such amendment enters into force.

VIII. Review

(A) During the year 2016 a review shall be carried out of the experience of claims for Pollution Damage in the ten years to 20 February 2016. The purpose of the review will be (1) to establish the approximate proportions in which the overall cost of such claims under the Liability Convention and/or the 1992 Fund Convention and/or the Protocol has been borne respectively by shipowners and by oil receivers in the period since 20 February 2006; and (2) to consider the efficiency, operation and performance of this Agreement. Such a review shall be repeated every five years thereafter.

(B) Representatives of oil receivers, and the Secretariat of the 1992 Fund and Supplementary Fund, are to be invited to participate in any review under this Clause on a consultative basis. The Participating Owners authorise the International Group to act on their behalf in the conduct of any such review.

(C) If a review under this Clause reveals that in the period since 20 February 2006 either shipowners or oil receivers have borne a proportion exceeding 60% of the overall cost referred to in Clause VIII(A) above, measures are to be taken to adjust the financial burden of such cost with the object of maintaining an approximately equal apportionment.

(D) Such measures may include –

    (1) amendment of this Agreement to provide for an increase or reduction in the amount of Indemnification payable under this Agreement;

    (2) amendment of this Agreement to improve its efficiency, operation and performance;

    (3) the conclusion or amendment of any other contractual agreement relating to the apportionment of the cost of oil pollution between shipowners and oil receivers; and

(4) any other measure or measures considered appropriate for the purpose of maintaining an approximately equal apportionment.

(E) If a review under this Clause reveals that either shipowners or oil receivers have borne a proportion exceeding 55% but not exceeding 60% of the overall cost referred to in Clause VIII(A) above, measures as referred to above may be (but are not bound to be) taken.

IX. Duration and termination

(A) This Agreement shall apply to any Incident occurring after noon GMT on 20 February 2006.

(B) Unless previously terminated in accordance with the provisions set out below, this Agreement shall continue in effect until the entry into force of any international instrument which materially and significantly changes the system of compensation established by the Liability Convention, the 1992 Fund Convention and the Protocol.

(C) Each Participating Owner agrees that the International Group shall be authorised to terminate this Agreement on behalf of all Participating Owners if –

(1) the Clubs cease to provide Insurance of the liability of Participating Owners to pay Indemnification under this Agreement; or

(2) the performance of the Agreement becomes illegal in a particular State or States (in which case this Agreement may be terminated in respect of such State or States whilst remaining in effect in respect of other States); or

(3) the International Group's reinsurers cease to provide adequate cover against the liabilities provided for by this Agreement, and cover for this risk is not reasonably available in the world market on equivalent terms; or

(4) the International Group is disbanded; or

(5) termination is authorised by his Club (and his Club has approved of the termination by the same procedure as that required for alteration of its Rules) due to any event or circumstance which prevents the performance of this Agreement and which is not within the reasonable contemplation of the Participating Owners.

(D) Termination of this Agreement shall not take effect until three months after the date on which the 1992 Fund is notified thereof in writing by the International Group.

(E) The termination of this Agreement shall not affect rights or obligations in respect of any Incident which occurs prior to the date of termination.

X. Withdrawal

(A) A Participating Owner may withdraw from this Agreement –

(1) on giving not less than 3 months' written notice of withdrawal to his Club; or

(2) by virtue of an amendment thereto, provided always –

(i) that he exercised any right to vote against the said amendment when his Club sought the approval thereto of its members; and

(ii) that within 60 days of the amendment being approved by the membership of his Club he gives written notice of withdrawal to his Club; and

(iii) that such withdrawal shall take effect simultaneously with the entry-into-effect of the amendment, or on the date on which his notice is received by his Club, whichever is later.

(B) If a Participating Owner ceases to be the owner of a Relevant Ship he shall be deemed, in respect of that ship only, to withdraw from this Agreement with immediate effect, and he or his Club shall give written notice to the 1992 Fund that he has ceased to be the owner of that Relevant Ship.

(C) A Participating Owner withdrawing from this Agreement shall have no further liability hereunder as from the date when his withdrawal takes effect; provided always that no withdrawal shall affect rights or obligations in respect of any Incident which occurs prior to that date.

XI. Legal rights of 1992 Fund

(A) Though not a Party to this Agreement, the 1992 Fund is intended to enjoy legally enforceable rights of Indemnification as described herein, and accordingly the 1992 Fund shall be entitled to bring proceedings in its own name against the Participating Owner in respect of any claim it may have hereunder. Such proceedings may include an action brought by the 1992 Fund against a Participating Owner to determine any issue relating to the construction, validity and/or performance of this Agreement.

(B) Notwithstanding Clause XI(A) and Clause VII(A) above, the consent of the 1992 Fund shall not be required to any amendment, termination or withdrawal made in accordance with the terms of this Agreement.

(C) The Parties to this Agreement authorise the International Group to agree terms with the 1992 Fund on which a claim for Indemnification under this Agreement in respect of an Entered Ship (or previously Entered Ship), or proceedings to determine any issue of construction, validity and/or performance of this Agreement, may be brought directly against the Club insuring the Ship at the time of the Incident. They also agree that in the event of the 1992 Fund bringing proceedings to enforce a claim against a Club in respect of an Entered Ship, the Club may require the Participating Owner to be joined in such proceedings.

XII. Law and jurisdiction

This Agreement shall be governed by English law and the English High Court of Justice shall have exclusive jurisdiction in relation to any disputes hereunder.

Tanker Oil Pollution Indemnification Agreement (TOPIA 2006)

Explanatory Note

This Note explains the purpose behind the Tanker Oil Pollution Indemnification Agreement (TOPIA) 2006 and gives a short summary of its main features. It does not form part of the Agreement but is intended to serve as an informal guide for those interested in understanding how it is intended to operate.

The Agreement establishes the TOPIA 2006 Scheme, the object of which is to provide a mechanism for shipowners to pay an increased contribution to the funding of the international system of compensation for oil pollution from ships, as established by the 1992 Civil Liability Convention (CLC 92), the 1992 Fund Convention and the 2003 Supplementary Fund Protocol.

The Scheme reflects the desire of shipowners to support efforts to ensure the continuing success of this international system. It also reflects the commitment they gave to the Assembly of the International Oil Pollution Compensation Fund 1992, at its 10th Session in October 2005, to put in place binding contractual schemes to ensure that the overall costs of claims falling within this system are shared approximately equally with oil receivers. TOPIA, together with the Small Tanker Oil Pollution Indemnification Agreement (STOPIA) 2006, is designed to achieve this. It is also intended to encourage widest possible ratification of the Supplementary Fund Protocol, and has been drawn up in recognition of the potential additional burden imposed by the Protocol on receivers of oil.

TOPIA provides for shipowners to indemnify the Supplementary Fund for 50% of the compensation it pays under the Protocol for Pollution Damage caused by tankers in Protocol States.

The Scheme is established by a legally binding Agreement between the owners of tankers which are insured against oil pollution risks by P&I Clubs in the International Group. In all but a relatively small number of cases, ships of this description will automatically be entered in the Scheme as a condition of Club cover. Their owners will be parties to the Agreement and are referred to as "Participating Owners".

As the Scheme is contractual it does not affect the legal position under the 1992 Conventions and Protocol, and the victims of oil spills continue to enjoy their existing rights against the 1992 Fund and Supplementary Fund. For this reason the Scheme provides for the owner of the ship involved in an incident to pay Indemnification to the Supplementary Fund, rather than to pay extra sums directly to claimants.

Although the Supplementary Fund is not a party to TOPIA, the Agreement is intended to confer legally enforceable rights on the Supplementary Fund, and it expressly provides that the Supplementary Fund may bring proceedings in its own name in respect of any claim under the Scheme. The Scheme is governed by English law, and English legislation enables legally enforceable rights to be conferred in this manner.

Insurers are not parties to the Agreement, but all Clubs in the International Group have amended (or agreed to amend) their Rules to provide shipowners with cover against liability to pay Indemnification under TOPIA. The Clubs are also authorised under the Scheme to enter into ancillary arrangements enabling the Supplementary Fund to enjoy a right of direct action against the relevant Club in respect of any claim under the Scheme. It is envisaged that these and other terms supporting the operation of the Scheme will be agreed between the Supplementary Fund and the International Group of P&I Clubs.

Whilst the above are the main features of the Scheme, its twelve clauses address numerous matters of detail. Clause I sets out various definitions, most of which are intended to dovetail with the terminology and provisions of the relevant international conventions. Clauses II and III contain general provisions relating to the Scheme and provide for it to apply to "Relevant Ships". Apart from a relatively small category of ships mentioned below, all tankers will be Relevant Ships if they are insured by an International Group Club. The Scheme provides that the owner of any such ship shall become a party to the Agreement when made a party by his Club in accordance with its Rules, and normally this will result in him automatically becoming a party as a condition of cover against oil pollution risks. The Agreement also provides for any Relevant Ship which he owns to be entered automatically in the Scheme.

An exception to these arrangements relates to ships which are insured by an International Group Club but are not reinsured through the Group's Pooling arrangements. A ship in this category is not automatically entered in the Scheme, but may nonetheless be deemed to be a Relevant Ship (and be entered in the Scheme) by written agreement between the owner and his Club. Certain Japanese coastal tankers are insured outside the International Group Pooling arrangements, but it appears that fewer than 200 of these exceed 200 gross tons.

Clause IV sets out the precise circumstances in which the Participating Owner is liable to pay Indemnification to the Supplementary Fund, and it includes detailed provisions affecting the calculation of the precise amount payable. The clause also contains provisions to prevent any recourse claim being prejudiced by a technical argument that Indemnification has reduced the loss for which the Supplementary Fund may claim recovery. For these reasons it is stipulated that Indemnification does not accrue until notice is given that no recourse (or further recourse) proceedings are contemplated, and in the meantime the Supplementary Fund is entitled to receive payment or payments on account equal to the amount of Indemnification which it expects to fall due. Such payments are to be made at the same time as payment of the levies on contributors to the Supplementary Fund. Clause IV also stipulates that Indemnification shall be payable for Pollution Damage caused by terrorist risks only to the extent, if any, that such amounts are covered by any insurance or reinsurance in force at the time of the Incident. This is due to the restrictions shipowners face in obtaining liability insurance cover for risks of this type.

Clause V deals in more detail with recourse against third parties. Credit is to be given to the Participating Owner for any sums recovered, but the Supplementary Fund retains an absolute discretion as to the commencement, conduct and any settlement of such proceedings.

Clause VI contains time bar provisions designed to dovetail with the 1992 Conventions (and to allow the Supplementary Fund a further 12 months in which to claim Indemnification after the time period for claims against it under the Supplementary Fund Protocol).

Clause VII deals with amendment of the Scheme and enables changes to be made by the International Group acting as agent for all Participating Owners. No amendment is to have retrospective effect, and the Clubs have agreed to consult with the Supplementary Fund in good time prior to any decision to amend the Scheme.

Clause VIII provides for a review to be carried out after ten years, and thereafter at five year intervals, in consultation with the 1992 Fund, the Supplementary Fund and representatives of oil receivers, to establish the approximate proportions in which the overall cost of oil pollution claims under the international compensation system has been borne respectively by shipowners and by oil receivers, and provides for measures which may be taken (including possible amendments of TOPIA) for the purpose of maintaining an approximately equal apportionment.

Clause IX deals with the duration of the Scheme, which is to apply to any Incident occurring after noon GMT on 20 February 2006, and is to continue until the current international compensation system is materially and significantly changed. The Clause also provides for termination of the Agreement in certain circumstances which may be expected to make the Agreement no longer workable. The Clubs have agreed to consult with the Supplementary Fund prior to any decision to terminate TOPIA.

Under Clause X a Participating Owner may withdraw from the Scheme, and the terms on which he may do so are set out. However, it is anticipated that the owner of a Relevant Ship will not normally be able to withdraw from TOPIA without prejudicing his Club cover in respect of oil pollution risks.

Clause XI sets out the legal rights of the Supplementary Fund under the Scheme, and the authority of the International Group to agree ancillary arrangements with the 1992 Fund in respect of direct actions. The Clubs have agreed to bear direct liability on a similar basis to that prescribed by CLC 92.

Finally the Agreement provides by Clause XII that it is to be governed by English law and that the English High Court of Justice shall have exclusive jurisdiction in relation to any disputes thereunder.

Tanker Oil Pollution Indemnification Agreement (TOPIA) 2006

Introduction

The Parties to this Agreement are the Participating Owners as defined herein.

The Participating Owners recognise the success of the international system of compensation for oil pollution from ships established by the 1992 Civil Liability and Fund Conventions, and they are aware that it may need to be revised or supplemented from time to time in order to ensure that it continues to meet the needs of society.

A Protocol has been adopted to supplement the 1992 Fund Convention by providing for additional compensation to be available from a Supplementary Fund for Pollution Damage in States which opt to accede to the Protocol. The Parties wish to encourage the widest possible ratification of the Protocol, with a view to facilitating the continuance of the existing compensation system in its current form (but as supplemented by the Protocol).

In consideration of the potential additional burden imposed by the Protocol on receivers of oil, the Participating Owners have agreed to establish the scheme set out herein, whereby the Participating Owners of tankers will indemnify the Supplementary Fund for 50% of its liability to pay compensation under the Protocol for Pollution Damage.

This indemnity is restricted in respect of Pollution Damage caused by terrorist risks, in recognition of the restrictions on cover against such risks in liability insurance available to shipowners.

This Agreement is intended to create legal relations and in consideration of their mutual promises Participating Owners of each Entered Ship have agreed with one another and do agree as follows ?

I. Definitions

(A) The following terms shall have the same meaning as in Article I of the Liability Convention:

"Incident", "Oil", "Owner", "Person", "Pollution Damage", "Preventive Measures", "Ship".

(B) "1992 Fund" means the International Oil Pollution Compensation Fund 1992 as established by the 1992 Fund Convention.

(C) "1992 Fund Convention" means the International Convention on the Establishment of an International Fund for Compensation for Oil Pollution Damage, 1992, as amended and/or supplemented from time to time, and any domestic legislation giving effect thereto.

(D) "Club" means a Protection and Indemnity (P&I) Association in the International Group; "the Owner's Club" means the Club by which a Relevant Ship owned by him is insured, or to which he is applying for Insurance; "his Club", "Club Party" and similar expressions shall be construed accordingly.

(E) "Entered Ship" means a Ship to which the Scheme applies, and "Entry" shall be construed accordingly.

(F) "Indemnification" means the indemnity payable under Clause IV of this Agreement.

(G) "Insurance", "insured" and related expressions refer to protection and indemnity cover against oil pollution risks.

(H) "International Group" means the International Group of P&I Clubs.

(I) "Liability Convention" means the International Convention on Civil Liability for Oil Pollution Damage, 1992, as amended from time to time, and any domestic legislation giving effect thereto.

(J) "Participating Owner" means the Owner of an Entered Ship who is a Party.

(K) "Party" means a party to this Agreement.

(L) "Protocol" means the Protocol of 2003 to supplement the 1992 Fund Convention, and any domestic legislation giving effect thereto; and "Protocol State" means a State in respect of which the said Protocol is in force.

(M) "Recourse Conclusion Notice" has the meaning set out in Clause V(C).

(N) "Relevant Ship" has the meaning set out in Clause III(B).

(O) "Scheme" means the Tanker Oil Pollution Indemnification Agreement (TOPIA) 2006 as established by this Agreement.

(P) "Supplementary Fund" means the Fund established by the Protocol.

(Q) "Tons" means the gross tonnage calculated in accordance with the tonnage measurement regulations contained in Annex I of the International Convention on Tonnage Measurement of Ships, 1969; the word "tonnage" shall be construed accordingly.

(R) "Unit of account" shall have the same meaning as that set out in Article V, paragraph 9 of the Liability Convention.

II. General

(A) This Agreement shall be known as the Tanker Oil Pollution Indemnification Agreement (TOPIA) 2006.

(B) The Owner of any Relevant Ship shall be eligible to become a Party and shall do so when made a Party by the Club insuring that Ship as the Rules of that Club may provide.

III. The TOPIA 2006 Scheme

(A) This Agreement is made to establish TOPIA for payment of Indemnification to the Supplementary Fund on the terms set out herein.

(B) A Ship shall be eligible for Entry in the scheme if:

(1) it is insured by a Club; and

(2) it is reinsured through the Pooling arrangements of the International Group.

Such a Ship is referred to herein as a "Relevant Ship".

(C) Any Relevant Ship owned by a Participating Owner shall automatically be entered in the Scheme upon his becoming a Party to this Agreement in accordance with Clause II(B) above.

(D) A Ship which is not a Relevant Ship by reason of the fact that it is reinsured independently of the said Pooling arrangements may nonetheless be deemed to be a Relevant Ship by written agreement between the Owner and his Club.

(E) Once a Relevant Ship has been entered in the Scheme it shall remain so entered until

(1) it ceases to be a Relevant Ship (as a result of ceasing to be insured or reinsured as stated in Clause III(B) above); or

(2) it ceases to be owned by a Participating Owner; or

(3) the Participating Owner has withdrawn from this Agreement in accordance with Clause X.

IV. Indemnification of the Supplementary Fund

(A) Where, as a result of an Incident, an Entered Ship causes Pollution Damage in respect of which (1) liability is incurred under the Liability Convention by the Participating Owner of that Ship and (2) the Supplementary Fund has paid or expects to pay compensation under the Protocol, the said Owner shall indemnify the Supplementary Fund in an amount calculated in accordance with this Clause.

(B) Indemnification shall not be payable for:

    (1) the costs of any Preventive Measures to the extent that the Participating Owner is exonerated from liability under Article III, paragraph 3 of the Liability Convention, and for which the Supplementary Fund is liable by virtue of the Protocol;

    (2) any other Pollution Damage to the extent that liability is incurred by the Supplementary Fund but not by the Participating Owner.

(C) The amount for which Indemnification is payable by the Participating Owner to the Supplementary Fund shall be 50% of the amount of compensation which the Supplementary Fund has paid or expects to pay for Pollution Damage caused by the Incident.

(D) Liability to pay Indemnification hereunder shall not affect any rights which the Participating Owner or his Club may have to recover from the Supplementary Fund any amounts in respect of the Incident, whether in their own right, by subrogation, assignment or otherwise. For the avoidance of doubt, any such amounts shall be included in the amount of compensation referred to in Clause IV(C) above.

(E) Unless otherwise agreed with the Supplementary Fund –

    (1) the entitlement of the Supplementary Fund to receive Indemnification from the Participating Owner accrues when it gives a Recourse Conclusion Notice as defined in Clause V(C) below;

    (2) prior to that time the Supplementary Fund shall be entitled to receive from the Participating Owner such payment or payments on account of Indemnification as the Supplementary Fund considers to be equal to the anticipated amount of Indemnification;

    (3) payment of any amounts which the Supplementary Fund is entitled to receive under this Agreement shall be made concurrent with payment of the levies on contributors for the Incident concerned in accordance with Articles 10 and 12 of the Protocol.

(F)(1) Any payment on account under Clause IV(E) above is made on the conditions that –

      (i) it is credited by the Supplementary Fund to a special account relating solely to Indemnification in respect of the Incident concerned;

      (ii) any surplus of the amount(s) paid by the Participating Owner remaining after all compensation payments by the Supplementary Fund have been made shall be refunded to the Participating Owner; and

      (iii) in so far as a surplus consists of amounts recovered by way of recourse from third parties it shall be credited to the Participating Owner in accordance with Clause V below.

    (2) Nothing in this Clause IV(F) shall prevent the Supplementary Fund from making use of any sums paid to it under this Agreement in the payment of claims for compensation arising from the Incident concerned; nor shall it require the Supplementary Fund to hold such sums (or any balance thereof) in a separate bank account or to invest them separately from other assets of the Supplementary Fund.

    (3) Save where the Supplementary Fund has been notified to the contrary, the Club insuring the Participating Owner shall be deemed to be authorised to act on his behalf in receiving any refund under this Clause.

(G) No Indemnification shall be payable under this Agreement for any amounts paid by the Supplementary Fund in respect of Pollution Damage caused by any act of terrorism save to the extent, if any, that such amounts are covered by any insurance or reinsurance in force at the time of the Incident. This provision shall apply irrespective of whether the Owner is exonerated from liability under the Liability Convention by virtue of Article III, paragraph 2 thereof.

(H) In the event of any dispute as to whether or not any act constitutes an act of terrorism for the purposes of this Agreement, Indemnification by the Participating Owner hereunder shall in any event be contingent on liability being accepted or established on the part of his Club to indemnify him in respect thereof.

V. Recourse against third parties

(A) Any decisions as to whether the Supplementary Fund is to take recourse action against any third parties, and as to the conduct of any such action, including any out-of-court settlement, are in the absolute discretion of the Supplementary Fund.

(B) Without prejudice to Clause V(A) above –

    (1) payment by the Participating Owner under this Agreement is made on the condition that he shall, in respect of any amount paid as Indemnification (or as payment on account thereof), acquire by subrogation any rights of recourse that the Supplementary Fund may enjoy against third parties, to the extent of the Participating Owner's interest in the benefit of any recoveries from such parties in accordance with this Agreement;

    (2) the Supplementary Fund may consult with the Participating Owner and/or his Club in relation to any recourse action in which they are actual or potential claimants;

    (3) nothing in this Agreement shall prevent the Supplementary Fund, the Owner and the Club from agreeing on any arrangements relating to such action as may be considered appropriate in the particular case, including any terms as to the apportionment of costs of funding such action, or as to the allocation of any recoveries made.

(C) For the purposes of this Agreement, a Recourse Conclusion Notice is notice to the Participating Owner that a final conclusion has been reached in relation to all and any recourse action taken or contemplated by the Supplementary Fund against any third parties in respect of the Incident. Such a conclusion may include a decision by the Supplementary Fund not to take a recourse action, or to discontinue any such action already commenced.

(D) Payment by the Participating Owner under this Agreement is made on the conditions that –

    (1) if the Supplementary Fund decides to take recourse action against any third party it will, unless otherwise agreed, either (a) seek recovery of compensation it has paid or expects to pay without deduction of any sums paid under this Agreement by the Participating Owner, or (b) on request, execute documentation as described in Clause V(D)(2) below;

    (2) if the Supplementary Fund decides not to take a recourse action (or to discontinue any such action already commenced) against any third party in respect of the incident, the Supplementary Fund will, on request, execute such reasonable documentation as may be required to transfer (or affirm the transfer) to the Participating Owner and/or his Club, by subrogation, assignment or otherwise, any rights of recourse which the Supplementary Fund may have against that third party, to the extent of any interest which the Participating Owner and/or his Club may have in recovering from that party any amounts paid under this Agreement;

    (3) if, after payment by the Participating Owner has been made, the Supplementary Fund recovers any sums from any third party, 50% of such recoveries (net of the costs incurred in making them) shall be retained by the Supplementary Fund and the remaining 50% shall be paid by the Supplementary Fund to the Participating Owner.

(E) Save where the Supplementary Fund has been notified to the contrary, the Club insuring the Participating Owner shall be deemed to be authorised to act on his behalf in receiving notice under Clause V(C) above; in receiving any sums payable to the Participating Owner under Clause V(D) above; and in agreeing all and any other matters relating to the operation of this Clause V.

VI. Procedure and miscellaneous

Any rights of the Supplementary Fund to Indemnification under this Agreement shall be extinguished unless an action is brought hereunder within four years from the date when the Pollution Damage occurred. However, in no case shall an action be brought after seven years from the date of the Incident which caused the damage. Where this Incident consists of a series of occurrences, the seven year period shall run from the date of the first such occurrence.

VII. Amendment

(A) This Agreement may be amended at any time by the International Group acting as agent for all Participating Owners. Any such amendment to this Agreement will take effect three months from the date on which written notice is given by the International Group to the Supplementary Fund.

(B) Each Participating Owner agrees that the International Group shall be authorised to agree on his behalf to an amendment of this Agreement if –

    (1) it is so authorised by his Club, and

    (2) his Club has approved of the amendment by the same procedure as that required for alteration of its Rules.

(C) Subject to Clause IX(A) below, any amendment of this Agreement shall not affect rights and obligations in respect of any Incident which occurred prior to the date when such amendment enters into force.

VIII. Review

(A) During the year 2016 a review shall be carried out of the experience of claims for Pollution Damage in the ten years to 20 February 2016. The purpose of the review will be (1) to establish the approximate proportions in which the overall cost of such claims under the Liability Convention and/or the 1992 Fund Convention and/or the Protocol has been borne respectively by shipowners and by oil receivers in the period since 20 February 2006; and (2) to consider the efficiency, operation and performance of this Agreement. Such a review shall be repeated every five years thereafter.

(B) Representatives of oil receivers, and the Secretariat of the 1992 Fund and Supplementary Fund, are to be invited to participate in any review under this Clause on a consultative basis. The Participating Owners authorise the International Group to act on their behalf in the conduct of any such review.

(C) If a review under this Clause reveals that in the period since 20 February 2006 either shipowners or oil receivers have borne a proportion exceeding 60% of the overall cost referred to in Clause VIII(A) above, measures are to be taken to adjust the financial burden of such cost with the object of maintaining an approximately equal apportionment.

(D) Such measures may include –

    (1) amendment of this Agreement to provide for an increase or reduction in the amount of Indemnification payable under this Agreement;

    (2) amendment of this Agreement to improve its efficiency, operation and performance;

    (3) the conclusion or amendment of any other contractual agreement relating to the apportionment of the cost of oil pollution between shipowners and oil receivers; and

    (4) any other measure or measures considered appropriate for the purpose of maintaining an approximately equal apportionment.

(E) If a review under this Clause reveals that either shipowners or oil receivers have borne a proportion exceeding 55% but not exceeding 60% of the overall cost referred to in Clause VIII(A), measures as referred to above may be (but are not bound to be) taken.

IX. Duration and termination

(A) This Agreement shall apply to any Incident occurring after noon GMT on 20 February 2006.

(B) Unless previously terminated in accordance with the provisions set out below, this Agreement shall continue in effect until the entry into force of any international instrument which materially and significantly changes the system of compensation established by the Liability Convention, the 1992 Fund Convention and the Protocol.

(C) Each Participating Owner agrees that the International Group shall be authorised to terminate this Agreement on behalf of all Participating Owners if –

    (1) the Clubs cease to provide Insurance of the liability of Participating Owners to pay Indemnification under this Agreement; or

(2) the performance of the Agreement becomes illegal in a particular State or States (in which case this Agreement may be terminated in respect of such State or States whilst remaining in effect in respect of other States); or

(3) the International Group's reinsurers cease to provide adequate cover against the liabilities provided for by this Agreement, and cover for this risk is not reasonably available in the world market on equivalent terms; or

(4) the International Group is disbanded; or

(5) termination is authorised by his Club (and his Club has approved of the termination by the same procedure as that required for alteration of its Rules) due to any event or circumstance which prevents the performance of this Agreement and which is not within the reasonable contemplation of the Participating Owners.

(D) Termination of this Agreement shall not take effect until three months after the date on which the Supplementary Fund is notified thereof in writing by the International Group.

(E) The termination of this Agreement shall not affect rights or obligations in respect of any Incident which occurs prior to the date of termination.

X. *Withdrawal*

(A) A Participating Owner may withdraw from this Agreement –

(1) on giving not less than 3 months' written notice of withdrawal to his Club; or

(2) by virtue of an amendment thereto, provided always –

(i) that he exercised any right to vote against the said amendment when his Club sought the approval thereof of its members; and

(ii) that within 60 days of the amendment being approved by the membership of his Club he gives written notice of withdrawal to his Club; and

(iii) that such withdrawal shall take effect simultaneously with the entry-into-effect of the amendment, or on the date on which his notice is received by his Club, whichever is later.

(B) If a Participating Owner ceases to be the owner of a Relevant Ship he shall be deemed, in respect of that ship only, to withdraw from this Agreement with immediate effect, and he or his Club shall give written notice to the Supplementary Fund that he has ceased to be the owner of that Relevant Ship.

(C) A Participating Owner withdrawing from this Agreement shall have no further liability hereunder as from the date when his withdrawal takes effect; provided always that no withdrawal shall affect rights or obligations in respect of any Incident which occurs prior to that date.

XI. *Legal rights of Supplementary Fund*

(A) Though not a Party to this Agreement, the Supplementary Fund is intended to enjoy legally enforceable rights of Indemnification as described herein, and accordingly the Supplementary Fund shall be entitled to bring proceedings in its own name against the Participating Owner in respect of any claim it may have hereunder. Such proceedings may include an action brought by the Supplementary Fund against a Participating Owner to determine any issue relating to the construction, validity and/or performance of this Agreement.

(B) Notwithstanding Clause XI(A) above and Clause VII(A) above, the consent of the Supplementary Fund shall not be required to any amendment, termination or withdrawal made in accordance with the terms of this Agreement.

(C) The Parties to this Agreement authorise the International Group to agree terms with the Supplementary Fund on which a claim for Indemnification under this Agreement in respect of an Entered Ship (or previously Entered Ship), or proceedings to determine any issue of construction, validity and/or performance of this Agreement, may be brought directly against the Club insuring the Ship at the time of the Incident. They also agree that in the event of the Supplementary Fund bringing proceedings to enforce a claim against a Club in respect of an Entered Ship, the Club may require the Participating Owner to be joined in such proceedings.

XII. *Law and jurisdiction*

This Agreement shall be governed by English law and the English High Court of Justice shall have exclusive jurisdiction in relation to any disputes hereunder.

International Convention on Civil Liability for Bunker Oil Pollution Damage, 2001

The States Parties to this Convention,

RECALLING article 194 of the United Nations Convention on the Law of the Sea, 1982,[1] which provides that States shall take all measures necessary to prevent, reduce and control pollution of the marine environment,

RECALLING ALSO article 235 of that Convention, which provides that, with the objective of assuring prompt and adequate compensation in respect of all damage caused by pollution of the marine environment, States shall co-operate in the further development of relevant rules of international law,

NOTING the success of the International Convention on Civil Liability for Oil Pollution Damage, 1992[2] and the International Convention on the Establishment of an International Fund for Compensation for Oil Pollution Damage, 1992[3] in ensuring that compensation is available to persons who suffer damage caused by pollution resulting from the escape or discharge of oil carried in bulk at sea by ships,

NOTING ALSO the adoption of the International Convention on Liability and Compensation for Damage in Connection with the Carriage of Hazardous and Noxious Substances by Sea, 1996[4] in order to provide adequate, prompt and effective compensation for damage caused by incidents in connection with the carriage by sea of hazardous and noxious substances,

RECOGNIZING the importance of establishing strict liability for all forms of oil pollution which is linked to an appropriate limitation of the level of that liability,

CONSIDERING that complementary measures are necessary to ensure the payment of adequate, prompt and effective compensation for damage caused by pollution resulting from the escape or discharge of bunker oil from ships,

DESIRING to adopt uniform international rules and procedures for determining questions of liability and providing adequate compensation in such cases,

HAVE AGREED as follows:

Article 1: Definitions

For the purposes of this Convention:
1. "Ship" means any seagoing vessel and seaborne craft, of any type whatsoever.
2. "Person" means any individual or partnership or any public or private body, whether corporate or not, including a State or any of its constituent subdivisions.

* © Crown Copyright 2005.
1. Treaty Series No. 81 (1999) Cm 4524.
2. Treaty Series No. 106 (1975) Cmnd 6183.
3. Treaty Series No. 95 (1978) Cmnd 7383.
4. Miscellaneous No.5 (1997) Cm 3580.

3. "Shipowner" means the owner, including the registered owner, bareboat charterer, manager and operator of the ship.

4. "Registered owner" means the person or persons registered as the owner of the ship or, in the absence of registration, the person or persons owning the ship. However, in the case of a ship owned by a State and operated by a company which in that State is registered as the ship's operator, "registered owner" shall mean such company.

5. "Bunker oil" means any hydrocarbon mineral oil, including lubricating oil, used or intended to be used for the operation or propulsion of the ship, and any residues of such oil.

6. "Civil Liability Convention" means the International Convention on Civil Liability for Oil Pollution Damage, 1992, as amended.

7. "Preventive measures" means any reasonable measures taken by any person after an incident has occurred to prevent or minimise pollution damage.

8. "Incident" means any occurrence or series of occurrences having the same origin, which causes pollution damage or creates a grave and imminent threat of causing such damage.

9. "Pollution damage" means:

(a) loss or damage caused outside the ship by contamination resulting from the escape or discharge of bunker oil from the ship, wherever such escape or discharge may occur, provided that compensation for impairment of the environment other than loss of profit from such impairment shall be limited to costs of reasonable measures of reinstatement actually undertaken or to be undertaken; and

(b) the costs of preventive measures and further loss or damage caused by preventive measures.

10. "State of the ship's registry" means, in relation to a registered ship, the State of registration of the ship and, in relation to an unregistered ship, the State whose flag the ship is entitled to fly.

11. "Gross tonnage" means gross tonnage calculated in accordance with the tonnage measurement regulations contained in Annex 1 of the International Convention on Tonnage Measurement of Ships, 1969.[5]

12. "Organization" means the International Maritime Organization.

13. "Secretary-General" means the Secretary-General of the Organization.

Article 2: Scope of application

This Convention shall apply exclusively:

(a) to pollution damage caused:
   (i) in the territory, including the territorial sea, of a State Party, and
   (ii) in the exclusive economic zone of a State Party, established in accordance with international law, or, if a State Party has not established such a zone, in an area beyond and adjacent to the territorial sea of that State determined by that State in accordance with international law and extending not more than 200 nautical miles from the baselines from which the breadth of its territorial sea is measured;
(b) to preventive measures, wherever taken, to prevent or minimise such damage.

Article 3: Liability of the shipowner

1. Except as provided in paragraphs 3 and 4, the shipowner at the time of an incident shall be liable for pollution damage caused by any bunker oil on board or originating from the ship, provided that, if an incident consists of a series of occurrences having the same origin, the liability shall attach to the shipowner at the time of the first of such occurrences.

2. Where more than one person is liable in accordance with paragraph 1, their liability shall be joint and several.

3. No liability for pollution damage shall attach to the shipowner if the shipowner proves that:

---

5. Treaty Series No. 50 (1982) Cmnd 8716.

(a) the damage resulted from an act of war, hostilities, civil war, insurrection or a natural phenomenon of an exceptional, inevitable and irresistible character; or

(b) the damage was wholly caused by an act or omission done with the intent to cause damage by a third party; or

(c) the damage was wholly caused by the negligence or other wrongful act of any Government or other authority responsible for the maintenance of lights or other navigational aids in the exercise of that function.

4. If the shipowner proves that the pollution damage resulted wholly or partially either from an act or omission done with intent to cause damage by the person who suffered the damage or from the negligence of that person, the shipowner may be exonerated wholly or partially from liability to such person.

5. No claim for compensation for pollution damage shall be made against the shipowner otherwise than in accordance with this Convention.

6. Nothing in this Convention shall prejudice any right of recourse of the shipowner which exists independently of this Convention.

Article 4: Exclusions

1. This Convention shall not apply to pollution damage as defined in the Civil Liability Convention, whether or not compensation is payable in respect of it under that Convention.

2. Except as provided in paragraph 3, the provisions of this Convention shall not apply to warships, naval auxiliary or other ships owned or operated by a State and used, for the time being, only on Government non-commercial service.

3. A State Party may decide to apply this Convention to its warships or other ships described in paragraph 2, in which case it shall notify the Secretary-General thereof specifying the terms and conditions of such application.

4. With respect to ships owned by a State Party and used for commercial purposes, each State shall be subject to suit in the jurisdictions set forth in article 9 and shall waive all defences based on its status as a sovereign State.

Article 5: Incidents involving two or more ships

When an incident involving two or more ships occurs and pollution damage results therefrom, the shipowners of all the ships concerned, unless exonerated under article 3, shall be jointly and severally liable for all such damage which is not reasonably separable.

Article 6: Limitation of liability

Nothing in this Convention shall affect the right of the shipowner and the person or persons providing insurance or other financial security to limit liability under any applicable national or international regime, such as the Convention on Limitation of Liability for Maritime Claims, 1976,[6] as amended.

Article 7: Compulsory insurance or financial security

1. The registered owner of a ship having a gross tonnage greater than 1000 registered in a State Party shall be required to maintain insurance or other financial security, such as the guarantee of a bank or similar financial institution, to cover the liability of the registered owner for pollution damage in an amount equal to the limits of liability under the applicable national or international limitation regime, but in all cases, not exceeding an amount calculated in accordance with the Convention on Limitation of Liability for Maritime Claims, 1976, as amended.

2. A certificate attesting that insurance or other financial security is in force in accordance with the provisions of this Convention shall be issued to each ship after the appropriate

6. Treaty Series No. 13 (1990) Cm 955.

authority of a State Party has determined that the requirements of paragraph 1 have been complied with. With respect to a ship registered in a State Party such certificate shall be issued or certified by the appropriate authority of the State of the ship's registry; with respect to a ship not registered in a State Party it may be issued or certified by the appropriate authority of any State Party. This certificate shall be in the form of the model set out in the annex to this Convention and shall contain the following particulars:

(a) name of ship, distinctive number or letters and port of registry;
(b) name and principal place of business of the registered owner;
(c) IMO ship identification number;
(d) type and duration of security;
(e) name and principal place of business of insurer or other person giving security and, where appropriate, place of business where the insurance or security is established;
(f) period of validity of the certificate which shall not be longer than the period of validity of the insurance or other security.

3. (a) A State Party may authorise either an institution or an organisation recognised by it to issue the certificate referred to in paragraph 2. Such institution or organisation shall inform that State of the issue of each certificate. In all cases, the State Party shall fully guarantee the completeness and accuracy of the certificate so issued and shall undertake to ensure the necessary arrangements to satisfy this obligation.

(b) A State Party shall notify the Secretary-General of :
(i) the specific responsibilities and conditions of the authority delegated to an institution or organisation recognised by it;
(ii) the withdrawal of such authority; and
(iii) the date from which such authority or withdrawal of such authority takes effect.

An authority delegated shall not take effect prior to three months from the date on which notification to that effect was given to the Secretary-General.

(c) The institution or organisation authorised to issue certificates in accordance with this paragraph shall, as a minimum, be authorised to withdraw these certificates if the conditions under which they have been issued are not maintained. In all cases the institution or organisation shall report such withdrawal to the State on whose behalf the certificate was issued.

4. The certificate shall be in the official language or languages of the issuing State. If the language used is not English, French or Spanish, the text shall include a translation into one of these languages and, where the State so decides, the official language of the State may be omitted.

5. The certificate shall be carried on board the ship and a copy shall be deposited with the authorities who keep the record of the ship's registry or, if the ship is not registered in a State Party, with the authorities issuing or certifying the certificate.

6. An insurance or other financial security shall not satisfy the requirements of this article if it can cease, for reasons other than the expiry of the period of validity of the insurance or security specified in the certificate under paragraph 2 of this article, before three months have elapsed from the date on which notice of its termination is given to the authorities referred to in paragraph 5 of this article, unless the certificate has been surrendered to these authorities or a new certificate has been issued within the said period. The foregoing provisions shall similarly apply to any modification which results in the insurance or security no longer satisfying the requirements of this article.

7. The State of the ship's registry shall, subject to the provisions of this article, determine the conditions of issue and validity of the certificate.

8. Nothing in this Convention shall be construed as preventing a State Party from relying on information obtained from other States or the Organization or other international organisations relating to the financial standing of providers of insurance or financial security for the purposes of this Convention. In such cases, the State Party relying on such information is not relieved of its responsibility as a State issuing the certificate required by paragraph 2.

9. Certificates issued or certified under the authority of a State Party shall be accepted by other States Parties for the purposes of this Convention and shall be regarded by other States Parties as having the same force as certificates issued or certified by them even if issued or certified in respect of a ship not registered in a State Party. A State Party may at any time request consultation with the issuing or certifying State should it believe that the insurer or guarantor named in the insurance certificate is not financially capable of meeting the obligations imposed by this Convention.

10. Any claim for compensation for pollution damage may be brought directly against the insurer or other person providing financial security for the registered owner's liability for pollution damage. In such a case the defendant may invoke the defences (other than bankruptcy or winding up of the shipowner) which the shipowner would have been entitled to invoke, including limitation pursuant to article 6. Furthermore, even if the shipowner is not entitled to limitation of liability according to article 6, the defendant may limit liability to an amount equal to the amount of the insurance or other financial security required to be maintained in accordance with paragraph 1. Moreover, the defendant may invoke the defence that the pollution damage resulted from the wilful misconduct of the shipowner, but the defendant shall not invoke any other defence which the defendant might have been entitled to invoke in proceedings brought by the shipowner against the defendant. The defendant shall in any event have the right to require the shipowner to be joined in the proceedings.

11. A State Party shall not permit a ship under its flag to which this article applies to operate at any time, unless a certificate has been issued under paragraphs 2 or 14.

12. Subject to the provisions of this article, each State Party shall ensure, under its national law, that insurance or other security, to the extent specified in paragraph 1, is in force in respect of any ship having a gross tonnage greater than 1000, wherever registered, entering or leaving a port in its territory, or arriving at or leaving an offshore facility in its territorial sea.

13. Notwithstanding the provisions of paragraph 5, a State Party may notify the Secretary-General that, for the purposes of paragraph 12, ships are not required to carry on board or to produce the certificate required by paragraph 2, when entering or leaving ports or arriving at or leaving from offshore facilities in its territory, provided that the State Party which issues the certificate required by paragraph 2 has notified the Secretary-General that it maintains records in an electronic format, accessible to all States Parties, attesting the existence of the certificate and enabling States Parties to discharge their obligations under paragraph 12.

14. If insurance or other financial security is not maintained in respect of a ship owned by a State Party, the provisions of this article relating thereto shall not be applicable to such ship, but the ship shall carry a certificate issued by the appropriate authority of the State of the ship's registry stating that the ship is owned by that State and that the ship's liability is covered within the limit prescribed in accordance with paragraph 1. Such a certificate shall follow as closely as possible the model prescribed by paragraph 2.

15. A State may, at the time of ratification, acceptance, approval of, or accession to this Convention, or at any time thereafter, declare that this article does not apply to ships operating exclusively within the area of that State referred to in article 2(a)(i).

Article 8: Time limits

Rights to compensation under this Convention shall be extinguished unless an action is brought thereunder within three years from the date when the damage occurred. However, in no case shall an action be brought more than six years from the date of the incident which caused the damage. Where the incident consists of a series of occurrences, the six-years' period shall run from the date of the first such occurrence.

Article 9: Jurisdiction

1. Where an incident has caused pollution damage in the territory, including the territorial sea, or in an area referred to in article 2(a)(ii) of one or more States Parties, or preven-

tive measures have been taken to prevent or minimise pollution damage in such territory, including the territorial sea, or in such area, actions for compensation against the shipowner, insurer or other person providing security for the shipowner's liability may be brought only in the courts of any such States Parties.

2. Reasonable notice of any action taken under paragraph 1 shall be given to each defendant.

3. Each State Party shall ensure that its courts have jurisdiction to entertain actions for compensation under this Convention.

Article 10: Recognition and enforcement

1. Any judgment given by a Court with jurisdiction in accordance with article 9 which is enforceable in the State of origin where it is no longer subject to ordinary forms of review, shall be recognised in any State Party, except:
   (a) where the judgement was obtained by fraud; or
   (b) where the defendant was not given reasonable notice and a fair opportunity to present his or her case.

2. A judgment recognised under paragraph 1 shall be enforceable in each State Party as soon as the formalities required in that State have been complied with. The formalities shall not permit the merits of the case to be re-opened.

Article 11: Supersession Clause

This Convention shall supersede any Convention in force or open for signature, ratification or accession at the date on which this Convention is opened for signature, but only to the extent that such Convention would be in conflict with it; however, nothing in this article shall affect the obligations of States Parties to States not party to this Convention arising under such Convention.

Article 12: Signature, ratification, acceptance, approval and accession

1. This Convention shall be open for signature at the Headquarters of the Organization from 1 October 2001 until 30 September 2002 and shall thereafter remain open for accession.

2. States may express their consent to be bound by this Convention by:
   (a) signature without reservation as to ratification, acceptance or approval;
   (b) signature subject to ratification, acceptance or approval followed by ratification, acceptance or approval; or
   (c) accession.

3. Ratification, acceptance, approval or accession shall be effected by the deposit of an instrument to that effect with the Secretary-General.

4. Any instrument of ratification, acceptance, approval or accession deposited after the entry into force of an amendment to this Convention with respect to all existing State Parties, or after the completion of all measures required for the entry into force of the amendment with respect to those State Parties shall be deemed to apply to this Convention as modified by the amendment.

Article 13: States with more than one system of law

1. If a State has two or more territorial units in which different systems of law are applicable in relation to matters dealt with in this Convention, it may at the time of signature, ratification, acceptance, approval or accession declare that this Convention shall extend to all its territorial units or only to one or more of them and may modify this declaration by submitting another declaration at any time.

2. Any such declaration shall be notified to the Secretary-General and shall state expressly the territorial units to which this Convention applies.

3. In relation to a State Party which has made such a declaration:
(a) in the definition of "registered owner" in article 1(4), references to a State shall be construed as references to such a territorial unit;
(b) references to the State of a ship's registry and, in relation to a compulsory insurance certificate, to the issuing or certifying State, shall be construed as referring to the territorial unit respectively in which the ship is registered and which issues or certifies the certificate;
(c) references in this Convention to the requirements of national law shall be construed as references to the requirements of the law of the relevant territorial unit; and
(d) references in articles 9 and 10 to courts, and to judgements which must be recognised in States Parties, shall be construed as references respectively to courts of, and to judgements which must be recognised in, the relevant territorial unit.

Article 14: Entry into Force

1. This Convention shall enter into force one year following the date on which 18 States, including five States each with ships whose combined gross tonnage is not less than 1 million, have either signed it without reservation as to ratification, acceptance or approval or have deposited instruments of ratification, acceptance, approval or accession with the Secretary-General.

2. For any State which ratifies, accepts, approves or accedes to it after the conditions in paragraph 1 for entry into force have been met, this Convention shall enter into force three months after the date of deposit by such State of the appropriate instrument.

Article 15: Denunciation

1. This Convention may be denounced by any State Party at any time after the date on which this Convention comes into force for that State.

2. Denunciation shall be effected by the deposit of an instrument with the Secretary-General.

3. A denunciation shall take effect one year, or such longer period as may be specified in the instrument of denunciation, after its deposit with the Secretary- General.

Article 16: Revision or amendment

1. A conference for the purpose of revising or amending this Convention may be convened by the Organization.

2. The Organization shall convene a conference of the States Parties for revising or amending this Convention at the request of not less than one-third of the States Parties.

Article 17: Depositary

1. This Convention shall be deposited with the Secretary-General.
2. The Secretary-General shall:
(a) inform all States which have signed or acceded to this Convention of:
   (i) each new signature or deposit of instrument together with the date thereof;
   (ii) the date of entry into force of this Convention;
   (iii) the deposit of any instrument of denunciation of this Convention together with the date of the deposit and the date on which the denunciation takes effect; and
   (iv) other declarations and notifications made under this Convention.
(b) transmit certified true copies of this Convention to all Signatory States and to all States which accede to this Convention.

Article 18: Transmission to United Nations

As soon as this Convention comes into force, the text shall be transmitted by the Secretary-General to the Secretariat of the United Nations for registration and publication in accordance with Article 102 of the Charter of the United Nations.

Article 19: Languages

This Convention is established in a single original in the Arabic, Chinese, English, French, Russian and Spanish languages, each text being equally authentic.

DONE AT LONDON this twenty-third day of March two thousand and one.

IN WITNESS WHEREOF the undersigned being duly authorised by their respective Governments for that purpose have signed this Convention.

Certificate of insurance or other financial security in respect of civil liability for bunker oil pollution damage

Issued in accordance with the provisions of article 7 of the International Convention on Civil Liability for Bunker Oil Pollution Damage, 2001

Name of Ship

Distinctive Number or letters

IMO Ship

Identification

Number Port of Registry

Name and full address of the principal place of business of the registered owner.

This is to certify that there is in force in respect of the above-named ship a policy of insurance or other financial security satisfying the requirements of article 7 of the International Convention on Civil Liability for Bunker Oil Pollution Damage, 2001.

Type of Security

....
....

Duration of Security

....
....

Name and address of the insurer(s)and/or guarantor(s)
Name

....
....

Address

....
....

This certificate is valid until

....

Issued or certified by the Government of

....
....

(Full designation of the State)
OR

The following text should be used when a State Party avails itself of article 7(3)
The present certificate is issued under the authority of the Government of ....
(full designation of the State) by .... (name of institution or organisation)
At ....
On ....
(Place) (Date)

....
....

(Signature and Title of issuing or certifying official)

Explanatory Notes:

1. If desired, the designation of the State may include a reference to the competent public authority of the country where the Certificate is issued.
2. If the total amount of security has been furnished by more than one source, the amount of each of them should be indicated.
3. If security is furnished in several forms, these should be enumerated.
4. The entry "Duration of Security" must stipulate the date on which such security takes effect.
5. The entry "Address" of the insurer(s) and/or guarantor(s) must indicate the principal place of business of the insurer(s) and/or guarantor(s). If appropriate, the place of business where the insurance or other security is established shall be indicated.

International Convention on Liability and Compensation for Damage in Connection with the Carriage of Hazardous and Noxious Substances by Sea, 1996

THE STATES PARTIES TO THE PRESENT CONVENTION,

CONSCIOUS of the dangers posed by the world-wide carriage by sea of hazardous and noxious substances,

CONVINCED of the need to ensure that adequate, prompt and effective compensation is available to persons who suffer damage caused by incidents in connection with the carriage by sea of such substances,

DESIRING to adopt uniform international rules and procedures for determining questions of liability and compensation in respect of such damage,

CONSIDERING that the economic consequences of damage caused by the carriage by sea of hazardous and noxious substances should be shared by the shipping industry and the cargo interests involved,

HAVE AGREED as follows:

CHAPTER I – GENERAL PROVISIONS

Definitions

Article 1

For the purposes of this Convention:

1. "Ship" means any seagoing vessel and seaborne craft, of any type whatsoever.
2. "Person" means any individual or partnership or any public or private body, whether corporate or not, including a State or any of its constituent subdivisions.
3. "Owner" means the person or persons registered as the owner of the ship or, in the absence of registration, the person or persons owning the ship. However, in the case of a ship owned by a State and operated by a company which in that State is registered as the ship's operator, "owner" shall mean such company.
4. "Receiver" means either:
   (a) the person who physically receives contributing cargo discharged in the ports and terminals of a State Party; provided that if at the time of receipt the person who physically receives the cargo acts as an agent for another who is subject to the jurisdiction of any State Party, then the principal shall be deemed to be the receiver, if the agent discloses the principal to the HNS Fund; or
   (b) the person in the State Party who in accordance with the national law of that State Party 17 is deemed to be the receiver of contributing cargo discharged in the ports and terminals provided that the total contributing cargo received according to such national law is substantially the same as that which would have been received under (a).
5. "Hazardous and noxious substances" (HNS) means:
   (a) any substances, materials and Articles carried on board a ship as cargo, referred to in (i) to (vii) below:

381

(i) oils carried in bulk listed in appendix I of Annex I to the International Convention for the Prevention of Pollution from Ships, 1973, as modified by the Protocol of 1978 relating thereto, as amended;

(ii) noxious liquid substances carried in bulk referred to in appendix II of Annex II to the International Convention for the Prevention of Pollution from Ships, 1973, as modified by the Protocol of 1978 relating thereto, as amended, and those substances and mixtures provisionally categorised as falling in pollution category A, B, C or D in accordance with regulation 3(4) of the said Annex II;

(iii) dangerous liquid substances carried in bulk listed in chapter 17 of the International Code for the Construction and Equipment of Ships Carrying Dangerous Chemicals in Bulk, 1983, as amended, and the dangerous products for which the preliminary suitable conditions for the carriage have been prescribed by the Administration and port administrations involved in accordance with paragraph 1.1.3 of the Code;

(iv) dangerous, hazardous and harmful substances, materials and articles in packaged form covered by the International Maritime Dangerous Goods Code, as amended;

(v) liquefied gases as listed in chapter 19 of the International Code for the Construction and Equipment of Ships Carrying Liquefied Gases in Bulk, 1983, as amended, and the products for which preliminary suitable conditions for the carriage have been prescribed by the Administration and port administrations involved in accordance with paragraph 1.1.6 of the Code;

(vi) liquid substances carried in bulk with a flashpoint not exceeding 60 C (measured by a closed cup test);

(vii) solid bulk materials possessing chemical hazards covered by appendix B of the Code of Safe Practice for Solid Bulk Cargoes, as amended, to the extent that these substances are also subject to the provisions of the International Maritime Dangerous Goods Code when carried in packaged form; and

(b) residues from the previous carriage in bulk of substances referred to in (a)(i) to (iii) and (v) to (vii) above.

6. "Damage" means:

(a) loss of life or personal injury on board or outside the ship carrying the hazardous and noxious substances caused by those substances;

(b) loss of or damage to property outside the ship carrying the hazardous and noxious substances caused by those substances;

(c) loss or damage by contamination of the environment caused by the hazardous and noxious substances, provided that compensation for impairment of the environment other than loss of profit from such impairment shall be limited to costs of reasonable measures of reinstatement actually undertaken or to be undertaken; and

(d) the costs of preventive measures and further loss or damage caused by preventive measures. Where it is not reasonably possible to separate damage caused by the hazardous and noxious substances from that caused by other factors, all such damage shall be deemed to be caused by the hazardous and noxious substances except if, and to the extent that, the damage caused by other factors is damage of a type referred to in Article 4, paragraph 3. In this paragraph, "caused by those substances" means caused by the hazardous or noxious nature of the substances.

7. "Preventive measures" means any reasonable measures taken by any person after an incident has occurred to prevent or minimise damage.

8. "Incident" means any occurrence or series of occurrences having the same origin, which 36 causes damage or creates a grave and imminent threat of causing damage.

9. "Carriage by sea" means the period from the time when the hazardous and noxious substances enter any part of the ship's equipment, on loading, to the time they cease to be present in any part of the ship's equipment, on discharge. If no ship's equipment is used, the period begins and ends respectively when the hazardous and noxious substances cross the ship's rail.

10. "Contributing cargo" means any hazardous and noxious substances which are carried by sea as cargo to a port or terminal in the territory of a State Party and discharged in that State. Cargo in transit which is transferred directly, or through a port or terminal, from one ship to another, either wholly or in part, in the course of carriage from the port or terminal of original loading to the port or terminal of final destination shall be considered as contributing cargo only in respect of receipt at the final destination.

11. The "HNS Fund" means the International Hazardous and Noxious Substances Fund established under Article 13.

12. "Unit of account" means the Special Drawing Right as defined by the International Monetary Fund.

13. "State of the ship's registry" means in relation to a registered ship the State of registration of the ship, and in relation to an unregistered ship the State whose flag the ship is entitled to fly.

14. "Terminal" means any site for the storage of hazardous and noxious substances received from waterborne transportation, including any facility situated off-shore and linked by pipeline or otherwise to such site.

15. "Director" means the Director of the HNS Fund.

16. "Organization" means the International Maritime Organization.

17. "Secretary-General" means the Secretary-General of the Organization.

Annexes

Article 2

The Annexes to this Convention shall constitute an integral part of this Convention.

Scope of application

Article 3

This Convention shall apply exclusively:

(a) to any damage caused in the territory, including the territorial sea, of a State Party;

(b) to damage by contamination of the environment caused in the exclusive economic zone of a State Party, established in accordance with international law, or, if a State Party has not established such a zone, in an area beyond and adjacent to the territorial sea of that State determined by that State in accordance with international law and extending not more than 200 nautical miles from the baselines from which the breadth of its territorial sea is measured;

(c) to damage, other than damage by contamination of the environment, caused outside the 54 territory, including the territorial sea, of any State, if this damage has been caused by a substance carried on board a ship registered in a State Party or, in the case of an unregistered ship, on board a ship entitled to fly the flag of a State Party; and

(d) to preventive measures, wherever taken.

Article 4

1. This Convention shall apply to claims, other than claims arising out of any contract for the carriage of goods and passengers, for damage arising from the carriage of hazardous and noxious substances by sea.

2. This Convention shall not apply to the extent that its provisions are incompatible with those of the applicable law relating to workers' compensation or social security schemes.

3. This Convention shall not apply:

(a) to pollution damage as defined in the International Convention on Civil Liability for Oil Pollution Damage, 1969, as amended, whether or not compensation is payable in respect of it under that Convention; and

(b) to damage caused by a radioactive material of class 7 either in the International Maritime Dangerous Goods Code, as amended, or in appendix B of the Code of Safe Practice for Solid Bulk Cargoes, as amended.

4. Except as provided in paragraph 5, the provisions of this Convention shall not apply to warships, naval auxiliary or other ships owned or operated by a State and used, for the time being, only on Government non-commercial service.

5. A State Party may decide to apply this Convention to its warships or other vessels described in paragraph 4, in which case it shall notify the Secretary-General thereof specifying the terms and conditions of such application.

6. With respect to ships owned by a State Party and used for commercial purposes, each State shall be subject to suit in the jurisdictions set forth in Article 38 and shall waive all defences based on its status as a sovereign State.

Article 5

1. A State may, at the time of ratification, acceptance, approval of, or accession to, this Convention, or any time thereafter, declare that this Convention does not apply to ships:
   (a) which do not exceed 200 gross tonnage; and
   (b) which carry hazardous and noxious substances only in packaged form; and
   (c) while they are engaged on voyages between ports or facilities of that State.

2. Where two neighbouring States agree that this Convention does not apply also to ships which are covered by paragraph 1(a) and (b) while engaged on voyages between ports or facilities of those States, the States concerned may declare that the exclusion from the application of this Convention declared under paragraph 1 covers also ships referred to in this paragraph.

3. Any State which has made the declaration under paragraph 1 or 2 may withdraw such declaration at any time.

4. A declaration made under paragraph 1 or 2, and the withdrawal of the declaration made under paragraph 3, shall be deposited with the Secretary-General who shall, after the entry into force of this Convention, communicate it to the Director.

5. Where a State has made a declaration under paragraph 1 or 2 and has not withdrawn it, hazardous and noxious substances carried on board ships covered by that paragraph shall not be considered to be contributing cargo for the purpose of application of Articles 18, 20, Article 21, paragraph 5 and Article 43.

6. The HNS Fund is not liable to pay compensation for damage caused by substances carried by a ship to which the Convention does not apply pursuant to a declaration made under paragraph 1 or 2, to the extent that:
   (a) the damage as defined in Article 1, paragraph 6(a), (b) or (c) was caused in:
      (i) the territory, including the territorial sea, of the State which has made the declaration, or in the case of neighbouring States which have made a declaration under paragraph 2, of either of them; or
      (ii) the exclusive economic zone, or area mentioned in Article 3(b), of the State or States referred to in (i);
   (b) the damage includes measures taken to prevent or minimise such damage.

Duties of state parties

Article 6

Each State Party shall ensure that any obligation arising under this Convention is fulfilled and shall take appropriate measures under its law including the imposing of sanctions as it may deem necessary, with a view to the effective execution of any such obligation.

CHAPTER II – LIABILITY

Liability of the owner

Article 7

1. Except as provided in paragraphs 2 and 3, the owner at the time of an incident shall be liable for damage caused by any hazardous and noxious substances in connection with their

carriage by sea on board the ship, provided that if an incident consists of a series of occurrences having the same origin the liability shall attach to the owner at the time of the first of such occurrences.

2. No liability shall attach to the owner if the owner proves that:

    (a) the damage resulted from an act of war, hostilities, civil war, insurrection or a natural phenomenon of an exceptional, inevitable and irresistible character; or

    (b) the damage was wholly caused by an act or omission done with the intent to cause damage by a third party; or

    (c) the damage was wholly caused by the negligence or other wrongful act of any Government or other authority responsible for the maintenance of lights or other navigational aids in the exercise of that function; or

    (d) the failure of the shipper or any other person to furnish information concerning the hazardous and noxious nature of the substances shipped either

        (i) has caused the damage, wholly or partly; or

        (ii) has led the owner not to obtain insurance in accordance with Article 12; provided that neither the owner nor its servants or agents knew or ought reasonably to have known of the hazardous and noxious nature of the substances shipped.

3. If the owner proves that the damage resulted wholly or partly either from an act or omission done with intent to cause damage by the person who suffered the damage or from the negligence of that person, the owner may be exonerated wholly or partially from liability to such person.

4. No claim for compensation for damage shall be made against the owner otherwise than in accordance with this Convention.

5. Subject to paragraph 6, no claim for compensation for damage under this Convention or otherwise may be made against:

    (a) the servants or agents of the owner or the members of the crew;

    (b) the pilot or any other person who, without being a member of the crew, performs services for the ship;

    (c) any charterer (howsoever described, including a bareboat charterer), manager or operator of the ship;

    (d) any person performing salvage operations with the consent of the owner or on the instructions of a competent public authority;

    (e) any person taking preventive measures; and

    (f) the servants or agents of persons mentioned in (c), (d) and (e);

unless the damage resulted from their personal act or omission, committed with the intent to cause such damage, or recklessly and with knowledge that such damage would probably result.

6. Nothing in this Convention shall prejudice any existing right of recourse of the owner against any third party, including, but not limited to, the shipper or the receiver of the substance causing the damage, or the persons indicated in paragraph 5.

Incidents involving two or more ships

Article 8

1. Whenever damage has resulted from an incident involving two or more ships each of which is carrying hazardous and noxious substances, each owner, unless exonerated under Article 7, shall be liable for the damage. The owners shall be jointly and severally liable for all such damage which is not reasonably separable.

2. However, owners shall be entitled to the limits of liability applicable to each of them under Article 9.

3. Nothing in this Article shall prejudice any right of recourse of an owner against any other owner.

Limitation of liability

Article 9

1. The owner of a ship shall be entitled to limit liability under this Convention in respect of any one incident to an aggregate amount calculated as follows:
   (a) 10 million units of account for a ship not exceeding 2,000 units of tonnage; and
   (b) for a ship with a tonnage in excess thereof, the following amount in addition to that mentioned in (a):

for each unit of tonnage from 2,001 to 50,000 units of tonnage, 1,500 units of account for each unit of tonnage in excess of 50,000 units of tonnage, 360 units of account provided, however, that this aggregate amount shall not in any event exceed 100 million units of account.

2. The owner shall not be entitled to limit liability under this Convention if it is proved that the damage resulted from the personal act or omission of the owner, committed with the intent to cause such damage, or recklessly and with knowledge that such damage would probably result.

3. The owner shall, for the purpose of benefiting from the limitation provided for in paragraph 1, constitute a fund for the total sum representing the limit of liability established in accordance with paragraph 1 with the court or other competent authority of any one of the States Parties in which action is brought under Article 38 or, if no action is brought, with any court or other competent authority in any one of the States Parties in which an action can be brought under Article 38. The fund can be constituted either by depositing the sum or by producing a bank guarantee or other guarantee, acceptable under the law of the State Party where the fund is constituted, and considered to be adequate by the court or other competent authority.

4. Subject to the provisions of Article 11, the fund shall be distributed among the claimants in proportion to the amounts of their established claims.

5. If before the fund is distributed the owner or any of the servants or agents of the owner or any person providing to the owner insurance or other financial security has as a result of the incident in question, paid compensation for damage, such person shall, up to the amount that person has paid, acquire by subrogation the rights which the person so compensated would have enjoyed under this Convention.

6. The right of subrogation provided for in paragraph 5 may also be exercised by a person other than those mentioned therein in respect of any amount of compensation for damage which such person may have paid but only to the extent that such subrogation is permitted under the applicable national law.

7. Where owners or other persons establish that they may be compelled to pay at a later date in whole or in part any such amount of compensation, with regard to which the right of subrogation would have been enjoyed under paragraphs 5 or 6 had the compensation been paid before the fund was distributed, the court or other competent authority of the State where the fund has been constituted may order that a sufficient sum shall be provisionally set aside to enable such person at such later date to enforce the claim against the fund.

8. Claims in respect of expenses reasonably incurred or sacrifices reasonably made by the owner voluntarily to prevent or minimise damage shall rank equally with other claims against the fund.

9. (a) The amounts mentioned in paragraph 1 shall be converted into national currency on the basis of the value of that currency by reference to the Special Drawing Right on the date of the constitution of the fund referred to in paragraph 3. The value of the national currency, in terms of the Special Drawing Right, of a State Party which is a member of the International Monetary Fund, shall be calculated in accordance with the method of valuation applied by the International Monetary Fund in effect on the date in question for its operations and transactions. The value of the national currency, in terms of the Special Drawing Right, of a State Party which is not a member of the International Monetary Fund, shall be calculated in a manner determined by that State.

(b) Nevertheless, a State Party which is not a member of the International Monetary Fund and whose law does not permit the application of the provisions of paragraph 9(a) may, at the time of ratification, acceptance, approval of or accession to this Convention or at any time thereafter, declare that the unit of account referred to in paragraph 9(a) shall be equal to 15 gold francs. The gold franc referred to in this paragraph corresponds to sixty-five-and-a-half milligrammes of gold of millesimal fineness nine hundred. The conversion of the gold franc into the national currency shall be made according to the law of the State concerned.

(c) The calculation mentioned in the last sentence of paragraph 9(a) and the conversion mentioned in paragraph 9(b) shall be made in such manner as to express in the national currency of the State Party as far as possible the same real value for the amounts in paragraph 1 as would result from the application of the first two sentences of paragraph 9(a). States Parties shall communicate to the Secretary-General the manner of calculation pursuant to paragraph 9(a), or the result of the conversion in paragraph 9(b) as the case may be, when depositing an instrument of ratification, acceptance, approval of or accession to this Convention and whenever there is a change in either.

10. For the purpose of this Article the ship's tonnage shall be the gross tonnage calculated in accordance with the tonnage measurement regulations contained in Annex I of the International Convention on Tonnage Measurement of Ships, 1969.

11. The insurer or other person providing financial security shall be entitled to constitute a fund in accordance with this Article on the same conditions and having the same effect as if it were constituted by the owner. Such a fund may be constituted even if, under the provisions of paragraph 2, the owner is not entitled to limitation of liability, but its constitution shall in that case not prejudice the rights of any claimant against the owner.

Article 10

1. Where the owner, after an incident, has constituted a fund in accordance with Article 9 and is entitled to limit liability:
   (a) no person having a claim for damage arising out of that incident shall be entitled to exercise any right against any other assets of the owner in respect of such claim; and
   (b) the court or other competent authority of any State Party shall order the release of any ship or other property belonging to the owner which has been arrested in respect of a claim for damage arising out of that incident, and shall similarly release any bail or other security furnished to avoid such arrest.

2. The foregoing shall, however, only apply if the claimant has access to the court administering the fund and the fund is actually available in respect of the claim.

Death and injury

Article 11

Claims in respect of death or personal injury have priority over other claims save to the extent that the aggregate of such claims exceeds two-thirds of the total amount established in accordance with Article 9, paragraph 1.

Compulsory insurance of the owner

Article 12

1. The owner of a ship registered in a State Party and actually carrying hazardous and noxious substances shall be required to maintain insurance or other financial security, such as the guarantee of a bank or similar financial institution, in the sums fixed by applying the limits of liability prescribed in Article 9, paragraph 1, to cover liability for damage under this Convention.

2. A compulsory insurance certificate attesting that insurance or other financial security is in force in accordance with the provisions of this Convention shall be issued to each ship after the appropriate authority of a State Party has determined that the requirements of paragraph 1 have been complied with. With respect to a ship registered in a State Party such compulsory insurance certificate shall be issued or certified by the appropriate authority of the State of the ship's registry; with respect to a ship not registered in a State Party it may be issued or certified by the appropriate authority of any State Party. This compulsory insurance certificate shall be in the form of the model set out in Annex I and shall contain the following particulars:

    (a) name of the ship, distinctive number or letters and port of registry;

    (b) name and principal place of business of the owner;

    (c) IMO ship identification number;

    (d) type and duration of security;

    (e) name and principal place of business of insurer or other person giving security and, where appropriate, place of business where the insurance or security is established; and

    (f) period of validity of certificate, which shall not be longer than the period of validity of the insurance or other security.

3. The compulsory insurance certificate shall be in the official language or languages of the issuing State. If the language used is neither English, nor French nor Spanish, the text shall include a translation into one of these languages.

4. The compulsory insurance certificate shall be carried on board the ship and a copy shall be deposited with the authorities who keep the record of the ship's registry or, if the ship is not registered in a State Party, with the authority of the State issuing or certifying the certificate.

5. An insurance or other financial security shall not satisfy the requirements of this Article if it can cease, for reasons other than the expiry of the period of validity of the insurance or security specified in the certificate under paragraph 2, before three months have elapsed from the date on which notice of its termination is given to the authorities referred to in paragraph 4, unless the compulsory insurance certificate has been surrendered to these authorities or a new certificate has been issued within the said period. The foregoing provisions shall similarly apply to any modification which results in the insurance or security no longer satisfying the requirements of this Article.

6. The State of the ship's registry shall, subject to the provisions of this Article, determine the conditions of issue and validity of the compulsory insurance certificate.

7. Compulsory insurance certificates issued or certified under the authority of a State Party in accordance with paragraph 2 shall be accepted by other States Parties for the purposes of this Convention and shall be regarded by other States Parties as having the same force as compulsory insurance certificates issued or certified by them even if issued or certified in respect of a ship not registered in a State Party. A State Party may at any time request consultation with the issuing or certifying State should it believe that the insurer or guarantor named in the compulsory insurance certificate is not financially capable of meeting the obligations imposed by this Convention.

8. Any claim for compensation for damage may be brought directly against the insurer or other person providing financial security for the owner's liability for damage. In such case the defendant may, even if the owner is not entitled to limitation of liability, benefit from the limit of liability prescribed in accordance with paragraph 1. The defendant may further invoke the defences (other than the bankruptcy or winding up of the owner) which the owner would have been entitled to invoke. Furthermore, the defendant may invoke the defence that the damage resulted from the wilful misconduct of the owner, but the defendant shall not invoke any other defence which the defendant might have been entitled to invoke in proceedings brought by the owner against the defendant. The defendant shall in any event have the right to require the owner to be joined in the proceedings.

9. Any sums provided by insurance or by other financial security maintained in accordance with paragraph 1 shall be available exclusively for the satisfaction of claims under this Convention.

10. A State Party shall not permit a ship under its flag to which this Article applies to trade unless a certificate has been issued under paragraph 2 or 12.

11. Subject to the provisions of this Article, each State Party shall ensure, under its national law, that insurance or other security in the sums specified in paragraph 1 is in force in respect of any ship, wherever registered, entering or leaving a port in its territory, or arriving at or leaving an offshore facility in its territorial sea.

12. If insurance or other financial security is not maintained in respect of a ship owned by a State Party, the provisions of this Article relating thereto shall not be applicable to such ship, but the ship shall carry a compulsory insurance certificate issued by the appropriate authorities of the State of the ship's registry stating that the ship is owned by that State and that the ship's liability is covered within the limit prescribed in accordance with paragraph 1. Such a compulsory insurance certificate shall follow as closely as possible the model prescribed by paragraph 2.

CHAPTER III – COMPENSATION BY THE INTERNATIONAL HAZARDOUS AND NOXIOUS SUBSTANCES FUND (HNS FUND) ESTABLISHMENT OF THE HNS FUND

Article 13

1. The International Hazardous and Noxious Substances Fund (HNS Fund) is hereby established with the following aims:
   (a) to provide compensation for damage in connection with the carriage of hazardous and noxious substances by sea, to the extent that the protection afforded by chapter II is inadequate or not available; and
   (b) to give effect to the related tasks set out in Article 15.

2. The HNS Fund shall in each State Party be recognised as a legal person capable under the 166 laws of that State of assuming rights and obligations and of being a party in legal proceedings before the courts of that State. Each State Party shall recognise the Director as the legal representative of the HNS Fund.

Compensation

Article 14

1. For the purpose of fulfilling its function under Article 13, paragraph 1(a), the HNS Fund shall pay compensation to any person suffering damage if such person has been unable to obtain full and adequate compensation for the damage under the terms of chapter II:
   (a) because no liability for the damage arises under chapter II;
   (b) because the owner liable for the damage under chapter II is financially incapable of meeting the obligations under this Convention in full and any financial security that may be provided under chapter II does not cover or is insufficient to satisfy the claims for compensation for damage; an owner being treated as financially incapable of meeting these obligations and a financial security being treated as insufficient if the person suffering the damage has been unable to obtain full satisfaction of the amount of compensation due under chapter II after having taken all reasonable steps to pursue the available legal remedies;
   (c) because the damage exceeds the owner's liability under the terms of chapter II.

2. Expenses reasonably incurred or sacrifices reasonably made by the owner voluntarily to prevent or minimise damage shall be treated as damage for the purposes of this Article.

3. The HNS Fund shall incur no obligation under the preceding paragraphs if:
   (a) it proves that the damage resulted from an act of war, hostilities, civil war or insurrection or was caused by hazardous and noxious substances which had escaped or been discharged from a warship or other ship owned or operated by a State and used, at the time of the incident, only on Government non-commercial service; or

(b) the claimant cannot prove that there is a reasonable probability that the damage resulted from an incident involving one or more ships.

4. If the HNS Fund proves that the damage resulted wholly or partly either from an act or omission done with intent to cause damage by the person who suffered the damage or from the negligence of that person, the HNS Fund may be exonerated wholly or partially from its obligation to pay compensation to such person. The HNS Fund shall in any event be exonerated to the extent that the owner may have been exonerated under Article 7, paragraph 3. However, there shall be no such exoneration of the HNS Fund with regard to preventive measures.

5. (a) Except as otherwise provided in subparagraph (b), the aggregate amount of compensation payable by the HNS Fund under this Article shall in respect of any one incident be limited, so that the total sum of that amount and any amount of compensation actually paid under chapter II for damage within the scope of application of this Convention as defined in Article 3 shall not exceed 250 million units of account.

(b) The aggregate amount of compensation payable by the HNS Fund under this Article for damage resulting from a natural phenomenon of an exceptional, inevitable and irresistible character shall not exceed 250 million units of account.

(c) Interest accrued on a fund constituted in accordance with Article 9, paragraph 3, if any, shall not be taken into account for the computation of the maximum compensation payable by the HNS Fund under this Article.

(d) The amounts mentioned in this Article shall be converted into national currency on the basis of the value of that currency with reference to the Special Drawing Right on the date of the decision of the Assembly of the HNS Fund as to the first date of payment of compensation.

6. Where the amount of established claims against the HNS Fund exceeds the aggregate amount of compensation payable under paragraph 5, the amount available shall be distributed in such a manner that the proportion between any established claim and the amount of compensation actually recovered by the claimant under this Convention shall be the same for all claimants. Claims in respect of death or personal injury shall have priority over other claims, however, save to the extent that the aggregate of such claims exceeds two-thirds of the total amount established in accordance with paragraph 5.

7. The Assembly of the HNS Fund may decide that, in exceptional cases, compensation in accordance with this Convention can be paid even if the owner has not constituted a fund in accordance with chapter II. In such cases paragraph 5(d) applies accordingly.

Related tasks of the HNS Fund

Article 15

For the purpose of fulfilling its function under Article 13, paragraph 1(a), the HNS Fund shall have the following tasks:

(a) to consider claims made against the HNS Fund;

(b) to prepare an estimate in the form of a budget for each calendar year of:

Expenditure:

(i) costs and expenses of the administration of the HNS Fund in the relevant year and any deficit from operations in the preceding years; and

(ii) payments to be made by the HNS Fund in the relevant year;

Income:

(iii) surplus funds from operations in preceding years, including any interest;

(iv) initial contributions to be paid in the course of the year;

(v) annual contributions if required to balance the budget; and

(vi) any other income;

(c) to use at the request of a State Party its good offices as necessary to assist that State to secure promptly such personnel, material and services as are necessary to enable the State to take measures to prevent or mitigate damage arising from an incident in respect of which the HNS Fund may be called upon to pay compensation under this Convention; and

(d) to provide, on conditions laid down in the internal regulations, credit facilities with a view to the taking of preventive measures against damage arising from a particular incident in respect of which the HNS Fund may be called upon to pay compensation under this Convention.

General provisions on contributions

Article 16

1. The HNS Fund shall have a general account, which shall be divided into sectors.

2. The HNS Fund shall, subject to Article 19, paragraphs 3 and 4, also have separate accounts in respect of:

(a) oil as defined in Article 1, paragraph 5(a)(i) (oil account);

(b) liquefied natural gases of light hydrocarbons with methane as the main constituent (LNG) (LNG account); and

(c) liquefied petroleum gases of light hydrocarbons with propane and butane as the main constituents (LPG) (LPG account).

3. There shall be initial contributions and, as required, annual contributions to the HNS 206 Fund.

4. Contributions to the HNS Fund shall be made into the general account in accordance with Article 18, to separate accounts in accordance with Article 19 and to either the general account or separate accounts in accordance with Article 20 or Article 21, paragraph 5. Subject to Article 19, paragraph 6, the general account shall be available to compensate damage caused by hazardous and noxious substances covered by that account, and a separate account shall be available to compensate damage caused by a hazardous and noxious substance covered by that account.

5. For the purposes of Article 18, Article 19, paragraph 1(a)(i), paragraph 1(a)(ii) and paragraph 1(c), Article 20 and Article 21, paragraph 5, where the quantity of a given type of contributing cargo received in the territory of a State Party by any person in a calendar year when aggregated with the quantities of the same type of cargo received in the same State Party in that year by any associated person or persons exceeds the limit specified in the respective subparagraphs, such a person shall pay contributions in respect of the actual quantity received by that person notwithstanding that that quantity did not exceed the respective limit.

6. "Associated person" means any subsidiary or commonly controlled entity. The question whether a person comes within this definition shall be determined by the national law of the State concerned.

General provisions on annual contributions

Article 17

1. Annual contributions to the general account and to each separate account shall be levied only as required to make payments by the account in question.

2. Annual contributions payable pursuant to Articles 18, 19 and Article 21, paragraph 5 shall be determined by the Assembly and shall be calculated in accordance with those Articles on the basis of the units of contributing cargo received or, in respect of cargoes referred to in Article 19, paragraph 1(b), discharged during the preceding calendar year or such other year as the Assembly may decide.

3. The Assembly shall decide the total amount of annual contributions to be levied to the general account and to each separate account. Following that decision the Director shall, in respect of each State Party, calculate for each person liable to pay contributions in accordance with Article 18, Article 19, paragraph 1 and Article 21, paragraph 5, the amount of that person's annual contribution to each account, on the basis of a fixed sum for each unit of contributing cargo reported in respect of the person during the preceding calendar year or such other year as the Assembly may decide. For the general account, the above-mentioned fixed sum per unit of contributing cargo for each sector shall be calculated pursuant to the regulations contained in Annex II to this Convention. For each separate account, the fixed sum per unit of contributing cargo referred to above shall be calculated by dividing the total annual contribution to be levied to that account by the total quantity of cargo contributing to that account.

4. The Assembly may also levy annual contributions for administrative costs and decide on the distribution of such costs between the sectors of the general account and the separate accounts.

5. The Assembly shall also decide on the distribution between the relevant accounts and sectors of amounts paid in compensation for damage caused by two or more substances which fall within different accounts or sectors, on the basis of an estimate of the extent to which each of the substances involved contributed to the damage.

Annual contributions to the general account

Article 18

1. Subject to Article 16, paragraph 5, annual contributions to the general account shall be made in respect of each State Party by any person who was the receiver in that State in the preceding calendar year, or such other year as the Assembly may decide, of aggregate quantities exceeding 20,000 tonnes of contributing cargo, other than substances referred to in Article 19, paragraph 1, which fall within the following sectors:
    (a) solid bulk materials referred to in Article 1, paragraph 5(a)(vii);
    (b) substances referred to in paragraph 2; and
    (c) other substances.

2. Annual contributions shall also be payable to the general account by persons who would have been liable to pay contributions to a separate account in accordance with Article 19, paragraph 1 had its operation not been postponed or suspended in accordance with Article 19. Each separate account the operation of which has been postponed or suspended under Article 19 shall form a separate sector within the general account.

Annual contributions to separate accounts

Article 19

1. Subject to Article 16, paragraph 5, annual contributions to separate accounts shall be made in respect of each State Party:
    (a) in the case of the oil account,
        (i) by any person who has received in that State in the preceding calendar year, or such other year as the Assembly may decide, total quantities exceeding 150,000 tonnes of contributing oil as defined in Article 1, paragraph 3 of the International Convention on the Establishment of an International Fund for Compensation for Oil Pollution Damage, 1971, as amended, and who is or would be liable to pay contributions to the International Oil Pollution Compensation Fund in accordance with Article 10 of that Convention; and
        (ii) by any person who was the receiver in that State in the preceding calendar year, or such other year as the Assembly may decide, of total quantities exceeding 20,000 tonnes of other oils carried in bulk listed in appendix I of

Annex I to the International Convention for the Prevention of Pollution from Ships, 1973, as modified by the Protocol of 1978 relating thereto, as amended;

(b) in the case of the LNG account, by any person who in the preceding calendar year, or such other year as the Assembly may decide, immediately prior to its discharge, held title to an LNG cargo discharged in a port or terminal of that State;

(c) in the case of the LPG account, by any person who in the preceding calendar year, or such other year as the Assembly may decide, was the receiver in that State of total quantities exceeding 20,000 tonnes of LPG.

2. Subject to paragraph 3, the separate accounts referred to in paragraph 1 above shall become effective at the same time as the general account.

3. The initial operation of a separate account referred to in Article 16, paragraph 2 shall be postponed until such time as the quantities of contributing cargo in respect of that account during the preceding calendar year, or such other year as the Assembly may decide, exceed the following levels:

(a) 350 million tonnes of contributing cargo in respect of the oil account;

(b) 20 million tonnes of contributing cargo in respect of the LNG account; and

(c) 15 million tonnes of contributing cargo in respect of the LPG account.

4. The Assembly may suspend the operation of a separate account if:

(a) the quantities of contributing cargo in respect of that account during the preceding calendar year fall below the respective level specified in paragraph 3; or

(b) when six months have elapsed from the date when the contributions were due, the total unpaid contributions to that account exceed ten per cent of the most recent levy to that account in accordance with paragraph 1.

5. The Assembly may reinstate the operation of a separate account which has been suspended in accordance with paragraph 4.

6. Any person who would be liable to pay contributions to a separate account the operation of which has been postponed in accordance with paragraph 3 or suspended in accordance with paragraph 4, shall pay into the general account the contributions due by that person in respect of that separate account. For the purpose of calculating future contributions, the postponed or suspended separate account shall form a new sector in the general account and shall be subject to the HNS points system defined in Annex II.

Initial contributions

Article 20

1. In respect of each State Party, initial contributions shall be made of an amount which shall for each person liable to pay contributions in accordance with Article 16, paragraph 5, Articles 18, 19 and Article 21, paragraph 5 be calculated on the basis of a fixed sum, equal for the general account and each separate account, for each unit of contributing cargo received or, in the case of LNG, discharged in that State, during the calendar year preceding that in which this Convention enters into force for that State.

2. The fixed sum and the units for the different sectors within the general account as well as for each separate account referred to in paragraph 1 shall be determined by the Assembly.

3. Initial contributions shall be paid within three months following the date on which the HNS Fund issues invoices in respect of each State Party to persons liable to pay contributions in accordance with paragraph 1.

Reports

Article 21

1. Each State Party shall ensure that any person liable to pay contributions in accordance with Articles 18, 19 or paragraph 5 of this Article appears on a list to be established and kept up to date by the Director in accordance with the provisions of this Article.

2. For the purposes set out in paragraph 1, each State Party shall communicate to the Director, at a time and in the manner to be prescribed in the internal regulations of the HNS Fund, the name and address of any person who in respect of the State is liable to pay contributions in accordance with Articles 18, 19 or paragraph 5 of this Article, as well as data on the relevant quantities of contributing cargo for which such a person is liable to contribute in respect of the preceding calendar year.

3. For the purposes of ascertaining who are, at any given time, the persons liable to pay contributions in accordance with Articles 18, 19 or paragraph 5 of this Article and of establishing, where applicable, the quantities of cargo to be taken into account for any such person when determining the amount of the contribution, the list shall be prima facie evidence of the facts stated therein.

4. Where a State Party does not fulfil its obligations to communicate to the Director the information referred to in paragraph 2 and this results in a financial loss for the HNS Fund, that State Party shall be liable to compensate the HNS Fund for such loss. The Assembly shall, on the recommendation of the Director, decide whether such compensation shall be payable by a State Party.

5. In respect of contributing cargo carried from one port or terminal of a State Party to another port or terminal located in the same State and discharged there, States Parties shall have the option of submitting to the HNS Fund a report with an annual aggregate quantity for each account covering all receipts of contributing cargo, including any quantities in respect of which contributions are payable pursuant to Article 16, paragraph 5. The State Party shall, at the time of reporting, either:

    (a) notify the HNS Fund that that State will pay the aggregate amount for each account in respect of the relevant year in one lump sum to the HNS Fund; or

    (b) instruct the HNS Fund to levy the aggregate amount for each account by invoicing individual receivers or, in the case of LNG, the title holder who discharges within the jurisdiction of that State Party, for the amount payable by each of them. These persons shall be identified in accordance with the national law of the State concerned.

Non-payment of contributions

Article 22

1. The amount of any contribution due under Articles 18, 19, 20 or Article 21, paragraph 5 and which is in arrears shall bear interest at a rate which shall be determined in accordance with the internal regulations of the HNS Fund, provided that different rates may be fixed for different circumstances.

2. Where a person who is liable to pay contributions in accordance with Articles 18, 19, 20 or Article 21, paragraph 5 does not fulfil the obligations in respect of any such contribution or any part thereof and is in arrears, the Director shall take all appropriate action, including court action, against such a person on behalf of the HNS Fund with a view to the recovery of the amount due. However, where the defaulting contributor is manifestly insolvent or the circumstances otherwise so warrant, the Assembly may, upon recommendation of the Director, decide that no action shall be taken or continued against the contributor.

Optional liability of states parties for the payment of contributions

Article 23

1. Without prejudice to Article 21, paragraph 5, a State Party may at the time when it deposits its instrument of ratification, acceptance, approval or accession or at any time thereafter declare that it assumes responsibility for obligations imposed by this Convention on any person liable to pay contributions in accordance with Articles 18, 19, 20 or Article 21, paragraph 5 in respect of hazardous and noxious substances received or discharged in the territory of that State. Such a declaration shall be made in writing and shall specify which obligations are assumed.

2. Where a declaration under paragraph 1 is made prior to the entry into force of this Convention in accordance with Article 46, it shall be deposited with the Secretary-General who shall after the entry into force of this Convention communicate the declaration to the Director.

3. A declaration under paragraph 1 which is made after the entry into force of this Convention shall be deposited with the Director.

4. A declaration made in accordance with this Article may be withdrawn by the relevant State giving notice thereof in writing to the Director. Such a notification shall take effect three months after the Director's receipt thereof.

5. Any State which is bound by a declaration made under this Article shall, in any proceedings brought against it before a competent court in respect of any obligation specified in the declaration, waive any immunity that it would otherwise be entitled to invoke.

Organisation and administration

Article 24

The HNS Fund shall have an Assembly and a Secretariat headed by the Director.

Assembly

Article 25

The Assembly shall consist of all States Parties to this Convention.

Article 26

The functions of the Assembly shall be:

(a) to elect at each regular session its President and two Vice-Presidents who shall hold office until the next regular session;

(b) to determine its own rules of procedure, subject to the provisions of this Convention;

(c) to develop, apply and keep under review internal and financial regulations relating to the aim of the HNS Fund as described in Article 13, paragraph 1(a), and the related tasks of the HNS Fund listed in Article 15;

(d) to appoint the Director and make provisions for the appointment of such other personnel as may be necessary and determine the terms and conditions of service of the Director and other personnel;

(e) to adopt the annual budget prepared in accordance with Article 15(b);

(f) to consider and approve as necessary any recommendation of the Director regarding the scope of definition of contributing cargo;

(g) to appoint auditors and approve the accounts of the HNS Fund;

(h) to approve settlements of claims against the HNS Fund, to take decisions in respect of the distribution among claimants of the available amount of compensation in accordance with Article 14 and to determine the terms and conditions according to which provisional payments in respect of claims shall be made with a view to ensuring that victims of damage are compensated as promptly as possible;

(i) to establish a Committee on Claims for Compensation with at least 7 and not more than 15 members and any temporary or permanent subsidiary body it may consider to be necessary, to define its terms of reference and to give it the authority needed to perform the functions entrusted to it; when appointing the members of such body, the Assembly shall endeavour to secure an equitable geographical distribution of members and to ensure that the States Parties are appropriately represented; the Rules of Procedure of the Assembly may be applied, mutatis mutandis, for the work of such subsidiary body;

(j) to determine which States not party to this Convention, which Associate Members of the Organization and which intergovernmental and international non-governmental organisations shall be admitted to take part, without voting rights, in meetings of the Assembly and subsidiary bodies;

(k) to give instructions concerning the administration of the HNS Fund to the Director and subsidiary bodies;

(l) to supervise the proper execution of this Convention and of its own decisions;

(m) to review every five years the implementation of this Convention with particular reference to the performance of the system for the calculation of levies and the contribution mechanism for domestic trade; and

(n) to perform such other functions as are allocated to it under this Convention or are otherwise necessary for the proper operation of the HNS Fund.

Article 27

1. Regular sessions of the Assembly shall take place once every calendar year upon convocation by the Director.

2. Extraordinary sessions of the Assembly shall be convened by the Director at the request of at least one third of the members of the Assembly and may be convened on the Director's own initiative after consultation with the President of the Assembly. The Director shall give members at least thirty days' notice of such sessions.

Article 28

A majority of the members of the Assembly shall constitute a quorum for its meetings.

Secretariat

Article 29

1. The Secretariat shall comprise the Director and such staff as the administration of the HNS Fund may require.

2. The Director shall be the legal representative of the HNS Fund.

Article 30

1. The Director shall be the chief administrative officer of the HNS Fund. Subject to the instructions given by the Assembly, the Director shall perform those functions which are assigned to the Director by this Convention, the internal regulations of the HNS Fund and the Assembly.

2. The Director shall in particular:

(a) appoint the personnel required for the administration of the HNS Fund;

(b) take all appropriate measures with a view to the proper administration of the assets of the HNS Fund;

(c) collect the contributions due under this Convention while observing in particular the provisions of Article 22, paragraph 2;

(d) to the extent necessary to deal with claims against the HNS Fund and to carry out the other functions of the HNS Fund, employ the services of legal, financial and other experts;

(e) take all appropriate measures for dealing with claims against the HNS Fund, within the limits and on conditions to be laid down in the internal regulations of the HNS Fund, including the final settlement of claims without the prior approval of the Assembly where these regulations so provide;

(f) prepare and submit to the Assembly the financial statements and budget estimates for each calendar year;

(g) prepare, in consultation with the President of the Assembly, and publish a report on the activities of the HNS Fund during the previous calendar year; and

(h) prepare, collect and circulate the documents and information which may be required for the work of the Assembly and subsidiary bodies.

Article 31

In the performance of their duties the Director and the staff and experts appointed by the Director shall not seek or receive instructions from any Government or from any authority external to the HNS Fund. They shall refrain from any action which might adversely reflect on their position as international officials. Each State Party on its part undertakes to respect the exclusively international character of the responsibilities of the Director and the staff and experts appointed by the Director, and not to seek to influence them in the discharge of their duties.

Finances

Article 32

1. Each State Party shall bear the salary, travel and other expenses of its own delegation to the Assembly and of its representatives on subsidiary bodies.

2. Any other expenses incurred in the operation of the HNS Fund shall be borne by the HNS Fund.

Voting

Article 33

The following provisions shall apply to voting in the Assembly:
  (a) each member shall have one vote;
  (b) except as otherwise provided in Article 34, decisions of the Assembly shall be made by a majority vote of the members present and voting;
  (c) decisions where a two-thirds majority is required shall be a two-thirds majority vote of members present; and
  (d) for the purpose of this Article the phrase "members present" means "members present at the meeting at the time of the vote", and the phrase "members present and voting" means "members present and casting an affirmative or negative vote". Members who abstain from voting shall be considered as not voting.

Article 34

The following decisions of the Assembly shall require a two-thirds majority:
  (a) a decision under Article 19, paragraphs 4 or 5 to suspend or reinstate the operation of a separate account;
  (b) a decision under Article 22, paragraph 2, not to take or continue action against a contributor;
  (c) the appointment of the Director under Article 26(d);
  (d) the establishment of subsidiary bodies, under Article 26(i), and matters relating to such establishment; and
  (e) a decision under Article 51, paragraph 1, that this Convention shall continue to be in force.

Tax exemptions and currency regulations

Article 35

1. The HNS Fund, its assets, income, including contributions, and other property necessary for the exercise of its functions as described in Article 13, paragraph 1, shall enjoy in all States Parties exemption from all direct taxation.

2. When the HNS Fund makes substantial purchases of movable or immovable property, or of services which are necessary for the exercise of its official activities in order to achieve its aims as set out in Article 13, paragraph 1, the cost of which include indirect taxes or sales taxes, the Governments of the States Parties shall take, whenever possible, appropriate measures for the remission or refund of the amount of such duties and taxes. Goods thus acquired shall not be sold against payment or given away free of charge unless it is done according to conditions approved by the Government of the State having granted or supported the remission or refund.

3. No exemption shall be accorded in the case of duties, taxes or dues which merely constitute payment for public utility services.

4. The HNS Fund shall enjoy exemption from all customs duties, taxes and other related taxes on articles imported or exported by it or on its behalf for its official use. Articles thus imported shall not be transferred either for consideration or gratis on the territory of the country into which they have been imported except on conditions agreed by the Government of that country.

5. Persons contributing to the HNS Fund as well as victims and owners receiving compensation from the HNS Fund shall be subject to the fiscal legislation of the State where they are taxable, no special exemption or other benefit being conferred on them in this respect.

6. Notwithstanding existing or future regulations concerning currency or transfers, States Parties shall authorise the transfer and payment of any contribution to the HNS Fund and of any compensation paid by the HNS Fund without any restriction.

Confidentiality of information

Article 36

Information relating to individual contributors supplied for the purpose of this Convention shall not be divulged outside the HNS Fund except in so far as it may be strictly necessary to enable the HNS Fund to carry out its functions including the bringing and defending of legal proceedings.

CHAPTER IV – CLAIMS AND ACTIONS

Limitation of actions

Article 37

1. Rights to compensation under chapter II shall be extinguished unless an action is brought thereunder within three years from the date when the person suffering the damage knew or ought reasonably to have known of the damage and of the identity of the owner.

2. Rights to compensation under chapter III shall be extinguished unless an action is brought thereunder or a notification has been made pursuant to Article 39, paragraph 7, within three years from the date when the person suffering the damage knew or ought reasonably to have known of the damage.

3. In no case, however, shall an action be brought later than ten years from the date of the incident which caused the damage.

4. Where the incident consists of a series of occurrences, the ten-year period mentioned in paragraph 3 shall run from the date of the last of such occurrences.

Jurisdiction in respect of action against the owner

Article 38

1. Where an incident has caused damage in the territory, including the territorial sea or in an area referred to in Article 3(b), of one or more States Parties, or preventive measures have been taken to prevent or minimise damage in such territory including the territorial sea or in such area, actions for compensation may be brought against the owner or other person providing financial security for the owner's liability only in the courts of any such States Parties.

2. Where an incident has caused damage exclusively outside the territory, including the territorial sea, of any State and either the conditions for application of this Convention set out in Article 3(c) have been fulfilled or preventive measures to prevent or minimise such damage have been taken, actions for compensation may be brought against the owner or other person providing financial security for the owner's liability only in the courts of:

    (a) the State Party where the ship is registered or, in the case of an unregistered ship, the State Party whose flag the ship is entitled to fly; or

    (b) the State Party where the owner has habitual residence or where the principal place of business of the owner is established; or

    (c) the State Party where a fund has been constituted in accordance with Article 9, paragraph 3.

3. Reasonable notice of any action taken under paragraph 1 or 2 shall be given to the defendant.

4. Each State Party shall ensure that its courts have jurisdiction to entertain actions for compensation under this Convention.

5. After a fund under Article 9 has been constituted by the owner or by the insurer or other person providing financial security in accordance with Article 12, the courts of the State in which such fund is constituted shall have exclusive jurisdiction to determine all matters relating to the apportionment and distribution of the fund.

Jurisdiction in respect of action against the HNS Fund or taken by the HNS Fund

Article 39

1. Subject to the subsequent provisions of this Article, any action against the HNS Fund for compensation under Article 14 shall be brought only before a court having jurisdiction under Article 38 in respect of actions against the owner who is liable for damage caused by the relevant incident or before a court in a State Party which would have been competent if an owner had been liable.

2. In the event that the ship carrying the hazardous or noxious substances which caused the damage has not been identified, the provisions of Article 38, paragraph 1, shall apply *mutatis mutandis* to actions against the HNS Fund.

3. Each State Party shall ensure that its courts have jurisdiction to entertain such actions against the HNS Fund as are referred to in paragraph 1.

4. Where an action for compensation for damage has been brought before a court against the owner or the owner's guarantor, such court shall have exclusive jurisdiction over any action against the HNS Fund for compensation under the provisions of Article 14 in respect of the same damage.

5. Each State Party shall ensure that the HNS Fund shall have the right to intervene as a party to any legal proceedings instituted in accordance with this Convention before a competent court of that State against the owner or the owner's guarantor.

6. Except as otherwise provided in paragraph 7, the HNS Fund shall not be bound by any judgement or decision in proceedings to which it has not been a party or by any settlement to which it is not a party.

7. Without prejudice to the provisions of paragraph 5, where an action under this Convention for compensation for damage has been brought against an owner or the owner's guarantor before a competent court in a State Party, each party to the proceedings shall be entitled under the national law of that State to notify the HNS Fund of the proceedings. Where such notification has been made in accordance with the formalities required by the law of the court seised and in such time and in such a manner that the HNS Fund has in fact been in a position effectively to intervene as a party to the proceedings, any judgement rendered by the court in such proceedings shall, after it has become final and enforceable in the State where the judgement was given, become binding upon the HNS Fund in the sense that the facts and findings in that judgement may not be disputed by the HNS Fund even if the HNS Fund has not actually intervened in the proceedings.

Recognition and enforcement

Article 40

1. Any judgment given by a court with jurisdiction in accordance with Article 38, which is enforceable in the State of origin where it is no longer subject to ordinary forms of review, shall be recognised in any State Party, except:

(a) where the judgment was obtained by fraud; or

(b) where the defendant was not given reasonable notice and a fair opportunity to present the case.

2. A judgment recognised under paragraph 1 shall be enforceable in each State Party as soon as the formalities required in that State have been complied with. The formalities shall not permit the merits of the case to be re-opened.

3. Subject to any decision concerning the distribution referred to in Article 14, paragraph 6, any judgment given against the HNS Fund by a court having jurisdiction in accordance with Article 39, paragraphs 1 and 3 shall, when it has become enforceable in the State of origin and is in that State no longer subject to ordinary forms of review, be recognised and enforceable in each State Party.

Subrogation and recourse

Article 41

1. The HNS Fund shall, in respect of any amount of compensation for damage paid by the HNS Fund in accordance with Article 14, paragraph 1, acquire by subrogation the rights that the person so compensated may enjoy against the owner or the owner's guarantor.

2. Nothing in this Convention shall prejudice any rights of recourse or subrogation of the HNS Fund against any person, including persons referred to in Article 7, paragraph 2(d), other than those referred to in the previous paragraph, in so far as they can limit their liability. In any event the right of the HNS Fund to subrogation against such persons shall not be less favourable than that of an insurer of the person to whom compensation has been paid.

3. Without prejudice to any other rights of subrogation or recourse against the HNS Fund which may exist, a State Party or agency thereof which has paid compensation for damage in accordance with provisions of national law shall acquire by subrogation the rights which the person so compensated would have enjoyed under this Convention.

Supersession clause

Article 42

This Convention shall supersede any convention in force or open for signature, ratification or accession at the date on which this Convention is opened for signature, but only to the extent that such convention would be in conflict with it; however, nothing in this Article shall affect the obligations of States Parties to States not party to this Convention arising under such convention.

CHAPTER V – TRANSITIONAL PROVISIONS

Information on contributing cargo

Article 43

When depositing an instrument referred to in Article 45, paragraph 3, and annually thereafter until this Convention enters into force for a State, that State shall submit to the Secretary General data on the relevant quantities of contributing cargo received or, in the case of LNG, discharged in that State during the preceding calendar year in respect of the general account and each separate account.

First Session of the Assembly

Article 44

The Secretary-General shall convene the first session of the Assembly. This session shall take place as soon as possible after the entry into force of this Convention and, in any case, not more than thirty days after such entry into force.

CHAPTER VI – FINAL CLAUSES

Signature, ratification, acceptance, approval and accession

Article 45

1. This Convention shall be open for signature at the Headquarters of the Organization from 1 October 1996 to 30 September 1997 and shall thereafter remain open for accession.
2. States may express their consent to be bound by this Convention by:
    (a) signature without reservation as to ratification, acceptance or approval; or
    (b) signature subject to ratification, acceptance or approval, followed by ratification, acceptance or approval; or
    (c) accession.
3. Ratification, acceptance, approval or accession shall be effected by the deposit of an instrument to that effect with the Secretary-General.

Entry into force

Article 46

1. This Convention shall enter into force eighteen months after the date on which the following conditions are fulfilled:
    (a) at least twelve States, including four States each with not less than 2 million units of gross tonnage, have expressed their consent to be bound by it, and
    (b) the Secretary-General has received information in accordance with Article 43 that those persons in such States who would be liable to contribute pursuant to Article 18, paragraphs 1(a) and (c) have received during the preceding calendar year a total quantity of at least 40 million tonnes of cargo contributing to the general account.
2. For a State which expresses its consent to be bound by this Convention after the conditions for entry into force have been met, such consent shall take effect three months after the date of expression of such consent, or on the date on which this Convention enters into force in accordance with paragraph 1, whichever is the later.

Revision and amendment

Article 47

1. A conference for the purpose of revising or amending this Convention may be convened by the Organization.
2. The Secretary-General shall convene a conference of the States Parties to this Convention for revising or amending the Convention, at the request of six States Parties or one-third of the States Parties, whichever is the higher figure.
3. Any consent to be bound by this Convention expressed after the date of entry into force of an amendment to this Convention shall be deemed to apply to the Convention as amended.

Amendment of limits

Article 48

1. Without prejudice to the provisions of Article 47, the special procedure in this Article shall apply solely for the purposes of amending the limits set out in Article 9, paragraph 1 and Article 14, paragraph 5.
2. Upon the request of at least one half, but in no case less than six, of the States Parties, any proposal to amend the limits specified in Article 9, paragraph 1, and Article 14, paragraph 5, shall be circulated by the Secretary-General to all Members of the Organization and to all Contracting States.

3. Any amendment proposed and circulated as above shall be submitted to the Legal Committee of the Organization (the Legal Committee) for consideration at a date at least six months after the date of its circulation.

4. All Contracting States, whether or not Members of the Organization, shall be entitled to participate in the proceedings of the Legal Committee for the consideration and adoption of amendments.

5. Amendments shall be adopted by a two-thirds majority of the Contracting States present and voting in the Legal Committee, expanded as provided in paragraph 4, on condition that at least one half of the Contracting States shall be present at the time of voting.

6. When acting on a proposal to amend the limits, the Legal Committee shall take into account the experience of incidents and, in particular, the amount of damage resulting there from changes in the monetary values and the effect of the proposed amendment on the cost of insurance. It shall also take into account the relationship between the limits established in Article 9, paragraph 1, and those in Article 14, paragraph 5.

7. (a) No amendment of the limits under this Article may be considered less than five years from the date this Convention was opened for signature nor less than five years from the date of entry into force of a previous amendment under this Article.

   (b) No limit may be increased so as to exceed an amount which corresponds to a limit laid down in this Convention increased by six per cent per year calculated on a compound basis from the date on which this Convention was opened for signature.

   (c) No limit may be increased so as to exceed an amount which corresponds to a limit laid down in this Convention multiplied by three.

8. Any amendment adopted in accordance with paragraph 5 shall be notified by the Organization to all Contracting States. The amendment shall be deemed to have been accepted at the end of a period of eighteen months after the date of notification, unless within that period no less than one-fourth of the States which were Contracting States at the time of the adoption of the amendment have communicated to the Secretary-General that they do not accept the amendment, in which case the amendment is rejected and shall have no effect.

9. An amendment deemed to have been accepted in accordance with paragraph 8 shall enter into force eighteen months after its acceptance.

10. All Contracting States shall be bound by the amendment, unless they denounce this Convention in accordance with Article 49, paragraphs 1 and 2, at least six months before the amendment enters into force. Such denunciation shall take effect when the amendment enters into force.

11. When an amendment has been adopted but the eighteen month period for its acceptance has not yet expired, a State which becomes a Contracting State during that period shall be bound by the amendment if it enters into force. A State which becomes a Contracting State after that period shall be bound by an amendment which has been accepted in accordance with paragraph 8. In the cases referred to in this paragraph, a State becomes bound by an amendment when that amendment enters into force, or when this Convention enters into force for that State, if later.

Denunciation

Article 49

1. This Convention may be denounced by any State Party at any time after the date on which it enters into force for that State Party.

2. Denunciation shall be effected by the deposit of an instrument of denunciation with the Secretary-General.

3. Denunciation shall take effect twelve months, or such longer period as may be specified in the instrument of denunciation, after its deposit with the Secretary-General.

4. Notwithstanding a denunciation by a State Party pursuant to this Article, any provisions of this Convention relating to obligations to make contributions under Articles 18, 19 or Article 21, paragraph 5 in respect of such payments of compensation as the Assembly may decide relating to an incident which occurs before the denunciation takes effect shall continue to apply.

Extraordinary Sessions of the Assembly

Article 50

1. Any State Party may, within ninety days after the deposit of an instrument of denunciation the result of which it considers will significantly increase the level of contributions from the remaining States Parties, request the Director to convene an extraordinary session of the Assembly. The Director shall convene the Assembly to meet not less than sixty days after receipt of the request.

2. The Director may take the initiative to convene an extraordinary session of the Assembly to meet within sixty days after the deposit of any instrument of denunciation, if the Director considers that such denunciation will result in a significant increase in the level of contributions from the remaining States Parties.

3. If the Assembly, at an extraordinary session, convened in accordance with paragraph 1 or 2 decides that the denunciation will result in a significant increase in the level of contributions from the remaining States Parties, any such State may, not later than one hundred and twenty days before the date on which the denunciation takes effect, denounce this Convention with effect from the same date.

Cessation

Article 51

1. This Convention shall cease to be in force:
   (a) on the date when the number of States Parties falls below 6; or
   (b) twelve months after the date on which data concerning a previous calendar year were to be communicated to the Director in accordance with Article 21, if the data shows that the total quantity of contributing cargo to the general account in accordance with Article 18, paragraphs 1(a) and (c) received in the States Parties in that preceding calendar year was less than 30 million tonnes.

Notwithstanding (b), if the total quantity of contributing cargo to the general account in accordance with Article 18, paragraphs 1(a) and (c) received in the States Parties in the preceding calendar year was less than 30 million tonnes but more than 25 million tonnes, the Assembly may, if it considers that this was due to exceptional circumstances and is not likely to be repeated, decide before the expiry of the above-mentioned twelve month period that the Convention shall continue to be in force. The Assembly may not, however, take such a decision in more than two subsequent years.

2. States which are bound by this Convention on the day before the date it ceases to be in force shall enable the HNS Fund to exercise its functions as described under Article 52 and shall, for that purpose only, remain bound by this Convention.

Winding up of the HNS Fund

Article 52

1. If this Convention ceases to be in force, the HNS Fund shall nevertheless:
   (a) meet its obligations in respect of any incident occurring before this Convention ceased to be in force; and
   (b) be entitled to exercise its rights to contributions to the extent that these contributions are necessary to meet the obligations under (a), including expenses for the administration of the HNS Fund necessary for this purpose.

2. The Assembly shall take all appropriate measures to complete the winding up of the HNS Fund including the distribution in an equitable manner of any remaining assets among those persons who have contributed to the HNS Fund.

3. For the purposes of this Article the HNS Fund shall remain a legal person.

Depositary

Article 53

1. This Convention and any amendment adopted under Article 48 shall be deposited with the Secretary-General.
2. The Secretary-General shall:
   (a) inform all States which have signed this Convention or acceded thereto, and all Members of the Organization, of:
      (i) each new signature or deposit of an instrument of ratification, acceptance, approval or accession together with the date thereof;
      (ii) the date of entry into force of this Convention;
      (iii) any proposal to amend the limits on the amounts of compensation which has been made in accordance with Article 48, paragraph 2;
      (iv) any amendment which has been adopted in accordance with Article 48, paragraph 5;
      (v) any amendment deemed to have been accepted under Article 48, paragraph 8, together with the date on which that amendment shall enter into force in accordance with paragraphs 9 and 10 of that Article;
      (vi) the deposit of any instrument of denunciation of this Convention together with the date on which it is received and the date on which the denunciation takes effect; and
      (vii) any communication called for by any Article in this Convention; and
   (b) transmit certified true copies of this Convention to all States which have signed this Convention or acceded thereto.
3. As soon as this Convention enters into force, a certified true copy thereof shall be transmitted by the depositary to the Secretary-General of the United Nations for registration and publication in accordance with Article 102 of the Charter of the United Nations.

Languages

Article 54

This Convention is established in a single original in the Arabic, Chinese, English, French, Russian and Spanish languages, each text being equally authentic.

[Post Provisions]

[Post Clauses (If any: Signed; Witnessed; Done; Authentic Texts; and Deposited Clauses)]

DONE AT LONDON this third day of May one thousand nine hundred and ninety-six.

IN WITNESS WHEREOF the undersigned, being duly authorised by their respective Governments for that purpose, have signed this Convention.

Federal Oil Pollution Act of 1990
[As Amended Through P.L. 106–580, 29 December 2000]

AN ACT To establish limitations on liability for damages resulting from oil pollution, to establish a fund for the payment of compensation for such damages, and for other purposes.

Be it enacted by the Senate and House of Representatives of the United States of America in Congress assembled,

Title I – Oil pollution liability and compensation

Sec. 1001. Definitions

For the purposes of this Act, the term–

(1) "act of God" means an unanticipated grave natural disaster or other natural phenomenon of an exceptional, inevitable, and irresistible character the effects of which could not have been prevented or avoided by the exercise of due care or foresight;

(2) "barrel" means 42 United States gallons at 60 degrees fahrenheit;

(3) "claim" means a request, made in writing for a sum certain, for compensation for damages or removal costs resulting from an incident;

(4) "claimant" means any person or government who presents a claim for compensation under this title;

(5) "damages" means damages specified in section 1002(b) of this Act, and includes the cost of assessing these damages;

(6) "deepwater port" is a facility licensed under the Deepwater Port Act of 1974 (33 U.S.C. 1501–1524);

(7) "discharge" means any emission (other than natural seepage), intentional or unintentional, and includes, but is not limited to, spilling, leaking, pumping, pouring, emitting, emptying, or dumping;

(8) "exclusive economic zone" means the zone established by Presidential Proclamation Numbered 5030, dated March 10, 1983, including the ocean waters of the areas referred to as "eastern special areas" in Article 3(1) of the Agreement between the United States of America and the Union of Soviet Socialist Republics on the Maritime Boundary, signed June 1, 1990;

(9) "facility" means any structure, group of structures, equipment, or device (other than a vessel) which is used for one or more of the following purposes: exploring for, drilling for, producing, storing, handling, transferring, processing, or transporting oil. This term includes any motor vehicle, rolling stock, or pipeline used for one or more of these purposes;

(10) "foreign offshore unit" means a facility which is located, in whole or in part, in the territorial sea or on the continental shelf of a foreign country and which is or was used for one or more of the following purposes: exploring for, drilling for, producing, storing, handling, transferring, processing, or transporting oil produced from the seabed beneath the foreign country's territorial sea or from the foreign country's continental shelf;

(11) "Fund" means the Oil Spill Liability Trust Fund, established by section 9509 of the Internal Revenue Code of 1986 (26 U.S.C. 9509);

(12) "gross ton" has the meaning given that term by the Secretary under part J of title 46, United States Code;

(13) "guarantor" means any person, other than the responsible party, who provides evidence of financial responsibility for a responsible party under this Act;

(14) "incident" means any occurrence or series of occurrences having the same origin, involving one or more vessels, facilities, or any combination thereof, resulting in the discharge or substantial threat of discharge of oil;

(15) "Indian tribe" means any Indian tribe, band, nation, or other organised group or community, but not including any Alaska Native regional or village corporation, which is recognized as eligible for the special programs and services provided by the United States to Indians because of their status as Indians and has governmental authority over lands belonging to or controlled by the tribe;

(16) "lessee" means a person holding a leasehold interest in an oil or gas lease on lands beneath navigable waters (as that term is defined in section 2(a) of the Submerged Lands Act (43 U.S.C. 1301(a))) or on submerged lands of the Outer Continental Shelf, granted or maintained under applicable State law or the Outer Continental Shelf Lands Act (43 U.S.C. 1331 *et seq.*);

(17) "liable" or "liability" shall be construed to be the standard of liability which obtains under section 311 of the Federal Water Pollution Control Act (33 U.S.C. 1321); (18) "mobile offshore drilling unit" means a vessel (other than a self-elevating lift vessel) capable of use as an offshore facility;

(19) "National Contingency Plan" means the National Contingency Plan prepared and published under section 311(d) of the Federal Water Pollution Control Act, as amended by this Act, or revised under section 105 of the Comprehensive Environmental Response, Compensation, and Liability Act (42 U.S.C. 9605);

(20) "natural resources" includes land, fish, wildlife, biota, air, water, ground water, drinking water supplies, and other such resources belonging to, managed by, held in trust by, appertaining to, or otherwise controlled by the United States (including the resources of the exclusive economic zone), any State or local government or Indian tribe, or any foreign government;

(21) "navigable waters" means the waters of the United States, including the territorial sea;

(22) "offshore facility" means any facility of any kind located in, on, or under any of the navigable waters of the United States, and any facility of any kind which is subject to the jurisdiction of the United States and is located in, on, or under any other waters, other than a vessel or a public vessel;

(23) "oil" means oil of any kind or in any form, including petroleum, fuel oil, sludge, oil refuse, and oil mixed with wastes other than dredged spoil, but does not include any substance which is specifically listed or designated as a hazardous substance under subparagraphs (A) through (F) of section 101(14) of the Comprehensive Environmental Response, Compensation, and Liability Act (42 U.S.C. 9601) and which is subject to the provisions of that Act;

(24) "onshore facility" means any facility (including, but not limited to, motor vehicles and rolling stock) of any kind located in, on, or under, any land within the United States other than submerged land;

(25) the term "Outer Continental Shelf facility" means an offshore facility which is located, in whole or in part, on the Outer Continental Shelf and is or was used for one or more of the following purposes: exploring for, drilling for, producing, storing, handling, transferring, processing, or transporting oil produced from the Outer Continental Shelf;

(26) "owner or operator" means (A) in the case of a vessel, any person owning, operating, or chartering by demise, the vessel, and (B) in the case of an onshore facility, and an offshore facility, any person owning or operating such onshore facility or offshore facility, and (C) in the case of any abandoned offshore facility, the person who owned or operated such facility immediately prior to such abandonment;

(27) "person" means an individual, corporation, partnership, association, State, municipality, commission, or political subdivision of a State, or any interstate body;

(28) "permittee" means a person holding an authorisation, license, or permit for geological exploration issued under section 11 of the Outer Continental Shelf Lands Act (43 U.S.C. 1340) or applicable State law;

(29) "public vessel" means a vessel owned or bareboat chartered and operated by the United States, or by a State or political subdivision thereof, or by a foreign nation, except when the vessel is engaged in commerce;

(30) "remove" or "removal" means containment and removal of oil or a hazardous substance from water and shorelines or the taking of other actions as may be necessary to minimise or mitigate damage to the public health or welfare, including, but not limited to, fish, shellfish, wildlife, and public and private property, shorelines, and beaches;

(31) "removal costs" means the costs of removal that are incurred after a discharge of oil has occurred or, in any case in which there is a substantial threat of a discharge of oil, the costs to prevent, minimise, or mitigate oil pollution from such an incident;

(32) "responsible party" means the following:

(A) VESSELS – In the case of a vessel, any person owning, operating, or demise chartering the vessel.

(B) ONSHORE FACILITIES – In the case of an onshore facility (other than a pipeline), any person owning or operating the facility, except a Federal agency, State, municipality, commission, or political subdivision of a State, or any interstate body, that as the owner transfers possession and right to use the property to another person by lease, assignment, or permit.

(C) OFFSHORE FACILITIES – In the case of an offshore facility (other than a pipeline or a deepwater port licensed under the Deepwater Port Act of 1974 (33 U.S.C. 1501 *et seq.*)), the lessee or permittee of the area in which the facility is located or the holder of a right of use and easement granted under applicable State law or the Outer Continental Shelf Lands Act (43 U.S.C. 1301–1356) for the area in which the facility is located (if the holder is a different person than the lessee or permittee), except a Federal agency, State, municipality, commission, or political subdivision of a State, or any interstate body, that as owner transfers possession and right to use the property to another person by lease, assignment, or permit.

(D) DEEPWATER PORTS – In the case of a deepwater port licensed under the Deepwater Port Act of 1974 (33 U.S.C. 1501–1524), the licensee.

(E) PIPELINES – In the case of a pipeline, any person owning or operating the pipeline.

(F) ABANDONMENT – In the case of an abandoned vessel, onshore facility, deepwater port, pipeline, or offshore facility, the persons who would have been responsible parties immediately prior to the abandonment of the vessel or facility.

(33) "Secretary" means the Secretary of the department in which the Coast Guard is operating;

(34) "tank vessel" means a vessel that is constructed or adapted to carry, or that carries, oil or hazardous material in bulk as cargo or cargo residue, and that:

(A) is a vessel of the United States;

(B) operates on the navigable waters; or

(C) transfers oil or hazardous material in a place subject to the jurisdiction of the United States;

(35) "territorial seas" means the belt of the seas measured from the line of ordinary low water along that portion of the coast which is in direct contact with the open sea and the line marking the seaward limit of inland waters, and extending seaward a distance of 3 miles;

(36) "United States" and "State" mean the several States of the United States, the District of Columbia, the Commonwealth of Puerto Rico, Guam, American Samoa, the United States Virgin Islands, the Commonwealth of the Northern Marianas, and any other territory or possession of the United States; and

(37) "vessel" means every description of watercraft or other artificial contrivance used, or capable of being used, as a means of transportation on water, other than a public vessel.

407

Sec. 1002. Elements of liability

(a) IN GENERAL – Notwithstanding any other provision or rule of law, and subject to the provisions of this Act, each responsible party for a vessel or a facility from which oil is discharged, or which poses the substantial threat of a discharge of oil, into or upon the navigable waters or adjoining shorelines or the exclusive economic zone is liable for the removal costs and damages specified in subsection (b) that result from such incident.

(b) COVERED REMOVAL COSTS AND DAMAGES:

   (1) REMOVAL COSTS – The removal costs referred to in subsection (a) are:

   (A) all removal costs incurred by the United States, a State, or an Indian tribe under subsection (c), (d), (e), or (l) of section 311 of the Federal Water Pollution Control Act (33 U.S.C. 1321), as amended by this Act, under the Intervention on the High Seas Act (33 U.S.C. 1471 *et seq.*), or under State law; and

   (B) any removal costs incurred by any person for acts taken by the person which are consistent with the National Contingency Plan.

   (2) DAMAGES – The damages referred to in subsection (a) are the following:

   (A) NATURAL RESOURCES – Damages for injury to, destruction of, loss of, or loss of use of, natural resources, including the reasonable costs of assessing the damage, which shall be recoverable by a United States trustee, a State trustee, an Indian tribe trustee, or a foreign trustee.

   (B) REAL OR PERSONAL PROPERTY – Damages for injury to, or economic losses resulting from destruction of, real or personal property, which shall be recoverable by a claimant who owns or leases that property.

   (C) SUBSISTENCE USE – Damages for loss of subsistence use of natural resources, which shall be recoverable by any claimant who so uses natural resources which have been injured, destroyed, or lost, without regard to the ownership or management of the resources.

   (D) REVENUES – Damages equal to the net loss of taxes, royalties, rents, fees, or net profit shares due to the injury, destruction, or loss of real property, personal property, or natural resources, which shall be recoverable by the Government of the United States, a State, or a political subdivision thereof.

   (E) PROFITS AND EARNING CAPACITY – Damages equal to the loss of profits or impairment of earning capacity due to the injury, destruction, or loss of real property, personal property, or natural resources, which shall be recoverable by any claimant.

   (F) PUBLIC SERVICES – Damages for net costs of providing increased or additional public services during or after removal activities, including protection from fire, safety, or health hazards, caused by a discharge of oil, which shall be recoverable by a State, or a political subdivision of a State.

(c) EXCLUDED DISCHARGES – This title does not apply to any discharge:

   (1) permitted by a permit issued under Federal, State, or local law;

   (2) from a public vessel; or

   (3) from an onshore facility which is subject to the Trans-Alaska Pipeline Authorization Act (43 U.S.C. 1651 *et seq.*).

(d) LIABILITY OF THIRD PARTIES:

   (1) IN GENERAL:

   (A) THIRD PARTY TREATED AS RESPONSIBLE PARTY – Except as provided in subparagraph (B), in any case in which a responsible party establishes that a discharge or threat of a discharge and the resulting removal costs and damages were caused solely by an act or omission of one or more third parties described in section 1003(a)(3) (or solely by such an act or omission in combination with an act of God or an act of war), the third party or parties shall be treated as the responsible party or parties for purposes of determining liability under this title.

   (B) SUBROGATION OF RESPONSIBLE PARTY – If the responsible party alleges that the discharge or threat of a discharge was caused solely by an act or omission of a third party, the responsible party –

(i) in accordance with section 1013, shall pay removal costs and damages to any claimant; and

(ii) shall be entitled by subrogation to all rights of the United States Government and the claimant to recover removal costs or damages from the third party or the Fund paid under this subsection.

(2) LIMITATION APPLIED:

(A) OWNER OR OPERATOR OF VESSEL OR FACILITY – If the act or omission of a third party that causes an incident occurs in connection with a vessel or facility owned or operated by the third party, the liability of the third party shall be subject to the limits provided in section 1004 as applied with respect to the vessel or facility.

(B) OTHER CASES – In any other case, the liability of a third party or parties shall not exceed the limitation which would have been applicable to the responsible party of the vessel or facility from which the discharge actually occurred if the responsible party were liable.

(33 U.S.C. 2702)

Sec. 1003. Defenses to liability

(a) COMPLETE DEFENSES – A responsible party is not liable for removal costs or damages under section 1002 if the responsible party establishes, by a preponderance of the evidence, that the discharge or substantial threat of a discharge of oil and the resulting damages or removal costs were caused solely by:

(1) an act of God;

(2) an act of war;

(3) an act or omission of a third party, other than an employee or agent of the responsible party or a third party whose act or omission occurs in connection with any contractual relationship with the responsible party (except where the sole contractual arrangement arises in connection with carriage by a common carrier by rail), if the responsible party establishes, by a preponderance of the evidence, that the responsible party:

(A) exercised due care with respect to the oil concerned, taking into consideration the characteristics of the oil and in light of all relevant facts and circumstances; and

(B) took precautions against foreseeable acts or omissions of any such third party and the foreseeable consequences of those acts or omissions; or

(4) any combination of paragraphs (1), (2), and (3).

(b) DEFENSES AS TO PARTICULAR CLAIMANTS – A responsible party is not liable under section 1002 to a claimant, to the extent that the incident is caused by the gross negligence or willful misconduct of the claimant.

(c) LIMITATION ON COMPLETE DEFENSE – Subsection (a) does not apply with respect to a responsible party who fails or refuses:

(1) to report the incident as required by law if the responsible party knows or has reason to know of the incident;

(2) to provide all reasonable cooperation and assistance requested by a responsible official in connection with removal activities; or

(3) without sufficient cause, to comply with an order issued under subsection (c) or (e) of section 311 of the Federal Water Pollution Control Act (33 U.S.C. 1321), as amended by this Act, or the Intervention on the High Seas Act (33 U.S.C. 1471 *et seq.*).

(33 U.S.C. 2702)

Sec. 1004. Limits on liability

(a) GENERAL RULE – Except as otherwise provided in this section, the total of the liability of a responsible party under section 1002 and any removal costs incurred by, or on behalf of, the responsible party, with respect to each incident shall not exceed:

(1) for a tank vessel, the greater of:
    (A) $1,200 per gross ton; or
    (B) (i) in the case of a vessel greater than 3,000 gross tons, $10,000,000; or
        (ii) in the case of a vessel of 3,000 gross tons or less, $2,000,000;
(2) for any other vessel, $600 per gross ton or $500,000, whichever is greater;
(3) for an offshore facility except a deepwater port, the total of all removal costs plus $75,000,000; and
(4) for any onshore facility and a deepwater port, $350,000,000.

(b) DIVISION OF LIABILITY FOR MOBILE OFFSHORE DRILLING UNITS:

(1) TREATED FIRST AS TANK VESSEL – For purposes of determining the responsible party and applying this Act and except as provided in paragraph (2), a mobile offshore drilling unit which is being used as an offshore facility is deemed to be a tank vessel with respect to the discharge, or the substantial threat of a discharge, of oil on or above the surface of the water.

(2) TREATED AS FACILITY FOR EXCESS LIABILITY – To the extent that removal costs and damages from any incident described in paragraph (1) exceed the amount for which a responsible party is liable (as that amount may be limited under subsection (a)(1)), the mobile offshore drilling unit is deemed to be an offshore facility. For purposes of applying subsection (a)(3), the amount specified in that subsection shall be reduced by the amount for which the responsible party is liable under paragraph (1).

(c) EXCEPTIONS:

(1) ACTS OF RESPONSIBLE PARTY – Subsection (a) does not apply if the incident was proximately caused by:
    (A) gross negligence or willful misconduct of, or
    (B) the violation of an applicable Federal safety, construction, or operating regulation by,
the responsible party, an agent or employee of the responsible party, or a person acting pursuant to a contractual relationship with the responsible party (except where the sole contractual arrangement arises in connection with carriage by a common carrier by rail).

(2) FAILURE OR REFUSAL OF RESPONSIBLE PARTY – Subsection (a) does not apply if the responsible party fails or refuses-
    (A) to report the incident as required by law and the responsible party knows or has reason to know of the incident;
    (B) to provide all reasonable cooperation and assistance requested by a responsible official in connection with removal activities; or
    (C) without sufficient cause, to comply with an order issued under subsection (c) or (e) of section 311 of the Federal Water Pollution Control Act (33 U.S.C. 1321), as amended by this Act, or the Intervention on the High Seas Act (33 U.S.C. 1471 *et seq.*).

(3) OCS FACILITY OR VESSEL – Notwithstanding the limitations established under subsection (a) and the defenses of section 1003, all removal costs incurred by the United States Government or any State or local official or agency in connection with a discharge or substantial threat of a discharge of oil from any Outer Continental Shelf facility or a vessel carrying oil as cargo from such a facility shall be borne by the owner or operator of such facility or vessel.

(4) CERTAIN TANK VESSELS – Subsection (a)(1) shall not apply to:
    (A) a tank vessel on which the only oil carried as cargo is an animal fat or vegetable oil, as those terms are used in section 2 of the Edible Oil Regulatory Reform Act; and (B) a tank vessel that is designated in its certificate of inspection as an oil spill response vessel (as that term is defined in section 2101 of title 46, United States Code) and that is used solely for removal.

(d) ADJUSTING LIMITS OF LIABILITY:

(1) ONSHORE FACILITIES – Subject to paragraph (2), the President may establish by regulation, with respect to any class or category of onshore facility, a limit of liability

under this section of less than $350,000,000, but not less than $8,000,000, taking into account size, storage capacity, oil throughput, proximity to sensitive areas, type of oil handled, history of discharges, and other factors relevant to risks posed by the class or category of facility.

(2) DEEPWATER PORTS AND ASSOCIATED VESSELS:

    (A) STUDY – The Secretary shall conduct a study of the relative operational and environmental risks posed by the transportation of oil by vessel to deepwater ports (as defined in section 3 of the Deepwater Port Act of 1974 (33 U.S.C. 1502)) versus the transportation of oil by vessel to other ports. The study shall include a review and analysis of offshore lightering practices used in connection with that transportation, an analysis of the volume of oil transported by vessel using those practices, and an analysis of the frequency and volume of oil discharges which occur in connection with the use of those practices.

    (B) REPORT – Not later than 1 year after the date of the enactment of this Act, the Secretary shall submit to the Congress a report on the results of the study conducted under subparagraph (A).

    (C) RULEMAKING PROCEEDING – If the Secretary determines, based on the results of the study conducted under this subparagraph (A), that the use of deepwater ports in connection with the transportation of oil by vessel results in a lower operational or environmental risk than the use of other ports, the Secretary shall initiate, not later than the 180th day following the date of submission of the report to the Congress under subparagraph (B), a rulemaking proceeding to lower the limits of liability under this section for deepwater ports as the Secretary determines appropriate. The Secretary may establish a limit of liability of less than $350,000,000, but not less than $50,000,000, in accordance with paragraph (1).

(3) PERIODIC REPORTS – The President shall, within 6 months after the date of the enactment of this Act, and from time to time thereafter, report to the Congress on the desirability of adjusting the limits of liability specified in subsection (a).

(4) ADJUSTMENT TO REFLECT CONSUMER PRICE INDEX – The President shall, by regulations issued not less often than every 3 years, adjust the limits of liability specified in subsection (a) to reflect significant increases in the Consumer Price Index.

(33 U.S.C. 2704)

Sec. 1005. Interest; partial payment of claims

(a) GENERAL RULE – The responsible party or the responsible party's guarantor is liable to a claimant for interest on the amount paid in satisfaction of a claim under this Act for the period described in subsection (b). The responsible party shall establish a procedure for the payment or settlement of claims for interim, short-term damages. Payment or settlement of a claim for interim, short-term damages representing less than the full amount of damages to which the claimant ultimately may be entitled shall not preclude recovery by the claimant for damages not reflected in the paid or settled partial claim.

(b) PERIOD:

    (1) IN GENERAL – Except as provided in paragraph (2), the period for which interest shall be paid is the period beginning on the 30th day following the date on which the claim is presented to the responsible party or guarantor and ending on the date on which the claim is paid.

    (2) EXCLUSION OF PERIOD DUE TO OFFER BY GUARANTOR – If the guarantor offers to the claimant an amount equal to or greater than that finally paid in satisfaction of the claim, the period described in paragraph (1) does not include the period beginning on the date the offer is made and ending on the date the offer is accepted. If the offer is made within 60 days after the date on which the claim is presented under section 1013(a), the period described in paragraph (1) does not include any period before the offer is accepted.

    (3) EXCLUSION OF PERIODS IN INTERESTS OF JUSTICE – If in any period a claimant is not paid due to reasons beyond the control of the responsible party or because it

would not serve the interests of justice, no interest shall accrue under this section during that period.

(4) CALCULATION OF INTEREST – The interest paid under this section shall be calculated at the average of the highest rate for commercial and finance company paper of maturities of 180 days or less obtaining on each of the days included within the period for which interest must be paid to the claimant, as published in the Federal Reserve Bulletin.

(5) INTEREST NOT SUBJECT TO LIABILITY LIMITS:

(A) IN GENERAL – Interest (including prejudgment interest) under this paragraph is in addition to damages and removal costs for which claims may be asserted under section 1002 and shall be paid without regard to any limitation of liability under section 1004.

(B) PAYMENT BY GUARANTOR – The payment of interest under this subsection by a guarantor is subject to section 1016(g).

(33 U.S.C. 2705)

Sec. 1006. Natural resources

(a) LIABILITY – In the case of natural resource damages under section 1002(b)(2)(A), liability shall be:

(1) to the United States Government for natural resources belonging to, managed by, controlled by, or appertaining to the United States;

(2) to any State for natural resources belonging to, managed by, controlled by, or appertaining to such State or political subdivision thereof;

(3) to any Indian tribe for natural resources belonging to, managed by, controlled by, or appertaining to such Indian tribe; and

(4) in any case in which section 1007 applies, to the government of a foreign country for natural resources belonging to, managed by, controlled by, or appertaining to such country.

(b) DESIGNATION OF TRUSTEES:

(1) IN GENERAL – The President, or the authorised representative of any State, Indian tribe, or foreign government, shall act on behalf of the public, Indian tribe, or foreign country as trustee of natural resources to present a claim for and to recover damages to the natural resources.

(2) FEDERAL TRUSTEES – The President shall designate the Federal officials who shall act on behalf of the public as trustees for natural resources under this Act.

(3) STATE TRUSTEES – The Governor of each State shall designate State and local officials who may act on behalf of the public as trustee for natural resources under this Act and shall notify the President of the designation.

(4) INDIAN TRIBE TRUSTEES – The governing body of any Indian tribe shall designate tribal officials who may act on behalf of the tribe or its members as trustee for natural resources under this Act and shall notify the President of the designation.

(5) FOREIGN TRUSTEES – The head of any foreign government may designate the trustee who shall act on behalf of that government as trustee for natural resources under this Act.

(c) FUNCTIONS OF TRUSTEES:

(1) FEDERAL TRUSTEES – The Federal officials designated under subsection (b)(2):

(A) shall assess natural resource damages under section 1002(b)(2)(A) for the natural resources under their trusteeship;

(B) may, upon request of and reimbursement from a State or Indian tribe and at the Federal officials' discretion, assess damages for the natural resources under the State's or tribe's trusteeship; and

(C) shall develop and implement a plan for the restoration, rehabilitation, replacement, or acquisition of the equivalent, of the natural resources under their trusteeship.

(2) STATE TRUSTEES – The State and local officials designated under subsection (b)(3):
    (A) shall assess natural resource damages under section 1002(b)(2)(A) for the purposes of this Act for the natural resources under their trusteeship; and
    (B) shall develop and implement a plan for the restoration, rehabilitation, replacement, or acquisition of the equivalent, of the natural resources under their trusteeship.
(3) INDIAN TRIBE TRUSTEES – The tribal officials designated under subsection (b)(4):
    (A) shall assess natural resource damages under section 1002(b)(2)(A) for the purposes of this Act for the natural resources under their trusteeship; and
    (B) shall develop and implement a plan for the restoration, rehabilitation, replacement, or acquisition of the equivalent, of the natural resources under their trusteeship.
(4) FOREIGN TRUSTEES – The trustees designated under subsection (b)(5):
    (A) shall assess natural resource damages under section 1002(b)(2)(A) for the purposes of this Act for the natural resources under their trusteeship; and
    (B) shall develop and implement a plan for the restoration, rehabilitation, replacement, or acquisition of the equivalent, of the natural resources under their trusteeship.
(5) NOTICE AND OPPORTUNITY TO BE HEARD – Plans shall be developed and implemented under this section only after adequate public notice, opportunity for a hearing, and consideration of all public comment.

(d) MEASURE OF DAMAGES:
(1) IN GENERAL – The measure of natural resource damages under section 1002(b)(2)(A) is:
    (A) the cost of restoring, rehabilitating, replacing, or acquiring the equivalent of, the damaged natural resources;
    (B) the diminution in value of those natural resources pending restoration; plus
    (C) the reasonable cost of assessing those damages.
(2) DETERMINE COSTS WITH RESPECT TO PLANS – Costs shall be determined under paragraph (1) with respect to plans adopted under subsection (c).
(3) NO DOUBLE RECOVERY – There shall be no double recovery under this Act for natural resource damages, including with respect to the costs of damage assessment or restoration, rehabilitation, replacement, or acquisition for the same incident and natural resource.

(e) DAMAGE ASSESSMENT REGULATIONS:
(1) REGULATIONS – The President, acting through the Under Secretary of Commerce for Oceans and Atmosphere and in consultation with the Administrator of the Environmental Protection Agency, the Director of the United States Fish and Wildlife Service, and the heads of other affected agencies, not later than 2 years after the date of the enactment of this Act, shall promulgate regulations for the assessment of natural resource damages under section 1002(b)(2)(A) resulting from a discharge of oil for the purpose of this Act.
(2) REBUTTABLE PRESUMPTION – Any determination or assessment of damages to natural resources for the purposes of this Act made under subsection (d) by a Federal, State, or Indian trustee in accordance with the regulations promulgated under paragraph (1) shall have the force and effect of a rebuttable presumption on behalf of the trustee in any administrative or judicial proceeding under this Act.

(f) USE OF RECOVERED SUMS – Sums recovered under this Act by a Federal, State, Indian, or foreign trustee for natural resource damages under section 1002(b)(2)(A) shall be retained by the trustee in a revolving trust account, without further appropriation, for use only to reimburse or pay costs incurred by the trustee under subsection (c) with respect to the damaged natural resources. Any amounts in excess of those required for these reimbursements and costs shall be deposited in the Fund.

(g) COMPLIANCE – Review of actions by any Federal official where there is alleged to be a failure of that official to perform a duty under this section that is not discretionary with that official may be had by any person in the district court in which the person resides or in which the alleged damage to natural resources occurred. The court may award costs of litigation (including reasonable attorney and expert witness fees) to any prevailing or substantially prevailing party. Nothing in this subsection shall restrict any right which any person may have to seek relief under any other provision of law.

(33 U.S.C. 2706)

Sec. 1007. Recovery by foreign claimants

   (a) REQUIRED SHOWING BY FOREIGN CLAIMANTS:

      (1) IN GENERAL – In addition to satisfying the other requirements of this Act, to recover removal costs or damages resulting from an incident a foreign claimant shall demonstrate that:

        (A) the claimant has not been otherwise compensated for the removal costs or damages; and

        (B) recovery is authorised by a treaty or executive agreement between the United States and the claimant's country, or the Secretary of State, in consultation with the Attorney General and other appropriate officials, has certified that the claimant's country provides a comparable remedy for United States claimants.

      (2) EXCEPTIONS – Paragraph (1)(B) shall not apply with respect to recovery by a resident of Canada in the case of an incident described in subsection (b)(4).

   (b) DISCHARGES IN FOREIGN COUNTRIES – A foreign claimant may make a claim for removal costs and damages resulting from a discharge, or substantial threat of a discharge, of oil in or on the territorial sea, internal waters, or adjacent shoreline of a foreign country, only if the discharge is from:

      (1) an Outer Continental Shelf facility or a deepwater port;

      (2) a vessel in the navigable waters;

      (3) a vessel carrying oil as cargo between 2 places in the United States; or

      (4) a tanker that received the oil at the terminal of the pipeline constructed under the Trans-Alaska Pipeline Authorization Act (43 U.S.C. 1651 *et seq.*), for transportation to a place in the United States, and the discharge or threat occurs prior to delivery of the oil to that place.

   (c) FOREIGN CLAIMANT DEFINED – In this section, the term "foreign claimant" means-

      (1) a person residing in a foreign country;

      (2) the government of a foreign country; and

      (3) an agency or political subdivision of a foreign country.

(33 U.S.C. 2707)

Sec. 1008. Recovery by responsible party

   (a) IN GENERAL – The responsible party for a vessel or facility from which oil is discharged, or which poses the substantial threat of a discharge of oil, may assert a claim for removal costs and damages under section 1013 only if the responsible party demonstrates that:

      (1) the responsible party is entitled to a defense to liability under section 1003; or

      (2) the responsible party is entitled to a limitation of liability under section 1004.

   (b) EXTENT OF RECOVERY – A responsible party who is entitled to a limitation of liability may assert a claim under section 1013 only to the extent that the sum of the removal costs and damages incurred by the responsible party plus the amounts paid by the responsible party, or by the guarantor on behalf of the responsible party, for claims asserted under section 1013 exceeds the amount to which the total of the liability under section 1002 and removal costs and damages incurred by, or on behalf of, the responsible party is limited under section 1004.

(33 U.S.C. 2708)

Sec. 1009. Contribution

A person may bring a civil action for contribution against any other person who is liable or potentially liable under this Act or another law. The action shall be brought in accordance with section 1017.

(33 U.S.C. 2709)

Sec. 1010. Indemnification agreements

(a) AGREEMENTS NOT PROHIBITED – Nothing in this Act prohibits any agreement to insure, hold harmless, or indemnify a party to such agreement for any liability under this Act.

(b) LIABILITY NOT TRANSFERRED – No indemnification, hold harmless, or similar agreement or conveyance shall be effective to transfer liability imposed under this Act from a responsible party or from any person who may be liable for an incident under this Act to any other person.

(c) RELATIONSHIP TO OTHER CAUSES OF ACTION – Nothing in this Act, including the provisions of subsection (b), bars a cause of action that a responsible party subject to liability under this Act, or a guarantor, has or would have, by reason of subrogation or otherwise, against any person.

(33 U.S.C. 2710)

Sec. 1011. Consultation on removal actions

The President shall consult with the affected trustees designated under section 1006 on the appropriate removal action to be taken in connection with any discharge of oil. For the purposes of the National Contingency Plan, removal with respect to any discharge shall be considered completed when so determined by the President in consultation with the Governor or Governors of the affected States. However, this determination shall not preclude additional removal actions under applicable State law.

(33 U.S.C. 2711)

Sec. 1012. Uses of the fund

(a) USES GENERALLY – The Fund shall be available to the President for:
  (1) the payment of removal costs, including the costs of monitoring removal actions, determined by the President to be consistent with the National Contingency Plan:
    (A) by Federal authorities; or
    (B) by a Governor or designated State official under subsection (d);
  (2) the payment of costs incurred by Federal, State, or Indian tribe trustees in carrying out their functions under section 1006 for assessing natural resource damages and for developing and implementing plans for the restoration, rehabilitation, replacement, or acquisition of the equivalent of damaged resources determined by the President to be consistent with the National Contingency Plan;
  (3) the payment of removal costs determined by the President to be consistent with the National Contingency Plan as a result of, and damages resulting from, a discharge, or a substantial threat of a discharge, of oil from a foreign offshore unit;
  (4) the payment of claims in accordance with section 1013 for uncompensated removal costs determined by the President to be consistent with the National Contingency Plan or uncompensated damages;
  (5) the payment of Federal administrative, operational, and personnel costs and expenses reasonably necessary for and incidental to the implementation, administration, and enforcement of this Act (including, but not limited to, sections 1004(d)(2), 1006(e), 4107, 4110, 4111, 4112, 4117, 5006, 8103, and title VII) and subsections (b), (c), (d), (j), and (l) of section 311 of the Federal Water Pollution Control Act (33 U.S.C. 1321), as amended by this Act, with respect to prevention, removal, and enforcement related to oil discharges, provided that:
    (A) not more than $25,000,000 in each fiscal year shall be available to the Secretary for operating expenses incurred by the Coast Guard;
    (B) not more than $30,000,000 each year through the end of fiscal year 1992 shall be available to establish the National Response System under section 311(j) of the Federal Water Pollution Control Act, as amended by this Act, including the purchase and prepositioning of oil spill removal equipment; and

415

(C) not more than $27,250,000 in each fiscal year shall be available to carry out title VII of this Act.

(b) DEFENSE TO LIABILITY FOR FUND – The Fund shall not be available to pay any claim for removal costs or damages to a particular claimant, to the extent that the incident, removal costs, or damages are caused by the gross negligence or willful misconduct of that claimant.

(c) OBLIGATION OF FUND BY FEDERAL OFFICIALS – The President may promulgate regulations designating one or more Federal officials who may obligate money in accordance with subsection (a).

(d) ACCESS TO FUND BY STATE OFFICIALS:

(1) IMMEDIATE REMOVAL – In accordance with regulations promulgated under this section, the President, upon the request of the Governor of a State or pursuant to an agreement with a State under paragraph (2), may obligate the Fund for payment in an amount not to exceed $250,000 for removal costs consistent with the National Contingency Plan required for the immediate removal of a discharge, or the mitigation or prevention of a substantial threat of a discharge, of oil.

(2) AGREEMENTS:

(A) IN GENERAL – The President shall enter into an agreement with the Governor of any interested State to establish procedures under which the Governor or a designated State official may receive payments from the Fund for removal costs pursuant to paragraph (1).

(B) TERMS – Agreements under this paragraph:

(i) may include such terms and conditions as may be agreed upon by the President and the Governor of a State;

(ii) shall provide for political subdivisions of the State to receive payments for reasonable removal costs; and

(iii) may authorise advance payments from the Fund to facilitate removal efforts.

(e) REGULATIONS – The President shall:

(1) not later than 6 months after the date of the enactment of this Act, publish proposed regulations detailing the manner in which the authority to obligate the Fund and to enter into agreements under this subsection shall be exercised; and

(2) not later than 3 months after the close of the comment period for such proposed regulations, promulgate final regulations for that purpose.

(f) RIGHTS OF SUBROGATION – Payment of any claim or obligation by the Fund under this Act shall be subject to the United States Government acquiring by subrogation all rights of the claimant or State to recover from the responsible party.

(g) AUDITS – The Comptroller General shall audit all payments, obligations, reimbursements, and other uses of the Fund, to assure that the Fund is being properly administered and that claims are being appropriately and expeditiously considered. The Comptroller General shall submit to the Congress an interim report one year after the date of the enactment of this Act. The Comptroller General shall thereafter audit the Fund as is appropriate. Each Federal agency shall cooperate with the Comptroller General in carrying out this subsection.

(h) PERIOD OF LIMITATIONS FOR CLAIMS:

(1) REMOVAL COSTS – No claim may be presented under this title for recovery of removal costs for an incident unless the claim is presented within 6 years after the date of completion of all removal actions for that incident.

(2) DAMAGES – No claim may be presented under this section for recovery of damages unless the claim is presented within 3 years after the date on which the injury and its connection with the discharge in question were reasonably discoverable with the exercise of due care, or in the case of natural resource damages under section 1002(b)(2)(A), if later, the date of completion of the natural resources damage assessment under section 1006(e).

(3) MINORS AND INCOMPETENTS – The time limitations contained in this subsection shall not begin to run:

(A) against a minor until the earlier of the date when such minor reaches 18 years of age or the date on which a legal representative is duly appointed for the minor, or

(B) against an incompetent person until the earlier of the date on which such incompetent's incompetency ends or the date on which a legal representative is duly appointed for the incompetent.

(i) LIMITATION ON PAYMENT FOR SAME COSTS – In any case in which the President has paid an amount from the Fund for any removal costs or damages specified under subsection (a), no other claim may be paid from the Fund for the same removal costs or damages.

(j) OBLIGATION IN ACCORDANCE WITH PLAN:

    (1) IN GENERAL – Except as provided in paragraph (2), amounts may be obligated from the Fund for the restoration, rehabilitation, replacement, or acquisition of natural resources only in accordance with a plan adopted under section 1006(c).

    (2) EXCEPTION – Paragraph (1) shall not apply in a situation requiring action to avoid irreversible loss of natural resources or to prevent or reduce any continuing danger to natural resources or similar need for emergency action.

(k) PREFERENCE FOR PRIVATE PERSONS IN AREA AFFECTED BY DISCHARGE:

    (1) IN GENERAL – In the expenditure of Federal funds for removal of oil, including for distribution of supplies, construction, and other reasonable and appropriate activities, under a contract or agreement with a private person, preference shall be given, to the extent feasible and practicable, to private persons residing or doing business primarily in the area affected by the discharge of oil.

    (2) LIMITATION – This subsection shall not be considered to restrict the use of Department of Defense resources.

(33 U.S.C. 2712)

Sec. 1013. Claims procedure

(a) PRESENTATION – Except as provided in subsection (b), all claims for removal costs or damages shall be presented first to the responsible party or guarantor of the source designated under section 1014(a).

(b) PRESENTATION TO FUND:

    (1) IN GENERAL – Claims for removal costs or damages may be presented first to the Fund-

        (A) if the President has advertised or otherwise notified claimants in accordance with section 1014(c);

        (B) by a responsible party who may assert a claim under section 1008;

        (C) by the Governor of a State for removal costs incurred by that State; or

        (D) by a United States claimant in a case where a foreign offshore unit has discharged oil causing damage for which the Fund is liable under section 1012(a).

    (2) LIMITATION ON PRESENTING CLAIM – No claim of a person against the Fund may be approved or certified during the pendency of an action by the person in court to recover costs which are the subject of the claim.

(c) ELECTION – If a claim is presented in accordance with subsection (a) and:

    (1) each person to whom the claim is presented denies all liability for the claim, or

    (2) the claim is not settled by any person by payment within 90 days after the date upon which (A) the claim was presented, or (B) advertising was begun pursuant to section 1014(b), whichever is later,

the claimant may elect to commence an action in court against the responsible party or guarantor or to present the claim to the Fund.

(d) UNCOMPENSATED DAMAGES – If a claim is presented in accordance with this section, including a claim for interim, short-term damages representing less than the full amount of damages to which the claimant ultimately may be entitled, and full and adequate compensation is unavailable, a claim for the uncompensated damages and removal costs may be presented to the Fund.

(e) PROCEDURE FOR CLAIMS AGAINST FUND – The President shall promulgate, and may from time to time amend, regulations for the presentation, filing, processing, settlement, and adjudication of claims under this Act against the Fund.

(33 U.S.C. 2713)

417

Sec. 1014. Designation of source and advertisement

(a) DESIGNATION OF SOURCE AND NOTIFICATION – When the President receives information of an incident, the President shall, where possible and appropriate, designate the source or sources of the discharge or threat. If a designated source is a vessel or a facility, the President shall immediately notify the responsible party and the guarantor, if known, of that designation.

(b) ADVERTISEMENT BY RESPONSIBLE PARTY OR GUARANTOR – (1) If a responsible party or guarantor fails to inform the President, within 5 days after receiving notification of a designation under subsection (a), of the party's or the guarantor's denial of the designation, such party or guarantor shall advertise the designation and the procedures by which claims may be presented, in accordance with regulations promulgated by the President. Advertisement under the preceding sentence shall begin no later than 15 days after the date of the designation made under subsection (a). If advertisement is not otherwise made in accordance with this subsection, the President shall promptly and at the expense of the responsible party or the guarantor involved, advertise the designation and the procedures by which claims may be presented to the responsible party or guarantor. Advertisement under this subsection shall continue for a period of no less than 30 days.

   (2) An advertisement under paragraph (1) shall state that a claimant may present a claim for interim, short-term damages representing less than the full amount of damages to which the claimant ultimately may be entitled and that payment of such a claim shall not preclude recovery for damages not reflected in the paid or settled partial claim.

(c) ADVERTISEMENT BY PRESIDENT – If:

   (1) the responsible party and the guarantor both deny a designation within 5 days after receiving notification of a designation under subsection (a),

   (2) the source of the discharge or threat was a public vessel, or

   (3) the President is unable to designate the source or sources of the discharge or threat under subsection (a),

the President shall advertise or otherwise notify potential claimants of the procedures by which claims may be presented to the Fund.

(33 U.S.C. 2714)

Sec. 1015. Subrogation [1]

(a) IN GENERAL – Any person, including the Fund, who pays compensation pursuant to this Act to any claimant for removal costs or damages shall be subrogated to all rights, claims, and causes of action that the claimant has under any other law.

(b) INTERIM DAMAGES:

   (1) IN GENERAL – If a responsible party, a guarantor, or the Fund has made payment to a claimant for interim, shortterm damages representing less than the full amount of damages to which the claimant ultimately may be entitled, subrogation under subsection (a) shall apply only with respect to the portion of the claim reflected in the paid interim claim.

   (2) FINAL DAMAGES – Payment of such a claim shall not foreclose a claimant's right to recovery of all damages to which the claimant otherwise is entitled under this Act or under any other law.

(c) ACTIONS ON BEHALF OF FUND – At the request of the Secretary, the Attorney General shall commence an action on behalf of the Fund to recover any compensation paid by the Fund to any claimant pursuant to this Act, and all costs incurred by the Fund by reason of the claim, including interest (including prejudgment interest), administrative and adjudicative costs, and attorney's fees. Such an action may be commenced against any responsible party or (subject to section 1016) guarantor, or against any other person who is liable,

---

1. Section 1142(d) of Public Law 104–324 (110 Stat. 3991) stated that "[s]ection 1015(a) of the Oil Pollution Act of 1990 (33 U.S.C. 2715(a)) is amended" by redesignating subsection (b) as subsection (c) and by inserting after subsection (a) a new subsection (b). The amendments were executed as amendments to section 1015.

pursuant to any law, to the compensated claimant or to the Fund, for the cost or damages for which the compensation was paid. Such an action shall be commenced against the responsible foreign government or other responsible party to recover any removal costs or damages paid from the Fund as the result of the discharge, or substantial threat of discharge, of oil from a foreign offshore unit.

(33 U.S.C. 2716)

Sec. 1016. Financial responsibility

(a) REQUIREMENT – The responsible party for:

    (1) any vessel over 300 gross tons (except a non-self-propelled vessel that does not carry oil as cargo or fuel) using any place subject to the jurisdiction of the United States; or

    (2) any vessel using the waters of the exclusive economic zone to transship or lighter oil destined for a place subject to the jurisdiction of the United States;

shall establish and maintain, in accordance with regulations promulgated by the Secretary, evidence of financial responsibility sufficient to meet the maximum amount of liability to which the responsible party could be subjected under section 1004(a) or (d) of this Act, in a case where the responsible party would be entitled to limit liability under that section. If the responsible party owns or operates more than one vessel, evidence of financial responsibility need be established only to meet the amount of the maximum liability applicable to the vessel having the greatest maximum liability.

(b) SANCTIONS:

    (1) WITHHOLDING CLEARANCE – The Secretary of the Treasury shall withhold or revoke the clearance required by section 4197 of the Revised Statutes of the United States of any vessel subject to this section that does not have the evidence of financial responsibility required for the vessel under this section.

    (2) DENYING ENTRY TO OR DETAINING VESSELS – The Secretary may –

        (A) deny entry to any vessel to any place in the United States, or to the navigable waters, or

        (B) detain at the place, any vessel that, upon request, does not produce the evidence of financial responsibility required for the vessel under this section.

    (3) SEIZURE OF VESSEL – Any vessel subject to the requirements of this section which is found in the navigable waters without the necessary evidence of financial responsibility for the vessel shall be subject to seizure by and forfeiture to the United States.

(c) OFFSHORE FACILITIES:

    (1) IN GENERAL:

        (A) EVIDENCE OF FINANCIAL RESPONSIBILITY REQUIRED – Except as provided in paragraph (2), a responsible party with respect to an offshore facility that:

            (i)(I) is located seaward of the line of ordinary low water along that portion of the coast that is in direct contact with the open sea and the line marking the seaward limit of inland waters; or

            (II) is located in coastal inland waters, such as bays or estuaries, seaward of the line of ordinary low water along that portion of the coast that is not in direct contact with the open sea;

            (ii) is used for exploring for, drilling for, producing, or transporting oil from facilities engaged in oil exploration, drilling, or production; and

            (iii) has a worst-case oil spill discharge potential of more than 1,000 barrels of oil (or a lesser amount if the President determines that the risks posed by such facility justify it),

        shall establish and maintain evidence of financial responsibility in the amount required under subparagraph (B) or (C), as applicable.

        (B) AMOUNT REQUIRED GENERALLY – Except as provided in subparagraph (C), the amount of financial responsibility for offshore facilities that meet the criteria of subparagraph (A) is:

(i) $35,000,000 for an offshore facility located seaward of the seaward boundary of a State; or

(ii) $10,000,000 for an offshore facility located landward of the seaward boundary of a State.

(C) GREATER AMOUNT – If the President determines that an amount of financial responsibility for a responsible party greater than the amount required by subparagraph (B) is justified based on the relative operational, environmental, human health, and other risks posed by the quantity or quality of oil that is explored for, drilled for, produced, or transported by the responsible party, the evidence of financial responsibility required shall be for an amount determined by the President not exceeding $150,000,000.

(D) MULTIPLE FACILITIES – In a case in which a person is a responsible party for more than one facility subject to this subsection, evidence of financial responsibility need be established only to meet the amount applicable to the facility having the greatest financial responsibility requirement under this subsection.

(E) DEFINITION – For the purpose of this paragraph, the seaward boundary of a State shall be determined in accordance with section 2(b) of the Submerged Lands Act (43 U.S.C. 1301(b)).

(2) DEEPWATER PORTS – Each responsible party with respect to a deepwater port shall establish and maintain evidence of financial responsibility sufficient to meet the maximum amount of liability to which the responsible party could be subjected under section 1004(a) of this Act in a case where the responsible party would be entitled to limit liability under that section. If the Secretary exercises the authority under section 1004(d)(2) to lower the limit of liability for deepwater ports, the responsible party shall establish and maintain evidence of financial responsibility sufficient to meet the maximum amount of liability so established. In a case in which a person is the responsible party for more than one deepwater port, evidence of financial responsibility need be established only to meet the maximum liability applicable to the deepwater port having the greatest maximum liability.

(e) METHODS OF FINANCIAL RESPONSIBILITY – Financial responsibility under this section may be established by any one, or by any combination, of the following methods which the Secretary (in the case of a vessel) or the President (in the case of a facility) determines to be acceptable: evidence of insurance, surety bond, guarantee, letter of credit, qualification as a self-insurer, or other evidence of financial responsibility. Any bond filed shall be issued by a bonding company authorised to do business in the United States. In promulgating requirements under this section, the Secretary or the President, as appropriate, may specify policy or other contractual terms, conditions, or defenses which are necessary, or which are unacceptable, in establishing evidence of financial responsibility to effectuate the purposes of this Act.

(f) CLAIMS AGAINST GUARANTOR:

(1) IN GENERAL – Subject to paragraph (2), a claim for which liability may be established under section 1002 may be asserted directly against any guarantor providing evidence of financial responsibility for a responsible party liable under that section for removal costs and damages to which the claim pertains. In defending against such a claim, the guarantor may invoke –

(A) all rights and defenses which would be available to the responsible party under this Act;

(B) any defense authorised under subsection (e); and

(C) the defense that the incident was caused by the willful misconduct of the responsible party.

The guarantor may not invoke any other defense that might be available in proceedings brought by the responsible party against the guarantor.

(2) FURTHER REQUIREMENT – A claim may be asserted pursuant to paragraph (1) directly against a guarantor providing evidence of financial responsibility under subsection (c)(1) with respect to an offshore facility only if –

(A) the responsible party for whom evidence of financial responsibility has been provided has denied or failed to pay a claim under this Act on the basis of being insolvent, as defined under section 101(32) of title 11, United States Code, and applying generally accepted accounting principles;

(B) the responsible party for whom evidence of financial responsibility has been provided has filed a petition for bankruptcy under title 11, United States Code; or

(C) the claim is asserted by the United States for removal costs and damages or for compensation paid by the Fund under this Act, including costs incurred by the Fund for processing compensation claims.

(3) RULEMAKING AUTHORITY – Not later than 1 year after the date of enactment of this paragraph, the President shall promulgate regulations to establish a process for implementing paragraph (2) in a manner that will allow for the orderly and expeditious presentation and resolution of claims and effectuate the purposes of this Act.

(g) LIMITATION ON GUARANTOR'S LIABILITY – Nothing in this Act shall impose liability with respect to an incident on any guarantor for damages or removal costs which exceed, in the aggregate, the amount of financial responsibility which that guarantor has provided for a responsible party pursuant to this section. The total liability of the guarantor on direct action for claims brought under this Act with respect to an incident shall be limited to that amount.

(h) CONTINUATION OF REGULATIONS – Any regulation relating to financial responsibility, which has been issued pursuant to any provision of law repealed or superseded by this Act, and which is in effect on the date immediately preceding the effective date of this Act, is deemed and shall be construed to be a regulation issued pursuant to this section. Such a regulation shall remain in full force and effect unless and until superseded by a new regulation issued under this section.

(i) UNIFIED CERTIFICATE – The Secretary may issue a single unified certificate of financial responsibility for purposes of this Act and any other law.

(33 U.S.C. 2717)

Sec. 1017. Litigation, jurisdiction, and venue

(a) REVIEW OF REGULATIONS – Review of any regulation promulgated under this Act may be had upon application by any interested person only in the Circuit Court of Appeals of the United States for the District of Columbia. Any such application shall be made within 90 days from the date of promulgation of such regulations. Any matter with respect to which review could have been obtained under this subsection shall not be subject to judicial review in any civil or criminal proceeding for enforcement or to obtain damages or recovery of response costs.

(b) JURISDICTION – Except as provided in subsections (a) and (c), the United States district courts shall have exclusive original jurisdiction over all controversies arising under this Act, without regard to the citizenship of the parties or the amount in controversy. Venue shall lie in any district in which the discharge or injury or damages occurred, or in which the defendant resides, may be found, has its principal office, or has appointed an agent for service of process. For the purposes of this section, the Fund shall reside in the District of Columbia.

(c) STATE COURT JURISDICTION – A State trial court of competent jurisdiction over claims for removal costs or damages, as defined under this Act, may consider claims under this Act or State law and any final judgment of such court (when no longer subject to ordinary forms of review) shall be recognized, valid, and enforceable for all purposes of this Act.

(d) ASSESSMENT AND COLLECTION OF TAX – The provisions of subsections (a), (b), and (c) shall not apply to any controversy or other matter resulting from the assessment or collection of any tax, or to the review of any regulation promulgated under the Internal Revenue Code of 1986.

(e) SAVINGS PROVISION – Nothing in this title shall apply to any cause of action or right of recovery arising from any incident which occurred prior to the date of enactment of this title. Such claims shall be adjudicated pursuant to the law applicable on the date of the incident.

(f) PERIOD OF LIMITATIONS:
  (1) DAMAGES – Except as provided in paragraphs (3) and (4), an action for damages under this Act shall be barred unless the action is brought within 3 years after –
    (A) the date on which the loss and the connection of the loss with the discharge in question are reasonably discoverable with the exercise of due care, or
    (B) in the case of natural resource damages under section 1002(b)(2)(A), the date of completion of the natural resources damage assessment under section 1006(c).
  (2) REMOVAL COSTS – An action for recovery of removal costs referred to in section 1002(b)(1) must be commenced within 3 years after completion of the removal action. In any such action described in this subsection, the court shall enter a declaratory judgment on liability for removal costs or damages that will be binding on any subsequent action or actions to recover further removal costs or damages. Except as otherwise provided in this paragraph, an action may be commenced under this title for recovery of removal costs at any time after such costs have been incurred.
  (3) CONTRIBUTION – No action for contribution for any removal costs or damages may be commenced more than 3 years after –
    (A) the date of judgment in any action under this Act for recovery of such costs or damages, or
    (B) the date of entry of a judicially approved settlement with respect to such costs or damages.
  (4) SUBROGATION – No action based on rights subrogated pursuant to this Act by reason of payment of a claim may be commenced under this Act more than 3 years after the date of payment of such claim.
  (5) COMMENCEMENT – The time limitations contained herein shall not begin to run –
    (A) against a minor until the earlier of the date when such minor reaches 18 years of age or the date on which a legal representative is duly appointed for such minor, or
    (B) against an incompetent person until the earlier of the date on which such incompetent's incompetency ends or the date on which a legal representative is duly appointed for such incompetent.

(33 U.S.C. 2717)

Sec. 1018. Relationship to other law

(a) PRESERVATION OF STATE AUTHORITIES; SOLID WASTE DISPOSAL ACT – Nothing in this Act or the Act of March 3, 1851 shall –
  (1) affect, or be construed or interpreted as preempting, the authority of any State or political subdivision thereof from imposing any additional liability or requirements with respect to –
    (A) the discharge of oil or other pollution by oil within such State; or
    (B) any removal activities in connection with such a discharge; or
  (2) affect, or be construed or interpreted to affect or modify in any way the obligations or liabilities of any person under the Solid Waste Disposal Act (42 U.S.C. 6901 *et seq.*) or State law, including common law.
(b) PRESERVATION OF STATE FUNDS – Nothing in this Act or in section 9509 of the Internal Revenue Code of 1986 (26 U.S.C. 9509) shall in any way affect, or be construed to affect, the authority of any State –
  (1) to establish, or to continue in effect, a fund any purpose of which is to pay for costs or damages arising out of, or directly resulting from, oil pollution or the substantial threat of oil pollution; or
  (2) to require any person to contribute to such a fund.
(c) ADDITIONAL REQUIREMENTS AND LIABILITIES; PENALTIES – Nothing in this Act, the Act of March 3, 1851 (46 U.S.C. 183 *et seq.*), or section 9509 of the Internal Revenue

Code of 1986 (26 U.S.C. 9509), shall in any way affect, or be construed to affect, the authority of the United States or any State or political subdivision thereof –
    (1) to impose additional liability or additional requirements; or
    (2) to impose, or to determine the amount of, any fine or penalty (whether criminal or civil in nature) for any violation of law;
relating to the discharge, or substantial threat of a discharge, of oil.

(d) FEDERAL EMPLOYEE LIABILITY – For purposes of section 2679(b)(2)(B) of title 28, United States Code, nothing in this Act shall be construed to authorise or create a cause of action against a Federal officer or employee in the officer's or employee's personal or individual capacity for any act or omission while acting within the scope of the officer's or employee's office or employment.

(33 U.S.C. 2718)

Sec. 1019. State financial responsibility

A State may enforce, on the navigable waters of the State, the requirements for evidence of financial responsibility under section 1016.

(33 U.S.C. 2719)

Sec. 1020. Application

This Act shall apply to an incident occurring after the date of the enactment of this Act.

(33 U.S.C. 2701 note)

Title II – Conforming amendments

*   *   *   *   *   *   *

Sec. 2002. Federal Water Pollution Control Act

(a) APPLICATION – Subsections (f), (g), (h), and (i) of section 311 of the Federal Water Pollution Control Act (33 U.S.C. 1321) shall not apply with respect to any incident for which liability is established under section 1002 of this Act.
    (b) * * *

(33 U.S.C. 1321 note)

Sec. 2003. Deepwater Port Act

    (a) * * *
    (b) AMOUNTS REMAINING IN DEEPWATER PORT FUND – Any amounts remaining in the Deepwater Port Liability Fund established under section 18(f) of the Deepwater Port Act of 1974 (33 U.S.C. 1517(f)) shall be deposited in the Oil Spill Liability Trust Fund established under section 9509 of the Internal Revenue Code of 1986 (26 U.S.C. 9509). The Oil Spill Liability Trust Fund shall assume all liability incurred by the Deepwater Port Liability Fund.

(26 U.S.C. 9509 note)

Sec. 2004. Outer Continental Shelf Lands Act amendments of 1978.

Title III of the Outer Continental Shelf Lands Act Amendments of 1978 (43 U.S.C. 1811-1824) is repealed. Any amounts remaining in the Offshore Oil Pollution Compensation Fund established under section 302 of that title (43 U.S.C. 1812) shall be deposited in the Oil Spill Liability Trust Fund established under section 9509 of the Internal Revenue Code of 1986 (26 U.S.C. 9509). The Oil Spill Liability Trust Fund shall assume all liability incurred by the Offshore Oil Pollution Compensation Fund.

(26 U.S.C. 9509 note)

Title III – International oil pollution prevention and removal

Sec. 3001. Sense of Congress regarding participation in international regime

It is the sense of the Congress that it is in the best interests of the United States to partici-pate in an international oil pollution liability and compensation regime that is at least as effective as Federal and State laws in preventing incidents and in guaranteeing full and prompt compensation for damages resulting from incidents.

Sec. 3002. United States-Canada Great Lakes Oil Spill Cooperation

(a) REVIEW – The Secretary of State shall review relevant international agreements and treaties with the Government of Canada, including the Great Lakes Water Quality Agreement, to determine whether amendments or additional international agreements are necessary to:

(1) prevent discharges of oil on the Great Lakes;

(2) ensure an immediate and effective removal of oil on the Great Lakes; and

(3) fully compensate those who are injured by a discharge of oil on the Great Lakes.

(b) CONSULTATION – In carrying out this section, the Secretary of State shall consult with the Department of Transportation, the Environmental Protection Agency, the National Oceanic and Atmospheric Administration, the Great Lakes States, the International Joint Commission, and other appropriate agencies.

(c) REPORT – The Secretary of State shall submit a report to the Congress on the results of the review under this section within 6 months after the date of the enactment of this Act.

Sec. 3003. United States-Canada Lake Champlain Oil Spill Cooperation

(a) REVIEW – The Secretary of State shall review relevant international agreements and treaties with the Government of Canada, to determine whether amendments or additional international agreements are necessary to:

(1) prevent discharges of oil on Lake Champlain;

(2) ensure an immediate and effective removal of oil on Lake Champlain; and

(3) fully compensate those who are injured by a discharge of oil on Lake Champlain.

(b) CONSULTATION – In carrying out this section, the Secretary of State shall consult with the Department of Transportation, the Environmental Protection Agency, the National Oceanic and Atmospheric Administration, the States of Vermont and New York, the International Joint Commission, and other appropriate agencies.

(c) REPORT – The Secretary of State shall submit a report to the Congress on the results of the review under this section within 6 months after the date of the enactment of this Act.

Sec. 3004. International inventory of removal equipment and personnel

The President shall encourage appropriate international organisations to establish an inter-national inventory of spill removal equipment and personnel.

Sec. 3005. Negotiations with Canada concerning tug escorts in Puget Sound

Congress urges the Secretary of State to enter into negotiations with the Government of Canada to ensure that tugboat escorts are required for all tank vessels with a capacity over 40,000 deadweight tons in the Strait of Juan de Fuca and in Haro Strait.

Title IV – Prevention and removal

Subtitle A – Prevention

★　★　★　★　★　★　★

Sec. 4102. Term of licenses, certificates of registry, and merchant mariners' documents; criminal record reviews in renewals

(a) ★ ★ ★

* * * * * * *

(d) TERMINATION OF EXISTING LICENSES, CERTIFICATES, AND DOCUMENTS – A license, certificate of registry, or merchant mariner's document issued before the date of the enactment of this section terminates on the day it would have expired if –

    (1) subsections (a), (b), and (c) were in effect on the date it was issued; and

    (2) it was renewed at the end of each 5-year period under section 7106, 7107, or 7302 of title 46, United States Code.

(46 U.S.C. 7106 note)

* * * * * * *

Sec. 4107. Vessel traffic service systems

    (a) * * *

    (b) DIRECTION OF VESSEL MOVEMENT –

        (1) STUDY – The Secretary shall conduct a study –

            (A) of whether the Secretary should be given additional authority to direct the movement of vessels on navigable waters and should exercise such authority; and

            (B) to determine and prioritise the United States ports and channels that are in need of new, expanded, or improved vessel traffic service systems, by evaluating –

                (i) the nature, volume, and frequency of vessel traffic;

                (ii) the risks of collisions, spills, and damages associated with that traffic;

                (iii) the impact of installation, expansion, or improvement of a vessel traffic service system; and

                (iv) all other relevant costs and data.

        (2) REPORT – Not later than 1 year after the date of the enactment of this Act, the Secretary shall submit to the Congress a report on the results of the study conducted under paragraph (1) and recommendations for implementing the results of that study.

* * * * * * *

Sec. 4109. Periodic gauging of plating thickness of commercial vessels

Not later than 1 year after the date of the enactment of this Act, the Secretary shall issue regulations for vessels constructed or adapted to carry, or that carry, oil in bulk as cargo or cargo residue –

    (1) establishing minimum standards for plating thickness; and

    (2) requiring, consistent with generally recognized principles of international law, periodic gauging of the plating thickness of all such vessels over 30 years old operating on the navigable waters or the waters of the exclusive economic zone.

(46 U.S.C. 3703 note)

Sec. 4110. Overfill and tank level or pressure monitoring devices

    (a) STANDARDS – Not later than 1 year after the date of the enactment of this Act, the Secretary shall establish, by regulation, minimum standards for devices for warning persons of overfills and tank levels of oil in cargo tanks and devices for monitoring the pressure of oil cargo tanks.

    (b) USE – Not later than 1 year after the date of the enactment of this Act, the Secretary shall issue regulations establishing, consistent with generally recognized principles of international law, requirements concerning the use of –

        (1) overfill devices, and

        (2) tank level or pressure monitoring devices, which are referred to in subsection (a) and which meet the standards established by the Secretary under subsection (a), on vessels constructed or adapted to carry, or that carry, oil in bulk as cargo or cargo residue on the navigable waters and the waters of the exclusive economic zone.

(46 U.S.C. 3703 note)

Sec. 4111. Study on tanker navigation safety standards

(a) IN GENERAL – Not later than 1 year after the date of enactment of this Act, the Secretary shall initiate a study to determine whether existing laws and regulations are adequate to ensure the safe navigation of vessels transporting oil or hazardous substances in bulk on the navigable waters and the waters of the exclusive economic zone.

(b) CONTENT – In conducting the study required under subsection (a), the Secretary shall –

    (1) determine appropriate crew sizes on tankers;

    (2) evaluate the adequacy of qualifications and training of crewmembers on tankers;

    (3) evaluate the ability of crewmembers on tankers to take emergency actions to prevent or remove a discharge of oil or a hazardous substance from their tankers;

    (4) evaluate the adequacy of navigation equipment and systems on tankers (including sonar, electronic chart display, and satellite technology);

    (5) evaluate and test electronic means of position-reporting and identification on tankers, consider the minimum standards suitable for equipment for that purpose, and determine whether to require that equipment on tankers;

    (6) evaluate the adequacy of navigation procedures under different operating conditions, including such variables as speed, daylight, ice, tides, weather, and other conditions;

    (7) evaluate whether areas of navigable waters and the exclusive economic zone should be designated as zones where the movement of tankers should be limited or prohibited;

    (8) evaluate whether inspection standards are adequate;

    (9) review and incorporate the results of past studies, including studies conducted by the Coast Guard and the Office of Technology Assessment;

    (10) evaluate the use of computer simulator courses for training bridge officers and pilots of vessels transporting oil or hazardous substances on the navigable waters and waters of the exclusive economic zone, and determine the feasibility and practicality of mandating such training;

    (11) evaluate the size, cargo capacity, and flag nation of tankers transporting oil or hazardous substances on the navigable waters and the waters of the exclusive economic zone –

        (A) identifying changes occurring over the past 20 years in such size and cargo capacity and in vessel navigation and technology; and

        (B) evaluating the extent to which the risks or difficulties associated with tanker navigation, vessel traffic control, accidents, oil spills, and the containment and cleanup of such spills are influenced by or related to an increase in tanker size and cargo capacity; and

    (12) evaluate and test a program of remote alcohol testing for masters and pilots aboard tankers carrying significant quantities of oil.

(c) REPORT – Not later than 2 years after the date of enactment of this Act, the Secretary shall transmit to the Congress a report on the results of the study conducted under subsection (a), including recommendations for implementing the results of that study.

(46 U.S.C. 3703 note)

Sec. 4112. Dredge modification study

(a) STUDY – The Secretary of the Army shall conduct a study and demonstration to determine the feasibility of modifying dredges to make them usable in removing discharges of oil and hazardous substances.

(b) REPORT – Not later than 1 year after the date of enactment of this Act, the Secretary of the Army shall submit to the Congress a report on the results of the study conducted under subsection (a) and recommendations for implementing the results of that study.

Sec. 4113. Use of liners

(a) STUDY – The President shall conduct a study to determine whether liners or other secondary means of containment should be used to prevent leaking or to aid in leak detection at onshore facilities used for the bulk storage of oil and located near navigable waters.

(b) REPORT – Not later than 1 year after the date of enactment of this Act, the President shall submit to the Congress a report on the results of the study conducted under subsection (a) and recommendations to implement the results of the study.

(c) IMPLEMENTATION – Not later than 6 months after the date the report required under subsection (b) is submitted to the Congress, the President shall implement the recommendations contained in the report.

Sec. 4114. Tank vessel manning

(a) RULEMAKING – In order to protect life, property, and the environment, the Secretary shall initiate a rulemaking proceeding within 180 days after the date of the enactment of this Act to define the conditions under, and designate the waters upon, which tank vessels subject to section 3703 of title 46, United States Code, may operate in the navigable waters with the auto-pilot engaged or with an unattended engine room.

(b) ★ ★ ★

★   ★   ★   ★   ★   ★   ★

(46 U.S.C. 3703 note)

Sec. 4115. Establishment of double hull requirement for tank vessels

(a) ★ ★ ★

(b) RULEMAKING – The Secretary shall, within 12 months after the date of the enactment of this Act, complete a rulemaking proceeding and issue a final rule to require that tank vessels over 5,000 gross tons affected by section 3703a of title 46, United States Code, as added by this section, comply until January 1, 2015, with structural and operational requirements that the Secretary determines will provide as substantial protection to the environment as is economically and technologically feasible.

(46 U.S.C. 3703a note)

★   ★   ★   ★   ★   ★   ★

(e) SECRETARIAL STUDIES –

    (1) OTHER REQUIREMENTS – Not later than 6 months after the date of enactment of this Act, the Secretary shall determine, based on recommendations from the National Academy of Sciences or other qualified organisations, whether other structural and operational tank vessel requirements will provide protection to the marine environment equal to or greater than that provided by double hulls, and shall report to the Congress that determination and recommendations for legislative action.

    (2) REVIEW AND ASSESSMENT – The Secretary shall –

        (A) periodically review recommendations from the National Academy of Sciences and other qualified organisations on methods for further increasing the environmental and operational safety of tank vessels;

        (B) not later than 5 years after the date of enactment of this Act, assess the impact of this section on the safety of the marine environment and the economic viability and operational makeup of the maritime oil transportation industry; and

        (C) report the results of the review and assessment to the Congress with recommendations for legislative or other action.

    (3) (A) The Secretary of Transportation shall coordinate with the Marine Board of the National Research Council to conduct the necessary research and development of a rationally based equivalency assessment approach, which accounts for the overall environmental performance of alternative tank vessel designs. Notwithstanding the Coast Guard opinion of the application of sections 101 and 311 of the Clean Water

Act (33 U.S.C. 1251 and 1321), the intent of this study is to establish an equivalency evaluation procedure that maintains a high standard of environmental protection, while encouraging innovative ship design. The study shall include:

 (i) development of a generalised cost spill data base, which includes all relevant costs such as clean-up costs and environmental impact costs as a function of spill size;

 (ii) refinement of the probability density functions used to establish the extent of vessel damage, based on the latest available historical damage statistics, and current research on the crash worthiness of tank vessel structures;

 (iii) development of a rationally based approach for calculating an environmental index, to assess overall outflow performance due to collisions and groundings; and

 (iv) application of the proposed index to double hull tank vessels and alternative designs currently under consideration.

(B) A Marine Board committee shall be established not later that 2 months after the date of the enactment of the Coast Guard Authorization Act of 1998. The Secretary of Transportation shall submit to the Committee on Commerce, Science, and Transportation of the Senate and the Committee on Transportation and Infrastructure in the House of Representatives a report on the results of the study not later than 12 months after the date of the enactment of the Coast Guard Authorization Act of 1998.

(C) Of the amounts authorised by section 1012(a)(5)(A) of this Act, $500,000 is authorised to carry out the activities under subparagraphs (A) and (B) of this paragraph.

(46 U.S.C. 3703a note)

★ ★ ★ ★ ★ ★ ★

Sec. 4116. Pilotage

 (a) ★ ★ ★

★ ★ ★ ★ ★ ★ ★

 (c) ESCORTS FOR CERTAIN TANKERS – Not later than 6 months after the date of the enactment of this Act, the Secretary shall initiate issuance of regulations under section 3703(a)(3) of title 46, United States Code, to define those areas, including Prince William Sound, Alaska, and Rosario Strait and Puget Sound, Washington (including those portions of the Strait of Juan de Fuca east of Port Angeles, Haro Strait, and the Strait of Georgia subject to United States jurisdiction), on which single hulled tankers over 5,000 gross tons transporting oil in bulk shall be escorted by at least two towing vessels (as defined under section 2101 of title 46, United States Code) or other vessels considered appropriate by the Secretary.

 (d) TANKER DEFINED – In this section the term "tanker" has the same meaning the term has in section 2101 of title 46, United States Code.

(46 U.S.C. 3703 note)

Sec. 4117. Maritime pollution prevention training program study

The Secretary shall conduct a study to determine the feasibility of a Maritime Oil Pollution Prevention Training program to be carried out in cooperation with approved maritime training institutions. The study shall assess the costs and benefits of transferring suitable vessels to selected maritime training institutions, equipping the vessels for oil spill response, and training students in oil pollution response skills. The study shall be completed and transmitted to the Congress no later than one year after the date of the enactment of this Act.

(46 U.S.C. app. 1295 note)

Sec. 4118. Vessel communication equipment regulations

The Secretary shall, not later than one year after the date of the enactment of this Act, issue regulations necessary to ensure that vessels subject to the Vessel Bridge-to-Bridge Radiotelephone Act of 1971 (33 U.S.C. 1203) are also equipped as necessary to –

428

(1) receive radio marine navigation safety warnings; and

(2) engage in radio communications on designated frequencies with the Coast Guard, and such other vessels and stations as may be specified by the Secretary.

(33 U.S.C. 1203 note)

Subtitle B – Removal

Sec. 4201. Federal Removal Authority

(a) ★ ★ ★

★   ★   ★   ★   ★   ★   ★

(c) REVISION OF NATIONAL CONTINGENCY PLAN[1] – Not later than one year after the date of the enactment of this Act, the President shall revise and republish the National Contingency Plan prepared under section 311(c)(2) of the Federal Water Pollution Control Act (as in effect immediately before the date of the enactment of this Act) to implement the amendments made by this section and section 4202.

(33 U.S.C. 1321 note)

Sec. 4202. National Planning and Response System

(a) ★ ★ ★

(b) IMPLEMENTATION –

(1) AREA COMMITTEES AND CONTINGENCY PLANS –

(A) Not later than 6 months after the date of the enactment of this Act, the President shall designate the areas for which Area Committees are established under section 311(j)(4) of the Federal Water Pollution Control Act, as amended by this Act. In designating such areas, the President shall ensure that all navigable waters, adjoining shorelines, and waters of the exclusive economic zone are subject to an Area Contingency Plan under that section.

(B) Not later than 18 months after the date of the enactment of this Act, each Area Committee established under that section shall submit to the President the Area Contingency Plan required under that section.

(C) Not later than 24 months after the date of the enactment of this Act, the President shall –

(i) promptly review each plan;

(ii) require amendments to any plan that does not meet the requirements of section 311(j)(4) of the Federal Water Pollution Control Act; and

(iii) approve each plan that meets the requirements of that section.

(2) NATIONAL RESPONSE UNIT – Not later than one year after the date of the enactment of this Act, the Secretary of the department in which the Coast Guard is operating shall establish a National Response Unit in accordance with section 311(j)(2) of the Federal Water Pollution Control Act, as amended by this Act.

(3) COAST GUARD DISTRICT RESPONSE GROUPS – Not later than 1 year after the date of the enactment of this Act, the Secretary of the department in which the Coast Guard is operating shall establish Coast Guard District Response Groups in accordance with section 311(j)(3) of the Federal Water Pollution Control Act, as amended by this Act.

(4) TANK VESSEL AND FACILITY RESPONSE PLANS; TRANSITION PROVISION; EFFECTIVE DATE OF PROHIBITION –

(A) Not later than 24 months after the date of the enactment of this Act, the President shall issue regulations for tank vessel and facility response plans under section 311(j)(5) of the Federal Water Pollution Control Act, as amended by this Act.

(B) During the period beginning 30 months after the date of the enactment of this paragraph and ending 36 months after that date of enactment, a tank vessel or

---

1. So in law. Probably should be redesignated as subsection (d).

facility for which a response plan is required to be prepared under section 311(j)(5) of the Federal Water Pollution Control Act, as amended by this Act, may not handle, store, or transport oil unless the owner or operator thereof has submitted such a plan to the President.

(C) Subparagraph (E) of section 311(j)(5) of the Federal Water Pollution Control Act, as amended by this Act, shall take effect 36 months after the date of the enactment of this Act.

(33 U.S.C. 1321 note)

* * * * * * *

Sec. 4203. Coast Guard vessel design

The Secretary shall ensure that vessels designed and constructed to replace Coast Guard buoy tenders are equipped with oil skimming systems that are readily available and operable, and that complement the primary mission of servicing aids to navigation.

* * * * * * *

Subtitle C – Penalties and Miscellaneous

* * * * * * *

Sec. 4303. Financial responsibility civil penalties

(a) ADMINISTRATIVE – Any person who, after notice and an opportunity for a hearing, is found to have failed to comply with the requirements of section 1016 or the regulations issued under that section, or with a denial or detention order issued under subsection (c)(2) of that section, shall be liable to the United States for a civil penalty, not to exceed $25,000 per day of violation. The amount of the civil penalty shall be assessed by the President by written notice. In determining the amount of the penalty, the President shall take into account the nature, circumstances, extent, and gravity of the violation, the degree of culpability, any history of prior violation, ability to pay, and such other matters as justice may require. The President may compromise, modify, or remit, with or without conditions, any civil penalty which is subject to imposition or which has been imposed under this paragraph. If any person fails to pay an assessed civil penalty after it has become final, the President may refer the matter to the Attorney General for collection.

(b) JUDICIAL – In addition to, or in lieu of, assessing a penalty under subsection (a), the President may request the Attorney General to secure such relief as necessary to compel compliance with this section 1016, including a judicial order terminating operations. The district courts of the United States shall have jurisdiction to grant any relief as the public interest and the equities of the case may require.

(33 U.S.C. 2716a)

Sec. 4304. Deposit of certain penalties into Oil Spill Liability Trust Fund

Penalties paid pursuant to section 311 of the Federal Water Pollution Control Act, section 309(c) of that Act, as a result of violations of section 311 of that Act, and the Deepwater Port Act of 1974, shall be deposited in the Oil Spill Liability Trust Fund created under section 9509 of the Internal Revenue Code of 1986 (26 U.S.C. 9509).

(26 U.S.C. 9509 note)

* * * * * * *

Title V – Prince William Sound Provisions

Sec. 5001. Oil Spill Recovery Institute

(a) ESTABLISHMENT OF INSTITUTE – The Secretary of Commerce shall provide for the establishment of a Prince William Sound Oil Spill Recovery Institute (hereinafter in this section referred to as the "Institute") through the Prince William Sound Science and Technology Institute located in Cordova, Alaska.

(b) FUNCTIONS – The Institute shall conduct research and carry out educational and demonstration projects designed to –

    (1) identify and develop the best available techniques, equipment, and materials for dealing with oil spills in the arctic and subarctic marine environment; and

    (2) complement Federal and State damage assessment efforts and determine, document, assess, and understand the long-range effects of Arctic or Subarctic oil spills on the natural resources of Prince William Sound and its adjacent waters (as generally depicted on the map entitled "EXXON VALDEZ oil spill dated March 1990"), and the environment, the economy, and the lifestyle and well-being of the people who are dependent on them, except that the Institute shall not conduct studies or make recommendations on any matter which is not directly related to Arctic or Subarctic oil spills or the effects thereof.

(c) ADVISORY BOARD:

    (1) IN GENERAL – The policies of the Institute shall be determined by an advisory board, composed of 16 members appointed as follows:

        (A) One representative appointed by each of the Commissioners of Fish and Game, Environmental Conservation, and Natural Resources of the State of Alaska, all of whom shall be State employees.

        (B) One representative appointed by each of the Secretaries of Commerce, the Interior, and Transportation, who shall be Federal employees.

        (C) Two representatives from the fishing industry appointed by the Governor of the State of Alaska from among residents of communities in Alaska that were affected by the EXXON VALDEZ oil spill, who shall serve terms of 2 years each. Interested organisations from within the fishing industry may submit the names of qualified individuals for consideration by the Governor.

        (D) Two Alaska Natives who represent Native entities affected by the EXXON VALDEZ oil spill, at least one of whom represents an entity located in Prince William Sound, appointed by the Governor of Alaska from a list of 4 qualified individuals submitted by the Alaska Federation of Natives, who shall serve terms of 2 years each.

        (E) Two representatives from the oil and gas industry to be appointed by the Governor of the State of Alaska who shall serve terms of 2 years each. Interested organisations from within the oil and gas industry may submit the names of qualified individuals for consideration by the Governor.

        (F) Two at-large representatives from among residents of communities in Alaska that were affected by the EXXON VALDEZ oil spill who are knowledgeable about the marine environment and wildlife within Prince William Sound, and who shall serve terms of 2 years each, appointed by the remaining members of the Advisory Board. Interested parties may submit the names of qualified individuals for consideration by the Advisory Board.

        (G) One nonvoting representative of the Institute of Marine Science.

        (H) One nonvoting representative appointed by the Prince William Sound Science and Technology Institute.

    (2) CHAIRMAN – The representative of the Secretary of Commerce shall serve as Chairman of the Advisory Board.

    (3) POLICIES – Policies determined by the Advisory Board under this subsection shall include policies for the conduct and support, through contracts and grants awarded on a nationally competitive basis, of research, projects, and studies to be supported by the Institute in accordance with the purposes of this section.

    (4) SCIENTIFIC REVIEW – The Advisory Board may request a scientific review of the research program every five years by the National Academy of Sciences which shall perform the review, if requested, as part of its responsibilities under section 7001(b)(2).

(d) SCIENTIFIC AND TECHNICAL COMMITTEE:

    (1) IN GENERAL – The Advisory Board shall establish a scientific and technical committee, composed of specialists in matters relating to oil spill containment and

cleanup technology, arctic and subarctic marine ecology, and the living resources and socioeconomics of Prince William Sound and its adjacent waters, from the University of Alaska, the Institute of Marine Science, the Prince William Sound Science and Technology Institute, and elsewhere in the academic community.

(2) FUNCTIONS – The Scientific and Technical Committee shall provide such advice to the Advisory Board as the Advisory Board shall request, including recommendations regarding the conduct and support of research, projects, and studies in accordance with the purposes of this section. The Advisory Board shall not request, and the Committee shall not provide, any advice which is not directly related to Arctic or Subarctic oil spills or the effects thereof.

(e) DIRECTOR – The Institute shall be administered by a Director appointed by the Advisory Board. The Prince William Sound Science and Technology Institute and the Scientific and Technical Committee may each submit independent recommendations for the Advisory Board's consideration for appointment as Director. The Director may hire such staff and incur such expenses on behalf of the Institute as are authorised by the Advisory Board.

(f) EVALUATION – The Secretary of Commerce may conduct an ongoing evaluation of the activities of the Institute to ensure that funds received by the Institute are used in a manner consistent with this section.

(g) AUDIT – The Comptroller General of the United States, and any of his or her duly authorised representatives, shall have access, for purposes of audit and examination, to any books, documents, papers, and records of the Institute and its administering agency that are pertinent to the funds received and expended by the Institute and its administering agency.

(h) STATUS OF EMPLOYEES – Employees of the Institute shall not, by reason of such employment, be considered to be employees of the Federal Government for any purpose.

(i) TERMINATION – The authorisation in section 5006(b) providing funding for the Institute shall terminate 10 years after the date of the enactment of the Coast Guard Authorization Act of 1996.

(j) USE OF FUNDS – No funds made available to carry out this section may be used to initiate litigation. No funds made available to carry out this section may be used for the acquisition of real property (including buildings) or construction of any building. No more than 20 percent of funds made available to carry out this section may be used to lease necessary facilities and to administer the Institute. The Advisory Board may compensate its Federal representatives for their reasonable travel costs. None of the funds authorised by this section shall be used for any purpose other than the functions specified in subsection (b).

(k) RESEARCH – The Institute shall publish and make available to any person upon request the results of all research, educational, and demonstration projects conducted by the Institute. The Administrator shall provide a copy of all research, educational, and demonstration projects conducted by the Institute to the National Oceanic and Atmospheric Administration.

(l) DEFINITIONS – In this section, the term "Prince William Sound and its adjacent waters" means such sound and waters as generally depicted on the map entitled "EXXON VALDEZ oil spill dated March 1990".

(33 U.S.C. 2731)

Sec. 5002. Terminal and tanker oversight and monitoring

(a) SHORT TITLE AND FINDINGS:
(1) SHORT TITLE – This section may be cited as the "Oil Terminal and Oil Tanker Environmental Oversight and Monitoring Act of 1990".
(2) FINDINGS – The Congress finds that:
(A) the March 24, 1989, grounding and rupture of the fully loaded oil tanker, the EXXON VALDEZ, spilled 11 million gallons of crude oil in Prince William Sound, an environmentally sensitive area;
(B) many people believe that complacency on the part of the industry and government personnel responsible for monitoring the operation of the Valdez terminal and vessel traffic in Prince William Sound was one of the contributing factors to the EXXON VALDEZ oil spill;

(C) one way to combat this complacency is to involve local citizens in the process of preparing, adopting, and revising oil spill contingency plans;

(D) a mechanism should be established which fosters the long-term partnership of industry, government, and local communities in overseeing compliance with environmental concerns in the operation of crude oil terminals;

(E) such a mechanism presently exists at the Sullom Voe terminal in the Shetland Islands and this terminal should serve as a model for others;

(F) because of the effective partnership that has developed at Sullom Voe, Sullom Voe is considered the safest terminal in Europe;

(G) the present system of regulation and oversight of crude oil terminals in the United States has degenerated into a process of continual mistrust and confrontation;

(H) only when local citizens are involved in the process will the trust develop that is necessary to change the present system from confrontation to consensus;

(I) a pilot program patterned after Sullom Voe should be established in Alaska to further refine the concepts and relationships involved; and

(J) similar programs should eventually be established in other major crude oil terminals in the United States because the recent oil spills in Texas, Delaware, and Rhode Island indicate that the safe transportation of crude oil is a national problem.

(b) DEMONSTRATION PROGRAMS:

(1) ESTABLISHMENT – There are established 2 Oil Terminal and Oil Tanker Environmental Oversight and Monitoring Demonstration Programs (hereinafter referred to as "Programs") to be carried out in the State of Alaska.

(2) ADVISORY FUNCTION – The function of these Programs shall be advisory only.

(3) PURPOSE – The Prince William Sound Program shall be responsible for environmental monitoring of the terminal facilities in Prince William Sound and the crude oil tankers operating in Prince William Sound. The Cook Inlet Program shall be responsible for environmental monitoring of the terminal facilities and crude oil tankers operating in Cook Inlet located South of the latitude at Point Possession and North of the latitude at Amatuli Island, including offshore facilities in Cook Inlet.

(4) SUITS BARRED – No program, association, council, committee or other organisation created by this section may sue any person or entity, public or private, concerning any matter arising under this section except for the performance of contracts.

(c) OIL TERMINAL FACILITIES AND OIL TANKER OPERATIONS ASSOCIATION:

(1) ESTABLISHMENT – There is established an Oil Terminal Facilities and Oil Tanker Operations Association (hereinafter in this section referred to as the "Association") for each of the Programs established under subsection (b).

(2) MEMBERSHIP – Each Association shall be comprised of 4 individuals as follows:

(A) One individual shall be designated by the owners and operators of the terminal facilities and shall represent those owners and operators.

(B) One individual shall be designated by the owners and operators of the crude oil tankers calling at the terminal facilities and shall represent those owners and operators.

(C) One individual shall be an employee of the State of Alaska, shall be designated by the Governor of the State of Alaska, and shall represent the State government.

(D) One individual shall be an employee of the Federal Government, shall be designated by the President, and shall represent the Federal Government.

(3) RESPONSIBILITIES – Each Association shall be responsible for reviewing policies relating to the operation and maintenance of the oil terminal facilities and crude oil tankers which affect or may affect the environment in the vicinity of their respective terminals. Each Association shall provide a forum among the owners and operators of the terminal facilities, the owners and operators of crude oil tankers calling at those facilities, the United States, and the State of Alaska to discuss and to make recommendations concerning all permits, plans, and site-specific regulations

governing the activities and actions of the terminal facilities which affect or may affect the environment in the vicinity of the terminal facilities and of crude oil tankers calling at those facilities.

(4) DESIGNATION OF EXISTING ORGANISATION – The Secretary may designate an existing nonprofit organisation as an Association under this subsection if the organisation is organised to meet the purposes of this section and consists of at least the individuals listed in paragraph (2).

(d) REGIONAL CITIZENS' ADVISORY COUNCILS:

(1) MEMBERSHIP – There is established a Regional Citizens' Advisory Council (hereinafter in this section referred to as the "Council") for each of the programs established by subsection (b).

(2) MEMBERSHIP – Each Council shall be composed of voting members and nonvoting members, as follows:

(A) VOTING MEMBERS – Voting members shall be Alaska residents and, except as provided in clause (vii) of this paragraph, shall be appointed by the Governor of the State of Alaska from a list of nominees provided by each of the following interests, with one representative appointed to represent each of the following interests, taking into consideration the need for regional balance on the Council:

(i) Local commercial fishing industry organisations, the members of which depend on the fisheries resources of the waters in the vicinity of the terminal facilities.

(ii) Aquaculture associations in the vicinity of the terminal facilities.

(iii) Alaska Native Corporations and other Alaska Native organisations the members of which reside in the vicinity of the terminal facilities.

(iv) Environmental organisations the members of which reside in the vicinity of the terminal facilities.

(v) Recreational organisations the members of which reside in or use the vicinity of the terminal facilities.

(vi) The Alaska State Chamber of Commerce, to represent the locally based tourist industry.

(vii) (I) For the Prince William Sound Terminal Facilities Council, one representative selected by each of the following municipalities: Cordova, Whittier, Seward, Valdez, Kodiak, the Kodiak Island Borough, and the Kenai Peninsula Borough.

(II) For the Cook Inlet Terminal Facilities Council, one representative selected by each of the following municipalities: Homer, Seldovia, Anchorage, Kenai, Kodiak, the Kodiak Island Borough, and the Kenai Peninsula Borough.

(B) NONVOTING MEMBERS – One ex-officio, nonvoting representative shall be designated by, and represent, each of the following:

(i) The Environmental Protection Agency.

(ii) The Coast Guard.

(iii) The National Oceanic and Atmospheric Administration.

(iv) The United States Forest Service.

(v) The Bureau of Land Management.

(vi) The Alaska Department of Environmental Conservation.

(vii) The Alaska Department of Fish and Game.

(viii) The Alaska Department of Natural Resources.

(ix) The Division of Emergency Services, Alaska Department of Military and Veterans Affairs.

(3) TERMS:

(A) DURATION OF COUNCILS – The term of the Councils shall continue throughout the life of the operation of the Trans-Alaska Pipeline System and so long as oil is transported to or from Cook Inlet.

(B) THREE YEARS – The voting members of each Council shall be appointed for a term of 3 years except as provided for in subparagraph (C).

(C) INITIAL APPOINTMENTS – The terms of the first appointments shall be as follows:

    (i) For the appointments by the Governor of the State of Alaska, one-third shall serve for 3 years, one-third shall serve for 2 years, and one-third shall serve for one year.

    (ii) For the representatives of municipalities required by subsection (d)(2)(A)(vii), a drawing of lots among the appointees shall determine that one-third of that group serves for 3 years, one-third serves for 2 years, and the remainder serves for 1 year.

(4) SELF-GOVERNING – Each Council shall elect its own chairperson, select its own staff, and make policies with regard to its internal operating procedures. After the initial organisational meeting called by the Secretary under subsection (i), each Council shall be self-governing.

(5) DUAL MEMBERSHIP AND CONFLICTS OF INTEREST PROHIBITED:

(A) No individual selected as a member of the Council shall serve on the Association.

(B) No individual selected as a voting member of the Council shall be engaged in any activity which might conflict with such individual carrying out his functions as a member thereof.

(6) DUTIES – Each Council shall –

(A) provide advice and recommendations to the Association on policies, permits, and site-specific regulations relating to the operation and maintenance of terminal facilities and crude oil tankers which affect or may affect the environment in the vicinity of the terminal facilities;

(B) monitor through the committee established under subsection (e), the environmental impacts of the operation of the terminal facilities and crude oil tankers;

(C) monitor those aspects of terminal facilities' and crude oil tankers' operations and maintenance which affect or may affect the environment in the vicinity of the terminal facilities;

(D) review through the committee established under subsection (f), the adequacy of oil spill prevention and contingency plans for the terminal facilities and the adequacy of oil spill prevention and contingency plans for crude oil tankers, operating in Prince William Sound or in Cook Inlet;

(E) provide advice and recommendations to the Association on port operations, policies and practices;

(F) recommend to the Association –

    (i) standards and stipulations for permits and site-specific regulations intended to minimise the impact of the terminal facilities' and crude oil tankers' operations in the vicinity of the terminal facilities;

    (ii) modifications of terminal facility operations and maintenance intended to minimise the risk and mitigate the impact of terminal facilities, operations in the vicinity of the terminal facilities and to minimise the risk of oil spills;

    (iii) modifications of crude oil tanker operations and maintenance in Prince William Sound and Cook Inlet intended to minimise the risk and mitigate the impact of oil spills; and

    (iv) modifications to the oil spill prevention and contingency plans for terminal facilities and for crude oil tankers in Prince William Sound and Cook Inlet intended to enhance the ability to prevent and respond to an oil spill; and

(G) create additional committees of the Council as necessary to carry out the above functions, including a scientific and technical advisory committee to the Prince William Sound Council.

435

(7) NO ESTOPPEL – No Council shall be held liable under State or Federal law for costs or damages as a result of rendering advice under this section. Nor shall any advice given by a voting member of a Council, or program representative or agent, be grounds for estopping the interests represented by the voting Council members from seeking damages or other appropriate relief.

(8) SCIENTIFIC WORK – In carrying out its research, development and monitoring functions, each Council is authorised to conduct its own scientific research and shall review the scientific work undertaken by or on behalf of the terminal operators or crude oil tanker operators as a result of a legal requirement to undertake that work. Each Council shall also review the relevant scientific work undertaken by or on behalf of any government entity relating to the terminal facilities or crude oil tankers. To the extent possible, to avoid unnecessary duplication, each Council shall coordinate its independent scientific work with the scientific work performed by or on behalf of the terminal operators and with the scientific work performed by or on behalf of the operators of the crude oil tankers.

(e) COMMITTEE FOR TERMINAL AND OIL TANKER OPERATIONS AND ENVIRONMENTAL MONITORING:

(1) MONITORING COMMITTEE – Each Council shall establish a standing Terminal and Oil Tanker Operations and Environmental Monitoring Committee (hereinafter in this section referred to as the "Monitoring Committee") to devise and manage a comprehensive program of monitoring the environmental impacts of the operations of terminal facilities and of crude oil tankers while operating in Prince William Sound and Cook Inlet. The membership of the Monitoring Committee shall be made up of members of the Council, citizens, and recognised scientific experts selected by the Council.

(2) DUTIES – In fulfilling its responsibilities, the Monitoring Committee shall –

(A) advise the Council on a monitoring strategy that will permit early detection of environmental impacts of terminal facility operations and crude oil tanker operations while in Prince William Sound and Cook Inlet;

(B) develop monitoring programs and make recommendations to the Council on the implementation of those programs;

(C) at its discretion, select and contract with universities and other scientific institutions to carry out specific monitoring projects authorised by the Council pursuant to an approved monitoring strategy;

(D) complete any other tasks assigned by the Council; and

(E) provide written reports to the Council which interpret and assess the results of all monitoring programs.

(f) COMMITTEE FOR OIL SPILL PREVENTION, SAFETY, AND EMERGENCY RESPONSE:

(1) TECHNICAL OIL SPILL COMMITTEE – Each Council shall establish a standing technical committee (hereinafter referred to as "Oil Spill Committee") to review and assess measures designed to prevent oil spills and the planning and preparedness for responding to, containing, cleaning up, and mitigating impacts of oil spills. The membership of the Oil Spill Committee shall be made up of members of the Council, citizens, and recognised technical experts selected by the Council.

(2) DUTIES – In fulfilling its responsibilities, the Oil Spill Committee shall –

(A) periodically review the respective oil spill prevention and contingency plans for the terminal facilities and for the crude oil tankers while in Prince William Sound or Cook Inlet, in light of new technological developments and changed circumstances;

(B) monitor periodic drills and testing of the oil spill contingency plans for the terminal facilities and for crude oil tankers while in Prince William Sound and Cook Inlet;

(C) study wind and water currents and other environmental factors in the vicinity of the terminal facilities which may affect the ability to prevent, respond to, contain, and clean up an oil spill;

(D) identify highly sensitive areas which may require specific protective measures in the event of a spill in Prince William Sound or Cook Inlet;

(E) monitor developments in oil spill prevention, containment, response, and cleanup technology;

(F) periodically review port organisation, operations, incidents, and the adequacy and maintenance of vessel traffic service systems designed to assure safe transit of crude oil tankers pertinent to terminal operations;

(G) periodically review the standards for tankers bound for, loading at, exiting from, or otherwise using the terminal facilities;

(H) complete any other tasks assigned by the Council; and

(I) provide written reports to the Council outlining its findings and recommendations.

(g) AGENCY COOPERATION – On and after the expiration of the 180-day period following the date of the enactment of this section, each Federal department, agency, or other instrumentality shall, with respect to all permits, site-specific regulations, and other matters governing the activities and actions of the terminal facilities which affect or may affect the vicinity of the terminal facilities, consult with the appropriate Council prior to taking substantive action with respect to the permit, site-specific regulation, or other matter. This consultation shall be carried out with a view to enabling the appropriate Association and Council to review the permit, site-specific regulation, or other matters and make appropriate recommendations regarding operations, policy or agency actions. Prior consultation shall not be required if an authorised Federal agency representative reasonably believes that an emergency exists requiring action without delay.

(h) RECOMMENDATIONS OF THE COUNCIL – In the event that the Association does not adopt, or significantly modifies before adoption, any recommendation of the Council made pursuant to the authority granted to the Council in subsection (d), the Association shall provide to the Council, in writing, within 5 days of its decision, notice of its decision and a written statement of reasons for its rejection or significant modification of the recommendation.

(i) ADMINISTRATIVE ACTIONS – Appointments, designations, and selections of individuals to serve as members of the Associations and Councils under this section shall be submitted to the Secretary prior to the expiration of the 120-day period following the date of the enactment of this section. On or before the expiration of the 180-day period following that date of enactment of this section, the Secretary shall call an initial meeting of each Association and Council for organisational purposes.

(j) LOCATION AND COMPENSATION:

(1) LOCATION – Each Association and Council established by this section shall be located in the State of Alaska.

(2) COMPENSATION – No member of an Association or Council shall be compensated for the member's services as a member of the Association or Council, but shall be allowed travel expenses, including per diem in lieu of subsistence, at a rate established by the Association or Council not to exceed the rates authorised for employees of agencies under sections 5702 and 5703 of title 5, United States Code. However, each Council may enter into contracts to provide compensation and expenses to members of the committees created under subsections (d), (e), and (f).

(k) FUNDING:

(1) REQUIREMENT – Approval of the contingency plans required of owners and operators of the Cook Inlet and Prince William Sound terminal facilities and crude oil tankers while operating in Alaskan waters in commerce with those terminal facilities shall be effective only so long as the respective Association and Council for a facility are funded pursuant to paragraph (2).

(2) PRINCE WILLIAM SOUND PROGRAM – The owners or operators of terminal facilities or crude oil tankers operating in Prince William Sound shall provide, on an annual basis, an aggregate amount of not more than $2,000,000, as determined by the Secretary. Such amount –

437

(A) shall provide for the establishment and operation on the environmental oversight and monitoring program in Prince William Sound;

(B) shall be adjusted annually by the Anchorage Consumer Price Index; and

(C) may be adjusted periodically upon the mutual consent of the owners or operators of terminal facilities or crude oil tankers operating in Prince William Sound and the Prince William Sound terminal facilities Council.

(3) COOK INLET PROGRAM – The owners or operators of terminal facilities, offshore facilities, or crude oil tankers operating in Cook Inlet shall provide, on an annual basis, an aggregate amount of not more than $1,000,000, as determined by the Secretary. Such amount –

(A) shall provide for the establishment and operation of the environmental oversight and monitoring program in Cook Inlet;

(B) shall be adjusted annually by the Anchorage Consumer Price Index; and

(C) may be adjusted periodically upon the mutual consent of the owners or operators of terminal facilities, offshore facilities, or crude oil tankers operating in Cook Inlet and the Cook Inlet Council.

(l) REPORTS:

(1) ASSOCIATIONS AND COUNCILS – Prior to the expiration of the 36-month period following the date of the enactment of this section, each Association and Council established by this section shall report to the President and the Congress concerning its activities under this section, together with its recommendations.

(2) GAO – Prior to the expiration of the 36-month period following the date of the enactment of this section, the General Accounting Office shall report to the President and the Congress as to the handling of funds, including donated funds, by the entities carrying out the programs under this section, and the effectiveness of the demonstration programs carried out under this section, together with its recommendations.

(m) DEFINITIONS – As used in this section, the term –

(1) "terminal facilities" means –

(A) in the case of the Prince William Sound Program, the entire oil terminal complex located in Valdez, Alaska, consisting of approximately 1,000 acres including all buildings, docks (except docks owned by the City of Valdez if those docks are not used for loading of crude oil), pipes, piping, roads, ponds, tanks, crude oil tankers only while at the terminal dock, tanker escorts owned or operated by the operator of the terminal, vehicles, and other facilities associated with, and necessary for, assisting tanker movement of crude oil into and out of the oil terminal complex; and

(B) in the case of the Cook Inlet Program, the entire oil terminal complex including all buildings, docks, pipes, piping, roads, ponds, tanks, vessels, vehicles, crude oil tankers only while at the terminal dock, tanker escorts owned or operated by the operator of the terminal, emergency spill response vessels owned or operated by the operator of the terminal, and other facilities associated with, and necessary for, assisting tanker movement of crude oil into and out of the oil terminal complex;

(2) "crude oil tanker" means a tanker (as that term is defined under section 2101 of title 46, United States Code) –

(A) in the case of the Prince William Sound Program, calling at the terminal facilities for the purpose of receiving and transporting oil to refineries, operating north of Middleston Island and bound for or exiting from Prince William Sound; and

(B) in the case of the Cook Inlet Program, calling at the terminal facilities for the purpose of receiving and transporting oil to refineries and operating in Cook Inlet and the Gulf of Alaska north of Amatuli Island, including tankers transiting to Cook Inlet from Prince William Sound;

    (3) "vicinity of the terminal facilities" means that geographical area surrounding the environment of terminal facilities which is directly affected or may be directly affected by the operation of the terminal facilities; and

    (4) "Secretary" means the Secretary of Transportation.

(n) SAVINGS CLAUSE:

    (1) REGULATORY AUTHORITY – Nothing in this section shall be construed as modifying, repealing, superseding, or preempting any municipal, State or Federal law or regulation, or in any way affecting litigation arising from oil spills or the rights and responsibilities of the United States or the State of Alaska, or municipalities thereof, to preserve and protect the environment through regulation of land, air, and water uses, of safety, and of related development. The monitoring provided for by this section shall be designed to help assure compliance with applicable laws and regulations and shall only extend to activities –

        (A) that would affect or have the potential to affect the vicinity of the terminal facilities and the area of crude oil tanker operations included in the Programs; and

        (B) are subject to the United States or State of Alaska, or municipality thereof, law, regulation, or other legal requirement.

    (2) RECOMMENDATIONS – This subsection is not intended to prevent the Association or Council from recommending to appropriate authorities that existing legal requirements should be modified or that new legal requirements should be adopted.

(o) ALTERNATIVE VOLUNTARY ADVISORY GROUP IN LIEU OF COUNCIL – The requirements of subsections (c) through (l), as such subsections apply respectively to the Prince William Sound Program and the Cook Inlet Program, are deemed to have been satisfied so long as the following conditions are met:

    (1) PRINCE WILLIAM SOUND – With respect to the Prince William Sound Program, the Alyeska Pipeline Service Company or any of its owner companies enters into a contract for the duration of the operation of the Trans-Alaska Pipeline System with the Alyeska Citizens Advisory Committee in existence on the date of enactment of this section, or a successor organisation, to fund that Committee or organisation on an annual basis in the amount provided for by subsection (k)(2)(A) and the President annually certifies that the Committee or organisation fosters the general goals and purposes of this section and is broadly representative of the communities and interests in the vicinity of the terminal facilities and Prince William Sound.

    (2) COOK INLET – With respect to the Cook Inlet Program, the terminal facilities, offshore facilities, or crude oil tanker owners and operators enter into a contract with a voluntary advisory organisation to fund that organisation on an annual basis and the President annually certifies that the organisation fosters the general goals and purposes of this section and is broadly representative of the communities and interests in the vicinity of the terminal facilities and Cook Inlet.

(33 U.S.C. 2732)

Sec. 5003. Bligh Reef Light

The Secretary of Transportation shall within one year after the date of the enactment of this title install and ensure operation of an automated navigation light on or adjacent to Bligh Reef in Prince William Sound, Alaska, of sufficient power and height to provide long-range warning of the location of Bligh Reef.

(33 U.S.C. 2733)

Sec. 5004. Vessel traffic service system

The Secretary of Transportation shall within one year after the date of the enactment of this title –

    (1) acquire, install, and operate such additional equipment (which may consist of radar, closed circuit television, satellite tracking systems, or other shipboard dependent surveillance), train and locate such personnel, and issue such final regulations as are nec-

essary to increase the range of the existing VTS system in the Port of Valdez, Alaska, sufficiently to track the locations and movements of tank vessels carrying oil from the Trans-Alaska Pipeline when such vessels are transiting Prince William Sound, Alaska, and to sound an audible alarm when such tankers depart from designated navigation routes; and

(2) submit to the Committee on Commerce, Science, and Transportation of the Senate and the Committee on Merchant Marine and Fisheries of the House of Representatives a report on the feasibility and desirability of instituting positive control of tank vessel movements in Prince William Sound by Coast Guard personnel using the Port of Valdez, Alaska, VTS system, as modified pursuant to paragraph (1).

(33 U.S.C. 2734)

Sec. 5005. Equipment and personnel requirements under tank vessel and facility response plans

(a) IN GENERAL – In addition to the requirements for response plans for vessels established by section 311(j) of the Federal Water Pollution Control Act, as amended by this Act, a response plan for a tanker loading cargo at a facility permitted under the Trans- Alaska Pipeline Authorization Act (43 U.S.C. 1651 *et seq.*),[1] shall provide for –

(1) prepositioned oil spill containment and removal equipment in communities and other strategic locations within the geographic boundaries of Prince William Sound, including escort vessels with skimming capability; barges to receive recovered oil; heavy duty sea boom, pumping, transferring, and lightering equipment; and other appropriate removal equipment for the protection of the environment, including fish hatcheries;

(2) the establishment of an oil spill removal organisation at appropriate locations in Prince William Sound, consisting of trained personnel in sufficient numbers to immediately remove, to the maximum extent practicable, a worst case discharge or a discharge of 200,000 barrels of oil, whichever is greater;

(3) training in oil removal techniques for local residents and individuals engaged in the cultivation or production of fish or fish products in Prince William Sound;

(4) practice exercises not less than 2 times per year which test the capacity of the equipment and personnel required under this paragraph; and

(5) periodic testing and certification of equipment required under this paragraph, as required by the Secretary.

(b) DEFINITIONS – In this section –

(1) the term "Prince William Sound" means all State and Federal waters within Prince William Sound, Alaska, including the approach to Hinchenbrook Entrance out to and encompassing Seal Rocks; and

(2) the term "worst case discharge" means –

(A) in the case of a vessel, a discharge in adverse weather conditions of its entire cargo; and

(B) in the case of a facility, the largest foreseeable discharge in adverse weather conditions.

(33 U.S.C. 2735)

Sec. 5006. Funding

(a) SECTIONS 5001, 5003 AND 5004 – Amounts in the Fund shall be available, without further appropriations and without fiscal year limitation, to carry out section 5001 in the amount as determined in section 5006(b), and to carry out sections 5003 and 5004, in an amount not to exceed $5,000,000.

(b) USE OF INTEREST ONLY – The amount of funding to be made available annually to carry out section 5001 shall be the interest produced by the Fund's investment of the

---

1. Section 354(2) of P.L. 102–388 attempted to amend section 5005(a) by inserting "and a response plan for such a facility," after "(43 U.S.C. 1651 *et seq.*).". The amendment probably should have made the insertion after "(43 U.S.C. 1651 *et seq.*),".

$22,500,000 remaining funding authorised for the Prince William Sound Oil Spill Recovery Institute and currently deposited in the Fund and invested by the Secretary of the Treasury in income producing securities along with other funds comprising the Fund. The National Pollution Funds Center shall transfer all such accrued interest, including the interest earned from the date funds in the Trans-Alaska Liability Pipeline Fund were transferred into the Oil Spill Liability Trust Fund pursuant to section 8102(a)(2)(B)(ii), to the Prince William Sound Oil Spill Recovery Institute annually, beginning 60 days after the date of enactment of the Coast Guard Authorization Act of 1996.

(c) USE FOR SECTION 1012[1] – Beginning with the eleventh year following the date of enactment of the Coast Guard Authorization Act of 1996, the funding authorised for the Prince William Sound Oil Spill Recovery Institute and deposited in the Fund shall thereafter be made available for purposes of section 1012 in Alaska.

(c) SECTION 5008[2] – Amounts in the Fund shall be available, without further appropriation and without fiscal year limitation, to carry out section 5008(b), in an amount not to exceed $5,000,000 of which up to $3,000,000 may be used for the lease payment to the Alaska SeaLife Center under section 5008(b)(2): *Provided,* That the entire amount is designated by the Congress as an emergency requirement pursuant to section 251(b)(2)(A) of the Balanced Budget and Emergency Deficit Control Act of 1985, as amended: *Provided further,* That the entire amount shall be available only to the extent an official budget request that includes designation of the entire amount of the request as an emergency requirement as defined in the Balanced Budget and Emergency Deficit Control Act of 1985, as amended, is transmitted by the President to the Congress.

(33 U.S.C. 2736)

Sec. 5007. Limitation

Notwithstanding any other law, tank vessels that have spilled more than 1,000,000 gallons of oil into the marine environment after March 22, 1989, are prohibited from operating on the navigable waters of Prince William Sound, Alaska.

(33 U.S.C. 2737)

Sec. 5008. North Pacific Marine Research Institute

(a) INSTITUTE ESTABLISHED – The Secretary of Commerce shall establish a North Pacific Marine Research Institute (hereafter in this section referred to as the "Institute") to be administered at the Alaska SeaLife Center by the North Pacific Research Board.

(b) FUNCTIONS – The Institute shall –
   (1) conduct research and carry out education and demonstration projects on or relating to the North Pacific marine ecosystem with particular emphasis on marine mammal, sea bird, fish, and shellfish populations in the Bering Sea and Gulf of Alaska including populations located in or near Kenai Fjords National Park and the Alaska Maritime National Wildlife Refuge; and
   (2) lease, maintain, operate, and upgrade the necessary research equipment and related facilities necessary to conduct such research at the Alaska SeaLife Center.

(c) EVALUATION AND AUDIT – The Secretary of Commerce may periodically evaluate the activities of the Institute to ensure that funds received by the Institute are used in a manner consistent with this section. The Federal Advisory Committee Act (5 U.S.C. App. 2) shall not apply to the Institute.

(d) STATUS OF EMPLOYEES – Employees of the Institute shall not, by reason of such employment, be considered to be employees of the Federal Government for any purpose.

(e) USE OF FUNDS – No funds made available to carry out this section may be used to initiate litigation, or for the acquisition of real property (other than facilities leased at the

---

1. First subsection (c) added by sec. 1102(b)(4) of P.L. 104–324, 110 Stat. 3965, Oct. 19, 1996. For second subsection (c), see note 5006–2.

2. Second subsection (c) added by sec. 2204(2) of P.L. 106–246, 114 Stat. 547, July 13, 2000. For first subsection (c), see note 5006–1.

Alaska SeaLife Center). No more than 10 percent of the funds made available to carry out subsection (b)(1) may be used to administer the Institute. The administrative funds of the Institute and the administrative funds of the North Pacific Research Board created under Public Law 105-83 may be used to jointly administer such programs at the discretion of the North Pacific Research Board.

(f) AVAILABILITY OF RESEARCH – The Institute shall publish and make available to any person on request the results of all research, educational, and demonstration projects conducted by the Institute. The Institute shall provide a copy of all research, educational, and demonstration projects conducted by the Institute to the National Park Service, the United States Fish and Wildlife Service, and the National Oceanic and Atmospheric Administration.

(33 U.S.C. 2738)

Title VI – Miscellaneous

Sec. 6001. Savings provisions

(a) CROSS-REFERENCES – A reference to a law replaced by this Act, including a reference in a regulation, order, or other law, is deemed to refer to the corresponding provision of this Act.

(b) CONTINUATION OF REGULATIONS – An order, rule, or regulation in effect under a law replaced by this Act continues in effect under the corresponding provision of this Act until repealed, amended, or superseded.

(c) RULE OF CONSTRUCTION – An inference of legislative construction shall not be drawn by reason of the caption or catch line of a provision enacted by this Act.

(d) ACTIONS AND RIGHTS – Nothing in this Act shall apply to any rights and duties that matured, penalties that were incurred, and proceedings that were begun before the date of enactment of this Act, except as provided by this section, and shall be adjudicated pursuant to the law applicable on the date prior to the date of the enactment of this Act.

(e) ADMIRALTY AND MARITIME LAW – Except as otherwise provided in this Act, this Act does not affect –

(1) admiralty and maritime law; or
(2) the jurisdiction of the district courts of the United States with respect to civil actions under admiralty and maritime jurisdiction, saving to suitors in all cases all other remedies to which they are otherwise entitled.

(33 U.S.C. 2751)

Sec. 6002. Annual appropriations

(a) REQUIRED – Except as provided in subsection (b), amounts in the Fund shall be available only as provided in annual appropriation Acts.

(b) EXCEPTIONS – Subsection (a) shall not apply to sections 1006(f), 1012(a)(4), or 5006, and shall not apply to an amount not to exceed $50,000,000 in any fiscal year which the President may make available from the Fund to carry out section 311(c) of the Federal Water Pollution Control Act, as amended by this Act, and to initiate the assessment of natural resources damages required under section 1006. Sums to which this subsection applies shall remain available until expended.

(33 U.S.C. 2752)

[Section 6003 – Repealed by section 109 of P.L. 104–134]

Sec. 6004. Cooperative development of common hydrocarbon-bearing areas

(a) * * *

(b) EXCEPTION FOR WEST DELTA FIELD – Section 5(j) of the Outer Continental Shelf Lands Act, as added by this section, shall not be applicable with respect to Blocks 17 and 18 of the West Delta Field offshore Louisiana.

(c) AUTHORISATION OF APPROPRIATIONS – There are hereby authorised to be appropri-ated such sums as may be necessary to provide compensation, including interest, to the State of Louisiana and its lessees, for net drainage of oil and gas resources as determined in the Third Party Factfinder Louisiana Boundary Study dated March 21, 1989. For purposes of this section, such lessees shall include those persons with an ownership interest in State of Louisiana leases SL10087, SL10088 or SL10187, or ownership interests in the production or proceeds therefrom, as established by assignment, contract or otherwise. Interest shall be computed for the period March 21, 1989 until the date of payment.

Title VII – Oil Pollution Research and Development Program

Sec. 7001. Oil Pollution Research and Development Program

(a) INTERAGENCY COORDINATING COMMITTEE ON OIL POLLUTION RESEARCH:

    (1) ESTABLISHMENT – There is established an Interagency Coordinating Committee on Oil Pollution Research (hereinafter in this section referred to as the "Interagency Committee").

    (2) PURPOSES – The Interagency Committee shall coordinate a comprehensive pro-gram of oil pollution research, technology development, and demonstration among the Federal agencies, in cooperation and coordination with industry, universities, research institutions, State governments, and other nations, as appropriate, and shall foster cost-effective research mechanisms, including the joint funding of research.

    (3) MEMBERSHIP – The Interagency Committee shall include representatives from the Department of Commerce (including the National Oceanic and Atmospheric Administration and the National Institute of Standards and Technology), the Department of Energy, the Department of the Interior (including the Minerals Management Service and the United States Fish and Wildlife Service), the Department of Transportation (including the United States Coast Guard, the Maritime Administration, and the Research and Special Projects Administration), the Department of Defense (including the Army Corps of Engineers and the Navy), the Environmental Protection Agency, the National Aeronautics and Space Administration, and the United States Fire Administration in the Federal Emergency Management Agency, as well as such other Federal agencies as the President may designate.

A representative of the Department of Transportation shall serve as Chairman.

(b) OIL POLLUTION RESEARCH AND TECHNOLOGY PLAN:

    (1) IMPLEMENTATION PLAN – Within 180 days after the date of enactment of this Act, the Interagency Committee shall submit to Congress a plan for the implementation of the oil pollution research, development, and demonstration program established pursuant to subsection (c). The research plan shall –

        (A) identify agency roles and responsibilities;

        (B) assess the current status of knowledge on oil pollution prevention, response, and mitigation technologies and effects of oil pollution on the environment;

        (C) identify significant oil pollution research gaps including an assessment of major technological deficiencies in responses to past oil discharges;

        (D) establish research priorities and goals for oil pollution technology develop-ment related to prevention, response, mitigation, and environmental effects;

        (E) estimate the resources needed to conduct the oil pollution research and devel-opment program established pursuant to subsection (c), and timetables for completing research tasks; and

        (F) identify, in consultation with the States, regional oil pollution research needs and priorities for a coordinated, multidisciplinary program of research at the regional level.

(2) ADVICE AND GUIDANCE – The Chairman, through the Department of Transportation, shall contract with the National Academy of Sciences to –
  (A) provide advice and guidance in the preparation and development of the research plan; and
  (B) assess the adequacy of the plan as submitted, and submit a report to Congress on the conclusions of such assessment.
The National Institute of Standards and Technology shall provide the Interagency Committee with advice and guidance on issues relating to quality assurance and standards measurements relating to its activities under this section.
(c) OIL POLLUTION RESEARCH AND DEVELOPMENT PROGRAM:
  (1) ESTABLISHMENT – The Interagency Committee shall coordinate the establishment, by the agencies represented on the Interagency Committee, of a program for conducting oil pollution research and development, as provided in this subsection.
  (2) INNOVATIVE OIL POLLUTION TECHNOLOGY – The program established under this subsection shall provide for research, development, and demonstration of new or improved technologies which are effective in preventing or mitigating oil discharges and which protect the environment, including –
    (A) development of improved designs for vessels and facilities, and improved operational practices;
    (B) research, development, and demonstration of improved technologies to measure the ullage of a vessel tank, prevent discharges from tank vents, prevent discharges during lightering and bunkering operations, contain discharges on the deck of a vessel, prevent discharges through the use of vacuums in tanks, and otherwise contain discharges of oil from vessels and facilities;
    (C) research, development, and demonstration of new or improved systems of mechanical, chemical, biological, and other methods (including the use of dispersants, solvents, and bioremediation) for the recovery, removal, and disposal of oil, including evaluation of the environmental effects of the use of such systems;
    (D) research and training, in consultation with the National Response Team, to improve industry's and Government's ability to quickly and effectively remove an oil discharge, including the long-term use, as appropriate, of the National Spill Control School in Corpus Christi, Texas, and the Center for Marine Training and Safety in Galveston, Texas;
    (E) research to improve information systems for decisionmaking, including the use of data from coastal mapping, baseline data, and other data related to the environmental effects of oil discharges, and cleanup technologies;
    (F) development of technologies and methods to protect public health and safety from oil discharges, including the population directly exposed to an oil discharge;
    (G) development of technologies, methods, and standards for protecting removal personnel, including training, adequate supervision, protective equipment, maximum exposure limits, and decontamination procedures;
    (H) research and development of methods to restore and rehabilitate natural resources damaged by oil discharges;
    (I) research to evaluate the relative effectiveness and environmental impacts of bioremediation technologies; and
    (J) the demonstration of a satellite-based, dependent surveillance vessel traffic system in Narragansett Bay to evaluate the utility of such system in reducing the risk of oil discharges from vessel collisions and groundings in confined waters.
  (3) OIL POLLUTION TECHNOLOGY EVALUATION – The program established under this subsection shall provide for oil pollution prevention and mitigation technology evaluation including –
    (A) the evaluation and testing of technologies developed independently of the research and development program established under this subsection;

(B) the establishment, where appropriate, of standards and testing protocols traceable to national standards to measure the performance of oil pollution prevention or mitigation technologies; and

(C) the use, where appropriate, of controlled field testing to evaluate real-world application of oil discharge prevention or mitigation technologies.

(4) OIL POLLUTION EFFECTS RESEARCH – (A) The Committee shall establish a research program to monitor and evaluate the environmental effects of oil discharges. Such program shall include the following elements:

(i) The development of improved models and capabilities for predicting the environmental fate, transport, and effects of oil discharges.

(ii) The development of methods, including economic methods, to assess damages to natural resources resulting from oil discharges.

(iii) The identification of types of ecologically sensitive areas at particular risk to oil discharges and the preparation of scientific monitoring and evaluation plans, one for each of several types of ecological conditions, to be implemented in the event of major oil discharges in such areas.

(iv) The collection of environmental baseline data in ecologically sensitive areas at particular risk to oil discharges where such data are insufficient.

(B) The Department of Commerce in consultation with the Environmental Protection Agency shall monitor and scientifically evaluate the long-term environmental effects of oil discharges if –

(i) the amount of oil discharged exceeds 250,000 gallons;

(ii) the oil discharge has occurred on or after January 1, 1989; and

(iii) the Interagency Committee determines that a study of the long-term environmental effects of the discharge would be of significant scientific value, especially for preventing or responding to future oil discharges.

Areas for study may include the following sites where oil discharges have occurred: the New York/New Jersey Harbor area, where oil was discharged by an Exxon underwater pipeline, the T/B CIBRO SAVANNAH, and the M/V BT NAUTILUS; Narragansett Bay where oil was discharged by the WORLD PRODIGY; the Houston Ship Channel where oil was discharged by the RACHEL B; the Delaware River, where oil was discharged by the PRESIDENTE RIVERA, and Huntington Beach, California, where oil was discharged by the AMERICAN TRADER.

(C) Research conducted under this paragraph by, or through, the United States Fish and Wildlife Service shall be directed and coordinated by the National Wetland Research Center.

(5) MARINE SIMULATION RESEARCH – The program established under this subsection shall include research on the greater use and application of geographic and vessel response simulation models, including the development of additional data bases and updating of existing data bases using, among others, the resources of the National Maritime Research Center. It shall include research and vessel simulations for –

(A) contingency plan evaluation and amendment;

(B) removal and strike team training;

(C) tank vessel personnel training; and

(D) those geographic areas where there is a significant likelihood of a major oil discharge.

(6) DEMONSTRATION PROJECTS – The United States Coast Guard, in conjunction with other such agencies in the Department of Transportation as the Secretary of Transportation may designate, shall conduct 4[1] port oil pollution minimisation demonstration projects, one each with (A) the Port Authority of New York and New Jersey, (B) the Ports of Los Angeles and Long Beach, California,[1] (C) the Port of New Orleans, Louisiana, and (D) a port on the Great Lakes[1] for the purpose of

---

1. Section 2002(1) of P.L. 101–537 and section 4002(1) of P.L. 101–646 made almost identical amendments to section 7001(c)(6). The amendments made by P.L. 101–537 have been executed.

developing and demonstrating integrated port oil pollution prevention and cleanup systems which utilise the information and implement the improved practices and technologies developed from the research, development, and demonstration program established in this section. Such systems shall utilise improved technologies and management practices for reducing the risk of oil discharges, including, as appropriate, improved data access, computerised tracking of oil shipments, improved vessel tracking and navigation systems, advanced technology to monitor pipeline and tank conditions, improved oil spill response capability, improved capability to predict the flow and effects of oil discharges in both the inner and outer harbor areas for the purposes of making infrastructure decisions, and such other activities necessary to achieve the purposes of this section.

(7) SIMULATED ENVIRONMENTAL TESTING – Agencies represented on the Interagency Committee shall ensure the longterm use and operation of the Oil and Hazardous Materials Simulated Environmental Test Tank (OHMSETT) Research Center in New Jersey for oil pollution technology testing and evaluations.

(8) REGIONAL RESEARCH PROGRAM:

(A) Consistent with the research plan in subsection (b), the Interagency Committee shall coordinate a program of competitive grants to universities or other research institutions, or groups of universities or research institutions, for the purposes of conducting a coordinated research program related to the regional aspects of oil pollution, such as prevention, removal, mitigation, and the effects of discharged oil on regional environments. For the purposes of this paragraph, a region means a Coast Guard district as set out in part 3 of title 33, Code of Federal Regulations (1989).

(B) The Interagency Committee shall coordinate the publication by the agencies represented on the Interagency Committee of a solicitation for grants under this subsection. The application shall be in such form and contain such information as may be required in the published solicitation. The applications shall be reviewed by the Interagency Committee, which shall make recommendations to the appropriate granting agency represented on the Interagency Committee for awarding the grant. The granting agency shall award the grants recommended by the Interagency Committee unless the agency decides not to award the grant due to budgetary or other compelling considerations and publishes its reasons for such a determination in the Federal Register. No grants may be made by any agency from any funds authorised for this paragraph unless such grant award has first been recommended by the Interagency Committee.

(C) Any university or other research institution, or group of universities or research institutions, may apply for a grant for the regional research program established by this paragraph. The applicant must be located in the region, or in a State a part of which is in the region, for which the project is proposed as part of the regional research program. With respect to a group application, the entity or entities which will carry out the substantial portion of the proposed research must be located in the region, or in a State a part of which is in the region, for which the project is proposed as part of the regional research program.

(D) The Interagency Committee shall make recommendations on grants in such a manner as to ensure an appropriate balance within a region among the various aspects of oil pollution research, including prevention, removal, mitigation, and the effects of discharged oil on regional environments. In addition, the Interagency Committee shall make recommendations for grants based on the following criteria:

(i) There is available to the applicant for carrying out this paragraph demonstrated research resources.

(ii) The applicant demonstrates the capability of making a significant contribution to regional research needs.

446

   (iii) The projects which the applicant proposes to carry out under the grant are consistent with the research plan under subsection (b)(1)(F) and would further the objectives of the research and development program established in this section.

  (E) Grants provided under this paragraph shall be for a period up to 3 years, subject to annual review by the granting agency, and provide not more than 80 percent of the costs of the research activities carried out in connection with the grant.

  (F) No funds made available to carry out this subsection may be used for the acquisition of real property (including buildings) or construction of any building.

  (G) Nothing in this paragraph is intended to alter or abridge the authority under existing law of any Federal agency to make grants, or enter into contracts or cooperative agreements, using funds other than those authorised in this Act for the purposes of carrying out this paragraph.

 (9) FUNDING – For each of the fiscal years 1991, 1992, 1993, 1994, and 1995, $6,000,000 of amounts in the Fund shall be available to carry out the regional research program in paragraph (8), such amounts to be available in equal amounts for the regional research program in each region; except that if the agencies represented on the Interagency Committee determine that regional research needs exist which cannot be addressed within such funding limits, such agencies may use their authority under paragraph (10) to make additional grants to meet such needs. For the purposes of this paragraph, the research program carried out by the Prince William Sound Oil Spill Recovery Institute established under section 5001, shall not be eligible to receive grants under this paragraph until the authorisation for funding under section 5006(b) expires.

 (10) GRANTS – In carrying out the research and development program established under this subsection, the agencies represented on the Interagency Committee may enter into contracts and cooperative agreements and make grants to universities, research institutions, and other persons. Such contracts, cooperative agreements, and grants shall address research and technology priorities set forth in the oil pollution research plan under subsection (b).

 (11) In carrying out research under this section, the Department of Transportation shall continue to utilise the resources of the Research and Special Programs Administration of the Department of Transportation, to the maximum extent practicable.

(d) INTERNATIONAL COOPERATION – In accordance with the research plan submitted under subsection (b), the Interagency Committee shall coordinate and cooperate with other nations and foreign research entities in conducting oil pollution research, development, and demonstration activities, including controlled field tests of oil discharges.

(e) BIENNIAL REPORTS – The Chairman of the Interagency Committee shall submit to Congress every 2 years on October 30 a report on the activities carried out under this section in the preceding 2 fiscal years, and on activities proposed to be carried out under this section in the current 2 fiscal year period.

(f) FUNDING – Not to exceed $22,000,000[1] of amounts in the Fund shall be available annually to carry out this section except for subsection (c)(8). Of such sums –

 (1) funds authorised to be appropriated to carry out the activities under subsection (c)(4) shall not exceed $5,000,000 for fiscal year 1991 or $3,500,000 for any subsequent fiscal year; and

 (2) not less than $3,000,000[1] shall be available for carrying out the activities in subsection (c)(6) for fiscal years 1992, 1993, 1994, and 1995.

All activities authorised in this section, including subsection (c)(8), are subject to appropriations.

(33 U.S.C. 2761)

---

1. Section 2002(2) of P.L. 101-537 and section 4002(2) of P.L. 101–646 made almost identical amendments to section 7001(f). The amendments made by P.L. 101–537 have been executed.

Title VIII – Trans-Alaska Pipeline System

Sec. 8001. Short Title

This title may be cited as the "Trans-Alaska Pipeline System Reform Act of 1990".

Subtitle A – Improvements to Trans-Alaska Pipeline System

★ ★ ★ ★ ★ ★ ★

Sec. 8102. Trans-Alaska Pipeline Liability Fund

(a) TERMINATION OF CERTAIN PROVISIONS:

  (1) ★ ★ ★

  (2) DISPOSITION OF FUND BALANCE:

    (A) RESERVATION OF AMOUNTS – The trustees of the Trans-Alaska Pipeline Liability Fund (hereafter in this subsection referred to as the "TAPS Fund") shall reserve the following amounts in the TAPS Fund –

      (i) necessary to pay claims arising under section 204(c) of the Trans-Alaska Pipeline Authorization Act (43 U.S.C. 1653(c)); and

      (ii) administrative expenses reasonably necessary for and incidental to the implementation of section 204(c) of that Act.

    (B) DISPOSITION OF THE BALANCE – After the Comptroller General of the United States certifies that the requirements of subparagraph (A) have been met, the trustees of the TAPS Fund shall dispose of the balance in the TAPS Fund after the reservation of amounts are made under subparagraph (A) by –

      (i) rebating the pro rata share of the balance to the State of Alaska for its contributions as an owner of oil, which, except as otherwise provided under article IX, section 15, of the Alaska Constitution, shall be used for the remediation of above-ground storage tanks; and then

      (ii) transferring and depositing the remainder of the balance into the Oil Spill Liability Trust Fund established under section 9509 of the Internal Revenue Code of 1986 (26 U.S.C. 9509).

    (C) DISPOSITION OF THE RESERVED AMOUNTS – After payment of all claims arising from an incident for which funds are reserved under subparagraph (A) and certification by the Comptroller General of the United States that the claims arising from that incident have been paid, the excess amounts, if any, for that incident shall be disposed of as set forth under subparagraphs (A) and (B).

    (D) AUTHORISATION – The amounts transferred and deposited in the Fund shall be available for the purposes of section 1012 of the Oil Pollution Act of 1990 after funding sections 5001 and 8103 to the extent that funds have not otherwise been provided for the purposes of such sections.

  (3) SAVINGS CLAUSE – The repeal made by paragraph (1) shall have no effect on any right to recover or responsibility that arises from incidents subject to section 204(c) of the Trans-Alaska Pipeline Authorization Act (43 U.S.C. 1653(c)) occurring prior to the date of enactment of this Act.

  (4) ★ ★ ★

  (5) EFFECTIVE DATE:

    (A) The repeal by paragraph (1) shall be effective 60 days after the date on which the Comptroller General of the United States certifies to the Congress that –

      (i) all claims arising under section 204(c) of the Trans- Alaska Pipeline Authorization Act (43 U.S.C. 1653(c)) have been resolved,

      (ii) all actions for the recovery of amounts subject to section 204(c) of the Trans-Alaska Pipeline Authorization Act have been resolved, and

      (iii) all administrative expenses reasonably necessary for and incidental to the implementation of section 204(c) of the Trans-Alaska Pipeline Authorization Act have been paid.

    (B) Upon the effective date of the repeal pursuant to subparagraph (A), the trustees of the TAPS Fund shall be relieved of all responsibilities under section 204(c) of the Trans-Alaska Pipeline Authorization Act, but not any existing legal liability.

  (6) TUCKER ACT – This subsection is intended expressly to preserve any and all rights and remedies of contributors to the TAPS Fund under section 1491 of title 28, United States Code (commonly referred to as the "Tucker Act").

* * * * * * *

Sec. 8103. Presidential Task Force

(a) ESTABLISHMENT OF TASK FORCE:

  (1) ESTABLISHMENT AND MEMBERS:

    (A) There is hereby established a Presidential Task Force on the Trans-Alaska Pipeline System (hereinafter referred to as the "Task Force") composed of the following members appointed by the President:

      (i) Three members, one of whom shall be nominated by the Secretary of the Interior, one by the Administrator of the Environmental Protection Agency, and one by the Secretary of Transportation.

      (ii) Three members nominated by the Governor of the State of Alaska, one of whom shall be an employee of the Alaska Department of Natural Resources and one of whom shall be an employee of the Alaska Department of Environmental Conservation.

      (iii) One member nominated by the Office of Technology Assessment.

    (B) Any member appointed to fill a vacancy occurring before the expiration of the term for which his or her predecessor was appointed shall be appointed only for the remainder of such term. A member may serve after the expiration of his or her term until a successor, if applicable, has taken office.

  (2) COCHAIRMEN – The President shall appoint a Federal cochairman from among the Federal members of the Task Force appointed pursuant to paragraph (1)(A) and the Governor shall designate a State cochairman from among the State members of the Task Force appointed pursuant to paragraph (1)(B).

  (3) COMPENSATION – Members shall, to the extent approved in appropriations Acts, receive the daily equivalent of the minimum annual rate of basic pay in effect for grade GS-15 of the General Schedule for each day (including travel time) during which they are engaged in the actual performance of duties vested in the Task Force, except that members who are State, Federal, or other governmental employees shall receive no compensation under this paragraph in addition to the salaries they receive as such employees.

  (4) STAFF – The cochairman of the Task Force shall appoint a Director to carry out administrative duties. The Director may hire such staff and incur such expenses on behalf of the Task Force for which funds are available.

  (5) RULE – Employees of the Task Force shall not, by reason of such employment, be considered to be employees of the Federal Government for any purpose.

(b) DUTIES OF THE TASK FORCE:

  (1) AUDIT – The Task Force shall conduct an audit of the Trans-Alaska Pipeline System (hereinafter referred to as "TAPS") including the terminal at Valdez, Alaska, and other related onshore facilities, make recommendations to the President, the Congress, and the Governor of Alaska.

  (2) COMPREHENSIVE REVIEW – As part of such audit, the Task Force shall conduct a comprehensive review of the TAPS in order to specifically advise the President, the Congress, and the Governor of Alaska concerning whether-

    (A) the holder of the Federal and State right-of-way is, and has been, in full compliance with applicable laws, regulations, and agreements;

    (B) the laws, regulations, and agreements are sufficient to prevent the release of oil from TAPS and prevent other damage or degradation to the environment and public health;

449

      (C) improvements are necessary to TAPS to prevent release of oil from TAPS and to prevent other damage or degradation to the environment and public health;

      (D) improvements are necessary in the onshore oil spill response capabilities for the TAPS; and

      (E) improvements are necessary in security for TAPS.

(3) CONSULTANTS:

      (A) The Task Force shall retain at least one independent consulting firm with technical expertise in engineering, transportation, safety, the environment, and other applicable areas to assist the Task Force in carrying out this subsection.

      (B) Contracts with any such firm shall be entered into on a nationally competitive basis, and the Task Force shall not select any firm with respect to which there may be a conflict of interest in assisting the Task Force in carrying out the audit and review. All work performed by such firm shall be under the direct and immediate supervision of a registered engineer.

(4) PUBLIC COMMENT – The Task Force shall provide an opportunity for public comment on its activities including at a minimum the following:

      (A) Before it begins its audit and review, the Task Force shall review reports prepared by other Government entities conducting reviews of TAPS and shall consult with those Government entities that are conducting ongoing investigations including the General Accounting Office. It shall also hold at least 2 public hearings, at least 1 of which shall be held in a community affected by the Exxon Valdez oil spill. Members of the public shall be given an opportunity to present both oral and written testimony.

      (B) The Task Force shall provide a mechanism for the confidential receipt of information concerning TAPS, which may include a designated telephone hotline.

(5) TASK FORCE REPORT – The Task Force shall publish a draft report which it shall make available to the public. The public will have at least 30 days to provide comments on the draft report. Based on its draft report and the public comments thereon, the Task Force shall prepare a final report which shall include its findings, conclusions, and recommendations made as a result of carrying out such audit. The Task Force shall transmit (and make available to the public), no later than 2 years after the date on which funding is made available under paragraph (7), its final report to the President, the Congress, and the Governor of Alaska.

(6) PRESIDENTIAL REPORT – The President shall, within 90 days after receiving the Task Force's report, transmit a report to the Congress and the Governor of Alaska outlining what measures have been taken or will be taken to implement the Task Force's recommendations. The President's report shall include recommended changes, if any, in Federal and State law to enhance the safety and operation of TAPS.

(7) EARMARK – Of amounts in the Fund, $5,000,000 shall be available, subject to appropriations, annually without fiscal year limitation to carry out the requirements of this section.

(c) GENERAL ADMINISTRATION AND POWERS OF THE TASK FORCE:

(1) AUDIT ACCESS – The Comptroller General of the United States, and any of his or her duly appointed representatives, shall have access, for purposes of audit and examination, to any books, documents, papers, and records of the Task Force that are pertinent to the funds received and expended by the Task Force.

(2) TERMINATION – The Task Force shall cease to exist on the date on which the final report is provided pursuant to subsection (b)(5).

(3) FUNCTIONS LIMITATION – With respect to safety, operations, and other matters related to the pipeline facilities (as such term is defined in section 202(4) of the Hazardous Liquid Pipeline Safety Act of 1979) of the TAPS, the Task Force shall not perform any functions which are the responsibility of the Secretary of Transportation under the Hazardous Liquid Pipeline Safety Act of 1979, as amended. The Secretary

may use the information gathered by and reports issued by the Task Force in carrying out the Secretary's responsibilities under that Act.

(4) POWERS – The Task Force may, to the extent necessary to carry out its responsibilities, conduct investigations, make reports, issue subpoenas, require the production of relevant documents and records, take depositions, and conduct directly or, by contract, or otherwise, research, testing, and demonstration activities.

(5) EXAMINATION OF RECORDS AND PROPERTIES – The Task Force, and the employees and agents it so designates, are authorised, upon presenting appropriate credentials to the person in charge, to enter upon, inspect, and examine, at reasonable times and in a reasonable manner, the records and properties of persons to the extent such records and properties are relevant to determining whether such persons have acted or are acting in compliance with applicable laws and agreements.

(6) FOIA – The information gathered by the Task Force pursuant to subsection (b) shall not be subject to section 552 of title 5, United States Code (commonly referred to as the "Freedom of Information Act"), until its final report is issued pursuant to subsection (b)(6).

(33 U.S.C. 1651 note)

* * * * * * *

International Convention on Salvage, 1989

THE STATES PARTIES TO THE PRESENT CONVENTION,

RECOGNISING the desirability of determining by agreement uniform international rules regarding salvage operations,

NOTING that substantial developments, in particular the increased concern for the protection of the environment, have demonstrated the need to review the international rules presently contained in the Convention for the Unification of Certain Rules of Law relating to Assistance and Salvage at Sea, done at Brussels, 23 September 1910,

CONSCIOUS of the major contribution which efficient and timely salvage operations can make to the safety of vessels and other property in danger and to the protection of the environment,

CONVINCED of the need to ensure that adequate incentives are available to persons who undertake salvage operations in respect of vessels and other property in danger,

HAVE AGREED as follows:

CHAPTER I: GENERAL PROVISIONS

Article 1 – Definitions

For the purpose of this Convention:

(a) "Salvage operation" means any act or activity undertaken to assist a vessel or any other property in danger in navigable waters or in any other waters whatsoever.

(b) "Vessel" means any ship or craft, or any structure capable of navigation.

(c) "Property" means any property not permanently and intentionally attached to the shoreline and includes freight at risk.

(d) "Damage to the environment" means substantial physical damage to human health or to marine life or resources in coastal or inland waters or areas adjacent thereto, caused by pollution, contamination, fire, explosion or similar major incidents.

(e) "Payment" means any reward, remuneration or compensation due under this Convention.

(f) "Organization" means the International Maritime Organization.

(g) "Secretary-General" means the Secretary-General of the Organization.

Article 2 – Application of the Convention

This Convention shall apply whenever judicial or arbitral proceedings relating to matters dealt with in this Convention are brought in a State Party.

Article 3 – Platforms and drilling units

This Convention shall not apply to fixed or floating platforms or to mobile offshore drilling units when such platforms or units are on location engaged in the exploration, exploitation or production of sea-bed mineral resources.

Article 4 – State-owned vessels

1. Without prejudice to article 5, this Convention shall not apply to warships or other non-commercial vessels owned or operated by a State and entitled, at the time of salvage operations, to sovereign immunity under generally recognised principles of international law unless that State decides otherwise.

2. Where a State Party decides to apply the Convention to its warships or other vessels described in paragraph 1, it shall notify the Secretary-General thereof specifying the terms and conditions of such application.

Article 5 – Salvage operations controlled by public authorities

1. This Convention shall not affect any provisions of national law or any international convention relating to salvage operations by or under the control of public authorities.

2. Nevertheless, salvors carrying out such salvage operations shall be entitled to avail themselves of the rights and remedies provided for in this Convention in respect of salvage operations.

3. The extent to which a public authority under a duty to perform salvage operations may avail itself of the rights and remedies provided for in this Convention shall be determined by the law of the State where such authority is situated.

Article 6 – Salvage contracts

1. This Convention shall apply to any salvage operations save to the extent that a contract otherwise provides expressly or by implication.

2. The master shall have the authority to conclude contracts for salvage operations on behalf of the owner of the vessel. The master or the owner of the vessel shall have the authority to conclude such contracts on behalf of the owner of the property on board the vessel.

3. Nothing in this article shall affect the application of article 7 nor duties to prevent or minimise damage to the environment.

Article 7 – Annulment and modification of contracts

A contract or any terms thereof may be annulled or modified if:

(a) the contract has been entered into under undue influence or the influence of danger and its terms are inequitable; or

(b) the payment under the contract is in an excessive degree too large or too small for the services actually rendered.

CHAPTER II: PERFORMANCE OF SALVAGE OPERATIONS

Article 8 – Duties of the salvor and of the owner and master

1. The salvor shall owe a duty to the owner of the vessel or other property in danger:
   (a) to carry out the salvage operations with due care;
   (b) in performing the duty specified in subparagraph (a), to exercise due care to prevent or minimise damage to the environment;
   (c) whenever circumstances reasonably require, to seek assistance from other salvors; and
   (d) to accept the intervention of other salvors when reasonably requested to do so by the owner or master of the vessel or other property in danger; provided however that the amount of his reward shall not be prejudiced should it be found that such a request was unreasonable.

2. The owner and master of the vessel or the owner of other property in danger shall owe a duty to the salvor:
   (a) to co-operate fully with him during the course of the salvage operations;
   (b) in so doing, to exercise due care to prevent or minimise damage to the environment; and

(c) when the vessel or other property has been brought to a place of safety, to accept redelivery when reasonably requested by the salvor to do so.

Article 9 – Rights of coastal States

Nothing in this Convention shall affect the right of the coastal State concerned to take measures in accordance with generally recognised principles of international law to protect its coastline or related interests from pollution or the threat of pollution following upon a maritime casualty or acts relating to such a casualty which may reasonably be expected to result in major harmful consequences, including the right of a coastal State to give directions in relation to salvage operations.

Article 10 – Duty to render assistance

1. Every master is bound, so far as he can do so without serious danger to his vessel and persons thereon, to render assistance to any person in danger of being lost at sea.

2. The States Parties shall adopt the measures necessary to enforce the duty set out in paragraph 1.

3. The owner of the vessel shall incur no liability for a breach of the duty of the master under paragraph 1.

Article 11 – Co-operation

A State Party shall, whenever regulating or deciding upon matters relating to salvage operations such as admittance to ports of vessels in distress or the provision of facilities to salvors, take into account the need for co-operation between salvors, other interested parties and public authorities in order to ensure the efficient and successful performance of salvage operations for the purpose of saving life or property in danger as well as preventing damage to the environment in general.

CHAPTER III: RIGHTS OF SALVORS

Article 12 – Conditions for reward

1. Salvage operations which have had a useful result give right to a reward.

2. Except as otherwise provided, no payment is due under this Convention if the salvage operations have had no useful result.

3. This chapter shall apply, notwithstanding that the salved vessel and the vessel undertaking the salvage operations belong to the same owner.

Article 13 – Criteria for fixing the reward

1. The reward shall be fixed with a view to encouraging salvage operations, taking into account the following criteria without regard to the order in which they are presented below:

    (a) the salved value of the vessel and other property;

    (b) the skill and efforts of the salvors in preventing or minimising damage to the environment;

    (c) the measure of success obtained by the salvor;

    (d) the nature and degree of the danger;

    (e) the skill and efforts of the salvors in saving the vessel, other property and life;

    (f) the time used and expenses and losses incurred by the salvors;

    (g) the risk of liability and other risks run by the salvors or their equipment;

    (h) the promptness of the services rendered;

    (i) the availability and use of vessels or other equipment intended for salvage operations;

    (j) the state of readiness and efficiency of the salvor's equipment and the value thereof.

2. Payment of a reward fixed according to paragraph 1 shall be made by all of the vessel and other property interests in proportion to their respective salved values. However, a State Party may in its national law provide that the payment of a reward has to be made by one of these interests, subject to a right of recourse of this interest against the other interests for their respective shares. Nothing in this article shall prevent any right of defence.

3. The rewards, exclusive of any interest and recoverable legal costs that may be payable thereon, shall not exceed the salved value of the vessel and other property.

Article 14 – Special compensation

1. If the salvor has carried out salvage operations in respect of a vessel which by itself or its cargo threatened damage to the environment and has failed to earn a reward under article 13 at least equivalent to the special compensation assessable in accordance with this article, he shall be entitled to special compensation from the owner of that vessel equivalent to his expenses as herein defined.

2. If, in the circumstances set out in paragraph 1, the salvor by his salvage operations has prevented or minimised damage to the environment, the special compensation payable by the owner to the salvor under paragraph 1 may be increased up to a maximum of 30% of the expenses incurred by the salvor. However, the tribunal, if it deems it fair and just to do so and bearing in mind the relevant criteria set out in article 13, paragraph 1, may increase such special compensation further, but in no event shall the total increase be more than 100% of the expenses incurred by the salvor.

3. Salvor's expenses for the purpose of paragraphs 1 and 2 means the out-of-pocket expenses reasonably incurred by the salvor in the salvage operation and a fair rate for equipment and personnel actually and reasonably used in the salvage operation, taking into consideration the criteria set out in article 13, paragraph 1(h), (i) and (j).

4. The total special compensation under this article shall be paid only if and to the extent that such compensation is greater than any reward recoverable by the salvor under article 13.

5. If the salvor has been negligent and has thereby failed to prevent or minimise damage to the environment, he may be deprived of the whole or part of any special compensation due under this article.

6. Nothing in this article shall affect any right of recourse on the part of the owner of the vessel.

Article 15 – Apportionment between salvors

1. The apportionment of a reward under article 13 between salvors shall be made on the basis of the criteria contained in that article.

2. The apportionment between the owner, master and other persons in the service of each salving vessel shall be determined by the law of the flag of that vessel. If the salvage has not been carried out from a vessel, the apportionment shall be determined by the law governing the contract between the salvor and his servants.

Article 16 – Salvage of persons

1. No remuneration is due from persons whose lives are saved, but nothing in this article shall affect the provisions of national law on this subject.

2. A salvor of human life, who has taken part in the services rendered on the occasion of the accident giving rise to salvage, is entitled to a fair share of the payment awarded to the salvor for salving the vessel or other property or preventing or minimising damage to the environment.

Article 17 – Services rendered under existing contracts

No payment is due under the provisions of this Convention unless the services rendered exceed what can be reasonably considered as due performance of a contract entered into before the danger arose.

Article 18 – The effect of salvor's misconduct

A salvor may be deprived of the whole or part of the payment due under this Convention to the extent that the salvage operations have become necessary or more difficult because of fault or neglect on his part or if the salvor has been guilty of fraud or other dishonest conduct.

Article 19 – Prohibition of salvage operations

Services rendered notwithstanding the express and reasonable prohibition of the owner or master of the vessel or the owner of any other property in danger which is not and has not been on board the vessel shall not give rise to payment under this Convention.

CHAPTER IV: CLAIMS AND ACTIONS

Article 20 – Maritime lien

1. Nothing in this Convention shall affect the salvor's maritime lien under any international convention or national law.

2. The salvor may not enforce his maritime lien when satisfactory security for his claim, including interest and costs, has been duly tendered or provided.

Article 21 – Duty to provide security

1. Upon the request of the salvor a person liable for a payment due under this Convention shall provide satisfactory security for the claim, including interest and costs of the salvor.

2. Without prejudice to paragraph 1, the owner of the salved vessel shall use his best endeavours to ensure that the owners of the cargo provide satisfactory security for the claims against them including interest and costs before the cargo is released.

3. The salved vessel and other property shall not, without the consent of the salvor, be removed from the port or place at which they first arrive after the completion of the salvage operations until satisfactory security has been put up for the salvor's claim against the relevant vessel or property.

Article 22 – Interim payment

1. The tribunal having jurisdiction over the claim of the salvor may, by interim decision, order that the salvor shall be paid on account such amount as seems fair and just, and on such terms including terms as to security where appropriate, as may be fair and just according to the circumstances of the case.

2. In the event of an interim payment under this article the security provided under article 21 shall be reduced accordingly.

Article 23 – Limitation of actions

1. Any action relating to payment under this Convention shall be time-barred if judicial or arbitral proceedings have not been instituted within a period of two years. The limitation period commences on the day on which the salvage operations are terminated.

2. The person against whom a claim is made at any time during the running of the limitation period extend that period by a declaration to the claimant. This period may in the like manner be further extended.

3. An action for indemnity by a person liable may be instituted even after the expiration of the limitation period provided for in the preceding paragraphs, if brought within the time allowed by the law of the State where proceedings are instituted.

Article 24 – Interest

The right of the salvor to interest on any payment due under this Convention shall be determined according to the law of the State in which the tribunal seized of the case is situated.

Article 25 – State-owned cargoes

Unless the State owner consents, no provision of this Convention shall be used as a basis for the seizure, arrest or detention by any legal process of, nor for any proceedings in rem against, non-commercial cargoes owned by a State and entitled, at the time of the salvage operations, to sovereign immunity under generally recognised principles of international law.

Article 26 – Humanitarian cargoes

No provision of this Convention shall be used as a basis for the seizure, arrest or detention of humanitarian cargoes donated by a State, if such State has agreed to pay for salvage services rendered in respect of such humanitarian cargoes.

Article 27 – Publication of arbitral awards

States Parties shall encourage, as far as possible and with the consent of the parties, the publication of arbitral awards made in salvage cases.

CHAPTER V: FINAL CLAUSES

Article 28 – Signature, ratification, acceptance, approval and accession

1. This Convention shall be open for signature at the Headquarters of the Organization from 1 July 1989 to 30 June 1990 and shall thereafter remain open for accession.
2. States may express their consent to be bound by this Convention by:
   (a) signature without reservation as to ratification, acceptance or approval; or
   (b) signature subject to ratification, acceptance or approval, followed by ratification, acceptance of approval; or
   (c) accession.
3. Ratification, acceptance, approval or accession shall be effected by the deposit of an instrument to that effect with the Secretary-General.

Article 29 – Entry into force

1. This Convention shall enter into force one year after the date on which 15 States have expressed their consent to be bound by it.
2. For a State which expresses its consent to be bound by this Convention after the conditions for entry into force thereof have been met, such consent shall take effect one year after the date of expression of such consent.

Article 30 – Reservations

1. Any State may, at the time of signature, ratification, acceptance, approval or accession, reserve the right not to apply the provisions of this Convention:
   (a) when the salvage operation takes place in inland waters and all vessels involved are of inland navigation;
   (b) when the salvage operations take place in inland waters and no vessel is involved;
   (c) when all interested parties are nationals of that State;
   (d) when the property involved is maritime cultural property of prehistoric, archaeological or historic interest and is situated on the sea-bed.
2. Reservations made at the time of signature are subject to confirmation upon ratification, acceptance or approval.
3. Any State which has made a reservation to this Convention may withdraw it at any time by means of a notification addressed to the Secretary-General. Such withdrawal shall take effect on the date the notification is received. If the notification states that the withdrawal of a reservation is to take effect on a date specified therein, and such date is later than the date the notification is received by the Secretary-General, the withdrawal shall take effect on such later date.

Article 31 – Denunciation

1. This Convention may be denounced by any State Party at any time after the expiry of one year from the date on which this Convention enters into force for that State.

2. Denunciation shall be effected by the deposit of an instrument of denunciation with the Secretary-General.

3. A denunciation shall take effect one year, or such longer period as may be specified in the instrument of denunciation, after the receipt of the instrument of denunciation by the Secretary-General.

Article 32 – Revision and amendment

1. A conference for the purpose of revising or amending this Convention may be convened by the Organization.

2. The Secretary-General shall convene a conference of the States Parties to this Convention for revising or amending the Convention, at the request of eight States Parties, or one fourth of the States Parties, whichever is the higher figure.

3. Any consent to be bound by this Convention expressed after the date of entry into force of an amendment to this Convention shall be deemed to apply to the Convention as amended.

Article 33 – Depositary

1. This Convention shall be deposited with the Secretary-General.

2. The Secretary-General shall:
   (a) inform all States which have signed this Convention or acceded thereto, and all Members of the Organization, of:
      (i) each new signature or deposit of an instrument of ratification, acceptance, approval or accession together with the date thereof;
      (ii) the date of the entry into force of this Convention;
      (iii) the deposit of any instrument of denunciation of this Convention together with the date on which it received and the date on which the denunciation takes effect;
      (iv) any amendment adopted in conformity with article 32;
      (v) the receipt of any reservation, declaration or notification made under this Convention;
   (b) transmit certified true copies of this Convention to all States which have signed this Convention or acceded thereto.

3. As soon as this Convention enters into force, a certified true copy thereof shall be transmitted by the Depositary to the Secretary-General of the United Nations for registration and publication in accordance with Article 102 of the Charter of the United Nations.

Article 34 – Languages

This Convention is established in a single original in the Arabic, Chinese, English, French, Russian and Spanish languages, each text being equally authentic.

IN WITNESS WHEREOF the undersigned being duly authorised by their respective Governments for that purpose have signed this Convention.

DONE AT LONDON this twenty-eighth day of April one thousand nine hundred and eighty-nine.

International Safety Management (ISM) Code 2002

Preamble

1. The purpose of this Code is to provide an international standard for the safe management and operation of ships and for pollution prevention.

2. The Assembly adopted resolution A.443(XI), by which it invited all Governments to take the necessary steps to safeguard the shipmaster in the proper discharge of his responsibilities with regard to maritime safety and the protection of the marine environment.

3. The Assembly also adopted resolution A.680(17), by which it further recognised the need for appropriate organisation of management to enable it to respond to the need of those on board ships to achieve and maintain high standards of safety and environmental protection.

4. Recognising that no two shipping companies or shipowners are the same, and that ships operate under a wide range of different conditions, the Code is based on general principles and objectives.

5. The Code is expressed in broad terms so that it can have a widespread application. Clearly, different levels of management, whether shore-based or at sea, will require varying levels of knowledge and awareness of the items outlined.

6 The cornerstone of good safety management is commitment from the top. In matters of safety and pollution prevention it is the commitment, competence, attitudes and motivation of individuals at all levels that determines the end result.

Part A – Implementation

1. GENERAL

1.1 Definitions

The following definitions apply to parts A and B of this Code.

1.1.1 "International Safety Management (ISM) Code" means the International Management Code for the Safe Operation of Ships and for Pollution Prevention as adopted by the Assembly, as may be amended by the Organization.

1.1.2 "Company" means the owner of the ship or any other organisation or person such as the manager, or the bareboat charterer, who has assumed the responsibility for operation of the ship from the shipowner and who, on assuming such responsibility, has agreed to take over all duties and responsibility imposed by the Code.

1.1.3 "Administration" means the Government of the State whose flag the ship is entitled to fly.

1.1.4 "Safety management system" means a structured and documented system enabling Company personnel to implement effectively the Company safety and environmental protection policy.

1.1.5 "Document of Compliance" means a document issued to a Company which complies with the requirements of this Code.

1.1.6 "Safety Management Certificate" means a document issued to a ship which signifies that the Company and its shipboard management operate in accordance with the approved safety management system.

1.1.7 "Objective evidence" means quantitative or qualitative information, records or statements of fact pertaining to safety or to the existence and implementation of a safety management system element, which is based on observation, measurement or test and which can be verified.

1.1.8 "Observation" means a statement of fact made during a safety management audit and substantiated by objective evidence.

1.1.9 "Non-conformity" means an observed situation where objective evidence indicates the non-fulfilment of a specified requirement.

1.1.10 "Major non-conformity" means an identifiable deviation that poses a serious threat to the safety of personnel or the ship or a serious risk to the environment that requires immediate corrective action and includes the lack of effective and systematic implementation of a requirement of this Code.

1.1.11 "Anniversary date" means the day and month of each year that corresponds to the date of expiry of the relevant document or certificate.

1.1.12 "Convention" means the International Convention for the Safety of Life at Sea, 1974, as amended.

1.2 Objectives

1.2.1 The objectives of the Code are to ensure safety at sea, prevention of human injury or loss of life, and avoidance of damage to the environment, in particular to the marine environment and to property.

1.2.2 Safety management objectives of the Company should, *inter alia*:

.1 provide for safe practices in ship operation and a safe working environment;

.2 establish safeguards against all identified risks; and

.3 continuously improve safety management skills of personnel ashore and aboard ships, including preparing for emergencies related both to safety and environmental protection.

1.2.3 The safety management system should ensure:

.1 compliance with mandatory rules and regulations; and

.2 that applicable codes, guidelines and standards recommended by the Organization, Administrations, classification societies and maritime industry organisations are taken into account.

1.3 Application

The requirements of this Code may be applied to all ships.

1.4 Functional requirements for a safety management system

Every Company should develop, implement and maintain a safety management system which includes the following functional requirements:

.1 a safety and environmental-protection policy;

.2 instructions and procedures to ensure safe operation of ships and protection of the environment in compliance with relevant international and flag State legislation;

.3 defined levels of authority and lines of communication between, and amongst, shore and shipboard personnel;

.4 procedures for reporting accidents and non-conformities with the provisions of this Code;

.5 procedures to prepare for and respond to emergency situations; and

.6 procedures for internal audits and management reviews.

2. SAFETY AND ENVIRONMENTAL-PROTECTION POLICY

2.1 The Company should establish a safety and environmental-protection policy which describes how the objectives given in paragraph 1.2 will be achieved.

2.2 The Company should ensure that the policy is implemented and maintained at all levels of the organisation, both ship-based and shore-based.

3. COMPANY RESPONSIBILITIES AND AUTHORITY

3.1 If the entity who is responsible for the operation of the ship is other than the owner, the owner must report the full name and details of such entity to the Administration.

3.2 The Company should define and document the responsibility, authority and interrelation of all personnel who manage, perform and verify work relating to and affecting safety and pollution prevention.

3.3 The Company is responsible for ensuring that adequate resources and shore-based support are provided to enable the designated person or persons to carry out their functions.

4. DESIGNATED PERSON(S)

To ensure the safe operation of each ship and to provide a link between the Company and those on board, every Company, as appropriate, should designate a person or persons ashore having direct access to the highest level of management. The responsibility and authority of the designated person or persons should include monitoring the safety and pollution-prevention aspects of the operation of each ship and ensuring that adequate resources and shore-based support are applied, as required.

5. MASTER'S RESPONSIBILITY AND AUTHORITY

5.1 The Company should clearly define and document the master's responsibility with regard to:

.1 implementing the safety and environmental-protection policy of the Company;

.2 motivating the crew in the observation of that policy;

.3 issuing appropriate orders and instructions in a clear and simple manner;

.4 verifying that specified requirements are observed; and

.5 reviewing the safety management system and reporting its deficiencies to the shore-based management.

5.2 The Company should ensure that the safety management system operating on board the ship contains a clear statement emphasising the master's authority. The Company should establish in the safety management system that the master has the overriding authority and the responsibility to make decisions with respect to safety and pollution prevention and to request the Company's assistance as may be necessary.

6. RESOURCES AND PERSONNEL

6.1 The Company should ensure that the master is:

.1 properly qualified for command;

.2 fully conversant with the Company's safety management system; and

.3 given the necessary support so that the master's duties can be safely performed.

6.2 The Company should ensure that each ship is manned with qualified, certificated and medically fit seafarers in accordance with national and international requirements.

6.3 The Company should establish procedures to ensure that new personnel and personnel transferred to new assignments related to safety and protection of the environment are given proper familiarisation with their duties. Instructions which are essential to be provided prior to sailing should be identified, documented and given.

6.4 The Company should ensure that all personnel involved in the Company's safety management system have an adequate understanding of relevant rules, regulations, codes and guidelines.

6.5 The Company should establish and maintain procedures for identifying any training which may be required in support of the safety management system and ensure that such training is provided for all personnel concerned.

6.6 The Company should establish procedures by which the ship's personnel receive relevant information on the safety management system in a working language or languages understood by them.

6.7 The Company should ensure that the ship's personnel are able to communicate effectively in the execution of their duties related to the safety management system.

7. *DEVELOPMENT OF PLANS FOR SHIPBOARD OPERATIONS*

The Company should establish procedures for the preparation of plans and instructions, including checklists as appropriate, for key shipboard operations concerning the safety of the ship and the prevention of pollution. The various tasks involved should be defined and assigned to qualified personnel.

8. *EMERGENCY PREPAREDNESS*

8.1 The Company should establish procedures to identify, describe and respond to potential emergency shipboard situations.

8.2 The Company should establish programmes for drills and exercises to prepare for emergency actions.

8.3 The safety management system should provide for measures ensuring that the Company's organisation can respond at any time to hazards, accidents and emergency situations involving its ships.

9. *REPORTS AND ANALYSIS OF NON-CONFORMITIES, ACCIDENTS AND HAZARDOUS OCCURRENCES*

9.1 The safety management system should include procedures ensuring that non-conformities, accidents and hazardous situations are reported to the Company, investigated and analysed with the objective of improving safety and pollution prevention.

9.2 The Company should establish procedures for the implementation of corrective action.

10. *MAINTENANCE OF THE SHIP AND EQUIPMENT*

10.1 The Company should establish procedures to ensure that the ship is maintained in conformity with the provisions of the relevant rules and regulations and with any additional requirements which may be established by the Company.

10.2 In meeting these requirements the Company should ensure that:

    .1 inspections are held at appropriate intervals;

    .2 any non-conformity is reported, with its possible cause, if known;

    .3 appropriate corrective action is taken; and

    .4 records of these activities are maintained.

10.3 The Company should establish procedures in its safety management system to identify equipment and technical systems the sudden operational failure of which may result in hazardous situations. The safety management system should provide for specific measures aimed at promoting the reliability of such equipment or systems. These measures should include the regular testing of stand-by arrangements and equipment or technical systems that are not in continuous use.

10.4 The inspections mentioned in 10.2 as well as the measures referred to in 10.3 should be integrated into the ship's operational maintenance routine.

11. *DOCUMENTATION*

11.1 The Company should establish and maintain procedures to control all documents and data which are relevant to the safety management system.

11.2 The Company should ensure that:

    .1 valid documents are available at all relevant locations;

    .2 changes to documents are reviewed and approved by authorised personnel; and

    .3 obsolete documents are promptly removed.

11.3 The documents used to describe and implement the safety management system may be referred to as the Safety Management Manual. Documentation should be kept in a form that the Company considers most effective. Each ship should carry on board all documentation relevant to that ship.

12. COMPANY VERIFICATION, REVIEW AND EVALUATION

12.1 The Company should carry out internal safety audits to verify whether safety and pollution-prevention activities comply with the safety management system.

12.2 The Company should periodically evaluate the efficiency of and, when needed, review the safety management system in accordance with procedures established by the Company.

12.3 The audits and possible corrective actions should be carried out in accordance with documented procedures.

12.4 Personnel carrying out audits should be independent of the areas being audited unless this is impracticable due to the size and the nature of the Company.

12.5 The results of the audits and reviews should be brought to the attention of all personnel having responsibility in the area involved.

12.6 The management personnel responsible for the area involved should take timely corrective action on deficiencies found.

PART B – CERTIFICATION AND VERIFICATION

13. CERTIFICATION AND PERIODICAL VERIFICATION

13.1 The ship should be operated by a Company which has been issued with a Document of Compliance or with an Interim Document of Compliance in accordance with paragraph 14.1, relevant to that ship.

13.2 The Document of Compliance should be issued by the Administration, by an organisation recognised by the Administration or, at the request of the Administration, by another Contracting Government to the Convention to any Company complying with the requirements of this Code for a period specified by the Administration which should not exceed five years. Such a document should be accepted as evidence that the Company is capable of complying with the requirements of this Code.

13.3 The Document of Compliance is only valid for the ship types explicitly indicated in the document. Such indication should be based on the types of ships on which the initial verification was based. Other ship types should only be added after verification of the Company's capability to comply with the requirements of this Code applicable to such ship types. In this context, ship types are those referred to in regulation IX/1 of the Convention.

13.4 The validity of a Document of Compliance should be subject to annual verification by the Administration or by an organisation recognised by the Administration or, at the request of the Administration, by another Contracting Government within three months before or after the anniversary date.

13.5 The Document of Compliance should be withdrawn by the Administration or, at its request, by the Contracting Government which issued the Document when the annual verification required in paragraph 13.4 is not requested or if there is evidence of major non-conformities with this Code.

13.5.1 All associated Safety Management Certificates and/or Interim Safety Management Certificates should also be withdrawn if the Document of Compliance is withdrawn.

13.6 A copy of the Document of Compliance should be placed on board in order that the master of the ship, if so requested, may produce it for verification by the Administration or by an organisation recognised by the Administration or for the purposes of the control referred to in regulation IX/6.2 of the Convention. The copy of the Document is not required to be authenticated or certified.

13.7 The Safety Management Certificate should be issued to a ship for a period which should not exceed five years by the Administration or an organisation recognised by the

Administration or, at the request of the Administration, by another Contracting Government. The Safety Management Certificate should be issued after verifying that the Company and its shipboard management operate in accordance with the approved safety management system. Such a Certificate should be accepted as evidence that the ship is complying with the requirements of this Code.

13.8 The validity of the Safety Management Certificate should be subject to at least one intermediate verification by the Administration or an organisation recognised by the Administration or, at the request of the Administration, by another Contracting Government. If only one intermediate verification is to be carried out and the period of validity of the Safety Management Certificate is five years, it should take place between the second and third anniversary dates of the Safety Management Certificate.

13.9 In addition to the requirements of paragraph 13.5.1, the Safety Management Certificate should be withdrawn by the Administration or, at the request of the Administration, by the Contracting Government which has issued it when the intermediate verification required in paragraph 13.8 is not requested or if there is evidence of major nonconformity with this Code.

13.10 Notwithstanding the requirements of paragraphs 13.2 and 13.7, when the renewal verification is completed within three months before the expiry date of the existing Document of Compliance or Safety Management Certificate, the new Document of Compliance or the new Safety Management Certificate should be valid from the date of completion of the renewal verification for a period not exceeding five years from the date of expiry of the existing Document of Compliance or Safety Management Certificate.

13.11 When the renewal verification is completed more than three months before the expiry date of the existing Document of Compliance or Safety Management Certificate, the new Document of Compliance or the new Safety Management Certificate should be valid from the date of completion of the renewal verification for a period not exceeding five years from the date of completion of the renewal verification."

14. INTERIM CERTIFICATION

14.1 An Interim Document of Compliance may be issued to facilitate initial implementation of this Code when:

 .1 a Company is newly established; or

 .2 new ship types are to be added to an existing Document of Compliance, following verification that the Company has a safety management system that meets the objectives of paragraph 1.2.3 of this Code, provided the Company demonstrates plans to implement a safety management system meeting the full requirements of this Code within the period of validity of the Interim Document of Compliance. Such an Interim Document of Compliance should be issued for a period not exceeding 12 months by the Administration or by an organisation recognised by the Administration or, at the request of the Administration, by another Contracting Government. A copy of the Interim Document of Compliance should be placed on board in order that the master of the ship, if so requested, may produce it for verification by the Administration or by an organisation recognised by the Administration or for the purposes of the control referred to in regulation IX/6.2 of the Convention. The copy of the Document is not required to be authenticated or certified.

14.2 An Interim Safety Management Certificate may be issued:

 .1 to new ships on delivery;

 .2 when a Company takes on responsibility for the operation of a ship which is new to the Company; or

 .3 when a ship changes flag.

Such an Interim Safety Management Certificate should be issued for a period not exceeding 6 months by the Administration or an organisation recognised by the Administration or, at the request of the Administration, by another Contracting Government.

14.3 An Administration or, at the request of the Administration, another Contracting Government may, in special cases, extend the validity of an Interim Safety Management

Certificate for a further period which should not exceed 6 months from the date of expiry.

14.4 An Interim Safety Management Certificate may be issued following verification that:

.1 the Document of Compliance, or the Interim Document of Compliance, is relevant to the ship concerned;

.2 the safety management system provided by the Company for the ship concerned includes key elements of this Code and has been assessed during the audit for issuance of the Document of Compliance or demonstrated for issuance of the Interim Document of Compliance;

.3 the Company has planned the audit of the ship within three months;

.4 the master and officers are familiar with the safety management system and the planned arrangements for its implementation;

.5 instructions, which have been identified as being essential, are provided prior to sailing; and

.6 relevant information on the safety management system has been given in a working language or languages understood by the ship's personnel.

15. VERIFICATION

15.1 All verifications required by the provisions of this Code should be carried out in accordance with procedures acceptable to the Administration, taking into account the guidelines developed by the Organization.

16. FORMS OF CERTIFICATES

16.1 The Document of Compliance, the Safety Management Certificate, the Interim Document of Compliance and the Interim Safety Management Certificate should be drawn up in a form corresponding to the models given in the appendix to this Code. If the language used is neither English nor French, the text should include a translation into one of these languages.

16.2 In addition to the requirements of paragraph 13.3, the ship types indicated on the Document of Compliance and the Interim Document of Compliance may be endorsed to reflect any limitations in the operations of the ships described in the safety management system.

APPENDIX K

The International Ship and Port Security Code (ISPS)

ANNEX 1
CONFERENCE RESOLUTION 2
(adopted on 12 December 2002)
ADOPTION OF THE INTERNATIONAL CODE FOR THE SECURITY OF SHIPS AND OF PORT FACILITIES

THE CONFERENCE,

HAVING ADOPTED amendments to the International Convention for the Safety of Life at Sea, 1974, as amended (hereinafter referred to as "the Convention"), concerning special measures to enhance maritime safety and security,

CONSIDERING that the new chapter XI-2 of the Convention makes a reference to an International Ship and Port Facility Security (ISPS) Code and requires that ships, companies and port facilities to comply with the relevant requirements of part A of the International Ship and Port Facility Security (ISPS) Code, as specified in part A of the ISPS Code,

BEING OF THE OPINION that the implementation by Contracting Governments of the said chapter will greatly contribute to the enhancement of maritime safety and security and safeguarding those on board and ashore,

HAVING CONSIDERED a draft of the International Code for the Security of Ships and of Port Facilities prepared by the Maritime Safety Committee of the International Maritime Organization (hereinafter referred to as "the Organization"), at its seventy-fifth and seventy-sixth session, for consideration and adoption by the Conference,

1. ADOPTS the International Code for the Security of Ships and of Port Facilities (hereinafter referred to as "the Code"), the text of which is set out in the Annex to the present resolution;

2. INVITES Contracting Governments to the Convention to note that the Code will take effect on 1 July 2004 upon entry into force of the new chapter XI-2 of the Convention;

3. REQUESTS the Maritime Safety Committee to keep the Code under review and amend it, as appropriate;

4. REQUESTS the Secretary-General of the Organization to transmit certified copies of the present resolution and the text of the Code contained in the Annex to all Contracting Governments to the Convention;

5. FURTHER REQUESTS the Secretary-General to transmit copies of this resolution and its Annex to all Members of the Organization, which are not Contracting Governments to the Convention.

ANNEX
INTERNATIONAL CODE FOR THE SECURITY OF SHIPS AND OF PORT FACILITIES
Preamble

1 The Diplomatic Conference on Maritime Security held in London in December 2002 adopted new provisions in the International Convention for the Safety of Life at Sea, 1974 and this Code* to enhance maritime security. These new requirements form the international

---

* The complete name of this Code is the International Code for the Security of Ships and of Port Facilities. The abbreviated name of this Code, as referred to in regulation XI-2/1 of SOLAS 74 as amended, is the International Ship and Port Facility Security (ISPS) Code or, in short, the ISPS Code.

framework through which ships and port facilities can co-operate to detect and deter acts which threaten security in the maritime transport sector.

2 Following the tragic events of 11th September 2001, the twenty-second session of the Assembly of the International Maritime Organization (the Organization), in November 2001, unanimously agreed to the development of new measures relating to the security of ships and of port facilities for adoption by a Conference of Contracting Governments to the International Convention for the Safety of Life at Sea, 1974 (known as the Diplomatic Conference on Maritime Security) in December 2002. Preparation for the Diplomatic Conference was entrusted to the Organization's Maritime Safety Committee (MSC) on the basis of submissions made by Member States, intergovernmental organisations and non-governmental organisations in consultative status with the Organization.

3 The MSC, at its first extraordinary session, held also in November 2001, in order to accelerate the development and the adoption of the appropriate security measures established an MSC Intersessional Working Group on Maritime Security. The first meeting of the MSC Intersessional Working Group on Maritime Security was held in February 2002 and the outcome of its discussions was reported to, and considered by, the seventy-fifth session of the MSC in March 2002, when an *ad hoc* Working Group was established to further develop the proposals made. The seventy-fifth session of the MSC considered the report of that Working Group and recommended that work should be taken forward through a further MSC Intersessional Working Group, which was held in September 2002. The seventy-sixth session of the MSC considered the outcome of the September 2002 session of the MSC Intersessional Working Group and the further work undertaken by the MSC Working Group held in conjunction with the Committee's seventy-sixth session in December 2002, immediately prior to the Diplomatic Conference and agreed the final version of the proposed texts to be considered by the Diplomatic Conference.

4 The Diplomatic Conference (9 to 13 December 2002) also adopted amendments to the existing provisions of the International Convention for the Safety of Life at Sea, 1974 (SOLAS 74) accelerating the implementation of the requirement to fit Automatic Identification Systems and adopted new Regulations in Chapter XI-1 of SOLAS 74 covering marking of the Ship's Identification Number and the carriage of a Continuous Synopsis Record. The Diplomatic Conference also adopted a number of Conference Resolutions including those covering implementation and revision of this Code, Technical Co-operation, and co-operative work with the International Labour Organization and World Customs Organization. It was recognised that review and amendment of certain of the new provisions regarding maritime security may be required on completion of the work of these two Organizations.

5 The provision of Chapter XI-2 of SOLAS 74 and this Code apply to ships and to port facilities. The extension of SOLAS 74 to cover port facilities was agreed on the basis that SOLAS 74 offered the speediest means of ensuring the necessary security measures entered into force and given effect quickly. However, it was further agreed that the provisions relating to port facilities should relate solely to the ship/port interface. The wider issue of the security of port areas will be the subject of further joint work between the International Maritime Organization and the International Labour Organization. It was also agreed that the provisions should not extend to the actual response to attacks or to any necessary clear-up activities after such an attack.

6 In drafting the provision care has been taken to ensure compatibility with the provisions of the International Convention on Standards of Training, Certification and Watchkeeping and Certification for Seafarers, 1978, as amended, the International Safety Management (ISM) Code and the harmonised system of survey and certification.

7 The provisions represent a significant change in the approach of the international maritime industries to the issue of security in the maritime transport sector. It is recognised that they may place a significant additional burden on certain Contracting Governments. The importance of Technical Co-operation to assist Contracting Governments implement the provisions is fully recognised.

8 Implementation of the provisions will require continuing effective co-operation and understanding between all those involved with, or using, ships and port facilities including ship's personnel, port personnel, passengers, cargo interests, ship and port management and those in National and Local Authorities with security responsibilities. Existing practices and procedures will have to be reviewed and changed if they do not provide an adequate level of security. In the interests of enhanced maritime security additional responsibilities will have to be carried by the shipping and port industries and by National and Local Authorities.

9 The guidance given in part B of this Code should be taken into account when implementing the security provisions set out in Chapter XI-2 of SOLAS 74 and in part A of this Code. However, it is recognised that the extent to which the guidance applies may vary depending on the nature of the port facility and of the ship, its trade and/or cargo.

10 Nothing in this Code shall be interpreted or applied in a manner inconsistent with the proper respect of fundamental rights and freedoms as set out in international instruments, particularly those relating to maritime workers and refugees including the International Labour Organization Declaration of Fundamental Principles and Rights at Work as well as international standards concerning maritime and port workers.

11 Recognising that the Convention on the Facilitation of Maritime Traffic, 1965, as amended, provides that foreign crew members shall be allowed ashore by the public authorities while the ship on which they arrive is in port, provided that the formalities on arrival of the ship have been fulfilled and the public authorities have no reason to refuse permission to come ashore for reasons of public health, public safety or public order, Contracting Governments when approving ship and port facility security plans should pay due cognisance to the fact that ship's personnel live and work on the vessel and need shore leave and access to shore based seafarer welfare facilities, including medical care.

Part A

MANDATORY REQUIREMENTS REGARDING THE PROVISIONS OF CHAPTER XI-2 OF THE INTERNATIONAL CONVENTION FOR THE SAFETY OF LIFE AT SEA, 1974, AS AMENDED

1 General

1.1 Introduction

This part of the International Code for the Security of Ships and Port Facilities contains mandatory provisions to which reference is made in chapter XI-2 of the International Convention for the Safety of Life at Sea, 1974 as amended.

1.2 Objectives

The objectives of this Code are:

.1 to establish an international framework involving co-operation between Contracting Governments, Government agencies, local administrations and the shipping and port industries to detect security threats and take preventive measures against security incidents affecting ships or port facilities used in international trade;

.2 to establish the respective roles and responsibilities of the Contracting Governments, Government agencies, local administrations and the shipping and port industries, at the national and international level for ensuring maritime security;

.3 to ensure the early and efficient collection and exchange of security-related information;

.4 to provide a methodology for security assessments so as to have in place plans and procedures to react to changing security levels; and

.5 to ensure confidence that adequate and proportionate maritime security measures are in place.

1.3 Functional requirements

In order to achieve its objectives, this Code embodies a number of functional requirements. These include, but are not limited to:

.1 gathering and assessing information with respect to security threats and exchanging such information with appropriate Contracting Governments;

.2 requiring the maintenance of communication protocols for ships and port facilities;

.3 preventing unauthorised access to ships, port facilities and their restricted areas;

.4 preventing the introduction of unauthorised weapons, incendiary devices or explosives to ships or port facilities;

.5 providing means for raising the alarm in reaction to security threats or security incidents;

.6 requiring ship and port facility security plans based upon security assessments; and

.7 requiring training, drills and exercises to ensure familiarity with security plans and procedures.

2 Definitions

2.1 For the purpose of this part, unless expressly provided otherwise:

.1 Convention means the International Convention for the Safety of Life at Sea, 1974 as amended.

.2 Regulation means a regulation of the Convention.

.3 Chapter means a chapter of the Convention.

.4 Ship security plan means a plan developed to ensure the application of measures on board the ship designed to protect persons on board, cargo, cargo transport units, ship's stores or the ship from the risks of a security incident.

.5 Port facility security plan means a plan developed to ensure the application of measures designed to protect the port facility and ships, persons, cargo, cargo transport units and ship's stores within the port facility from the risks of a security incident.

.6 Ship security officer means the person on board the ship, accountable to the master, designated by the Company as responsible for the security of the ship, including implementation and maintenance of the ship security plan and for liaison with the company security officer and port facility security officers.

.7 Company security officer means the person designated by the Company for ensuring that a ship security assessment is carried out; that a ship security plan is developed, submitted for approval, and thereafter implemented and maintained and for liaison with port facility security officers and the ship security officer.

.8 Port facility security officer means the person designated as responsible for the development, implementation, revision and maintenance of the port facility security plan and for liaison with the ship security officers and company security officers.

.9 Security level 1 means the level for which minimum appropriate protective security measures shall be maintained at all times.

.10 Security level 2 means the level for which appropriate additional protective security measures shall be maintained for a period of time as a result of heightened risk of a security incident.

.11 Security level 3 means the level for which further specific protective security measures shall be maintained for a limited period of time when a security incident is probable or imminent, although it may not be possible to identify the specific target.

2.2 The term "ship", when used in this Code, includes mobile offshore drilling units and high-speed craft as defined in regulation XI-2/1.

2.3 The term "Contracting Government" in connection with any reference to a port facility, when used in sections 14 to 18, includes a reference to the "Designated Authority".

2.4 Terms not otherwise defined in this part shall have the same meaning as the meaning attributed to them in chapters I and XI-2.

3 Application

3.1 This Code applies to:
  .1 the following types of ships engaged on international voyages:
    .1 passenger ships, including high-speed passenger craft;
    .2 cargo ships, including high-speed craft, of 500 gross tonnage and upwards; and
    .3 mobile offshore drilling units; and
  .2 port facilities serving such ships engaged on international voyages.

3.2 Notwithstanding the provisions of section 3.1.2, Contracting Governments shall decide the extent of application of this Part of the Code to those port facilities within their territory which, although used primarily by ships not engaged on international voyages, are required, occasionally, to serve ships arriving or departing on an international voyage.
  3.2.1 Contracting Governments shall base their decisions, under section 3.2, on a port facility security assessment carried out in accordance with this Part of the Code.
  3.2.2 Any decision which a Contracting Government makes, under section 3.2, shall not compromise the level of security intended to be achieved by chapter XI-2 or by this Part of the Code.

3.3 This Code does not apply to warships, naval auxiliaries or other ships owned or operated by a Contracting Government and used only on Government non-commercial service.

3.4 Sections 5 to 13 and 19 of this part apply to Companies and ships as specified in regulation XI-2/4.

3.5 Sections 5 and 14 to 18 of this part apply to port facilities as specified in regulation XI-2/10.

3.6 Nothing in this Code shall prejudice the rights or obligations of States under international law.

4 Responsibilities of Contracting Governments

4.1 Subject to the provisions of regulation XI-2/3 and XI-2/7, Contracting Governments shall set security levels and provide guidance for protection from security incidents. Higher security levels indicate greater likelihood of occurrence of a security incident. Factors to be considered in setting the appropriate security level include:
  .1 the degree that the threat information is credible;
  .2 the degree that the threat information is corroborated;
  .3 the degree that the threat information is specific or imminent; and
  .4 the potential consequences of such a security incident.

4.2 Contracting Governments, when they set security level 3, shall issue, as necessary, appropriate instructions and shall provide security related information to the ships and port facilities that may be affected.

4.3 Contracting Governments may delegate to a recognised security organisation certain of their security related duties under chapter XI-2 and this Part of the Code with the exception of:
  .1 setting of the applicable security level;
  .2 approving a Port Facility Security Assessment and subsequent amendments to an approved assessment;
  .3 determining the port facilities which will be required to designate a Port Facility Security Officer;
  .4 approving a Port Facility Security Plan and subsequent amendments to an approved plan;
  .5 exercising control and compliance measures pursuant to regulation XI-2/9; and
  .6 establishing the requirements for a Declaration of Security.

4.4 Contracting Governments shall, to the extent they consider appropriate, test the effectiveness of the Ship or the Port Facility Security Plans, or of amendments to such plans, they have approved, or, in the case of ships, of plans which have been approved on their behalf.

5 Declaration of security

5.1 Contracting Governments shall determine when a Declaration of Security is required by assessing the risk the ship/port interface or ship to ship activity poses to persons, property or the environment.

5.2 A ship can request completion of a Declaration of Security when:
 .1 the ship is operating at a higher security level than the port facility or another ship it is interfacing with;
 .2 there is an agreement on a Declaration of Security between Contracting Governments covering certain international voyages or specific ships on those voyages;
 .3 there has been a security threat or a security incident involving the ship or involving the port facility, as applicable;
 .4 the ship is at a port which is not required to have and implement an approved port facility security plan; or
 .5 the ship is conducting ship to ship activities with another ship not required to have and implement an approved ship security plan.

5.3 Requests for the completion of a Declaration of Security, under this section, shall be acknowledged by the applicable port facility or ship.

5.4 The Declaration of Security shall be completed by:
 .1 the master or the ship security officer on behalf of the ship(s); and, if appropriate,
 .2 the port facility security officer or, if the Contracting Government determines otherwise, by any other body responsible for shore-side security, on behalf of the port facility.

5.5 The Declaration of Security shall address the security requirements that could be shared between a port facility and a ship (or between ships) and shall state the responsibility for each.

5.6 Contracting Governments shall specify, bearing in mind the provisions of regulation XI-2/9.2.3, the minimum period for which Declarations of Security shall be kept by the port facilities located within their territory.

5.7 Administrations shall specify, bearing in mind the provisions of regulation XI-2/9.2.3, the minimum period for which Declarations of Security shall be kept by ships entitled to fly their flag.

6 Obligations of the Company

6.1 The Company shall ensure that the ship security plan contains a clear statement emphasising the master's authority. The Company shall establish in the ship security plan that the master has the overriding authority and responsibility to make decisions with respect to the safety and security of the ship and to request the assistance of the Company or of any Contracting Government as may be necessary.

6.2 The Company shall ensure that the company security officer, the master and the ship security officer are given the necessary support to fulfil their duties and responsibilities in accordance with chapter XI-2 and this Part of the Code.

7 Ship security

7.1 A ship is required to act upon the security levels set by Contracting Governments as set out below.

7.2 At security level 1, the following activities shall be carried out, through appropriate measures, on all ships, taking into account the guidance given in part B of this Code, in order to identify and take preventive measures against security incidents:
 .1 ensuring the performance of all ship security duties;
 .2 controlling access to the ship;
 .3 controlling the embarkation of persons and their effects;

.4 monitoring restricted areas to ensure that only authorised persons have access;

.5 monitoring of deck areas and areas surrounding the ship;

.6 supervising the handling of cargo and ship's stores; and

.7 ensuring that security communication is readily available.

7.3 At security level 2, the additional protective measures, specified in the ship security plan, shall be implemented for each activity detailed in section 7.2, taking into account the guidance given in part B of this Code.

7.4 At security level 3, further specific protective measures, specified in the ship security plan, shall be implemented for each activity detailed in section 7.2, taking into account the guidance given in part B of this Code.

7.5 Whenever security level 2 or 3 is set by the Administration, the ship shall acknowledge receipt of the instructions on change of the security level.

7.6 Prior to entering a port or whilst in a port within the territory of a Contracting Government that has set security level 2 or 3, the ship shall acknowledge receipt of this instruction and shall confirm to the port facility security officer the initiation of the implementation of the appropriate measures and procedures as detailed in the ship security plan, and in the case of security level 3, in instructions issued by the Contracting Government which has set security level 3. The ship shall report any difficulties in implementation. In such cases, the port facility security officer and ship security officer shall liase and co-ordinate the appropriate actions.

7.7 If a ship is required by the Administration to set, or is already at, a higher security level than that set for the port it intends to enter or in which it is already located, then the ship shall advise, without delay, the competent authority of the Contracting Government within whose territory the port facility is located and the port facility security officer of the situation.

    7.7.1 In such cases, the ship security officer shall liaise with the port facility security officer and co-ordinate appropriate actions, if necessary.

7.8 An Administration requiring ships entitled to fly its flag to set security level 2 or 3 in a port of another Contracting Government shall inform that Contracting Government without delay.

7.9 When Contracting Governments set security levels and ensure the provision of security level information to ships operating in their territorial sea, or having communicated an intention to enter their territorial sea, such ships shall be advised to maintain vigilance and report immediately to their Administration and any nearby coastal States any information that comes to their attention that might affect maritime security in the area.

    7.9.1 When advising such ships of the applicable security level, a Contracting Government shall, taking into account the guidance given in the part B of this Code, also advise those ships of any security measure that they should take and, if appropriate, of measures that have been taken by the Contracting Government to provide protection against the threat.

8 Ship security assessment

8.1 The ship security assessment is an essential and integral part of the process of developing and updating the ship security plan.

8.2 The company security officer shall ensure that the ship security assessment is carried out by persons with appropriate skills to evaluate the security of a ship, in accordance with this section, taking into account the guidance given in part B of this Code.

8.3 Subject to the provisions of section 9.2.1, a recognised security organisation may carry out the ship security assessment of a specific ship.

8.4 The ship security assessment shall include an on-scene security survey and, at least, the following elements:

.1 identification of existing security measures, procedures and operations;

.2 identification and evaluation of key ship board operations that it is important to protect;

.3 identification of possible threats to the key ship board operations and the likelihood of their occurrence, in order to establish and prioritise security measures; and

.4 identification of weaknesses, including human factors in the infrastructure, policies and procedures.

8.5 The ship security assessment shall be documented, reviewed, accepted and retained by the Company.

9 Ship security plan

9.1 Each ship shall carry on board a ship security plan approved by the Administration. The plan shall make provisions for the three security levels as defined in this Part of the Code.

> 9.1.1 Subject to the provisions of section 9.2.1, a recognised security organisation may prepare the ship security plan for a specific ship.

9.2 The Administration may entrust the review and approval of ship security plans, or of amendments to a previously approved plan, to recognised security organisations.

> 9.2.1 In such cases the recognised security organisation, undertaking the review and approval of a ship security plan, or its amendments, for a specific ship shall not have been involved in either the preparation of the ship security assessment or of the ship security plan, or of the amendments, under review.

9.3 The submission of a ship security plan, or of amendments to a previously approved plan, for approval shall be accompanied by the security assessment on the basis of which the plan, or the amendments, have been developed.

9.4 Such a plan shall be developed, taking into account the guidance given in part B of this Code and shall be written in the working language or languages of the ship. If the language or languages used is not English, French or Spanish, a translation into one of these languages shall be included. The plan shall address, at least, the following:

.1 measures designed to prevent weapons, dangerous substances and devices intended for use against persons, ships or ports and the carriage of which is not authorised from being taken on board the ship;

.2 identification of the restricted areas and measures for the prevention of unauthorised access to them;

.3 measures for the prevention of unauthorised access to the ship;

.4 procedures for responding to security threats or breaches of security, including provisions for maintaining critical operations of the ship or ship/port interface;

.5 procedures for responding to any security instructions Contracting Governments may give at security level 3;

.6 procedures for evacuation in case of security threats or breaches of security;

.7 duties of shipboard personnel assigned security responsibilities and of other shipboard personnel on security aspects;

.8 procedures for auditing the security activities;

.9 procedures for training, drills and exercises associated with the plan;

.10 procedures for interfacing with port facility security activities;

.11 procedures for the periodic review of the plan and for updating;

.12 procedures for reporting security incidents;

.13 identification of the ship security officer;

.14 identification of the company security officer including 24-hour contact details;

.15 procedures to ensure the inspection, testing, calibration, and maintenance of any security equipment provided on board;

.16 frequency for testing or calibration of any security equipment provided on board;

.17 identification of the locations where the ship security alert system activation points are provided[1]; and

.18 procedures, instructions and guidance on the use of the ship security alert system, including the testing, activation, deactivation and resetting and to limit false alerts.

9.4.1 Personnel conducting internal audits of the security activities specified in the plan or evaluating its implementation shall be independent of the activities being audited unless this is impracticable due to the size and the nature of the Company or of the ship.

9.5 The Administration shall determine which changes to an approved ship security plan or to any security equipment specified in an approved plan shall not be implemented unless the relevant amendments to the plan are approved by the Administration. Any such changes shall be at least as effective as those measures prescribed in chapter XI-2 and this Part of the Code.

9.5.1 The nature of the changes to the ship security plan or the security equipment that have been specifically approved by the Administration, pursuant to section 9.5, shall be documented in a manner that clearly indicates such approval. This approval shall be available on board and shall be presented together with the International Ship Security Certificate (or the Interim International Ship Security Certificate). If these changes are temporary, once the original approved measures or equipment are reinstated, this documentation no longer needs to be retained by the ship.

9.6 The plan may be kept in an electronic format. In such a case, it shall be protected by procedures aimed at preventing its unauthorised deletion, destruction or amendment.

9.7 The plan shall be protected from unauthorised access or disclosure.

9.8 Ship security plans are not subject to inspection by officers duly authorised by a Contracting Government to carry out control and compliance measures in accordance with regulation XI-2/9, save in circumstances specified in section 9.8.1.

9.8.1 If the officers duly authorised by a Contracting Government have clear grounds to believe that the ship is not in compliance with the requirements of chapter XI-2 or part A of this Code, and the only means to verify or rectify the non-compliance is to review the relevant requirements of the ship security plan, limited access to the specific sections of the plan relating to the noncompliance is exceptionally allowed, but only with the consent of the Contracting Government of, or the master of, the ship concerned. Nevertheless, the provisions in the plan relating to section 9.4 subsections .2, .4, .5, .7, .15, .17 and .18 of this Part of the Code are considered as confidential information, and cannot be subject to inspection unless otherwise agreed by the Contracting Governments concerned.

10 Records

10.1 Records of the following activities addressed in the ship security plan shall be kept on board for at least the minimum period specified by the Administration, bearing in mind the provisions of regulation XI-2/9.2.3:

.1 training, drills and exercises;

.2 security threats and security incidents;

.3 breaches of security;

.4 changes in security level;

.5 communications relating to the direct security of the ship such as specific threats to the ship or to port facilities the ship is, or has been; .6 internal audits and reviews of security activities;

1. Administrations may allow, in order to avoid compromising in any way the objective of providing on board the ship security alert system, this information to be kept elsewhere on board in a document known to the master, the ship security officer and other senior shipboard personnel as may be decided by the Company.

.7 periodic review of the ship security assessment;

.8 periodic review of the ship security plan;

.9 implementation of any amendments to the plan; and

.10 maintenance, calibration and testing of any security equipment provided on board including testing of the ship security alert system.

10.2 The records shall be kept in the working language or languages of the ship. If the language or languages used are not English, French or Spanish, a translation into one of these languages shall be included.

10.3 The records may be kept in an electronic format. In such a case, they shall be protected by procedures aimed at preventing their unauthorised deletion, destruction or amendment.

10.4 The records shall be protected from unauthorised access or disclosure.

11 Company security officer

11.1 The Company shall designate a company security officer. A person designated as the company security officer may act as the company security officer for one or more ships, depending on the number or types of ships the Company operates provided it is clearly identified for which ships this person is responsible. A Company may, depending on the number or types of ships they operate designate several persons as company security officers provided it is clearly identified for which ships each person is responsible.

11.2 In addition to those specified elsewhere in this Part of the Code, the duties and responsibilities of the company security officer shall include, but are not limited to:

.1 advising the level of threats likely to be encountered by the ship, using appropriate security assessments and other relevant information;

.2 ensuring that ship security assessments are carried out;

.3 ensuring the development, the submission for approval, and thereafter the implementation and maintenance of the ship security plan;

.4 ensuring that the ship security plan is modified, as appropriate, to correct deficiencies and satisfy the security requirements of the individual ship;

.5 arranging for internal audits and reviews of security activities;

.6 arranging for the initial and subsequent verifications of the ship by the Administration or the recognised security organisation;

.7 ensuring that deficiencies and non-conformities identified during internal audits, periodic reviews, security inspections and verifications of compliance are promptly addressed and dealt with;

.8 enhancing security awareness and vigilance;

.9 ensuring adequate training for personnel responsible for the security of the ship;

.10 ensuring effective communication and co-operation between the ship security officer and the relevant port facility security officers;

.11 ensuring consistency between security requirements and safety requirements;

.12 ensuring that, if sister-ship or fleet security plans are used, the plan for each ship reflects the ship-specific information accurately; and

.13 ensuring that any alternative or equivalent arrangements approved for a particular ship or group of ships are implemented and maintained.

12 Ship security officer

12.1 A ship security officer shall be designated on each ship.

12.2 In addition to those specified elsewhere in this Part of the Code, the duties and responsibilities of the ship security officer shall include, but are not limited to:

.1 undertaking regular security inspections of the ship to ensure that appropriate security measures are maintained;

.2 maintaining and supervising the implementation of the ship security plan, including any amendments to the plan;

.3 co-ordinating the security aspects of the handling of cargo and ship's stores with other shipboard personnel and with the relevant port facility security officers;

.4 proposing modifications to the ship security plan;

.5 reporting to the company security officer any deficiencies and non-conformities identified during internal audits, periodic reviews, security inspections and verifications of compliance and implementing any corrective actions;

.6 enhancing security awareness and vigilance on board;

.7 ensuring that adequate training has been provided to shipboard personnel, as appropriate;

.8 reporting all security incidents;

.9 co-ordinating implementation of the ship security plan with the company security officer and the relevant port facility security officer; and

.10 ensuring that security equipment is properly operated, tested, calibrated and maintained, if any.

13 Training, drills and exercises on ship security

13.1 The company security officer and appropriate shore-based personnel shall have knowledge and have received training, taking into account the guidance given in part B of this Code.

13.2 The ship security officer shall have knowledge and have received training, taking into account the guidance given in part B of this Code.

13.3 Shipboard personnel having specific security duties and responsibilities shall understand their responsibilities for ship security as described in the ship security plan and shall have sufficient knowledge and ability to perform their assigned duties, taking into account the guidance given in part B of this Code.

13.4 To ensure the effective implementation of the ship security plan, drills shall be carried out at appropriate intervals taking into account the ship type, ship personnel changes, port facilities to be visited and other relevant circumstances, taking into account the guidance given in part B of this Code.

13.5 The company security officer shall ensure the effective coordination and implementation of ship security plans by participating in exercises at appropriate intervals, taking into account the guidance given in part B of this Code.

14 Port facility security

14.1 A port facility is required to act upon the security levels set by the Contracting Government within whose territory it is located. Security measures and procedures shall be applied at the port facility in such a manner as to cause a minimum of interference with, or delay to, passengers, ship, ship's personnel and visitors, goods and services.

14.2 At security level 1, the following activities shall be carried out through appropriate measures in all port facilities, taking into account the guidance given in part B of this Code, in order to identify and take preventive measures against security incidents:

.1 ensuring the performance of all port facility security duties;

.2 controlling access to the port facility;

.3 monitoring of the port facility, including anchoring and berthing area(s);

.4 monitoring restricted areas to ensure that only authorised persons have access;

.5 supervising the handling of cargo;

.6 supervising the handling of ship's stores; and

.7 ensuring that security communication is readily available.

14.3 At security level 2, the additional protective measures, specified in the port facility security plan, shall be implemented for each activity detailed in section 14.2, taking into account the guidance given in part B of this Code.

14.4 At security level 3, further specific protective measures, specified in the port facility security plan, shall be implemented for each activity detailed in section 14.2, taking into account the guidance given in part B of this Code.

14.4.1 In addition, at security level 3, port facilities are required to respond to and implement any security instructions given by the Contracting Government within whose territory the port facility is located.

14.5 When a port facility security officer is advised that a ship encounters difficulties in complying with the requirements of chapter XI-2 or this part or in implementing the appropriate measures and procedures as detailed in the ship security plan, and in the case of security level 3 following any security instructions given by the Contracting Government within whose territory the port facility is located, the port facility security officer and ship security officer shall liase and co-ordinate appropriate actions.

14.6 When a port facility security officer is advised that a ship is at a security level, which is higher than that of the port facility, the port facility security officer shall report the matter to the competent authority and shall liase with the ship security officer and co-ordinate appropriate actions, if necessary.

15 Port facility security assessment

15.1 The port facility security assessment is an essential and integral part of the process of developing and updating the port facility security plan.

15.2 The port facility security assessment shall be carried out by the Contracting Government within whose territory the port facility is located. A Contracting Government may authorise a recognised security organisation to carry out the port facility security assessment of a specific port facility located within its territory.

15.2.1 When the port facility security assessment has been carried out by a recognised security organisation, the security assessment shall be reviewed and approved for compliance with this section by the Contracting Government within whose territory the port facility is located.

15.3 The persons carrying out the assessment shall have appropriate skills to evaluate the security of the port facility in accordance with this section, taking into account the guidance given in part B of this Code.

15.4 The port facility security assessments shall periodically be reviewed and updated, taking account of changing threats and/or minor changes in the port facility and shall always be reviewed and updated when major changes to the port facility take place.

15.5 The port facility security assessment shall include, at least, the following elements:

.1 identification and evaluation of important assets and infrastructure it is important to protect;

.2 identification of possible threats to the assets and infrastructure and the likelihood of their occurrence, in order to establish and prioritise security measures;

.3 identification, selection and prioritisation of counter measures and procedural changes and their level of effectiveness in reducing vulnerability; and

.4 identification of weaknesses, including human factors in the infrastructure, policies and procedures.

15.6 The Contracting Government may allow a port facility security assessment to cover more than one port facility if the operator, location, operation, equipment, and design of these port facilities are similar. Any Contracting Government, which allows such an arrangement shall communicate to the Organization particulars thereof.

15.7 Upon completion of the port facility security assessment, a report shall be prepared, consisting of a summary of how the assessment was conducted, a description of each vulnerability found during the assessment and a description of counter measures that could be used to address each vulnerability. The report shall be protected from unauthorised access or disclosure.

16 Port facility security plan

16.1 A port facility security plan shall be developed and maintained, on the basis of a port facility security assessment, for each port facility, adequate for the ship/port interface. The plan shall make provisions for the three security levels, as defined in this Part of the Code.

    16.1.1 Subject to the provisions of section 16.2, a recognised security organisation may prepare the port facility security plan of a specific port facility.

16.2 The port facility security plan shall be approved by the Contracting Government in whose territory the port facility is located.

16.3 Such a plan shall be developed taking into account the guidance given in part B of this Code and shall be in the working language of the port facility. The plan shall address, at least, the following:

    .1 measures designed to prevent weapons or any other dangerous substances and devices intended for use against persons, ships or ports and the carriage of which is not autho- . rised, from being introduced into the port facility or on board a ship;

    .2 measures designed to prevent unauthorised access to the port facility, to ships moored at the facility, and to restricted areas of the facility;

    .3 procedures for responding to security threats or breaches of security, including provisions for maintaining critical operations of the port facility or ship/port interface;

    .4 procedures for responding to any security instructions the Contracting Government, in whose territory the port facility is located, may give at security level 3;

    .5 procedures for evacuation in case of security threats or breaches of security;

    .6 duties of port facility personnel assigned security responsibilities and of other facility personnel on security aspects;

    .7 procedures for interfacing with ship security activities;

    .8 procedures for the periodic review of the plan and updating;

    .9 procedures for reporting security incidents;

    .10 identification of the port facility security officer including 24-hour contact details;

    .11 measures to ensure the security of the information contained in the plan;

    .12 measures designed to ensure effective security of cargo and the cargo handling equipment at the port facility;

    .13 procedures for auditing the port facility security plan;

    .14 procedures for responding in case the ship security alert system of a ship at the port facility has been activated; and

    .15 procedures for facilitating shore leave for ship's personnel or personnel changes, as well as access of visitors to the ship including representatives of seafarers' welfare and labour organisations.

    16.3.1 Personnel conducting internal audits of the security activities specified in the plan or evaluating its implementation shall be independent of the activities being audited unless this is impracticable due to the size and the nature of the port facility.

16.4 The port facility security plan may be combined with, or be part of, the port security plan or any other port emergency plan or plans.

16.5 The Contracting Government in whose territory the port facility is located shall determine which changes to the port facility security plan shall not be implemented unless the relevant amendments to the plan are approved by them.

16.6 The plan may be kept in an electronic format. In such a case, it shall be protected by procedures aimed at preventing its unauthorised deletion, destruction or amendment.

16.7 The plan shall be protected from unauthorised access or disclosure.

16.8 Contracting Governments may allow a port facility security plan to cover more than one port facility if the operator, location, operation, equipment, and design of these port facilities are similar. Any Contracting Government, which allows such an alternative arrangement, shall communicate to the Organization particulars thereof.

17 Port facility security officer

17.1 A port facility security officer shall be designated for each port facility. A person may be designated as the port facility security officer for one or more port facilities.

17.2 In addition to those specified elsewhere in this Part of the Code, the duties and responsibilities of the port facility security officer shall include, but are not limited to:

.1 conducting an initial comprehensive security survey of the port facility taking into account the relevant port facility security assessment;

.2 ensuring the development and maintenance of the port facility security plan;

.3 implementing and exercising the port facility security plan;

.4 undertaking regular security inspections of the port facility to ensure the continuation of appropriate security measures;

.5 recommending and incorporating, as appropriate, modifications to the port facility security plan in order to correct deficiencies and to update the plan to take into account of relevant changes to the port facility;

.6 enhancing security awareness and vigilance of the port facility personnel;

.7 ensuring adequate training has been provided to personnel responsible for the security of the port facility;

.8 reporting to the relevant authorities and maintaining records of occurrences which threaten the security of the port facility;

.9 co-ordinating implementation of the port facility security plan with the appropriate Company and ship security officer(s);

.10 co-ordinating with security services, as appropriate;

.11 ensuring that standards for personnel responsible for security of the port facility are met;

.12 ensuring that security equipment is properly operated, tested, calibrated and maintained, if any; and

.13 assisting ship security officers in confirming the identity of those seeking to board the ship when requested.

17.3 The port facility security officer shall be given the necessary support to fulfil the duties and responsibilities imposed by chapter XI-2 and this Part of the Code.

18 Training, drills and exercises on port facility security

18.1 The port facility security officer and appropriate port facility security personnel shall have knowledge and have received training, taking into account the guidance given in part B of this Code.

18.2 Port facility personnel having specific security duties shall understand their duties and responsibilities for port facility security, as described in the port facility security plan and shall have sufficient knowledge and ability to perform their assigned duties, taking into account the guidance given in part B of this Code.

18.3 To ensure the effective implementation of the port facility security plan, drills shall be carried out at appropriate intervals taking into account the types of operation of the port facility, port facility personnel changes, the type of ship the port facility is serving and other relevant circumstances, taking into account guidance given in part B of this Code.

18.4 The port facility security officer shall ensure the effective coordination and implementation of the port facility security plan by participating in exercises at appropriate intervals, taking into account the guidance given in part B of this Code.

19 Verification and certification for ships

19.1 Verifications

19.1.1 Each ship to which this Part of the Code applies shall be subject to the verifications specified below:

.1 an initial verification before the ship is put in service or before the certificate required under section 19.2 is issued for the first time, which shall include a complete verification of its security system and any associated security equipment covered by the relevant provisions of chapter XI-2, this Part of the Code and the approved ship security plan. This verification shall ensure that the security system and any associated security equipment of the ship fully complies with the applicable requirements of chapter XI-2 and this Part of the Code, is in satisfactory condition and fit for the service for which the ship is intended;

.2 a renewal verification at intervals specified by the Administration, but not exceeding five years, except where section 19.3 is applicable. This verification shall ensure that the security system and any associated security equipment of the ship fully complies with the applicable requirements of chapter XI-2, this Part of the Code and the approved ship security plan, is in satisfactory condition and fit for the service for which the ship is intended;

.3 at least one intermediate verification. If only one intermediate verification is carried out it shall take place between the second and third anniversary date of the certificate as defined in regulation I/2(n). The intermediate verification shall include inspection of the security system and any associated security equipment of the ship to ensure that it remains satisfactory for the service for which the ship is intended. Such intermediate verification shall be endorsed on the certificate;

.4 any additional verifications as determined by the Administration.

19.1.2 The verifications of ships shall be carried out by officers of the Administration. The Administration may, however, entrust the verifications to a recognised security organisation referred to in regulation XI-2/1.

19.1.3 In every case, the Administration concerned shall fully guarantee the completeness and efficiency of the verification and shall undertake to ensure the necessary arrangements to satisfy this obligation.

19.1.4 The security system and any associated security equipment of the ship after verification shall be maintained to conform with the provisions of regulations XI-2/4.2 and XI-2/6, this Part of the Code and the approved ship security plan. After any verification under section 19.1.1 has been completed, no changes shall be made in security system and in any associated security equipment or the approved ship security plan without the sanction of the Administration.

19.2 Issue or endorsement of certificate

19.2.1 An International Ship Security Certificate shall be issued after the initial or renewal verification in accordance with the provisions of section 19.1.

19.2.2 Such certificate shall be issued or endorsed either by the Administration or by a recognised security organisation acting on behalf of the Administration.

19.2.3 Another Contracting Government may, at the request of the Administration, cause the ship to be verified and, if satisfied that the provisions of section 19.1.1 are complied with, shall issue or authorise the issue of an International Ship Security Certificate to the ship and, where appropriate, endorse or authorise the endorsement of that certificate on the ship, in accordance with this Code.

19.2.3.1 A copy of the certificate and a copy of the verification report shall be transmitted as soon as possible to the requesting Administration.

19.2.3.2 A certificate so issued shall contain a statement to the effect that it has been issued at the request of the Administration and it shall have the same force and receive the same recognition as the certificate issued under section 19.2.2.

19.2.4 The International Ship Security Certificate shall be drawn up in a form corresponding to the model given in the appendix to this Code. If the language used is not English, French or Spanish, the text shall include a translation into one of these languages.

19.3 Duration and validity of certificate

19.3.1 An International Ship Security Certificate shall be issued for a period specified by the Administration which shall not exceed five years.

19.3.2 When the renewal verification is completed within three months before the expiry date of the existing certificate, the new certificate shall be valid from the date of completion of the renewal verification to a date not exceeding five years from the date of expiry of the existing certificate.

19.3.2.1 When the renewal verification is completed after the expiry date of the existing certificate, the new certificate shall be valid from the date of completion of the renewal verification to a date not exceeding five years from the date of expiry of the existing certificate.

19.3.2.2 When the renewal verification is completed more than three months before the expiry date of the existing certificate, the new certificate shall be valid from the date of completion of the renewal verification to a date not exceeding five years from the date of completion of the renewal verification.

19.3.3 If a certificate is issued for a period of less than five years, the Administration may extend the validity of the certificate beyond the expiry date to the maximum period specified in section 19.3.1, provided that the verifications referred to in section 19.1.1 applicable when a certificate is issued for a period of five years are carried out as appropriate.

19.3.4 If a renewal verification has been completed and a new certificate cannot be issued or placed on board the ship before the expiry date of the existing certificate, the Administration or recognised security organisation acting on behalf of the Administration may endorse the existing certificate and such a certificate shall be accepted as valid for a further period which shall not exceed five months from the expiry date.

19.3.5 If a ship at the time when a certificate expires is not in a port in which it is to be verified, the Administration may extend the period of validity of the certificate but this extension shall be granted only for the purpose of allowing the ship to complete its voyage to the port in which it is to be verified, and then only in cases where it appears proper and reasonable to do so. No certificate shall be extended for a period longer than three months, and the ship to which an extension is granted shall not, on its arrival in the port in which it is to be verified, be entitled by virtue of such extension to leave that port without having a new certificate. When the renewal verification is completed, the new certificate shall be valid to a date not exceeding five years from the expiry date of the existing certificate before the extension was granted.

19.3.6 A certificate issued to a ship engaged on short voyages which has not been extended under the foregoing provisions of this section may be extended by the Administration for a period of grace of up to one month from the date of expiry stated on it. When the renewal verification is completed, the new certificate shall be valid to a date not exceeding five years from the date of expiry of the existing certificate before the extension was granted.

19.3.7 If an intermediate verification is completed before the period specified in section 19.1.1, then:

.1 the expiry date shown on the certificate shall be amended by endorsement to a date which shall not be more than three years later than the date on which the intermediate verification was completed;

.2 the expiry date may remain unchanged provided one or more additional verifications are carried out so that the maximum intervals between the verifications prescribed by section 19.1.1 are not exceeded.

19.3.8 A certificate issued under section 19.2 shall cease to be valid in any of the following cases:

   .1 if the relevant verifications are not completed within the periods specified under section 19.1.1;

   .2 if the certificate is not endorsed in accordance with section 19.1.1.3 and 19.3.7.1, if applicable;

   .3 when a Company assumes the responsibility for the operation of a ship not previously operated by that Company; and

   .4 upon transfer of the ship to the flag of another State.

19.3.9 In the case of:

   .1 a transfer of a ship to the flag of another Contracting Government, the Contracting Government whose flag the ship was formerly entitled to fly shall, as soon as possible, transmit to the receiving Administration copies of, or all information relating to, the International Ship Security Certificate carried by the ship before the transfer and copies of available verification reports, or

   .2 a Company that assumes responsibility for the operation of a ship not previously operated by that Company, the previous Company shall as soon as possible, transmit to the receiving Company copies of any information related to the International Ship Security Certificate or to facilitate the verifications described in section 19.4.2.

19.4 Interim certification

19.4.1 The certificates specified in section 19.2 shall be issued only when the Administration issuing the certificate is fully satisfied that the ship complies with the requirements of section 19.1. However, after 1 July 2004, for the purposes of:

   .1 a ship without a certificate, on delivery or prior to its entry or re-entry into service;

   .2 transfer of a ship from the flag of a Contracting Government to the flag of another Contracting Government;

   .3 transfer of a ship to the flag of a Contracting Government from a State which is not a Contracting Government; or

   .4 when a Company assumes the responsibility for the operation of a ship not previously operated by that Company; until the certificate referred to in section 19.2 is issued, the Administration may cause an Interim International Ship Security Certificate to be issued, in a form corresponding to the model given in the Appendix to this Part of the Code.

19.4.2 An Interim International Ship Security Certificate shall only be issued when the Administration or recognised security organisation, on behalf of the Administration, has verified that:

   .1 the ship security assessment required by this Part of the Code has been completed,

   .2 a copy of the ship security plan meeting the requirements of chapter XI-2 and part A of this Code is provided on board, has been submitted for review and approval, and is being implemented on the ship;

   .3 the ship is provided with a ship security alert system meeting the requirements of regulation XI-2/6, if required,

   .4 the company security officer:

      .1 has ensured:

         .1 the review of the ship security plan for compliance with this Part of the Code,

         .2 that the plan has been submitted for approval, and

         .3 that the plan is being implemented on the ship, and

      .2 has established the necessary arrangements, including arrangements for drills, exercises and internal audits, through which the company security officer is satisfied that the ship will successfully complete the required verification in accordance with section 19.1.1.1, within 6 months;

   .5 arrangements have been made for carrying out the required verifications under section 19.1.1.1;

.6 the master, the ship's security officer and other ship's personnel with specific security duties are familiar with their duties and responsibilities as specified in this Part of the Code; and with the relevant provisions of the ship security plan placed on board; and have been provided such information in the working language of the ship's personnel or languages understood by them; and

.7 the ship security officer meets the requirements of this Part of the Code.

19.4.3 An Interim International Ship Security Certificate may be issued by the Administration or by a recognised security organisation authorised to act on its behalf.

19.4.4 An Interim International Ship Security Certificate shall be valid for 6 months, or until the certificate required by section 19.2 is issued, whichever comes first, and may not be extended.

19.4.5 No Contracting Government shall cause a subsequent, consecutive Interim International Ship Security Certificate to be issued to a ship if, in the judgment of the Administration or the recognised security organisation, one of the purposes of the ship or a Company in requesting such certificate is to avoid full compliance with chapter XI-2 and this Part of the Code beyond the period of the initial interim certificate as specified in section 19.4.4.

19.4.6 For the purposes of regulation XI-2/9, Contracting Governments may, prior to accepting an Interim International Ship Security Certificate as a valid certificate, ensure that the requirements of sections 19.4.2.4 to 19.4.2.6 have been met.

APPENDIX TO PART A
Appendix 1

Form of the International Ship Security Certificate

INTERNATIONAL SHIP SECURITY CERTIFICATE

(official seal)   *(State)*

Certificate Number

Issued under the provisions of the

INTERNATIONAL CODE FOR THE SECURITY OF SHIPS AND OF PORT FACILITIES (ISPS CODE)

Under the authority of the Government of _____

(name of State)

by _____

(persons or organisation authorised)

Name of ship   :...

Distinctive number or letters   :...

Port of registry   :...

Type of ship   :...

Gross tonnage   :...

IMO Number   :...

Name and address of the Company   :...

THIS IS TO CERTIFY:

1 that the security system and any associated security equipment of the ship has been verified in accordance with section 19.1 of part A of the ISPS Code;

2 that the verification showed that the security system and any associated security equipment of the ship is in all respects satisfactory and that the ship complies with the applicable requirements of chapter XI-2 of the Convention and part A of the ISPS Code;

3 that the ship is provided with an approved Ship Security Plan.

Date of initial/renewal verification on which this certificate is based ....

This Certificate is valid until ....

subject to verifications in accordance with section 19.1.1 of part A of the ISPS Code.

Issued at ....

(place of issue of the Certificate)

Date of issue ....

*(signature of the duly authorised official
issuing the Certificate)*

(Seal or stamp of issuing authority, as appropriate)

ENDORSEMENT FOR INTERMEDIATE VERIFICATION

THIS IS TO CERTIFY that at an intermediate verification required by section 19.1.1 of part A of the ISPS Code the ship was found to comply with the relevant provisions of chapter XI-2 of the Convention and part A of the ISPS Code.

Intermediate verification   Signed ....

(Signature of authorised official)

Place ....

Date ....

(Seal or stamp of the authority, as appropriate)

487

ENDORSEMENT FOR ADDITIONAL VERIFICATIONS*

Additional verification

Signed ....
(Signature of authorised official)
Place ....
Date ....

(Seal or stamp of the authority, as appropriate)

Additional verification

Signed ....
(Signature of authorised official)
Place ....
Date ....

(Seal or stamp of the authority, as appropriate)

Additional verification

Signed ....
(Signature of authorised official)
Place ....
Date ....

(Seal or stamp of the authority, as appropriate)

---

* This part of the certificate shall be adapted by the Administration to indicate whether it has established additional verifications as provided for in section 19.1.1.4.

ADDITIONAL VERIFICATION IN ACCORDANCE WITH SECTION A/19.3.7.2 OF THE ISPS CODE

THIS IS TO CERTIFY that at an additional verification required by section 19.3.7.2 of part A of the ISPS Code the ship was found to comply with the relevant provisions of chapter XI-2 of the Convention and part A of the ISPS Code.

Signed ....
(Signature of authorised official)
Place ....
Date ....

(Seal or stamp of the authority, as appropriate)

ENDORSEMENT TO EXTEND THE CERTIFICATE IF VALID FOR LESS THAN 5 YEARS WHERE SECTION A/19.3.3 OF THE ISPS CODE APPLIES

The ship complies with the relevant provisions of part A of the ISPS Code, and the Certificate shall, in accordance with section 19.3.3 of part A of the ISPS Code, be accepted as valid until ....

Signed ....
(Signature of authorised official)
Place ....
Date ....

(Seal or stamp of the authority, as appropriate)

ENDORSEMENT WHERE THE RENEWAL VERIFICATION HAS BEEN COMPLETED AND SECTION A/19.3.4 OF THE ISPS CODE APPLIES

The ship complies with the relevant provisions of part A of the ISPS Code, and the Certificate shall, in accordance with section 19.3.4 of part A of the ISPS Code, be accepted as valid until ....

Signed ....
(Signature of authorised official)
Place ....
Date ....

(Seal or stamp of the authority, as appropriate)

ENDORSEMENT TO EXTEND THE VALIDITY OF THE CERTIFICATE UNTIL REACHING THE PORT OF VERIFICATION WHERE SECTION A/19.3.5 OF THE ISPS CODE APPLIES OR FOR A PERIOD OF GRACE WHERE SECTION A/19.3.6 OF THE ISPS CODE APPLIES

This Certificate shall, in accordance with section 19.3.5/19.3.6[*] of part A of the ISPS Code, be accepted as valid until ....

Signed ....
(Signature of authorised official)
Place ....
Date ....

(Seal or stamp of the authority, as appropriate)

[*] Delete as appropriate.

ENDORSEMENT FOR ADVANCEMENT OF EXPIRY DATE WHERE SECTION A/19.3.7.1 OF THE ISPS CODE APPLIES

In accordance with section 19.3.7.1 of part A of the ISPS Code, the new expiry date[**] is ....

Signed ....
(Signature of authorised official)
Place ....
Date ....

(Seal or stamp of the authority, as appropriate)

[**] In case of completion of this part of the certificate the expiry date shown on the front of the certificate shall also be amended accordingly.

Appendix 2

Form of the International Ship Security Certificate

INTERIM INTERNATIONAL SHIP SECURITY CERTIFICATE

(official seal)   *(State)*

Certificate Number

Issued under the provisions of the

INTERNATIONAL CODE FOR THE SECURITY OF SHIPS AND OF PORT FACILITIES (ISPS CODE)

Under the authority of the Government of _____

(name of State)

by _____

(persons or organisation authorised)

Name of ship	:..
Distinctive number or letters	:..
Port of registry	:..
Type of ship	:..
Gross tonnage	:..
IMO Number	:..
Name and address of the Company	:..

Is this a subsequent, consecutive interim certificate? Yes/No*

If Yes, date of issue of initial interim certificate ....

THIS IS TO CERTIFY THAT the requirements of section A/19.4.2 of the ISPS Code have been complied with.

This certificate is issued pursuant to section A/19.4 of the ISPS Code.

This Certificate is valid until ....

Issued at ....

(place of issue of the Certificate)

Date of issue ....

                                        (signature of the duly authorised official issuing the Certificate)

(Seal or stamp of issuing authority, as appropriate)

* Delete as appropriate.

Athens Convention Relating to the Carriage of Passengers and their Luggage by Sea, 2002

(Consolidated text of the Athens Convention relating to the
Carriage of Passengers and their Luggage by Sea, 1974
and the Protocol of 2002 to the Convention)

Article 1 – Definitions

In this Convention the following expressions have the meaning hereby assigned to them:

1
  (a) "carrier" means a person by or on behalf of whom a contract of carriage has been concluded, whether the carriage is actually performed by that person or by a performing carrier;
  (b) "performing carrier" means a person other than the carrier, being the owner, charterer or operator of a ship, who actually performs the whole or a part of the carriage;
  (c) "carrier who actually performs the whole or a part of the carriage" means the performing carrier, or, in so far as the carrier actually performs the carriage, the carrier;
2 "contract of carriage" means a contract made by or on behalf of a carrier for the carriage by sea of a passenger or of a passenger and his luggage, as the case may be;
3 "ship" means only a seagoing vessel, excluding an air-cushion vehicle;
4 "passenger" means any person carried in a ship,
  (a) under a contract of carriage, or
  (b) who, with the consent of the carrier, is accompanying a vehicle or live animals which are covered by a contract for the carriage of goods not governed by this Convention;
5 "luggage" means any article or vehicle carried by the carrier under a contract of carriage, excluding:
  (a) articles and vehicles carried under a charter party, bill of lading or other contract primarily concerned with the carriage of goods, and
  (b) live animals;
6 "cabin luggage" means luggage which the passenger has in his cabin or is otherwise in his possession, custody or control. Except for the application of paragraph 8 of this Article and Article 8, cabin luggage includes luggage which the passenger has in or on his vehicle;
7 "loss of or damage to luggage" includes pecuniary loss resulting from the luggage not having been re-delivered to the passenger within a reasonable time after the arrival of the ship on which the luggage has been or should have been carried, but does not include delays resulting from labour disputes;
8 "carriage" covers the following periods:
  (a) with regard to the passenger and his cabin luggage, the period during which the passenger and/or his cabin luggage are on board the ship or in the course of embarkation or disembarkation, and the period during which the passenger and his cabin lugga ge are transported by water from land to the ship or vice-versa, if the cost of such transport is included in the fare or if the vessel used for this purpose of auxiliary transport has been put at the disposal of the passenger by the carrier. However, with regard to the passenger, carriage does not include the period during which he is in a marine terminal or station or on a quay or in or on any other port installation;
  (b) with regard to cabin luggage, also the period during which the passenger is in a marine terminal or station or on a quay or in or on any other port installation if that

luggage has been taken over by the carrier or his servant or agent and has not been re-delivered to the passenger;

   (c) with regard to other luggage which is not cabin luggage, the period from the time of its taking over by the carrier or his servant or agent on shore or on board until the time of its re-delivery by the carrier or his servant or agent;

9 "international carriage" means any carriage in which, according to the contract of carriage, the place of departure and the place of destination are situated in two different States, or in a single State if, according to the contract of carriage or the scheduled itinerary, there is an intermediate port of call in another State;

10 "Organization" means the International Maritime Organization.

11 "Secretary-General" means the Secretary-General of the Organization.

Article 1bis – Annex

The annex to this Convention shall constitute an integral part of the Convention.

Article 2 – Application

1 This Convention shall apply to any international carriage if:

   (a) the ship is flying the flag of or is registered in a State Party to this Convention, or

   (b) the contract of carriage has been made in a State Party to this Convention, or

   (c) the place of departure or destination, according to the contract of carriage, is in a State Party to this Convention.

2 Notwithstanding paragraph 1 of this Article, this Convention shall not apply when the carriage is subject, under any other international convention concerning the carriage of passengers or luggage by another mode of transport, to a civil liability regime under the provisions of such convention, in so far as those provisions have mandatory application to carriage by sea.

Article 3 – Liability of the carrier

1 For the loss suffered as a result of the death of or personal injury to a passenger caused by a shipping incident, the carrier shall be liable to the extent that such loss in respect of that passenger on each distinct occasion does not exceed 250,000 units of account, unless the carrier proves that the incident:

   (a) resulted from an act of war, hostilities, civil war, insurrection or a natural phenomenon of an exceptional, inevitable and irresistible character; or

   (b) was wholly caused by an act or omission done with the intent to cause the incident by a third party.

If and to the extent that the loss exceeds the above limit, the carrier shall be further liable unless the carrier proves that the incident which caused the loss occurred without the fault or neglect of the carrier.

2 For the loss suffered as a result of the death of or personal injury to a passenger not caused by a shipping incident, the carrier shall be liable if the incident which caused the loss was due to the fault or neglect of the carrier. The burden of proving fault or neglect shall lie with the claimant.

3 For the loss suffered as a result of the loss of or damage to cabin luggage, the carrier shall be liable if the incident which caused the loss was due to the fault or neglect of the carrier. The fault or neglect of the carrier shall be presumed for loss caused by a shipping incident.

4 For the loss suffered as a result of the loss of or damage to luggage other than cabin luggage, the carrier shall be liable unless the carrier proves that the incident which caused the loss occurred without the fault or neglect of the carrier.

5 For the purposes of this article:

   (a) "shipping incident" means shipwreck, capsizing, collision or stranding of the ship, explosion or fire in the ship, or defect in the ship;

(b) "fault or neglect of the carrier" includes the fault or neglect of the servants of the carrier, acting within the scope of their employment;

(c) "defect in the ship" means any malfunction, failure or non-compliance with applicable safety regulations in respect of any part of the ship or its equipment when used for the escape, evacuation, embarkation and disembarkation of passengers, or when used for the propulsion, steering, safe navigation, mooring, anchoring, arriving at or leaving berth or anchorage, or damage control after flooding; or when used for the launching of life saving appliances; and

(d) "loss" shall not include punitive or exemplary damages.

6 The liability of the carrier under this Article only relates to loss arising from incidents that occurred in the course of the carriage. The burden of proving that the incident which caused the loss occurred in the course of the carriage, and the extent of the loss, shall lie with the claimant.

7 Nothing in this Convention shall prejudice any right of recourse of the carrier against any third party, or the defence of contributory negligence under Article 6 of this Convention. Nothing in this Article shall prejudice any right of limitation under Articles 7 or 8 of this Convention.

8 Presumptions of fault or neglect of a party or the allocation of the burden of proof to a party shall not prevent evidence in favour of that party from being considered.

Article 4 – Performing carrier

1 If the performance of the carriage or part thereof has been entrusted to a performing carrier, the carrier shall nevertheless remain liable for the entire carriage according to the provisions of this Convention. In addition, the performing carrier shall be subject and entitled to the provisions of this Convention for the part of the carriage performed by him.

2 The carrier shall, in relation to the carriage performed by the performing carrier, be liable for the acts and omissions of the performing carrier and of his servants and agents acting within the scope of their employment.

3 Any special agreement under which the carrier assumes obligations not imposed by this Convention or any waiver of rights conferred by this Convention shall affect the performing carrier only if agreed by him expressly and in writing.

4 Where and to the extent that both the carrier and the performing carrier are liable, their liability shall be joint and several.

5 Nothing in this Article shall prejudice any right of recourse as between the carrier and the performing carrier.

Article 4bis – Compulsory insurance

1 When passengers are carried on board a ship registered in a State Party that is licensed to carry more than twelve passengers, and this Convention applies, any carrier who actually performs the whole or a part of the carriage shall maintain insurance or other financial security, such as the guarantee of a bank or similar financial institution, to cover liability under this Convention in respect of the death of and persona l injury to passengers. The limit of the compulsory insurance or other financial security shall not be less than 250,000 units of account per passenger on each distinct occasion.

2 A certificate attesting that insurance or other financial security is in force in accordance with the provisions of this Convention shall be issued to each ship after the appropriate authority of a State Party has determined that the requirements of paragraph 1 have been complied with. With respect to a ship registered in a State Party, such certificate shall be issued or certified by the appropriate authority of the State of the ship's registry; with respect to a ship not registered in a State Party it may be issued or certified by the appropriate authority of any State Party. This certificate shall be in the form of the model set out in the annex to this Convention and shall contain the following particulars:

(a) name of ship, distinctive number or letters and port of registry;

(b) name and principal place of business of the carrier who actually performs the whole or a part of the carriage;

(c) IMO ship identification number;

(d) type and duration of security;

(e) name and principal place of business of insurer or other person providing financial security and, where appropriate, place of business where the insurance or other financial security is established; and

(f) period of validity of the certificate, which shall not be longer than the period of validity of the insurance or other financial security.

3 (a) A State Party may authorise an institution or an organisation recognised by it to issue the certificate. Such institution or organisation shall inform that State of the issue of each certificate. In all cases, the State Party shall fully guarantee the completeness and accuracy of the certificate so issued, and shall undertake to ensure the necessary arrangements to satisfy this obligation.

(b) A State Party shall notify the Secretary-General of:

(i) the specific responsibilities and conditions of the authority dele gated to an institution or organisation recognised by it;

(ii) the withdrawal of such authority; and

(iii) the date from which such authority or withdrawal of such authority takes effect. An authority delegated shall not take effect prior to three months from the date from which notification to that effect was given to the Secretary-General.

(c) The institution or organisation authorised to issue certificates in accordance with this paragraph shall, as a minimum, be authorised to withdraw these certificates if the conditions under which they have been issued are not complied with. In all cases the institution or organisation shall report such withdrawal to the State on whose behalf the certificate was issued.

4 The certificate shall be in the official language or languages of the issuing State. If the language used is not English, French or Spanish, the text shall include a translation into one of these languages, and, where the State so decides, the official language of the State may be omitted.

5 The certificate shall be carried on board the ship, and a copy shall be deposited with the authorities who keep the record of the ship's registry or, if the ship is not registered in a State Party, with the authority of the State issuing or certifying the certificate.

6 An insurance or other financial security shall not satisfy the requirements of this Article if it can cease, for reasons other than the expiry of the period of validity of the insurance or security specified in the certificate, before three months have elapsed from the date on which notice of its termination is given to the authorities referred to in paragraph 5, unless the certificate has been surrendered to these authorities or a new certificate has been issued within the said period. The foregoing provisions shall similarly apply to any modification which results in the insurance or other financial security no longer satisfying the requirements of this Article.

7 The State of the ship's registry shall, subject to the provisions of this Article, determine the conditions of issue and validity of the certificate.

8 Nothing in this Convention shall be construed as preventing a State Party from relying on information obtained from other States or the Organization or other international organisations relating to the financial standing of providers of insurance or other financial security for the purposes of this Convention. In such cases, the State Party relying on such information is not relieved of its responsibility as a State issuing the certificate.

9 Certificates issued or certified under the authority of a State Party shall be accepted by other States Parties for the purposes of this Convention and shall be regarded by other States Parties as having the same force as certificates issued or certified by them, even if issued or certified in respect of a ship not registered in a State Party. A State Party may at any time request consultation with the issuing or certifying State should it believe that the insurer or guarantor named in the insurance certificate is not financially capable of meeting the obligations imposed by this Convention.

10 Any claim for compensation covered by insurance or other financial security pursuant to this Article may be brought directly against the insurer or other person providing financial security. In such case, the amount set out in paragraph 1 applies as the limit of liability of the insurer or other person providing financial security, even if the carrier or the performing carrier is not entitled to limitation of liability. The defendant may further invoke the defences (other than the bankruptcy or winding up) which the carrier referred to in paragraph 1 would have been entitled to invoke in accordance with this Convention. Furthermore, the defendant may invoke the defence that the damage resulted from the wilful misconduct of the assured, but the defendant shall not invoke any other defence which the defendant might have been entitled to invoke in proceedings brought by the assured against the defendant. The defendant shall in any event have the right to require the carrier and the performing carrier to be joined in the proceedings.

11 Any sums provided by insurance or by other financial security maintained in accordance with paragraph 1 shall be available exclusively for the satisfaction of claims under this Convention, and any payments made of such sums shall discharge any liability arising under this Convention to the extent of the amounts paid.

12 A State Party shall not permit a ship under its flag to which this Article applies to operate at any time unless a certificate has been issued under paragraphs 2 or 15.

13 Subject to the provisions of this Article, each State Party shall ensure, under its national law, that insurance or other financial security, to the extent specified in paragraph 1, is in force in respect of any ship that is licensed to carry more than twelve passengers, wherever registered, entering or leaving a port in its territory in so far as this Convention applies.

14 Notwithstanding the provisions of paragraph 5, a State Party may notify the Secretary-General that, for the purposes of paragraph 13, ships are not required to carry on board or to produce the certificate required by paragraph 2 when entering or leaving ports in its territory, provided that the State Party which issues the certificate has notified the Secretary-General that it maintains records in an electronic format, accessible to all States Parties, attesting the existence of the certificate and enabling States Parties to discharge their obligations under paragraph 13.

15 If insurance or other financial security is not maintained in respect of a ship owned by a State Party, the provisions of this Article relating thereto shall not be applicable to such ship, but the ship shall carry a certificate issued by the appropriate authorities of the State of the ship's registry, stating that the ship is owned by that State and that the liability is covered within the amount prescribed in accordance with paragraph 1. Such a certificate shall follow as closely as possible the model prescribed by paragraph 2.

Article 5 – Valuables

The carrier shall not be liable for the loss of or damage to monies, negotiable securities, gold, silverware, jewellery, ornaments, works of art, or other valuables, except where such valuables have been deposited with the carrier for the agreed purpose of safe-keeping in which case the carrier shall be liable up to the limit provided for in paragraph 3 of Article 8 unless a higher limit is agreed upon in accordance with paragraph 1 of Article 10.

Article 6 – Contributory fault

If the carrier proves that the death of or personal injury to a passenger or the loss of or damage to his luggage was caused or contributed to by the fault or neglect of the passenger, the Court seized of the case may exonerate the carrier wholly or partly from his liability in accordance with the provisions of the law of that court.

Article 7 – Limit of liability for death and personal injury

1 The liability of the carrier for the death of or personal injury to a passenger under Article 3 shall in no case exceed 400,000 units of account per passenger on each distinct occa-

sion. Where, in accordance with the law of the court seized of the case, damages are awarded in the form of periodical income payments, the equivalent capital value of those payments shall not exceed the said limit.

2 A State Party may regulate by specific provisions of national law the limit of liability prescribed in paragraph 1, provided that the national limit of liability, if any, is not lower than that prescribed in paragraph 1. A State Party, which makes use of the option provided for in this paragraph, shall inform the Secretary-General of the limit of liability adopted or of the fact that there is none.

Article 8 – Limit of liability for loss of or damage to luggage and vehicles

1 The liability of the carrier for the loss of or damage to cabin luggage shall in no case exceed 2,250 units of account per passenger, per carriage.

2 The liability of the carrier for the loss of or damage to vehicles including all luggage carried in or on the vehicle shall in no case exceed 12,700 units of account per vehicle, per carriage.

3 The liability of the carrier for the loss of or damage to luggage other than that mentioned in paragraphs 1 and 2 shall in no case exceed 3,375 units of account per passenger, per carriage.

4 The carrier and the passenger may agree that the liability of the carrier shall be subject to a deductible not exceeding 330 units of account in the case of damage to a vehicle and not exceeding 149 units of account per passenger in the case of loss of or damage to other luggage, such sum to be deducted from the loss or damage.

Article 9 – Unit of Account and conversion

1 The Unit of Account mentioned in this Convention is the Special Drawing Right as defined by the International Monetary Fund. The amounts mentioned in Article 3, paragraph 1, Article 4bis, paragraph 1, Article 7, paragraph 1, and Article 8 shall be converted into the national currency of the State of the court seized of the case on the basis of the value of that currency by reference to the Special Drawing Right on the date of the judgment or the date agreed upon by the parties. The value of the national currency, in terms of the Special Drawing Right, of a State Party which is a member of the International Monetary Fund, shall be calculated in accordance with the method of valuation applied by the International Monetary Fund in effect on the date in question for its operations and transactions. The value of the national currency, in terms of the Special Drawing Right, of a State Party which is not a member of the International Monetary Fund, shall be calculated in a manner determined by that State Party.

2 Nevertheless, a State which is not a member of the International Monetary Fund and whose law does not permit the application of the provisions of paragraph 1 may, at the time of ratification, acceptance, approval of or accession to this Convention or at any time thereafter, declare that the Unit of Account referred to in paragraph 1 shall be equal to 15 gold francs. The gold franc referred to in this paragraph corresponds to sixty-five and a half milligrams of gold of millesimal fineness nine hundred. The conversion of the gold franc into the national currency shall be made according to the law of the State concerned.

3 The calculation mentioned in the last sentence of paragraph 1, and the conversion mentioned in paragraph 2 shall be made in such a manner as to express in the national currency of the States Parties, as far as possible, the same real value for the amounts in Article 3, paragraph 1, Article 4bis, paragraph 1, Article 7, paragraph 1, and Article 8 as would result from the application of the first three sentences of paragraph 1. States shall communicate to the Secretary-General the manner of calculation pursuant to paragraph 1, or the result of the conversion in paragraph 2, as the case may be, when depositing an instrument of ratification, acceptance, approval of or accession to this Convention and whenever there is a change in either.

Article 10 – Supplementary provisions on limits of liability

1 The carrier and the passenger may agree, expressly and in writing, to higher limits of liability than those prescribed in Articles 7 and 8.
2 Interest on damages and legal costs shall not be included in the limits of liability prescribed in Articles 7 and 8.

Article 11 – Defences and limits for carriers' servants

If an action is brought against a servant or agent of the carrier or of the performing carrier arising out of damage covered by this Convention, such servant or agent, if he proves that he acted within the scope of his employment, shall be entitled to avail himself of the defences and limits of liability which the carrier or the performing carrier is entitled to invoke under this Convention.

Article 12 – Aggregation of claims

1 Where the limits of liability prescribed in Articles 7 and 8 take effect, they shall apply to the aggregate of the amounts recoverable in all claims arising out of the death of or personal injury to any one passenger or the loss of or damage to his luggage.
2 In relation to the carriage performed by a performing carrier, the aggregate of the amounts recoverable from the carrier and the performing carrier and from their servants and agents acting within the scope of their employment shall not exceed the highest amount which could be awarded against either the carrier or the performing carrier under this Convention, but none of the persons mentioned shall be liable for a sum in excess of the limit applicable to him.
3 In any case where a servant or agent of the carrier or of the performing carrier is entitled under Article 11 of this Convention to avail himself of the limits of liability prescribed in Articles 7 and 8, the aggregate of the amounts recoverable from the carrier, or the performing carrier as the case may be, and from that servant or agent, shall not exceed those limits.

Article 13 – Loss of right to limit liability

1 The carrier shall not be entitled to the benefit of the limits of liability prescribed in Articles 7 and 8 and paragraph 1 of Article 10, if it is proved that the damage resulted from an act or omission of the carrier done with the intent to cause such damage, or recklessly and with knowledge that such damage would probably result.
2 The servant or agent of the carrier or of the performing carrier shall not be entitled to the benefit of those limits if it is proved that the damage resulted from an act or omission of that servant or agent done with the intent to cause such damage, or recklessly and with knowledge that such damage would probably result.

Article 14 – Basis for claims

No action for damages for the death of or persona l injury to a passenger, or for the loss of or damage to luggage, shall be brought against a carrier or performing carrier otherwise than in accordance with this Convention.

Article 15 – Notice of loss or damage to luggage

1 The passenger shall give written notice to the carrier or his agent:
   (a) in the case of apparent damage to luggage:
       (i) for cabin luggage, before or at the time of disembarkation of the passenger;
       (ii) for all other luggage, before or at the time of its re-delivery;
   (b) in the case of damage to luggage which is not apparent, or loss of luggage, within fifteen days from the date of disembarkation or re-delivery or from the time when such re-delivery should have taken place.

497

2 If the passenger fails to comply with this Article, he shall be presumed, unless the contrary is proved, to have received the luggage undamaged.

3 The notice in writing need not be given if the condition of the luggage has at the time of its receipt been the subject of joint survey or inspection.

Article 16 – Time-bar for actions

1 Any action for damages arising out of the death of or personal injury to a passenger or for the loss of or damage to luggage shall be time-barred after a period of two years.

2 The limitation period shall be calculated as follows:

    (a) in the case of personal injury, from the date of disembarkation of the passenger;

    (b) in the case of death occurring during carriage, from the date when the passenger should have disembarked, and in the case of personal injury occurring during carriage and resulting in the death of the passenger after disembarkation, from the date of death, provided that this period shall not exceed three years from the date of disembarkation;

    (c) in the case of loss of or damage to luggage, from the date of disembarkation or from the date when disembarkation should have taken place, whichever is later.

3 The law of the Court seized of the case shall govern the grounds for suspension and interruption of limitation periods, but in no case shall an action under this Convention be brought after the expiration of any one of the following periods of time:

    (a) A period of five years beginning with the date of disembarkation of the passenger or from the date when disembarkation should have taken place, whichever is later; or, if earlier

    (b) a period of three years beginning with the date when the claimant knew or ought reasonably to have known of the injury, loss or damage caused by the incident.

4 Notwithstanding paragraphs 1, 2 and 3 of this Article, the period of limitation may be extended by a declaration of the carrier or by agreement of the parties after the cause of action has arisen. The declaration or agreement shall be in writing.

Article 17 – Competent jurisdiction

1 An action arising under Articles 3 and 4 of this Convention shall, at the option of the claimant, be brought before one of the courts listed below, provided that the court is located in a State Party to this Convention, and subject to the domestic law of each State Party governing proper venue within those States with multiple possible forums:

    (a) the Court of the State of permanent residence or principal place of business of the defendant, or

    (b) the Court of the State of departure or that of the destination according to the contract of carria ge, or

    (c) the Court of the State of the domicile or permanent residence of the claimant, if the defendant has a place of business and is subject to jurisdiction in that State, or

    (d) the Court of the State where the contract of carriage was made, if the defendant has a place of business and is subject to jurisdiction in that State.

2 Actions under article 4bis of this Convention shall, at the option of the claimant, be brought before one of the courts where action could be brought against the carrier or performing carrier according to paragraph 1.

3 After the occurrence of the incident which has caused the damage, the parties may agree that the claim for damages shall be submitted to any jurisdiction or to arbitration.

Article 17bis – Recognition and enforcement

1 Any judgment given by a court with jurisdiction in accordance with Article 17 which is enforceable in the State of origin where it is no longer subject to ordinary forms of review, shall be recognised in any State Party, except

    (a) where the judgment was obtained by fraud; or

(b) where the defendant was not given reasonable notice and a fair opportunity to present his or her case.

2 A judgment recognised under paragraph 1 shall be enforceable in each State Party as soon as the formalities required in that State have been complied with. The formalities shall not permit the merits of the case to be re-opened.

3 A State Party to this Protocol may apply other rules for the recognition and enforcement of judgments, provided that their effect is to ensure that judgments are recognised and enforced at least to the same extent as under paragraphs 1 and 2.

Article 18 – Invalidity of contractual provisions

Any contractual provision concluded before the occurrence of the incident which has caused the death of or personal injury to a passenger or the loss of or damage to the passenger's luggage, purporting to relieve any person liable under this Convention of liability towards the passenger or to prescribe a lower limit of liability than that fixed in this Convention except as provided in Article 8, paragraph 4, and any such provision purporting to shift the burden of proof which rests on the carrier or performing carrier, or having the effect of restricting the options specified in Article 17, paragraphs 1 or 2, shall be null and void, but the nullity of that provision shall not render void the contract of carriage which shall remain subject to the provisions of this Convention.

Article 19 – Other conventions on limitation of liability

This Convention shall not modify the rights or duties of the carrier, the performing carrier, and their servants or agents provided for in international conventions relating to the limitation of liability of owners of seagoing ships.

Article 20 – Nuclear damage

No liability shall arise under this Convention for damage caused by a nuclear incident:

(a) if the operator of a nuclear installation is liable for such damage under either the Paris Convention of 29 July 1960 on Third Party Liability in the Field of Nuclear Energy as amended by its Additional Protocol of 28 January 1964, or the Vienna Convention of 21 May 1963 on Civil Liability for Nuclear Damage, or any amendment or Protocol thereto which is in force; or

(b) if the operator of a nuclear installation is liable for such damage by virtue of a national law governing the liability for such damage, provided that such law is in all respects as favourable to persons who may suffer damage as either the Paris or the Vienna Conventions or any amendment or Protocol thereto which is in force.

Article 21 – Commercial carriage by public authorities

This Convention shall apply to commercial carriage undertaken by States or Public Authorities under contract of carriage within the meaning of Article 1.

Article 22 – Declaration of non-application

1 Any Party may at the time of signing, ratifying, accepting, approving or acceding to this Convention, declare in writing that it will not give effect to this Convention when the passenger and the carrier are subjects or nationals of that Party.

2 Any declaration made under paragraph 1 of this Article may be withdrawn at any time by a notification in writing to the Secretary-General.

Article 22bis – Final clauses of the Convention

The final clauses of this Convention shall be Articles 17 to 25 of the Protocol of 2002 to the Athens Convention relating to the Carriage of Passengers and their Luggage by Sea, 1974.

References in this Convention to States Parties shall be taken to mean references to States Parties to that Protocol.

Final Clauses

[Articles 17 to 25 of the Protocol of 2002 to the Athens Convention relating to the Carriage of Passengers and their Luggage by Sea, 1974.]

Article 17 – Signature, ratification, acceptance, approval and accession

1 This Protocol shall be open for signature at the Headquarters of the Organization from 1 May 2003 until 30 April 2004 and shall thereafter remain open for accession.
2 States may express their consent to be bound by this Protocol by:
    (a) signature without reservation as to ratification, acceptance or approval; or
    (b) signature subject to ratification, acceptance or approval followed by ratification, acceptance or approval; or
    (c) accession.
3 Ratification, acceptance, approval or accession shall be effected by the deposit of an instrument to that effect with the Secretary-General.
4 Any instrument of ratification, acceptance, approval or accession deposited after the entry into force of an amendment to this Protocol with respect to all existing States Parties, or after the completion of all measures required for the entry into force of the amendment with respect to those States Parties shall be deemed to apply to this Protocol as modified by the amendment.
5 A State shall not express its consent to be bound by this Protocol unless, if Party thereto, it denounces:
    (a) the Athens Convention relating to the Carriage of Passengers and their Luggage by Sea, done at Athens on 13 December 1974;
    (b) the Protocol to the Athens Convention relating to the Carriage of Passengers and their Luggage by Sea, done at London on 19 November 1976; and
    (c) the Protocol of 1990 to amend the Athens Convention relating to the Carriage of Passengers and their Luggage by Sea, done at London on 29 March 1990,
with effect from the time that this Protocol will enter into force for that State in accordance with Article 20.

Article 18 – States with more than one system of law

1 If a State has two or more territorial units in which different systems of law are applicable in relation to matters dealt with in this Protocol, it may at the time of signature, ratification, acceptance, approval or accession declare that this Protocol shall extend to all its territorial units or only to one or more of them, and may modify this declaration by submitting another declaration at any time.
2 Any such declaration shall be notified to the Secretary-General and shall state expressly the territorial units to which this Protocol applies.
3 In relation to a State Party which has made such a declaration:
    (a) references to the State of a ship's registry and, in relation to a compulsory insurance certificate, to the issuing or certifying State, shall be construed as referring to the territorial unit respectively in which the ship is registered and which issues or certifies the certificate;
    (b) references to the requirements of national law, national limit of liability and national currency shall be construed respectively as references to the requirements of the law, the limit of liability and the currency of the relevant territorial unit; and
    (c) references to courts, and to judgments which must be recognised in States Parties, shall be construed as references respectively to courts of, and to judgments which must be recognised in, the relevant territorial unit.

Article 19 – Regional Economic Integration Organisations

1 A Regional Economic Integration Organisation, which is constituted by sovereign States that have transferred competence over certain matters governed by this Protocol to that Organisation, may sign, ratify, accept, approve or accede to this Protocol. A Regional Economic Integration Organisation which is a Party to this Protocol shall have the rights and obligations of a State Party, to the extent that the Regional Economic Integration Organisation has competence over matters governed by this Protocol.

2 Where a Regional Economic Integration Organisation exercises its right of vote in matters over which it has competence, it shall have a number of votes equal to the number of its Member States which are Parties to this Protocol and which have transferred competence to it over the matter in question. A Regional Economic Integration Organisation shall not exercise its right to vote if its Member States exercise theirs, and vice versa.

3 Where the number of States Parties is relevant in this Protocol, including but not limited to Articles 20 and 23 of this Protocol, the Regional Economic Integration Organisation shall not count as a State Party in addition to its Member States which are States Parties.

4 At the time of signature, ratification, acceptance, approval or accession the Regional Economic Integration Organisation shall make a declaration to the Secretary-General specifying the matters governed by this Protocol in respect of which competence has been transferred to that Organisation by its Member States which are signatories or Parties to this Protocol and any other relevant restrictions as to the scope of that competence. The Regional Economic Integration Organisation shall promptly notify the Secretary-General of any changes to the distribution of competence, including new transfers of competence, specified in the declaration under this paragraph. Any such declarations shall be made available by the Secretary-General pursuant to Article 24 of this Protocol.

5 States Parties which are Member States of a Regional Economic Integration Organisation which is a Party to this Protocol shall be presumed to have competence over all matters governed by this Protocol in respect of which transfers of competence to the Organisation have not been specifically declared or notified under paragraph 4.

Article 20 – Entry into force

1 This Protocol shall enter into force twelve months following the date on which 10 States have either signed it without reservation as to ratification, acceptance or approval or have deposited instruments of ratification, acceptance, approval or accession with the Secretary-General.

2 For any State which ratifies, accepts, approves or accedes to this Protocol after the conditions in paragraph 1 for entry into force have been met, this Protocol shall enter into force three months after the date of deposit by such State of the appropriate instrument, but not before this Protocol has entered into force in agreement with paragraph 1.

Article 21 – Denunciation

1 This Protocol may be denounced by any State Party at any time after the date on which this Protocol comes into force for that State.

2 Denunciation shall be effected by the deposit of an instrument to that effect with the Secretary-General.

3 A denunciation shall take effect twelve months, or such longer period as may be specified in the instrument of denunciation, after its deposit with the Secretary-General.

4 As between the States Parties to this Protocol, denunciation by any of them of the Convention in accordance with Article 25 thereof shall not be construed in any way as a denunciation of the Convention as revised by this Protocol.

Article 22 – Revision and Amendment

1 A Conference for the purpose of revising or amending this Protocol may be convened by the Organization.

2 The Organization shall convene a Conference of States Parties to this Protocol for revising or amending this Protocol at the request of not less than one-third of the States Parties.

Article 23 – Amendment of limits

1 Without prejudice to the provisions of Article 22, the special procedure in this Article shall apply solely for the purposes of amending the limits set out in Article 3, paragraph 1, Article 4*bis*, paragraph 1, Article 7, paragraph 1 and Article 8 of the Convention as revised by this Protocol.

2 Upon the request of at least one half, but in no case less than six, of the States Parties to this Protocol, any proposal to amend the limits, including the deductibles, specified in Article 3, paragraph 1, Article 4bis, paragraph 1, Article 7, paragraph 1, and Article 8 of the Convention as revised by this Protocol shall be circulated by the Secretary-General to all Members of the Organization and to all States Parties.

3 Any amendment proposed and circulated as above shall be submitted to the Legal Committee of the Organization (hereinafter referred to as "the Legal Committee") for consideration at a date at least six months after the date of its circulation.

4 All States Parties to the Convention as revised by this Protocol, whether or not Members of the Organization, shall be entitled to participate in the proceedings of the Legal Committee for the consideration and adoption of amendments.

5 Amendments shall be adopted by a two-thirds majority of the States Parties to the Convention as revised by this Protocol present and voting in the Legal Committee expanded as provided for in paragraph 4, on condition that at least one half of the States Parties to the Convention as revised by this Protocol shall be present at the time of voting.

6 When acting on a proposal to amend the limits, the Legal Committee shall take into account the experience of incidents and, in particular, the amount of damage resulting therefrom, changes in the monetary values and the effect of the proposed amendment on the cost of insurance.

7 (a) No amendment of the limits under this Article may be considered less than five years from the date on which this Protocol was opened for signature nor less than five years from the date of entry into force of a previous amendment under this Article.

   (b) No limit may be increased so as to exceed an amount which corresponds to the limit laid down in the Convention as revised by this Protocol increased by six per cent per year calculated on a compound basis from the date on which this Protocol was opened for signature.

   (c) No limit may be increased so as to exceed an amount which corresponds to the limit laid down in the Convention as revised by this Protocol multiplied by three.

8 Any amendment adopted in accordance with paragraph 5 shall be notified by the Organization to all States Parties. The amendment shall be deemed to have been accepted at the end of a period of eighteen months after the date of notification, unless within that period not less than one fourth of the States that were States Parties at the time of the adoption of the amendment have communicated to the Secretary-General that they do not accept the amendment, in which case the amendment is rejected and shall have no effect.

9 An amendment deemed to have been accepted in accordance with paragraph 8 shall enter into force eighteen months after its acceptance.

10 All States Parties shall be bound by the amendment, unless they denounce this Protocol in accordance with Article 21, paragraphs 1 and 2 at least six months before the amendment enters into force. Such denunciation shall take effect when the amendment enters into force.

11 When an amendment has been adopted but the eighteen- month period for its acceptance has not yet expired, a State which becomes a State Party during that period shall be bound by the amendment if it enters into force. A State which becomes a State Party after that period shall be bound by an amendment which has been accepted in accor-

dance with paragraph 8. In the cases referred to in this paragraph, a State becomes bound by an amendment when that amendment enters into force, or when this Protocol enters into force for that State, if later.

Article 24 – Depositary

1 This Protocol and any amendments adopted under Article 23 shall be deposited with the Secretary-General.
2 The Secretary-General shall:
    (a) inform all States which have signed or acceded to this Protocol of:
        (i) each new signature or deposit of an instrument of ratification, acceptance, approval or accession together with the date thereof;
        (ii) each declaration and communication under Article 9, paragraphs 2 and 3, Article 18, paragraph 1 and Article 19, paragraph 4 of the Convention as revised by this Protocol;
        (iii) the date of entry into force of this Protocol;
        (iv) any proposal to amend the limits which has been made in accordance with Article 23, paragraph 2 of this Protocol;
        (v) any amendment which has been adopted in accordance with Article 23, paragraph 5 of this Protocol;
        (vi) any amendment deemed to have been accepted under Article 23, paragraph 8 of this Protocol, together with the date on which that amendment shall enter into force in accordance with paragraphs 9 and 10 of that Article;
        (vii) the deposit of any instrument of denunciation of this Protocol together with the date of the deposit and the date on which it takes effect;
        (viii) any communication called for by any Article of this Protocol;
    (b) transmit certified true copies of this Protocol to all States which have signed or acceded to this Protocol.
3 As soon as this Protocol comes into force, the text shall be transmitted by the Secretary-General to the Secretariat of the United Nations for registration and publication in accordance with Article 102 of the Charter of the United Nations.

Article 25 – Languages

This Protocol is established in a single original in the Arabic, Chinese, English, French, Russian and Spanish languages, each text being equally authentic.

DONE AT LONDON this first day of November 2002.

IN WITNESS WHEREOF the undersigned, being duly authorised by their respective Governments for that purpose, have signed this Protocol.

ANNEX

CERTIFICATE OF INSURANCE OR OTHER FINANCIAL SECURITY IN RESPECT OF LIABILITY FOR THE DEATH OF AND PERSONAL INJURY TO PASSENGERS

Issued in accordance with the provisions of Article 4*bis* of the Athens Convention relating to the Carriage of Passengers and their Luggage by Sea, 2002

Name of Ship	Distinctive number or letters	IMO Ship Identification Number	Port of Registry	Name and full address of the principal place of business of the carrier who actually performs the carriage.

This is to certify that there is in force in respect of the above-named ship a policy of insurance or other financial security satisfying the requirements of Article 4bis of the Athens Convention relating to the Carriage of Passengers and their Luggage by Sea, 2002.

Type of Security ....

Duration of Security ....

Name and address of the insurer(s) and/or guarantor(s)

Name ....,,,,,,,,,,.................................

Address ....

....

      This certificate is valid until ....

      Issued or certified by the Government of ....

....

(Full designation of the State)

OR

The following text should be used when a State Party avails itself of Article 4*bis*, paragraph 3:

The present certificate is issued under the authority of the Government of ....
(full designation of the State) by .... (name of institution or organisation)

At .... On ....
     (Place)   (Date)

....
(Signature and Title of issuing or certifying official)

Explanatory Notes:

1 If desired, the designation of the State may include a reference to the competent public authority of the country where the Certificate is issued.
2 If the total amount of security has been furnished by more than one source, the amount of each of them should be indicated.
3 If security is furnished in several forms, these should be enumerated.
4 The entry "Duration of Security" must stipulate the date on which such security takes effect.
5 The entry "Address" of the insurer(s) and/or guarantor(s) must indicate the principal place of business of the insurer(s) and/or guarantor(s). If appropriate, the place of business where the insurance or other security is established shall be indicated.

International Convention on Limitation of Liability for Maritime Claims for 1976 and 1996 Protocol

Convention on Limitation of Liability for Maritime Claims, 1976
(London, 19 November 1976)

THE STATES PARTIES TO THIS CONVENTION,

HAVING RECOGNISED the desirability of determining by agreement certain uniform rules relating to the limitation of liability for maritime claims,

HAVE DECIDED to conclude a Convention for this purpose and have thereto agreed as follows:

Chapter I: The right of limitation

Article 1 – Persons entitled to limit liability

1. Shipowners and salvors, as hereinafter defined, may limit their liability in accordance with the rules of this Convention for claims set out in Article 2.
2. The term "shipowner" shall mean the owner, charterer, manager and operator of a seagoing ship.
3. Salvor shall mean any person rendering services in direct connexion with salvage operations. Salvage operations shall also include operations referred to in Article 2, paragraph 1(d), (e) and (f).
4. If any claims set out in Article 2 are made against any person for whose act, neglect or default the shipowner or salvor is responsible, such person shall be entitled to avail himself of the limitation of liability provided for in this Convention.
5. In this Convention the liability of a shipowner shall include liability in an action brought against the vessel itself.
6. An insurer of liability for claims subject to limitation in accordance with the rules of this Convention shall be entitled to the benefits of this Convention to the same extent as the assured himself.
7. The act of invoking limitation of liability shall not constitute an admission of liability.

Article 2 – Claims subject to limitation

1. Subject to Articles 3 and 4 the following claims, whatever the basis of liability may be, shall be subject to limitation of liability:
   (a) claims in respect of loss of life or personal injury or loss of or damage to property (including damage to harbour works, basins and waterways and aids to navigation), occurring on board or in direct connexion with the operation of the ship or with salvage operations, and consequential loss resulting therefrom;
   (b) claims in respect of loss resulting from delay in the carriage by sea of cargo, passengers or their luggage;
   (c) claims in respect of other loss resulting from infringement of rights other than contractual rights, occurring in direct connexion with the operation of the ship or salvage operations;
   (d) claims in respect of the raising, removal, destruction or the rendering harmless of a ship which is sunk, wrecked, stranded or abandoned, including anything that is or has been on board such ship;

(e) claims in respect of the removal, destruction or the rendering harmless of the cargo of the ship;

(f) claims of a person other than the person liable in respect of measures taken in order to avert or minimise loss for which the person liable may limit his liability in accordance with this Convention, and further loss caused by such measures.

2. Claims set out in paragraph 1 shall be subject to limitation of liability even if brought by way of recourse or for indemnity under a contract or otherwise. However, claims set out under paragraph 1(d), (e) and (f) shall not be subject to limitation of liability to the extent that they relate to remuneration under a contract with the person liable.

Article 3 – Claims excepted from limitation

The rules of this Convention shall not apply to:

(a) claims for salvage or contribution in general average;

(b) claims for oil pollution damage within the meaning of the International Convention on Civil Liability for Oil Pollution Damage, dated 29 November 1969 or of any amendment or Protocol thereto which is in force;

(c) claims subject to any international convention or national legislation governing or prohibiting limitation of liability for nuclear damage;

(d) claims against the shipowner of a nuclear ship for nuclear damage;

(e) claims by servants of the shipowner or salvor whose duties are connected with the ship or the salvage operations, including claims of their heirs, dependants or other persons entitled to make such claims, if under the law governing the contract of service between the shipowner or salvor and such servants the shipowner or salvor is not entitled to limit his liability in respect of such claims, or if he is by such law only permitted to limit his liability to an amount greater than that provided for in Article 6.

Article 4 – Conduct barring limitation

A person liable shall not be entitled to limit his liability if it is proved that the loss resulted from his personal act or omission, committed with the intent to cause such loss, or recklessly and with knowledge that such loss would probably result.

Article 5 – Counterclaims

Where a person entitled to limitation of liability under the rules of this Convention has a claim against the claimant arising out of the same occurrence, their respective claims shall be set off against each other and the provisions of this Convention shall only apply to the balance, if any.

Chapter II: Limits of liability

Article 6 – The general limits

1. The limits of liability for claims other than those mentioned in Article 7, arising on any distinct occasion, shall be calculated as follows:

(a) in respect of claims for loss of life or personal injury,

(i) 333,000 Units of Account for a ship with a tonnage not exceeding 500 tons,

(ii) for a ship with a tonnage in excess thereof, the following amount in addition to that mentioned in (i):

for each ton from 501 to 3,000 tons, 500 Units of Account;

for each ton from 3,001 to 30,000 tons, 333 Units of Account;

for each ton from 30,001 to 70,000 tons, 250 Units of Account; and

for each ton in excess of 70,000 tons, 167 Units of Account,

(b) in respect of any other claims,

    (i) 167,000 Units of Account for a ship with a tonnage not exceeding 500 tons,

    (ii) for a ship with a tonnage in excess thereof the following amount in addition to that mentioned in (i):

        for each ton from 501 to 30,000 tons, 167 Units of Account;

        for each ton from 30,001 to 70,000 tons, 125 Units of Account; and

        for each ton in excess of 70,000 tons, 83 Units of Account.

2. Where the amount calculated in accordance with paragraph 1(a) is insufficient to pay the claims mentioned therein in full, the amount calculated in accordance with paragraph 1(b) shall be available for payment of the unpaid balance of claims under paragraph 1(a) and such unpaid balance shall rank rateably with claims mentioned under paragraph 1(b).

3. However, without prejudice to the right of claims for loss of life or personal injury according to paragraph 2, a State Party may provide in its national law that claims in respect of damage to harbour works, basins and waterways and aids to navigation shall have such priority over other claims under paragraph 1(b) as is provided by that law.

4. The limits of liability for any salvor not operating from any ship or for any salvor operating solely on the ship to, or in respect of which he is rendering salvage services, shall be calculated according to a tonnage of 1,500 tons.

5. For the purpose of this Convention the ship's tonnage shall be the gross tonnage calculated in accordance with the tonnage measurement rules contained in Annex I of the International Convention on Tonnage Measurement of Ships, 1969.

Article 7 – The limit for passenger claims

1. In respect of claims arising on any distinct occasion for loss of life or personal injury to passengers of a ship, the limit of liability of the shipowner thereof shall be an amount of 46,666 Units of Account multiplied by the number of passengers which the ship is authorised to carry according to the ship's certificate, but not exceeding 25 million Units of Account.

2. For the purpose of this Article "claims for loss of life or personal injury to passengers of a ship" shall mean any such claims brought by or on behalf of any person carried in that ship:

    (a) under a contract of passenger carriage, or

    (b) who, with the consent of the carrier, is accompanying a vehicle or live animals which are covered by a contract for the carriage of goods.

Article 8 – Unit of Account

1. The Unit of Account referred to in Articles 6 and 7 is the Special Drawing Right as defined by the International Monetary Fund. The amounts mentioned in Articles 6 and 7 shall be converted into the national currency of the State in which limitation is sought, according to the value of that currency at the date the limitation fund shall have been constituted, payment is made, or security is given which under the law of that State is equivalent to such payment. The value of a national currency in terms of the Special Drawing Right, of a State Party which is a member of the International Monetary Fund, shall be calculated in accordance with the method of valuation applied by the International Monetary Fund in effect at the date in question for its operations and transactions. The value of a national currency in terms of the Special Drawing Right, of a State Party which is not a member of the International Monetary Fund, shall be calculated in a manner determined by that State Party.

2. Nevertheless, those States which are not members of the International Monetary Fund and whose law does not permit the application of the provisions of paragraph 1 may, at the time of signature without reservation as to ratification, acceptance or approval or at the time of ratification, acceptance, approval or accession or at any time thereafter, declare that the limits of liability provided for in this Convention to be applied in their territories shall be fixed as follows:

   (a) in respect of Article 6, paragraph 1(a) at an amount of:
       (i) 5 million monetary units for a ship with a tonnage not exceeding 500 tons,
      (ii) for a ship with a tonnage in excess thereof, the following amount in addition to
            that mentioned in (i):
                for each ton from 501 to 3,000 tons, 7,500 monetary units;
                for each ton from 3,001 to 30,000 tons, 5,000 monetary units;
                for each ton from 30,001 to 70,000 tons, 3,750 monetary units; and
                for each ton in excess of 70,000 tons, 2,500 monetary units; and
   (b) in respect of Article 6, paragraph 1(b), at an amount of:
       (i) 2.5 million monetary units for a ship with a tonnage not exceeding 500 tons,
      (ii) for a ship with a tonnage in excess thereof, the following amount in addition to
            that mentioned in (i):
                for each ton from 501 to 30,000 tons, 2,500 monetary units;
                for each ton from 30,001 to 70,000 tons, 1,850 monetary units; and
                for each ton in excess of 70,000 tons, 1,250 monetary units; and
   (c) in respect of Article 7, paragraph 1, at an amount of 700,000 monetary units mul-
        tiplied by the number of passengers which the ship is authorised to carry according
        to its certificate, but not exceeding 375 million monetary units.
   Paragraphs 2 and 3 of Article 6 apply correspondingly to sub-paragraphs (a) and (b) of
   this paragraph.
3. The monetary unit referred to in paragraph 2 corresponds to sixty-five and a half milligrammes of gold of millesimal fineness nine hundred. The conversion of the amounts
   referred to in paragraph 2 into the national currency shall be made according to the law
   of the State concerned.
4. The calculation mentioned in the last sentence of paragraph 1 and the conversion mentioned in paragraph 3 shall be made in such a manner as to express in the national currency of the State Party as far as possible the same real value for the amounts in Articles
   6 and 7 as is expressed there in units of account. States Parties shall communicate to the
   depositary the manner of calculation pursuant to paragraph 1, or the result of the conversion in paragraph 3, as the case may be, at the time of the signature without reservation as to ratification, acceptance or approval, or when depositing an instrument referred
   to in Article 16 and whenever there is a change in either.

Article 9 – Aggregation of claims

1. The limits of liability determined in accordance with Article 6 shall apply to the aggregate
   of all claims which arise on any distinct occasion:
   (a) against the person or persons mentioned in paragraph 2 of Article 1 and any person
        for whose act, neglect or default he or they are responsible; or
   (b) against the shipowner of a ship rendering salvage services from that ship and the
        salvor or salvors operating from such ship and any person for whose act, neglect or
        default he or they are responsible; or
   (c) against the salvor or salvors who are not operating from a ship or who are operating
        solely on the ship to, or in respect of which, the salvage services are rendered and
        any person for whose act, neglect or default he or they are responsible.
2. The limits of liability determined in accordance with Article 7 shall apply to the aggregate
   of all claims subject thereto which may arise on any distinct occasion against the person
   or persons mentioned in paragraph 2 of Article 1 in respect of the ship referred to in
   Article 7 and any person for whose act, neglect or default he or they are responsible.

Article 10 – Limitation of liability without constitution of a limitation fund

1. Limitation of liability may be invoked notwithstanding that a limitation fund as mentioned in Article 11 has not been constituted. However, a State Party may provide in its
   national law that, where an action is brought in its Courts to enforce a claim subject to
   limitation, a person liable may only invoke the right to limit liability if a limitation fund

has been constituted in accordance with the provisions of this Convention or is constituted when the right to limit liability is invoked.

2. If limitation of liability is invoked without the constitution of a limitation fund, the provisions of Article 12 shall apply correspondingly.
3. Questions of procedure arising under the rules of this Article shall be decided in accordance with the national law of the State Party in which action is brought.

Chapter III: The Limitation Fund

Article 11 – Constitution of the fund

1. Any person alleged to be liable may constitute a fund with the Court or other competent authority in any State Party in which legal proceedings are instituted in respect of claims subject to limitation. The fund shall be constituted in the sum of such of the amounts set out in Articles 6 and 7 as are applicable to claims for which that person may be liable, together with interest thereon from the date of the occurrence giving rise to the liability until the date of the constitution of the fund. Any fund thus constituted shall be available only for the payment of claims in respect of which limitation of liability can be invoked.
2. A fund may be constituted, either by depositing the sum, or by producing a guarantee acceptable under the legislation of the State Party where the fund is constituted and considered to be adequate by the Court or other competent authority.
3. A fund constituted by one of the persons mentioned in paragraph 1(a), (b) or (c) or paragraph 2 of Article 9 or his insurer shall be deemed constituted by all persons mentioned in paragraph 1(a), (b) or (c) or paragraph 2, respectively.

Article 12 – Distribution of the fund

1. Subject to the provisions of paragraphs 1, 2 and 3 of Article 6 and of Article 7, the fund shall be distributed among the claimants in proportion to their established claims against the fund.
2. If, before the fund is distributed, the person liable, or his insurer, has settled a claim against the fund such person shall, up to the amount he has paid, acquire by subrogation the rights which the person so compensated would have enjoyed under this Convention.
3. The right of subrogation provided for in paragraph 2 may also be exercised by persons other than those therein mentioned in respect of any amount of compensation which they may have paid, but only to the extent that such subrogation is permitted under the applicable national law.
4. Where the person liable or any other person establishes that he may be compelled to pay, at a later date, in whole or in part any such amount of compensation with regard to which such person would have enjoyed a right of subrogation pursuant to paragraphs 2 and 3 had the compensation been paid before the fund was distributed, the Court or other competent authority of the State where the fund has been constituted may order that a sufficient sum shall be provisionally set aside to enable such person at such later date to enforce his claim against the fund.

Article 13 – Bar to other actions

1. Where a limitation fund has been constituted in accordance with Article 11, any person having made a claim against the fund shall be barred from exercising any right in respect of such claim against any other assets of a person by or on behalf of whom the fund has been constituted.
2. After a limitation fund has been constituted in accordance with Article 11, any ship or other property, belonging to a person on behalf of whom the fund has been constituted, which has been arrested or attached within the jurisdiction of a State Party for a claim which may be raised against the fund, or any security given, may be released by order of the Court or other competent authority of such State. However, such release shall always be ordered if the limitation fund has been constituted:

(a) at the port where the occurrence took place, or, if it took place out of port, at the first port of call thereafter; or
(b) at the port of disembarkation in respect of claims for loss of life or personal injury; or
(c) at the port of discharge in respect of damage to cargo; or
(d) in the State where the arrest is made.

3. The rules of paragraphs 1 and 2 shall apply only if the claimant may bring a claim against the limitation fund before the Court administering that fund and the fund is actually available and freely transferable in respect of that claim.

Article 14 – Governing law

Subject to the provisions of this Chapter the rules relating to the constitution and distribution of a limitation fund, and all rules of procedure in connexion therewith, shall be governed by the law of the State Party in which the fund is constituted.

Chapter IV: Scope of application

Article 15

1. This Convention shall apply whenever any person referred to in Article 1 seeks to limit his liability before the Court of a State Party or seeks to procure the release of a ship or other property or the discharge of any security given within the jurisdiction of any such State. Nevertheless, each State Party may exclude wholly or partially from the application of this Convention any person referred to in Article 1 who at the time when the rules of this Convention are invoked before the Courts of that State does not have his habitual residence in a State Party or does not have his principal place of business in a State Party or any ship in relation to which the right of limitation is invoked or whose release is sought and which does not at the time specified above fly the flag of a State Party.
2. A State Party may regulate by specific provisions of national law the system of limitation of liability to be applied to vessels which are:
    (a) according to the law of that State, ships intended for navigation on inland waterways
    (b) ships of less than 300 tons.
   A State Party which makes use of the option provided for in this paragraph shall inform the depositary of the limits of liability adopted in its national legislation or of the fact that there are none.
3. A State Party may regulate by specific provisions of national law the system of limitation of liability to be applied to claims arising in cases in which interests of persons who are nationals of other States Parties are in no way involved.
4. The Courts of a State Party shall not apply this Convention to ships constructed for, or adapted to, and engaged in, drilling:
    (a) when that State has established under its national legislation a higher limit of liability than that otherwise provided for in Article 6; or
    (b) when that State has become party to an international convention regulating the system of liability in respect of such ships.
   In a case to which sub-paragraph (a) applies that State Party shall inform the depositary accordingly.
5. This Convention shall not apply to:
    (a) air-cushion vehicles;
    (b) floating platforms constructed for the purpose of exploring or exploiting the natural resources of the sea-bed or the subsoil thereof.

Chapter V: Final clauses

Article 16 – Signature, ratification and accession

1. This Convention shall be open for signature by all States at the Headquarters of the Inter-Governmental Maritime Consultative Organization (hereinafter referred to as "the

Organization") from 1 February 1977 until 31 December 1977 and shall thereafter remain open for accession.

2. All States may become parties to this Convention by:
   (a) signature without reservation as to ratification, acceptance or approval; or
   (b) signature subject to ratification, acceptance or approval followed by ratification, acceptance or approval; or
   (c) accession.
3. Ratification, acceptance, approval or accession shall be effected by the deposit of a formal instrument to that effect with the Secretary-General of the Organization (hereinafter referred to as "the Secretary-General").

Article 17 – Entry into force

1. This Convention shall enter into force on the first day of the month following one year after the date on which twelve States have either signed it without reservation as to ratification, acceptance or approval or have deposited the requisite instruments of ratification, acceptance, approval or accession.
2. For a State which deposits an instrument of ratification, acceptance, approval or accession, or signs without reservation as to ratification, acceptance or approval, in respect of this Convention after the requirements for entry into force have been met but prior to the date of entry into force, the ratification, acceptance, approval or accession or the signature without reservation as to ratification, acceptance or approval, shall take effect on the date of entry into force of the Convention or on the first day of the month following the ninetieth day after the date of the signature or the deposit of the instrument, whichever is the later date.
3. For any State which subsequently becomes a Party to this Convention, the Convention shall enter into force on the first day of the month following the expiration of ninety days after the date when such State deposited its instrument.
4. In respect of the relations between States which ratify, accept, or approve this Convention or accede to it, this Convention shall replace and abrogate the International Convention relating to the Limitation of the Liability of Owners of Sea-going Ships, done at Brussels on 10 October 1957, and the International Convention for the Unification of certain Rules relating to the Limitation of Liability of the Owners of Sea-going Vessels, signed at Brussels on 25 August 1924.

Article 18 – Reservations

1. Any State may, at the time of signature, ratification, acceptance, approval or accession, reserve the right to exclude the application of Article 2 paragraph 1(d) and (e). No other reservations shall be admissible to the substantive provisions of this Convention.
2. Reservations made at the time of signature are subject to confirmation upon ratification, acceptance or approval.
3. Any State which has made a reservation to this Convention may withdraw it at any time by means of a notification addressed to the Secretary-General. Such withdrawal shall take effect on the date the notification is received. If the notification states that the withdrawal of a reservation is to take effect on a date specified therein, and such date is later than the date the notification is received by the Secretary-General, the withdrawal shall take effect on such later date.

Article 19 – Denunciation

1. This Convention may be denounced by a State Party at any time one year from the date on which the Convention entered into force for that Party.
2. Denunciation shall be effected by the deposit of an instrument with the Secretary-General.
3. Denunciation shall take effect on the first day of the month following the expiration of one year after the date of deposit of the instrument, or after such longer period as may be specified in the instrument.

Article 20 – Revision and amendment

1. A Conference for the purpose of revising or amending this Convention may be convened by the Organization.
2. The Organization shall convene a Conference of the States Parties to this Convention for revising or amending it at the request of not less than one-third of the Parties.
3. After the date of the entry into force of an amendment to this Convention, any instrument of ratification, acceptance, approval or accession deposited shall be deemed to apply to the Convention as amended, unless a contrary intention is expressed in the instrument.

Article 21 – Revision of the limitation amounts and of Unit of Account or monetary unit

1. Notwithstanding the provisions of Article 20, a Conference only for the purposes of altering the amounts specified in Articles 6 and 7 and in Article 8, paragraph 2, or of substituting either or both of the Units defined in Article 8, paragraphs 1 and 2, by other units shall be convened by the Organization in accordance with paragraphs 2 and 3 of this Article. An alteration of the amounts shall be made only because of a significant change in their real value.
2. The Organization shall convene such a Conference at the request of not less than one fourth of the States Parties.
3. A decision to alter the amounts or to substitute the Units by other units of account shall be taken by a two-thirds majority of the States Parties present and voting in such Conference.
4. Any State depositing its instrument of ratification, acceptance, approval or accession to the Convention, after entry into force of an amendment, shall apply the Convention as amended.

Article 22 – Depositary

1. This Convention shall be deposited with the Secretary-General.
2. The Secretary-General shall:
    (a) transmit certified true copies of this Convention to all States which were invited to attend the Conference on Limitation of Liability for Maritime Claims and to any other States which accede to this Convention;
    (b) inform all States which have signed or acceded to this Convention of:
        (i) each new signature and each deposit of an instrument and any reservation thereto together with the date thereof;
        (ii) the date of entry into force of this Convention or any amendment thereto;
        (iii) any denunciation of this Convention and the date on which it takes effect;
        (iv) any amendment adopted in conformity with Articles 20 or 21;
        (v) any communication called for by any Article of this Convention.
3. Upon entry into force of this Convention, a certified true copy thereof shall be transmitted by the Secretary-General to the Secretariat of the United Nations for registration and publication in accordance with Article 102 of the Charter of the United Nations.

Article 23 – Languages

This Convention is established in a single original in the English, French, Russian and Spanish languages, each text being equally authentic.

DONE AT LONDON this nineteenth day of November one thousand nine hundred and seventy-six.

IN WITNESS WHEREOF the undersigned being duly authorised for that purpose have signed this Convention.

**Protocol of 1996 to amend the Convention on Limitation of Liability
for Maritime Claims of 19 November 1976**
(London, 2 May 1996)

THE PARTIES TO THE PRESENT PROTOCOL,

CONSIDERING that it is desirable to amend the Convention on Limitation of Liability for Maritime Claims, done at London on 19 November 1976, to provide for enhanced compensation and to establish a simplified procedure for updating the limitation amounts,

HAVE AGREED as follows:

Article 1

For the purposes of this Protocol:

1. "Convention" means the Convention on Limitation of Liability for Maritime Claims, 1976.
2. "Organization" means the International Maritime Organization.
3. "Secretary-General" means the Secretary-General of the Organization.

Article 2

Article 3, subparagraph (a) of the Convention is replaced by the following text:

    (a) claims for salvage, including, if applicable, any claim for special compensation under Article 14 of the International Convention on Salvage 1989, as amended, or contribution in general average;

Article 3

Article 6, paragraph 1 of the Convention is replaced by the following text:

1. The limits of liability for claims other than those mentioned in Article 7, arising on any distinct occasion, shall be calculated as follows:
   (a) in respect of claims for loss of life or personal injury,
      (i) 2 million Units of Account for a ship with a tonnage not exceeding 2,000 tons,
      (ii) for a ship with a tonnage in excess thereof, the following amount in addition to that mentioned in (i):
         for each ton from 2,001 to 30,000 tons, 800 Units of Account;
         for each ton from 30,001 to 70,000 tons, 600 Units of Account; and
         for each ton in excess of 70,000 tons, 400 Units of Account,
   (b) in respect of any other claims,
      (i) 1 million Units of Account for a ship with a tonnage not exceeding 2,000 tons,
      (ii) for a ship with a tonnage in excess thereof, the following amount in addition to that mentioned in (i):
         for each ton from 2,001 to 30,000 tons, 400 Units of Account;
         for each ton from 30,001 to 70,000 tons, 300 Units of Account; and
         for each ton in excess of 70,000 tons, 200 Units of Account.

Article 4

Article 7, paragraph 1 of the Convention is replaced by the following text:

1. In respect of claims arising on any distinct occasion for loss of life or personal injury to passengers of a ship, the limit of liability of the shipowner thereof shall be an amount of 175,000 Units of Account multiplied by the number of passengers which the ship is authorised to carry according to the ship's certificate.

Article 5

Article 8, paragraph 2 of the Convention is replaced by the following text:

    2. Nevertheless, those States which are not members of the International Monetary Fund and whose law does not permit the application of the provisions of paragraph 1 may, at the time of signature without reservation as to ratification, acceptance or approval or at the time of ratification, acceptance, approval or accession or at any time thereafter, declare that the limits of liability provided for in this Convention to be applied in their territories shall be fixed as follows:

       (a) in respect of Article 6, paragraph 1(a), at an amount of

         (i) 30 million monetary units for a ship with a tonnage not exceeding 2,000 tons;

         (ii) for a ship with a tonnage in excess thereof, the following amount in addition to that mentioned in (i):

            for each ton from 2,001 to 30,000 tons, 12,000 monetary units;

            for each ton from 30,001 to 70,000 tons, 9,000 monetary units; and

            for each ton in excess of 70,000 tons, 6,000 monetary units; and

       (b) in respect of Article 6, paragraph 1(b), at an amount of:

         (i) 15 million monetary units for a ship with a tonnage not exceeding 2,000 tons;

         (ii) for a ship with a tonnage in excess thereof, the following amount in addition to that mentioned in (i):

            for each ton from 2,001 to 30,000 tons, 6,000 monetary units;

            for each ton from 30,001 to 70,000 tons, 4,500 monetary units; and

            for each ton in excess of 70,000 tons, 3,000 monetary units; and

       (c) in respect of Article 7, paragraph 1, at an amount of 2,625,000 monetary units multiplied by the number of passengers which the ship is authorised to carry according to its certificate.

Paragraphs 2 and 3 of Article 6 apply correspondingly to subparagraphs (a) and (b) of this paragraph.

Article 6

The following text is added as paragraph 3*bis* in Article 15 of the Convention:

    3*bis* Notwithstanding the limit of liability prescribed in paragraph 1 of Article 7, a State Party may regulate by specific provisions of national law the system of liability to be applied to claims for loss of life or personal injury to passengers of a ship, provided that the limit of liability is not lower than that prescribed in paragraph 1 of Article 7. A State Party which makes use of the option provided for in this paragraph shall inform the Secretary-General of the limits of liability adopted or of the fact that there are none.

Article 7

Article 18, paragraph 1 of the Convention is replaced by the following text:

    1. Any State may, at the time of signature, ratification, acceptance, approval or accession, or at any time thereafter, reserve the right:

       (a) to exclude the application of Article 2, paragraphs 1(d) and (e);

       (b) to exclude claims for damage within the meaning of the International Convention on Liability and Compensation for Damage in Connection with the Carriage of Hazardous and Noxious Substances by Sea, 1996 or of any amendment or protocol thereto.

No other reservations shall be admissible to the substantive provisions of this Convention.

Article 8 – Amendment of limits

    1. Upon the request of at least one half, but in no case less than six, of the States Parties to this Protocol, any proposal to amend the limits specified in Article 6, paragraph 1,

Article 7, paragraph 1 and Article 8, paragraph 2 of the Convention as amended by this Protocol shall be circulated by the Secretary-General to all Members of the Organization and to all Contracting States.

2. Any amendment proposed and circulated as above shall be submitted to the Legal Committee of the Organization (the Legal Committee) for consideration at a date at least six months after the date of its circulation.

3. All Contracting States to the Convention as amended by this Protocol, whether or not Members of the Organization, shall be entitled to participate in the proceedings of the Legal Committee for the consideration and adoption of amendments.

4. Amendments shall be adopted by a two-thirds majority of the Contracting States to the Convention as amended by this Protocol present and voting in the Legal Committee expanded as provided for in paragraph 3, on condition that at least one half of the Contracting States to the Convention as amended by this Protocol shall be present at the time of voting.

5. When acting on a proposal to amend the limits, the Legal Committee shall take into account the experience of incidents and, in particular, the amount of damage resulting therefrom, changes in the monetary values and the effect of the proposed amendment on the cost of insurance.

6. (a) No amendment of the limits under this Article may be considered less than five years from the date on which this Protocol was opened for signature nor less than five years from the date of entry into force of a previous amendment under this Article.

 (b) No limit may be increased so as to exceed an amount which corresponds to the limit laid down in the Convention as amended by this Protocol increased by six percent per year calculated on a compound basis from the date on which this Protocol was opened for signature.

 (c) No limit may be increased so as to exceed an amount which corresponds to the limit laid down in the Convention as amended by this Protocol multiplied by three.

7. Any amendment adopted in accordance with paragraph 4 shall be notified by the Organization to all Contracting States. The amendment shall be deemed to have been accepted at the end of a period of eighteen months after the date of notification, unless within that period not less than one-fourth of the States that were Contracting States at the time of the adoption of the amendment have communicated to the Secretary-General that they do not accept the amendment, in which case the amendment is rejected and shall have no effect.

8. An amendment deemed to have been accepted in accordance with paragraph 7 shall enter into force eighteen months after its acceptance.

9. All Contracting States shall be bound by the amendment, unless they denounce this Protocol in accordance with paragraphs 1 and 2 of Article 12 at least six months before the amendment enters into force. Such denunciation shall take effect when the amendment enters into force.

10. When an amendment has been adopted but the eighteen-month period for its acceptance has not yet expired, a State which becomes a Contracting State during that period shall be bound by the amendment if it enters into force. A State which becomes a Contracting State after that period shall be bound by an amendment which has been accepted in accordance with paragraph 7. In the cases referred to in this paragraph, a State becomes bound by an amendment when that amendment enters into force, or when this Protocol enters into force for that State, if later.

Article 9

1. The Convention and this Protocol shall, as between the Parties to this Protocol, be read and interpreted together as one single instrument.

2. A State which is Party to this Protocol but not a Party to the Convention shall be bound by the provisions of the Convention as amended by this Protocol in relation to other States Parties hereto, but shall not be bound by the provisions of the Convention in relation to States Parties only to the Convention.

3. The Convention as amended by this Protocol shall apply only to claims arising out of occurrences which take place after the entry into force for each State of this Protocol.

4. Nothing in this Protocol shall affect the obligations of a State which is a Party both to the Convention and to this Protocol with respect to a State which is a Party to the Convention but not a Party to this Protocol.

Final clauses

Article 10 – Signature, ratification, acceptance, approval and accession

1. This Protocol shall be open for signature at the Headquarters of the Organization from 1 October 1996 to 30 September 1997 by all States.
2. Any State may express its consent to be bound by this Protocol by:
   (a) signature without reservation as to ratification, acceptance or approval; or
   (b) signature subject to ratification, acceptance or approval followed by ratification, acceptance or approval; or
   (c) accession.
3. Ratification, acceptance, approval or accession shall be effected by the deposit of an instrument to that effect with the Secretary-General.
4. Any instrument of ratification, acceptance, approval or accession deposited after the entry into force of an amendment to the Convention as amended by this Protocol shall be deemed to apply to the Convention so amended, as modified by such amendment.

Article 11 – Entry into force

1. This Protocol shall enter into force ninety days following the date on which ten States have expressed their consent to be bound by it.
2. For any State which expresses its consent to be bound by this Protocol after the conditions in paragraph 1 for entry into force have been met, this Protocol shall enter into force ninety days following the date of expression of such consent.

Article 12 – Denunciation

1. This Protocol may be denounced by any State Party at any time after the date on which it enters into force for that State Party.
2. Denunciation shall be effected by the deposit of an instrument of denunciation with the Secretary-General.
3. A denunciation shall take effect twelve months, or such longer period as may be specified in the instrument of denunciation, after its deposit with the Secretary-General.
4. As between the States Parties to this Protocol, denunciation by any of them of the Convention in accordance with Article 19 thereof shall not be construed in any way as a denunciation of the Convention as amended by this Protocol.

Article 13 – Revision and amendment

1. A conference for the purpose of revising or amending this Protocol may be convened by the Organization.
2. The Organization shall convene a conference of Contracting States to this Protocol for revising or amending it at the request of not less than one-third of the Contracting States.

Article 14 – Depositary

1. This Protocol and any amendments adopted under Article 8 shall be deposited with the Secretary General.
2. The Secretary-General shall:
   (a) inform all States which have signed or acceded to this Protocol of:
       (i) each new signature or deposit of an instrument together with the date thereof;

(ii) each declaration and communication under Article 8, paragraph 2 of the Convention as amended by this Protocol, and Article 8, paragraph 4 of the Convention;

(iii) the date of entry into force of this Protocol;

(iv) any proposal to amend limits which has been made in accordance with Article 8, paragraph 1;

(v) any amendment which has been adopted in accordance with Article 8, paragraph 4;

(vi) any amendment deemed to have been accepted under Article 8, paragraph 7, together with the date on which that amendment shall enter into force in accordance with paragraphs 8 and 9 of that Article;

(vii) the deposit of any instrument of denunciation of this Protocol together with the date of the deposit and the date on which it takes effect;

(b) transmit certified true copies of this Protocol to all Signatory States and to all States which accede to this Protocol.

3. As soon as this Protocol enters into force, the text shall be transmitted by the Secretary-General to the Secretariat of the United Nations for registration and publication in accordance with Article 102 of the Charter of the United Nations.

Article 15 – Languages

This Protocol is established in a single original in the Arabic, Chinese, English, French, Russian and Spanish languages, each text being equally authentic

DONE at London this second day of May one thousand nine hundred and ninety-six.

IN WITNESS WHEREOF the undersigned, being duly authorised by their respective Governments for that purpose, have signed this Protocol.

International Convention for the Unification of Certain Rules Relating to the Arrest of Sea-Going Ships, 1952

THE HIGH CONTRACTING PARTIES,

HAVING RECOGNISED the desirability of determining by agreement certain uniform rules of law relating to the arrest of sea-going ships,

HAVE DECIDED to conclude a convention for this purpose and thereto have agreed as follows:

Article 1

In this Convention the following words shall have the meanings hereby assigned to them:
1. "Maritime Claim" means a claim arising out of one or more of the following:
   a. damage caused by any ship either in collision or otherwise;
   b. loss of life or personal injury caused by any ship or occurring in connection with the operation of any ship;
   c. salvage;
   d. agreement relating to the use or hire of any ship whether by charterparty or otherwise;
   e. agreement relating to the carriage of goods in any ship whether by charterparty or otherwise;
   f. loss of or damage to goods including baggage carried in any ship;
   g. general average;
   h. bottomry;
   i. towage;
   j. pilotage;
   k. goods or materials wherever supplied to a ship for her operation or maintenance;
   l. construction, repair or equipment of any ship or dock charges and dues;
   m. wages of masters, officers, or crew;
   n. master's disbursements, including disbursements made by shippers, charterers or agents on behalf of a ship or her owner;
   o. disputes as to the title to or ownership of any ship;
   p. disputes between co-owners of any ship as to the ownership, possession employment or earnings of that ship;
   q. the mortgage or hypothecation of any ship.
2. "Arrest" means the detention of a ship by judicial process to secure a maritime claim, but does not include the seizure of a ship in execution or satisfaction of a judgment.
3. "Person" includes individuals, partnerships and bodies corporate, Governments, their Departments, and Public Authorities.
4. "Claimant" means a person who alleges that a maritime claim exists in his favour.

Article 2

A ship flying the flag of one of the contracting States may be arrested in the jurisdiction of any of the contracting States in respect of any maritime claim, but in respect of no other claim but nothing in this Convention shall be deemed to extend or restrict any right or powers vested in any Governments or their Departments, Public Authorities, or Dock or Harbour Authorities under their existing domestic laws or regulations to arrest, detain or otherwise prevent the sailing of vessels within their jurisdiction.

Article 3

1. Subject to the provisions of paragraph 4 of this Article and of Article 10, a claimant may arrest either the particular ship in respect of which the maritime claim arose, or any other ship which is owned by the person who was, at the time when the maritime claim arose, the owner of the particular ship, even though the ship arrested be ready to sail but no ship, other than the particular ship in respect of which the claim arose, may be arrested in respect of any of the maritime claims enumerated in Article 1(1)(o), (p) or (q).
2. Ships shall be deemed to be in the same ownership when all the shares therein are owned by the same person or persons.
3. A ship shall not be arrested, nor shall bail or other security be given more than once in any one or more of the jurisdictions of any of the Contracting States in respect of the same maritime claim by the same claimant and, if a ship has been arrested in any one of such jurisdictions, or bail or other security has been given in such jurisdiction either to release the ship or to avoid a threatened arrest, any subsequent arrest of the ship or of any ship in the same ownership by the same claimant for the same maritime claim shall be set aside, and the ship released by the Court or other appropriate judicial authority of that State, unless the claimant can satisfy the Court or other appropriate judicial authority that the bail or other security had been finally released before the subsequent arrest or that there is good cause for maintaining that arrest.
4. When in the case of a charter by demise of a ship the charterer and not the registered owner is liable in respect of a maritime claim relating to that ship, the claimant may arrest such ship or any other ship in the ownership of the charterer by demise, subject to the provisions of this Convention, but no other ship in the ownership of the registered owner shall be liable to arrest in respect of such maritime claims. The provisions of this paragraph shall apply to any case in which a person other than the registered owner of a ship is liable in respect of a maritime claim relating to that ship.

Article 4

A ship may only be arrested under the authority of a Court or of the appropriate judicial authority of the Contracting State in which the arrest is made.

Article 5

The Court or other appropriate judicial authority within whose jurisdiction the ship has been arrested shall permit the release of the ship upon sufficient bail or other security being furnished, save in cases in which a ship has been arrested in respect of any of the maritime claims enumerated in Article 1(1)(o) and (p). In such cases the Court or other appropriate judicial authority may permit the person in possession of the ship to continue trading the ship, upon such person furnishing sufficient bail or other security, or may otherwise deal with the operation of the ship during the period of the arrest.

In default of agreement between the Parties as to the sufficiency of the bail or other security the Court or other appropriate judicial authority shall determine the nature and amount thereof.

The request to release the ship against such security shall not be construed as an acknowledgment of liability or as a waiver of the benefit of the legal limitation of liability of the owner of the ship.

Article 6

All questions whether in any case the claimant is liable in damages for the arrest of a ship or for the costs of the bail or other security furnished to release or prevent the arrest of a ship, shall be determined by the law of the Contracting State in whose jurisdiction the arrest was made or applied for.

The rules of procedure relating to the arrest of a ship, to the application for obtaining the authority referred to in Article 4, and all matters of procedure which the arrest may entail, shall be governed by the law of the Contracting State in which the arrest was made or applied for.

Article 7

1. The Courts of the country in which the arrest was made shall have jurisdiction to determine the case upon its merits:
    - if the domestic law of the country in which the arrest is made gives jurisdiction to such Courts
    - or in any of the following cases namely:
        a. if the claimant has his habitual residence or principal place of business in the country in which the arrest was made;
        b. if the claim arose in the country in which the arrest was made;
        c. if the claim concerns the voyage of the ship during which the arrest was made;
        d. if the claim arose out of a collision or in circumstances covered by Article 13 of the International Convention for the unification of certain rules of law with respect to collisions between vessels, signed at Brussels on 23rd September 1910;
        e. if the claim is for salvage;
        f. if the claim is upon a mortgage or hypothecation of the ship arrested.
2. If the Court within whose jurisdiction the ship was arrested has not jurisdiction to decide upon the merits, the bail or other security given in accordance with Article 5 to procure the release of the ship shall specifically provide that it is given as security for the satisfaction of any judgment which may eventually be pronounced by a Court having jurisdiction so to decide and the Court or other appropriate judicial authority of the country in which the arrest is made shall fix the time within which the claimant shall bring an action before a Court having such jurisdiction.
3. If the parties have agreed to submit the dispute to the jurisdiction of a particular Court other than that within whose jurisdiction the arrest was made or to arbitration, the Court or other appropriate judicial authority within whose jurisdiction the arrest was made may fix the time within which the claimant shall bring proceedings.
4. If, in any of the cases mentioned in the two preceding paragraphs, the action or proceedings are not brought within the time so fixed, the defendant may apply for the release of the ship or of the bail or other security.
5. This Article shall not apply in cases covered by the provisions of the revised Rhine Navigation Convention of 17 October 1868.

Article 8

1. The provisions of this Convention shall apply to any vessel flying the flag of a Contracting State in the jurisdiction of any Contracting State.
2. A ship flying the flag of a non-Contracting State may be arrested in the jurisdiction of any Contracting State in respect of any of the maritime claims enumerated in Article 1 or of any other claim for which the law of the Contracting State permits arrest.
3. Nevertheless any Contracting State shall be entitled wholly or partly to exclude from the benefits of this Convention any Government of a non-Contracting State or any person who has not, at the time of the arrest, his habitual residence or principal place of business in one of the Contracting States.
4. Nothing in this Convention shall modify or affect the rules of law in force in the respective Contracting States relating to the arrest of any ship within the jurisdiction of the State or her flag by a person who has his habitual residence or principal place of business in that State.

5. When a maritime claim is asserted by a third party other than the original claimant, whether by subrogation, assignment or otherwise, such third party shall, for the purpose of this Convention, be deemed to have the same habitual residence or principal place of business as the original claimant.

Article 9

Nothing in this Convention shall be construed as creating a right of action, which, apart from the provisions of this Convention, would not arise under the law applied by the Court which had seisin of the case, nor as creating any maritime liens which do not exist under such law or under the Convention on Maritime Mortgages and Liens, if the latter is applicable.

Article 10

The High Contracting Parties may at the time of signature, deposit of ratification or accession, reserve
   a. the right not to apply this Convention to the arrest of a ship for any of the claims enumerated in paragraphs (o) and (p) of Article 1, but to apply their domestic laws to such claims;
   b. the right not to apply the first paragraph of Article 3 to the arrest of a ship, within their jurisdiction, for claims set out in Article 1, paragraph (q).

Article 11

The High Contracting Parties undertake to submit to arbitration any disputes between States arising out of the interpretation or application of this Convention, but this shall be without prejudice to the obligations of those High Contracting Parties who have agreed to submit their disputes to the International Court of Justice.

Article 12

This Convention shall be open for signature by the States represented at the Ninth Diplomatic Conference on Maritime Law. The protocol of signature shall be drawn up through the good offices of the Belgian Ministry of Foreign Affairs.

Article 13

This Convention shall be ratified and the instruments of ratification shall be deposited with the Belgian Ministry of Foreign Affairs which shall notify all signatory and acceding States of the deposit of any such instruments.

Article 14

   a. This Convention shall come into force between the two States which first ratify it, six months after the date of the deposit of the second instrument of ratification.
   b. This Convention shall come into force in respect of each signatory State which ratifies it after the deposit of the second instrument of ratification six months after the date of the deposit of the instrument of ratification of that State.

Article 15

Any State not represented at the Ninth Diplomatic Conference on Maritime Law may accede to this Convention.

The accession of any State shall be notified to the Belgian Ministry of Foreign Affairs which shall inform through diplomatic channels all signatory and acceding States of such notification.

The Convention shall come into force in respect of the acceding State six months after the date of the receipt of such notification but not before the Convention has come into force in accordance with the provisions of Article 14(a).

Article 16

Any High Contracting Party may three years after the coming into force of this Convention in respect of such High Contracting Party or at any time thereafter request that a conference be convened in order to consider amendments to the Convention.

Any High Contracting Party proposing to avail itself of this right shall notify the Belgian Government which shall convene the conference within six months thereafter.

Article 17

Any High Contracting Party shall have the right to denounce this Convention at any time after the coming into force thereof in respect of such High Contracting Party. This denunciation shall take effect one year after the date on which notification thereof has been received by the Belgian government which shall inform through diplomatic channels all the other High Contracting Parties of such notification.

Article 18

    a. Any High Contracting Party may at the time of its ratification of or accession to this Convention or at any time thereafter declare by written notification to the Belgian Ministry of Foreign Affairs that the Convention shall extend to any of the territories for whose international relations it is responsible. The Convention shall six months after the date of the receipt of such notification by the Belgian Ministry of Foreign Affairs extend to the territories named therein, but not before the date of the coming into force of the Convention in respect of such High Contracting Party.

    b. A High Contracting Party which has made a declaration under (a) of this Article extending the Convention to any territory for whose international relations it is responsible may at any time thereafter declare by notification given to the Belgian Ministry of Foreign Affairs that the Convention shall cease to extend to such territory and the Convention shall one year after the receipt of the notification by the Belgian Ministry of Foreign Affairs cease to extend thereto.

    c. The Belgian Ministry of Foreign Affairs shall inform through diplomatic channels all signatory and acceding States of any notification received by it under this Article.

Done at Brussels, on May 10, 1952 in the French and English languages, the two texts being equally authentic.

APPENDIX O

International Convention on the Arrest of Ships, 1999

(Geneva, 12 March 1999)

The States Parties to this Convention, Recognising the desirability of facilitating the harmonious and orderly development of world seaborne trade, Convinced of the necessity for a legal instrument establishing international uniformity in the field of arrest of ships which takes account of recent developments in related fields,

Have agreed as follows:

Article 1 – Definitions

For the purposes of this Convention:
1. "Maritime Claim" means a claim arising out of one or more of the following:
   (a) loss or damage caused by the operation of the ship;
   (b) loss of life or personal injury occurring, whether on land or on water, in direct connection with the operation of the ship;
   (c) salvage operations or any salvage agreement, including, if applicable, special compensation relating to salvage operations in respect of a ship which by itself or its cargo threatened damage to the environment;
   (d) damage or threat of damage caused by the ship to the environment, coastline or related interests; measures taken to prevent, minimise, or remove such damage; compensation for such damage; costs of reasonable measures of reinstatement of the environment actually undertaken or to be undertaken; loss incurred or likely to be incurred by third parties in connection with such damage; and damage, costs, or loss of a similar nature to those identified in this subparagraph (d);
   (e) costs or expenses relating to the raising, removal, recovery, destruction or the rendering harmless of a ship which is sunk, wrecked, stranded or abandoned, including anything that is or has been on board such ship, and costs or expenses relating to the preservation of an abandoned ship and maintenance of its crew;
   (f) any agreement relating to the use or hire of the ship, whether contained in a charter party or otherwise;
   (g) any agreement relating to the carriage of goods or passengers on board the ship, whether contained in a charter party or otherwise;
   (h) loss of or damage to or in connection with goods (including luggage) carried on board the ship;
   (i) general average;
   (j) towage;
   (k) pilotage;
   (l) goods, materials, provisions, bunkers, equipment (including containers) supplied or services rendered to the ship for its operation, management, preservation or maintenance;
   (m) construction, reconstruction, repair, converting or equipping of the ship;
   (n) port, canal, dock, harbour and other waterway dues and charges;

(o) wages and other sums due to the master, officers and other members of the ship's complement in respect of their employment on the ship, including costs of repatriation and social insurance contributions payable on their behalf;

(p) disbursements incurred on behalf of the ship or its owners;

(q) insurance premiums (including mutual insurance calls) in respect of the ship, payable by or on behalf of the shipowner or demise charterer;

(r) any commissions, brokerages or agency fees payable in respect of the ship by or on behalf of the shipowner or demise charterer;

(s) any dispute as to ownership or possession of the ship;

(t) any dispute between co-owners of the ship as to the employment or earnings of the ship;

(u) a mortgage or a "hypothèque" or a charge of the same nature on the ship;

(v) any dispute arising out of a contract for the sale of the ship.

2. "Arrest" means any detention or restriction on removal of a ship by order of a Court to secure a maritime claim, but does not include the seizure of a ship in execution or satisfaction of a judgment or other enforceable instrument.

3. "Person" means any individual or partnership or any public or private body, whether corporate or not, including a State or any of its constituent subdivisions.

4. "Claimant" means any person asserting a maritime claim.

5. "Court" means any competent judicial authority of a State.

Article 2 – Powers of arrest

1. A ship may be arrested or released from arrest only under the authority of a Court of the State Party in which the arrest is effected.

2. A ship may only be arrested in respect of a maritime claim but in respect of no other claim.

3. A ship may be arrested for the purpose of obtaining security notwithstanding that, by virtue of a jurisdiction clause or arbitration clause in any relevant contract, or otherwise, the maritime claim in respect of which the arrest is effected is to be adjudicated in a State other than the State where the arrest is effected, or is to be arbitrated, or is to be adjudicated subject to the law of another State.

4. Subject to the provisions of this Convention, the procedure relating to the arrest of a ship or its release shall be governed by the law of the State in which the arrest was effected or applied for.

Article 3 – Exercise of right of arrest

1. Arrest is permissible of any ship in respect of which a maritime claim is asserted if:

(a) the person who owned the ship at the time when the maritime claim arose is liable for the claim and is owner of the ship when the arrest is effected; or

(b) the demise charterer of the ship at the time when the maritime claim arose is liable for the claim and is demise charterer or owner of the ship when the arrest is effected; or

(c) the claim is based upon a mortgage or a "hypothèque" or a charge of the same nature on the ship; or

(d) the claim relates to the ownership or possession of the ship; or

(e) the claim is against the owner, demise charterer, manager or operator of the ship and is secured by a maritime lien which is granted or arises under the law of the State where the arrest is applied for.

2. Arrest is also permissible of any other ship or ships which, when the arrest is effected, is or are owned by the person who is liable for the maritime claim and who was, when the claim arose:

(a) owner of the ship in respect of which the maritime claim arose; or

(b) demise charterer, time charterer or voyage charterer of that ship.

This provision does not apply to claims in respect of ownership or possession of a ship.

3. Notwithstanding the provisions of paragraphs 1 and 2 of this article, the arrest of a ship which is not owned by the person liable for the claim shall be permissible only if, under the law of the State where the arrest is applied for, a judgment in respect of that claim can be enforced against that ship by judicial or forced sale of that ship.

Article 4 – Release from arrest

1. A ship which has been arrested shall be released when sufficient security has been provided in a satisfactory form, save in cases in which a ship has been arrested in respect of any of the maritime claims enumerated in article 1, paragraphs 1 (s) and (t). In such cases, the Court may permit the person in possession of the ship to continue trading the ship, upon such person providing sufficient security, or may otherwise deal with the operation of the ship during the period of the arrest.

2. In the absence of agreement between the parties as to the sufficiency and form of the security, the Court shall determine its nature and the amount thereof, not exceeding the value of the arrested ship.

3. Any request for the ship to be released upon security being provided shall not be construed as an acknowledgement of liability nor as a waiver of any defence or any right to limit liability.

4. If a ship has been arrested in a non-party State and is not released although security in respect of that ship has been provided in a State Party in respect of the same claim, that security shall be ordered to be released on application to the Court in the State Party.

5. If in a non-party State the ship is released upon satisfactory security in respect of that ship being provided, any security provided in a State Party in respect of the same claim shall be ordered to be released to the extent that the total amount of security provided in the two States exceeds:

    (a) the claim for which the ship has been arrested, or

    (b) the value of the ship, whichever is the lower. Such release shall, however, not be ordered unless the security provided in the non-party State will actually be available to the claimant and will be freely transferable.

6. Where, pursuant to paragraph 1 of this article, security has been provided, the person providing such security may at any time apply to the Court to have that security reduced, modified, or cancelled.

Article 5 – Right of rearrest and multiple arrest

1. Where in any State a ship has already been arrested and released or security in respect of that ship has already been provided to secure a maritime claim, that ship shall not thereafter be rearrested or arrested in respect of the same maritime claim unless:

    (a) the nature or amount of the security in respect of that ship already provided in respect of the same claim is inadequate, on condition that the aggregate amount of security may not exceed the value of the ship; or

    (b) the person who has already provided the security is not, or is unlikely to be, able to fulfil some or all of that person's obligations; or

    (c) the ship arrested or the security previously provided was released either:

        (i) upon the application or with the consent of the claimant acting on reasonable grounds, or

        (ii) because the claimant could not by taking reasonable steps prevent the release.

2. Any other ship which would otherwise be subject to arrest in respect of the same maritime claim shall not be arrested unless:

    (a) the nature or amount of the security already provided in respect of the same claim is inadequate; or

    (b) the provisions of paragraph 1 (b) or (c) of this article are applicable.

3. "Release" for the purpose of this article shall not include any unlawful release or escape from arrest.

Article 6 – Protection of owners and demise charterers of arrested ships

1. The Court may as a condition of the arrest of a ship, or of permitting an arrest already effected to be maintained, impose upon the claimant who seeks to arrest or who has procured the arrest of the ship the obligation to provide security of a kind and for an amount, and upon such terms, as may be determined by that Court for any loss which may be incurred by the defendant as a result of the arrest, and for which the claimant may be found liable, including but not restricted to such loss or damage as may be incurred by that defendant in consequence of:

    (a) the arrest having been wrongful or unjustified; or
    (b) excessive security having been demanded and provided.

2. The Courts of the State in which an arrest has been effected shall have jurisdiction to determine the extent of the liability, if any, of the claimant for loss or damage caused by the arrest of a ship, including but not restricted to such loss or damage as may be caused in consequence of:

    (a) the arrest having been wrongful or unjustified, or
    (b) excessive security having been demanded and provided.

3. The liability, if any, of the claimant in accordance with paragraph 2 of this article shall be determined by application of the law of the State where the arrest was effected.

4. If a Court in another State or an arbitral tribunal is to determine the merits of the case in accordance with the provisions of article 7, then proceedings relating to the liability of the claimant in accordance with paragraph 2 of this article may be stayed pending that decision.

5. Where pursuant to paragraph 1 of this article security has been provided, the person providing such security may at any time apply to the Court to have that security reduced, modified or cancelled.

Article 7 – Jurisdiction on the merits of the case

1. The Courts of the State in which an arrest has been effected or security provided to obtain the release of the ship shall have jurisdiction to determine the case upon its merits, unless the parties validly agree or have validly agreed to submit the dispute to a Court of another State which accepts jurisdiction, or to arbitration.

2. Notwithstanding the provisions of paragraph 1 of this article, the Courts of the State in which an arrest has been effected, or security provided to obtain the release of the ship, may refuse to exercise that jurisdiction where that refusal is permitted by the law of that State and a Court of another State accepts jurisdiction.

3. In cases where a Court of the State where an arrest has been effected or security provided to obtain the release of the ship:

    (a) does not have jurisdiction to determine the case upon its merits; or
    (b) has refused to exercise jurisdiction in accordance with the provisions of paragraph 2 of this article, such Court may, and upon request shall, order a period of time within which the claimant shall bring proceedings before a competent Court or arbitral tribunal.

4. If proceedings are not brought within the period of time ordered in accordance with paragraph 3 of this article then the ship arrested or the security provided shall, upon request, be ordered to be released.

5. If proceedings are brought within the period of time ordered in accordance with paragraph 3 of this article, or if proceedings before a competent Court or arbitral tribunal in another State are brought in the absence of such order, any final decision resulting therefrom shall be recognised and given effect with respect to the arrested ship or to the security provided in order to obtain its release, on condition that:

(a) the defendant has been given reasonable notice of such proceedings and a reasonable opportunity to present the case for the defence; and

(b) such recognition is not against public policy (*ordre public*).

6. Nothing contained in the provisions of paragraph 5 of this article shall restrict any further effect given to a foreign judgment or arbitral award under the law of the State where the arrest of the ship was effected or security provided to obtain its release.

Article 8 – Application

1. This Convention shall apply to any ship within the jurisdiction of any State Party, whether or not that ship is flying the flag of a State Party.

2. This Convention shall not apply to any warship, naval auxiliary or other ships owned or operated by a State and used, for the time being, only on government non-commercial service.

3. This Convention does not affect any rights or powers vested in any Government or its departments, or in any public authority, or in any dock or harbour authority, under any international convention or under any domestic law or regulation, to detain or otherwise prevent from sailing any ship within their jurisdiction.

4. This Convention shall not affect the power of any State or Court to make orders affecting the totality of a debtor's assets.

5. Nothing in this Convention shall affect the application of international conventions providing for limitation of liability, or domestic law giving effect thereto, in the State where an arrest is effected.

6. Nothing in this Convention shall modify or affect the rules of law in force in the States Parties relating to the arrest of any ship physically within the jurisdiction of the State of its flag procured by a person whose habitual residence or principal place of business is in that State, or by any other person who has acquired a claim from such person by subrogation, assignment or otherwise.

Article 9 – Non-creation of maritime liens

Nothing in this Convention shall be construed as creating a maritime lien.

Article 10 – Reservations

1. Any State may, at the time of signature, ratification, acceptance, approval, or accession, or at any time thereafter, reserve the right to exclude the application of this Convention to any or all of the following :

(a) ships which are not seagoing;

(b) ships not flying the flag of a State Party;

(c) claims under article 1, paragraph 1 (s).

2. A State may, when it is also a State Party to a specified treaty on navigation on inland waterways, declare when signing, ratifying, accepting, approving or acceding to this Convention, that rules on jurisdiction, recognition and execution of court decisions provided for in such treaties shall prevail over the rules contained in article 7 of this Convention.

Article 11 – Depositary

This Convention shall be deposited with the Secretary-General of the United Nations.

Article 12 – Signature, ratification, acceptance, approval and accession

1. This Convention shall be open for signature by any State at the Headquarters of the United Nations, New York, from 1 September 1999 to 31 August 2000 and shall thereafter remain open for accession.

2. States may express their consent to be bound by this Convention by:

(a) signature without reservation as to ratification, acceptance or approval; or

(b) signature subject to ratification, acceptance or approval, followed by ratification, acceptance or approval; or

(c) accession.

3. Ratification, acceptance, approval or accession shall be effected by the deposit of an instrument to that effect with the depositary.

Article 13 – States with more than one system of law

1. If a State has two or more territorial units in which different systems of law are applicable in relation to matters dealt with in this Convention, it may at the time of signature, ratification, acceptance, approval or accession declare that this Convention shall extend to all its territorial units or only to one or more of them and may modify this declaration by submitting another declaration at any time.

2. Any such declaration shall be notified to the depositary and shall state expressly the territorial units to which the Convention applies.

3. In relation to a State Party which has two or more systems of law with regard to arrest of ships applicable in different territorial units, references in this Convention to the Court of a State and the law of a State shall be respectively construed as referring to the Court of the relevant territorial unit within that State and the law of the relevant territorial unit of that State.

Article 14 – Entry into force

1. This Convention shall enter into force six months following the date on which 10 States have expressed their consent to be bound by it.

2. For a State which expresses its consent to be bound by this Convention after the conditions for entry into force thereof have been met, such consent shall take effect three months after the date of expression of such consent.

Article 15 – Revision and amendment

1. A conference of States Parties for the purpose of revising or amending this Convention shall be convened by the Secretary-General of the United Nations at the request of one-third of the States Parties.

2. Any consent to be bound by this Convention, expressed after the date of entry into force of an amendment to this Convention, shall be deemed to apply to the Convention, as amended.

Article 16 – Denunciation

1. This Convention may be denounced by any State Party at any time after the date on which this Convention enters into force for that State.

2. Denunciation shall be effected by deposit of an instrument of denunciation with the depositary.

3. A denunciation shall take effect one year, or such longer period as may be specified in the instrument of denunciation, after the receipt of the instrument of denunciation by the depositary.

Article 17 – Languages

This Convention is established in a single original in the Arabic, Chinese, English, French, Russian and Spanish languages, each text being equally authentic.

DONE AT Geneva this twelfth day of March, one thousand nine hundred andninety-nine.

IN WITNESS WHEREOF the undersigned being duly authorised by their respective Governments for that purpose have signed this Convention.

Index

(All references are to paragraph number.)